Douglas DC-3/C-47

in Latin American Military Service

Douglas DC-3/C-47
in Latin American Military Service

Dan Hagedorn and Mario Overall

Crécy Publishing Ltd

Published in 2021 by Crécy Publishing Limited

A CIP record for this book is available from the British Library

ISBN 9781910809471

Printed and bound in Turkey by Pelikan Print

Crécy Publishing Limited
1a Ringway Trading Estate, Shadowmoss Road,
Manchester M22 5LH

www.crecy.co.uk

Front cover: C-47 of the Honduran Air Force, photographed at Toncontín Airbase, Tegucigalpa, in April, 1986. *R.E.G. Davies, via Dan Hagedorn*

Front flap (top): Douglas VC-47D serial T-37 of the Paraguayan Air Force, photographed sometime in 1964. *Via Gary Kuhn*

Front flap (bottom): Douglas C-47B serial 6007, sporting the Galeana name, photographed in 1967. *Pete Bulban via Jay Miller*

Back cover, top to bottom: Douglas C-47 serial 0653 of the Guatemalan Air Force, parked at La Aurora Airbase's northern ramp in 1949. *Guatemalan Air Force Photo Archives via LAAHS*
C-47A serial 304 of the Honduran Air Force, photographed at Howard AFB, in the Panama Canal Zone, on 2 December 1969. *Dan Hagedorn*
C-47 serial 103 of the Salvadoran Air Force, photographed at Howard AFB, in the Panama Canal Zone, on February 1969. *Dan Hagedorn*

Contents

Introduction

I F YOU ARE READING this specialised volume dedicated to one of the most significant aircraft families of the first century of practical manned flight, you will almost certainly need no introduction to the genesis of the Douglas DC-2, DC-3 and its inevitable military equivalents that emerged starting in the 1930s. A richly deserved body of literature has become available since the 1960s, crafted both for the layman and the enthusiast, including the monumental – and, it must be observed – ongoing efforts of the International Association of Aviation Historians (better known as Air-Britain) to document, in its several monographs, the service lives of each and every aircraft built.

The accounts of the Second World War contributions of the C-47, C-53 and a bewildering array of former civil DC-3s drafted into military service, as well as the Navy and Marine Corps R4Ds and British Commonwealth Dakotas, are legion and it is particularly significant that variants of the extremely versatile Douglas twin served in every single theatre of that greatest of human conflagrations – and, it should be remembered, on both sides.

But while the C-47 and Dakota have long since disappeared from the inventory of every one of the great Second World War Allied powers, and only a few soldier on in civilian hands as painted ladies striving valiantly to memorialise the exertions of their sisters in the hands of the Greatest Generation, a dwindling few still soldier on in Latin America at the time of writing. Although overwhelmingly re-engined or Basler Turbo conversions, the end for even these, the longest-serving of the entire breed, is finally in sight.

And so, after a fashion, this labour of love and respect will serve as a valedictory for the significant number of DC-2s, DC-3s, C-47s and variants that saw service in what we collectively refer to as Latin America – the very youngest of which is now more than seventy-five years old.

Some readers will be surprised that we have elected to include a full chapter devoted to US military use of these aircraft in Latin America, primarily those stationed permanently in the region starting as early as June 1940 when two sleek, brilliantly polished and state-of-the-art Douglas C-33s arrived at the US Army Air Corps stations at either extremity of the former Panama Canal Zone in June 1940. They caused a sensation among Army Air Corps personnel in Central America and it was not long before they were plying that region's skies, ranging far and wide to not only 'show the colours' but to transport ranking officials in the final stages of arrangements for the momentous 'destroyers for bases' deal with Great Britain, intent on examining exactly what the US was getting from the deal. Of course, Pan American and Panagra had been operating DC-2s and DC-3s in the region for some time, and while they did much to establish the primacy of the design in the minds of many air-minded Latin Americans, their value as military assets had yet to be appreciated.

The commercial DC-2s and DC-3s, and the USAAC's prized C-33s, were followed during the war years by a very hard-working and far-ranging fleet of C-39s, C-47s, exotic C-49s and examples of the C-53 and C-68. Post-war, the evolution of an extensive US Air Force Mission system to virtually every established air arm in the region saw numerous C-47s assigned, and a single example stationed with the important Inter-American Air Forces Academy at Albrook Field, in the Panama Canal Zone, may lay claim to having been one of the most influential of all C-47s in the region, as will be described in the text.

Events in Europe soon impacted Latin America, and as France succumbed to the German juggernaut, a totally unintended result of that conquest saw the very first DC-3 pass to military service in Latin America when a former Air France aircraft was confiscated by the Argentine government in 1941, not long after the USAAC first introduced its C-33s in Panama.

Lend-Lease was arguably the most transformative assistance programme in the history of Latin American military aviation, but, primarily because of their extremely high value to the far-flung Allied cause, few Latin American nations successfully included C-47s in their Lend-Lease requisitions, no matter how compelling a case they made. Brazil and, oddly, Colombia, were they only military benefactors of C-47s via this means.

However, as victory became obvious, none other than General Henry H. 'Hap' Arnold himself, the wartime Commander of the USAAF, shaped an early post-war programme known as the American Republics Projects (ARP) with the prime objective of not only building on the success of the Lend-Lease programme, but bringing the Western Hemispheric nations of Latin America deeply into the fold by providing nearly all with additional tactical types – including the first of a wave of C-47s.

The war-surplus boom period added to the largesse of the ARP as air arms that, mainly for political reasons, did not fully qualify for the benefits of that programme found that they could acquire not only combat aircraft but transports as well at bargain-basement prices for the first time. For many, acquiring C-47s was high on their list of priorities.

The late 1940s was also a period of political instability in the region, as the long-standing dictatorial regimes were targeted by elements who saw the Allied victory as a worldwide swing towards democratic ideals. Perhaps not surprisingly, surplus DC-3s and C-47s, as well as some that were seized from established airlines in the region, became extremely valuable tools for both sides. These often shadowy activities are chronicled in these pages, including instances in which DC-3s and C-47s were used, for the first time, as ad hoc ground attack assets and even interceptors during the Costa Rica civil war of 1948. Much further south, both civil and military DC-3s and C-47s actually engaged in aerial combat during the bitter Bolivian civil war of 1948, providing evidence that it had not taken Latin Americans long to not only field and maintain these aircraft, but to appreciate their versatility as well.

The 1950s might well be described as 'the Decade of the DC-3 and C-47' in Latin American aviation history. As rapidly as they could, virtually every established air arm, even if they could not afford anything else, acquired at least a few C-47s or variants. Soon, it became a maxim that, if no other aircraft of a given nation's military establishment was flying every single day, the C-47 would be the sole exception. US aid programmes of the 1950s and '60s, including the so-called Rio Pact, and including the Reimbursable Aid (RA) elements of MDAP, MAP, Foreign Military Sales (FMS) and Grant Aid (GA) programmes, saw ever increasing numbers of C-47s heading south, not to mention direct commercial acquisitions, assumptions of former civil aircraft by default by military operators as in Argentina and elsewhere, and even recovery of abandoned US aircraft, which happened more than once.

By the 1960s, Latin American operators could reasonably lay claim to possessing some of the highest time C-47 crews anywhere in the world. Indeed, in some air arms, most pilots and first officers by the end of the 1960s had never flown any other operational type, and the resulting prowess and familiarity with long-serving aircraft often approached legendary proportions. The same could be said for the hard-pressed ground crews who maintained these durable airframes, often literally bringing some aircraft back from the brink of oblivion after what would, in almost any other setting, have been described as a complete write-off.

Latin America also saw the use of military DC-3s and C-47s on what nearly anyone would describe as the dark side of their existence, especially in Argentina, where the brutal suppression of dissent involved the use of aircraft to deliver an untold number of men, women and children to oblivion during the period of 'the Dirty War', roughly 1976–83, when and unknowable number of *los desaparecidos* almost certainly spent their final moments alive in the cold, roaring interior of military C-47s, among other types, as they awaited their fate.

Ironically, US Air Force use of C-47s in Latin America actually experienced a renaissance during the late 1960s and early '70s, as the era of counter-insurgency warfare gained currency, and the 605th Air Commando Squadron, based at Howard AFB in the Panama Canal Zone, gained the seldom recognised distinction being the last large US military operating unit for a surprising number of veteran C-47s – nearly all of which eventually passed to Latin American operators when the USAF finally found the demands of Southeast Asia a far more compelling way of using its resources. It was during this period that the first of the 'Spooky' gunships emerged, and it did not take long for similar modifications to make their way into Latin American air force inventories, notably in Colombia, the Dominican Republic and El Salvador.

By the 1980s, C-47s were still to be found in substantial numbers throughout the military establishments of Latin America, but spares and maintenance issues inevitably started to emerge, as the US aid pipeline for some came to an end. Cast upon their own resources, some

air arms found that by then they had sufficient experience with the type to keep them going into the 1990s, but with increasing frequency, replacements were being sought. The so-called Basler BT-67 turbo conversions, seizures of otherwise airworthy airframes from drug-runners and the occasional largesse of failed 'tramp' airlines provided occasional supplementary aircraft, but the glory days were all but over.

For the 'number bashers' who may navigate these pages, just a few words of explanation for some of the conventions that we found it necessary to include in our data tables. As will be quickly evident, we have gone to considerable trouble to identify the Manufacturer's Serial Number (MSN, the term used by the US FAA, 'Constructor's Number' or 'c/n' for most European enthusiasts) as well as all known previous identities. We have also attempted to identify the root variant and subsequent modification variants for each aircraft, as these often have a direct bearing on the capabilities of an aircraft. Use of simplistic terms 'DC-3' and 'C-47' often fail to convey the significance of many of these substantial modifications. Similarly, in quite a few instances, we have identified aircraft that we regard as candidates for specific identities by using italicised text, while those which are confirmed are in normal font. In nearly every such instance, these entries are the best candidates that can be nominated, and usually, the dates and circumstances 'fit' the known sequences. We take full responsibility for these assumptions, and sincerely hope that in the fullness of time our fraternity will be able to put the open questions to rest, once and for all.

At the time of writing, C-47s and BT-67s are still flying with a small number of Latin American operators, and while the end has not yet been reached, you can see it from here. It is thus an appropriate moment to review these splendid aircraft and their very intensive use in a region of the world with which their shape, sound and longevity have become synonymous. There is an old saying that when the first manned vessel returns from a mission to Mars it will be number two in the pattern behind a DC-3, and this will almost certainly be one from Latin America.

Dan Hagedorn and **Mario Overall**
Maple Valley and Guatemala City 2020

CHAPTER ONE

United States Military Service in Latin America

N O HISTORY of the military use of the DC-2, DC-3 and C-47 series in the region of the Western Hemisphere usually described as Latin America would be complete or truly comprehensible without at least a summary of the activities of aircraft of these classic series that were actually stationed with elements of the United States armed forces south of the Rio Grande.

United States Army Air Corps and United States Navy and Marine Corps aviation had gained an early appreciation for the potential of the aircraft of this series and, it must be observed, placed small but timely orders with Douglas at a time when the manufacturer could truly benefit from the financial as well as endorsement value of such acquisitions. Although the numbers involved could hardly be described as pivotal, they were nonetheless 'cash on the barrel head' during the last years of the Great Depression and certainly contributed to Douglas being able to cite these purchases to potential customers in what quickly evolved into a worldwide market and demand.

Perhaps to everyone's surprise, the Navy stepped up first, however, with an order for three R2D-1s, which were essentially DC-2-125s, all delivered in mid-December 1934, barely more than a year after the first flight of DC-1-109 X223Y. These were followed by two more in September 1935, although none of these were known to have actually been stationed at what were then the only two US Navy air facilities in Latin America, Guantanamo Bay, Cuba, and Coco Solo Naval Air Station, Panama Canal Zone.

Commencing with a single XC-32, a DC-2 variant, also in September 1935, and then, oddly two C-34s in March and April 1936, the Air Corps took the extraordinary follow-on step of acquiring no fewer than eighteen C-33s with a pair of Wright R-1820-25 engines. These fourteen-place aircraft, variants of the DC-2-145, had been strengthened to meet rather stringent service requirements as cargo aircraft and were handed over to their very

proud new Air Corps operators starting in May 1936 as serial numbers AC36-70 to AC36-87. They were dispersed across the country as single units to a service that was in the throes of coping with Depression budget restraints, in part to cloak the actual size of the small fleet from critics of excess governmental spending at a crucial juncture in the national recovery.

In the midst of the 1920s and '30s, and in spite of the pervasive peacetime economy of the 1920s and the Depression that commenced in 1929, both the US Army and Navy had quietly but very deliberately devoted major percentages of their annual budgets to the defence of what was arguably the capstone element of between-the-wars US defence planning, the Panama Canal.

Indeed, since its completion, the United States Army, in particular, which held the overarching responsibility for the defence of this national asset, had gradually constructed defence installations that, per square mile, matched or exceeded any to be found anywhere else on earth at the time. These included massive coastal artillery installations and associated fortifications on both the Atlantic as well as the Pacific approaches, highly mobile ground forces to support

The first of many to follow. Douglas C-33 AC36-72 shortly after arrival at Albrook Field, Canal Zone, near the Pacific terminus of the strategic defence asset, with an impromptu mix of Panamanian football players and Air Corps personnel gathering on a hot and humid 11 June 1940 to take in the shiny new marvel. The distinctive landing lights, RDF loop and antenna array mark her as a DC-2-145 variant. *Maj. Jesse W. Miller*

them, and Air Corps installations that, by the end of the 1930s, represented nearly 25 per cent of the standing Order of Battle of the entire service. Indeed, as world events once again seemed to be inevitably heading for yet another conflagration, none other than General Henry H. 'Hap' Arnold, himself a veteran of the pioneering days of the 7th Aero Squadron in Panama in 1917–18, used his VIP-configured Douglas C-41A (AC40-70), the Army designation for the DC-3A-253A, to fly direct from Florida to the Canal Zone on Tuesday, 7 May 1940, arriving at 1920 hours to inspect at first hand the rapidly expanding air defence arrangements then under way there. It was the very first known military Douglas twin-engined transport to venture into Latin America. Such was the value placed on defending the canal at the time.

Later that same month, twenty-five officer pilots and twenty-nine enlisted crew members of the resident Panama Canal Department Air Force's 19th Wing, as it was known at that juncture, led by the Wing Executive Officer, LTC Francis M. Brady, took part in what by then had become a fairly routine process: the aerial reinforcement of the Air Corps units in the Canal Zone directly from the Continental United States, via intermediary stops in Mexico and Central America. The result of some very challenging diplomatic manoeuvring, this procedure had actually commenced some years earlier, and paved the way for the aerial reinforcement of the canal clear through the war years.

The contingent flew to the San Antonio Air Depot (SAAD) in Texas, starting with six 'straight' Douglas B-18s carrying most of the men. Four of these were exchanged at the SAAD for improved B-18As, as well as two Douglas C-33s (by then about four years old) and a number of North American O-47As. Upon return with the 'new' aircraft on 11 and 17 June, one of the C-33s was assigned to each of the major Airbase Squadrons, AC36-72 to the 15th at Albrook Field on the Pacific side and AC36-78 to the 16th at Old France Field on the Atlantic side. These two aircraft thus gained the distinction of having been the very first Douglas twin-engine transports to actually be stationed in Latin America.[1]

Although the Air Corps had managed to assign transport and utility aircraft to the small garrison in the Canal Zone previously,[2] most of them had consisted of variants of the amphibious Douglas Dolphin and, while these had provided excellent service throughout the isthmus, they came nowhere close to the capabilities that were soon exhibited by the two C-33s, which suddenly seemed to be in demand everywhere. Evidence of this new flexibility was not long in coming.

During one of the pre-war 19th Wing manoeuvres in Central America that were being routinely conducted by June 1940, a Boeing P-26A fighter flown by 2Lt John B. Henry had been obliged to make a forced landing on a soft, sandy beach near Managua, Nicaragua. It had nosed over and was substantially damaged, but repairable. Crews from the legendary TACA airline in Nicaragua had managed to extricate the aircraft from the beach and transport it via a barge to Corinto, Nicaragua, and then, very laboriously, via a narrow-gauge railway to Managua. None other than Col Adlai H. Gilkeson, a Maj. Randall and a Lt Darcy cleared Albrook Field with C-33 AC36-72 on 19 July, carrying mechanics and equipment to recover the P-26A. Flying at about 11,000ft – a real luxury for the crews at the time – en route to Managua, the crew encountered a most unusual phenomenon for them: very cold weather. The flight engineer, having not anticipated such weather in the tropics, had not filled the C-33's relative luxury of a steam-heating system with water and thus, in their tropical khaki uniforms, the crew became quite uncomfortable by the time they arrived at Managua. There, with the aid of the Nicaraguan Guardia Nacional, the P-26 was essentially reconstructed, using the spares, tools and skills brought in aboard the C-33 and, when completed, was escorted back to the Canal Zone via San Jose, Costa Rica. This excursion was the first known use of a Douglas twin-engine transport in Latin America in this manner – the first of many that were to follow. While in Managua, Col Gilkeson was a guest of honour of President Somoza, and the Air Corps crew gave Somoza a flight over and around Managua in the C-33, in the process not only polishing Somoza's vanity, but accomplishing the first known flight by a sitting head of state in a military Douglas twin in Latin America.

Both of the newly arrived 19th Wing C-33s, AC36-72 and AC36-78, grace the apron at Albrook Field for their first formal arrival reception, with a third C-33, a visitor from Randolph Field, Texas, in the background. This was the solitary military concrete apron in all of Central America at the time, and the three hangars to the right still exist. *Maj. Jesse W. Miller*

The rigors of operating in Panama, where the only hard-surfaced Army runway was at Albrook Field, soon caught up with the hard-worked C-33s. AC36-78, the France Field, 16th Airbase Squadron aircraft, met her end at Puntarenas, Costa Rica, on 13 January 1941 when she was obliged to make a forced landing due to engine failure, although this loss was also reported as having been at Punta Vargas, located in the Caribbean coast of Costa Rica, close to the border with Panama, in June 1941.[3] The Costa Rica site is shown on the Individual Aircraft Record Card, however, and this aircraft thus must be accorded the dubious distinction of having been the first military Douglas DC-2/DC-3 variant to be lost in Latin America – the first of many to follow. She had a very creditable 3,066 hours total time at the date of her loss. So far as can be determined, her remains are still there, although her engines were recovered with some exertions.

In fact, the highly conversational *Air Corps Newsletter* (V.8680) actually provided more specific information about this loss than the Individual Aircraft Record Card and Sixth Air Force scattered accounts. According to the *Newsletter*, the loss was actually on 7 December 1940 when her starboard engine caught fire and the pilot, Major Harold A. Bartron, was forced to make an emergency landing at what was described as an 'abandoned airfield' at Puntarenas, Costa Rica, near the edge of the coast. The aircraft had flown to Guatemala City and was returning at the time with parts salvaged from two Douglas B-18s that had crashed. The co-pilot was Capt. R.L. Wood, the Crew Chief S/Sgt Peter Wegley and the Radio Operator Sgt Berlin F. Wells, all of whom escaped without any serious injuries. Maj. Bartron was the Air Corps Supply Officer for the Panama Canal Department (PCD) and Capt. Wood, the Panama Air Depot (PAD) adjutant.

The 20th Transport Squadron

The impact of the two C-33s had been profound, and the Air Corps leadership in Panama managed, via their example, the establishment of a dedicated unit with the sole function of providing air transport and air cargo support for the PCD. This was formalised as a component of the pre-war USAAC expansion programme by the creation of the 20th Transport Squadron, the first such unit established by the service overseas.

Activated at France Field on 15 December 1940, with initially only one officer and one NCO, and at first attached for command and control to the PAD there, one of the unit's first aircraft was the surviving C-33, AC36-72, which was reassigned to the squadron from the 16th Airbase Squadron on 1 February 1941 with Unit Number '1'.[4] It had actually joined two brand-new Douglas C-39s, AC38-510 and 38-524, which were nominally 'owned' by the squadron, starting in December 1940, but one of which had been detached to Headquarters and Headquarters Squadron (HHS), Panama Canal Department Air Force (PCDAF), for the exclusive use of the Department Commander, General Van Voorhis, at Albrook Field.

This small establishment was augmented in late March 1941 by the assignment of an exotic Douglas C-49 (41-7689) and, with the departure of C-33 AC36-72 back to the continental United States (CONUS) to Olmsted Field on 9 May 1941, the organic C-39 retroactively gained Unit Number '1'. By 1 July 1941, the unit had finally grown to four officers (all pilots) and eighty-seven NCOs and enlisted men. Initially, as the defence establishment surrounding the canal grew by leaps and

The approved unit insignia of the 20th Troop Carrier Squadron, designed by (then) Lt Kenneth E. Marts, a pilot in the unit. Although not officially approved by the Institute of Heraldry until 13 January 1943, it is known to have been painted on unit aircraft as early as mid-1942. *Col Kenneth E. Marts*

bounds, the unit's primary operations involved daily flights from France Field to Albrook Field and then on to the new, secret auxiliary base at Rio Hato, Republic of Panama, about 70 air miles to the west of the canal. The unit made its first foreign flight on 11 May 1941, when it transported a new engine for a C-39 grounded at Managua, Nicaragua, which had in fact been en route to the unit from the CONUS when it experienced engine trouble. The two C-39s were assigned Unit Numbers '3' and '4' by August 1941 and, later that same month, were joined by two more C-39s (AC38-504 and 38-534), although it should be noted that these Unit Numbers were rather fluid and, as the strength of the unit grew and its fleet dispersed throughout the rapidly expanding command, they were changed at least twice. Known details of these are provided in the 'Notes' section of the aircraft tables at the end of this chapter.

The first of many, long-distance, cross-country flights by the unit was on 2 June 1941, to distant Trinidad, a two-day journey – one day out and one day back. Two organic C-39s (AC38-524 and AC38-510) were used, the former flown by then Lt R.O. Good, with Lt W.W. Weldon as his co-pilot, and AC38-510 flown by Lt Harry C. Morrison (the flight commander, who became the squadron commander between 2 September and 17 October 1942) and co-pilot Lt C.W. Larson. There were no navigational aids whatsoever, and the maps provided to the crews were commercially acquired Shell Oil tourist brochures! The crews, however, made the excursion look routine. The unit also started making long-distance flights to the San Antonio Air Depot (SAAD) in the CONUS, as vitally needed additional aircraft engine overhaul capability for the hard-pressed PAD became evident. The first such flight took place on 26 September 1941.

By October 1941, by which time the Panama Canal Department Air Force had been redesignated as the Caribbean Air Force, the 20th Transport Squadron, like many of the tactical units of the command, found many of its aircraft and crews dispersed to the far-flung reaches of the Caribbean and, during the course of the month, its hard-pressed quartet of C-39s was augmented by the arrival of a Douglas C-49C (41-7721) and five C-49Ds (41-7716 to 41-7720), followed by C-49B 41-7692 in November for the exclusive use of General Johnson, the CAF Commander by then. That same month, the squadron sent Flight B to the newly completed Howard Field on the Pacific side of the isthmus while, for the time being, the main body remained at France Field. Flight B (Reinforced), with six C-49s, was transferred to Howard Field on 22 November 1941, to work specifically with the newly arrived 501st Parachute Infantry Battalion and the 550th Airborne Infantry garrisoned there, part of the so-called Panama Mobile Force. By the end of 1941, the hard-pressed unit had already flown 2,082 hours and carried 2,032,127lb of war materiel and no fewer than 9,633 passengers.

With the sudden entry of the US into the war on 7 December 1941, the unit immediately dispatched two C-39s (AC38-510 and 38-534) to Trinidad, formalising this distant dispatch on 22 December as a detachment, while others were based out of Losey Field, Puerto Rico. By February 1942, France Field had become far too crowded with fighter and bomber units charged with defending the Atlantic and Caribbean approaches from what was expected to be an imminent attack from Axis forces, and the 20th Transport Squadron was moved lock, stock and barrel to Howard Field (although the actual order read Fort Kobbe, which is adjacent to Howard Field, and where co-scribe Hagedorn was stationed in 1966–69).

It was only the second time that any unit had moved by motor convoy across the isthmus, and, as a measure of the difficulties of travel in the Canal Zone at the time, it took between 0700 and 1700 hours to make the 53-mile journey. The unit suffered its first wartime accident on 29 March 1942 when C-49C 41-7715 was wrecked at Tejería, Veracruz, Mexico, while being flown by Charles W. Larson, although it was repaired and later returned to CONUS in May 1943.

The unit was continuously reinforced as the early wartime emergency left the defenders of the canal, all too aware of what had happened in Hawaii and the Philippines, with the overwhelming belief that they would certainly be next on the Japanese avalanche of conquests. In fact, as on the west of coast of the US, there were constant alerts and warnings, as well as a plethora of false sightings, and what soon became the Sixth Air Force occupied its pre-planned auxiliary network of airfields throughout Panama, Central America and the Antilles, and as far west as the remote Galapagos. These deployments placed an enormous strain on the 20th Transport Squadron, which was, accordingly, reinforced yet again in April with the arrival of ten brand-new C-47s, bringing unit strength to eighteen aircraft.

Air transport soon became critical to the Sixth Air Force that, geographically, had responsibility for an enormous area, including virtually everything from the border between Guatemala and Mexico south to Tierra del Fuego, as far east as the Greater and Lesser Antilles, and west to the Galapagos. Besides its fleet of mixed Douglas twins, in order to support this vast network of stations, the unit was among the first USAAF units to acquire Consolidated OA-10 flying boats, Fairchild UC-61s (to support the jungle Air Warning Service, or AWS radar and ground observer stations), Stinson L-1s, and the solitary examples of the USAAF Hamilton UC-89, Junkers C-79, Stinson UC-91, and the huge XB-15 (later XC-105). These were, during the course of 1943, augmented even further by at least one venerable North American BC-1 (AC38-361), at least one Piper L-4C (42-79557), Luscombe UC-90A (42-79549), Stinson UC-81, Beech UC-43A, a rare Douglas C-68 and several Beech UC-45Fs. The squadron thus flew one of the most cosmopolitan assorts of aircraft types of any unit of the war years, but was, in the process, equipped with an assortment that could fulfill nearly every one of its very diverse mission requirements. The assignment of these unusual, non-standard aircraft was a measure of how hard-pressed the unit was by late 1942, virtually the entire civil register of Panamanian aircraft having been purchased – not 'impressed' as has so often been reported – in August 1942. Indeed, the Sixth Air Force Chief of Staff at the time, Brigadier General H.A. Johnson, was so disturbed by the proposed assignment of yet another oddball aircraft, a former LATI Savoia-Marchetti S.M.76, to the unit, which he judged would only add even further to the demands already being placed on the ground crews, that he sent a memo to the Commanding General, Caribbean Defence Command (CDC) in which he did not mince words. He said, 'the assignment of the Savoia-Marchetti airplane to this command would, in our opinion, aggravate an already unsatisfactory maintenance problem with reference to operating aircraft of foreign manufacture and aircraft manufactured according to commercial specifications. In this connection, it is desired to point out that we now have assigned a Junkers [the one-and-only C-79], Stinson Tri-Motor (C-91), Stinson Reliant (C-81), Hamilton (UC-89), Beechcraft (UC-43A), Cubs, Taylorcraft, Luscombes etc.'

Fortunately for all concerned, the S.M.76 was lost at Jaqué, Republic of Panama, when being ferried from the Panagra overhaul facility at Lima, Peru, or the unit would certainly have been burdened with yet another maintenance nightmare at a very poor juncture, with but only limited actual transport value.[5]

On 10 July 1942, the squadron was formally redesignated as the 20th Troop Carrier Squadron and was subordinated to the Sixth Air Force Base Command, which later became the Sixth Air Force Service Command. The unit was subsequently redesignated once more during the war, becoming the 20th Troop Carrier Squadron (Special) on 12 November 1943 – so far as can be determined, the only wartime USAAF transport unit to gain this suffix.[6]

By early 1943, the now highly prized and extremely competent unit was commanded by Capt. Raynold A. Berg and he counted thirty-six officers and 234 NCOs and enlisted ranks in his widely dispersed unit. Usually flying lonely, one-aircraft, long-distance flights far and wide without any possibility of rescue over vast stretches of tropical, shark-infested waters or trackless jungle, the unit conducted its first 'all-hands' mission on 17 May 1943, when the entire unit was ordered to Borinquen Field, Puerto Rico, to ferry an entire infantry regiment from there to Morrison Field, Florida, which the unit completed without incident on 3 June.

On 1 May 1943, suffered its first fatal casualty when a unit C-49D 41-7717 being flown out of Waller Field, Trinidad, by Lt Richard F. Sturges and his co-pilot, Lt Holland, with a crew of two others, crashed sometime between 2100 and 2200 hours as she was returning from Puerto Rico after dark into mountains north of Waller Field. Then in June 1943, Flight 'A', serial number unconfirmed, piloted by 1Lt J.M. Mulvehill departed Howard Field and crashed at 0615, only fifteen minutes after take-off, just north of Howard, killing all five on board. This was followed by the alarming loss of a unit C-47A, 42-23596, on 10 July without a trace while on a flight between Waller Field and Atkinson Field, British Guiana. Some sources, for some reason, give this loss as having occurred on 8 July. Speculation at the time was that the crew had spotted a submarine in the twilight, dropped down to investigate, and were shot down by anti-aircraft fire – a tactic then coming into vogue with the hard-pressed Kriegsmarine.

Besides its mundane, day-to-day direct support to the far-flung Caribbean Defence Command stations, Air Warning Service (Radar) stations and the like, the unit also occasionally got to 'show the colours', and in the process undoubtedly impressed upon Latin American observers the value of such a dedicated air transport unit. On 1 September 1943, the unit sent two C-47As to Santiago, Chile, where they boarded thirty-five Chilean Army, Air Force and Cadet officers to the Canal Zone to attend a special CDC course.

The squadron enjoyed the attentions of a very special guest indeed for dinner in their mess hall on 26 March 1944, when none other than the First Lady, Eleanor Roosevelt, dined with all ranks.

Labeled as the 20th Troop Carrier Squadron (Special) between 1 March and 31 December 1944, the unit was unusual within the USAAF as operating, in addition to its heterogeneous landplanes, several OA-10 Catalina flying boats, which were utilised to fly highly classified missions to San José Island in the Bay of Panama, known as the 'San Jose Project'. This classified project is believed to have involved the testing and storage of chemical weapons.

The 20th was tasked with a most unusual and seldom-reported mission during the first two weeks of May 1944 when a mix of five new C-47s, four C-49s and a single C-39 (AC38-534, which went along to carry spares, plus a C-47 loaned to the organisation from an unknown operator) – some camouflaged and some not – flew to distant La Paz, Bolivia, each aircraft carrying two military policemen armed with Thompson .45 calibre submachine guns, with 300 extra rounds, while each crew member was issued a .45 calibre pistol.

Rather ominously, no parachutes were to be carried aboard the aircraft whatsoever, which caused no small measure of anxiety, and all equipment regarded as 'non-essential' was stripped from the aircraft. As if this were not enough, when the crews arrived at their aircraft, they saw that non-transparent covers had been placed over all of the fuselage windows of each aircraft. For the purposes of the 'Manoeuvres', the aircraft were arbitrarily divided into three flights,

'A' Flight led by Maj. Raynold A. Berg (comprising C-47s 41-7770, C-47A 42-93102, and C-47 41-7761), the Squadron Commander, 'B' Flight led by Maj. Charles W. Larson (with C-47 41-7782, C-47A 42-23597 and C-47 41-7785) and 'C' Flight led by Capt. Frederick A. Sanders (with C-49Cs 41-7715 and 41-7721, and C-49Ds 41-7719 and 41-7720). Each of the eleven aircraft was to carry sufficient Field Rations to feed eighteen people for four days. This nearly total effort was referred to only as 'Secret manoeuvres' at the time.

The crews were issued very specific orders, and, because of the unusual nature of this mission, they are quoted here at length. They were told that, 'this manoeuvre will not, repeat not be discussed with any other person. Instructions as to destination will be furnished you verbally by the Commanding General, Sixth Air Force prior to departure. Flight Commanders may be given the itinerary, next destination only, immediately before take-off from home stations, but they will be cautioned not to inform any other members of the flight as to destinations. Flight Leaders will inform the pilots and co-pilots of their next destination only immediately prior to time set for take-off. All personnel assigned to accompany these planes will be directed prior to departure that they are not to discuss with anyone their flight plans, next destination, or to give any information as to possible routes or next landing places, except the Flight Element Leaders authorised to arrange for clearances with the flight control section of airports in accordance with normal procedures. Radio silence will be observed during flights, except the necessary communications by the Flight Leaders with airdromes and for emergency communication between aircraft in flight which should be by voice if possible.'

In fact, the 'Manoeuvres' got off to a shaky start and did not finally launch until 0655 hours on 16 May, the initial destination given as Talara, Peru, where there was a very well-established USAAF base, and then on to Arequipa the next day. To the astonishment of all, the aircraft were refuelled at Arequipa with pumps carried by the C-39. C-49C 41-7715 nosed up while taxiing at Arequipa and had to be left behind for repairs, although it soon returned to service. Shortly after arrival at the high-altitude El Alto field at La Paz around 0845 on 18 May, following the midway refuelling stop at Arequipa, Peru, to the surprise of most of the crews and under very strict security constraints, they were loaded in almost complete silence with German, Japanese and Italian men, women and children who had been interned by the Bolivian authorities. These were then transported back to Panama, where some of them were confined for the duration of the war in internment camps while others were moved on to the US. This was all completed very efficiently and quickly and, by 0930, after not quite forty-five minutes on the ground, they departed. To the surprise of the twenty-two officers involved, all were presented, on the spot, with honorary Fuerza Aérea Boliviana (FAB, or Bolivian Air Force) wings.[7]

The armada arrived back at Albrook Field, after an overnight in Peru, where the crews were ordered to remain aboard their aircraft while their mysterious passengers were hastily disembarked. They had stopped for the night at Talara on the return flight, however, where the 'passengers' were all herded into a building inside a barbed-wire fence, complete with searchlights and guards. Apparently, General 'Hap' Arnold himself was briefed in detail on the preparations for this highly sensitive mission, and noted with concern that the unit would be obliged to use such a mix of equipment to execute it. Possibly as a direct result, he issued an order on 7 June, directing that the last of the 20th TCS's C-39s (AC38-534), one C-49 (41-7689) and C-49B (41-7692), two C-49Cs (41-7715 and 41-7720) and three C-49Ds (41-7716, 41-7719 and 41-7721) be replaced at the earliest possible date by brand-new, standard C-47s.

Struggling to bring its invaluable and solitary transport unit 'into the fold' to ease manning and supply issues, the War Department issued instructions on 4 July 1944 that the 20th Troop Carrier Squadron was to be reorganised 'at the earliest practicable date' to some semblance of 'normal' Table of Organisation and Equipment (TO&E) standard, and settle on an authorised strength of forty-one officers, one warrant officer and 217 NCOs and enlisted ranks. Not long afterwards, on 1 December, the distant detachments at Waller Field, Trinidad (BWI), and Borinquen Field, Puerto Rico, were finally recalled. By the end of that month, the unit had been relieved from assignment to the Sixth Air Force Service Command and was subordinated to the PAD. It had a total of sixteen aircraft on strength, consisting of two C-47s, nine C-47As, and single examples of the C-47B, UC-45F, UC-61, L-1, and OA-10. One final wartime administrative change occurred 5 May 1945, when the unit was subordinated directly to Headquarters, Sixth Air Force, an oblique gesture of official respect for the value of this extremely versatile and supremely flexible unit. By the end of June, the unit had completely re-equipped with brand-new Curtiss C-46As, much to the disgust of the crews.

Perhaps most significant to the story of the DC-3 and C-47 in Latin American military service, the unit served to provide unique On the Job Training (OJT) to twenty-six Bolivian ground crews and maintainers, who started to arrive at Albrook for this first-of-its-kind tuition in Latin America on 7 February 1945, followed by sixteen FAB pilots, who trained intensively with the 20th TCS later on. Indeed, one of the Lend-Lease Bolivian C-47As was actually attached to the 20th TCS to help facilitate this training.

While the training programme for the Bolivians was under way, a 20th TCS C-47 flew to Guatemala City on 26 April 1945, to survey the possibility of using the aircraft in fighting a forest fire in the Petén region, the very first such notion recorded in Latin American aviation history.

This C-33, clearly on the apron at Albrook Field, Canal Zone, bears an unidentified insignia on her starboard fuselage. It has been speculated that this was either an unofficial unit insignia of the 15th or 16th Air Base Squadron, but another source associates it with Randolph Field, Texas. *Maj. Jesse W. Miller*

As of 31 March 1945, Sixth Air Force all but concluded the frantic supply and resupply missions that had dominated late 1941, 1942, 1943 and most of 1944. As a direct result, the command was at last able to distribute some of the C-47 largesse that it had recently enjoyed to ease the strain on the 20th TCS and provide local commands with transport capability they had never enjoyed. This left the 20th TCS with a total of eight C-47As (four at Albrook, one at Miami, one detached to the Galapagos Islands and two, for some reason, at Santiago, Chile) and one C-47B at Albrook. Aircraft that had formerly been with the 20th TCS were distributed and assigned as follows:

- Headquarters and Headquarters, XXVIth Fighter Command, based at Albrook Field, CZ, had a single C-47, in addition to other administrative aircraft.

- The 350th Base Headquarters and Airbase Squadron at Río Hato Airbase, Republic of Panama, had one C-47, in addition to other administrative aircraft.

- The 538th Base Headquarters and Airbase Squadron, Albrook Field, CZ, had a C-47.

- The veteran 16th Base Headquarters and Airbase Squadron, where it had all started in 1940, had two C-47As at Albrook Field, CZ, serving alongside single examples of the North American B-25D, Beech UC-45, UC-45F and North American RO-47A (which was detached to Rey Island).

- Headquarters and Headquarters Squadron, Sixth Air Force, also at Albrook, had a C-47A as well as a rare Luscombe UC-90, a North American RO-47A and two Beech UC-45Fs, while a Douglas C-49B was detached, for some reason, to Arequipa, Peru.

- The 20th Troop Carrier Squadron itself possessed eight C-47As and one new C-47B.

- The Caribbean Defence Command-Panama Canal Department (CDC-PCD) Flight Section at Albrook Field had one veteran Douglas C-49, a Beech UC-45F, the legendary Boeing RB-17D Swoose, and a Douglas UC-67 – the solitary example in the command.

By the end of June 1945, the C-39s, C-49s and C-47s that had served so well with the 20th TCS had been dispersed to other operating organisations or returned to the CONUS. In spite of this, Sixth Air Force at long last, in response to nearly constant pleas throughout the course of the war, received three brand-new C-47As. One of these was assigned to the Army Airways Communication System, replacing a stripped-down North American B-25D, which was poorly suited to the tasks being placed upon it. The other two were assigned to the Tropical Weather School, a luxury that could surely not have been afforded earlier, and a clear demonstration that the war had truly been won.

As the war mercifully came to an end, new aircraft 'in the pipeline' for Sixth Air Force continued to arrive. These included a brand-new C-47B, due to be completed (for some reason) at Chico, California, on 10 September 1945 under Assignment Project #426, which, oddly, was designated for assignment to the Airport Engineering Mission to Chile. Another brand-new C-47B, on Project #425, was also received in September for direct assignment to the US Military Air Attaché in La Paz, Bolivia – the first known such specific assignment of many to follow.

A few words regarding the manner in which we have elected to present either known Unit Numbers or Serials (actually called Radio Call Numbers as of the late war years and immediate post-war period) in the first column. These are noted based on photographic evidence or as noted in either Sixth Air Force Assignment Orders or unit dispatch documents, or a mix of these sources. While purists may challenge some of these as excessively pedantic, it is our sincere hope that they will prove helpful to researchers unfamiliar with the vagaries of the USAAF serial system of the period that, to the casual observer, can prove confusing in the extreme. While we do not have photographic evidence to support our presentations for every aircraft, a sufficient number have been amassed or examined to establish general standards. For example, images have been located showing C-47B-1-DK 43-48296 wearing both '348296' and, in other instances, '3-48296' on her vertical fin, which appears to support the notion that even units in the field at numbered air force level were having difficulty understanding exactly how they should be painted on!

Finally, a few words regarding gender.

Throughout the more than fifty years that co-author Hagedorn has been conducting research into the Sixth Air Force, a very large number of in-person interviews were conducted with veterans of the war there. Without a single exception, he noted, without any prompting whatsoever, that all of them, to a man, invariably referred to the aircraft they served aboard as having been a member of the female gender, usually using the word 'her', but occasionally less endearing terms!

That the Douglas twins were, and indeed remain, ladies in practically every sense, we have herein perpetuated the notion, which of late has become so grossly perverted. They were not 'it' or 'them'. They were, invariably, and often with profound fondness, 'she' and 'her'.

Only four C-39s were assigned to the 20th Transport Squadron, as the unit was known when AC38-510 was photographed arriving at Albrook Field, Canal Zone, in April 1941. Eventually camouflaged in the distinctive scheme shown on accompanying C-49 images, AC38-510 became unit No. 1 (second use) and was initially detached to France Field on the Atlantic side. She deployed to Trinidad four days before Pearl Harbor and remained in the Antilles until 4 April 1944, when she was wrecked at Vernam Field, Jamaica. *Fred Young, USAFSO*

USAAC AND USAAF 1939–45

Unit Number or Serial as Worn	Full US Serial	Type as Built	MSN	Assigned and Notes
1	AC36-72	C-33	1505	Douglas design DC-2-145. Arrived Albrook Fld 11 Jun 40. Assigned to 15th Airbase Squadron. To 20th Transport Squadron 1 Feb 41 as Unit Number '1'. Returned to CONUS 9 May 41.
–	AC36-78	C-33	1511	Douglas design DC-2-145. Arrived France Fld 17 Jun 40. Assigned to 16th Airbase Squadron. Lost in forced landing Puntarenas, Costa Rica, 7 Dec 40 (although, for some reason, 13 Jan 41 has also been repeatedly cited) while being flown by Lt Harold A. Bartron.
4	AC38-504	C-39	2061	Douglas design DC-2-243. Arrived France Fld 21 Apr 41. 20th Transport Squadron, Unit Number '4'. To Albrook Fld, CZ. To Howard Fld, CZ, by May 42. PAD completed work on this aircraft Aug 42. To Borinquen Fld, Puerto Rico, 8 Oct 42. To Antilles Air Command (AAC) Troop Carrier Detachment, Borinquen Fld, PR, by 31 Dec 43. Condemned PRAD 1 Apr 44 and broken up.
1	AC38-510	C-39	2067	Douglas design DC-2-243. Arrived France Fld Apr 41. 20th Transport Squadron, Unit Number '1' (second use). To Detachment, Waller Fld, Trinidad, 3 Dec 41. Returned to Howard Fld, CZ, 26 Mar 42. To Detachment, Waller Fld, Trinidad, 31 May 42. PAD completed work on this aircraft Aug 42. To Howard Fld, CZ, 23 Nov 42. To Detachment, Waller Fld, Trinidad, 1 Feb 43. Borinquen Fld, PR, 30 Nov 43. Accident 4 Apr 44 at Vernam Fld, Jamaica, while being flown by David A. West. Condemned PRAD 2 May 44 and broken up.
2	AC38-524	C-39	2081	Douglas design DC-2-243. Arrived France Fld 25 Oct 40. HHS, Panama Canal Department Air Force. 20th Transport Squadron, Unit Number '2'. To Losey Fld, PR, 12 Feb 41. To Waller Fld, Trinidad, Jan 42. To Losey Fld, PR, by May 42. Crashed at approximately 0330hrsZ 15 miles north-west of Coamo, PR, while being flown by Capt. Francis H. Durant, hit a mountain top. Crew and all on board perished. However, an accident website states that this aircraft was lost 15 Mar 44 at Pito, Republic of Panama, while based at APO825, while being flown by Jack H. Eichler. The former report is believed accurate. Not finally condemned and surveyed, however, until 4 Jan 44 for some reason, although 7 Apr 44 is also cited!
3	AC38-534	C-39	2091	Douglas design DC-2-243. Arrived France Fld 21 Jul 41. 20th Transport Squadron, Unit Number '3'. To Detachment, Waller Field, Trinidad, 21 Dec 41 and suffered an accident there 6 Apr 42 while being flown by 1Lt Edward D. Bacci when his port brake locked up but was repaired. Returned to Howard Fld, CZ, 12 Apr 43. Wrecked there. Repaired after extensive work at PAD Nov 43. Returned to Canal Zone 4 Dec 43. Returned to CONUS (reported available) Jun 44 but not actually flown out until 24 Aug 44. To Mexico 24 Aug 44 as XA-DOS, CMA.
7689	41-7689	C-49	3274	Built as DC-3-384 for TWA but not delivered. To 20th Transport Squadron, Albrook Fld, CZ, 27 Mar 41. General Andrews' aircraft, operated for him by the 20th but actually assigned to HHS, Panama Canal Department Air Force, and for other duties as assigned. Survived the war and returned to the CONUS 10 Aug 45.

Serial AC41-7716, built as a DC-3-201G for Eastern, became a C-49D and joined the 20th Transport Squadron as part of the pre-war build-up on 17 October 1941. Unit No. 6, she became the personal aircraft of General House, but spent much of the war in Puerto Rico and the Antilles, returning to the CONUS in late August 1944 from Losey Field. *Woodson Van Osdol*

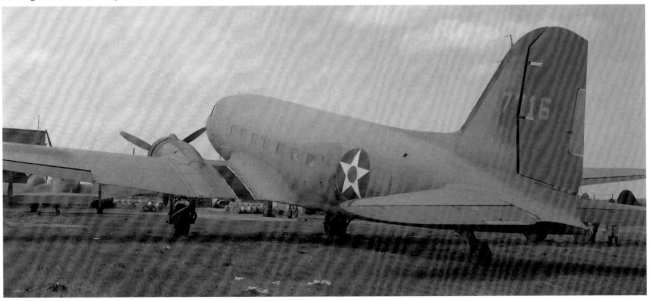

7692	41-7692	C-49B	4095	Built as DC-3-201F as NC-28387 for Eastern A/L but not delivered. To DC-3-387 and C-49B. To 20th Transport Squadron, Albrook Fld, CZ, 29 Nov 41. Personal aircraft of General Johnson, operated for him and other duties by 20th. Undercarriage collapsed on take-off from San Jose AAB, Guatemala, 20 Jan 42 while being flown by Dudley D. Hale but, after considerable exertions, it was recovered and repaired. Accident 17 Aug 44 somewhere in the Canal Zone, probably at Albrook Fld, while parked. Survived the war and returned to the US 11 Mar 45 but Air-Britain reported her in Ecuador as of 31 Mar 45. If so, this was probably at the USAAF base at Salinas, Ecuador.
7697	41-7697	C-50	4119	Built as DC-3-277D for American but not delivered. Reported to Fifth Air Force, Australia, 20 Oct 42 but also reported (in error) as a C-49B and experiencing an accident 5 miles east of Vernam Field, Jamaica, 3 Sep 45 while being flown by H. A. Hindert. This would make it the last-known C-49 or C-50 in the Caribbean and Sixth Air Force, but an error in the serial number cannot be discounted.
7700	41-7700	C-50	4122	Built as a DC-3-277D NC-33662 for American and then converted to a DC-3-396, this aircraft was noted temporarily assigned to Mexico City, Mexico as of 27 Nov 42 but had returned to the US by 1 Jan 43. The reason for this unusual assignment is unknown.
17715/5	41-7715	C-49C	4814	Built as a DC-3-357A for Delta but not delivered. To 20th Transport Squadron, Howard Fld, CZ, 9 Sep 41 as Unit Number '5'. Wrecked at Tejeria, Veracruz, Mexico, 29 Mar 42 while being flown by Charles W. Larson but repaired. Accident 23 Jul 44 at Rey Island, Republic of Panama, while being flown by Gerald Linscheid. Surveyed in the Canal Zone (but also reported as Vera Cruz, PR, which is highly questionable) 27 Jul 44. Survived to become NC-45396 with PAA in 1945.
7716/6	41-7716	C-49D	4141	Built as a DC-3-201G as NC-33635 for Eastern but not delivered. To 20th Transport Squadron 17 Oct 41 Unit Number '6'. General House's aircraft, operated for him by the 20th and for other duties as assigned. To Borinquen Fld, PR, 31 May 42. Returned to CONUS 29 Aug 44 from Losey Fld, PR.
17717/7	41-7717	C-49D	4142	Built as a DC-3-201G as NC-33636 for Eastern but not delivered. To 20th Transport Squadron, Howard Fld, CZ, 7 Oct 41 as Unit Number '7'. Wrecked at Pacora Auxiliary Aerodrome, Republic of Panama, 27 May 42, while being flown by 1Lt Kenneth Marts while formation flying with another aircraft. Repaired. Another accident 7 Jun 42 at Managua, Nicaragua, while being flown by Charles Montgomery. Yet another accident 3 Aug 42 at Naranjo Field, Costa Rica, apparently involving 41-7718 (q.v.) while being flown by Richard F. Sturges. Accident just after take-off from Howard Fld, CZ, in Jan 43 while being flown by 1Lt J.M. Mulvehill, all five on board fatal. The aircraft involved in this accident has also been incorrectly cited as having been 41-7718. However, 41-7717 also reported as assigned to Flight 'B' of the 20th TCS and lost in an accident 1 May 43 at Waller Fld, Trinidad, while being flown by Richard F. Sturges. Air-Britain gives the aircraft involved in this accident as 41-7718 (q.v. next) however. Condemned and surveyed at the PAD 5 Feb 43.
17718/8	41-7718	C-49D	4143	Built as a DC-3-201G as NC-33637 for Eastern but not delivered. To 20th Transport Squadron, Howard Fld, CZ, 7 Oct 41 as Unit Number '8'. Accident 3 Aug 42 at Naranjo Field, Costa Rica, while being flown by Frederick A. Sanders. Condemned and surveyed at PAD 11 May 43.
7719/9	41-7719	C-49D	4144	Built as a DC-3-201G as NC-33638 for Eastern but not delivered. To 20th Transport Squadron, Howard Fld, CZ, 7 Oct 41 as Unit Number '9'. Assigned to Salinas AAB, Ecuador, 31 May 42. To PAD by 8 Jul 42. Accident 19 Nov 42 at Albrook Fld, CZ, while being flown by Richard T. Pierce. Repaired by PAD by the end of Dec 42. Returned to CONUS 14 Dec 43 but was back in Panama by 5 Jan 44 and next at Morrison Field, Florida, by 1 Sep 44.
7720/10	41-7720	C-49D	4145	Built as a DC-3-201G as NC-33639 for Eastern but not delivered. To 20th Transport Squadron, Albrook Fld, CZ, 22 Oct 41 as Unit Number '10' and attached to Headquarters, Sixth Air Force. Accident 23 Oct 43 at Rey Island, Republic of Panama, while being flown by Lewis R. Rule. Recovered and repaired after enormous exertions. Returned to CONUS 3 Jun 43 but was back in Panama by 15 Jul 43. To Morrison Field, Florida, by 31 Aug 44.
17721/11	41-7721	C-49C	4815	Built as a DC-3-3567A as NC-28347 for Delta but not delivered. To 20th Transport Squadron, Albrook Fld, CZ, 12 Oct 41, Unit Number '11'. General Gilkeson's aircraft operated for him by the 20th and for other duties as assigned. Returned to CONUS 23 May 43.
7731	41-7731	C-47-DL	4210	Borinquen Fld, PR, 30 Mar 42. To Destination Code MAGPIE (Bombay, India) 13 Apr 42 and on to Tenth Air Force, CBI.
7761/14	41-7761	C-47-DL	4248	Howard Fld, CZ, 25 Mar 42, 20th Troop Carrier Squadron, Unit Number '14'. Salinas AAB, Ecuador, 10 Sep 42. Returned to Howard Fld 30 Sep 42. Returned to Salinas AAB, Ecuador, 9 Oct 42. PAD completed some form of work on this aircraft Apr 43 and again in Feb 44. Assigned to HHS, XXVIth Fighter Command, Albrook Fld, CZ, 16 Mar 45. Survived the war and salvaged in the Canal Zone 17 Aug 46.
7762/12	41-7762	C-47-DL	4249	Howard Fld, CZ, 7 Apr 42, 20th Troop Carrier Squadron, Unit Number '12'. To Losey Fld, PR, 8 Jun 42. PAD completed some form of work on this aircraft Dec 43. Accident 19 Jan 44 at Beane Fld, St Lucia, home based at Borinquen Fld, PR, at the time, 2Lt Malcolm E. Starkloff, pilot.

7763	41-7763	C-47-DL	4250	Howard Fld, CZ, 8 Apr 42, 20th Troop Carrier Squadron. To Detachment, Waller Fld, Trinidad, 31 May 42. Returned to Howard Fld, CZ, 3 Feb 43. Back to Waller Fld, Trinidad, 31 Jul 43. Returned to the CONUS 29 May 43. This aircraft has also been reported repeatedly as having been assigned to the 29th Transport Squadron, Patterson Fld, OH, but USAFSO records clearly show that it was with the Sixth Air Force unit until returned to the CONUS in May 43.
7764	41-7764	C-47-DL	4251	Howard Fld, CZ, 9 Apr 42, 20th Troop Carrier Squadron. To Losey Fld, PR, 5 May 42 but apparently to Detachment, Waller Fld, Trinidad, the same day. Wrecked 30 May 42 north-west coast of Jamaica, 2Lt James Roberts commanding (but see 41-7784).
7765	41-7765	C-47-DL	4252	Howard Fld, CZ, 14 Apr 42, 20th Troop Carrier Squadron. To Detachment, Waller Fld, Trinidad, 21 May 42. Returned to Howard Fld, CZ, 12 Apr 43. Back to Trinidad 31 Jul 43. Returned to CONUS, date uncertain.
7770/13	41-7770	C-47-DL	4257	Howard Fld, CZ, 7 Apr 42, 20th Troop Carrier Squadron, Unit Number '13'. Accident 19 Aug 42 at San Jose, Costa Rica (although cited as 'CZ' in some sources), while being flown by 2Lt Elbert C. Jenkins. Repaired by PAD the same month. Back to PAD Mar 43 for IRAN, work completed May 43. She was reassigned from 16th Airbase Squadron (APO 825) back to the 20th TCS 10 Jan 45. Written off at La Sabana Field, San Jose, Costa Rica, 20 or 26 Apr 46, home based at Rio Hato Aerodrome, Republic of Panama, at the time.
7775	41-7775	C-47-DL	4262	Assigned to the Caribbean Wing, Air Transport Command 1 May 43, operated for PAA by American A/L. Not Sixth Air Force asset. Returned to CONUS 12 Apr 45. RFC 7 Oct 45 to NC-54327. To Haitian Air Corps by 1954.
7778	41-7778	C-47-DL	4265	Assigned to the Caribbean Wing, Air Transport Command 1 May 43. To African/Middle East Wing 15 Dec 43. Not Sixth Air Force asset.
7782/15	41-7782	C-47-DL	4269	Howard Fld, CZ, 22 Apr 42, 20th Troop Carrier Squadron, Unit Number '15' and immediately to Detachment, Waller Fld, Trinidad. PAD completed some form of work on this aircraft Apr 43 and again in Jul 43. Accident 22 Sep 43 at APO 839 (La Aurora Field, Guatemala City, Guatemala), home based at APO 832 (Howard Fld, CZ) at the time, 2Lt D.K. Mumma. Repaired. Survived the war to FLC 15 Jul 47. To Avensa as YV-C-AVL.
7783/16	41-7783	C-47-DL	4270	Howard Fld, CZ, 22 Apr 42, 20th Troop Carrier Squadron, Unit Number '16' and immediately to Detachment, Waller Fld, Trinidad. Reported condemned and salvaged 4 Sep 46 but also reported to Puerto Rico Air Transport as NC-66001.
7784/17	41-7784	C-47-DL	4271	Howard Fld, CZ, 22 Apr 42, 20th Troop Carrier Squadron, Unit Number '17' and immediately to Detachment, Losey Fld, PR, and crashed 30 May 42 1 mile west of Fish River on the north-west coast of Jamaica, pilot in command also cited as 2Lt James Roberts (but also see 41-7764).
7785/18	41-7785	C-47-DL	4272	Howard Fld, CZ, 22 Apr 42, 20th Troop Carrier Squadron, Unit Number '18'. PAD completed some form of work on this aircraft Apr 43. To Losey Fld, PR, 2 Nov 44. Sold via FLC to Transair, Inc. as NC-66112.

To the layman, C-49s were visually indistinguishable from C-47s. AC41-7717 behind the jeep is a C-49D, however, at Howard Field, and is marked in the olive drab over light grey she arrived in, while a sister aircraft, further down the apron, wears the distinctive Sixth Air Force camouflage. This aircraft was damaged in a mid-air collision at Pacora, Panama, on 27 May 1942 while being flown by (then) 1Lt Kenneth E. Marts but was repaired by the PAD. It was wrecked again after take-off from Howard in January 1943 with 1Lt J.M. Mulvehile at the controls, all five on board being killed. The relaxed 20th Transport Squadron officers in the jeep are West and Van Osdol.
Col Kenneth E. Marts

Proof-positive that the former airliners were in fact used as paratroop transports, 20th Troop Carrier Squadron C-49A 41-7718 is seen at Howard Field, CZ, preparing to load officers and men of the 501st Parachute Infantry, part of the so-called Panama Mobile Force, garrisoned at neighbouring Fort Kobbe, CZ, in 1942. This aircraft was lost with Flight 'B' of the unit on 1 May 1943 when she crashed into mountains north of Waller Field, Trinidad, with Lts Sturges and Holland at the controls.
Col Kenneth E. Marts

7834	41-7834	C-47-DL	4333	Assigned to 'Panama' 6 Jun 43. Returned to CONUS 24 Aug 43. This aircraft is known to have been assigned for use by PAA by 14 May 42 and is not shown on any Sixth Air Force documents, and thus must be regarded as probably having been operated on high-priority flights on the former PAA/Panagra routes based out of Albrook Field, CZ.
7839	41-7839	C-47-DL	4338	Assigned to 'Panama' 27 Jan 44 and not reported again until 23 Jan 45 at San Bernardino, California. Oddly, no Sixth Air Force documents note this aircraft.
7860	41-7860	C-47-DL	4359	Assigned to 'Panama' 1 May 43. Returned to CONUS 20 Dec 43. This aircraft is known to have been assigned for use by Braniff from 11 Sep 42 and is not shown on any Sixth Air Force documents, and thus must be regarded as probably having been operated on high-priority flights on former Braniff routes based out of Albrook Field, CZ.
31967	43-1967	C-49J	4992	Built as a DC-3-454 as NC-14282 for American but not delivered. Known assigned to Sixth Air Force 10 Oct 43 and assumed to 20th Troop Carrier Squadron (Sp). Returned to CONUS 30 Jan 44.
31968	43-1968	C-49J	4997	Built as a DC-3-454 for the Netherlands East Indies Army but not delivered. Known to Sixth Air Force 11 Jan 44 but returned to CONUS very quickly on 13 Jan 44.
31969	43-1969	C-49J	4993	Built as a DC-3-454 as NC-34970 for Braniff but not delivered. Known to Sixth Air Force 12 Oct 43. Returned to CONUS 28 Feb 44.
31978	43-1978	C-49J	6318	Built as a DC-3-454 for American but not delivered. Known to Sixth Air Force 12 Oct 43. Returned to CONUS 22 Feb 44.
31982	43-1982	C-49J	5000	Built as a DC-3-454 for the Netherlands East Indies Army but not delivered. Known to Sixth Air Force 10 Dec 43 but returned to CONUS 4 Jan 44.
31988	43-1988	C-49J	6343	Built as a DC-3-454 as NC-30046 for Delta but not delivered. Known to Sixth Air Force 13 Oct 43. Returned to CONUS 21 Jan 44.
31998/998	43-1998	C-49K	4985	Built as a DC-3-455 as NC-34976 for TWA but not delivered. Known to Sixth Air Force 20 Nov 43 but returned to the CONUS by 16 Dec 43. Passed to RFC 24 Jan 45 and to NC-19134.
32002	43-2002	C-49K	6327	Built as a DC-3-455 as NC-34980 for TWA. Known to Sixth Air Force but apparently diverted to the South Atlantic Wing of Air transport Command. To CONUS 31 Aug 44.
32010	43-2010	C-49K	6335	Built as a DC-3-455 as NC-30033 for Eastern. Known to Sixth Air Force 10 Oct 43 but returned to CONUS 28 Feb 44.
32016	43-2016	C-49K	6340	Built as a DC-3-455 as NC-30038 for Eastern but not delivered. Known to Sixth Air Force 17 Oct 43. Returned to CONUS 28 Feb 44.
'1-13475'	'41-13475'	C-47		A Sixth Air Force document shows this as a C-47 assigned to the 20th Troop Carrier Squadron *c*.21 May 44. However, this is a Curtiss P-40C serial number!
2-23471	42-23471	C-47A-5-DL	9333	Assigned to Sixth Air Force, Trinidad (Waller Field) 31 Dec 45. To Borinquen Field, PR, 5 Jul 46. To Albrook Field, CZ, 30 Apr 47. Returned to 48th Service Group, Borinquen Field, PR, 1 Jan 48. Assigned to the 6th Fighter Wing, Howard Field, CZ, 20 Feb 48, the 582nd Service Group 5 May 48 and the 5605th Airbase Group 28 Jul 48. To the 5702nd Foreign Mission Squadron, Albrook AFB, CZ, 27 Sep 48, the 5701st Foreign Mission Group 23 Mar 49 and the 5700th Airbase Group 1 May 49. Returned to CONUS 17 Nov 49.

A rare underside view of a C-49C, in this case 41-7721 of the 20th TCS along the Pacific coast of Panama in 1942. Having arrived in Panama on 12 October 1941, she became Unit No. 11 and was for a time assigned as the personal aircraft of General Gilkeson. She returned to CONUS in June 1944. *Col Kenneth E. Marts*

A starboard view of C-49C 41-7721. Unit No. 11 was not worn on the exterior by this time, but inside the passenger door. This view also affords a look at the random-pattern upper port-wing camouflage of a sister aircraft of the 20th TCS as of 1942. *Col Kenneth E. Marts*

C-49C 41-7721 undergoing line maintenance at Howard Field, Canal Zone, the home station for the unit for most of the war. One of the distinctive, permanent barracks and administration buildings is visible in the background, the three massive hangars remembered by many veterans of Howard not having been finished yet. Sixth Air Force aircraft were authorised a flat white underside with blue splotches or 'clouds' randomly applied as well. *Col Kenneth E. Marts*

Built as a DC-3-455 for TWA, this is a rare Douglas C-49K, 43-1998/998, which was loaned to the 20th TCS, Sixth Air Force, briefly between 20 November and 16 December 1943. Pictured here at Rio Hato Auxiliary Aerodrome, Republic of Panama, she still wears her Air Transport Command insignia on her rear fuselage. *Jim Dias*

Few 20th TCS (Sp) aircraft wore any special insignia, other than the approved unit badge. Aircraft detached to Headquarters and Headquarters Squadron (HHS), Sixth Air Force, were another matter however. Here, C-49 AC41-7689, named 'Phoenix Bird 2' is pictured at New France Field, CZ, while assigned to LTG H.R. Harmon, Sixth Air Force CG from June 1944. The aircraft survived to return to the US on 10 August 1945. *Col Ole Griffith*

Above: By mid-1944, the remaining C-39s and C-49s assigned to the (by then) 20th TCS (Sp) had been scrubbed clean of their 1942–43 unique camouflage schemes. As described in the text, this is one of the four C-49s that, together with one C-39 and five brand new C-47s, flew to La Paz, Bolivia, under strict security to transport enemy aliens to internment on 18 May 1944. Here, this C-49, unique in having a top-side navigator's hatch, is being used as a mobile control tower at La Paz, with Captain Charles A. Montgomery directing the landings of the detachment. This C-49 had actually been flown to Bolivia by Colonel Homer W. Ferguson a day ahead of the rest of the task force to co-ordinate timing and arrangements with the Bolivian government and US Military Mission there. Barely noticeable on the port forward fuselage side is the 20th TCS unit insignia. *Unit History, May–October 1944, USAFHRA*

Right: Despite the huge geographic area covered, aircraft of the wartime 20th TCS (Sp) suffered only a relatively small number of accidents, but of them all, the one suffered by C-49C AC41-7715, Unit No. 10 on Rey Island, Republic of Panama, on 23 July 1944 must rate as the most memorable. Incredibly, of the crew (pilot Capt. Gerald Linscheid and co-pilot Lt Sweeney) and ten passengers aboard, there was only one fatality – S/Sgt Milton W. Hagen, although one other sustained serious injuries, three experienced major injuries and the remainder were unscathed. While landing on the short grass strip on the island, the hydraulic brakes failed, and she plummeted over an embankment at the end. Incredibly, she was somehow recovered and became NC-45396 with PAA late in 1945! *Unit History, USAFHRA*

2-23596	42-23596	C-47A-30-DL	9458	To 20th Troop Carrier Squadron, Howard Fld, CZ, 21 Jun 43 on Project 94034R, formerly with Trinidad Detachment, VI Fighter Command, Antilles Air Command. While with Flight 'B', 20th Troop Carrier Squadron, this aircraft was lost without trace on 8 Jul 43 somewhere between Waller Fld, Trinidad and Atkinson Fld, British Guiana, while being flown by 2Lt Isador Gruber.
2-23597	42-23597	C-47A-30-DL	9459	Assigned to PAD 19 Jun 43. To 20th Troop Carrier Squadron, Howard Fld, CZ, 21 Jun 43 on Project 94034R. To PAD 19 Jun 43 to 24 Jun 43. 20th Troop Carrier Squadron as late as 16 May 44 through at least 28 Mar 45, when it was assigned to 16th Airbase Squadron, Albrook Fld, CZ. To ARP Venezuela (FAV) 28 Aug 47, formally handed over 5 Dec 47.
2-24324	42-24324	C-47A-50-DL	10186	Assigned to Borinquen Field, PR, apparently upon return from service in North Africa but excluded 31 Dec 45.
2-38331	42-38331	C-49H	4107	Built as DC-3-314B for Braniff as NC-28363. To Sixth Air Force[8] between 1 and 29 May 43. Returned to CONUS 25 Jul 43.
2-65581	42-65581	C-49H	2203	Built as DC-3-277B as NC-21799 for American. To Sixth Air Force 24 Jul 43. Returned to CONUS 28 Oct 43.
2-68687	42-68687	C-49H	2179	Built as DC-3-314 as NC-21773 for Braniff. To Sixth Air Force 1 May 43. Returned to CONUS 28 Oct 43.
2-68688	42-68688	C49H C-68	2180	Built as DC-3-214 as NC-21774 for Braniff. To Sixth Air Force 1 May 43 but actually departed US at New York 18 Jun 43. Sixth Air Force records, for some reason, show this aircraft as a C-68. Returned to CONUS 1 or 18 Oct 43 according to differing sources.
2-68689	42-68689	C-49H/C-68	2181	Built as a DC-3-314 for Braniff as NC-21775. To Sixth Air Force 1 May 43. Returned to CONUS either 1 or 28 Oct 43, according to different sources. Sixth Air Force records, for some reason, show this aircraft as a C-68.
2-68839	42-68839	C-53D-DO	11766	Borinquen Field, PR, 21 Apr 44 assigned to HHS, Antilles Air Command. This was the solitary C-53 known assigned within the two Commands. To Howard Field, CZ, by 2 Jul 47. To WAA 15 Jul 47, sold to the Dominican Republic as HI-12 and may have subsequently passed to the FAD.
2-92772	42-92772	C-47A-15-DK	12610	An Eighth Air Force veteran, this aircraft was apparently redeployed to Borinquen Field, PR. It was then released to CAC 30 Apr 47 for onward sale via the FLC 26 Oct 47 but after that date, the trail goes completely cold.
2-93094	42-93094	C-47A-20-DK	12967	Known with the Caribbean Wing of ATC after delivery 8 Apr 44 and suffered an accident 14 May 44 at Waller Field, Trinidad. However, this aircraft is also linked to the Ninth Air Force in Europe. It has been suggested as having become Chilean 962.
2-93102	42-93102	C-47A-20-DK	12976	To 20th Troop Carrier Squadron, Howard Fld, CZ, 26 Apr 44 through at least 31 Dec 44. To Antilles Air Command (AAC) Apr 45, Borinquen Fld, PR. To Division of Military Intelligence, Chile, 18 Sep 46, ARP and apparently to the FACh as 952 (1), although 962 has also been suggested.
2-93281	42-93281	C-47A-20-DK	13175	To 20th Troop Carrier Squadron, Howard Fld, CZ, 18 May 44 through at least 31 Dec 44. To Chile 3 Sep 46 under ARP.
2-101002	42-101002	C-47A-75-DL	19465	Assigned to the Army Air Forces Tropical Weather Unit, Howard Fld, CZ, via the PAD 22 Jun 45, having arrived in Sixth Air Force the previous day. To Division of Military Intelligence, Chile (probably ARP), 3 Oct 46. Reports that this aircraft was assigned to Europe ATC probably refer to a deleted assignment.
3-15226	43-15226	C-47A-80-DL	19692	Assigned to the Caribbean Wing, Air Transport Command after Eighth Air Force assignment and based at Waller Field, Trinidad. Crashed 16 Aug 45 4 miles from Waller Field, Trinidad, 1Lt James J. Byrne commanding.
3-15942	43-15942	C-47A-90-DL	20408	To 20th Troop Carrier Squadron, Howard Fld, CZ, 12 Jun 44 through at least 23 Aug 45. Accident 23 Aug 45 5 miles south-west of Limatambo Field, Lima, Peru, home based at Albrook Fld, CZ, 2Lt John T. O'Boyle commanding. Apparently recovered and repaired as Reclamation was not complete until 4 Apr 48. This aircraft may have been intended for Peru under ARP.
3-16124	43-16124	C-47A-90-DL	20590	Departed the US for Natal, Brazil, 30 Jun 45 but diverted to Howard Fld, CZ. Sold via FEA to RX-76 (COPA, Panama).
3-16142	43-16142	C-47B-1-DL	20608	Sixth Air force and then to Antilles Air Command, Borinquen Fld, PR, 14 Apr 45.
3-16148	43-16148	C-47B-1-DL	20614	CAC 30 Apr 45. To USAAF Mission to Colombia Jun 45. Crashed 3 Jun 45 at Bogota, Colombia, while being flown by Ramsey Habeich, rank not given, condemned after Survey 1 Aug 45 and remains sold via FEA to a Colombian airline.
3-16153	43-16153	C-47B-1-DL	20619	Via Morrison Fld, FL, to either Albrook or Howard Fld, CZ, 30 Apr 45. To USAF Mission to Bolivia. Accident 18 Jan 48 at El Alto, La Paz, Bolivia, while being flown by John M. Turner. Sold via FLC to Bolivia as CB-36 (LAB) by 15 Apr 48.
3-16284	43-16284	C-47B-1-DL	20750	To Howard Fld, CZ, 20th Troop Carrier Squadron 1945, formerly South Atlantic Wing, Air Transport Command. Excess Inventory list, sold via FEA to YV-AZP TACA de Venezuela and via intermediate owners to Chile as FACh-960 (q.v.).
3-16285	43-16285	C-47B-1-DL	20751	To Howard Fld, CZ, after South Atlantic Wing, Air Transport Command c.30 Jul 44. To Rio Hato AB, Republic of Panama, by 1 Jan 48. France AFB, CZ, 5 Mar 48. CAC 10 Feb 49. Reclaimed and salvaged, Canal Zone 1 Mar 50.

Above: With the empennage of 20th TCS (Sp) C-49B 41-7692 visible in the background, the other stars accompanying Bob Hope on his USO tour of Panama in March 1945 stroll with their Sixth Air Force escort towards the cantonment area. From left to right, they are Vera Vagne, Francis Langford and Jerry Colona. *Raymond A. Glorioso*

Left: The never-ending tedium of far-ranging personnel and cargo flights during the war years was occasionally punctuated with moments of pure delight. Here, none other than Bob Hope deplanes at Rio Hato Aerodrome for a show from rare 20th TCS (Sp) C-49B AC41-7692 on 10 March 1944. The aircraft was nominally assigned to the use of Gen. Johnson at the time. She also survived the war and returned to the US later the same month. *Raymond A. Glorioso*

Below: This 20th TCS (Sp) C-49 was nicknamed 'Worrybird' and, unfortunately, has eluded identification, although she may be AC41-7716, a C-49D, which had been assigned to Puerto Rico in May 1942. Assigned at the time to Flight 'B' at Waller Field, Trinidad, she is being positioned on a taxiway there around April 1943. *Col Kenneth E. Marts*

3-16286	43-16286	C-47B-1-DL	20752	To Howard Fld, CZ, after South Atlantic Wing, Air Transport Command, *c*.30 Jul 44. To Rio Hato AB, Republic of Panama, 1 Jan 48. To France AFB, CZ, 27 Jan 48. To CAC 20 Mar 49. Returned to CONUS 29 Oct 49.
3-48000	43-48000	C-47A-30-DK	13816/25261	Assigned to the 20th Troop Carrier Squadron, Howard Fld, CZ, 29 Jul 44 and as late as 14 Aug 45 when a wing tip was damaged while she was being taxied on the ramp at Howard Field. To Rio Hato Auxiliary Airbase, Republic of Panama, 5th BCS, 1 Jan 48. To France AFB, CZ, 4th BCS, 9 Jan 48. To the 5621st Foreign Mission Group 26 Jul 48, 5625th Airbase Group 1 Oct 48, 5620th Airbase Squadron 25 Jul 49 and the 5700th Airbase Group, Albrook AFB, CZ, 24 Oct 49. This aircraft then became a Class 26 instructional airframe and may, in fact, been among the first aircraft assigned to what was then known as the USAF School for Latin America – later the Inter-American Air Forces Academy.
3-48001	43-48001	C-47A-30-DK	13817/25262	To Howard Fld, CZ, 20th Troop Carrier Squadron 3 Aug 44. Passed to FLC 20 Aug 47 but, instead of onward sale, Reclaimed and salvaged in the Canal Zone 4 Apr 48.
3-48002	43-48002	C-47A-30-DK	13818/25263	To Howard Fld, CZ, 7 Aug 44 probably to the 20th Troop Carrier Squadron. To Borinquen Fld, PR, 2 Oct 44. To Division of Military Intelligence, Chile, 15 Oct 47. To FAC-954.
3-48003/03	43-48003	C-47A-30-DK	13819/25264	To Howard Fld, CZ, 4 Aug 44 probably to the 20th Troop Carrier Squadron. Accident 20 Jun 45 4 miles north/north-west of Arequipa, Peru, 1Lt Glenn W. Pederson commanding. Repaired. Returned to CONUS 1946. To FAV 18 Sep 46.
3-48004	43-48004	C-47A-30-DK	13820/25265	To Howard Fld, CZ, 5 Jul 44 probably to the 20th Troop Carrier Squadron. To Borinquen Fld, PR, 2 Oct 44. To Division of Military Intelligence, Chile, 15 Oct 47 but not known to have gone to the Chilean Air Force, although FACh-952 is a possibility. Possibly a spares source? No subsequent known history.
3-48005	43-48005	C-47A-30-DK VC-47A	13821/25266	To Sixth Air Force, probably for the 20th TCS 3 Aug 44. To PAD 7 Nov 44 for 'minor adjustments', and then assigned to the personal use of General Butler the next day. Still in Sixth Air Force 31 Dec 44. To 3rd BCS, Albrook Field, CZ, 30 Apr 47. To the 5702nd Foreign Mission Squadron 26 Jul 48 and redesignated as a VC-47A 6 Dec 48. To the 5701st Foreign Mission Group 25 Feb 49 and the 5602nd Foreign Mission Group at Howard AFB, CZ, 7 Apr 49. Returned to CONUS 22 Sep 49.
3-48006	43-48006	C-47A-30-DK	13822/25267	Assigned to the 20th Troop Carrier Squadron, Howard Fld, CZ, 3 Aug 44 and as late as March 1945. To the 5th BCS, Rio Hato Auxiliary Aerodrome, Republic of Panama, 30 Apr 47. Accident 12 Aug 47 approximately 165 miles and at a position 280° from home base, Rio Hato, Republic of Panama, while being flown by Karuba Carnahan. Apparently recovered and repaired as assigned to France Field, CZ, 4th BCS 8 Jan 48. To the 5621st Foreign Mission Group 26 Jul 48 and 5625th Airbase Group 21 Mar 49. To the 5620th Airbase Squadron 25 Apr 49. Returned to CONUS 27 Oct 49.
3-48007	43-48007	C-47A-30-DK	13823/25268	To Howard Fld, CZ, probably to the 20th Troop Carrier Squadron 2 Aug 44 and as late as 31 Dec 44. To Division of Military Intelligence, Uruguay, 31 Oct 47, ARP FAU-507 where, for a time, she became the Uruguayan Presidential VIP aircraft.
3-48296	43-48296	C-47B-1-DK	14112/25557	Departed the US via Miami 3 Jul 45 for either Albrook Fld, CZ, or Howard Field. Condemned and dropped from the inventory as excess 1 Aug 45 but regained 15 Aug 47. Redesignated as a C-47D and crashed 10 Oct 47 50 miles South of Borja, Peru, while being flown by John R. Hawkins. Not clear if it was recovered, but reclamation administratively complete in the Canal Zone 9 Jun 48.
3-48301	43-48301	C-47B-1-DK C-47D	14117/25562	From PAD to 20th Troop Carrier Squadron, Howard Fld, CZ, 10 Apr 45. To the 48th SRG, Borinquen Field, PR, as a C-47D 1 Jan 48. To the 7406th Foreign Mission Squadron, Bolivia, 1 Dec 48. Remained in CAC as late as 5 Oct 49 when returned to CONUS.
3-48799	43-48799	C-47B-5-DK	14615/26060	Assigned to PAD and Sixth Air Force 7 Jul 45 and to the 3rd BCS at Albrook Field. See post-war table.

This extraordinary 1942 image at an unknown location shows not only the mix of camouflage schemes worn by a mix of at least nine 20th TCS C-47s and C-49s by this time, but the fact that the aircraft at right does in fact have some form of elaborate nose art on her. The nearest aircraft is a nearly brand-new C-47, 41-7761, while C-49C 41-7715 is also visible. This may be Waller Field, Trinidad, while still under construction. *Col Kenneth E. Marts*

The C-47-DL, 41-7770 of the 20th TCS is shown being unloaded at Seymour Field, Galapagos Islands, and was apparently taken during the brief period after June 1943 when the US national insignia had a red border. The frequent and high-priority trips to 'The Rock' were real nail-bitters for 20th TCS crews, as they had to stage from Albrook to either Salinas, Ecuador, or Talara, Peru, before making the long flight to the islands. A navigational error of only a few miles would end in disaster. Although wearing the distinctive Sixth Air Force three-tone camouflage scheme, 17770 appears to have had her engine cowlings either scrubbed free or painted a different colour. *Merton R. Hoch*

Above: An exceptionally rare image for two reasons. First, this 20th TCS (Sp) image is in colour, dating from 1945, and second because she wears full unit titles on her fuselage in yellow – as well as the unit insignia on her port nose, just visible near the antenna. *'Watchdogs With Wings', USAAF*

Below: The 20th Troop Carrier Squadron was pioneering in every respect, and the thousands of flights made by the Douglas twins of this unit throughout Latin America between 1940 and 1945 undoubtedly left a lasting impression. Here the 'First Shirt' of the squadron and a rather motley assortment of officers and other ranks pose by the unit's brand-new insignia at their Howard Field, Canal Zone, headquarters in mid-1942. *Woodson van Osdol*

Although the exploits of the 20th TCS (Sp) during the war involved many bizarre episodes, none rose to the level of the 'Top Secret' maximum effort to distant La Paz, Bolivia, in May 1944, as described in the text. Here, one of the unit C-47s involved in that movement takes off from lofty Arequipa, Peru, a refuelling layover en route, with a typical Andean backdrop. *Unit History, March–October 1944, USAFHRA*

A mix of one C-39, four C-49s (one not in the picture) and five C-47s at La Paz's El Alto airfield in May 1944 waiting to board Axis prisoners – a mix of men, women and children of German, Italian and Japanese nationality. Note the Thompson .45 calibre submachine gun-totting MP with a Bolivian policeman in the foreground. All of the windows on the aircraft had been covered over. That this image has survived is remarkable, as photography of the proceedings was strictly prohibited. *M.J. Dignin*

Below: Unfortunately, the serial number of this 20th TCS C-47, 'Bushwhackin' Klootch', has not been identified, but she clearly has the attention of this ground crewman at Howard Field, CZ, some time in 1944. *James L. Jenkins*

Above: As the war dragged on, slowly but surely nose art started to appear on 20th TCS aircraft. Here, 'Escape' is believed to have been C-47-DL 41-7782, Unit No. 15, seen here at Howard Field in 1944. *James L. Jenkins*

Below: This C-47-DL, believed to be 41-7761, was reassigned from her lengthy assignment to the 20th TCS to HHS, XXVIth Fighter Command at Albrook Field in March 1945. Pictured here visiting Howard Field, besides the stylised bulldog on the nose and chequered cowlings, a red outlined diamond with a white field and a red, circled question mark can just be seen on the vertical fin. *Via Colby R. Karr*

3-48906	43-48906	C-47B-6-DK C-47D C-47B VC-47D C-47E	14722/26167	This aircraft is unique in that she was dispatched, almost brand new, to the large US Military Mission in Chile (the assignment on the Individual Aircraft Record Card states 'Military Intelligence Division-MID Chile', which was shorthand for the mission activity of the period) out of Kelly Field, TX, as early as 23 Nov 44, and may qualify as the very first 'official' mission aircraft as a consequence. She was formally assigned to CAC 4 Jun 47, having apparently remained in Chile throughout the intervening period. She was then assigned to the 7411th Special Mission Squadron, US Mission to Ecuador, 1 Jan 48 and then on the US Mission to Colombia 1 Jul 48, being redesignated as a C-47D 9 Nov 48. She was another of the former C-47Ds redesignated as C-47B 20 Oct 50 but became a VC-47D 1 Jul 52 then, unusually, a C-47E while in the US briefly 3 Oct 56. She apparently remained with the USAF Mission to Ecuador through 14 Feb 61 when she went to the USAF Mission to Bolivia. She was returned to CONUS 27 Oct 63, having spent her entire service life to that time in Latin America, aside from several short periods for overhaul work.
3-48962	43-48962	C-47B-10-DK C-47D	14778/26223	To Howard Fld, CZ, 23 Oct 44 probably to the 20th Troop Carrier Squadron. To Borinquen Fld, PR, 26 Oct 45. Redesignated as C-47D 1948. To Havana, Cuba, 25 May 48, probably with US Air Attaché. To French AF under MDAP 15 Jun 50 but also reported to Cuba under late ARP as FAEC-206 (q.v.), which seems more likely.
'34943'		C-47		Photo evidence of this aircraft, marked as such, with USAF Mission to Cuba c.June 1954. Possibly 43-49433 mis-marked.
3-49141	43-49141	C-47B-10-DK	14957/26402	To Howard Fld, CZ, 20th Troop Carrier Squadron 11 Jun 44 through at least 6 Nov 44. To Borinquen Fld, PR, 7 Nov 44 to at least 31 Dec 44. To the 334th Troop Carrier Squadron by 2 Nov 46. Lost in accident 2 Nov 46 on or after departure from Vernam Fld, Jamaica, bound for San Juan, PR, while being flown by Joseph W. Logsdon.
3-49143	43-49143	C-47B-10-DK C-47D	14959/26404	To Howard Fld, CZ, 20th Troop Carrier Squadron 11 May 44 through at least 5 Nov 44. To Borinquen Fld, PR, 6 Nov 44. To C-47D by 24 Jun 48. Accident 4 Feb 50 at NAS Roosevelt Roads, PR, while being flown by Robert M. Thompson, home based at Ramey AFB, PR, at the time and Reclaimed.
3-49144	43-49144	C-47B-10-DK C-47D	14960/26405	Assigned to Sixth Air Force 5 Nov 44, probably to the 20th Troop Carrier Squadron. To Borinquen Field, PR, the next day, probably to the 20th TCS detachment there. To the 4th BCS, France Field, CZ, 1 Jan 48. Redesignated as C-47D. To the 24th Air-Sea Rescue Squadron detachment, Vernam Field, Jamaica, 23 Jan 48. To Ramey AFB, PR, 12 Dec 49, 5900th ABS. Returned to CONUS 12 Jan 50.
3-49145	43-49145	C-47B-10-DK	14961/26406	To Howard Fld, CZ, 20th Troop Carrier Squadron 11 May 44 through at least 5 Nov 44. To Borinquen Fld, PR, 6 Nov 44. Had returned to Albrook Fld, CZ, by 1 Jan 48. To CONUS 11 Nov 49.
3-49226	43-49226	C-47B-13-DK	15042/26487	Assigned to the Caribbean Defence Command/Panama Canal Department Flight Section, Albrook Fld, CZ, by May 45. Oddly, there is no known subsequent history for this aircraft.
3-49356	43-49356	C-47B-15-DK	15172/26617	Assigned to Sixth Air Force for personal use of General Wooten c.9 Nov 44. To South Atlantic Wing, Air Transport Command by 10 Jan 45. Redesignated as a C-47D post-war and returned to Howard Field, CZ, 1 Jan 48 and as late as 10 Jul 48. To CONUS 6 Jun 50.
3-49366	43-49366	C-47B-15-DK	15182/26627	Assigned to Sixth Air Force, probably 20th TCS, 13 Feb 45. Returned to CONUS 10 Dec 45.
4-76219	44-76219	C-47B-25-DK	15803/32551	To Howard Fld, CZ, 20th Troop Carrier Squadron 10 Feb 45. To Division of Military Intelligence Uruguay 10 Feb 46. To PLUNA as CX-AFE.
4-77258	44-77258	C-47B-40-DK	16842/33590	To Sixth Air Force after 16 Jul 45. Crashed 11 Oct 46 somewhere in Colombia while being flown by a USAAF officer, Joel C. Lee, home based at Albrook Fld, CZ, but detached to Bogota. This was almost certainly an ARP aircraft intended for the FAC.

This C-47B, possibly 43-48799, was assigned to the Panama Air Depot (PAD) directly from the US on 7 1945 and has had an RDF loop added at some point on a pylon under her nose. Named 'Jackie', she also sports scalloped engine cowlings and is seen here at France Field, CZ, not far from a line-up of XXVIth Fighter Command Lockheed P-38Ls. *Gabriel G. O'Doherty*

By the time that C-47A-30-DL was assigned to the 20th TCS on 21 June 1943, the former, straightforward Unit Numbers had been dropped in favour of simply the last two digits of the USAAF serial number, in this case 42-23597/'97'. Camouflage had also been eliminated on some aircraft, while others retained various arrangements. This aircraft served on with the 20th TCS (Sp) until 25 March 1945, when she was transferred to the Albrook Field (APO 825) Base Unit. *Col Ole Griffith*

1Lt Glenn W. Pederson and his 20th TCS (Sp) crew were extremely lucky on 21 June 1945 when they were obliged to make a forced landing on take-off after stopping to refuel at Arequipa, Peru, on a flight from Lima to La Paz, Bolivia. Their aircraft, C-47A-30-DK 43-48003, Unit Number '03' (on her nose), had been assigned to the squadron on 4 August 1944 and, somehow, she was repaired and flown out of the mountains and back to Howard Field, CZ. She later went to Venezuela in 1946. Note once again that her engine cowlings have been either scrubbed free of paint or painted yellow. *Unit History, USAFHRA*

The Antilles Air Command (AAC) Troop Carrier Detachment and the 330th Transport Squadron (Cargo and Mail)

By 31 December 1943, the 20th TCS Detachment, which had been operating nearly autonomously out of Waller Field, Trinidad, for almost two years was officially cited, for the first time, as the AAC Troop Carrier Detachment,[9] but was headquartered at distant Borinquen Field, PR, and had a single very tired C-39 and three only slightly less weary C-47s. The Antilles Air Command had been officially relieved from direct subordination to the Sixth Air Force effective from 16 June 1943, although it had been shaped as a separate force effective from 27 May, in the process inheriting sixty-five aircraft, of all types, from the Sixth Air Force. Having been formally designated as the Antilles Air Task Force on 20 February 1943, it remained a major subordinate command of Caribbean Defence Command.

By July 1944, when the theatre asset 20th Troop Carrier Squadron described above had finally become so dispersed throughout Latin America as to become administratively untenable, the War Department finally recognised that the outlying Antilles Air Command (AAC), which, until then, had been an element of the Panama-based Sixth Air Force, in fact required its own, organic transport unit. As a direct consequence, the 330th Transport Squadron was constituted. The assignment and numeric designation of this unit to the AAC is not reflected in the official USAAF volume dedicated to wartime units, but it was, in fact, nothing more than the former 20th Transport Squadron Detachment, which had already been the *de facto* Antilles transport element for some time.

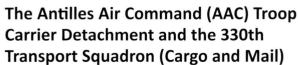

This late-model C-47B-13-DK, 43-49226 was delivered factory fresh to the Caribbean Defense Command-Panama Canal Department (CDC-PCD) Flight Section in late November 1944 but, oddly, there is absolutely no known service history for the aircraft after the war. The CDC-PCD Flight Section adopted horizontal red bands on the vertical fins of their VIP aircraft. She was photographed here at Albrook Field, CZ, and wore the CDC insignia on her nose as well. *Jerry Sympson*

The same aircraft, C-47B-13-DK 43-49226 in May 1945, by which time she had experienced a few markings detail changes. The CDC emblem on her nose, a Spanish galleon on a blue disc, has been augmented by the upper section of her nose cone being painted red, in addition to the two horizontal red bands on her vertical fin, and her former abbreviated USAAF serial, which had been '349226', had been shortened to just '26' in much larger numerals. *Jerry Sympson*

The last-known photo of CDC-PCD Flight Section C-47B-13-DK 43-49226, by which time her abbreviated serial (349226) had been repainted between the red horizontal bands on her vertical fin but the odd code 'CE226' added to the fuselage behind the national insignia. The CDC badge remains on her nose in this Rio Hato Auxiliary Aerodrome image, and suggests she may have been detached to the Corps of Engineers by this time, who were engaged in deactivating bases throughout the former Sixth Air Force area. *Stephen Franklin*

Some USAAF C-47s that operated in Latin America within the Sixth Air Force area of responsibility were obviously there on other assignments. Here, C-47A-90-DL 43-15983 sits next to a rare Fuerza Aérea Ecuatoriana Junkers Ju 52/3m at Quito in August 1944. This aircraft was never assigned to Sixth Air Force and, at the time was assigned to the 503rd Base Unit, Gravely Point, Washington National Airport, an Air Transport Command organisation. She ended her days in Vietnam. *NARA 18-AM-264M-32*

Caribbean Air Command, the American Republics Projects and the 24th Composite Wing

Almost immediately after the victorious end of the war, as elsewhere in the emasculated post-war USAAF establishment, the Sixth Air Force was virtually dismantled as the service struggled to reorganise in a drastically reduced budgetary environment, and the remains were redesignated as the Caribbean Air Command (CAC). By 1950 it was authorised a total of twenty-six C-47s, although in fact only twenty-four were actually assigned. Nearly all of these were assigned to the major operational organ of the CAC, the 24th Composite Wing, although other manoeuvre elements comprised the 6th Fighter Wing (25 August 1946 to 28 July 1948), the 4th Tactical Reconnaissance Squadron (25 August 1946 to 1 February 1948) and, most notably, none other than the remnants of the wartime 20th Troop Carrier Squadron, which continued to function as such between 5 May 1945 and 17 June 1948. For a brief period, CAC also included several understrength transport units in Puerto Rico, including the 334th Troop Carrier Squadron at Borinquen Field, PR, as of May 1946. Of the C-47s that remained in the CAC, one of these, significantly, was one of the very first aircraft assigned to what would become the Inter-American Air Forces Academy (IAAFA) at Albrook Field. Additionally, the CAC had three VC-47s, although, curiously, these were not officially authorised. Some of these aircraft were undoubtedly assigned to the emerging US Latin American Air Missions System, concurrent with the growth of the American Republics Projects (ARP) throughout the region, which had commenced in earnest in 1946, and very few were actually assigned to any numbered unit at the three remaining stations in the Canal Zone.

The Latin American Mission System was formally constituted by CAC by General Orders No. 71 dated 15 September 1949. Each of thirteen nations (Argentina, Bolivia, Chile, Colombia, Ecuador, El Salvador, Guatemala, Haiti, Honduras, Mexico, Paraguay, Peru and Venezuela) was authorised a Mission, which – with the exception of Mexico – was designated as, for example, the USAF Mission to Argentina, etc. The designation for the unit in Mexico was USAF Liaison Office to Mexico. It is noteworthy that Brazil and Nicaragua were noticeably absent from the initial cadre. These were all assigned

to the 5506th USAF Latin American Mission Squadron, Headquartered at Albrook AFB, CZ, with each nation unit identified as a flight of the squadron. In terms of personnel, the largest was by far that in Peru with seventeen officers, twenty NCOs and two civilians, while the smallest was, ironically, that to Mexico, with but two officers, three NCOs and one civilian secretary. By December 1949, however, a J.B.USM.C. (Joint Brazil–US Military Commission) Flight had been added.

Between July and December 1949, with the establishment of the Mission System, CAC C-47 strength changed drastically, and the command found itself in possession of no fewer than sixty-five assorted C-47s as well as eight VC-47s. Most sat idle, however, awaiting assignments to undermanned units or onward to Latin America under some form of US aid. A significant number, about 30 per cent, were eventually assigned to the various USAF Missions, as noted in the accompanying table. The sudden and priority demands of what became known as the Berlin Airlift, however, soon saw nearly all of these otherwise capable aircraft dispatched to that effort. However, by 1 July 1948, the CAC could count an astonishing seventy-two assorted C-47s on its Order of Battle, although many of these were awaiting transfer and were essentially in open storage. By 30 June 1949, this had remained essentially unchanged, as the roster reflected at that time a total of sixty-two C-47s, but did not include two C-47s assigned to the National Guard based in the Canal Zone (which almost certainly were those in the possession of the Puerto Rican National Guard, the solitary National Guard organisation in the Caribbean) and eight assorted VC-47s.

CAC also possessed, briefly, the 36th Fighter Wing (from 2 July 1948 until 13 August 1948) and its subordinate 23rd Fighter Group, which survived autonomously for a brief period from 25 April until 24 September 1949. For command and control, these were all grouped under the 5700th Composite Wing.

With the end of Second World War, one of the primary mission objectives of the CAC, after defence of the Canal, was the promotion of US aircraft, doctrine and procedures in Latin America. General Henry H. Arnold himself had travelled extensively in the region, and what became the American Republics Projects (ARP) was one of his 'pet' projects, as he prepared to turn over the reins of the world air power organisation he had created. Nodding to the success of the

This 20th TCS (Sp) C-47A, photographed while loading at Howard Field, CZ, after October 1944, poses a minor mystery. Clearly showing a red numeral '3' on her rear fuselage, this suggests that either the unit reassigned Unit Numbers to later aircraft, before adopting the simpler scheme of using just the last two digits of the USAAF serial, or there was another interim scheme. *Col Ole Griffith*

Photos of US C-47s in the Caribbean Air Command (CAC) in the immediate post-war years are surprisingly rare. This 'plain vanilla' C-47B-28-DK, 44-76382, had been assigned to CAC on 31 May 1946 and is pictured here at Borinquen Field, Puerto Rico, after 1 January 1948 while assigned to the 24th Composite Wing. She remained in Puerto Rico with various units until 11 February 1965, when she was transferred to the US Army. *Sam Smith*

The extraordinary markings on this USAF C-47, pictured at Albrook Air Force base, Canal Zone, include the flags of many of the Latin American nations interspersed down the fuselage by the windows, with a special insignia on the nose with the words 'US Air Force South – For Latin America'. Unfortunately, her serial is unknown. *Capt. George G. Farinas*

No discussion of US C-47s in Latin America would be complete without noting the aircraft assigned from 12 May 1949 to the Puerto Rican National Guard's 198th Fighter Interceptor Squadron at Isla Grande. Here, '315605' (43-15604, a C-47A-85-DL) shares the apron with other unit aircraft, including a B-26B, UC-45F, and T-6G. Note that the C-47 sports 'PR-ANG' on either side of the national insignia but simply 'Puerto Rico National Guard' titles on the upper fuselage. She remained with the unit until June 1961, when she returned to CONUS. *via Luis Santos*

wartime Lend-Lease programme in the region, his vision entailed what he described as 'Tab Forces' to augment the resources of the US in hemispheric defence. The term 'Tab Force' gained a life of its own, based on the master plan itself, a huge document, which had an index page 'Tab' in the actual document volumes for each of the regional, national air forces that were to not only be the beneficiaries of ARP, but organised 'in depth' according to their individual national capabilities, for overall hemispheric defence. It was, in effect, Arnold's aviation vision of the Monroe Doctrine.

Initially described merely as 'Allocation of Aircraft to Latin America' as early as 8 June 1945, the Army Air Force's plans for what became the ARP was met by what Maj. General R.L. Walsh, Special Assistant to Arnold for this programme, described as 'internal disagreement within the State Department, resulting in indistinct and negative policy on aircraft allocations, virtually nullifying AAF efforts to develop those Air Forces pursuant to expressed War Department size'.

To say that the USAAF's plans for ARP were ambitious may be an understatement. These included what was referred to as the 'Interim Latin American Aircraft Requirements' allocations, which set down country-by-country objectives of the AAF, including organising each national air arm under AAF Tables of Organisation and Equipment

(T/O&E) that were in use by the AAF itself at the time – right down to the personnel strength required of each, aircraft, side arms and uniforms. Brazil, for example, was to get one complete fighter squadron (T/O&E 1-27) with either P-47Ds or P-47Ns, four complete bombardment squadrons (T/O&E 1-127) with North American B-25Js, no fewer than ten transport squadrons (under T/O&E 1-347) with a mix of ninety Douglas C-47s and twenty-five Beech C-45s, an advanced twin-engine training squadron with a mix of five Beech AT-11s and five AT-7s, and three complete airbase units (T/O&E 20-1). The total programme, at the beginning, was set to comprise at least 1,530 aircraft, combined, for all projected Latin American recipients.

Besides Assistant Secretary of State Braden, the AAF encountered staunch opposition to its programme, to its surprise, from the powerful Aircraft Industries Association (AIA), which, not unexpectedly, was anxious not to repeat the disastrous surplus environment that had confronted the US aeronautical industry at the end of the First World War. The AIA wanted to sell both new (and used) aircraft to Latin American operators, a market that had proven the salvation of some of them in the between-the-wars period. Specifically, the AIA was

Built as a C-47B-6-DK, this aircraft, 43-48906, is unique in that she was dispatched, almost brand new, to the US Military Mission in Chile in late November 1944 – and remained in Latin America in various assignments until October 1963. She is seen here with the CAC badge on her fin while assigned to the USAF Mission to Ecuador as noted in our accompanying table. Redesignated, successively, as C-47D, C-47B, VC-47D and C-47E, she wore her Day-Glo rear fuselage and nose markings only briefly. *Douglas C40294*

Assigned to the CAC's 5700th Air Base Wing in April 1953, C-47B-10-DK 43-49110 was assigned to the USAF Mission to Nicaragua six days later – where she remained, with minor trips back to the Canal Zone for IRAN, until August 1967! Pictured here early in that period, she went to a Military Assistance Program (MAP) assignment on 23 January 1970, possibly to the Fuerza Aérea de Nicaragua, which would have been entirely appropriate. *Harold G. Martin*

concerned about the wholesale 'giveaway' of competent air transport aircraft and, most notably, C-47s and C-54s. As a direct result of this combination of staunch political opposition, the Interim ARP was slashed on practically a daily basis to accommodate these realities. In one instance, the State Department, in a letter to Col R.L. Vittrup, General Staff Corps, who was trying to run interference between State, the War Department and Arnold, stated bluntly that 'this department desires to make it absolutely clear that no authority is given at this time for the sale of military equipment under this programme [ARP] to the Dominican Republic, Haiti, Nicaragua, Honduras, Argentina and Panama, and no aircraft whatsoever to Bolivia and Paraguay'. Clearly, the State Department was determined that the US should not be seen to be equipping dictatorial regimes at a time when democratic forces were on the rise, while Arnold and his staff took the view – arguably justified – that the provision of modern equipment to the very same air arms that the State Department had approved for Lend-Lease offsets (with the exception of Argentina) would in fact bolster change, especially within the several national aviation establishments, which had already been intensively exposed to US military, cultural and philosophical viewpoints.

By 9 January 1946, the State Department and AIA had prevailed, however and, instead of the 1,530 aircraft the AAF had budgeted for, the total number to be allocated region wide under ARP had dropped to 597, of which, significantly, 185 would be C-47 variants. Notably, only Bolivia (9), Brazil (46), Chile (9), Colombia (6), Cuba (4), Ecuador (4), Guatemala (4), Mexico (7), Peru (8), Uruguay (4) and Venezuela (3) were to get C-47s but, as it turned out, even these numbers were optimistic.

Arnold, however, did an 'end-run' on both the AIA and the State Department. While they could exert authority to preclude direct country-to-country transfers under ARP as originally envisaged, they could not prevent him from assigning aircraft to USAAF overseas commands, and this is precisely what he did. Not surprisingly, CAC was one of the principal destinations. At the same time, he went to work expanding the US Mission structure in Latin America, and often, while State Department approval for deliveries were being hammered out, the aircraft, in many instances, were actually in the recipient nations being used to train local crews by US Mission personnel. Thus, even though official handover dates prevail within this volume, in the case of ARP-supplied C-47s, they were very often actually 'in country' far in advance of those formal delivery dates. Arnold also, concurrently, used the considerable experience of the large PAD installation at Albrook Field to overhaul ARP

aircraft, and tend to them while pending transfer to recipient nations. All the while, these aircraft were being carried 'on the books' of CAC, thus accounting for the large numbers shown on period Order of Battle documents.

But even earlier, Arnold had directed in mid-September 1945 that a 'programme be set up to provide C-47 aircraft for Latin America' specifically. Quite without consulting with the State Department, Arnold set his staff to work co-ordinating with of the Office of the Army-Navy Liquidation Commissioner (better known by the acronym FLC) 'in conjunction with the State Department', which apparently was so consumed with other priorities at the time that they shuffled this action off to relatively minor officers, to set up a schedule of aircraft available for sale, specifically, to Latin American military as well as civil operators – nearly all of whom were hungry for modern aircraft. The schedule that was established provided for the allocation of no fewer than eighty-four assorted C-47s. Of these, about twenty were to be concentrated at the so-called Miami sales centre between September and December 1947, and about thirteen more in the Panama Canal Zone. The remainder, however, were to be concentrated at a separate sales centre located at Natal, Brazil, a major Air Transport Command hub during the war. Arnold directed, apparently in an effort to 'get ahead' of State Department concerns, that C-47s would be delivered by USAAF crews to the sales centres at Natal and at Albrook Field in the Canal Zone 'against specific requests from the Theatre Commanders' and which had been, conveniently, declared surplus by the same commanders, and then sold by the field representatives of the FLC. Arnold also ensured that the aircraft set aside for this purpose were not merely in 'as-is/where-is' condition, and further directed that 'all aircraft delivered to the Sales Centres be reconditioned and modified as requested by the Theatre Commanders'. By 14 September, the US Ambassador to Brazil had been the solitary official to submit a request on behalf of an overture from Brazil, which had asked for a staggering thirty-three aircraft. Of these, twelve were actually either physically at or en route to the ATC base at Morrison Field, Florida, and ATC had been ordered to deliver twenty-five more there as soon as possible. The first increment of these aircraft, modified and thoroughly reconditioned, left for Natal on 17 September, and the remainder were to follow as rapidly as they could thereafter. It should be understood, however, that not all of these aircraft were for military end-users: quite a few went to established Latin American airlines, such as PLUNA in Uruguay, which obtained two. This was almost certainly Arnold's way of making the programme more palatable to the State Department.

Yet another very well-travelled aircraft, C-47B-1-DL 43-16381, marked here as 0-16381 with the USAF Mission to Chile at Howard AFB, CZ, on 10 July 1966, had arrived in CAC in April 1949. While redesignated as a C-47D, at the time of this photo her data block clearly read VC-47B. Note that her engine cowlings and underside had been painted light grey. She went to Chile under MAP as FACh-972 in November 1970. *Hagedorn*

The portable crane in the foreground notwithstanding, this C-47D, built as C-47B-1-DK 43-48496, shares a portion of the apron at Howard AFB, CZ, on 29 September 1966 with a Boeing C-97 of the Illinois ANG. Assigned to US Air Forces Southern Command (USAFSO), whose badge she wears on her fin in January 1963, she had just returned from the USAF Mission to Guatemala and was bound next for the USAF Mission to the Dominican Republic. She became T-71 with the Fuerza Aérea Paraguaya under MAP in November 1970. *Hagedorn*

No two of the large number of C-47s assigned to the USAF Mission system in Latin America were painted or marked identically. Here 43-49404A, marked as 0-49404, loading at Howard AFB, CZ, on 9 December 1966 – undoubtedly with Christmas gifts for Mission personnel and their families acquired at the BX – was by this point a VC-47D, and had been in Latin America since 1949. At one time or another she served with the USAF Mission system in Argentina, Bolivia, Chile, Colombia, Cuba, Honduras, Mexico, Nicaragua, Paraguay, Peru and Venezuela! She was transferred under MAP o an unknown recipient on 28 January 1970, possibly Colombia. *Hagedorn*

Although many of the images in this book show C-47s in Latin America with beautiful blue sky and towering cloud banks, the truth is that the majority of the aircraft in the region operated 500 miles north or south of the Equator, and very much in the tropics for as much as nine months of the year. Here, C-47D 44-76448, marked as 0-76448 near Hangar 1 at Howard AFB, CZ, prepares to return to Honduras on 9 December 1966 on a typical rainy season day. This aircraft, like so many of the USAFSO Mission aircraft, went to Ecuador under MAP as FAE-76448 on 31 May 1970. *Hagedorn*

Posing in immaculate condition aged twenty-one, 45-1114, marked as 0-51114 at Howard AFB, CZ, on 11 November 1966 had been redesignated as VC-47B by this time but with stencilled 'United States of America' titles. Although nominally assigned to the USAF Mission to Venezuela, she was probably actually supporting US Embassy-Caracas activities at the time. She went to MAP on 20 February 1969 from Davis-Monthan but her ultimate operator remains unknown. *Hagedorn*

Throughout the table below, the reader will also note the emergence, as early as 1948, of four-digit USAF units, such as the 5500th Foreign Mission Squadron,[10] which was assigned to support the Força Aérea Brasileira (FAB, see Chapter Four). Although 'home based' at either Albrook or Howard AFB in the Panama Canal Zone, every Latin American air arm that contracted for a USAF Mission had such an organisation resident, usually at or near their main operating air field, during nearly all of the decades of the 1950s, '60s and '70s. Many of the C-47s assigned to these Missions performed yeoman service and were often shifted from one Mission to another as requirements changed. Their impact on 'showing the flag' throughout Latin America cannot be overstated.

These Missions, ARP and the historical impact of the wartime Lend-Lease programme on Latin American military aviation was, indeed, profound. But it was a combination of the ARP and the extensive Mission system, which has been largely ignored or swept into the convenient 'Rio Pact' arrangements orchestrated by the State Department, proved to be the 'booster shot' needed to truly bring these national air forces into modern maturity. The C-47s supplied and supported played no small part in all of this.

Rarely seen or photographed, this VC-47D, 45-1128, marked as 0-51128, bears the joint English–Portuguese titles of the United States–Brazil Military Commission when seen at Howard AFB, CZ, on 20 February 1967. She was handed over to Guatemala under MAP on 20 August 1970 as FAG-560 and was later converted to Basler BT-67 configuration as TG-FAG-4/560 in 1994. *Hagedorn*

US Air Force Southern Command (USAFSO) and the 605th Air Commando Squadron

By the early 1960s, US military doctrine had shifted to the counter-insurgency (COIN) and concurrent Civic Action model, spurred in no small measure by the lessons of the Korean War and the plethora of insurgency actions that seemed to be surfacing everywhere, notably in Southeast Asia and Latin America.

Initially, USAFSO included, as its major manoeuvre element, the reorganised 5700th Composite Airbase between 24 October 1954 and 8 November 1967, supplemented from 1967 by the 24th Composite Wing, which included the extraordinary 605th Air Commando Squadron (ACS).

By 1966, the 605th ACS must certainly have been one of the largest squadrons in the USAF, and, based entirely at Howard Air Force Base on the Pacific side, included separate sections equipped with On-Mark (Douglas) B-26Ks, Helio U-10s, North American T-28D-5s,

Curtiss C-46Ds and assorted Douglas C-47s. USAFSO could count a total of twenty-three assorted C-47s and VC-47s on its inventory as of 8 October 1964, not all of which have been identified.

On any given day between 1965 and 1969, the main ramp at Howard was populated with row upon row of C-47s assigned to the 605th, which, with its other tactical aircraft, was intended to serve as, essentially, a 'model air force' tailored for COIN functions, and a working example for Latin American air arms to study and emulate. The unit certainly must have constituted the last major grouping of C-47s in one unit in USAF history and, not surprisingly, a significant number of the well-maintained survivors of this unit later passed to Latin American operators, as can be seen in the accompanying table. By the end of the 1960s, however, the venerable T-28s, B-26s, C-46s and C-47s had given way to Cessna A-37s, Fairchild C-123s and Sikorsky HH-3s, and the incredible sound of large numbers of radial engines at Howard Field, after nearly thirty years, finally fell silent.

An extraordinary organisation, the 605th Air Commando Squadron was almost certainly the last active duty USAF organisation to operate C-47s in unit strength. Recognisable by their uniform colour schemes and special antenna array, they included, by August 1968, 0-48499 (43-48499) which, oddly, was still designated at the time as a VC-47B. She went to a MAP recipient on 4 September 1970, possibly Nicaragua. *Hagedorn*

Another 605th ACS aircraft, 43-16379 (marked as 0-16379) has just about everything hanging out in this January 1968 image at Howard and shows ample evidence of her experimental use as a field-modified gunship along her port window line. Officially a C-47D by this time, she went to the Dominican Republic as FAD-3407 on 27 August 1970 and may well have been the same aircraft that the FAD modified into a gunship. *Hagedorn*

Post-War USAF C-47s in Latin America

Serial as Worn	Full US Serial	Type as Built	MSN	Assigned and Notes
G-4	44-76691 0-76691	TC-47B-30-DK TC-47D C-47D TC-47D C-47D GC-47D	16275/33023	To Class 26 at Albrook AFB, CZ, 30 Nov 65 to Inter-American Air Forces Academy, Albrook AFB, CZ, as GC-47D by Dec 68 and as late as Mar 74. Fate unknown.
G-18	42-92079	GC-47D	11840	Former 605th ACS aircraft (see 0-92079) Inter-American Air Forces Academy, Albrook AFB, CZ, as GC-47D by Mar 74. Fate unknown.
G-19	45-967	C-47B-45-DK C-47D GC-47D	16970/34230	Inter-American Air Forces Academy, Albrook AFB, CZ, as GC-47D 16 Jun 70 and as late as 1 Jan 75. Fate unknown.
0-00597	43-100597	C-47A-65-DL	19060	Ex-Air National Guard. To 24th ACW, Howard AFB, CZ, 21 Jun 68. Noted at Howard AFB, CZ, with plain white upper decking 8 Jul 68. Returned to CONUS 19 Sep 68.
0-00805	42-100805	C-47A-70-DL C-47D	19268	Assigned 72nd Airbase Group, Ramey AFB, PR, 1 Dec 58. Returned to CONUS 12 Feb 59.
0-15369	43-15369	C-47A-80-DL	19835	Assigned to SAO 72nd Airbase Group, Ramey AFB, PR, 16 Nov 55. To CONUS 20 Dec 55. Much later to MAP 8 Oct 64, destination untraced.
0-15497	43-15497	C-47A-85-DL C-47D	19963	Ex-Alaska Air National Guard. Assigned to SOU 24th ACW, Howard AFB, CZ, 11 Jun 68. To 24th SOW, same station 31 Jul 68. Noted at Howard AFB, CZ, with 605th Air Commando Squadron as C-47D by 13 Nov 68. To MAP 29 Jan 70, destination not traced.
0-15970	43-15970	C-47A-90-DL C-47D	20436	605th Air Commando Squadron, via 24th ACW 25 May 68, ex-Maryland Air National Guard, Jun 68. Redesignated as C-47D 3 Feb 69. To plain white upper decking by Nov 69. To FAP-203 (Panama) 17 Jan 70.
0-16075	43-16075	C-47A-90-DL	20541	To 605th Air Commando Squadron, Howard AFB, CZ, 1 Jul 64. Redesignated as C-47D 26 May 67 and to 24th ACW 31 Mar 68, 24th SOW 31 Jul 68. Apparently intended for MAP to Uruguay, and had arrived in Montevideo by 15 May 70 but to FAA (Argentina) instead 4 Sep 70. However, there is no record of the FAA having received this aircraft. Contrary to other published accounts, she in fact became the second Uruguayan aircraft to bear FAU-508.
0-16139	43-16139	C-47A-90-DL	20605	Assigned to the 1127th Foreign Assistance Group, Havana, Cuba, 7 Oct 59 but returned to CONUS 13 Oct 60.
0-16282	43-16282	C-47B-1-DL C-47D	20748	605th Air Commando Squadron, Howard AFB, CZ, 24 Apr 64. Accident 28 Aug 67 and apparently stricken as a result.
0-16379	43-16379	C-47B-1-DL C-47D	20845	605th Air Commando Squadron 1 Jul 64 till at least 15 Apr 68 as C-47D. Repainted Feb 68. To 24th ACW, Howard AFB, CZ, 15 Apr 68. Detailed to Guatemala City, Guatemala, probably on an MTT 26 May 70. To FAD-3407 under MAP 27 Aug 70.

Seen being painted with yet another variation on a Mission aircraft titles, 43-49887 (marked as 0-49887) had been in Latin America since 1948 when photographed at Howard in June 1969, as a VC-47D. She went to Paraguay as T-69 under MAP on 27 August 1970. *Hagedorn*

0-16381	43-16381	C-47B-1-DL C-47D VC-47B	20847	Assigned to CAC and with the Joint US-Brazil Military Commission 2 Apr 49, when it suffered an accident at Guaratingueta Airport, Brazil, while being flown by Roy L. Ferguson, Jr. Cited in error on some accident reports as s/n '45-16381'. To USAF Mission to Chile 11 Aug 53 and as late as 28 Jul 55. To USAF Mission to Peru 8 Aug 57 but returned to the Chilean Mission by 15 Dec 57. Although nominally assigned to the 24th SOW at Howard AFB, CZ, she was in fact in Chile most of the time and went to the FACh under MAP 13 Nov 70 as FACh-972 and then N2782N by Nov 82.
0-24405	42-24405	C-47A-60-DL	10267	605th Air Commando Squadron by Nov 69 as C-47D. To Panamanian FAP-204 Jan 70.
0-45967	45-967	C-47B-45-DK C-47D GC-47D	16970/34230	To USAF Mission to El Salvador 6 Jul 50. To USAF Mission to Colombia 31 Jan 51. To USAF Mission to Chile 8 Dec 51. USAF Mission to Guatemala 4 Jun 52. To USAF Mission to Honduras 6 Jun 53. To USAF Mission to Argentina 1 Aug 53. To USAF Mission to Ecuador 17 Dec 53. To USAF Mission to Venezuela 11 Jan 55. To USAF Mission to Colombia 29 May 55. To USAF Mission to Bolivia 14 Jul 56. To USAF Mission to Colombia 12 Aug 57. To USAF Mission to Guatemala again 6 Mar 58 and as late as June 1969. To the Inter-American Air Forces Academy, Albrook AFB, CZ, 16 Jun 70 as a GC-47D (G-19).
0-48275	43-48275	C-47B-1-DK C-47D VC-47D	14091/25536	To CAC 7405th SU 1 Jan 48 and apparently detailed to the US Mission to Argentina with the 7405th Military Mission Squadron by 26 Apr 48. Redesignated as a C-47D 5 Apr 49. Accident 19 Aug 50 at Rosario de la Frontera, Salta, Argentina, while being flown by Robert D. Knapp, home based at Albrook AFB, CZ, suggesting it may have been assigned to the USAF Mission to Argentina at the time. Redesignated as a VC-47D 12 Mar 51. To the USAF Mission to Paraguay 31 Jan 52. To USAF Mission to Uruguay as VC-47D 12 Dec 52. Noted at Rio de Janeiro, Brazil 21 Dec 68. To the 5700th Airbase Wing, Howard AFB, CZ, by 31 Aug 67 and to the 24th Composite Wing 1 Dec 67. Returned to the USAF Mission to Uruguay by 17 Jul 68 and to MAP via Howard AFB, CZ, 27 Oct 70 although the recipient nation is unknown.
0-48466	43-48466	C-47B-1-DK VC-47B	14282/25727	Assigned to CAC's 5700th ABG, Albrook AFB, CZ, 16 May 62. To the 1127th FAG, USAF Mission to Peru, 17 Nov 62. Returned to CONUS 23 Jun 63.
0-48472	43-48472	C-47B-1-DK	14288/25733	USAF Mission to Guatemala by 1949. Reportedly crashed 31 Jan 50 near Guatemala City, four killed. However, assigned to Base Flight, Howard AFB, CZ, USAFSO by 31 Dec 64 as a C-47D and also reported to FAU-522 by 1967.
0-48496	43-48496	C-47B-1-DK C-47D	14312/25757	To CAC 5700th ABG, Albrook AFB, CZ, 24 Jan 63. To 5500th Foreign Mission Squadron, USAF Mission to Honduras 25 Aug 63. Base Flight, Howard AFB, CZ, USAFSO as C-47D as early as 9 Dec 64. To USAF Mission to Uruguay 20 Apr 65. To USAF Mission to Chile 4 Aug 65. To 1127th FAG, USAF Mission to Guatemala 23 Feb 66. To USAF Mission to the Dominican Republic 20 Jul 67. To 605th Air Commando Squadron. To 24th ACW 31 Mar 68 and deployed to Lima, Peru c.9 Jun 68. MAP to Paraguay 9 Nov 70 as T-71.
0-48499	43-48499	C-47B-1-DK C-47D VC-47B	14315/25760	TAO 1st ACW, Howard AFB, CZ, 19 Jan 64. 605th Air Commando Squadron 1 Jul 64 and as late as Aug 68, oddly as a VC-47B. To 24th SOW 31 Jul 68 and to Managua, Nicaragua 25 Nov 69, possibly on TDY. Returned to Howard AFB, CZ, 2 Mar 70 and to MAP 4 Sep 70, possibly to Nicaragua.

Another immaculate 605th ACS aircraft, 0-15497 was one of the oldest C-47Ds in the USAFSO inventory. Having previously served with the Alaskan Air National Guard, she had been recalled to active duty and went to MAP on 29 January 1970, although her final operator remains unknown. *Hagedorn*

Right: A rare sight in the late 1960s, a line-up of 605th ACS C-47s on the west taxiway at Howard AFB, CZ, in November 1969. The nearest aircraft, C-47D 0-15970 (43-15970), was a former Maryland ANG aircraft and became the Panamanian FAP-203 under MAP on 17 January 1970. *Hagedorn*

Below: Awaiting her next mission, 605th ACS C-47D 0-16075 poses on the apron in front of Base Operations at Howard AFB, CZ, in 1968 shortly after the punctual 1332hrs rainy season deluge. Built as a C-47A-90-DL, this aircraft went to Uruguay as FAU-508 under MAP. *Jimmy Stark*

0-48501	43-48501	C-47B-1-DK C-47D	14317/25762	MTO Albrook AFB, CZ, 1806th AACG 5 Jan 57. Returned to CONUS 14 Jul 57.
0-48799	43-48799	C-47B-5-DK C-47D VC-47D	14615/26060	Had been in Sixth Air Force and CAC since 9 Jul 45. Redesignated as C-47D 6 Apr 48 and VC-47D 1 Dec 48. To USAF Mission to El Salvador as VC-47D by 7 Jul 52. To USAF Mission to Ecuador 15 May 64 but returned to the Mission in El Salvador by 16 Feb 67. From 1 Dec 67 with 24th ACW, Howard AFB, CZ, and to MAP 1 Feb 70, recipient unknown.
0-48912	43-48912	C-47B-5-DK C-47D	14728/26173	C-47D 605th Air Commando Squadron 1 Jul 64, Howard AFB, CZ, as late as Aug 68 by which time she had passed to the 24th ACW. By Oct 69 noted at Howard wearing 'XI Posta Aérea Militar de las Americas' titles. To the USAF Mission to the Dominican Republic 23 Sep 70 and to MAP 2 Nov 70, possibly to the FAD.
0-49108	43-49108M	C-47B-11-DK	14924/26369	Was loaned to the US Air Attaché to Chile by Bolling AFB, DC, *c.*26 May 50. It was returned to CONUS to Norton AFB, CA, 16 Aug 50.
0-49110	43-49110	C-47B-10-DK	14926/26371	Assigned to CAC 5700th ABG, Albrook AFB 11 Apr 53. To Managua, Nicaragua, 16 Jun 54. Where she remained for many years with the USAF Mission. Had been stripped and completely repainted with 'white cap' during Oct 64. USAF Mission to Nicaragua as VC-47D by 31 Dec 64 (also see entry for 3-49110).
0-49205	43-49205	C-47B-10-DK C-47D	15021/26466	Assigned to 24th ACW 9 Apr 68. C-47D, noted at Howard AFB, CZ. To MAP Colombia 29 Jan 70.
0-49251	43-49251	C-47B-10-DK C-47D	15067/26512	Assigned to 5620th ABS, CAC France Field, CZ, 10 Jul 49. To US Mission to Haiti 27 Jul 49 where it remained, incredibly, with but short visits back to its home station in the Canal Zone, until 19 Oct 63. To the USAF Mission to Colombia 16 Apr 64. Base Flight, Howard AFB, CZ, USAFSO by 31 Dec 64 and briefly detached to the USAF Mission to Brazil *c.*25 May 65 and had been redesignated by Aug 66 as C-47D. To the USAF Mission to Uruguay 4 Jun 67. To 605th Air Commando Squadron 10 Dec 67 and as late as Nov 69, and element of the 24th ACW. To unknown MAP recipient 22 Jan 70.
0-49280	43-49280	C-47B-15-DK C-47D VC-47D	15096/26541	Assigned for use by the US Air Attaché in Paraguay 30 Jan 47. Returned to CONUS 21 Apr 49 but returned to CAC as a VC-47D to USAF Mission to Guatemala 24 Feb 50 where she remained through 30 Jun 666. Her assignment between that date and MAP transfer to Honduras 5 Dec 75, probably as FAH-319 has always been cited as 'LOG Kelly, SAAMA' and Robins WRAMA' but in fact she was about other business in South America. Noted, for instance, at Belize in 1968 and at Howard AFB, CZ, with 'United States of America' titles Nov 69 and non-standard colour scheme.

0-49404	43-49404A	C-47B-15-DK C-47D VC-47D	15220/26665	Assigned to CAC PAD 30 Jun 49. Was US Air Attaché's aircraft in Argentina c.8 Sep 49 as a C-47D while his normal aircraft, 44-76252 was at the PAD for overhaul. To USAF Mission to Bolivia 14 Sep 54. To USAF Mission to Nicaragua 12 Aug 55. To USAF Mission to Mexico 17 Feb 56. To USAF Mission to Colombia 19 Oct 56. To USAF Mission to Honduras 13 Mar 57. To USAF Mission to Cuba 18 Nov 57. To USAF Mission to Venezuela 12 Feb 58. To USAF Mission to Peru 14 Aug 58. To USAF Mission to Paraguay 4 Dec 58. Returned to USAF Mission to Nicaragua 11 Mar 59 and on to the USAF Mission to Uruguay 12 May 59. To USAF Mission to Chile 29 Jun 59. To USAF Mission to Venezuela 17 Nov 59. Returned to USAF Mission to Colombia 18 Aug 60 where she remained until at least 31 Aug 67 as VC-47D. To the 24th ACW, Howard AFB, CZ, 8 Dec 67 and to unknown recipient, MAP 28 Jan 70.
0-49504	43-49504	C-47B-15-DK C-47D	15320/26765	Assigned to USAFSO 605th Air Commando Squadron, Howard AFB, CZ, 1 Jul 64. Suffered a ground accident 16 Oct 67 at Santa Rosa de Capon, Honduras but apparently repaired and to FAH-307 17 Jun 68.
3-49513 0-49513	43-49513	C-47B-15-DK C-47D	15329/26774	Assigned to the Joint Brazil-US Military Commission, Rio de Janeiro, Brazil, 28 Feb 49. To CAC Albrook AFB, CZ, 20 Apr 56 as C-47D. To USAF Mission to Colombia 11 Feb 56. To USAF Mission to Ecuador 2 Jul 56. Returned to CONUS 17 Jul 57. Back to 24th ACW, Howard AFB, CZ, 3 Apr 68 and noted at Howard AFB, CZ, as C-47D with plain white upper decking Nov 69 assigned to the 24th SOW. To unknown recipient, MAP 22 Jan 70.
0-49556	43-49556	C-47B-15-DK C-47D	15372/26817	To 23rd ABG, Albrook Field, CZ, 19 Jul 49. To USAF Mission to Chile 23 Oct 52. To USAF Mission to Colombia 29 Sep 55. To USAF Mission to Paraguay 9 Dec 55. To USAF Mission to Guatemala 31 Oct 56. To USAF Mission to Venezuela 15 Jul 57. To USAF Mission to Brazil 13 Dec 57. To USAF Mission to Chile 6 Nov 58. To USAF Mission to Venezuela 9 Apr 59. To USAF Mission to Argentina 17 Jul 59. To USAF Mission to Bolivia 13 Sep 60. To USAF Mission to Ecuador 22 Nov 60. To USAF Mission to Paraguay 14 Mar 63. Noted at Howard AFB, CZ, still marked as such 21 Apr 68. Returned to CONUS 7 Nov 69.
0-49567	43-49567	C-47B-15-DK C-47D SC-47D	15383/26828	63rd Air Rescue Squadron, Ramey AFB, PR, 26 Nov 57. To CONUS 23 May 58.
0-49785	43-49785	C-47B-20-DK C-47D	15601/27046	To 24th ACW, Howard AFB, CZ, 31 Mar 68 as C-47D. To MAP FAE-49785 21 Aug 70.
3-49887	0-49887 43-49887 43-49887A	C-47B-20-DK C-47D VC-47D VC-47B VC-47D	15703/27148	To CAC's 7409th Foreign Mission Squadron, Bogota, Colombia, 1 Jan 48. USAF Mission to Peru as VC-47B 12 Feb 48. To USAF Mission to Chile 8 Apr 56. Returned to USAF Mission to Peru 28 May 56. Redesignated as VC-47D 30 Apr 60 but reverted to VC-47B 13 Mar 61 but changed back to VC-47D 7 Jun 65! To USAF Mission to Paraguay 30 Oct 69. MAP to Paraguay as T-69 27 Aug 70.
0-50916	45-916	C-47B-45-DK	16919/34177	See 5-916 below. MAAG Brazil, VC-47D. Stationed at Rio de Janeiro between Mar 61 and Feb 65.
0-50967	45-967	C-47B-45-DK	16970/34230	See 5-967 below. USAF Mission to Guatemala by 1961 and Jun 69. To IAAFA as G-19 by Mar 74 (q.v.).

Pictured on 11 April 1969 at Howard AFB, C-47D 0-16379 of the 605th ACS, which had been assigned in July 1964, has the name 'Super Puff' in the last two cabin windows, painted on by some wag for unknown reasons – the solitary known instance of a 605th aircraft bearing any special markings. She went to the Dominican Republic as FAD-3407 under MAP on 27 August 1970. *John Mercier*

Very rare and worn for only a week, C-47D 0-48912 bears the titles and nose insignia of the 'XI Posta Aérea Militar de las Americas' at Howard AFB in October 1969. Assigned to the 24th ACW at the time, she went to the USAF Mission to the Dominican Republic next and then to MAP on 2 November 1970, although the recipient has not been identified. *Hagedorn*

Marked strictly in accordance with T.O.s of the day in this November 1969 image, 0-49513 (built as C-47B-15-DK 43-49513) was assigned to the 24th SOW at the time but went to an unknown MAP recipient on 22 January 1970. She had been in Latin America exclusively since February 1949 and had served in Brazil, Colombia, and Ecuador previously. *Hagedorn*

0-51032	45-1032	C-47B-45-DK	17035/34300	MAAG to the Dominican Republic as early as 14 Sep 64 to at least 1967 as C-47D. Repainted Oct 67, plain white upper decking.
0-51110	45-1110	C-47B-50-DK C-47D	17113/34380	To CAC after Oct 45. Accident at Mariscal Estigarribia Field, Asunción, Paraguay, 6 Nov 46 while being flown by Karl T. Barthelmess. Probably marked as 5-1110 at the time. Recovered and repaired. Noted at Rio de Janeiro, Brazil, between Mar 61 and Aug 62 as 0-51110, probably with US Air Attaché. To MAP Paraguay as T-51 after being donated following an accident.
0-51111	45-1111	C-47B-50-DK	17114/34381	To MAAG Brazil by Sep 63, C-47D. To USAF Mission to the Republic of Argentina by 31 Oct 64 then back to MAAG Brazil by 31 Jun 66.
0-51114	45-1114	C-47B-50-DK VC-47B	17117/34384	Assigned to USAF Air Attaché, Lima, Peru, 24 Sep 64 as VC-47B. USAFSO, USAF Air Attaché Venezuela, by 12 Jan 65 'United States of America' titles as VC-47B by 11 Nov 66. Noted as such at Lima, Peru, by 1967. Stored at Davis-Monthan AFB, AZ, by 3 Dec 67 and to MAP unknown recipient 20 Feb 69.
0-51115	45-1115	C-47B-50-DK	17118/34385	US Air Attaché to Colombia's aircraft *c.*11 Jun 48 as VC-47D. To US Air Attaché Cuba *c.*26 Nov 49. To DMAFB, AZ. by Dec 60. However, assigned as VC-47D to the USAF Air Attaché for Venezuela by 31 Dec 64.
0-51119	45-1119	C-47B-50-DK	17122/34389	US Air Attaché Peru as VC-47B by 12 Jan 65 but reclaimed due to extensive corrosion. To George T. Baker Aviation School, Miami, FL, by Sep 70 however.
0-51128	45-1128	C-47B-50-DK VC-47D	17131/34398	Assigned to the Base Flight, Howard AFB, CZ, USAFSO as of 31 Dec 64. To United States-Brazil Military Commission as VC-47D from Jan 66 (with Portuguese language titles as well 'Comissao Militar Mista Brasil Estados Unidos') and by 20 Feb 67 as a VC-47D. To plain white upper decking at Howard by Oct 67 through at least 24 Dec 69 however. To Guatemala as FAG-560 under MAP 20 Aug 70 and later converted to Basler BT-67 configuration as TG-FAG-4/560 in 1994.
0-51131	45-1131	C-47B-50-DK	17134/34401	US Air Attaché to Bolivia's aircraft *c.*15 Dec 48.
0-51132	45-1132	C-47B-50-DK	17135/34402	USAF Mission to Venezuela as C-47D by 31 Dec 64. Noted at Howard AFB, CZ, Nov 69 with 'United States of America' titles only.
0-51138	45-1138	C-47B-50-DK	17141/34408	US Air Attaché's aircraft in Argentina between 5 Jun 46 and at least 30 Jun 48. Was written off 17 Feb 49.
0-52549	45-2549	C-117A-5-DK	18552/34133	To US Air Attaché, Brazil as C-117B.
0-76252	44-76252A	C-47B-28-DK C-47D VC-47D	15836/32584	Assigned to Albrook Field, CZ, CAC, 1 Jan 48 as VC-47D assigned as US Air Attaché's aircraft in Argentina between 28 Apr 49 and at least 14 Jan 56. To CONUS 22 Jul 63.
0-76385	44-76385	C-47B-25-DK	15969/32717	Former RAF Dakota KN354 returned to US control. Assigned to Base Flight, Howard AFB, CZ, USAFSO as C-47D as of 31 Dec 64. To MAAG Brazil by Sep 65 and 13 Nov 67.
0-76395	44-76395	C-47B-27-DK	15979/32727	Arrived Havana, Cuba, 7 Nov 48 for TDY as the US Air Attaché Cuba's aircraft, as a VC-47D, following the wreck of his regular aircraft, 42-23346 in a hurricane.
0-76443	43-76443	C-47B-25-DK	16027/32775	605th Air Commando Squadron. However, this aircraft has also been reported to have been surveyed in Germany 30 Jan 48!
4-76448 0-76448	44-76448	C-47B-25-DK C-47D	16032/32780	Assigned to CAC and detailed to Tegucigalpa, Honduras, 1 Jan 48. Apparently to joint duty to the USAF Mission to Guatemala and Colombia briefly, before returning to Honduras to the newly installed USAF Mission and remained there, incredibly, until 19 Jul 66. Day-Glo removed, completely repainted and corrosion control exercised Oct 64. To Base Flight, Howard AFB, CZ, USAFSO as C-47D by 31 Dec 64. Noted at Howard AFB, CZ, as C-47D 4 Mar 68 and 26 Oct 68 with simply 'United States of America' titles. To FAE-76448 MAP 31 May 70.

0-76451	44-76451	C-47B-25-DK	16035/32783	To SAO, Ramey AFB, PR, 305th Bomb Wing 7 Mar 54. Returned to CONUS 6 Apr 54.
4-76455 0-76455	44-76455	C-47B-25-DK C-47D	16039/32787	Joint Brazil-US Military Commission 12 Sep 47. MAAG to Brazil from Feb 61. To Base Flight, Howard AFB, CZ, USAFSO as C-47D by 31 Dec 64 but back to MAAG Brazil by Oct 65. To plain white upper decking at Howard AFB, CZ, 24th SOW, by 31 Jul 68. To MAP unknown recipient 29 Jan 70.
0-77051	44-77051	C-47B-35-DK	16635/33383	605th Air Commando Squadron, Howard AFB, CZ, by 1964. However, this aircraft has also been reported to have gone to the USSR under Lend-Lease 6 Jun 45!
0-92079	42-92079	C-47A-DK	11840	605th Air Commando Squadron by 16 Oct 65 and redesignated as C-47D 31 May 67. To 24th ACW 31 Mar 68 and the 24th SOE 31 Jul 68. To Puerto Rico Air National Guard by 1970. To IAAFA as G-18 14 Nov 73 (q.v.).
0-92104	42-92104	C-47A-1-DK	11867	605th Air Commando Squadron, USAFSO by 1 Jul 64 and redesignated as C-47D 29 Sep 67. Noted wearing a sub-standard size US fuselage national insignia as of 8 Jan 67. To 24th ACW, Howard AFB, CZ, 31 Mar 68 and 24th SOW there also 31 Jul 68. To El Salvador as FAS-106 4 Sep 70 after having apparently been 'in country' for training as early as 24 Nov 69.
0-224405	42-24405	C-47A-60-DL	10267	Ex-Air National Guard. Noted at Howard AFB, CZ, with plain white upper decking 18 Jul 68.
0-316331	43-16331	C-47B-1-DL	20797	Reported at Rio de Janeiro/Galeão Airport Aug 1962. However, this aircraft has always been reported to have been salvaged in Australia 15 Nov 44!
3-49533 0-349533	43-49533 43-49533A	C-47B-15-DK C-47D	15349/26794	To 7421st Foreign Mission Squadron, Lima, Peru 1 Jan 48. To USAF Mission to Ecuador 21 Feb 52. To USAF Mission to Argentina 9 May 52. Returned to USAF Mission to Peru 5 Feb 53. To USAF Mission to Chile 21 Oct 56. Back to USAF Mission to Peru 8 Dec 56. To USAF Mission to Argentina 4 Aug 57 and sustained damage at Cordoba in 1959. To FAA as T-35 17 May 60 (q.v.).
0-476442	44-76442	C-47B-25-DK C-47D	16026/32774	605th Air Commando Squadron, Howard AFB, CZ, 1 Jul 64, all grey by 26 Oct 68. To USAF Mission to Venezuela 15 Nov 69. Returned to Canal Zone 22 Jul 70. To FAP T-73 under MAP 9 Nov 70.
0-476445	44-76445	C-47B-25-DK	16029/32777	605th Air Commando Squadron, Howard AFB, CZ, by 1964.
0-476449	44-76449	C-47B-27-DK	16033/32781	605th Air Commando Squadron, Howard AFB, CZ, by Sep 64. To DMAFB storage by 11 Jan 71.
1-18491	41-18491	C-47-DL	4583	To Howard Fld, CZ, 10 Feb 46 To War Assets Administration (WAA) 25 Jul 46 and became NC-4111.
2-23346	42-23346	C-47A-1-DL	9208	To Division of Military Intelligence, Cuba, 9 Dec 46. To Albrook Fld, CZ, 18 Dec 46. To Havana, Cuba (Air Attaché's aircraft), 25 Oct 48. Assigned to HQC-MAA 14 Feb 49. To Havana, Cuba, 25 Mar 49. Reclaimed as the result of damage in a hurricane at Havana 25 Oct 49 (see 44-76395).
2-23384	42-23384	C-47A-15-DL	9246	To Division of Military Intelligence, Brazil 8 Oct 46. To FAB same date.

Wearing a decidedly non-regulation colour scheme, including scalloping around the nose and engine cowlings, and an unusual dual cheatline, 0-49280 was built as a C-47B-15-DK (43-49280) and by the time of this November 1969 photograph at Howard AFB, was a VC-47D assigned to USAFSO Headquarters. She had been in Latin America since January 1947, pioneering mission activity in Paraguay, and passed via MAP to Honduras, probably as FAH-319 on 5 December 1975. *Hagedorn*

2-23398	42-23398	C-47A-5-DL	9260	Assigned to CAC PAD 30 Apr 47. To Borinquen Field, PR, temporarily 25 May 48. To Ramey AFB, PR, 1 Jul 48. Returned to 5702nd Foreign Missions Squadron, Albrook AFB, CZ, 26 Jul 48. To the 5713th Airbase Squadron, San Jose Airbase, Guatemala, 16 Oct 48 and to the USAF Mission to Guatemala 1 Jan 49. To the 5701st Foreign Missions Group 4 Apr 49 and 5700th Airbase Group 1 May 49. Returned to CONUS 17 Nov 49.
2-23771	42-23771	C-47A-30-DL	9633	To CAC 5700th Airbase Group, Albrook AFB, CZ, 15 Sep 49. Accident 6 Mar 48 at Columbia, Republic of Panama, home based at Howard AFB, CZ, while being flown by Jack W. McCamic. Repaired. To USAF Mission to El Salvador 7 Feb 52. To USAF Mission to Honduras 9 Jul 52. Returned to CONUS 24 Mar 56.
2-24124	42-24124	C-47A-45-DL	9986	Assigned to the Joint Brazil-US Commission at Rio de Janeiro, Brazil, 22 Dec 48. Returned to CONUS 31 Mar 49.
2-24311	42-24311	C-47A-50-DL	10173	Assigned to 785th Airbase Unit, Borinquen Field, PR, 13 Aug 46. To the 73rd ACG, Ramey AFB, PR, 1 Jun 48 and the 1806th AACG 1 Oct 48. To Albrook AFB, CZ, 3 Jun 49. Returned to CONUS 5 May 50.
2-32926	42-32926	C-47-DL	9152	To Howard Fld, CZ, ex-Bolling Fld, DC, 22 Jan 46 for Chief of (illegible). Accident 16 May 47 at Quito, Ecuador, while being flown by Stanley J. Buinicky, home based at Albrook Fld, CZ. Probably intended for ARP Ecuador. To FLC 10 Jul 47 to 9 Sep 47. Fate from there unknown.
2-93731	42-93731	C-47A-25-DK	13675	Assigned to Caribbean TSP, Borinquen Field, PR, a veteran of the Ninth Air Force in Europe. Crashed 10 Sep 45 6 miles north-west of Borinquen Field, PR, 1Lt Gilbert R. Forbas commanding.
2-100604	42-100604	C-47A-65-DL	19067	Assigned ex-Kelly to CAC by 11 Feb 48. To ARP Project No. 94548 Venezuela 5 Sep 48.
3-15556	43-15556	C-47A-85-DL	20022	Assigned MTO to the 1806th AACG, Albrook AFB, CZ, 15 Jul 54. Returned to CONUS 10 Jan 57.
3-15605	43-15605 0-15605	C-47A-85-DL	20071	198th Fighter Interceptor Squadron, Puerto Rico Air National Guard, Borinquen Field, PR, 12 May 49. Stayed until returned to CONUS 10 Jun 61.
3-15688	43-15688	C-47A-90-DL C-47B C-47E	20154	Assigned to the Joint Brazil-US Commission, Rio de Janeiro, Brazil, 1 Jan 48. Transferred to USAF Mission to Bolivia 21 Jan 49. To 5700th Airbase Group, Albrook AFB, CZ, 5 Dec 49 but effectively detached to La Paz. Redesignated as a C-47B for some reason 12 Apr 51. Redesignated as a C-47E 26 Aug 56, remaining in Bolivia until 16 Dec 60. To USAF Mission to Ecuador 17 Feb 63 but returned to Albrook 23 Mar 63. Returned to CONUS and transferred to the US Army 27 Apr 63.
3-15772	43-15772	C-47A-90-DL C-47B	20238	Assigned to the 1130th Special Advisory Group, Caracas, Venezuela, 17 Aug 52. Apparently redesignated as a C-47B 21 Mar 53. To the USAF Mission to Cuba 30 Oct 57. Returned to CONUS 22 Dec 57.
3-15975	43-15975	C-47A-90-DL	20441	Assigned to the MTO, 521st ATG, Ramey AFB, PR, 20 Jul 48. Returned to CONUS by 4 Feb 49.
3-16161	43-16161 43-16161A	C-47A-90-DL	20627	Assigned to CAC and then the USAF Mission to Peru 5 Nov 49, replacing 43-49533A. To the USAF Mission to Ecuador 28 Feb 50. Returned to CONUS 5 Jul 50.
3-16278	43-16278	C-47B-1-DL	20744	CAC and PAD 1 Jan 48. Redesignated as C-47D 16 Jul 48. To USAF Mexico Liaison Flight 1 Nov 49 and apparently remained there with the USAAF/USAF Training Detachment as late as 24 Jun 53. To the 5700th Airbase Group, Albrook AFB, CZ, 7 Oct 54. To HQO Havana, Cuba, 1130th Special Actions Group 15 Mar 56. Returned to 5700th ABG, Albrook AFB, CZ, 25 May 56. Returned to CONUS by 1 Jul 57.
3-16400	43-16400	C-47B-1-DL C-47D	20866	Assigned to the 1st Rescue Squadron, Waller AFB, Trinidad, 1 Feb 49. To Howard AFB, CZ, 1 Jun 49. Redesignated as C-47D and to Ramey AFB, PR, 10 Nov 49. Returned to CONUS 15 Mar 50.

A sight never to be repeated, at least nine former USAFSO, Mission and 605th ACS C-47s await their fate at sunset on the west taxiway at Howard AFB, CZ, in November 1969. Most were transferred to Latin American air arms under MAP. *Hagedorn*

3-48270	43-48270	C-47B-1-DK C-47D	14086/25531	Assigned to CAC and detached to the infant US Mission to Bolivia 1 Jan 48. Formally assigned to the 7406th Foreign Mission Squadron at La Paz 20 Apr 48. Redesignated as C-47D 10 Mar 49 and to the 5700th Airbase Group, Albrook AFB, CZ, 10 Dec 49. To the USAF Mission to Haiti 25 Mar 52 but returned to the 5700th ABG 5 Jun 52. Then to the USAF Mission to El Salvador 5 Feb 53. Once again recalled to the 5700th ABG but then to the USAF Mission to Venezuela as part of the 1130th SAG 13 Apr 54. Once again to the USAF Mission to Haiti 23 Dec 55 and then on to the USAF Mission to Uruguay 7 May 56. Returned to CONUS 17 Apr 57.
3-48301	43-48301	C-47B-1-DK	14117/25562	To CAC, 48th Rescue Squadron, Borinquen Field, PR, 30 Apr 47. Redesignated as a C-47D with that unit at, by then, Ramey AFB, PR by 3 Apr 48. To Albrook Field, CZ, and then attached to the USAF Mission to Bolivia 1 May 49. Returned to the PAD, Albrook AFB, CZ, 22 Jul 49 and from there back to Kelly AFB, TX. It appears to have returned to the USAF Mission to Bolivia briefly 17 Jul 50 before going to Kadena AFB, Japan.
3-48398	43-48398	C-47B-1-DK C-47D SC-47D	14214/25659	Assigned to the 1st Rescue Squadron, CAC, Howard Field, CZ, 1 Jan 48 as a C-47D. To MTO 5700th Airbase Group, Albrook AFB, CZ, 9 Oct 50. To Far East 6 Dec 50 due to the Korean conflict. However, returned to the 63rd ARS, Ramey AFB, PR, 1 Nov 57 as an SC-47D. She returned to CONUS 9 Dec 57 however.
3-48402	43-48402	C-47B-1-DK	14218/25663	Assigned to CAC, PAD 30 Jun 49. To the 1130th SAG, Quito, Ecuador 26 Sep 49. To the USAF Mission to Bolivia 21 Dec 49. To the USAF Mission to Venezuela 31 Jul 50. Returned to CONUS 7 Mar 51.
3-48404	43-48404	C-47B-1-DK	14220/25665	Assigned to the 1130th SAG, Rio de Janeiro, Brazil, 8 Dec 49. Returned to CONUS 7 Feb 50.
3-48472	43-48472	C-47B-1-DK C-47D	14288/25733	Assigned to the US Mission to Guatemala 13 Nov 46. To the CAC's 7414th SU 1 Jan 48 then the 7414th Foreign Mission Squadron, probably at Guatemala City, 20 Mar 48. Redesignated as a C-47D 23 Aug 48. To the Joint Brazil-US Military Commission 10 Mar 59 then the 1130th SAG, USAF Mission to Peru 23 May 59. Returned to the USAF Mission to Guatemala 1 Oct 59, then the USAF Mission to Colombia 10 Dec 59. Next to the 5500th Foreign Mission Squadron, USAF Mission to Ecuador 5 Oct 61. Then the USAF Mission to Uruguay 28 Feb 63, back to Ecuador 8 Apr 63. MAP to Uruguay as FAU-522 10 Mar 65.
3-48483	43-48483	C-47B-1-DK	14299/25744	To CAC, CZ, after having served in Europe with Ninth AF and in Italy after 19 Feb 46. To Brazil 1 Jan 48. This aircraft suffered an accident at Rio-Galeao 30 Aug 48 while being flown by Jerome C. Eicholz and was based at Rio at the time, probably on Mission or Air Attaché duty. She was apparently repaired as she returned to CONUS 3 Jan 49.
3-48601	43-48601	C-47B-5-DK	14417/25862	To CAC, CZ, 20 Sep 45 but had returned to CONUS by 24 Apr 46.
3-48602	43-48602	C-47B-5-DK	14418/25863	To CAC, CZ, 20 Sep 45. Accident 3 Dec 45 10 miles south-east of Colonia Carlos Pellegrini, Corrientes, Argentina, home based at Howard Fld, CZ, 1Lt Orville A. Michelsen commanding. Recovered and repaired, becoming 0-348602 but fate unknown.
3-48699	43-48699	C-47B-5-DK C-47D VC-47D	14515/25960	Joint Brazil-US Commission, Rio de Janeiro, Brazil, 1 Jan 48 as C-47D, VC-47D from 1 Sep 50. Returned to CONUS 1 Mar 53.
3-48715	43-48715	C-47B-5-DK	14531/25976	Sixth Air Force, PAD 29 Oct 45, probably positioned for possible ARP distribution. To the US Mission to Bolivia but returned to the CONUS by 4 Dec 46 instead.
3-48725	43-48725	C-47B-5-DK C-47D VC-47D VC-47B	14541/25986	Apparently intended for ARP Chile, as in country by 17 Sep 45. Her whereabouts between then and 1 Jan 48 are unknown, but she then reappeared with CAC and nominally assigned to Atkinson Field, British Guiana, with the 7408th SU there. She then returned to the USAF Mission to Chile 23 Dec 48 and was redesignated as a C-47D 1 Jan 49. She was then outfitted as a VC-47D 16 Oct 50 and VC-47B 4 Jan 51, all the while shuttling between Santiago, Chile, and home station at Albrook AFB, CZ. She suffered an unspecified accident and was 'reclaimed' 1 Jun 53 but then sold for rebuild. It is not clear who did this or how it was accomplished, but she was then sold to the FAP in Peru as 53-307 sometime in 1953, a most unusual metamorphosis. It has been speculated that Panagra performed this rebuild, and this seems to fit the known circumstances.
3-48758	43-48758	C-47B-8-DK C-47D VC-47D	14574/26019	Assigned CAC's 3rd BCS, Albrook Field, CZ, 1 Jan 48 and had been redesignated as a C-47D by 16 Jul 48. To the 5702nd Mission Group 26 Jul 48. Redesignated as a VC-47D 17 Nov 48. To the 5701st Mission Group 23 Mar 49 and apparently detailed to the USAF Mission to Chile by 22 Feb 54. To the USAF Mission to Cuba by 19 Jun 54. Suffered an accident 23 May 1958 and apparently sold 'as is/where is' and became PP-NAR in Brazil by 7 Aug 58.
3-48810	43-48810	C-47B-5-DK	14626/26071	To Howard Fld, CZ, 6 Jun 46 and assigned to the 6th Weather Squadron. Accident 9 Oct 47 at Albrook Fld, CZ, while being flown by William P. Nash. Repaired. Redesignated as a C-47D by Jan 48. Reclaimed by 24 Mar 48 in the Canal Zone.
3-49873	43-49873	C-47B-23-DK	15689/27134	To CAC after 25 Nov 45, Eighth AF veteran. Probably pre-positioned for surplus sale at Albrook Field, CZ. To FLC 5 Feb 46 to unknown recipient.
3-48923	43-48923	C-47B-10-DK	14739/26184	To Atkinson Field, British Guiana, 1 Jan 48. To either Albrook or Howard Fld, CZ, 28 Jul 49. Reclamation complete 9 Jul 49, however, some sources claim was sold and rebuilt to become N75290.

Arguably one of the most significant C-47s in Latin American aviation history – and certainly the best maintained – GC-47D 'G-4' sits the apron at the Inter-American Air Forces Academy at Albrook AFB, CZ, in December 1968. She was the former 44-76691A and was assigned to USAFO on 30 November 1965 as 'Class 26', specifically for instructional use. Her fate remains unknown following the return of the Canal Zone and Albrook to the Republic of Panama. *Hagedorn*

3-49016	43-49016	C-47B-13-DK	14832/26277	Passed to the FLC at Albrook Field, CZ, 1 Jan 46 for surplus sale. Acquired by LAN Chile as CC-CLK-0001 18 Feb 46.
3-49018	43-49018	C-47B-11-DK	14834/26279	To either Albrook or Howard Field, CZ. Dropped on Excess Inventory List 1 Feb 47.
3-49035	43-49035	C-47B-10-DK C-47D	14851/26296	Assigned to the CAC's 26th Air-Sea Rescue Squadron detachment at Beane Field, St. Lucia after 27 Nov 45 and redesignated as a C-47D 22 Jan 46. To the 5916th Airbase Squadron 16 Aug 48, probably Beane Field, then to the 5904th Airbase Group, Ramey AFB, PR, 19 Apr 49. To 23rd Airbase Group, Howard AFB, CZ, 20 Aug 49 and the 5601st Airbase Squadron 24 Sep 49. To the 1st Rescue Squadron, Albrook AFB, CZ, 1 Nov 49 but returned to CONUS 28 Feb 50.
3-49039	43-49039	C-47B-10-DK 'TC-47B' C-47D	14855/26300	Assigned to CAC, probably Albrook Field, CZ, 20 Aug 46 and almost immediately assigned to the ARP cadre in Chile, where she was perhaps informally referred to as a 'TC-47B'. Redesignated as C-47D 27 Apr 48. To the 7409th Military Mission Squadron, Bogota, Colombia, 28 Apr 48. This aircraft suffered an accident 5 Feb 49 3 miles east of Bogota while apparently stationed with the USAF Mission at Cali while being commanded by Capt J. MacBeall. It was apparently recovered and repaired as it returned to CONUS 3 Jul 50.
3-49041	43-49041	C-47B-10-DK	14857/26302	To either Albrook or Howard Field, CZ. Declared excess 4 Jun 47 but to FLC 23 Jul 48. Redesignated as a C-47D 28 Feb 47 and VC-47D 14 Jan 49. Salvaged 16 Oct 50.
3-49043	43-49043	C-47B-10-DK 'TC-47B'	14859/26304	To CAC after 6 Jun 46, and almost immediately detailed to the ARP Cadre in Chile, where she was identified, perhaps informally, as a 'TC-47B'. This aircraft suffered a landing accident at Los Cerrillos, Santiago, Chile, 29 Aug 47 while being flown by Donald C. Dickson but was apparently returned to service. Via FLC to unknown buyer 23 Jul 48, possibly the FACh. No subsequent history known.
3-49080	43-49080	C-47B-10-DK C-47D	14896/26341	European theatre Ninth AF veteran. Returned to the US and departed for Albrook Fld, CZ, Jun 46 where it remained as late as 1 Jan 48, by which time it had been redesignated as a C-47D. Accident 26 Jul 49 at Tiquisate, Guatemala, while being flown by Harry H. Roddenberry. Home based at Albrook AFB, CZ, at the time. To CONUS 11 Nov 49.
3-49081	43-49081	C-47B-10-DK	14897/26342	Assigned to CAC 26 Nov 45 and to the 26th Air-Sea Rescue Squadron detachment at Beane Field, St Lucia by 1 Jan 48. Redesignated as a C-47D and assigned to the 5916th Airbase Squadron 26 Jul 48. To the 5900th Airbase Squadron, Ramey AFB, PR, 7 May 49. There with the 55th Strategic Reconnaissance Wing as late as 2 Nov 50. Returned to CONUS by 20 May 51.
3-49089	43-49089	C-47B-10-DK	14905/26350	Assigned to Borinquen Field, PR, 10 Dec 45. To Atkinson Field, British Guiana, by 1 Jan 48 but returned to Borinquen 6 Apr 48. To Ramey AFB, PR, 1 Jul 48. To Coolidge Field, BWI, 11 Oct 48 and back to Ramey by 1 Aug 49. Returned to CONUS 4 Nov 49.
3-49105	43-49105	C-47B-10-DK	14921/26366	To Sixth Air Force after 15 Sep 45, a veteran of the Twelfth Air Force in Italy. At Howard AFB, CZ, by 1 Nov 49 and to Albrook AFB, CZ, by 17 Aug 50. As a C-47D, suffered an accident 19 Aug 50 at La Sabana Airport, San Jose, Costa Rica, while being flown by Owen C. Brickford. Was home based at Albrook AFB, CZ, at the time. Although official reclaimed, it apparently survived to become N75391 by Jan 58 with an owner who gave residence, perhaps significantly, as San Jose, Costa Rica.

3-49108	43-49108	C-47B-11-DK	14924/26369	Assigned to the US Mission to Guatemala 14 Apr 47 and to the 1134th SAS, US Air Attaché Venezuela *c.*6 Aug 48. Redesignated as VC-47D by Sep 54. To DMAFB, AZ, by Sep 67.
3-49110 0-49110	43-49110	C-47B-10-DK C-47D VC-47D	14926/26371	Assigned to 5700th Airbase Group, Albrook AFB, CZ, 11 Apr 53. To the USAF Mission to Nicaragua 17 Apr 53 where it remained, although home based at Albrook and Howard AFB, CZ, as late as 31 Aug 67. To the 24th Composite Wing 31 May 68 at Howard AFB and to MAP 23 Jan 70, recipient unknown.
3-49146	43-49146	C-47B-10-DK VC-47D	14962/26407	Assigned to Sixth Air Force 17 Aug 47 and with the 3rd BCS at Albrook Field, CZ, by 1 Jan 48. To the 5702nd Mission Group 26 Jul 48 and redesignated as a VC-47D 2 Nov 48. To the 5701st Mission Group 23 Mar 49 and returned to CONUS 8 May 50.
3-49280 0-49280	43-49280	C-47B-15-DK C-47D VC-47D	15096/26541	To DMI, US Air Attaché Paraguay 30 Jan 47 and as late as 25 Oct 48. To US Air Attaché Guatemala 24 Feb 50 as VC-47D. Noted in Belize as 0-49280 by 1968. To CONUS 30 Nov 72 and then MAP to FAH-319 5 Dec 75.
3-49339	43-49339	C-47B-15-DK	15155/26600	US Air Attaché to Guatemala by 6 Sep 49 as VC-47D. Reassigned to Brookley AFB, AL, 5 Dec 49 and replaced by 45-1113 (q.v.).
3-49356	43-49356	C-47B-15-DK C-47D	15172/26617	See wartime list. To Howard AFB, CZ, 1 Jul 48. Returned to CONUS 6 Jun 50.
3-49438	43-49438	C-47B-15-DK C-47D	15254/26699	Assigned to 5701st Mission Group, CAC Albrook AFB, CZ, 19 Mar 49 as a C-47D. To the USAF Mission to Cuba 11 Apr 51. Returned to CONUS 3 Jan 61.
3-49497	43-49497	C-47B-15-DK	15313/26758	Accident 23 Jun 49 at Kanama Field, Varadero, Cuba, while being flown by Clarence C. Rarick, Assigned to US Air Attaché, Cuba, at the time. Around 26 Nov 49, the Cuban Attaché exchanged this aircraft with the US Air Attaché to Colombia. The Cuban Attaché got 45-1115 (q.v.) and Colombia got VC-47D 43-49497.
3-49537	43-49537	C-47B-15-DK	15353/26798	To Howard Fld, CZ, 19 Dec 45, probably pre-positioned for surplus sale at Albrook Field, CZ. Dropped on Excess Inventory List 1 Jun 46 and sold to LAV as YV-C-AFE.
3-49746	43-49746	C-47B-20-DK	15562/27007	Assigned to Borinquen Field, PR, 1 Jan 48 and Ramey AFB, PR, 1 Jul 48. Apparently suffered an unidentified accident in the Caribbean and reclaimed 8 Sep 48.
4-76326	44-76326	C-47B-28-DK C-47D VC-47D	15910/32658	Assigned to CAC 31 May 46 to Borinquen Field, PR. To 24th Composite Wing as C-47D 1 Jan 48. Ramey AFB, PR, 1 Jul 48. To USAF Mission to El Salvador 11 Jan 49. Redesignated as VC-47D 1 Sep 49. To 5700th ABG, Albrook AFB, CZ, 6 Feb 52. Returned to CONUS 5 Apr 52.
4-76342	44-76342	C-47B-28-DK C-47D VC-47D	15926/32674	Assigned to CAC 31 May 46, to 24th Composite Group, Ramey AFB, PR, as C-47D 1 Jan 48. Redesignated as VC-47D 7 Apr 49. To 5601st Airbase Squadron, Howard AFB, CZ, 20 Aug 49. Returned to CONUS 9 May 50.
4-76382 0-76382	44-76382	C-47B-28-DK C-47D VC-47D	15966/32714	To CAC 31 May 46. To 24th Composite Wing, Borinquen Field, PR, as C-47D 1 Jan 48 To Ramey AFB, PR, 1 Jul 48. Redesignated as VC-47D 7 Apr 49. To US Army 11 Feb 65.
4-76385 0-76385	44-76385 KN354 VMYBZ 44-76385	C-47B-25-DK Dakota IV C-47D	15969/32717	To CAC, 5700th ABG, Albrook AFB, CZ, 19 Feb 61. To USAF Mission (or Air Attaché) to Haiti 29 Jun 61. To USAF Mission to Venezuela 18 Aug 61. To USAF Mission to El Salvador 31 Jul 62. To USAF Mission to Haiti 20 Feb 63. To USAF Mission to Nicaragua 3 Apr 63. To USAF Mission to Ecuador 11 May 63. To USAF Mission to Colombia 1 Aug 63. To USAF Mission to Ecuador 24 Oct 63. To USAF Mission to El Salvador 4 May 64. To USAF Mission to the Dominican Republic 9 Sep 64. To USAF Mission to Brazil 7 Sep 65. To USAF Mission to Venezuela 29 Mar 66. To USAF Mission to Brazil 20 Feb 67. To 24th SOW, Howard AFB, CZ, 1 Dec 67. To unknown recipient, MAP 28 Jan 70.
4-77262A	44-77262A	C-47B-40-DK C-47D	16846/33594	To CAC after 2 Jul 45. Assigned to Borinquen Field, PR, 27 Nov 45. Redesignated as a C-47D and assigned to Waller Field, Trinidad, by 1Jan 48. Accident 5 May 49 at Waller Fld, Trinidad as C-47D while being flown by Leon Reed. Home based there at the time and reclaimed 1 Oct 49.
4-77276	44-77276	C-47B-40-DK	16860/33608	To CAC after Jul 45. Accident 19 Sep 47 at Albrook Fld, CZ, while being flown by William P. Nash. Repaired and to CONUS and SAC. Possibly to USAAF Mission to Argentina briefly. To 5904th Airbase Group, Ramey AFB, PR, 1 Feb 49 as C-47D.
4-77282	44-77282	C-47B-40-DK C-47D	16866/33614	To CAC, Borinquen Field, PR, 12 Dec 45. As C-47D by 1 Jan 48, accident 19 Nov 48 at Atkinson AFB, British Guiana, while being flown by George H. Walsh. Based there at the time. Presumed lost, as reclamation approved 25 Jan 50 and no further known service history.
4-77275	44-77275	C-47B-35-DK C-47D	16859/33607	Assigned to 521st ATG, Ramey AFB, PR, 14 Jul 47.
4-77276	44-77276	C-47B-35-DK C-47D	16860/33608	Assigned to CAC after 21 Aug 46 and to the US Mission to Argentina by 1 Jan 48 as a C-47D. To Ramey AFB, PR, 1 Feb 49. Returned to CONUS by 20 Aug 51.
4-77294	44-77294	C-47B-35-DK C-47D	16878/33626	Assigned to 55th SRW, Ramey AFB, PR, 14 Feb 52 as C-47D. Returned to CONUS but back to 72nd ABG, Ramey AFB, PR, 31 Oct 56.
5-876	45-876	C-47B-45-DK C-47D VC-47D C-47D	16879/34134	Assigned to CAC 13 Dec 45. To 25th ARS, Coolidge AFB, BWI, 1 Jan 48. Redesignated as a C-47D 1 Sep 48. To 5920th ABS, Waller AFB, Trinidad, 24 May 49. Redesignated as a VC-47D 1 Jun 49. Assigned to the 5900th Composite Wing, Ramey AFB, PR, 24 Feb 50 and reverted to C-47D 14 Apr 50. Returned to CONUS 12 Jun 52.

5-878	45-878	C-47B-45-DK	16881/34137	To Albrook Fld, CZ, by 1 Jan 48. Accident 7 May 48 at Vernam Fld, Jamaica, while being flown by Basil E. Palmer, Jr., home based at Albrook AFB, CZ. To War Assets Administration (WAA) 3 Dec 49. To Haitian Air Corps by 1950 as serial 5878.
5-890	45-890	C-47B-45-DK	16893/34150	Assigned briefly to Howard AFB, CZ, 1 Jan 48 but returned to CONUS by 14 Jan.
5-916	45-916	C-47B-45-DK C-47D	16919/34177	To CAC 23 May 46. Accident 8 Mar 47 at Las Mercedes Airport, Managua, Nicaragua, while being flown by Lloyd C. Romine. Home based at Albrook Fld, CZ, at the time. Redesignated as C-47D 8 Apr 48. Assigned to Joint Brazil-US Military Commission, Rio de Janeiro 2 Jul 48. Redesignated as VC-47D 20 Sep 48 and was assigned to the JBUSMC between Mar 61 and Feb 65 as 0-50916. Returned to CONUS by 5 Jun 65.
5-932	45-932	C-47B-45-DK C-47D	16935/34194	Assigned to 783rd Base Unit, Albrook AFB, CZ, 1 Jan 48. To the 153rd Army Airways Communications Squadron 1 Jun 48. To the 1806th AACG, Ramey AFB, PR, 29 Nov 48 but returned to Albrook AFB, CZ, 3 Jun 49. Returned to CONUS 5 Nov 50.
5-967	45-967	C-47B-45-DK C-47D	16970/34230	To CAC 14 May 46. Assigned to the San Jose, Guatemala Auxiliary Aerodrome, 1 Jan 48. To the 3rd BCS, Albrook AFB, CZ, 7 Jan 48. To the 1st Rescue Squadron, Howard AFB, CZ, 28 Feb 48. Redesignated as C-47D 2 Nov 48. Accident 16 Feb 49 at Toncontín Field, Tegucigalpa, Honduras, while being flown by William O. Butler. Home based at Albrook Fld, CZ, at the time but in actuality probably assigned to the 5701st Mission Group, USAF Mission to Honduras at the time. See 0-50967 above for subsequent history.
5-994	45-994	C-47B-45-DK C-47D	16997/34259	To CAC 14 May 46. Assigned to the 4th Tactical Reconnaissance Squadron, Rio Hato, Republic of Panama, 1 Jan 48. Redesignated as C-47D 17 Mar 48. Still with the 4th TRS, reassigned to New France AFB, CZ, 26 Jul 48 and Howard AFB, CZ, 16 Aug 48. To the USAF Mission to Paraguay 17 Feb 49. Accident 12 May 49 at Albrook AFB, CZ, home based there, while being flown by Carl W. Leisering. Returned to CONUS 19 Apr 50.
5-1002	45-1002	C-47B-45-DK	17005/34268	Assigned to 785th BU, Borinquen Field, PR, 16 Jun 47. To 73rd AACG, Ramey AFB, PR, 1 Jun 48. Returned to CONUS 1 Oct 48.
5-1007	45-1007	C-47B-45-DK C-47D	17010/34273	To CAC, 3rd BC, Albrook Field, CZ, 14 May 46. Redesignated as C-47D 1 Jan 48. Accident 5 Oct 49 'in flight' over Albrook AFB, CZ, while being flown by F.C. Gass. Assumed a bird strike or mid-air collision. Apparently survived to become 0-51007 and to the 7531st ABS at Bovingdon, UK, by Feb 56.
5-1009	45-1009	C-47B-45-DK C-47D	17012/34275	Assigned to CAC, 334th Troop Carrier Squadron, Borinquen Field, PR, 14 May 46. Redesignated as C-47D 1 Jan 48. To the 582nd SRG, Howard AFB, CZ, 23 May 48. To the 55th SRW, Ramey AFB, PR, 1 Nov 50. Returned to CONUS 28 Nov 51.
5-1021	45-1021	C-47B-45-DK C-47D	17024/34288	Assigned to CAC, Albrook Field, CZ, 14 May 46. To 20th Troop Carrier Squadron 1 Jan 48. Redesignated as C-47D 4 Mar 48. To the 18th Troop Carrier Squadron 1 Sep 48. To 5912th ABS, Vernam AFB, Jamaica, 20 Dec 48. Returned to CONUS 19 Apr 50.
5-1029	45-1029	C-47B-45-DK C-47D	17032/34297	To CAC 14 May 46. Accident 2 Jan 47 at Pocrí AAD, Republic of Panama, home based at Howard Field, CZ, while being flown by Richard E. Brasington. To the 582nd ASG, Howard AFB, CZ, 1 Jan 48. Redesignated as C-47D 2 Jan 48. Returned to CONUS 5 May 50.
5-1030	45-1030	C-47B-45-DK C-47D	17033/34298	Assigned to CAC 14 May 46. To the 20th Troop Carrier Squadron, Albrook AFB, CZ, 1 Jan 48. Redesignated as C-47D 17 Mar 48. To 18th Troop Carrier Squadron 1 Sep 48. To 5925th ABS, Waller AFB, Trinidad, 1 Oct 48. To 5918th ABS, Atkinson AFB, British Guiana, 27 Dec 48. Returned to 5920th ABG, Waller AFB, Trinidad, 1 May 49. To CONUS 15 May 50.
5-1032	45-1032	C-47B-45-DK C-47D	17035/34300	Assigned to CAC, 20th Troop Carrier Squadron, Albrook Field, CZ, 14 May 46. Redesignated as C-47D 2 May 48. To 18th Troop Carrier Squadron 1 Sep 48. To USAF Mission to Bolivia 12 Jul 55. To USAF Mission to Colombia 5 Jan 56. To USAF Mission to Ecuador 17 May 56. To USAF Mission to Peru 16 Aug 57. To USAF Mission to Colombia 2 Jul 58. To USAF Mission to Brazil 1 Oct 58. To USAF Mission to Haiti 29 Jan 59. To USAF Mission to El Salvador 4 Apr 59. To USAF Mission to Haiti 9 Jun 61. To USAF Mission to the Dominican Republic 31 Jul 62 through at least 30 Nov 69. To Honduras MAP as FAH-308 (q.v.) 19 Aug 70.
5-1064	45-1064	C-47B-50-DK VC-47B	17067/34334	There is some evidence that this aircraft had been set aside under ARP for Uruguay, as she was assigned to the Division of Military Intelligence/Montevideo 25 Jun 47 but had passed to the USAF Mission to Uruguay by 25 Oct 48. To the USAF Mission to Venezuela 15 Feb 50 and redesignated as VC-47B 2 Mar 51. Returned to CONUS 18 Aug 52.
5-1084	45-1084	C-47B-50-DK C-47D	17087/34354	Assigned to USAF Mission to Ecuador as C-47D 19 Apr 48. To USAF Mission to Colombia 1 Jul 48 but back to Ecuador 23 Dec 48. Returned to CONUS 11 Aug 50.
5-1087	45-1087	C-47B-5p-DK	17090/34357	Assigned to CAC 2 Dec 46. To 1st Rescue Squadron, Howard Field, CZ, 8 Oct 47. To Albrook AFB, CZ, 12 Oct 49. To Far East Air Force 16 Jan 51.
5-1089	45-1089	C-47B-50-DK C-47D	17092/34359	Assigned to 3rd BC, Albrook Field, CZ, CAC 1 Mar 48. To the San Jose Auxiliary Air Field, Guatemala, 9 Mar 48. Returned to 3rd BC, Albrook AFB, CZ, 24 Mar 48 as C-47D. To Far East Air Force 30 Jun 50.
5-1090	45-1090	C-47B-50-DK	17093/34360	This aircraft was briefly assigned to Natal, Brazil, 12 Dec 45, probably prepositioned for potential sale in Latin America but had returned to CONUS by 29 Apr 46.

5-1093	45-1093	C-47B-50-DK	17096/34363	Assigned to the 785th Base Unit, Borinquen Field, PR, CAC, 26 Jun 47 and to the 783rd Base Unit, Albrook Field, CZ, by 21 Feb 48. To the 153rd AACS 1 Jun 48. To the 1937th AACS 1 Oct 48 and the 1806th AACG, Ramey AFB, PR, 1 Feb 49. Returned to the 5700th ABS, Albrook AFB, CZ, 26 Jan 50 before returning to CONUS 28 Apr 50 due to the Korean War.
5-1099	45-1099	C-47B-50-DK C-47D	17102/34369	Assigned to CAC 1 Jan 48. Redesignated as C-47D 24 May 48. 5602nd Mission Group, Howard AB, CZ, 9 Jan 49. USAF Mission to Peru 26 Jun 52. USAF Mission to Bolivia 21 Oct 52. USAF Mission to Ecuador 28 Apr 53. USAF Mission to Bolivia again 6 Jun 53. Back to Ecuador 6 Jan 55. Salvaged 30 Nov 56 for reasons unknown, but rebuilt and to Peru as FAP-677 (q.v.) 1958.
5-1101	45-1101	C-47B-50-DK C-47D	17104/34371	Assigned to 20th Troop Carrier Squadron, CAC, Albrook Field, CZ, 23 May 46. To 18th Troop Carrier Squadron 1 Sep 48. To Ramey AFB, PR, 28 Oct 48. Redesignated as C-47D 6 Jan 49. To CONUS 14 Dec 58.
5-1102	45-1102	C-47B-50-DK	17105/34372	Assigned to US Mission to Ecuador 10 Jun 46, possibly a candidate for the ARP but instead returned to CONUS 17 Sep 46.
5-1105	45-1105	C-47B-50-DK	17108/34375	Assigned CAC 30 Apr 47. Stationed at Borinquen Fld, PR, with the 48th SR/ADG later 5904th Airbase Group Ramey AFB, PR, 26 Jul 48. Accident 22 Dec 47 at Borinquen Fld, PR, while being flown by Clarence L. Lollar. Repaired. Returned to CONUS 24 Sep 50.
5-1109	45-1109	C-47B-50-DK C-47D	17112/34379	Assigned to CAC 6 Jun 46. To USAF Mission to Colombia 1 Jan 48 as a C-47D. To PAA as C-47E, Brownsville, TX, 1 Aug 56.
5-1110 0-51110	45-1110	C-47B-50-DK C-47D	17113/34380	Assigned to CAC 6 Jun 46. To 7419th Foreign Mission Squadron, USAF Mission to Paraguay 18 Jan 48. To USAF Mission to Bolivia 18 Jul 48. Returned to Paraguay 28 Dec 48. Redesignated as C-47D 31 Jan 49. Remained with USAF Mission to Paraguay as late as 10 Jan 61. Was reclaimed in country but donated to the FAP as T-51 around Feb 64.
5-1111 0-51111	45-1111	C-47B-50-DK C-47D	17114/34381	Assigned to 3rd BC, Albrook Field, CZ, 14 May 46. To San Jose Auxiliary Airbase, Guatemala 9 Jan 48 until at least 30 Sep 49. Redesignated as C-47D 3 Jul 48. To USAF Mission to Paraguay 1 Jun 50. To USAF Mission to Venezuela 17 Mar 52. To USAF Mission to Ecuador 29 Jul 52. To USAF Mission to Venezuela 22 No52. To USAF Mission to Nicaragua 6 May 54. To USAF Mission to Haiti 18 Jun 54. Returned to Nicaragua 8 Dec 54. To USAF Mission to Ecuador 5 Feb 55. To USAF Mission to Argentina 14 Dec 59. To USAF Mission to Brazil 30 Jan 61. To MAAG Brazil September 1963 to at least March 1966. To Uruguay as FAU-511 (q.v.) via MAP 27 Sep 70.
5-1113	45-1113	C-47B-50-DK	17116/34383	To Division of Military Intelligence Ecuador via Canal Zone, arrived Quito, Ecuador 25 Oct 46 for US Air Attaché as late as 9 Jul 48. To Guatemala, US Air Attaché 14 Dec 49. Accident 31 Jan 50 at La Tinta, Alta Verapaz, Guatemala, four killed including the pilot, Harold W. Woodson. The aircraft was cited, in error, at the time as s/n '46-1113'. Was replaced by VC-47D 43-49280 (q.v.). Reclamation recommended 31 Jan 50 and completed 31 May 50 on site in Guatemala.
5-1114 0-51114	45-1114	C-47B-50-DK C-47D VC-47D VC-47B	17117/34384	Assigned to Division of Military Intelligence Chile 15 Aug 46, a candidate for ARP to Chile but redirected to Colombia by 27 Jul 47. Retained by the USAF and assigned to the USAF Mission to Chile 25 Oct 48 and redesignated as a C-47D 12 Dec 49. Redesignated as VC-47D 14 Apr 50. To USAF Mission to Bolivia as VC-47B 29 Aug 50. To USAF Mission to Chile 24 Aug 51. To USAF Mission to Venezuela 14 Apr 64. To USAF Mission to Peru 16 Dec 64. To MAP via Miami 20 Feb 69, recipient unknown.
5-1115 0-51115	45-1115	C-47B-50-DK C-47D VC-47D	17118/34385	To Division of Military Intelligence Colombia 23 Sep 46 and a candidate for ARP to Colombia. Instead, to US Mission to Colombia 25 Oct 48. To USAF Mission to Cuba 23 Nov 49. Returned to CONUS 21 Feb 50 and redesignated as C-47D 2 Mar 50. Returned to Cuba 9 Mar 50. Redesignated as VC-47D 13 Sep 50. To USAF Mission to Venezuela 30 Oct 57. Returned to CONUS by 8 Jun 68.
5-1119 0-51119	45-1119	C-47B-50-DK C-47D	17122/34389	Assigned to Division of Military Intelligence Peru 18 Nov 46 and a candidate for ARP to Peru. Retained by USAF and redesignated as C-47D 12 Dec 49. Remained with USAF Mission to Peru, despite intermittent returns to the Canal Zone 'home station' for periodic inspections, etc, as late as 13 Sep 64.
5-1128 0-51128	45-1128	C-47B-50-DK C-47D	17131/34398	Assigned to CAC 5700th ABG, Albrook AFB, CZ, 15 Nov 63. To USAF Mission to Peru 13 Sep 64. To USAF Mission to Brazil 14 Jan 66. To FAG-560 (q.v.) by 20 Aug 70.
5-1129	45-1129	C-47B-50-DK	17132/34399	Assigned to Division of Military Intelligence Venezuela 17 Jun 46, a candidate for ARP to Venezuela. Apparently transferred to either the FAV or a Venezuelan government agency 11 May 48.
5-1131	45-1131	C-47B-50-DK	17134/34401	Assigned to the Division of Military Intelligence Uruguay 15 Jan 46, a candidate for ARP for Uruguay. Instead, retained by the USAF and to the USAF Mission to Guatemala 25 Oct 48. To the USAF Mission to Bolivia 17 Jun 49. Returned to CONUS 4 Jan 50.
5-1132 0-51132	45-1132	C-47B-50-DK C-47D	17135/34402	Assigned to the Division of Military Intelligence via CAC 4 Mar 46, a candidate for ARP to Venezuela. Retained by the USAF and redesignated as C-47D 9 Aug 48 and to USAF Mission to Venezuela where it remained as late as 1 Feb 65. To MAP 23 Jan 70, unknown recipient.

5-1136	45-1136	C-47B-50-DK	17139/34406	To CAC after Nov 45. Accident 24 Jan 47 at Managua, Nicaragua, while being flown by Willis F. Lewis, home based at La Aurora Airport, Guatemala City, Guatemala, where it had been based since 10 Dec 46, possibly with the USAAF Mission. To TACA as XH-TAF.
5-1138	45-1138	C-47B-50-DK	17141/34408	To CAC after 19 Nov 45 and to Division of Military Intelligence Argentina 5 Jun 46, a candidate for ARP to Argentina. Retained by the USAF, however. Accident 17 Feb 49 approximately 75 miles west/south-west of Salta, Argentina, while being flown by Gerald E. Williams. Assumed to have been with the USAF Mission to Argentina at the time, as noted home based at Buenos Aires since 5 Jun 46. Reclamation completed 12 Apr 49.
5-1139	45-1139	C-47B-50-DK C-47D VC-47D	17142/34409	The last C-47 built. Assigned to Division of Military Intelligence Mexico and thus a candidate for ARP to Mexico. Instead to the US Air Attaché Mexico c.5 Aug 48. Redesignated as C-47D 12 Dec 49. Became a VC-47D 14 Apr 50. Returned to CONUS 28 Jan 61.

Such was the demand for C-47 crew training in Latin America that the IAAFA was obliged to lay in a second C-47 to accommodate trainees. This, the former 0-50967 (45-967) had arrived in the CAC on 14 May 1946 and last served with the USAF Mission to Guatemala. She joined the Class 26 airframes at Albrook by 25 November 1970 as a GC-47D. *John Mercier*

United States Navy and United States Marine Corps

Nearly always overlooked, and very poorly documented in public literature, US Naval aviation has also had a long-term presence in Latin America, commencing with the airfields carved out of Guantanamo Bay, Cuba, and the amphibious and flying boat establishment at Coco Solo Naval Air Station contiguous with France Field on the Atlantic side of the Panama Canal.

During the Second World War, Naval and Marine Corps aviation in the region was deeply engaged in the intensive anti-submarine campaign, and comprised mainly patrol bomber, blimp and convoy escort units stationed from Guantanamo Bay south through the Antilles (Roosevelt Roads NAS in Puerto Rico) to the MCAS on St

Thomas, US Virgin Islands, Chaguaramas Bay Naval Air Station, Trinidad (actually commissioned as an element of the 'Destroyers-for-Bases' agreement on 1 August 1941), and little-known Naval Air Stations and bases in Nicaragua, the Galapagos Islands, down the 'hump' of Brazil and as far south as Montevideo, Uruguay.

While overwhelmingly tactical in nature, these widely dispersed and largely independent organisations required priority resupply on occasion, as well as practical means of communication and personnel medevac and transfer. The Navy and Marines did not have the resources of the USAAF for these purposes and, consequently, did not maintain squadron-size R4D operating units in the region. However, a number of R4Ds were apparently attached at Fleet level to support the far-flung assets, as well as dispersed US Navy missions and attachés in Latin America, and those known are described in the accompanying table.

Known US Navy and Marine Corps R4Ds Stationed in Latin America

Serial as Worn	Full US Serial	Type as Built and US Navy Bureau of Aeronautics Number	MSN	Assigned and Notes
3134	BuA3134	R4D-1	4224	To VR-7 3 Mar 43. Crashed on take-off at Zandery Field, Surinam, 12 Oct 43, six killed. As VR-7 had detachments far and wide, it is not clear exactly where this aircraft was home based at the time of the crash.
01984	BuA01984	R4D-1	4440	Air-Britain reported this aircraft made a forced landing in the sea 29 Jun 43 1 mile east of San Cristobal Island. If this is correct, this was one of the Galapagos Archipelago islands and the aircraft may have been flying in support of the Naval Air Station in the Galapagos, although her last known assignment was with VMJ-153, a Marine utility squadron.
01986	BuA01986	R4D-1	4550	Assigned to MCAS St Thomas, US Virgin Islands, 11 Oct 42 to 8 Feb 43 and again 15 Nov 43 to 3 Jun 44. Returned to CONUS.
01988	BuA01988	R4D-1	4552	VR-7 from 3 Apr 43, NATS. Hit mountain 30 miles east of Rio de Janeiro, Brazil, 19 Nov 43, eighteen killed. The location of this loss must be in error, as there is only ocean 30 miles 'east' of Rio!
12420	BuA12420	R4D-5	9442	Assigned to FASRON 108 at NAS Coco Solo, CZ, Jul 48. This is one of only a few Navy or Marine Corps R4Ds positively known to have been assigned in the Canal Zone.
12436	BuA12436	R4D-5	9619	With US Navy Mission to Ecuador at Quito by 3 Jun 53. To CONUS 9 Jul 55.
12442	BuA12442	R4D-5 C-47H	9675	Assigned to the Naval Advisory Group, Buenos Aires, Argentina, as of 1 Apr 60. Reclassified as a C-47H 18 Sep 62. To CONUS 28 Dec 62.
17094	BuA17094 (42-108796)	R4D-5 (C-47A-DK)	11808	Assigned to NAS Coco Solo, Canal Zone, in Nov 46. To CONUS by January 1947.
17105	BuA17105 (42-108807)	R4D-5 (C-47A-1-DK) C-47H	11918	US Navy Mission to Peru 8 May 60. Redesignated as C-47H 18 Sep 62. To US Navy Mission to Ecuador 8 Oct 63. Crashed into the side of Antisana Volcano, Ecuador 15 May 64 while on an unspecified US Navy 'cargo' supply mission to the interior and destroyed by fire; ten survivors, but one fatality.
17128	BuA17128 (42-92461)	R4D-5 (C-47A-5-DK)	12264	VR-7. Written off 22 Jul 44 when it hit high ground at Alegria near Recife, Brazil.
17134	BuA17134 (42-92478)	R4d-5 (C-47A-5-DK)	12283	Assigned to US Navy Mission to Peru 2 Aug 53. Returned to CONUS but later assigned to US Naval Attaché Mexico City 30 Jan 50. Returned to CONUS 11 Aug 61.
17146	BuA17146 (42-92526)	R4D-5 (C-47A-5-DK)	12336	Assigned to US Naval Attaché Mexico City 25 Aug 52. Returned to CONUS 7 Sep 54.
17175	BuA17175	R4D-8Z R4D-8	(12779) 43301	Assigned to NAS Roosevelt Roads, PR, 20 Sep 59. To CONUS 9 Oct 61.
17181	BuA17181 (42-92925)	R4D-5 (C-47A-20-DK)	12780	Assigned to COM-15 Panama 3 Aug 60 but returned to CONUS 25 Oct 60. Much later to FAN-417 (May 76, q.v.).
17199	BuA17199 (42-93194)	R4D-5 (C-47A-20-DK)	13079	Assigned to VU-10 at NAS Guantanamo Bay, Cuba, 10 Oct 58. To CONUS 9 Nov 59.
17201	BuA17201 (42-93214)	R4D-5 (C-47A-20-DK)	13101	Assigned to US Navy Mission to Brazil, Rio de Janeiro, 11 Jul 58. Returned to CONUS 21 Nov 58.
17211	BuA17211 (42-93322)	R4D-5 (C-47A-25-DK)	13221	Assigned to MAW-2 Detachment at NAS Roosevelt Roads, PR, 10 Oct 51. Returned to CONUS 10 Nov 51. Possibly only TDY.
17212	BuA17212 (42-93323)	R4D-5 (C-47A-25-DK)	13222	Assigned to US Navy Mission to Peru 31 Jan 58. Returned to CONUS 2 Sep 60.
17213	BuA17213 (42-93324)	R4D-5 (C-47A-25-DK)	13223	Assigned to US Navy Mission to Colombia 1 Aug 53. To US Naval Attaché Melbourne, Australia, 15 Aug 56. However, returned to the US Navy Mission to Colombia again 12 Feb 60. To CONUS 12 Mar 62.
17214	BuA17214 (42-93325)	R4D-5 (C-47A-25-DK) C-47M	13224	Assigned to US Navy Mission to Chile, Valparaiso, Chile, 31 Oct 67. To US Navy Mission to Ecuador 6 Feb 68 and US Navy Mission to Brazil 16 Oct 68. Returned to CONUS 20 Feb 69.
17251	BuA17251 (43-48365)	R4D-5 R4D-6 (C-47B-1-DK) C-47J C-47M	14181/25626	Assigned to the US Navy Mission to Chile 28 May 60. To the US Navy Mission to Peru 12 Feb 63. Redesignated as C-47J 18 Sep 62 and C-47M 30 Mar 65. To US Navy Mission to Nationalist China 2 Jul 66.
17252	BuA17252 (43-48366)	R4D-6 (C-47B-1-DK)	14182/25627	Assigned to US Navy Aviation Facility Rio de Janeiro, Brazil, Aug 45. Assigned to Joint Caribbean/US Mission Jun 46. To Quonset NAS Dec 46.
17255	BuA17255 43-48369	R4D-6 (C-47B-1-DK)	14185/25630	NAS San Juan, PR, Aug 44. To VE-2 Dec 44.
17256	BuA17256 (43-48370)	R4D-6 (C-47B-1-DK)	14186/25631	Assigned to FASRON-109, NAS Roosevelt Roads, PR, May 47. To 10th Naval District, NAS Guantanamo Bay, Cuba, 29 Apr 50. To 10th Naval District, San Juan, PR, Aug 50. Returned to CONUS 28 Jul 52.
17257	BuA17257 (43-48371)	R4D-6 (C-47B-1-DK)	14187/25632	NAS Guantánamo Bay, Cuba, after Apr 48.

Two US Navy R4D-1s load a mix of personnel, at left and cargo, right, on the tarmac at NAS Guantanamo Bay, Cuba, on 1 December 1942. Assigned to VR-1, nominally home-based at NAS Norfolk, Virginia, aside from units codes, such as 1-R-8 at right, wartime Navy serials, or Bureau Numbers, were very small and seldom noted by photographers. *NARA RG 80-G-33465 via Dana Bell*

17260	BuA17260 (43-48374)	R4D-6 (C-47B-1-DK) C-47M	14190/25635	NAS Coco Solo, CZ, Jan 47. To US Navy Mission to Brazil 20 Jan 53 and remained there, intermittently, until 30 Nov 62 by which time it had been redesignated as a C-47M. To DMAFB, AZ, Dec 69.
17262	BuA17262 (43-48376)	R4D-6 (C-47B-1-DK)	14192/25637	Assigned to US Naval Assistance Group Buenos Aires, Argentina, 12 Oct 53. To CONUS Dec 56.
17269	BuA17269 (43-48511)	R4D-6 (C-47B-1-DK)	14327/25772	Assigned to US Navy Mission to Ecuador 12 Dec 57. To US Naval Attaché Cape Town, South Africa, 28 Feb 61.
17282	BuA17282 (43-48685)	R4D-6 (C-47B-5-DK)	14501/25946	HAMRON-24, NAS Roosevelt Roads, PR, May 52. To CONUS August 1952.
17283	BuA17283 (43-48687)	R4D-6 (C-47B-5-DK) C-47J C-47M	14503/25948	US Navy Mission to Venezuela 29 Sep 62 as C-47J. Redesignated as C-47M 17 May 65. US Navy Mission to Brazil 20 May 69. To Chilean Navy as NAVAL 125 30 Jul 70.
17284	BuA17284 (43-48688)	R4D-6 (C-47B-5-DK)	14504/25949	NAS Coco Solo, CZ, Oct 44. To NAS Quonset Nov 46.
17291	BuA17291 (43-48695)	R4D-6 (C-47B-5-DK) R4D-6R	14511/25956	Assigned to US Navy Aviation Facility Rio de Janeiro, Brazil, Feb 47. To Cherry Point Aug 48.
39071	BuA39071 (42-24159)	C-117D (R4D-5) (C-47A-40-DL)	10021	NAS Bermuda as C-117D from 11 Jun 70.
39080	BuA39080	R4D-8	(10207) 43354	Assigned to the 10th Naval District, San Juan, PR, 22 May 56. To CONUS 4 Jan 58.
50740	BuA50740 (43-48696)	R4D-6 (C-47B-5-DK)	14512/25957	US Naval Attaché Mexico City, Mexico, 1 Sep 54. To CONUS 3 Aug 57.
50742	BuA50742 (43-48763)	R4D-6 (C-47B-5-DK)	14579/26024	US Navy Mission to Brazil by 6 Jan 56 and then to US Navy Mission to Chile 1 Oct 56. Returned to CONUS 11 Jan 58.
50747	BuA50747 (43-48837)	R4D-6 (C-47B-5-DK)	14653/26098	US Navy Mission to Ecuador 10 May 55. To US Navy Mission to Colombia 11 Dec 57.
50752	BuA50752 (43-48863)	R4D-6 (C-47B-5-DK) C-47J	14679/26124	US Naval Attaché Mexico City 28 Apr 61. Redesignated as a C-47J 18 Sep 62. To US Naval Attaché New Delhi, India, 25 Nov 64.
50753	BuA50753 (43-48867)	R4D-6 (C-47B-5-DK) C-47M C-47J	14683/26128	NAS Roosevelt Roads, PR, 22 Mar 60. Via intermediate assignments, to Senior Naval Advisor, Buenos Aires, Argentina, 10 Jan 65 as a C-47M from 4 Jun 65 and C-47J from 6 Aug 65. To US Naval Mission to Brazil 1 Nov 65.
50769	BuA50769 (43-49063)	R4D-6 (C-47B-10-DK)	14879/26324	Assigned to the Naval Advisory Group, Buenos Aires, Argentina, 5 Jan 56. Returned to CONUS 21 Mar 58.
50787	BuA50787 (43-49263)	R4D-6 (C-47B-15-DK) C-47M	15079/26524	Assigned to the US Navy Mission to Venezuela 30 Jan 65. To CONUS 12 Mar 65.
50790	BuA50790 (43-49307)	R4D-6 (C-47B-15-DK)	15123/26568	US Navy Mission to Brazil by Aug 48. Redesignated as R4D-6R by 3 Mar 49 and returned to CONUS by 1 Aug 51.
50794	BuA50794 (43-49327)	R4D-6 (C-47B-15-DK) C-47J C-47M	15143/26588	US Navy Mission to Colombia 12 Oct 55. US Navy Mission to Ecuador 20 Sep 61. US Navy Mission to Venezuela 21 Oct 67 by which time she had been redesignated as C-47J. To SENNAVADV Buenos Aires, Argentina, 14 Mar 68. After storage at Davis-Monthan AFB, AZ, was acquired via MAS by the Chilean Navy as NAVAL 122 Feb 69.
50802	BuA50802 (43-49397)	R4D-6 (C-47B-15-DK)	15213/26658	Assigned to NAS Guantanamo Bay, Cuba, 12 Jul 67. Returned to CONUS 17 Sep 68.
50806	BuA50806 (43-49417)	R4D-6 (C-47B-15-DK)	15233/26678	Assigned to the 10th Naval District, Guantanamo Bay, Cuba, 22 Nov 58. Returned to CONUS 17 Nov 59.

50809	BuA50809 (43-49432)	R4D-6 C-47B-15-DK	15248/26693	Assigned to the US Naval Mission to Chile, Valparaiso, Chile, 30 Nov 59. Returned to CONUS 22 Apr 60.
50811	BuA50811 (43-49442)	R4D-6 (C-47B-15-DK)	15255/26703	Assigned to the US Naval Mission to Chile, Valparaiso, Chile, Jan 58. Returned to CONUS 15 Mar 63.
50817	BuA50817 (43-49563)	R4D-6 (C-47B-15-DK) C-47J	15379/26824	Assigned to NAS Guantanamo Bay, Cuba, 26 Apr 61. To CONUS 18 Nov 62.
50827	BuA50827 (43-49697) N79961	R4D-6 (C-47B-20-DK) C-47J C-47M	15513/26958	US Navy Attaché (S. NavAdv) to Argentina, 24 Jan 66. To Chilean Navy NAVAL 124 23 Jul 69 from storage.
50837	BuA50837 (43-49747)	R4D-6 (C-47B-20-DK)	15563/27008	Assigned to the US Naval Mission to Chile, Valparaiso, Chile, 27 Jul 52. To Naval Advisory Group Argentina 28 Feb 58. To N7998A 29 Aug 60.
99830	BuA99830 (44-76828)	(TC-47B-30-DK) R4D-7 R4D-6 C-47J C-47M R4D-7 (TC-47B-30-DK) C-47R	16412/33160	US Naval Advisory Group Buenos Aires, Argentina 31 Aug 62 and redesignated as C-47J 18 Sep 62. Redesignated C-47M 27 Apr 65. US Navy Mission to Ecuador 6 Jul 67 and redesignated as C-47R 31 Dec 68. To Argentine Navy as 0652 (q.v.) 1 Jul 70.
99839	(44-76895) BuA99839	(TC-47B-35-DK) R4D-7 R4D-6	16479/33227	Assigned to NAS Roosevelt Roads, PR. Feb 48 as an R4D-6. To CONUS 10 Oct 50.
99844	(44-76935) BuA99844	(TC-47B-354-DK) R4D-7 C-47J	16519/33267	Assigned to US Naval Attaché Mexico City 4 Jan 57. To US Navy Mission to Ecuador 31 Aug 59. To US Navy Mission to Colombia 11 Mar 62 and redesignated as a C-47J 18 Sep 62. To CONUS 30 Nov 63.
99855	BuA99855 (44-77019)	R4D-7 (TC-47B-35-DK)	16603/33351	NAS San Juan, PR, 26 Jul 46.

Left: This Navy R4D-1, possibly BuA01986, is unusual in having been scrubbed free of its blue camouflage and may in fact have been a US Marine Corps aircraft, as it was photographed at St Thomas, US Virgin Islands, where the USMC had maintained an VMS aviation detachment for some time. Other than the national insignia, however, the aircraft is completely devoid of markings. *Gerard Casius*

Below: Resplendent in wartime Navy blue camouflage, this R4D-1 poses on the tarmac at General Andrews Field, Ciudad Trujillo, in the Dominican Republic early in the war. Unfortunately, only a portion of her unit codes can be seen, 7-R-xx6, but at least establishes that she was assigned to VR-7 which ranged far and wide throughout the hemisphere. *NARA RG 80-G-15360 via Dana Bell*

CHAPTER TWO

Argentina

IN RETROSPECT, it is particularly appropriate that our account of Latin American operators of Douglas twin-engine transports should begin with Argentina, quite aside from the fact that alphabetically the operating armed forces of that nation come first. This is because, after pre-Pearl Harbor US armed forces use of examples of the series, primarily in defence of the Panama Canal in the pre-Second World War period, Argentina became the very first nation in Latin America to acquire an example, although via decidedly non-traditional means, as will be seen.

During the decade of the 1930s, both the Argentine Army and Navy had evolved what were arguably the best equipped, best trained and most professional air arms in all of Latin America, only neighbouring Chile challenging them for this distinction. Shaped by a combination of influential major powers, notably the United States, Germany and to some extent Great Britain, both services had fielded modest air transport elements within their establishments since the 1920s.

The country remained officially neutral during the course of the Second World War, which, as it turned out, resulted in most of her armed forces suffering from shortages of every kind, as the ready supply of spares from both Allied and Axis sources evaporated quickly. The preponderance of pro-Axis sympathies among the large and influential German and Italian colonies that existed in the country unquestionably contributed to this from the Allied perspective and, as a result, Argentina only offered up a purely cosmetic declaration of war against the Axis powers when it became abundantly clear that Allied victory was

One of the first 'stock' C-47As acquired by the FAA, T-20 was ferried home as LV-XFP in February 1947 and, between July and November 1951, was modified for use in the Antarctic, although she in fact never flew there. Pictured here in 1952 completely kitted out, including ample high-visibility red on her nose, wing tips and empennage, and details of the ski installation are illustrated in the annex. Argentina was the only Latin American military operator to equip C-47s with skis, although both air force and naval aircraft were so equipped. These were similar to those of US Navy R4D-5S aircraft. *Steeneck via Dr Gary Kuhn*

assured, in April 1945. On the other hand, the nation as a whole had profited enormously during the war, principally by supplying food stuffs to a beleaguered Britain for cash on the barrelhead.

The declaration of war did result in potentially beneficial avenues of procurement for Argentina, however, as due to US policy as of 16 April 1945, any nation so aligned was basically eligible to apply to the Foreign Economic Administration (FEA) for allocation of surplus aeronautical equipment, including aircraft of virtually every kind.

Availing itself of these promising avenues, by 11 July 1947, the various branches of the Argentine government and armed forces had purchased no fewer than 129 aircraft, the vast majority purchased by the Argentine Purchasing Commission, headed by Comodoro Edgardo Accinelli, and, besides the civil airlines in existence at the time (Aeroposta Argentina, FAMA, ALFA and ZONDA) some of these were destined to see service with the Argentine military and naval aviation services, although not all via direct acquisition. These included nine highly prized surplus Douglas C-54s, which the Commission arranged to have converted to DC-4s before delivery by Martin in Baltimore, eight C-47s (which, similarly, were converted to DC-3 variants before delivery), thirty-two Beech AT-11s (of which twenty were bound for the Army), ten unidentified 'ambulance' aircraft and two aerial photographic aircraft (also unidentified) as well as eighty assorted Piper J3 variants. Significantly, and as a direct result of the long Second World War spares hiatus, the Commission also scrambled to spend some $3 million on an incredible list of spares of every description.

The earliest known image of a truly historic aircraft, the former Air France DC-3-294 after being acquired by the Argentine Army in 1942 – the very first DC-2, DC-3 or C-47 series aircraft to enter military service, other than the United States, in Latin America. She was reserialed as T-169 on 8 July 1944. *Santiago Rivas*

To put all of this into perspective, as of 1945, the Argentine Army, on paper, had possessed a total of 244 aircraft of all types, of which some forty-four were fighters, forty-one bombers, and 159 reconnaissance, transport and trainer types. Of the total, seventeen had been indigenously designed and constructed, while 109 were a mix of vintage pre-war US, British, French and German designs

In the midst of all of this, a seemingly endless series of military coups and political turmoil within the country eventually resulted in the accession of Coronel Juan Domingo Perón to the Presidency in 1946, just after the end of the war, ushering in a spending spree of its wartime bounty of Pounds Sterling that largely benefited the armed forces. The United Kingdom offered to settle its wartime debts to Argentina with manufactured products – including aircraft – as the war had nearly exhausted its cash reserves. Not wasting any time, by October 1945, Argentina had submitted a preliminary list of aircraft that it required, amounting to some 175 liaison and training aircraft, followed by the dispatch of a Commission in June 1946 led by a respected flag officer. Diplomatically, the British were in a difficult spot in all of this. The United States, which had managed to array almost total hemispheric co-operation during the war – Argentina having been the solitary, glaring exception – was politically opposed to enabling any combat aircraft deliveries, primarily because of the nature of the South American country's openly fascist government, which had been solidly entrenched since 1943. Ironically, the rise of Perón helped ease the US stance and, aided by the hemispheric notions of wartime US Army Air Forces Commander General Henry H. 'Hap' Arnold, the US State Department's stance and its agreement with Britain not to supply Argentina with any aircraft 'capable of being used in combat operations' was simply ignored.

In retrospect, the aircraft acquisitions that followed, which primarily benefited the air force, are very nearly without parallel in aviation history. Aero-historian Santiago Rivas, in his seminal work *British Combat Aircraft in Latin America* (Crécy, Manchester, UK, 2019) described not only what actually materialised as a result of these negotiations, but the equally staggering aspirations and negotiations that did not see fruition. Besides 100 Gloster Meteor F.Mk.IV jet fighters – the first in Latin America – as well as thirty mighty Avro Lincoln B.Mk.II four-engine heavy bombers and fifteen Lancaster B.Mk.Is to partially re-equip and enlarge the combat elements, a total of 104 dedicated transport types were also acquired from Britain. These comprised fifteen impressive Bristol Type 170 Mk.21 and 31M *Freighter* heavy-lifters, twenty-three Vickers 615 Viking I and Ib personnel transports, seventy de Havilland D.H.104 Dove I light transports, ten Airspeed AS.65 Consul utility transports, communications and training aircraft and three each of long-range, four engine Avro Lancastrian C.Mk.IVs and Avro Yorks. As these started arriving, they at first supplemented surviving pre-war transport types, among which, ironically, the venerable Junkers Ju 52/3m were by far the most numerous, with at least fifteen still being nominally on strength as late as 1949.

A snapshot of the Argentine air arm as of 1951, by which time the majority of the aircraft acquired during the post-war shopping spree had somehow been integrated into the existing establishment, reveals an incredibly diverse air force, which must certainly have taxed the ingenuity (and patience) of its crews and maintainers and which, for the purposes of our account, helps set the stage for what followed. It is worth note that, between 1946 and 1951, no fewer than twenty-three DC-3s and C-47s had joined the force via rather diverse routes, retrospectively and with the foregoing transport types already on hand or on order as noted above, and this appears to be a testament to the fact that, with all of their assorted qualities, nothing could quite meet existing requirements like the Douglas twins. Indeed, some aviation historians have contended that, mainly because of the influence during the war years of several successive USAAF Missions to the Argentine Army Aviation Command, had the highly advantageous arrangement with the British not been operative, the service's preferences would have been for state-of-the-art US types from the start.

So here is how the air arm actually looked at that juncture:

Grupo 1 de Bombardeo
(BAM Coronel Pringles, Villa Reynolds, San Luis Province)

25 – Avro Lincoln B.Mk.II (of which two had already been cannibalised for spares)

5 – Martin Model 139WAA

Grupo 2 de Bombardeo
(BAM Coronel Pringles, Villa Reynolds, San Luis Province)

15 – Avro Lancaster B.Mk.I (all of which had been grounded for lack of spares)

Grupo 1 de Caza
(BAM El Plumerillo, Mendoza)

39 – Fiat G-55 (from an original total of 30 G-55A and 15 G-55B)

21 – Curtiss Hawk 75-0

Grupos 2 & 3 de Caza
(BAM Tandil)

46 – Gloster Meteor F.Mk.IV (with another 46 in reserve)

Grupo 1 de Ataque
(BAM El Plumerillo, Mendoza)

16 – Northrop/Douglas 8A-2

30 – FMA I.Ae.24 Calquin

Grupo 1 de Observación
(BAM General Urquiza, Paraná)

32 – FMA I.Ae.DL-22

4 – Beech AT-11

Grupo 2 de Ataque
(BAM Reconquista)

20 – FMA I.Ae.24 Calquin

15 – Fiat G-46-2B

4 – Beech AT-11

Grupo 1 de Transporte
(BAM El Palomar, Buenos Aires)

9 – Junkers Ju 52/3m

6 – Vickers 615 Viking I

1 – Lockheed Model 10-E

1 – Lockheed Model 12-A

3 – Beech AT-11

12 – Douglas DC-3 and C-47

10 – de Havilland D.H.104 Dove I

7 – Bristol Type 170

10 – Focke-Wulf Fw-44J

10 – Airspeed AS.65 Consul

Grupo 2 de Transporte
(BAM Morón, Buenos Aires)

3 – Junkers Ju-52/3m

4 – Beech AT-11

5 – Douglas DC-4 and C-54

10 – Douglas DC-3 and C-47

60 – de Havilland D.H.104 Dove I

5 – Vickers 615 Viking I

As the significance of this listing portrays graphically, the mathematics of this huge influx of new aircraft, to put it simply, quickly overwhelmed the Argentine Army's ability to absorb, let alone maintain and man, such fleets. Transition training alone, from legacy types, required concurrent expansions in the infrastructure of the service, not least its training establishments, which was also assimilating large numbers of new aircraft, not to mention base facilities, depot maintenance and repair, communications and organisation.

Capacity, especially in air transport, was certainly well beyond the needs of Argentina's defence needs and of the service itself at the time, and probably accounts for the fact that some of the problematical types, notably the efficacious but rapidly obsolescing Avro Lancastrians and Yorks, had disappeared from the Air Order of Battle by this time, less than four years after acquisition. passing to quasi-civil us. These were replaced by significant quantities of DC-3s, C-47s and DC-4s, which in the post-war market were plentiful, capable, cheap and which promised more standardised day-to-day capabilities, maintenance, spares support, reliability and value.

Having set the stage, let us now examine how, in the face of its pre-war maturity and post-war largesse, the several Argentine military establishments came to acquire Douglas twins, a story that begins with a solitary DC-3.

The First Latin American Military DC-3 and the Comando de las Fuerzas Aéreas Militares del Ejército de Argentina

There is no small amount of irony in the provenance of the first Douglas twin-engine transport to gain Latin American military markings.

Built as a DC-3-294, Manufacturer's Serial Number (MSN)[11] 2122 for its European distributor, Fokker in the Netherlands, this aircraft was delivered to Fokker on 26 May 1939 but the company almost immediately sold it to Air France, on 7 June, where she gained the French marks F-ARQJ. Air France had commenced efforts to assimilate the very successful Aéropostale route system in Latin America, which, as early as 1931, had rather overextended itself, using mainly elderly between-the-wars French types over a nine-nation route system, competing with German and US interests all the while. When Air France finally secured all of Aéropostale's routes, starting with Brazil in March 1939, the decision was made to supplement the old Aéropostale equipment that had been inherited, which saw large flying boats being used for routine South Atlantic crossings, with a few state-of-the-art aircraft to compete head-to-head with a very ambitious Pan American system. This included F-ARQJ, which, even in the face of all that had happened with its parent organisation at home following the German assault on France, managed to continue limited operations for a time, the solitary DC-3 in the entire fleet. With the German occupation of the Vichy French territory on 11 November 1942, however, the remaining Air France equipment, personnel and infrastructure in Latin America was suddenly an organisation without a country.

At the same time, the United States was engaged in a determined programme to eliminate Axis influence in Latin American aviation, and after the fall of France, the isolated French airline interests in the region were left to continue on as best they could, as events back home deteriorated daily.

The common wisdom has always been that the best of the remaining Air France equipment, to evade being seized by neighbouring nations (especially Brazil) at the behest of the US, eloped to Argentina, where at least three of its most modern and efficacious aircraft were incorporated into the Argentine Comando de las Fuerzas Aéreas Militares del Ejército on 5 May 1943. These included Dewoitine D.338s F-AQBT (msn 20) and F-AQBR (msn 18), which gained Army serials 170 and 171, Dewoitine D.333 F-ANQC (msn 2) and F-ANQB (msn 1), which became 172 and 173 – and DC-3-294 F-ARQJ (msn 2122), which became serial 169.

The pride of the service, the former F-ARQJ became T-169 in July 1944 and, in November 1946, T-16. Note the line-up of North American NA-16-4Ps in the left background. *Santiago Rivas*

Although of marginal quality, this was the special emblem worn on either side of the nose of T-169 while she served, essentially, as 'Air Force One' for Argentina between 1942 and 1946. *Alexander P. de Seversky*

However, more recent research suggests that the transfer of these five very capable and valuable aircraft to Argentine governmental control may have in fact taken place more than a year earlier. The 31 January 1942 issue of the reliable periodical *Interavia* (No. 801) reported the following: 'The accident involving the special aeroplane of the Argentine Foreign Minister, Dr. Ruiz Guiñazú on January 29th, following the close of the Pan American Conference, is probably known from the daily press. The aeroplane, which was controlled by Dr. Samuel Bosch, the new Director of Argentine Civil Aviation, carried the Argentine six-man delegation to the Conference as well as a crew of four: it crashed immediately after the take-off from Santos Dumont Airport, Rio de Janeiro. The difficulties which the machine experienced during the take-off and which forced the pilot to make an emergency landing on the water in the immediate vicinity of the airfield, are explained by damage to a tyre incurred during the take-off and with an excessive payload. No fatal casualties were suffered.'

The very next issue of *Interavia,* for 10 February 1942, expanded on the first report, advising that, 'the airliner concerned was a Douglas DC-3 twin-engined aircraft which had been purchased from the South American branch of Air France by the Argentine Government only a short while previously. The machine was piloted by Capt. Antoine, who formerly was employed by Air France in South America.'

This intriguing report, from a usually very reliable source, led a number of historians on a merry chase, but the Dean of Argentine aviation historians, Dr Francisco Halbritter, was finally able to determine that, wishful thinking notwithstanding, *Interavia* had actually got it all wrong: the aircraft that crashed was, indeed, a former Air France machine, but she wasn't the sole DC-3. She was Potez 62-1 LV-SEC, the former F-ANQQ (MSN 11/4030), which had also been

acquired by the Argentine DGAC, her French marks, significantly, having been cancelled administratively on 30 June 1941.

At any rate, the DC-3 was initially assigned to the Army's II Escuadrilla de la Agrupación Transporte around 2 July 1943 and, along with the four tri-motored Dewoitines, had her serial prefixed with a 'T' (for Transporte) on 8 July 1944, becoming T-169. Needless to say, the five aircraft quickly became symbols of power and prestige, and T-169 may well have altered Argentine history had it not been for the professionalism of pilots Tte G. Ruzo and Cdte. L. Ríos on 4 September 1945, when the aircraft collided with Army Curtiss Hawk 75-0, serial number C-607, near Villa María, Córdoba. The VIP passenger on board at the time was none other than the sitting Minister of War, one Coronel Juan D. Perón. As it was, T-169 suffered damage to one of her engines and the central fuselage area, but her crew managed to land safely and repairs were eventually carried out at BAM El Palomar.

The pre-war serial issued to this aircraft confounded subsequent generations of historians, as the wartime Argentine Army could scarcely imagine that the post-war service would eventually acquire large numbers of DC-3s and C-47s, with a confusing series of numbering systems, which stubbornly resisted their attempts to accommodate the 'out-of-sequence' serial T-169.

As if that were not enough, on 2 November 1946, the DC-3-294 was reserialed in the first, new post-war system, becoming T-16, by which time she had accumulated a respectable 1,907 hours 20 minutes total flight time.

But her trek was hardly over. After many adventures with the post-war Fuerza Aérea Argentina (FAA) she was donated to Paraguay on 27 May 1969, where she became T-67. Her new owners could scarcely have imagined her provenance.

Logic would suggest that T-10 was in the first serial sequence put into use as the Fuerza Aérea Argentina started acquiring significant numbers of DC-3s and C-47s in the post-war years. In fact, it was in the second series, assigned in 1966, and a former ZONDA and Aerolineas Argentinas DC-3C, MSN 13336, shown here while assigned to the I Brigada Aérea. She became VR-10 in 1970. *via Dr Gary Kuhn*

Another I Brigada Aérea DC-3C, T-11 was also inducted into the FAA in 1966 and her markings are interesting in that the serial code is worn on the upper starboard with the national insignia on the upper port wing extremity. Her service was only brief, however, being stricken and offered for sale in February 1968. *Air-Britain*

Initial Post-War Acquisitions

Despite the plethora of new and refurbished aircraft arriving from Britain, Argentina apparently wasted little time in taking advantage of the post-war surplus bonanza in the US to expand even further the swollen ramps of the Agrupación de Transporte. As the US State Department remained steadfastly opposed to Argentine participation in the American Republics Projects (ARP) sponsored by the USAAF, the country would almost certainly otherwise have benefited from direct C-47 offsets. However, in view of the huge influx of capable British aircraft at virtually the same juncture, supplying even modest numbers of USAAF types would have been difficult to justify at the time. Thus, Argentina acquired its first post-war C-47s through strictly commercial means.

In August 1946, two surplus aircraft, C-47A-80-DL MSN 19659 and C-47A-90-DL MSN 20406, were bought by the Commission on behalf of the Secretaría de Aeronáutica from qualified US civil owners and, bearing temporary Argentine ferry marks LV-XEO and LV-XEP, were flown home as the first two post-war Douglas twins destined for military service, becoming T-151 and T-172 in the pre-war and wartime serial system. As it turned out, they became the first of many to follow, as our accompanying table illustrates.

By the time of this image, the historic ex-Air France DC-3-294, formerly 169 and T-169, was just another line aircraft with I Brigada Aérea. However, note that the curtains in the cabin windows have been retained, indicating she was still an 'Admiral's Barge'. She survived to be donated to the Fuerza Aérea Paraguaya as T-67 in May 1969 – that operator having no appreciation whatsoever of her unique lineage. *via Dr Gary Kuhn*

First 'T' Series Prefix Serials Sequence Aircraft – 1943–47

Argentine Army Serial	Previous Identity	Type as Built	MSN	Assignments and Notes
169 T-169	F-ARQJ	DC-3-294	2122	Acquired in early 1942. Issued 169 on 2 Jul 43. Modified to T-169 8 Jul 44. Reserialed as T-16 2 Nov 46 (q.v.).
T-151	43-15193 NC-39354 LV-XEO	C-47A-80-DL	19659	Acquired via civil purchase before 29 Aug 46. Reserialed almost immediately as T-174 9 Oct 46 (q.v.).
T-172	43-15940 NC-41761 LV-XEP	C-47A-90-DL	20406	Acquired via civil purchase before 29 Aug 46. Reserialed almost immediately as T-175 9 Oct 46 (q.v.).
T-174	43-15193 NC-39354 LV-XEO T-151	C-47A-80-DL	19659	The former T-151 (see above) serialed 9 Oct 46. Reserialed into the second series as T-17 2 Nov 46 (q.v.).
T-175	43-15940 NC-41761 LV-XEP T-172	C-47A-90-DL	20406	The former T-172 (see above) serialed 9 Oct 46. Reserialed into the second series as T-18 2 Nov 46 (q.v.).

Besides illustrating one of the very few known used of RATO by a Latin American military aircraft, this view also reveals that C-47A T-20 wore her underwing codes in accordance with pre-war Argentine directives and, apparently, that the undersides of her horizontal tail surfaces were also painted red. *via Leif Hëllstrom*

By the time this photo was taken, T-20 had divested all of her special Antarctic markings and modifications and returned to standard service with the GIT. As she was lost to an accident while landing at Curuzú Cuatiá, Corrientes, on 19 March 1956, this image was taken some time between 1952 and then. *Gordon S. Williams*

Following those first modest acquisitions, and combined with these, the FAA eventually operated a total of fifty-five Douglas DC-3 series twin-engine transports, comprising an extraordinarily diverse mix of variants, modifications and hybrid aircraft. These included three built from the start as DC-3s or DC-3As, three C-4's, thirty-eight C-47As of virtually every major block, five C-47Bs, one C-53, three R4D-1s and one R4D-5. Of these, no fewer than twenty-five had been converted at some point to DC-3C or DC-3D (or DC-3C-like) configuration, presenting the FAA logistics and maintenance organisation with an exceptionally challenging array of support problems.

The peak years of service were in 1966 and 1967, when between thirty-seven and thirty-eight assorted aircraft were counted among the active inventory. The accompanying table describing the individual service lives of each aircraft, it must be observed, will be found to differ in large part with the accepted wisdom, and many assumptions previously recorded in print will be noticeably absent. The summaries presented here, while they may be regarded as somewhat confusing to the casual observer, are arranged in such a way as to aid the understanding of the incredibly convoluted FAA serial and coding systems that often changed after only brief use. These summaries have been assembled through a combination of primary research by the pioneering and excellent work of the team of Javier Mosquera, Guillermo Gebel and Atilio Marino, and has been verified via primary documents located by the authors over a period of more than fifty years at the US National Archives and the USAF Historical Research Agency. Additionally, the findings of John M. Davis, the extraordinary work of Air-Britain over the years, and John and Maureen Woods of the highly regarded 'Friends of the DC-3' clan, have enabled extensive cross-checks and the solutions to a very large number of assumptions and outstanding questions.

USAAF and USAF Air Order of Battle documents have been found to be remarkably reliable over the years and, while lacking in detailed specifics at times, have served to confirm findings from other sources, and to challenge yet others. The earliest report found was for 21 August 1943, when it showed the Army with one DC-3, which, as can be seen, reveals that not only had the US made note of the acquisition of Number 169 (the former F-ARQJ) by that date, it had also done so in a timely manner. Oddly, two follow-on reports, for 15 June and 28 August 1944, cited the solitary aircraft as type DC-3A, probably because the US Army Air Attaché had not as of that date yet learned of the actual provenance

of the aircraft. With a change of personnel, by 17 July 1945, the AOB cited the aircraft as a 'C-47', probably the earliest of many 'spotting errors' to follow, but certainly referring to the DC-3-294.

The FAA had actually started casting around for more Douglas twins as early as 6 May 1946, when the US Embassy queried the State Department in Washington, DC, as to whether there would be any objections to the Argentine Army or Navy acquiring two surplus PLUNA (Uruguay) Douglas DC-2s,[12] a sale that was not consummated, the Army instead opting for 'younger' aircraft then becoming available in large numbers on the US surplus market.

The following month, on 3 June 1946, the FAA was awaiting approval of export licences for two C-47s found in Miami (almost certainly T-151 and T-172), the broker for which had appealed to the State Department for quick action on these, as they feared that if they were not forthcoming that 'the sale of four more C-47s and two C-54s may be broken off otherwise'.

Despite the ambivalent attitude towards Argentina within the US State Department, besides these two aircraft, Export Licence No. 146 was finally issued on 14 January 1947, for eight more C-47s, with the 'customer' cited as the FAA. These almost certainly included the aircraft that received ferry registrations between LV-XEO and LV-XFV, although the export licence made no mention of their conversion prior to delivery to DC-3C configuration.

As mentioned earlier, Argentina was eventually excluded from the USAAF-sponsored American Republics Projects (ARP), but not before a single C-47A-65-DL, 42-100537 (MSN 19000) had been formally set aside by the USAAF for offset to the FAA. The State Department interceded at the last minute, however (the aircraft was actually being readied for delivery from Panama around 18 December 1947), and the aircraft ended up in Venezuela instead.

In spite of the plethora of new and reconditioned British transport types entering its inventory during this period, by 31 January 1948, the FAA had drastically expanded the number of Douglas twins in its inventory, which, by that date, stood at eighteen, all assigned to the II Grupo de la Agrupación de Transporte at BAM El Palomar, which was fairly bursting at the seams with new aircraft. An AOB of later the same year, 1 October, still reflected a total of eighteen, but noted that four of these were non-operational for minor repairs, but should be returned to service within a week which, given the number of transport aircraft types being serviced at the time, was rather remarkable.

Photos of FAA C-47s and DC-3s acquired on the US surplus market and bearing the briefly worn ferry marks are very rare. Here, LV-XFS is seen at the Miami FLC Sales Centre with a former RCAF Fairchild PT-26 in the foreground. Built as a C-47A-75-DL, she has clearly already been converted to a DC-3C and was taken up on 3 February 1947, becoming T-22 (first use). *Hagedorn Collection*

Here is LV-XFS after she had her full FAA marks and titles applied as T-22. Note the 'air stair' installation and, just visible, her I Brigada Aérea titles. As she was a total loss in an accident at the FMA in Córdoba in July 1958, this images dates prior to that date. It is interesting to note that, of the C-47s and DC-3s in this four-aircraft line-up, no two have the same colour scheme on their empennage! *via Dr Gary Kuhn*

Between 1 January 1949 and 1 April 1950, the FAA DC-3 and C-47 strength remained constant at exactly eighteen aircraft, all still at El Palomar. In light of this, it is somewhat surprising that the FAA submitted a request via the Argentine Embassy in Washington, dated 28 February 1950 for '27 two-engine medium transports', using as its justification a carefully worded statement that the Argentine government intended to use these to modernise 'all branches of service', and although the request did not specify C-47s, there is little doubt that they were the preferred type. The request, significantly, also included a request for a very lengthy list of spare parts for sixteen 'DC-3s', five Douglas DC-4s or C-54s, and no fewer than thirty-two Beech AT-11s. The work on most of these was performed by the Aviation Maintenance Corporation (AMC).

The next detailed FAA Order of Battle, dated 26 November 1951 reflected a total then of twenty-two 'DC-3s' in the inventory, of which only twelve remained at El Palomar (as noted earlier, with

fifty-seven other assorted types) and ten at BAM Morón (alongside an astonishing seventy-seven other types). From that date until 1960, FAA DC-3/C-47 strength remained almost precisely constant, although dipping slightly to fifteen in 1959, attrition having been made up by the acquisition of at least three refurbished aircraft from the Texas Engineering & Manufacturing Company, Inc., of Dallas, known historically as simply TEMCO, by September 1954. During 1960, however, this surged to twenty-eight as the FAA was suddenly presented with the motley assortment of aircraft that had been acquired by the ill-advised Army campaign to create its own organic transport element, in defiance of the FAA, the two services often finding themselves at opposite extremes of the political spectrum. Here then is a by-serial listing of the eventual total of thirty-two mixed types that fleshed out these numbers between roughly 1947 and 1969.

Acquired at exactly the same time and from the same source as T-22, her sister T-23 was also a DC-3C conversion and, when photographed, was also assigned to the I Brigada Aérea when photographed. She had the duty of escorting the first fifteen brand-new Beech T-34s home from Wichita, Kansas, in May 1957, when this image was taken. *Steve Kraus*

Another March 1947 DC-3C acquisition, T-25 was photographed here twenty years later at the Aeroparque in August 1967, by which time her nose had been modestly modified to incorporate a Bendix RD-1R weather radar. At this time, she was assigned to the exclusive use of the Comandante en Jefe de la FAA, probably explaining her high-visibility markings and the national flag on her nose. *Jean Magendie*

Second 'T' Series Prefix Serials Sequence Aircraft – 1947–69

FAA Serial	Previous Identity	Type as Built	MSN	Assignments and Notes
T-16	F-ARQJ 169 T-169	DC-3-294	2122	The former T-169 (see above) serialed 2 Nov 46. Assigned to the Subsecretaría de Aviación Civil, Dirección General de Circulación Aérea y Aeródromos on 28 Jun 51. Although frequently being cited as having been written off 5 May 70 at Río Cuarto, she was in fact donated to the Fuerza Aérea Paraguaya (FAP) as T-67 on 27 May 69 (q.v.).
T-17(1)	43-15193 NC-39354 LV-XEO T-151 T-174	C-47A-80-DL	19659	The former T-174 (see above) serialed 2 Nov 46. Assigned to II Grupo de la Agrupación Transporte at BAM El Palomar. Suffered an accident 1 Jul 49 while operating for LADE at Los Cinco Jagüeles, La Pampa and repaired using parts from T-18 (q.v.) by 1950. Temporarily assigned to the Industrias Aeronáuticas y Mecánicas del Estado (I.A.M.E.) during 1952. Damaged on landing at Taller Regional Río Cuarto 16 Sep 55. Reserialed as T-31 Nov 59 (q.v.).
T-18(1)	43-15940 NC-41761 LV-XEP T-172 T-175	C-47A-90-DL	20406	The former T-175 (see above) serialed 2 Nov 46. Assigned to II Grupo de la Agrupación Transporte at BAM El Palomar. Assigned to the Regimiento I de Transporte (RITA) 13 May 48. Suffered a serious accident 28 Nov 47 on landing at Bahía Blanca, the first FAA C-47 lost, as she was deemed uneconomically repairable. Parts of this aircraft were subsequently used in repairs to T-17 and T-89 (q.v.).
T-19(1)	44-77206 LV-ACG	C-47B-40-DK	16790/33538	Originally to FAMA as LV-ACG but incorporated into the FAA as T-19 10 Jan 47 and assigned to the II Grupo de la Agrupación Transporte at BAM El Palomar. Transferred to the Comando de Institutos Militares and the Escuela de Aviación Militar (EAM) as a trainer in 1948 but returned to the Grupo I de Transporte (GIT) in 1956. This aircraft was destroyed on the night of 12 Aug 58 at Trelew, Chubut, when the crew apparently incorrectly read their instruments.
T-20(1)	43-16013 NC-67562 LV-XFP	C-47A-90-DL	20479	Acquired via civil purchase and became T-20 3 Feb 47 (some sources cite 27 Feb 47). Assigned to the II Grupo de la Agrupación Transporte at BAM El Palomar 18 Mar 47. Transferred to the RITA 13May 48 and then the GIT 9 Jan 51. Modified for operations in the Antarctic in Alaska between 20 Jul 51 and 15 Nov 51, similar to the modifications to US Navy R4D-5S aircraft and assigned to the Grupo de Tareas a la Antártida Nov 51 but, in the event, even though sporting high-visibility Day-Glo paint on her nose and empennage, was never actually used in Antarctica.[13] Returned to the GIT. Lost on 19 Mar 56 on landing at Curuzú Cuatiá, Corrientes, while engaged in civic action medical support.
T-21	42-24074 LV-XFR[14]	C-47A-40-DL DC-3C	9936	Acquired via civil purchase after modification as a DC-3C in the US and incorporated into the FAA as T-21 3 Feb 47 (some sources state 27 Feb 47). Assigned to the II Grupo de la Agrupación Transporte at BAM El Palomar 30 Apr 47. Assigned to the RITA 13 May 48 and then the GIT 9 Jan 51. This aircraft was totally destroyed on 3 Jul 59 6km north-east of the Córdoba airport. Her remains were used to test the Marbore IIC rocket motor in her empennage as later installed in TA-05 (q.v.).
T-22(1)	42-101016 LV-XFS	C-47A-75-DL DC-3C	19479	Acquired via civil purchase after modification as a DC-3C in the US and incorporated into the FAA as T-22 3 Feb 47. Assigned to the II Grupo de la Agrupación Transporte at BAM El Palomar 6 Mar 47. Transferred to the RITA 13 May 48 and the GIT 9 Jan 51. This aircraft was totally destroyed 17 Jul 58 at the FMA in Córdoba.

T-23	43-15531 LV-XFT	C-47A-85-DL DC-3C	19997	Acquired via civil purchase after modification as a DC-3C in the US and incorporated into the FAA as T-23 3 Feb 47. Assigned to the II Grupo de la Agrupación Transporte at BAM El Palomar 19 Apr 47. Transferred to the RITA 13 May 48 and the GIT 9 Jan 51. This was one of the aircraft employed by the so-called Grupo Aéreo de Transporte Revolucionario[15] during the revolt of September 1955. During this unfortunate event, the aircraft was crudely marked with the 'Cristo Vence' emblem on her fuselage. Returned to the FAA fold, it suffered a forced landing at Florianópolis, Brazil, 20 May 62 but was recovered and repaired. Another accident on 22 May 63 at Punta de Agua, Córdoba, was also repaired but the aircraft was officially withdrawn from service in Dec 67, last assigned to I Brigada Aérea since at least 18 Nov 66., one of the longest serving of the initial batch of post-war acquisitions. This aircraft had the distinction of having served as escort for the first fifteen Beech T-34 Mentors flown down from the US in May 57.
T-24	43-15076 LV-XFU	C-47A-80-DL DC-3C	19542	Acquired via civil purchase after modification as a DC-3C in the US and incorporated into the FAA as T-24 6 Mar 47. The identity of this aircraft has been associated with NC-53376 of Challenger Airlines in the US as late as 1965, but apparently official Argentine records consistently identify her as having joined the FAA. Assigned to the II Grupo de la Agrupación Transporte at BAM El Palomar 19 Apr 47. Transferred to the RITA 13 May 48 and suffered an accident 31 May 48 when it struck a telephone pole at El Palomar but was repaired. Transferred to the GIT 9 Jan 51. Suffered damage at Córdoba 20 Jul 55 but repaired. Stricken from the inventory 17 Oct 69 and, although reportedly donated (some sources say she was sold) to the Dirección Provincial de Aviación de la Provincia de Buenos Aires 10 Feb 70 (some sources cite 17 Oct 69), there is no record of it having received any subsequent civil identity with that organisation. At some point it flew LADE routes and was named 'El Patagónic'. She was broken up some time after Feb 70.
T-25	42-100563 LV-XFV	C-47A-65-DL DC-3C	19026	Acquired via civil purchase after modification as a DC-3C in the US and incorporated into the FAA as T-25 6 Mar 47. Assigned to the II Grupo de la Agrupación Transporte at BAM El Palomar 19 Apr 47. Transferred to the RITA 13 May 48 and the GIT 9 Jan 51. Although a 'line' DC-3C, the aircraft was locally outfitted as a VIP transport and assigned to the exclusive use of the Ministerio de Aeronáutica. The aircraft suffered damage during a landing at the Aeródromo Militar Aeroparque at Buenos Aires 15 Nov 54 but was repaired. Sometime during the 1960s, the aircraft received a most unusual installation, when a Bendix RD-1R weather radar was installed. Still in VIP configuration, she was assigned to use by the Comandante en Jefe de la FAA in 1965. On 31 May 69 she was transferred to the VII Brigada Aérea but was stricken from the inventory in Dec 69. The aircraft was donated to the Automóvil Club Argentino 12 Mar 70 and civil registered as LV-JTC but suffered an accident 25 Feb 71 at Tucumán and was not repaired. Apparently, her Bendix radar was recovered and installed in another aircraft.
T-26	42-100932 LV-XFX	C-47A-75-DL DC-3C	19395	Acquired via civil purchase after modification as a DC-3C in the US and incorporated into the FAA as T-26 on 10 Apr 47 (some sources cite July 1947). Assigned to the II Grupo de la Agrupación Transporte at BAM El Palomar 6 May 47. Transferred to the RITA 13 May 48 and the GIT 9 Jan 51. Like T-23 above, she was utilised by the Grupo Aéreo de Transporte Revolucionario in Sep 55 but returned to the fold of the FAA for the next fourteen years. She was stricken from the inventory 31 May 69 and donated to the Fuerza Aérea Boliviana's TAME (Transportes Aéreos Militares) as TAM-32 (q.v., although it has also been cited, apparently erroneously, as having become TAM-31) on 12 Jul 69, subsequently being sold and becoming CP-1470.

An exceptionally well-travelled aircraft, T-27 was built as a C-47A-25-DK but was modified early post-war to DC-3C configuration, then seeing service with airlines in the US, Argentina and Brazil, and briefly serving with the Ejercito Argentino as EA-8T. After further adventures, she was donated to Paraguay as T-65 in May 1969. *via Dr Gary Kuhn*

Unusual in having been an R4D-1, T-38 arrived in the FAA via the Army in September 1960. Here, pictured with unusually large format service titles, she was with the DINFIA but was, at the time photographed, undergoing extensive work. Her engines are missing, as are her wing root fairings. Oddly, she was reserialed around December 1967 when the service changed its system not to TC-38, as would seem appropriate, but TC-27. *Georg von Roitberg*

T-27	42-93682 NC-62567 LV-ABH PP-XES PP-YQA EA-8T	C-47A-25-DK DC-3C	13621	In a rather confusing administrative action, the FAA arbitrarily decided to 'reactivate' its early post-war 'T' series in 1960, and T-27 was the first aircraft to resume that series, after an extraordinary odyssey of prior civil use and the short-lived Army aviation experiment, from which the aircraft was transferred to FAA control via Executive Resolution No. 89/60 on 20 Sep 60. She was immediately repainted and assigned to the GIT of the I Brigada Aérea, a decidedly 'non-standard' aircraft if there ever was one. She did not survive long, however, and was stricken from the inventory on 8 Mar 63 but, surprisingly, was taken up once again on 29 Jan 65 and returned to the IBA inventory. She was once again stricken in 1968 but was donated to Paraguay as T-65 (q.v., although some sources cite T-61) on 27 May 69.
T-28	43-47967 NC-90908 PP-YQJ EA-10T	C-47A-30-DK DC-3C	13783/25228	Like T-27, this aircraft was transferred from the Army to the FAA on 20 Sep 60 and was assigned to the GIT of I Brigada Aérea (IBA). The aircraft was stricken on 8 Mar 63 but then modified to joint passenger/cargo configuration and described officially as a 'C-47A' on 22 Sep 64, being reserialed in the next series as TC-28 (q.v.) in 1965 as a result.
T-29	41-20055 YS-24 PP-AVI EA-4T	C-53-DO	4825	Another former Army aircraft with an extensive civil history, this aircraft passed to the FAA 20 Sep 60 and also joined the GIT of the IBA. Although administratively stricken on 8 Mar 63, this was set aside, and she re-entered the FAA inventory 26 Sep 63. Serving only a little more than three more years, she was once again stricken in Dec 66 and officially abandoned on 12 Feb 68 (some sources cited 8 Mar 63). A spotting report dated 23 Jan 68 was apparently in error for another aircraft.
T-30	43-48610 NC-79005 PP-PCV PP-YQM EA-12T	C-47B-5-DK DC-3C	14426/25871	Yet another former Army aircraft with a lengthy civil career, starting with the redoubtable Pan Am in 1946, this aircraft passed to the FAA on 20 Sep 60 and was assigned to GIT of IBA. She was declared excess on 8 Mar 63 but was recalled to active duty on 26 Sep 63. A landing accident was suffered on 23 Jun 64 (one source gave the date as 26 Jun 64) at Santiago del Estero and incurred more than 58 per cent damage, the aircraft deemed uneconomically repairable and stricken from the inventory.
T-31	43-15193 NC-39354 LV-XEO T-151 T-174 T-17	C-47A-80-DL	19659	Swept up in what was actually the second service-wide, post-war, reserialing programme, this aircraft gained marks T-31 'out of sequence' in November 1959, but these were changed to TC-31 (q.v.) in Nov 61.
T-32	BuA04705 NC-9399H PP-KAB PP-ANM EA-2T	R4D-1	4365	Another of the aircraft that had been acquired for the abortive Army aviation element gained the next serial in line, T-32 on 20 Sep 60. Like its sister, she was assigned to the GIT of the IBA, but was almost immediately reissued serial TC-32 sometime in 1961, although one source cites 8 Mar 63. (q.v.).
T-33	42-23392 NC-79014 N91228 N148A	C-47A-5-DL DC-3C C-47A	9254	This aircraft was acquired commercially by the FAA from the William C. Wold and Associates, ex-Allegheny Airlines, and was reconverted from passenger-configured DC-3C standard to C-47A standard prior to delivery around 8 Feb 60. Upon arrival in Argentina, the aircraft was initially assigned to the Fábrica Militar de Aviones (FMA) but soon moved to the GIT. She was reserialed TC-33 in Nov 61 (q.v.).
T-34	42-92936 NC-63400 N91229 N149A	C-47A-20-DK DC-3C C-47A	12792	Also acquired via the William C. Wold and Associates, this aircraft was reconverted from DC-3C passenger configuration to C-47A-like standard by Slinn & Campbell and became T-34 in Feb 60. Initially assigned to the FMA for further work, she then was assigned to the GIT. She was reserialed as TC-34 in 1962 (q.v.), although one source cites 8 Mar 63.
T-35	43-49533 3-49533 0-349533	C-47B-15-DK C-47D	15349/26794	The first militarily modernised C-47 acquired by the FAA, this aircraft had served extensively in Latin America, in turn, with the USAF Mission to Peru, then that of Ecuador, Chile, Argentina, Peru again and finally Argentina (see Chapter 1). She had suffered an accident on 22 May 59 at the FAA's EAM while being flown by a mixed FAA/USAF crew. Ruled uneconomical to recover and repair by the USAF, she was offered to the FAA 'as is/where is' for a bargain $5,000. The FAA made her airworthy again and assigned her in 1960 to the IV Brigada Aérea. She was reserialed as TC-35 in 1962 (q.v.), although one source cites 8 Mar 63.
T-36	42-92246 FL614 (RAF) NC-34985 LV-AFS PP-XEP PP-YQB EA-9T	C-47A-1-DK Dakota III DC-3C	12025	Yet another of the former Argentine Army aircraft transferred to the FAA on 20 Sep 60 (one source cites 21 Nov 60), this was another exceptionally well-travelled (and rather weary) aircraft, Like the others, it was assigned to the GIT of the IBA but was intended to have become TC-36 in 1962, but this did not happen. She was declared redundant on or about 8 Mar 63 and transferred to the FAA's Escuela de Suboficiales de la Fuerza Aérea on 29 Jan 65 and eventually scrapped.
T-37	NC-34925 TI-16 PP-AXW PP-NBJ EA-6T	DC-3A-345	4957	One of only three 'straight' DC-3s without a military history prior to arriving in Argentina, this was another former Army aircraft passed to the FAA on 20 Sep 60 (one source cites Aug 61). She was assigned to the GIT of the IBA and, like T-36, was intended to have become TC-37, and instead was only operated briefly as T-37 between Jul 61 and Nov 62. She was stricken from the inventory on 8 Mar 63 and scrapped, despite persistent reports that she was donated to Paraguay in 1969.

T-38	BuA03140 PP-KAA PP-ANS EA-8T	R4D-1	4280	Another former Army aircraft, T-38 was transferred to the FAA on 20 Sep 60 with the others and assigned to the GIT of IBA. Intended to have become TC-38, she soldiered on briefly as T-38 before being offered for sale on 8 Mar 63. After having set idle for some time, she was acquired by DINFIA (the successor of FMA) in 1965, registered with the quasi-governmental marks LQ-IPC on 4 May 66 and modified with a mixed cargo/passenger interior. In the event, DINFIA did not initially operate the aircraft as such, instead she was intended to have passed to the Dirección General de Agua y Energía Eléctrica. However, she remained with DINFIA, where she performed duties for the Área Material Córdoba and the Centro de Ensayos en Vuelo. She remained assigned to these duties until Dec 67, when she returned to FAA control and, in fact, was oddly reserialed as TC-27 and not TC-38 as often cited (q.v.).
T-39(1)	42-100975 NC-19135 PP-SVA PP-ANF EA-1T	C-47A-75-DL	19438	The first of the former Army aircraft, this veteran also passed to the FAA on 20 Sep 60 (although one source cites November 1961) as T-39, being assigned to the GIT of the IBA. Although instructions were issued to reserial her as TC-39 during 1962, she was overtaken by events when she suffered a landing accident at BAM Tandil. Following her rather tortured recovery, parts of her were used in the rebuild of T-19(2) during 1968. This aircraft had frequently been cited as having been donated to Paraguay as T-39 in 1961 or 1965.
T-48	42-100881 LV-XFW	C-47A-75-DL DC-3C	19344	Acquired directly by the FAA from a commercial broker in the US, where she had been converted to DC-3C configuration, this aircraft was ferried to Argentina as LV-XFW and became T-48 far earlier than her serial would suggest, on 3 Feb 47 (some sources cite Apr 47). She was assigned to the II Grupo de la Agrupación Transporte at BAM El Palomar 27 Feb 47. She was transferred to the RITA on 13 May 48 and then to the GIT on 9 Jan 51. She was reserialed in the third FAA C-47 series as T-02 (q.v.) in Sep 59.
T-49	42-100505 LV-XFY	C-47A-65-DL DC-3C	18968	Acquired directly by the FAA from a commercial broker in the US, where she had been converted to DC-3C configuration, this aircraft was ferried to Argentina as LV-XFY and became T-49 on 24 May 47. Like her sisters, she was initially assigned to the II Grupo de la Agrupación Transporte at BAM El Palomar on 17 Jun 47. Initially outfitted in a VIP configuration, with a DC-3-style passenger door, she was for a time detailed for the exclusive use of the Comandante en Jefe de la FAA. She then passed to the RITA 13 May 48 and the GIT 9 Jan 51. She was reserialed in the third series as T-01 (q.v.) in Sep 59.
T-50	42-93174 NC-88726	C-47A-20-DK	13056	A former Panagra aircraft, the FAA acquired her on 24 May 47 as T-50 and initially assigned the aircraft to the II Grupo de la Agrupación Transporte at BAM El Palomar. Like nearly all of her sisters, she then moved to the RITA on 13 May 48 and the GIT on 9 Jan 51. She suffered an emergency landing on 24 Jun 48 at Gualeguaychú, Entre Rios, but was recovered and repaired. She was severely damaged again by severe weather while en route to Córdoba in 1952 and was withdrawn from service, passing to the care of the EAM. In August 1955, she was handed over to the Escuela de Tropas Aerotransportadas del Ejército Argentino where she became an instructional airframe, her fuselage mounted on a concrete plinth and used to train paratroopers. Her fuselage was still in existence by 2008, and the commander and staff of the IV Brigada Paracaidista have decided to make modest conservation efforts to preserve it as an exhibit.
T-51	41-18454 NC-86565	C-47-DL	4516	Another Panagra veteran, T-51 was also acquired by the FAA on 24 May 47 and followed the exact same assignments as T-50 above. Between 27 Feb 53 and 21 May 53, however, she was being used in connection with tests of the PAT-1 projectile, along with Avro Lancaster B.Mk.I B-036. She suffered an accident in the Chaco in Oct 53 which was sufficiently severe to see her dropped from the inventory by Dec 53.
T-52	42-23912 NC-30016	C-47A-35-DL	9774	This aircraft was purchased commercially in the US by 12 Jun 47 and followed the same assignment path as T-50 and T-51. By the early 1950s, she had been locally modified to a configuration roughly equivalent to DC-3C. She suffered an accident and minor damage at San Antonio de Areco, Buenos Aires, on 19 Jun 55, was repaired and reserialed T-03 (q.v.) in Jun 60.
T-53	41-38722 NC-68219	C-47-DL	6181	Also acquired from commercial interests in the US by 12 Jun 47, this veteran aircraft had originally entered the USAAF inventory on 28 Dec 42, making her one of the oldest C-47s acquired by the FAA. After becoming T-53, she followed the usual assignment track. She was involved supporting forces loyal to the government during the September 1955 revolution and was damaged on the 17th at Deán Funes, Cordoba, while engaged in a resupply mission. Recovered and repaired, she suffered another accident on 28 Jul 59 at Vicente Casares, Buenos Aires, involving a forced landing following an in-flight fire. Although plans were in place to restore her to service and assign serial T-32, these were never completed and she was stricken instead.
T-67	43-15327 NC-67776 LV-NQU	C-47A-85-DL	20093	Acquired locally in Argentina from J. Wasserman around 7 Aug 48 (some sources cite Apr 48), and actually accepted at BAM El Palomar on 6 Sep 48, this aircraft was destined for the Taller Regional Quilmes, then to the II Grupo de la Agrupación Transporte for use by the Ministerio de Aeronáutica. She suffered a landing accident on 2 Jul 49 at Ascochinga, Córdoba, but was recovered and repaired, and remained at the service of the Ministerio even after transfer to the GIT. She experienced an in-flight fire on 20 Jul 53 in the vicinity of Villa Martelli but landed safely and was repaired. She was reserialed as T-04 (q.v.) in Aug 59.

T-89	43-15499	C-47A-85-DL	19965	Acquired from Aeronaves Dodero on 10 Jul 50 (some sources cite 11 Feb 50) and issued
	NC-65283	DC-3C		out-of-sequence serial T-89, this aircraft was almost immediately assigned to the RITA
	LV-ABF			on 18 Jul. Not long after being acquired, however, extensive corrosion was discovered
				and apparently parts of T-18 (q.v.) were used to almost completely rebuild the aircraft,
				gaining a VIP interior in the process. She was flown by the Grupo Aéreo de Transporte
				Revolucionario during the September 1955 revolution but was reserialed as T-05 (q.v.) in
				Oct 59.

By the end of June 1969, the FAA strength in Douglas twins is perhaps best described as a mix of ten C-47 cargo variants and nine assorted DC-3 passenger variants. USAF MAP documents show that the FAA had lost three DC-3s through attrition (which seems to coincide with known crash information, including TC-28 on 5 May 69) but that six others had been deleted from the inventory as merely 'other losses', (these included the three donated to Bolivia and Paraguay each) and that, combined, the nineteen aircraft had accumulated a total of 1,405 flying hours, total, during the preceding quarter that, given the age and diversity of the fleet, was quite respectable. What is more surprising, however, was the fact that all but three of the C-47s and two of the DC-3s were being supported actively by the MAP spares pipeline at the time, which must certainly have involved enormous exertions on the part of the logistics staff. The non-MAP supported aircraft had all been ex-Aerolíneas Argentinas hand-me-downs acquired in 1966.

Of the nineteen, a mix of thirteen C-47s and DC-3s were assigned to the I Brigada Aérea at BAM El Palomar and had been assigned a Combat Readiness Code of C-3, this having been based on the fact that 50 per cent or more of the unit's assigned aircraft were out of commission at any one time. The unit also had a total of twenty-nine trained crews for these aircraft, which was clearly disproportionate. Interestingly, one C-47 was also assigned to the IV Brigada Aérea at BAM El Plumerillo, Mendoza, to support that unit's nineteen North American F-86Fs and another to the V Brigada Aérea at BAM General Pringles, Villa Mercedes, in support of the twenty-three Douglas A-4Bs that had been received by that time. The two MAP-supplied HC-47s, and a 'straight' C-47, were assigned alongside the FAA's three MAP-supplied Grumman HU-16B Albatross amphibians at BAM Tandil in a unit identified in MAP reports as the '1st Long-Range Surveillance (SAR) Squadron'.

The FAA had, by 22 July 1969, let it be known that it was commencing the process of withdrawing its long-serving C-47s and DC-3s from the inventory and, indeed, some were withdrawn and, as noted, others donated to Bolivia and Paraguay. However, few among the leadership at the time could foresee that, in fact, the type was destined to soldier on in some numbers for another twenty-one years!

Third 'T' Series Serials Sequence Aircraft – 1960–70

FAA Serial	Previous Identity	Type as Built	MSN	Assignments and Notes
T-01	42-100505 LV-XFY T-49	C-47A-65-DL DC-3C	18968	When the FAA reviewed and refreshed its transport aircraft serialing system in 1959, this aircraft was selected to gain the distinction of the 'new' T-01 in conjunction with its VIP condition and the fact that she was destined to serve as the 'Admiral's Barge' for none other than the Comandante en Jefe of the FAA himself and, on occasion, for the President and other dignitaries. She apparently made a number of foreign sojourns as such, as she was issued a Permit to Overfly Brazilian territory in Oct 59. The interior was made even more luxurious by the talented staff of the Taller Regional Quilmes (TRQ) and a Bendix RDR-1R weather radar was installed. Serving in this capacity for some time until supplanted by more modern aircraft, she was reserialed once again as T-40 (q.v.) in Nov 66.
T-02	42-100881 LV-XFW T-48	C-47A-75-DL DC-3C	19344	Gaining her second FAA serial in September 1959, this well-maintained airframe served with distinction and was with the I Brigada Aérea by 1967, continuing in service until 31 May 69 and, after some modest work, was donated on to the Fuerza Aérea Boliviana on 12 Jul 69, where she became TAM-31 (q.v.).
T-03	42-23912 NC-30016 T-52	C-47A-35-DL DC-3C (config.)	9774	Although reserialed as T-03 in Jun 60, this aircraft served only for only eight more years, and was stricken from the inventory in Dec 68. She served with the I Brigada Aérea as of 13 Apr 67.
T-04(1)	43-15327 NC-67776 LV-NQU T-67	C-47A-85-DL	20093	Oddly, this aircraft appears to have received her 'new' serial, T-04, almost a year ahead of her numeric predecessors, in Aug 59 and was apparently modified from an earlier, unidentified passenger interior back to a C-47 type mixed cargo/paratrooper capable interior. She wore these new marks only relatively briefly, however, being reserialed – probably because of these modifications – as TC-04 (q.v.) in 1962.
T-04(2)	42-93258 KG558 LV-ADJ	C-47A-20-DK Dakota III DC-3C	13150	Causing no end of confusion for both spotters and historians over the years, this former ZONDA and Aerolíneas Argentinas passenger-configured airliner was transferred to the FAA when the airline finally said goodbye to its old faithful mounts on 12 May 66. Assigned to the GIT, she actually operated on LADE routes as late as December 1967. A USAF document reported that she was lost from the inventory between Jul 68 and Jun 69, but the exact circumstances have not been identified. Often reported, in error, as having been T-09, which muddied the waters even further, photographic evidence has proven otherwise.
T-05	43-15499 NC-65283 LV-ABF T-89	C-47A-85-DL DC-3C	19965	This aircraft gained these second set of marks in Oct 59 and, initially, remained in her passenger-style DC-3C configuration. In 1962, however, she was converted to cargo configuration, including the reinstallation of a cargo-style, double door on the port rear fuselage, and became TC-05 (q.v.) as a result.

T-08	42-92988 CF-DSW LV-ABY	C-47A-20-DK DC-3C	12850	Another former ZONDA and Aerolíneas Argentinas aircraft, T-08 was integrated into the FAA on 22 Mar 66 (some sources cite 22 Jun 66) and was assigned to the GIT flying routes for LADE. She experienced a landing accident on 26 Mar 66, not long after changing colours at I Brigada Aérea but was only comparatively slightly damaged. T-08 was stricken from the inventory in May 1969 and donated the same month to the Fuerza Aérea Paraguaya on the 27th, becoming T-63 (q.v.).
T-09	42-93549 KG656 LV-ABZ	C-47A-25-DK Dakota III DC-3C	13473	Another former ZONDA and Aerolíneas Argentinas airliner, she passed to the FAA on 14 Mar 66 (some sources cite 22 Jun 66) and was assigned to the GIT flying LADE routes. Her tenure was very brief, however, being offered for sale by Aug 67 and actually dropped from the inventory between Jul 68 and Jun 69.
T-10	42-93426 KG605 LV-ACJ	C-47A-25-DK Dakota III DC-3C	13336	Another former ZONDA and Aerolíneas Argentinas airliner, this aircraft became T-10 on 9 Mar 66 (some sources cite 22 Jun 66) and was assigned identically to T-08 and T-09 above. Although withdrawn in Sep 69 at I Brigada Aérea (with which she had served as early as 3 Dec 67), she was reportedly modified by BOAC[16] as an airways verification and radio aids platform and, as a consequence, was reserialed as VR-10 (q.v.) on 13 Mar 70.
T-11	42-92445 FZ666 LV-CAN	C-47A-5-DK Dakota III DC-3C	12246	Another of the ex-ZONDA and Aerolíneas Argentinas airliners, T-11 was taken up by the FAA on 19 May 66 (some sources cite 22 Jun 66) and was assigned as T-08 to T-10. She was stricken and offered for sale in Feb 68.
T-12	42-92151 FL599 LV-ACP	C-47A-1-DK Dakota III DC-3C	11920	Another of the ex-ZONDA and Aerolíneas Argentinas airliners, T-12 entered FAA service on 25 Mar 66 and followed the same assignment path as T-08 to T-11. Withdrawn in July 1969, she was donated to the Fuerza Aérea Boliviana on 12 Jul 69, becoming TAM-30 (q.v.).
T-13	41-38717 NC-14271 CF-FVX LV-AFE	C-47-DL DC-3C	6176	One of the oldest C-47s operated by the FAA, this aircraft had originally arrived in Argentina for Aeroposta Argentina on 9 Dec 47 as LV-AFE. When Aerolíneas Argentinas was created on 7 Dec 50, it passed to their colours and finally to the FAA on 24 Mar 66 (some sources cite 22 Jun 66), then being operated and assigned as the other former Aerolíneas Argentinas DC-3Cs. She served a brief three months with the FAA, being offered for sale in May 1966, thus qualifying as the shortest service FAA DC-3 or C-47.
T-14	42-23300 NC-86592 LV-AGD	C-47A-1-DL DC-3C	9162	One of the shortest service FAA C-47s, this aircraft was passed to the FAA's control on 22 Jun 66 and was assigned to the GIT for service on LADE routes. After barely three years of service under FAA control, she was stricken on 2 Oct 69.
T-17(2)	43-15694 CA50 (CATC) XT-T36 NC-8328C N1797B ETA-101 ME-1T MG-1T	C-47A-90-DL	20160	Unquestionably one of the most travelled of all Latin American C-47s, this aircraft, after having served no fewer than six previous masters, found her way into the FAA inventory in October 1960 and served with the GIT as part of PAA61 (the Programmea de Actividad Aérea 1961, a Civic Action Programme) briefly as T-17, the second use of this serial, before being reserialed as TC-17 (q.v.) in Nov 61.
T-18(2)	43-15922 CA3 (CATC) XT-T24 NC-8324C N1795B ETA-103 ME-3T MG-3T	C-47A-90-DL	20388	Like her sister T-17(2) described above, this aircraft was very well used when acquired by the FAA in Oct 60, after which she was assigned to the GIT also with the PAA61 programme. She was reserialed as TC-18 (q.v.) in Nov 61.
T-19(2)	BuA05062 NC-36815 PP-AVW EA-5T	R4D-1	4754	Another of the former Army aircraft, this aircraft was taken up by the FAA 20 Sep 60 (although some sources cite Aug 61) and almost immediately assigned to the GIT of I Brigada Aérea. She was declared excess on 8 Mar 63 and offered for sale. However, she was recalled to active duty in 1968 and reserialed as T-39(2). References to her having become LQ-JNB are questionable.
T-20(2)	NC-18937 C-100 (AVIANCA) PP-BHD PP-YQL EA-11T	DC-3-228	2012	The oldest DC-3 series aircraft to serve with the FAA, this one also came to the service via the Army, being taken up on 20 Sep 60 and, like her sisters, assigned to the GIT of the I Brigada Aérea. She experienced an accident on 25 Oct 61 at BAM Aeroparque but was quickly repaired and returned to service. She was declared surplus and offered for sale on 8 Mar 63 but was subsequently excluded from this action and was outfitted for radio aids verification duties with the RACA and was assigned to the Dirección General de Circulación Aérea y Aeródromos (DGCAA) as LQ-CAA in a governmental role. For some reason, these marks were changed to LQ-IOS on 17 Feb 66 before being returned to FAA control in July 1970 as VR-12 (q.v.). Remarkably, this very high-time aircraft was once again returned to passenger configuration in 1972 and reserialed a final time, as T-102 (q.v.).
T-22(2)	42-92394 FZ633 PP-JAC PP-YPB EA-7T	C-47A-1-DK Dakota III DC-3C	12190	The last of the former Army aircraft, T-22(2) passed to the FAA on 20 Sep 60 (some sources cite 4 Oct 60) like her sisters and followed the exact same assignment sequence as T-19(2). She was not in use between 8 Mar 63 and 26 Sep 63. She survived rather longer in service, however, and was not declared surplus and offered for sale until May 69. Suggestions persist that this aircraft was acquired by the Fuerza Aérea Paraguaya initially as T-22 around 8 Mar 63 or, according to some sources, as T-67 (in 1968) and later T-16, but this has eluded convincing verification.

Rarely illustrated, DC-3C T-40 was the 'highest' serial code issued in the FAA's third series. She was formerly the VIP-configured T-01, and only wore T-40 from November 1966 until stricken in December 1970. The Day-Glo nose and fuselage band is also unusual. *MAP 1985-114 #141*

T-39(2)	BuA05062 NC-36815 PP-AVW EA-5T T-19	R4D-1	4754	Another very storied aircraft, these marks were taken up in the FAA in Aug 68 after having been T-19, and the aircraft was assigned to the GIT. She was transferred to quasi-government civil marks LQ-JNB 17 Jan 1969 (some sources cite 15 Apr 69), however.
T-40	42-100505 LV-XFY T-49 T-01	C-47A-65-DL DC-3C	18968	These marks were taken up in Nov 66. She was stricken from the inventory in Dec 70. Although made available to provincial and civil operators, she never flew again.

By mid-1971, the FAA had commenced applying camouflage on many of its C-47s, usually engaging colours nearly identical to those that had been applied to its new Douglas A-4B Skyhawks when first delivered. In the midst of these changes, it is not generally noted that very experienced FAA C-47 crews took an active part in the ONUC – United Nations Operations in the Congo – starting after 14 July 1960, and extending through January 1961, using C-47s seconded to the UN from the USAF, AVIANCA and Transair. Although no actual FAA-owned C-47s took part in these operations, the contributions of the FAA's crews, pilots, crews and maintainers, were exceptional, and provided them with a wealth of foreign and combat support operational experience which they had never experienced before.

Fourth 'T' Series Serials – 1971–90

FAA Serial	Previous Identity	Type as Built	MSN	Assignments and Notes
T-101	43-48194 KG778 LV-ACF LQ-ACF S-3 TS-03	C-47A-30-DK Dakota III DC-3D	14010/25455	Another veteran aircraft, this aircraft was not serialed as T-101 until Dec 71 and, initially, was assigned to the Grupo Aéreo Estatal, passing to the INAC on 3 Nov 72 and as late as Oct 74 and for exclusive use of the Comandante General. Even with a lot of time on the clock, this aircraft, despite her earlier multiple owners, was maintained in a very high state of maintenance, with a locally styled VIP interior. She even became a movie star, featuring in *Highlander II*. Still configured as a VIP transport, she was reassigned to the V Brigada Aérea in 1990, one of the last FAA C-47s in service. She then went to static display at the Aeropuerto El Calafate marked as LQ-GJT (which she had never actually worn) and has since passed into the custody of the Museo Nacional de Aéronautica (MNA) for long-term preservation. One source claims she was actually displayed at Villa Reynolds at a V Brigada Aérea museum there.
T-102	NC-18937 C-100 (AVIANCA) PP-BHD PP-YQL EA-11T T-20 LQ-CAA LQ-IOS VR-12	DC-3-228	2012	With yet another lengthy pedigree, this aircraft survived numerous changes to be returned to passenger configuration in 1972 as T-102 and was assigned for the use of the Instituto Nacional de Aviación Civil (INAC) upon its formation on 3 Nov 72 and until at least Oct 74. Although she experienced an in-flight incident on 21 Mar 73, she suffered only modest damage and was repaired. She was assigned to PAA1981 briefly on 18 Sep 81 before being assigned to Área Material Quilmes (AMQ) where she made her final flight on 8 Aug 72 with in incredible 32,711:07 on the clock. At last report, she had been made into a bar in Santa Clara.
T-103	43-48194 KG778 N123S 0490/CTA-25 LQ-MSP S-4 TS-04 E-301	C-47B-5-DK Dakota III	14669/26114	Yet another most unusual provenance, this aircraft had been outfitted as a flying clinic after acquisition by the Navy (q.v.) in 1958 and continued in that role after passing to governmental and then Sanitario (ambulance) marks with the FAA. After use as a multi-engine trainer at the EAM, she gained the marks T-103 in December 1975 as a pure passenger transport. Transferred to the INAC in 1982, she was subsequently assigned to the II Brigada Aérea in 1985. In 1989, she moved to the V Brigada Aérea but was surplused on 28 Dec 90. She was subsequently displayed on elevated plinths in Paraná but devoid of most of her markings and engines.
T-104	42-93459 KG614 LV-ACE VR-14	C-47A-25-DK Dakota III DC-3C	13373	Another long-serving aircraft, this aircraft moved from airways verification duties as VR-14 to T-104 as a dedicated passenger transport as T-104 in 1977 (although one report claims she was in service as early as 1975). By 1984, she was assigned to the V Brigada Aérea. She was withdrawn from service on 28 Dec 90 and was subsequently displayed in excellent condition at the Museo Interfuerzas de Santa Romana, San Luis.

DC-3s and C-47s gained a new lease on life in the FAA in the early 1970s, and DC-3D T-101, which gained these marks in December 1971, had a lengthy pedigree. Seen here on 17 December 1985 at Moron AB with the INAC badge on her nose, she was highly polished and, despite her age, very well maintained and had a locally outfitted VIP interior. She had a bit part in the movie *Highlander II* and survived to go to a museum setting, although exactly where is in dispute. *Carlos A. Ay*

Seen here with stylized Presidencia de la Nacion titles and named 'Independencia' (just visible in script under the cockpit window), LQ-GJT was built as a C-47A-10-DK (MSN 12678) and, although she did not have an FAA serial code was very much operated and maintained for the executive branch by the air force. Ironically, she eventually passed to the Navy as 5-T-10 and, somewhere along the line, had clearly been converted to Hyper-DC3 configuration – one of a very few such conversions in quasi military service. *via Dr Gary Kuhn*

Another high-time aircraft and a former RAF Dakota III, T-103 retained most of her C-47B-5-DK characteristics, clear through US, RAF, Argentine Navy, governmental and prior FAA identities. She gained T-103 in December 1975 and, even though using her original cargo door with a sill-mounted portable ladder, was a passenger transport when pictured here with II Brigada Aérea at Moron AB in December 1985. She survived mounted on a plinth in Paraná but is devoid of any identity. *Carlos A. Ay*

With a slightly different colour scheme and cheatline, T-104 is seen here with V Brigada Aérea subtitles and the INAC badge on her nose at BAM Villa Reynolds in April 1986. She is currently on display at the Museo Interfuerzas in Santa Romana, San Luis, in excellent condition. *Carlos A. Ay*

Evidence of the convoluted *FAA* DC-3 and C-47 serialing systems, T-01 was built as a C-47A-65-DL, converted to DC-3C configuration, ferried home as LV-XFY and initially serialed as T-49. A VIP-configured aircraft and, at the time of this image assigned to the use of the Comandante en Jefe de la FAA she ranged as such far and wide. Retaining essentially the same colour scheme, she was again reserialed as T-40 in November 1966, as pictured earlier. *via Dr Gary Kuhn*

The *FAA* commenced using 'TC' (Transporte y Carga) codes in the autumn of 1959 in order to identify aircraft that had mixed passenger and cargo interiors, a local adaptation. TC-15, a C-47A-80-DL, was the first MAP-supplied C-47 for the service, having been withdrawn from storage at Davis-Monthan in September 1964 and, apparently, never converted to C-47D configuration. Wearing I Brigada Aérea subtitles and with her starboard engine removed and covered with a tarp in the foreground, this may have been after the accident she suffered on 14 April 1970. She was written off on 13 June 1977 at Mendoza. *via Dr Gary Kuhn*

Another instance of unusually large format service titles, T-03 is best described as a 'DC-3C-like' configuration, and had gained these marks, from the earlier T-52 in June 1960. She was stricken from the inventory in December 1968. *via Dr Gary Kuhn*

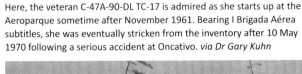

Here, the veteran C-47A-90-DL TC-17 is admired as she starts up at the Aeroparque sometime after November 1961. Bearing I Brigada Aérea subtitles, she was eventually stricken from the inventory after 10 May 1970 following a serious accident at Oncativo. *via Dr Gary Kuhn*

The 'TC' Series – 1961–90

FAA Serial	Previous Identity	Type as Built	MSN	Assignments and Notes
TC-04	43-15327 NC-67776 LV-NQU T-67 T-04	C-47A-85-DL	20093	Possessing a rather tortured lineage, this aircraft had become T-04 with the FAA in Aug 59, at which time it was retrofitted as a dedicated paratroop carrier. She was reserialed in 1962 as TC-04, then to E-304 (q.v.) in Aug 63.
(TC-05)	43-15499 NC-65283 LV-ABF T-89 T-05	C-47A-85-DL DC-3C	19965	Although this aircraft was assigned the serial TC-05 in October 1959, it was never actually painted on and her subsequent history involved her modification to operate on the Glaciar Upsala between Nov 63 and Jun 64 and her reserialing as TA-05 in Sep 64, apparently
TC-11	BuA05052 NC-79087 NC-49363 ZP-CCF LV-GIX LQ-GIX	R4D-1	4556	Although actually acquired by the FAA after an extraordinary civil exodus as LQ-GIX (q.v.) on 10 Oct 61, this aircraft did not become fully 'militarised' as TC-11 until December 1969 when her status was formalised with the Base Oficial de Aviacíon Civil (BOAC), latterly known as the INAC. An accident on 5 May 72 at the remote Aeródromo Gordillo in La Rioja Province resulted in about 7 per cent damage, but she was repaired after some exertions. Another accident, during a night landing at the INAC base on 23 May 77, resulted in her being stricken.
TC-15	43-15330	C-47A-80-DL	19796	The first C-47 to reach the FAA via MAP direct from USAF service, she was pulled from storage at the legendary Davis-Monthan AFB, AZ, delivered to the FAA in Sep 64 and immediately assigned to the GIT. After brief service with the PAA1964 Civic Action programme, she was transferred to the IV Brigada Aérea in January 1969. Although she suffered significant damage in an accident on 14 Apr 70 at the home station of her operator, she was written off in a second incident on 13 Jun 77 at Mendoza and scrapped, having by that time shed her earlier camouflage.
TC-17	43-15694 CA50 (CATC) XT-T36 NC-8328C N1797B ETA-101 ME-1T MG-1T T-17	C-47A-90-DL	20160	Briefly marked as T-17(2), this long-serving aircraft became TC-17 in Nov 61. She suffered minor damage in an accident on 16 Jan 68 at BAM Mar del Plata and, after repairs, was transferred to the GAE of the EAM, where she was apparently utilised as a multi-engine conversion aircraft. She was wrecked again on 10 May 70, this time seriously, at Oncativo, Córdoba, while performing at an airshow there and was stricken as a result.
TC-18	43-15922 CA3 (CATC) XT-T24 NC-8324C N1795B ETA-103 ME-3T MG-3T T-18	C-47A-90-DL	20388	Briefly marked as T-18(2), this well-travelled aircraft became TC-18 in Nov 61 and, like TC-17, was assigned to the GAE of the EAM near the end of 1962 where she remained through Dec 78 when she was reassigned to the VI Brigada Aérea. There she had the nearly unique distinction of supporting the integration of the advanced IAI M-5 Dagger jet fighters into that line unit. She had been camouflaged by 16 Jun 77. Withdrawn from use in Dec 81, she was apparently broken up for parts by 1990.
TC-19	43-48016 KG733 LV-ACO	C-47A-30-DK Dakota III	13832/25277	A former Aerolíneas Argentinas airliner, this aircraft was incorporated into the FAA on 22 Mar 66 and was assigned to the GIT to fly LADE services. She was stricken from the inventory in Jun 68.

Rarely illustrated in colour, TC-18 was wearing Direccion de Aeronautica subtitles when photographed here. Note also the numbers on the vertical fin, which appear to be '241-18', a rarely seen form of FAA 'permanent' serial number. She was later used to aid the integration of IAI M-5 Daggers into V Brigada Aérea. *Air-Britain*

A former Aerolineas Argentinas aircraft as LV-ADF, TC-20 was taken up by the FAA in September 1966. One of the first to be camouflaged in MAP-supplied, Vietnam War-era camouflage colours, she is seen here with the badge of the Grupo V de Caza on her starboard nose after 1971 and a very small national insignia far inboard under her starboard wing. Stricken in December 1990, she unusually was sold to Chile as CC-CLK. *Carlos A. Ay*

TC-20	43-15692 NC-60942 LV-ADF	C-47A-90-DL	20158	Another former Aerolíneas Argentinas airliner, TC-20 was incorporated into the FAA in September 1966 (some sources cite 22 Jun 66) and assigned initially to the GIT, but by November had moved to support LADE services. In 1969, she was assigned to Grupo Aéreo 7 of the VII Brigada Aérea and then on to the V Brigada Aérea in 1971. She was damaged in a most unusual manner on 25 Oct 90 near BAM Mar del Plata when she was hit by anti-aircraft fire from Argentine Army units exercising in the area. She was stricken from the inventory in Dec 90, one of the last FAA C-47s, and was subsequently sold into Chile as CC-CLK.
TC-21	43-15495 NC-86547 LV-AET	C-47A-85-DL DC-3C	19961	Another former Aerolíneas Argentinas airliner, TC-21 was taken up by the FAA 9 Mar 66 and assigned to the GIT. Eight days later, she commenced performing LADE services but was reassigned to the EAM in 1968. By Aug 75, she was assigned to the Area Material Río IV, where she was maintained in excellent condition with white upper decking. She was dropped from the inventory in Apr 90 and was acquired by a museum in Brazil on 28 Apr 92.
TC-27	BuA03140 PP-KAA PP-ANS EA-8T T-38 (TC-38) LQ-IPC	R4D-1	4280	Another very well-travelled aircraft, this aircraft was unusual in having exited FAA service to quasi-governmental marks and then reentered as TC-27 in Dec 67. By 15 Feb 79 she had been transferred to the EAM and then to the INAC in 1982, and finally V Brigada Aérea in 1988. She was stricken from the inventory in Jan 89 and was last noted stored at the Área Material Quilmes on 31 May 91.
TC-28	43-47967 NC-90908 PP-YQJ EA-10T T-28	C-47A-30-DK DC-3C	13783/25228	One of the former Army aircraft, this aircraft gained codes TC-28 in 1965 concurrent with her assignment to the División Ensayos en Vuelo del Taller Regional Río Cuarto. She sustained slight damage in an accident on 10 Oct 66 at the EAM and although repaired, met her end on 5 May 69 on landing at Las Higueras, Río Cuarto, Cordoba, about 420 miles west of Buenos Aires with eleven fatalities.
TC-31	43-15193 NC-39354 LV-XEO T-151 T-174 T-17(1) T-31	C-47A-80-DL	19659	After service in Argentina from 1946, this weary aircraft was finally reserialed as TC-31 in Nov 61 and assigned to the V Brigada Aérea in Nov 66. The aircraft experienced an in-flight engine fire on 7 Aug 71 (some published accounts have given the date as 8 Aug 71) near BAM General Pringles, although the pilot managed to land the aircraft on a highway with 50 per cent damage. She had been camouflaged by 13 Jul 71. This aircraft was, in fact, the first C-47 acquired by the FAA after the end of the Second World War.

Right: The port-side nose of TC-20 reveals additional details in this July 1989 view. In addition to the Grupo V de Caza badge at bottom, she also sports the capper V Brigada Aérea badge above it, and a most unusual blade antenna under her nose. *Gustavo F. Guevloa via Eduardo Luzardo*

Below: TC-21 was a DC-3C and another former Aerolineas Argentinas aircraft (LV-AET) taken up on 9 March 1966. Seen here taxiing at the Aeroparque on 18 July 1974, she served on into April 1990 when she was stricken and acquired by a museum in Brazil. *Michael Magnusson*

TC-32	BuA04705 NC-9399H PP-KAB PP-ANM EA-2T T-32	R4D-1	4365	Although assigned the serial TC-32 not long after joining the FAA as T-32, this was not immediately taken up. In fact, the aircraft was withdrawn from use as T-32 around 8 Mar 63 but was recalled on 22 Sep 64, after which she was converted to joint passenger/cargo configuration as TC-32. A landing accident on 20 Aug 67 at BAM Tandil incurred only slight damage, and she was repaired. Although officially withdrawn again in Dec 67, the I Brigada Aérea apparently continued to make use of her as late as 19 Apr 68.
TC-33(2)	43-15327 NC-67776 LV-NQU T-67 T-04 TC-04 E-304	C-47A-85-DL	20093	The final identity of one of the longest-serving FAA C-47s, these marks were taken up late in Dec 69 and she was assigned to Grupo Aéreo 7 of the VII Brigada Aérea. She was then transferred to the V Brigada Aérea on 6 Jul 72 and finally withdrawn from service in Jul 88. She was then donated to the Aeroclub Baradero as a gate guardian, although she was cosmetically restored into her final operational colour scheme by the club members, and was last noted stored at the Área Material Quilmes on 31 May 91.
TC-33(1)	42-23392 NC-79014 N91228 N148A T-33	C-47A-5-DL DC-3C	9254	Formally T-33 from 8 Feb 60, this was actually the first C-47 to be reserialed as TC-33 in Nov 61. In May 62, she was selected to take part in Operación Upsala and was suitably modified to undertake missions in Antarctica starting in Jun 62. It was subsequently modified extensively by the Grupo Técnico I (GT-1) in Jul 62 and, after completion, was reserialed as TA-33 (q.v.).
TC-34	42-92936 NC-63400 N91229 N149A T-34	C-47A-20-DK DC-3C	12792	Another of the longest-serving FAA C-47s, she did not assume marks TC-34 until 1962. She was transferred to the V Brigada Aérea in May 69 and to II Brigada Aérea in 1971. She was finally withdrawn from service in Dec 88 and, perhaps uniquely in aviation history, was donated to the Club de Aeromodelismo Río de la Plata in Feb 96 who situated her at Ezpeleta, Buenos Aires, where she remains in good condition.
TC-35	43-49533 T-35	C-47B-15-DK C-47D	15349/26794	Chronologically the longest serving of all FAA C-47s, this aircraft entered service as T-35 in 1960 and was stricken from the inventory in Dec 90 as TC-35, having assumed these marks in 1962. She was assigned to the II Brigada Aérea between 1981 and 1983 and then to the V Brigada Aérea in 1990. After being surplused, she was sold into Chile as CC-CLL.
TC-36	43-49353 TA-06	C-47B-15-DK C-47D SC-47D EC-47D HC-47D 'HC-47A'	15169/26614	A highly specialised and modified aircraft, TC-36 was one of the very few MAP-supplied C-47s acquired by the FAA, in Apr 66 as TA-06, where she was identified, for some reasons, as a HC-47A. Her first assignment was to the I Brigada Aérea but moved to the specialised Escuadrón de Tareas Especiales de la BAM Tandil on 26 Dec 67. She was then transferred to the VII Brigada Aérea in 1972. The aircraft suffered a fire while on the ground on 31 Jul 73, but after extensive work was repaired and then became TC-36 in Dec 73. She was transferred concurrently to the BAM Reconquista, where she was assigned to the Escuadrilla de Servicios. She was stricken from the inventory in Nov 81.
TC-37	43-15541 TA-07	C-47A-85-DL C-47D SC-47A HC-47A	20007	The former specialised TA-07, another of the MAP-supplied and distinctive 'Hawk-nosed' C-47s, this aircraft gained marks TC-37 in Dec 74 and her initial assignment was to the VII Brigada Aérea, where she gained an unusual three-tone camouflage. She was detailed to the INAC to replace its former mount, TC-11, and after several stand-down periods, was finally stricken on 12 Nov 90 with 18,713:20 hours total time.
(TC-38)	BuA03140 PP-KAA PP-ANS EA-8T T-38	R4D-1	4280	Although the marks TC-38 were officially issued to this aircraft after T-38, they were not actually taken up and the aircraft became LQ-IPC in May 66.

Photographed after August 1975, by which time she had also been camouflaged and assigned to the *Area Material Rio IV,* the subtitles for which she wears here. Smaller size – but not subdued – national insignia are, unusually, placed in all four positions, and her camouflage is noticeably weathered. *Carlos A. Ay*

Compare this image with the earlier view of T-38, the same R4D-1. Wearing a locally procured, and very distressed, camouflage paint scheme, TC-27 (outlined in white) is seen in 1981 with, unusually, her INAC subtitles fully spelled out. *via Eduardo Luzardo*

A busy apron at Buenos Aires Aeroparque in September 1973 shows TC-33 appearing decidedly venerable next to an HS 748, BAC-111 and Bölkow Bö105. Here, she is wearing the subtitles of the V Brigada Aérea and, for some reason, has had her nose painted either light blue or grey. One of the longest-serving FAA C-47As, she was placed in storage in May 1991. *George G.J. Kamp*

Assigned to the I Brigada Aérea by the time of this photograph, TC-31 was actually the very first C-47 acquired by the FAA after the end of the Second World War as T-151. Once again, looking down the line at the other three aircraft, no two wear the exact same colour schemes or antenna arrangements, aside from the nose ventral RDF loops. *via Dr Gary Kuhn*

TC-33 again, this time wearing yet another variation on camouflage and markings. Still assigned to V Brigada Aérea, she is pictured at BA Villa Reynolds in April 1986. *Carlos A. Ay*

Specialised Markings Assigned to DC-3s and C-47 Operated by the FAA 1961–76

FAA Serial or Registration	Previous Identity	Type as Built	MSN	Assignments and Notes
E-301	43-48194 KJ940 N123S 0490/CTA-25 LQ-MSP S-4 TS-04	C-47B-5-DK Dakota III	14669/26114	Gained this trainer serial in Dec 71 and assigned to the Grupo Aéreo Escuela of the EAM for multi-engine training. Reserialed for the final time as T-103 (q.v.) Dec 75.
E-304	43-15327 NC-67776 LV-NQU T-67 T-04 TC-04	C-47A-85-DL	20093	Gaining 'E' (for Escuela) trainer marks as E-304 in Aug 63, after TC-04, these were retained as she was usually engaged as a crew and transition trainer until becoming TC-33 (q.v.) in Dec 69. It should be noted that this aircraft has also been identified, erroneously, as MSN 20013 the former USAAF 43-15547 and this has resulted in substantial confusion.
TA-05	43-15499 NC-65283 LV-ABF T-89 T-05 TC-05	C-47A-85-DL DC-3C	19965	This aircraft was virtually unique in FAA service in having been converted, between Sep 63 and Jun 64, for operations from the Upsala Glacier between 15 June and 5 Jul 64, and in having been baptised with a nickname, El Montañés, by Sep 64. Seldom reported, she was also modified to tri-motor configuration by the installation of a Turbomeca Marboré IIIC-3 engine for extra power during take-offs between Oct and Dec 64, making her first flight in this mode on 14 Dec. She subsequently made at least twelve Antarctic flights between 18 Sep 64 and 29 Oct 69. She made her final flight on 25 Apr 70, passed to the custody of what was then the FAA Museum on 22 May 70 and is now in a place of honour at the MNA. A curious Dutch spotting report has led many researchers on a merry chase, claiming that this aircraft was spotted at Buenos Aires Ezeiza airport on 5 Feb 79!
TA-06	43-49353	C-47B-15-DK C-47D SC-47D EC-47D HC-47D HC-47A	15169/26614	This was a MAP-supplied aircraft transferred direct from the USAF stocks on 19 Mar 66, and oddly, was described at the time as a HC-47A, initially assigned to the I Brigada Aérea. She then moved to the Escuadrón de Tareas Especiales de la BAM Tandil on 26 Dec 67 and then to the VII Brigada Aérea in 1972. She caught fire after landing on 31 Jul 73, requiring major repairs and, following the completion of these, was reserialed as TC-36 (q.v.) in Dec 73.
TA-07	43-15541	C-47A-85-DL C-47D SC-47D EC-47D SC-47A HC-47A	20007	Another of the few MAP-supplied specialty aircraft, this aircraft was received in Jul 66 and assigned to I Brigada Aérea. She was then reassigned to the Escuadrón de Tareas Especiales de la BAM Tandil on 26 Dec 67, and remained there until 1972, when she moved to the VII Brigada Aérea. She was reserialed as TC-37 (q.v.) in Dec 74.
TA-33	42-23392 NC-79014 N91228 N148A T-33 TC-33 LC-47A	C-47A-5-DL DC-3C	9254	This aircraft received this serial on 26 Oct 62 after being modified for duty in the Antarctic, becoming the second FAA C-47 so modified (although the first, T-20, was not actually used as such), as described in TC-33 (q.v.). She made her first landing on the ice continent sometime after 2 Nov 62. She was certainly one of the most colourful of all FAA C-47s, sporting Day-Glo paint on her nose, wing tips, most of her empennage, and along her upper spine, besides the brilliant Argentine rudder markings and a large letter 'A' edged in white on her vertical fin. Unfortunately, she was destroyed on 10 Dec 62 when her JATO units caused a fire during take-off bound for the South Pole from the Ellsworth Scientific Station. Most of the aircraft remains in Antarctica to this day.

The FAA decided in early 1960s to specially mark and code aircraft that were detailed specifically to Antarctic duty, and TA-06, an HC-47A supplied under MAP on 19 March 1966, was the second of four such aircraft. Note her extended, radar nose. She was recoded in December 1973 as TC-36 in the standard cargo/passenger series. *via Ken F. Measures*

Chronologically the longest serving of the FAA's C-47s, even at that C-47D TC-35 did not gain this serial until 1960 – and was not stricken from the inventory until December 1990. Once again, considerable variations are noted in the camouflage scheme on final approach to the Aeroparque on 4 January 1977, including a larger national insignia and flat white instead of light blue undersurfaces. She was sold after withdrawal to Chile, becoming CC-CLL there. *Michael Magnusson*

LQ-ACF	43-48194 KG778 LV-ACF	C-47A-30-DK Dakota III DC-3D	14010/25455	This aircraft had been acquired for use by the Ministerio de Asistencia Social y Salud Pública on 1 Nov 62, who modified her as a dedicated ambulance aircraft named 'Ministro Tiburcio Padilla'. She was transferred as such to the FAA on 16 Aug 67 and her quasi-governmental registration finally cancelled in favour of S-3 (q.v.) on 15 Feb 68.
LQ-GIX	BuA05052 NC-79087 NC-49363 ZP-CCF LV-GIX	R4D-1	4556	This aircraft was transferred from the Argentine state petroleum entity YPF to the FAA on 10 Oct 61 and was operated by the service as LQ-GIX on behalf of the Dirección General de Instrucción y Habitación. It became TC-11 (q.v.) in Dec 69.
LQ-GJT	42-108883 NC-63689	C-47A-10-DK	12678	Strictly speaking, this aircraft, at one time wearing the titles Presidencia de la Nacion, was not on the FAA AOB, although it was operated by the Air Force on behalf of the head of state in immaculate condition and named 'Independencia'. It eventually passed to the Navy as 0652/5-T-10 (q.v.).
LQ-INL	43-48514 BuA17272 N7633C N44 LV-PDJ	(C-47B-1-DK) R4D-5 R4D-6E R4D-6S SC-47J	14330/25775	This aircraft entered FAA service with quasi-governmental markings as LQ-INL on 21 Jun 65, after modifications by BOAC, and operated for the Secretaría de Aeronáutica as a VIP transport. She became VR-11 (q.v.) in Dec 69.
LQ-IOS	NC-18937 C-100 (AVIANCA) PP-BHD PP-YQL EA-11T T-20 LQ-CAA	DC-3-228	2012	By the time this veteran aircraft received these quasi-governmental marks on 17 Feb 66, she was twenty-nine years old. She was operated as such by the FAA on behalf of the Dirección General de Circulación Aérea y Aeródromos (DGCAA) until gaining military marks VR-12 in Jul 70.
LQ-IPC	BuA03140 PP-KAA PP-ANS EA-8T T-38 TC-38	R4D-1	4280	After being modified as a combination passenger and cargo interior, these quasi-government marks were assigned to this aircraft briefly on 4 May 66, and was planned to be operated by the FAA as such on behalf of the Dirección General de Agua y Energía Eléctrica but, in the event, remained attached to the DINFIA instead. Following the creation of the Área Material Córdoba, passed to its dependent Centro de Ensayos en Vuelo. It finally gained serial TC-27 (q.v.) in Dec 67.
LQ-MSP	43-48194 KJ940 N123S 0490/CTA-25	C-47B-5-DK Dakota III	14669/26114	Originally acquired by the Argentine Navy in 1958, this aircraft was transferred to the Ministerio de Asistencia Social y Salud Pública as LQ-MSP on 20 Sep 60 and converted to an ambulance aircraft. Initially named 'Esperanza', it was later renamed as 'Malaespina' and was again transferred, this time to the FAA on 16 Aug 67, although not officially taken up until 7 Feb 68. Her governmental marks were cancelled on 15 Feb 68 and she became S-4 (q.v.) briefly, before becoming TS-04, E-301 and finally T-103.
S-3	43-48194 KG778 LV-ACF LQ-ACF	C-47A-30-DK Dakota III DC-3D	14010/25455	After LQ-ACF (see above) this aircraft was marked as S-3 in FAA service on 15 Feb 68 and assigned to I Brigada Aérea. It was then transferred to the BOAC and reserialed as TS-03 in 1969.
S-4	43-48194 KJ940 N123S 0490/CTA-25 LQ-MSP	C-47B-5-DK Dakota III	14669/26114	History as LQ-MSP shown above but was reserialed as S-4 by the FAA on 15 Feb 68 and assigned to I Brigada Aérea before being transferred to the BOAC and then reserialed as TS-04 (q.v.) in 1969.

The first FAA aircraft to gain special Antarctic marks in the 1960s was TA-05, which had been acquired as a DC-3C, formerly LV-ABF, T-89, T-05 and TC-05. Converted to Antarctic configuration between September 1963 and June 1964, she made a number of flights on the ice continent, aided by the installation of a Turbomeca Marboré IIIC-3 jet engine in her rear fuselage, as shown on our accompanying drawing. She is seen here preserved in fair condition at the MNA on 7 March 1972. *Peter Hayes*

Another view of HC-47A TA-06 with incomplete Antarctic markings while still nominally assigned to the I Brigada Aérea on 18 November 1966. *Andreas Kelemen*

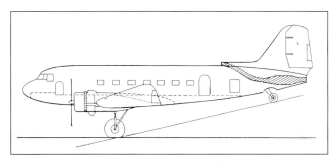

This drawing shows the manner in which the 880lb maximum thrust Turbomeca Marboré IIC-3 gas turbine engine was installed in DC-3C TA-05, making her a tri-motor. *Hagedorn Collection*

TA-07/A wearing complete Escuadrón de Tareas Especiales colours and markings, also an HC-47A supplied under MAP with the extended radar nose in July 1966. She reverted to TC-37 in December 1974. *via Roger Eberle*

TS-03	43-48194 KG778 LV-ACF LQ-ACF S-3	C-47A-30-DK Dakota III DC-3D	14010/25455	History as S-3 above but reserialed as TS-03 in 1969 (some sources cite 15 Feb 68), and then again in Dec 71 when she became T-101 (q.v.).
TS-04	43-48194 KJ940 N123S 0490/CTA-25 LQ-MSP S-4	C-47B-5-DK Dakota III	14669/26114	Reserialed from S-2 (q.v.) effective 1969 (some sources cite 7 Feb 68) and reconverted from ambulance to conventional passenger transport to become E-301 (q.v.) in Dec 71.
VR-10	42-93426 LV-ACJ T-10	C-47A-25-DK DC-3C	13336	After her last flight as T-10 on 9 Mar 70, this aircraft was remarked as VR-10 and made her first flight as such four days later, continuing her radio aids and airways verification duties as such. She was stricken in Aug 71 and was transferred to the Gobierno de la Provincia de Salta and then the Provincia de la Rioja in turn, but apparently these transfers were not consummated. Instead, she was sold to a private owner and, incredibly, became LV-ACJ again after more than twenty-five years. She was then sold into Bolivia as CP-1622.
VR-11	43-48514 BuA17272 N7633C N44 LV-PDJ LQ-INL	(C-47B-1-DK) R4D-5 R4D-6E R4D-6S SC-47J	14330/25775	This is one of the few FAA C-47 series aircraft that had only incidental prior service with the air arm, passing from quasi-governmental marks LQ-INL to VR-11 in Dec 69. Assigned initially to the BOAC, she was stricken by Dec 72 and was eventually sold into Guatemala as TG-BAC in Nov 75.
VR-12	NC-18937 C-100 (AVIANCA) PP-BHD PP-YQL EA-11T T-20 LQ-CAA LQ-IOS	DC-3-228	2012	A seemingly odd candidate for radio and airways verification duties, this aircraft only wore such appropriate marks, VR-12, from Jul 70 until 72, when she was converted to passenger configuration once again and remarked as T-102 (q.v.).
VR-14	42-93459 KG614 LV-ACE	C-47A-25-DK Dakota III DC-3C	13373	The last C-47 series aircraft acquired by the FAA, she was at first assigned to the Comando de Regiones Aéreas as part of the PAA1970 in 1970, but has also been reliably reported to have been taken up by the FAA on 22 Jun 66, not gaining marks VR-14 for some reason until 1968, and was assigned to radio and airways verification tasks. When the INAC was created on 3 Nov 72, VR-14 was one of its first aircraft. She was reconverted to passenger configuration in 1977 and passed to marks T-104 (q.v.).

Four FAA DC-3s and C-47s were detailed starting around 1968 to radio and airways verification duties, including VR-14, the very last C-47 series aircraft acquired by the service in 1970 – modified earlier in her career for Aerolineas Argentinas as a DC-3C as LV-ACE. Seen here at the Aeroparque on 18 July 1974, she subsequently became T-104 with the INAC, illustrated earlier. *Michael Magnusson*

Another view of VR-14 showing her Comando de Regiones Aéreas subtitles, in her rather attractive high-visibility colour scheme. *ALPS*

Only two FAA C-47s gained dedicated Escuela (school or training) codes, including E-304, built as a C-47A-85-DL with no fewer than five previous identities, the last being TC-04. Marked as such in August 1963, she reverted to TC-33 in December 1969. Note that her subtitles showed her assigned to I Brigada Aérea, in spite of her trainer function at the time. *via Dr Gary Kuhn*

The Argentine Navy

The Argentine Navy has maintained a naval aviation service since 11 February 1916, when the genesis of what was to follow was established as the Parque y Escuela de Aerostación y Aviación de la Armada at Fuerte Barragán near La Plata.

Guided initially by a short-lived Italian mission, by 1919, the Navy had made a conscious decision in 1921 to pattern its establishment after that of the US Navy and, with only minor ripples, did exactly that for the following thirty years.[17] Being a South Atlantic coastal nation, with important interest in the lengthy Rio Plata as well, the Navy quickly established itself within Argentine society as a professionally desirable career path for sons of the Republic and, historically, something of a defender of the Constitution politically.

Throughout the inter-war period, the Aviación Naval, as it was commonly framed, methodically established dedicated pursuit, bombardment, patrol, training and transport/utility units roughly paralleling the US Navy practices of the period. In many respects, the Navy's air arm was regarded by foreign observers of the day as being, at least, on a nearly equal par with the rival Army establishment and, also echoing the US between-the-wars experience, these two emerging aviation establishments competed for funding, recognition and resources.

Like the Army aviation establishment, the Navy's air arm, which had arrived at the end of the 1930s as unquestionably the best and most balanced Naval aviation establishment in Latin America, suffered from Argentina's virtual isolation during the Second World War, while attempting at the same time to carry on neutrality patrols

of its territory and waters. During the course of its rather quiet and low-profile expansion, the service, which had initially been largely concentrated at three major Naval coastal operating bases, Punta Indio, Puerto Belgrano and Comandante Espora, expanded its reach through the establishment of a series of Bases Aeronavales, Estaciones Aeronavales and Aeródromos Aeronavales Auxiliares. By the end of the 1950s, besides the key bases noted, these included Trelew, Ezeiza at Buenos Aires, Río Grande, Ushuaia, Río Gallegos, Comandante Luis Piedrabuena, Corti, Calderón, Cabecera Lago Fagnano, Martín García, Mar del Plata, Madryn, Isla Verde, Camarones, Punta Ninfas, Puerto Rosales and Deseado.

These widely separated installations, regarded as essential to support a coastal defence fleet, would obviously have benefited from rapid liaison, communications, resupply, personnel movement and reinforcement as necessary and, as a direct result the Navy started acquiring a small series of dedicated transports and utility aircraft as early as 1931 when a very versatile Fokker Super Universal, bought with interchangeable wheel or float undercarriage, started carrying out flights linking the various and expanding Naval installations. This was augmented by other types as its value came to be appreciated, including three mighty Curtiss-Wright CT-32 Condor twin-engine transports in July 1937. These served exceptionally well and, in the process, cemented the Navy's understanding of the potential of multi-engine, purpose-built heavy transports. Besides logistical support to the fleet, these provided the Navy with the means of rapidly deploying its highly regarded Marine infantry, a luxury that the service had never before enjoyed.

An extraordinary photograph by any measure, for the purposes of our story, the star in this eclectic line-up is the C-39 next to last in line, still wearing her former AVENSA cheatlines. As the first PBY-5As were acquired shortly before the C-39s, it dates this image as late 1946 or early 1947. From left to right, the aircraft pictured at BAN Comandante Espora include an eleven-year-old Curtiss-Wright CW-16E Kelito, Stearman Model 76D-1, Grumman G-20, Junkers W.34, Curtiss-Wright T-32 Condor, the C-39 and the PBY-5A. *Jorge Nũnez Padin*

From their vantage point throughout the Second World War, the Argentine Naval Aviation leadership was able to observe the exceptional value of aviation in support of every aspect of Naval operations, and set about ensuring that, as soon as the hostilities had ended, the Aviación Naval would, like its Army rivals, commence the process of modernising its equipment. Unlike the Army, however, the Navy did not directly benefit from the infusion of British types, other than the second-hand acquisition of a number of, at best, obsolescent Supermarine Walrus biplanes with which to outfit her catapult launch-fitted capital ships.

For the purposes of our story, however, one of her priority acquisitions, via a rather unusual series of events, was a mix of five[18] former AVENSA Venezuela passenger-configured Douglas C-39s (and two exotic C-42s, one of them converted in USAAC service from a C-39) around 16 August 1946, at almost the same moment that the Army was acquiring its first surplus C-47s. Frequently cited as 'DC-2 ½s', all five arrived at BAM Morón on 16 August 1946. Reportedly acquired at bargain prices, the oldest of these was already seven years old and had seen hard use with the USAAC/USAAF before being sold surplus to AVENSA in September 1944. As noted in the FAA section, an attempt had been made as early as 6 May 1946 to acquire two former PLUNA (Uruguay) DC-2s for either the Army or the Navy, but this arrangement did not advance. Of the five actually acquired from Venezuela, three were intended for issue to BAN Comandante Espora and the other two for BAN Punta Indio.

The codes shown reflect assignments to various Naval aviation units and have been frequently misreported over the years.

The various code presentations shown in the following table denote assignments to the following units and, as will be noted, several were reused, leading to considerable confusion over the years:

2-Gt-5, 2-Gt-6 – denoted assignment to the Escuadra Aeronaval No. 2

3-Gt-5, 3-Gt-6, 3-Gt-7, 3-Gt-8, 3-Gt-14, 3-Gt-15 and 3-Gt-16 – denotes an aircraft assigned to the Agrupación de Servicios Auxiliares.

TA-30, TA-31, TA-32, TA-33, TA-34, 3-T-31, 3-T-32, 3-T-33 and 3-T-34 – was used while the aircraft were assigned to Base Aeronaval Punta Indio.

1-E-301, 1-E-302, 1-E-303 and 1-E-304 – denotes assignment to the Escuela de Aviacion Naval

CTA-37, CTA-38, CTA-39 and CTA-40 – denotes aircraft assigned to the 3º Escuadrilla de Transporte.

Some sources have quoted the Navy C-39s and C-42s as having initially worn 'O' for Observacion codes initially, such as 3-O-1 to 3-O-5, but this is completely without foundation.

A detailed summary of these, the solitary DC-2 variants to see conventional service with any Latin American air arm, follows.

Navy C-39 3-Gt-5 was the former USAAC AC38-526 and, when this image was taken, was already eight years old. Assigned initially to the Escuadra Aeronaval No. 2 she became TA-30 on 27 November 1949 and eventually passed to civil marks LV-GGV in 1958. *Jorge Nũnez Padin*

The value of the Navy C-39/DC-2s as trainers was considerable, and 1-E-302, which had previously worn codes 3-Gt-14, 3-Gt-5, 3-Gt-6, TA-32 and 3-T-32 by the time of this image after 1957, was changed once again to CTA-38 before suffering an accident on 21 March 1957. *Jorge Nũnez Padin*

Built as a C-47A-1-DL, 3-Gt-3, pictured here at Ushuaia in the far south of Argentina around 1948, had been acquired in mid-August 1947. She later was converted to a flying hospital and dispensary. *Jorge Nũnez Padin*

Below: This view of '3Gt-9' reveals her previously unknown conversion prior to delivery as a DC-3C. On the original image, the titles 'Aircraft Radio Corporation' are barely visible on the fuselage above the window line, also a previously unknown operator. *Hagedorn Collection*

Acquired on 28 December 1946 after an undocumented conversion to DC-3C configuration, this C-47A-30-DL (42-23716) had originally been coded 2-Gt-15 but, unusually, had been recoded as '3Gt-9' without the normal 'dash' after the first digit. Argentine Navy aircraft carried the anchor symbol in all four wing positions and were unusual internationally in also wearing the blue/white/blue national colours on the horizontal tail surfaces, top and bottom, in addition to on the rudder. This aircraft has been preserved in Ushuaia since 1978, last bearing the codes 5-T-22. *William C. Haines*

Aviación Naval PSN and Codes Worn	Previous Identity	Type as Built	MSN	Assignments and Notes
0103 (psn) 2-Gt-5 TA-30 3-T-30 1-E-301 CTA-37	AC38-526 YV-AVK	C-39 (DC-2-243)	2083	Acquired from Venezuela 13 Jul 46 and assigned initial codes 2-Gt-5 by 25 Jul 46 but did not actually arrive in country until 16 Aug 46. Recoded as TA-30 27 Nov 49 and 3-T-30 on 1 Jan 51. To the Escuela de Aviacion Naval in 1952 as 1-E-301. To CTA-37 in 1957. She was withdrawn from use and offered for sale on 19 Aug 58 as CTA-37 with 4,135 hours recorded (probably only with the AN, as her previous USAAC and AVENSA time was probably not available). Sold to Carlos A. Fantini 19 Aug 58 as scrap, she in fact became LV-GGV with Transaer sometime in 1959.
0104 (psn) 2-Gt-6 TA-31 3-T-31	AC38-528 YV-AVL	C-39 C-42 (DC-2-243)	2085	Acquired from Venezuela 13 Jul 46 and assigned initial codes 2-Gt-6 by 25 Jul 46 but did not arrive in country until 16 Aug 46. Recoded TA-31 27 Nov 49 and 3-T-31 1 Jan 51. Stricken from the inventory later that year.
0105 (psn) 3-Gt-14 3-Gt-5 3-Gt-6 TA-32 3-T-32 1-E-302 CTA-38	AC38-499 YV-AVG	C-39 (DC-2-243)	2057	Acquired from Venezuela 16 Aug 46 and issued codes 3-Gt-14 1 Dec 46 but changed to 3-Gt-5 31 Dec 46. Recoded as 3-Gt-6 3 Nov 48. To TA-32 27 Nov 49 and then 3-T-32 1 Jan 51. To the EAN as 1-E-302 in 1952. To CTA-38 in 1957, by which time she had a medium blue nose cone and engine cowlings. Accident at 0900 21 Mar 57 while landing at the auxiliary aerodrome at La Payanca, Buenos Aires, under the command of Tte De Corbeta Luis Suárez and was apparently not repaired.
0106 (psn) 3-Gt-15 3-Gt-6 3-Gt-7 TA-33 3-T-33 1-E-304 CTA-39	AC38-517 YV-AVH	C-39 (DC-2-243)	2074	Acquired from Venezuela 16 Aug 46 coded initially as 3-Gt-15 but changed to 3-Gt-6 31 Dec 46 then 3-Gt-7 on 3 Nov 48. Recoded as TA-33 27 Nov 49 and then 3-T-33 1 Jan 51. To the EAN as 1-E-304 in 1952 and finally CTA-39 in 1957. Withdrawn from use in 1958 and offered for sale on 19 Aug 58 with 5,003 hours total Navy time, this aircraft was destined to be the only long-term survivor of the five, being sold to a civil owner as scrap – and who promptly sold her on to the airline Transaer on 20 May 60 as LV-GGU. Last known when CofA expired sometime later.

Yet another variation on Navy code presentation, 3-Gt-12 has a very small-format, lower-case letter 't' indeed. She had been converted to DC-3C-S1C3G configuration prior to delivery and later was recoded as 4-T-12 and CTA-12. Note the curtains in the windows. *Warren Shipp via Dr Gary Kuhn*

0107 (psn)	AC38-503	C-42 (DC-2-267)	2060	Acquired from Venezuela 16 Aug 46 and initially coded as 3-Gt-16. Recoded as 3-Gt-7
3-Gt-16	YV-AVJ			3 Dec 46 and then 3-Gt-8 3 Nov 48. To TA-34 by 18 Aug 49 and 3-T-34 1 Jan 51. To the
3-Gt-7				EAN in 1952 as 1-E-303 but to CTA-40 in 1957. Like 0106, this aircraft was also
3-Gt-8				withdrawn from Navy service in 1958 and sold as scrap on 19 Aug 58. In fact, she became
TA-34				LV-GGT with Transaer on 20 Dec 59 with 8,698 hours recorded but was subsequently
3-T-34				wrecked on 17 May 60 at El Sonseado.
1-E-303				
CTA-40				

Although the C-39s and single C-42 had rendered fairly good service to the Navy, they were clearly very tired and labour intensive to maintain. What was worse was that, as of the end of the Second World War, they were very difficult to support from a spares standpoint, although through the ingenuity and resourcefulness that had become almost legendary among its dedicated support personnel, the service managed to keep them active into the autumn of 1958.

The post-war surplus bonanza enabled the Navy, like the Army, to avail itself of much 'younger' war-build C-47s, however, and by 28 December 1946, the first three acquisitions had arrived and joined the force. These were joined by four more between 13 June and 14 August 1947 (most of these from the Aero Corporation of Atlanta, Georgia, which also supplied ten Beech AT-11s and at least sixty assorted Boeing-Stearman PT-17/N2S series aircraft at the same time), having been flown home by Argentine Navy crews, and the final examples, for a total of sixteen, between 13 February and 16 August 1948.

By 1 October 1948, the CAN could count a total of 205 aircraft on hand of seventeen basic types, of which twenty were the mix of C-47s and C-39s. Although fairly well off with late-model Second World War surplus types, including six Consolidated PBY-5 flying boats and eighteen amphibious PBY-5As, nine Douglas C-54s, two Grumman JRF-6Bs, six Beech AT-11s, twenty-seven Vultee BT-13As and the first three of a large number of North American AT-6A Standards to follow, the service also still operated and maintained an astonishing number of vintage pre-war types and biplanes. These included eighteen surviving Vought V-142As, six Supermarine Walruses, ten Martin 139WANs, at least sixteen Grumman J2F-5 and J2F-6 Ducks, single examples of the venerable Douglas 116 Dolphin, and Junkers W.34, two equally veteran Curtiss-Wright CT-20 Condors, at least two licence-built Focke-Wulf Fw-44Js, several eleven-year-old Curtiss-Wright CW-16E-3 Kelitos and Stearman

Model 76D-1s, and twenty-one assorted Boeing-Stearman PT-17 and N2S series Kaydets.

The principal operating units for the C-39s and C-47s were the 2ª and 3ª Escuadrillas, which, by 10 October 1949 were very cosmopolitan units indeed, based at the two main Naval air stations at Punta del Indio and Bahia Blanca. Besides the eleven C-39s and C-47s, the *2ª* Escuadrilla possessed an astonishing twenty-nine other aircraft (including three C-54s, three AT-11s, eighteen Grumman J2F-5 and seven Vultee BT-13As) but had but seven commissioned pilots on strength. The 3ª Escuadrilla was equally flush with aircraft, possessing, in addition to its own mix of eleven C-39s and C-47s, twenty-seven other aircraft (two C-54s, three AT-11s, eighteen J2F-5s and five North American AT-6A Standard aircraft). This unit was also, however, seriously undermanned, with only seven commissioned aviators.

This strength remained constant through 1 April 1950. Following is a detailed examination of the sixteen aircraft acquired by the Navy between 1946 and the end of 1948 that, unlike the Army and FAA, did not include any foreign aid-supplied aircraft in the conventional sense, the Navy going it alone and on its own resources. The rather complex Argentine Naval Aviation coding system was similar to that used by the US Navy in the pre-1941 period, and denoted operating unit in the first characters or numeral, function in the second, and number-within-unit in the third. After the Second World War, all transport types were recoded within the Comando de Transportes Aeronavales (CTA) series as, for example, CTA-20. This umbrella organisation was disbanded in April 1963 and replaced by the Escuadra Aeronaval 5, accounting for most of the subsequent codes, such as 5-T-23. Although all aircraft were supposed to have been changed, some, perhaps as the result of being displaced for overhaul or extensive work elsewhere, retained their earlier coding. An example is CTA-15, which was still being observed as late as October 1970 for some reason.

Probably the last C-47 acquired by the Navy, 5-T-10 has obviously been converted to 'Hi-Per DC-3' configuration and was last designated as a C-47R in US Navy service. Named 'Stella Maris', this name does not appear to be painted on the aircraft in this view. *MAP 1985-118 #35*

Aviación Naval

PSN and Codes Worn	Previous Identity	Type as Built	MSN	Assignment and Notes
0117 (psn) 2-Gt-13 2-Gt-7/'45' TA-20 3-T-20 4-T-20 CTA-20 5-T-23	42-100661	C-47A-70-DL	'19124'	Acquired from the FLC at Ontario, California, 29 May 46 and issued Export Licence No. 1797 on 7 Jun 46. Her first flight as 2-Gt-13 was on 7 Nov 46. Recoded as 2-Gt-7 28 Dec 46 with, for some reason, tail number '45'. Following an accident and extended repairs, was recoded as TA-20 27 Nov 49 and then 3-T-20 1 Jan 51. Passed to codes 4-t-20 1 Jan 53 and then CTA-20 in 1957. To the 2º Escuadrilla Aeronaval de Sosten Logístico Móvil as 5-T-23. Unquestionably the first Navy C-47, the reported MSN for this aircraft has always presented a dilemma, as it remained in USAF service well into the 1960s! She was deactivated 15 Apr 75.
0171 (psn) 2-Gt-14 2-Gt-8 TA-21 3-T-21 CTA-21 5-T-21	41-18555	C-47-DL	4680	Acquired via the FLC and issued Export Licence No. 1797 7 Jun 46. She suffered a collision prior to delivery at Van Nuys, California, but finally departed for home as 2-Gt-14 8 Apr 47. Recoded as 2-Gt-8 28 Dec 47. Experienced an accident in Paraguay 21 Jan 48 and apparently components of this aircraft were used to rebuild another aircraft that had crashed at Iquique. Finally re-entered service as TA-21 but then became 3-T-21 1 Jan 51, then CTA-21 in 1957. To 5-T-21 in cargo configuration by 30 Dec 63. A veteran of the wartime Tenth Air Force in the CBI, this aircraft was finally withdrawn on 15 Apr 1975 with 16,048 hours total time.
0172 (psn) 2-Gt-15 2-Gt-9 TA-22 3-T-22 4-T-22 CTA-22 5-T-22	42-23716	C-47A-30-DL DC-3C C-47A	9578	Acquired via the FLC and issued Export Licence No. 1797 on 7 Jun 46 as 2-Gt-15. Recoded as 2-Gt-9 28 Dec 46 and TA-22 on 27 Nov 49. Was modified as a dedicated photographic aircraft at BAN Punta Indio around 21 Jun 50. Recoded as 3-T-22 1 Jan 51. Recoded as 4-T-22 1 Jan 53 and as CTA-22 by 1957. Reassigned to the 2º Escuadrilla Aeronaval de Sostén Logístico Móvil as 5-T-22 as a pure cargo aircraft after 1964. By the time she had been recoded as 5-T-22, this aircraft was named 'Cabo de Hornos' and steps were introduced to transfer this aircraft to the Uruguayan Navy, but this did not materialise. She made her final flight on 28 Jul 79 and is now preserved on display at the Aero Club Ushuaia.

Note that, in addition to other markings peculiarities, Argentine naval aircraft usually carried the upper blue horizontal stripe of the rudder markings forward over the tip of the vertical fin as well. This aircraft, 5-T-21, marks adopted around April 1963, looks exceptionally well cared for here after twenty-two years of service and at least four previous codes in this 1968 view. Note her 'psn' (0171) in small numerals on the vertical fin as well. *Air-Britain*

0187 (psn) 2-Gt-17 2-Gt-10 TA-23 3-T-23	43-15564	C-47A-85-DL	20030	Acquired via the FLC and the Aviation Maintenance Company and issued Export Licence No. 1797 7 Jun 46 as 2-Gt-17. Commenced her ferry flight home from Van Nuys, CA, 10 May 47. Recoded as 2-Gt-10 28 Aug 47 and TA-23 27 Nov 49. Recoded as 3-T-23 1 Jan 51. Crashed at 1630hrs on 30 Apr 51 at BAN Punta Indio on a test flight while being commanded by Capt. de Corbeta Carlos Jorge Mutt.
0188 (psn) 2-Gt-16 3-Gt-4 TA-26 3-T-26 4-T-26 CTA-24 5-T-24	42-23494	C-47A-1-DL	9356	Acquired via the FLC and issued Export Licence No. 1797 7 Jun 46 via the Aviation Maintenance Company as 2-Gt-16. Commenced her ferry flight home from Van Nuys, CA, 10 May 47 in company with 2-Gt-17 noted above. Recoded as 3-Gt-4 in 1948 and TA-26 27 Nov 49. Recoded as 3-T-26 1 Jan 51 and 4-T-26 1 Jan 53. Recoded as CTA-24 in 1957. Operated by the 2° Escuadrilla Aeronaval de Sostén Logístico Móvil, Escuadra Aeronaval No. 5 and, confusingly, was also named 'Cabo de Hornos' by Dec 78 and camouflaged operating from Ushuaia in the islands of Tierra del Fuego. Recoded as 5-T-24, however, and named 'Beagle'. Officially withdrawn from service 24 Nov 81.
0220 (psn) 3-Gt-1 TA-10 3-T-10 4-T-10 CTA-10 LQ-GJT 5-T-10	42-108883 NC-63689	C-47A-10-DK DC-3C-S1C3G	12678	Apparently acquired from Michael Patrick Efferson & Associates and assigned to BAN Punta Indio as 3-Gt-1 8 Aug 47. Recoded as TA-10 27 Nov 49 but changed to 3-T-10 1 Jan 51. Recoded as 4-T-10 1 Jan 53. To CTA-10 in 1957. This aircraft was unique in passing from Navy control to governmental control in Ma 60 as LQ-GJT, where she served as a Presidential aircraft as such, named Independencia. Unusually, she then reverted to Navy marks again as PSN 0220 5-T-10 and named Stella Maris when LQ-GJT was cancelled 22 Nov 67. She was officially stricken 4 May 79 and offered for sale 24 Nov 81.
0232 (psn) 2-Gt-18 3-Gt-3 TA-25 3-T-25 4-T-25 CTA-23	42-23309	C-47A-1-DL	9171	Acquired via the Aviation Maintenance Company and issued Export Licence No. 3004 on 23 Sep 46 as 2-Gt-18. Arrived home in Argentina 5 Aug 47 and recoded as 3-Gt-3. Recoded as TA-25 27 Nov 49 and then 3-T-25 by July 1950. To 4-T-25 1 Jan 53. Reconfigured as an ambulance aircraft during 1957 and to CTA-23 named Esperanza. This aircraft suffered an accident 29 Oct 63 and made a forced landing on the coast near Bahia Aguirre, Tierra del Fuego and was stricken as a result.
0260 (psn) 2-Gt-19/'49'	42-24037	C-47A-40-DL	9899	Acquired via the Aviation Maintenance Company and issued Export Licence No. 3004 on 23 Sep 46. Arrived home in Argentina 29 Jan 48 as 2-Gt-19 with tail number '49'. This aircraft was lost on 8 Jul 48 under the command of Tte De Navío Juan Carlos Gil while home based at BAN Comandante Espora, crashing into a hill near Coronel Pringles which was obscured by darkness and extreme cloud cover. It exploded and burned and was fatal to all five Navy personnel on board.
0264 (psn) 3-Gt-9/'48' 3-Gt-2 TA-11 3-T-11 4-T-11 CTA-11 5-T-11	42-108906 NC-58216	C-47A-20-DK 'DC3 ejecutiva'	12908	Acquired 23 Sep 47 and issued codes 3-Gt-9, tail number '48'. Recoded as 3-Gt-2 during 1947 and then TA-11 27 Nov 49. To 3-T-11 1 Jan 51 and 4-T-11 1 Jan 53. To CTA-11 in 1957 and then 5-T-11 Withdrawn from service with 9,041:30 hours total time 5 Feb 75.
0278 (psn) 2-Gt-20 3-Gt-5 TA-27 3-T-23 4-T-23 CTA-14 5-T-26	42-93545 KG652 NC-95488	C-47A-25-DK Dakota III	13469	Acquired from Michael Patrick Efferson & Associates after 12 Dec 46 as 2-Gt-20 (some sources suggest 16 Aug 48). However, she is known to have been undergoing test flight as 2-Gt-20 as early as 27 Apr 48, casting that date into doubt. Recoded as 3-Gt-5 16 Aug 48. Recoded as TA-27 27 Nov 49 and then 3-T-23 1 Jan 51. Became 4-T-23 1 Jan 53 and CTA-14 in 1957. To 5-T-26. This aircraft was ceded to the small Paraguayan Naval aviation force as T-26 in Nov 79.

Code 5-T-23 was, in fact, 'psn' 0117, the very first Navy C-47, but has confounded historians by invariably being cited as MSN 19124. She was finally retired in 1975 after twenty-nine years of continuous service. *Jorge Núñez Padin via Eduardo Luzardo*

Another long-serving Navy C-47A-1-DL, the former 42-23494, 5-T-24 had been acquired in June 1947 and initially marked as 3-Gt-4. Note again her blue engine cowlings, prop spinner caps and nose cone. *via Will Blount*

0281 (psn) 3-Gt-12 TA-12 3-T-12 4-T-12 CTA-12	42-92882 NC-57674	C-47A-15-DK DC-3C-S1C3G LC-47	12732	Acquired in 1948 via the William Reilly & Co., she was a Second World War Eight and Ninth Air Force veteran. Initially coded 3-Gt-12, this was changed to TA-12 27 Nov 49 and then 3-T-12 1 Jan 51. Recoded as 4-T-12 1 Jan 53 and to CTA-12 in 1957. This aircraft was extensively modified for service around Nov 61 with the Grupo Naval Antártico and assigned to the Unidad de Exploración y Reconocimiento Aerofotográfico at Estación Aeronaval Río Gallegos, Santa Cruz by 21 Jan 62, including high-visibility Day-Glo-style red areas on her nose, empennage and wing tips, as well as skis. This aircraft was lost to air action at her home station, BAN Punta de Indio, on 3 Apr 63 when she was strafed by FAA aircraft during the revolutionary action that autumn.
0282 (psn) 3-Gt-13 TA-13 3-T-13 4-T-13 CTA-13 5-T-12	41-18479 NC-54228	C-47-DL DC-3C-S1C3G	4571	Acquired via the L.B. Smith Aircraft Corp. 28 Jul 48 as 3-Gt-13. Recoded as TA-13 27 Nov 49 and 3-T-13 1 Jan 51. Recoded 4-T-13 1 Jan 53 and CTA-13 in 1957, at which time she sported a deep blue nose cone and engine cowlings. To 5-T-12 30 Dec 63. Withdrawn 27 Dec 71.
0296 (psn) 2-Gt-22 2-Gt-12 TA-24 3-T-24 4-T-24 CTA-15	'VHCCL' 'VHCFD' NC-68180	C-47-DL 'LC-47' config.	4664	Apparently acquired 2 Jun 48 via Arrow Airways, Inc. of Torrance, CA, as 2-Gt-22 and, if her identity is correct, a very rare combat veteran of the Fifth Air Force in the Southwest Pacific Area. After a forced landing in Chile near Iquique 18 Oct 48, apparently on her way home, she was recovered, repaired and recoded as 2-Gt-12. Converted initially to a camera aircraft she became TA-24 27 Nov 49. Recoded as 3-T-24 1 Jan 51 and 4-T-24. To CTA-15 in 1957. Modified for South Pole operations by Dec 61 in the Antarctic with the U.T.7.8 Unidad de Exploración y Reconocimiento Aerofotográfica of the Grupo Naval Antartico and equipped with skis and a high-visibility colour scheme, marked as CTA-15. This aircraft was withdrawn in 1971 and is now preserved in Buenos Aires.
0490 (psn) CTA-25	43-48853 KJ940 SAAF 6845 N123S LV-PKP	C-47B-5-DK Dakota III	14669/26114	Acquired by the Navy 9 Aug 58 as CTA-25. Passed to LQ-MSP on 20 Sep 60 and operated by the Ministerio de Asistencia Social y Salud Pública but still owned by the Navy and actually carried on the strength of the 2ª Escuadrilla Aeronaval de Transporte, as a replacement for PSN 0232 (q.v.) and was reportedly the most advanced 'flying hospital' in the world at the time. She reportedly carried two nicknames during this period, 'Esperanza' and 'Malaspina', the latter derived from her quasi-governmental marks. Probably to the chagrin of the Navy, she passed to the FAA as S-4 (q.v.) 7 Feb 68.
0652 (psn) 5-T-13 5-T-10	(44-76828) BuA99830 N30 BuA99830	TC-47B-30-DK R4D-7 R4D-6 C-47J C-47M C-47R	16412/33160	Although frequently cited in error as somehow having been the former PSN 0260 (q.v.), this was actually an entirely different aircraft, added to the inventory late on 6 Jul 70. She was deactivated 9 Feb 72 and sold 24 Nov 81. The use of codes 5-T-10 have been cast into doubt.

Ski-equipped and painted in high-visibility colours, CTA-15 has been unofficially cited as an 'LC-47,' formerly 2-Gt-12 and 4-T-24. If her identity is correct, she possessed a wartime service record. She is now preserved in questionable condition in Buenos Aires. *Georg von Roitberg*

Argentine politics after the rise of Perón in 1946 often pitted the conservative Navy leadership against the regime. The Navy was the principal instigator of an unsuccessful revolt on 28 September 1951, in which the Naval air arm played a central role. As a direct result, drastic purges of the commissioned officer corps of the service followed and, by the end of 1951, the AN was down to about twenty-five commissioned officer pilots to man a force then comprising some eighty-seven aircraft of all types – including C-47s and C-39s. By late 1952, by careful vetting and recalls of retirees to active duty, and the best efforts of the Naval aviation school, it had bounced back to around 150. It should be noted that, at the time, Naval aviators were often sent 'to sea' to ensure that they were well-rounded and, as a result, were not permanently assigned to aviation billets. NCOs and enlisted ratings, on the other hand were and, with about 2,000 such highly experienced and fiercely loyal personnel, mainly at Punta del Indio and Bahia Blanca, this included at least twenty trained aerial gunners.

Yet another revolution, this time involving elements of all of the armed forces, boiled over on 16 June 1955. Naval aviation was deeply involved, including the valuable transport element. Details of this nationwide and exceptionally convoluted series of events can be found in Hagedorn's *Latin American Air Wars and Aircraft, 1912–1969* (Hikoki/Crecy, 2006) but, for the purposes of this account, of the thirty-nine 'rebel' aircraft that sought refuge and asylum in neighbouring Uruguay as the revolt unraveled, seven were Navy C-47s. The first to arrive was 4-T-12 at 1743hrs, landing at Montevideo's Carrasco airfield, with 4-T-22 right behind her. Then, as the astonished Fuerza Aérea Uruguaya looked on, yet another, 4-T-11 coasted in three minutes later at 1746hrs. Code 4-T-23 followed at 1757hrs and one more, with her codes partially obscured by hastily applied rebel markings, at 1810hrs. As if this were not enough, 4-T-24 also fled to Uruguay, landing instead at the Colonia airfield at 1745hrs, and was found to be carrying, in addition to her Navy crew, a number of FAA rebel pilots as well. Five minutes later, she was followed in there by 4-T-20 that, besides her Navy crew, carried a number of FAA rebel pilots, three NCOs and Dr Zabala Ortiz. Thus, seven Navy C-47s had been obliged to flee their homeland – nearly every airworthy example at the time – along with six air force Gloster Meteor F.Mk4s, (two of which crash landed), a single Fiat G.55A, two Navy Douglas C-54s, three PBY-5As (one with combat damage), sixteen armed North American AT-6A Standards, and four Navy Beech AT-11s (one with combat damage). All of the Navy aircraft had fled from BAN Punta del Indio, which is located about 80 air miles south-east of Buenos Aires. It is significant to note that, of the twenty-eight FAA commissioned pilots who sought refuge in Uruguay, the majority arrived in Navy C-47s at Colonia (opposite Buenos Aires across the Rio de la Plata estuary) and had been the last two aircraft to depart BAM Morón before it was retaken by armed forces elements loyal to the regime.

The departure of the last Navy C-47s from BAM Morón on the afternoon of 16 June was very nearly prevented by loyal forces remaining behind there. One intrepid FAA officer identified only as Tte Fernández, volunteered to stay behind and cover the escape. In doing so, he was killed in action by approaching loyal FAA NCOs. Other loyal forces hastily drove a vehicle across the runway at its midway point but somehow the C-47 was able to get off the ground and just clear it.

The day after the tumultuous revolt, the Uruguayan Presidential Council voted to notify the Argentine Government that it could recover their aircraft whenever it desired. The following day, Brigadier Alfredo R. González Filguera, who identified himself as 'Director of the Argentine Air Force Command School', arrived with an array of engineers to survey the fleet of escaped aircraft. Between 20 and 25 June, nearly all of the Argentine aircraft had been flown back to their stations by FAA crews, the FAU providing guards and even some mechanics and supplies to aid this operation.

But this was not the end of this episode. Late on the evening of 3 August 1955, an unidentified Navy C-47 once again arrived unannounced at Carrasco near Montevideo, this time transporting the two-man crew and their families, and immediately requested asylum. The Argentine Naval Ministry immediately attempted to put its 'spin' on this incident, telling the press that, while on a 'test flight' of the aircraft out of BAN Comandante Espora at Bahía Blanca, the pilot, Tte George E. Collet and his co-pilot, Tte Ramón A. Corvera, had landed in a 'nearby' open field and took aboard the wives and children of both of them, after which they suddenly flew to Uruguay, apparently being in fear of reprisals for their part in the June revolution.

The repercussions of this escape flight very nearly had catastrophic consequences for the CAN and its transport force. Perón, apparently

outraged, summarily ordered that all surviving Naval transport-type aircraft were to be immediately surrendered to the FAA, totalling by this time four C-54s and nine C-47s. In fact, cooler heads prevailed, and the transfer never took place, but it was a very near thing.

Argentine Army

Like many evolving air forces worldwide, the service that emerged as the Fuerza Aérea Argentina (FAA) in January 1945 had initially been created as an element of the Army (Ejército) and, as elsewhere, the process of independence as a separate and equal branch of service was only accomplished after contentious political turmoil. In most such instances, the seething post-partum experience eventually resolved into tolerance and grudging co-operation. In Argentina, however, where the armed forces represented a dominant force in the political reality, the three major branches of service, as evidenced by the descriptions above of the 1951 and 1955 revolutions, in the absence of any genuine foreign threat other than the unlikely ambitions of neighbouring Chile, the concept of inter-service co-operation and joint operations was, at best, secondary to vested interests.

Like the United States, the Army (Ejército) did not take long to recognise that the surrender of all of its aviation components to the new FAA in 1945 had placed it in the position of having to 'play nicely' with the air force in order to modernise its strategic and tactical evolution – especially the advent, during and after the Second World War, of the huge advantages of aerial movement and insertion of forces and materiel, not to mention communications, liaison, and artillery support. The Army had actually acquired its first three C-47s in December 1945, as purely administrative and support aircraft, followed by three more around November 1956. But as experiments in aerial mobility worldwide started to command notice, and also just like the US Army, the Argentine ground forces leadership chaffed at the often-divergent stance of the air force leadership, and decided to create their own, organic aviation element – and it was something more than just a few support types. This, the Comando de Aviación del Ejército (CAE), was established in 1957, and, at least at the beginning, presented little concern to the air force, acquiring a small number of liaison aircraft, light transports and small helicopters.

The Army had ambitions to create a genuine and modernised 'air mobile' capability, however, and when it became clear that the FAA was either unable or unwilling to support this objective with its own exceptionally mixed transport fleet, the Army decided to go at it alone. So, it came to pass that the Army started casting around for available, relatively inexpensive DC-3 or C-47 types with which to organise its own air transport capability.

An exceptionally rare colour image of an Ejercito Argentino C-47B-1-DL, E.T.A.102 displaying the Army's variation on the national insignia roundel. Probably a TEMCO rehab, she became ME-2T by November 1956, then MG-2T, AE-12E and AE-100, then passed to civil marks LV-JIG in November 1968. *Atilio Marino*

The first Army aircraft, E.T.A.101, also acquired via TEMCO in December 1954, displaying the hand-applied 'Cristo Vence' rebel markings of the so-called 'Revolución Libertadora' while operating with the Grupo Aéreo de Transporte Revolucionario in September 1955. This aircraft later became ME-1T and MG-1T before passing to the air force as T-17. *Atilio Marino*

Another of the September 1955 MR aircraft, E.T.A.103 was another Army TEMCO overhaul and, unusually, has the lower rear fuselage area painted in a rather unusual manner. This aircraft also eventually went to the air force as T-18 in October 1960. *Atilio Marino*

In retrospect, the aircraft acquired were a motley crew, at best, coming principally from former Brazilian commercial operators and from CATC. Exactly how the Army was going to man, maintain and engage these aircraft isn't clear, and, since nearly all of them were, in fairly short order, transferred to a rather surprised FAA, which, upon learning earlier of the Army's gambit, had immediately asserted that this capability was clearly an air force remit, things had gone full circle. At least one historian has speculated that the entire enterprise had actually been nothing more than an Army tactic to get what it wanted from the FAA in the first place. As events unfolded, this view appears to have some validity.

Comando de Aviación del Ejército Argentino DC-3s and C-47s – 1954–60

CAE Serial Code	Previous Identity	Built As	MSN	Assignments and Notes
E.T.A.101 ME-1T MG-1T	43-15694 CA50 (CATC) XT-T36 NC-8328C N1797B	C-47A-90-DL	20160	Acquired by the Ejército from TEMCO in Texas in December 1954, which converted her back to paratroop configuration for use by the Escuela de Tropas Aerotransportadas. This aircraft was marked as such when used by the so-called Grupo Aéreo de Transporte Revolucionario in Sep 55. She was recoded as ME-1T in Nov 56, MG-1T in March 1958 and went to the FAA as T-17 (q.v.) in Oct 60.
E.T.A.102 ME-2T MG-2T AE-12E AE-100	43-16351 XT-??? NC-8334C N1798B	C-47B-1-DL	20817	Probably acquired from TEMCO as E.T.A.101 above. Recoded as ME-2T in Nov 56 and MG-2T in Mar 58. Became AE-12E sometime afterwards and AE-100 in Sep 68, passing to LV-JIG 7 Nov 68.
E.T.A.103 ME-3T MG-3T	43-15922 CA3 (CATC) XT-T24 NC-8324C N1795B	C-47A-90-DL	20388	Acquired from TEMCO as E.T.A.101 above, subsequently being remarked as ME-3T in Nov 56 and MG-3T in March 1958. To the FAA as T-18 (q.v.) in Oct 60.
EA-1T	42-100975 NC-19135 PP-SVA PP-ANF	C-47A-75-DL	19438	Acquired for the CAE by the Secretaría de Guerra from REAL in Brazil in 1960. To the FAA as T-39 (q.v.) on 20 Sep 60.
EA-2T	BuA04705 NC-9399H PP-KAB PP-ANM	R4D-1	4365	Acquired for the CAE by the Secretaría de Guerra from REAL in Brazil in 1960, although the Brazilian marks (PP-ANM) were not actually cancelled until 17 Aug 61. To the FAA as T-32 (q.v.) on 20 Sep 60.
EA-3T	BuA03140 PP-KAA PP-ANS	R4D-1	4280	Acquired for the CAE by the Secretaria de Guerra from REAL in Brazil in 1960, although the Brazilian marks (PP-ANS) were not actually cancelled until 12 Nov 61. To the FAA as T-39 (q.v.) on 20 Sep 60.
EA-4T	41-20055 YS-24 PP-AVI	C-53-DO	4825	Identical to EA-2T above. To the FAA as T-29 (q.v.) on 20 Sep 60.
EA-5T	BuA05062 NC-36815 PP-AVW	R4D-1	4754	Identical to EA-2T above. Her Brazilian marks (PP-AVW) were not cancelled until 18 Aug 61. To the FAA a T-19 (q.v.) on 20 Sep 60.
EA-6T	NC-34925 TI-16 PP-AXW PP-NBJ	DC-3A-345	4957	Identical to EA-2T above. To the FAA as T-37 (q.v.) on 20 Sep 60.

EA-7T	42-92394 FZ633 PP-JAC PP-YPB	C-47A-1-DK Dakota III DC-3C	12190	Identical to EA-2T above. To the FAA as T-22 (q.v.) on 20 Sep 60.
EA-8T	42-93682 NC-62567 LV-ABH PP-XES PP-YQA	C-47A-25-DK DC-3C	13621	Identical to EA-2T above. To the FAA as T-27 (q.v.) on 20 Sep 60.
EA-9T	42-92246 FL614 NC-34985 LV-AFS PP-XEP PP-YQB	C-47A-1-DK Dakota III DC-3C	12025	Identical to EA-2T above. To the FAA as T-36 (q.v.) on 20 Sep 60.
EA-10T	43-47967 NC-90908 PP-YQJ	C-47A-30-DK DC-3C	13783/25228	Identical to EA-2T above, the former PP-YQJ. To the FAA as T-28 (q.v.) on 20 Sep 60.
EA-11T	NC-18937 C-100 (AVIANCA) PP-BHD PP-YQL	DC-3-228	2012	Acquired for the CAE by the Secretaría de Guerra from REAL in Brazil in 1960, although the Brazilian marks (PP-YQL) were not actually cancelled until 29 Jun 61. To the FAA as T-20 (q.v.) on 20 Sep 60.
EA-12T	43-48610 NC-79005 PP-PCV PP-YQM	C-47B-5-DK DC-3C	14426/25871	Identical to EA-2T above. To the FAA as T-30 (q.v.) on 20 Sep 60.

C-47s with the Prefectura Nacional Maritima

Performing many of the functions of what is often termed a Coast Guard, this small but efficient organisation had evolved from the Capitanía de Puertos and then the Prefectura de Puertos. In the early 1900s, the service was brought under the control of the Commander-in-Chief of the Navy, and its scope extended to coastal patrol, fishery protection and the interdiction of smuggling activities. In 1970, the name was changed once again to simply Prefectura Naval Argentina and, when the service had acquired two C-47s in 1962, Argentina

completed the hat-trick replicated only by the United States in the Western Hemisphere, and by only a handful of nations worldwide: every uniformed branch of the Argentine military had operated Douglas twins.

Inevitably, the service created a División de Aviación to provide valuable services to its small and isolated outposts, mainly among the exceptionally long Argentine coastal frontiers and, between 31 October and 26 December 1962, added two C-47s to that force. Little is known of their actual day-to-day use, and there do not appear to have been any recorded political or revolutionary excursions. These are described here:

Prefectura Code	Previous Identity	Built As	MSN	Assignments and Notes
LQ-ADG (26Dec 62) PM-15 (22Aug 63) PA-15 (1970)	44-77098 KP216 A.7931 CF-DXT LV-ADG	C-47B-35-DK Dakota IV	16682/33430	After rather extensive service for eight years, this aircraft was transferred to the Provincia de Formosa government by 26 Dec 62, once again as LQ-ADG. Apparently, they both legally retained their quasi-governmental marks, as LQ-ADG was not official cancelled until 19 Sep 63, while LQ-ACW was not cancelled until 23 May 63. Marked as PM-15 from 22 Aug 63 and PA-15 from 1970. Returned to LV-ADG once again 22 Aug 72.
LQ-ACW (26Dec 62) PM-16 (6Mar 63) PA-16 (1970)	42-92275 FL631 LV-ACW LQ-ACW	C-47A-1-DK Dakota III	12057	Military marks taken up 6 Mar 63 as PM-16 changed to PA-16 in 1970. This aircraft had almost the exact same service experience as LQ-ADG, passing to the same provincial government in 29 Aug 72 as LQ-ACW.

Unique to Argentine, the Prefectura Nacional Maritima – a Coast Guard-like organisation – also operated a pair of C-47s. PM-15 was a former RAF Dakota IV (KP216) and is seen here undergoing open-air engine maintenance. The distinctive ventral nose radio loop marks her as a C-47B, as noted in our Annex documents. She subsequently passed to civil marks once again as LV-ADG in August 1972. *via Dr Gary Kuhn*

With a much more well-defined cheatline than PM-15, the other Prefectura aircraft, PM-16 also saw RAF service as Fl631, but was a C-47A. She went to provincial government marks LQ-ACW in August 1972 after less than nine years of service with the PNM. *APN157 via Ken F. Measures*

CHAPTER THREE

Bolivia

O F ALL OF THE MAINLAND South American nations that employed DC-3 and C-47 aircraft in significant numbers, those obtained by Bolivia certainly experienced the most tumultuous and convoluted service experience.

To the surprise of many, Bolivia ended up being one of only three Latin American air arms to actually take delivery of C-47s under the provisions of the highly successful Lend-Lease Programme during the course of the war years, thus joining a very exclusive club that comprised giant, neighbouring Brazil and Colombia to the far north. The reasoning behind this seemingly odd allocation will be discussed at length later in this narrative.

Bolivia's exertions during the well-documented Chaco War of the 1930s with neighbouring Paraguay have been well documented, and certainly represented one of the golden eras of Bolivian military aviation, one of the principal lessons of which for Bolivian military doctrine having been the highly successful use and value of air transport during much of the conflict. Indeed, it may be fairly said that, in a nation as geographically challenged as Bolivia, she was the

earliest to take this lesson to heart not just in Latin America, but internationally. Despite enormous spending during the conflict, and the creation of what was, by the end of 1934, one of the best-equipped and experienced air arms in all of Latin America, by 7 December 1941, the once-lethal force had shrivelled on the vine in the absence of a credible threat to the succession of sitting regimes that changed with alarming frequency.

Pioneers in every sense, these six Bolivian Army airmen were the first Latin American military aviators to be trained to fly C-47s, and are pictured in front of E.T.A.I at Albrook Field, Canal Zone, while attached to the Sixth Air Force's 20th Troop Carrier Squadron. The crews received a total of between fifty and seventy hours of intensive training per month while attached. Unfortunately, their names were not recorded at the time. *USAFHRA*

The Bolivian crews at Albrook Field, Canal Zone, arrayed on either side of a visiting senior officer in the middle who had travelled from La Paz to attend their graduation, and then return home with them in the first Latin American military C-47 actually entered into service in 1945. Note the rudder markings, just visible. The four aircraft were all 'used', and at least one of them was camouflaged when delivered. Interestingly, some of the pilots wear Bolivian wings, while at least one has USAAF wings. *USAFHRA*

Ironically, it was the very power demonstrated by the Bolivian air arm during the Chaco War that gave what was seemingly a nation of politicians pause. This was especially true in the lofty regions of the centre of government in La Paz[19] where, for all intents and purposes, the Cuerpo de Aviación literally hovered at its central and most important station, El Alto, within very short striking distance of friend or foe in the city. As a direct consequence, the service was the subject of endless 'micromanagement', usually consisting of purges of loyal or recalcitrant crews every time the balloon went up. This obviously impacted training, the establishment of a disciplined force, pay and allowances, and a sense of sustainability. Hapless ground crews, almost universally of indigenous origin, were often poorly treated, badly led and fed, and yet were expected to perform miracles of maintenance on aircraft that had long since passed their prime, and for which spares were a shambles of deteriorating parts in a completely disorganised assortment of sheds. The government, which was decidedly pro-Fascist, much to the alarm of the US, like Peru, engaged an Italian air mission between 1937 and 1941, while the local German population, many of whom occupied positions of wealth and business in the tightly compacted capitol and principal cities, were overtly National Socialists in outlook. By 1942, the FBI estimated that there were only about 500 Italians in Bolivia. However, they put the number of German nationals at a staggering 5,000, in addition to some 8,000 Jews of German extraction. Although the Italian Military Mission had a ground component, they

quickly realised that the Bolivian Army had a tradition of German influence. The FBI also found that Nazi influence had penetrated the leadership of the Bolivian Army, as well as several other key government agencies. The highly prolific Bolivian news media of the day was found to be 'emphatically under Nazi influence' and that the small and poorly financed newspapers were 'generally purchasable, with the majority of the Bolivian press subsidised by German interests, either directly by cash subsidies or indirectly through Transocean News Service and local advertising pressures'.

The disappointing performance of the Italian Air Mission led the Bolivian government to approach the US for both a ground and air force Mission replacement, a need that even the most ethnocentric of the Bolivian military leadership grudgingly recognised. This was substantially more attractive because of the successful relationship that Bolivia had enjoyed with none other than the Curtiss-Wright Export Corporation, which had supplied the overwhelming majority of the Bolivians' most efficacious aircraft during the Chaco War, and which continued – much to the chagrin of the Italian Mission – when Bolivia acquired ten Curtiss-Wright A19R 'all-metal' light combat aircraft in June 1938, its first truly modern mounts.

The US Army Ground and Air Missions arrived in September 1941 – the first in Latin America – and the small air component was immediately shuttled off to distant Cochabamba and Santa Cruz, where the Bolivians maintained their nearly dormant training activities at the time. They brought with them three brand-new North American AT-6As

An exceptionally rare image of the substantial Panagra maintenance facility erected in Bolivia by the end of 1945, with at least four Panagra DC-2s and DC-3s visible and, at right, just visible, one of the first four Bolivian Army C-47s, still camouflaged. These aircraft, the fuel stocks there, and trained mechanics proved pivotal during the 1949 revolution. *NARA RG18-AO-322R-35*

– also the first in Latin America – and set about rebuilding an air force. At the same time, with the US entry into the war shortly after the Missions' arrival, the US embassy, as elsewhere in Latin America, immediately commenced a never-ending campaign to encourage the Bolivian government to gain control of powerful German and Italian elements within its society – a process that the Bolivians, unashamedly, used to their advantage, not gaining momentum until 1944. The classified 20th Troop Carrier Squadron missions to Bolivia, described in Chapter 1, were one of the final acts of that process.

At the same time, Bolivia was regarded as being very rich in untapped natural resources, not least of which was tin, but the most important of which was tungsten – seldom recognised – and all of which was coveted by both the emerging Axis and Allied powers. German propaganda and intelligence activities within Bolivia were rampant during the first three years of the war years, and the US FBI, which held counter-intelligence responsibility for all of Latin America, had a disproportionately large contingent resident at the US Embassy early on.

In the midst of all of this, Bolivia's senior leadership became aware of the largesse represented by the Lend-Lease Programme and noted via its own intelligence and diplomatic apparatus that neighbouring Latin American republics were leveraging this programme to their benefit. They wasted little time requesting that the US Missions bend all efforts towards assisting the Bolivian General Staff in assembling a hefty requisition for all manner of equipment, ground, naval and air under the provisions of the programme. To the credit of the Mission staff, they did in fact attempt to counsel moderation, as Bolivia's standing Army at the time consisted of only about 1,000 officers, a similar number of NCOs, and about 7,280 conscripts, and the air arm, which on a really good day could count seventy-five officers of all ranks, was still very much a component of the Army. Indeed, the Fuerza Aérea Boliviana (FAB), a formal descriptor that had been encouraged into general use by the Air Mission, did not become an independent branch of service until August 1957. Key to the entire requisition, however, was a component dedicated to improving air transportation within the Republic, as the long-standing – but German-controlled – national airline, Lloyd Aéreo Boliviano (LAB) had been almost entirely equipped with German aircraft as late as August 1941, the airline not having been nationalised by the government until May 1941. Quite aside from Lend-Lease, the US mounted a concerted effort, via the Defence Supplies Corporation, to essentially eliminate Axis influence in Latin American air transportation concurrent with the emergence of Lend-Lease.

And so, Bolivia started receiving Lend-Lease supplied aircraft as early as May 1942, although getting them to the landlocked and remote FAB stations was a story in itself. The aircraft requisitioned and actually approved by the Munitions Assignment Board (Air), it should be observed, were considerably in excess of the FAB's ability to absorb and operate, and the overwhelmed Air Mission at Santa Cruz could only watch and marvel as shipping cases started arriving both at their station and El Alto.

In the midst of all of this, in December 1943 yet another revolution erupted in Bolivia and, this time, promulgated largely by young Army officers, resulted in the final elimination of senior Army and FAB officers who had been trained by the Germans and Italians, as well as Nazi-inclined Ministers of the former regime, who were summarily imprisoned almost to a man. The irony in all of this is that it was this very former leadership that had championed the large Lend-Lease bounty, most of the machinations for which had been well above the pay grades of the junior officers who then assumed power. Indeed, most of them had no idea how this process worked and, had it not been for the Air Mission, under the leadership of Maj. Bruce Baumgardner, who was very highly regarded by the young officers (many of whom he had trained), the entire air arm may have been thrown into hopeless disarray. Baumgardner had been designated as an honorary coronel in the FAB and, significantly, technical chief of all FAB operations. In this capacity, he was responsible only to the newly designated Minister of Defence and the President of Bolivia, certainly a status unparalleled until this time.

As a direct result of the energetic Mission's efforts in the few months following the organisation (and move) of the training centre from Cochabamba to BAM El Trompillo, Santa Cruz, the FAB had flown more total hours, service-wide, than it had for a combined total of the prior ten years. The Mission also assisted the FAB in establishing subordinate headquarters and operating bases at BAM La Florida, Sucre, and BAM El Tejar, Tarija. The younger cadets, many of whom were either involved in or directly supported the December 1943 revolution, had been trained in interception techniques, navigation problems, instrument flying and night formation flying, none of which the FAB had ever previously attempted.

The Mission and the electrified FAB had big plans. They vowed to train 600 pilots, and to then maintain that strength, which would have made the service one of the largest in Latin America. Considering that they only had about seventy-five, all told, at the time of the revolution, of which about twenty had been trained in USAAF or US civil schools, this was a very lofty ambition indeed. But perhaps

The earliest known colour image of a Bolivian TAM C-47, in this instance TAM-01, complete with the coat of arms of the Presidencia over one of the cabin windows. It appears that at least two different aircraft wore this code, three if E.T.A.I is included. *via Jonathan Olguin*

The second C-47 known to have worn codes TAM-01. In complete and relatively standardised TAM colours and markings, apparently after having been put out to pasture. Note the presence of an astrodome on the forward cabin roof of this aircraft and the antenna array, completely different from the preceding aircraft marked TAM-01 pictured. This photo was taken prior to 1986. *MAP1985-129 #5913*

more importantly, they had also trained some 175 mechanics – the very first formal training any of them had ever received – and, of these, the USAAF Mission regarded forty-five as 'excellent', nearly 'natural' mechanics, another fifteen as 'good' and the remaining 115 as possessing varying degrees of aptitude and training. The service, as of ten months following the revolution, had a total of sixty-eight aircraft of seventeen different types, of which a quite respectable total of sixty were operational, ranging from two Junkers Ju 86Zs (both undergoing repair) and a mix of eight survivors of the Chaco War (two examples each of the Curtiss Model 35-A Hawk Type I, Curtiss Falcon, Curtiss-Wright C14R Osprey, A19R and CW-16E and a quite impressive array of nearly brand-new Lend-Lease types. These included two each Beech AT-7s and AT-11s, eight Curtiss-Wright SNC-1 Falcons, ten Vultee BT-13As, five Boeing-Stearman PT-17s, nine North American AT-6Cs, eight each Interstate L-8As and Stinson L-9As, and a solitary Grumman JRF-5. Subsequently, significant additional PT-17s, BT-13As and AT-6Ds would follow.

But in keeping with the previous Bolivian government's objective of improving internal communications and transportation, and possibly as a quietly orchestrated quid pro quo for the new government's tardy co-operation in the internment of German Nazis

in the country, a little known Lend-Lease requisition, BL-305, showed up at the MAB (Air), and received almost instantaneous high-level support. This was for four 'used' Douglas C-47As specifically for the FAB, and quite apart from the DSC's ongoing efforts to rebuild LAB. These were in fact and rather surprisingly listed as 'substitutes' for the original requisition, which had been for four Beech UC-45Fs, and the MAB apparently attempted to assuage the concerns of some of the critics of this approval, who argued that the Allies had far more urgent wartime demands for these highly prized transports, by suggesting that of the four that it approved, all would be 'used' aircraft and that one of these 'could' be diverted to LAB. This was a quite extraordinary action by the MAB (Air), and the implication is that it had received support for approval from the very highest levels. The supply of 'used' aircraft was clearly meant to take the 'sting' out of the arrangement for other contenders, as usually, only factory-fresh, new-build aircraft were supplied against approved Lend-Lease requisitions.

These four aircraft are significant in that they were the first mass transfer of C-47s approved and actually delivered to any Latin American air arm, although Colombia was first to receive a single

Here, TAM-02 was captured on the rough surface of El Alto near La Paz, with two other service aircraft nearby. In this case, her TAM titles are worn in white inside the weathered cheatline, a similar but different style than usually seen, and at least her starboard engine is missing completely. She is also unusual in having two RDF loops on the forward cabin roof. *Hagedorn Collection*

Yet another variation on early TAM colours and markings, TAM-04 is otherwise natural metal, but has the code repeated under the port wing and on the starboard upper wing – with national roundels on opposite wing locations. This photo dates from prior to 1956. *via William Green*

example in October 1944, and being concurrent with a Brazilian requisition that saw actual delivery about a month after the first Bolivian aircraft. It is also important to note that these were, after having been identified by the USAAF from its existing fleet, actually legally signed for by the Bolivian Army Purchasing Commission on 22 January 1945, and then flown, individually, to the San Antonio Air Depot (SAAD) in Texas for preparation to depart. The first one, and the others shown in the table below, departed for Albrook Field, Canal Zone, on 28 January, and the other three followed on 5 April. It is believed that at least two of the aircraft still wore USAAF-style wartime olive drab over light grey camouflage, and SAAD was instructed to paint on the FAB national insignia and, it is assumed, their initial operating serials, before departure from Texas. It appears from available records that, for some reason, the FAB elected to mark these aircraft starting with the codes and Roman numerals E.T.A.I to E.T.A.IV. The acronym E.T.A. denoted what was, essentially a unit in the process of creation, the Escuadrón de Transporte Aéreo, although US Intelligence Report IR-43-51 had defined it, instead, as denoting Ejército Transporte Aéreo that, given the nature of the service at that time, may be more accurate. In fact, when the first aircraft arrived at Albrook Field, Canal Zone, they wore the titles Transportes Militares de Bolivia.

Another very unusual aspect of this initial quartet was that, upon the arrival of the first aircraft (42-23345) at Albrook Field, Canal Zone, it was administratively attached to the 20th Troop Carrier Squadron of the Sixth Air Force, the solitary occasion known in which a Latin American C-47 was actually attached to an active duty USAAF or USAF unit. There, four of the most experienced FAB pilots and seventeen NCOs were to undergo an intensive transition and training programme with the personnel of the 20th TCS and, by 7 April 1945, all four had arrived and the programme commenced immediately. Expected to end on 30 April, since the cadre of twenty-one FAB personnel were not scheduled to depart home until the middle of May, their training was extended to include more link trainer time, a novelty for the Bolivians, as well as additional crew-building and transition flights over extended distances. Another, group of carefully selected FAB pilots followed after the first group returned to La Paz. By 17 July 1945, with the aid of 20th TCS crews, all four of the C-47s were home at La Paz, the pride of the service.

Between V-J Day and 6 February 1948, the FAB acquired at least four more identified C-47s and it was with these aircraft that the service endured the events of 27 August to 17 September 1949, yet another revolution, in which they played most unusual and crucial roles.

A typical scene at one of TAM's numerous rural, lowland request stop locations, with a combination of diverse cargo, crew and curious bystanders evident. TAM-05 is either a C-47 or C-47A and has eluded identification and went missing on 8 November 1958 – the third TAM C-47 lost that year. *via Henk Kavelaars*

Compare this nearly identical view of TAM-14 with that of TAM-02 pictured earlier. While the cheatline is similar, the white upper decking is arrange differently and, on TAM-14, the acronym 'FAB' is worn on the starboard upper wing instead of the TAM code. Photographed at El Alto, this may in fact have been the second aircraft to wear these codes, as the original TAM-14 was written off on 26 April 1969 and this image is dated in November 1973. *Dr Jean Magendie*

On Saturday, 27 August, the revolution broke out at Cochabamba, Santa Cruz and Potosi, led by elements of the militant Movimiento Nacionalista Revolucionario (MNR), both within the country and from exile. Rebel forces seized control of eight LAB aircraft (probably a mix of Lockheed 18-10 Lodestars, including CB-25, CB-27 and CB-28, and DC-3s CB-29 to at least CB-33), one of the FAB's C-47s, which was away from La Paz at the time, and at least nine North American AT-6Cs and AT-6Ds, nine Vultee BT-13As, one Curtiss-Wright SNC-1, the Grumman JRF-5 and all of the Boeing-Stearman PT-17s that were, at the time, based at BAM El Trompillo and at Cochabamba. The FAB and loyal government forces had five active duty C-47s (of the eight that had been acquired to that time, suggesting that, besides the one seized by MNR forces, two had already been lost). They also had six North American AT-6Ds, five BT-13As and two Curtiss C-46Ds commandeered from the Corporación Boliviana de Fomento (almost certainly CB-40 and CB-41), as well as an unidentified C-47 commandeered from the Aramayo Mining Company – plus some non-airworthy Curtiss-Wright SNC-1s and assorted older aircraft languishing and awaiting maintenance work at El Alto.

Part of the FAB garrison, including some cadets at Cochabamba, went over to the MNR but, as far as can be determined, none of the serving FAB pilots or officers there took part in the revolutionary activities. The CO, Mayor García, was, in fact, jailed by the rebels. The CO and most of his staff at BAM El Trompillo, Santa Cruz, were also put under armed guard during the entirety of the revolution, and it is not known with any degree of certainty exactly how many of the FAB NCOs and enlisted ranks stationed there assisted the rebels.

Aircrews and pilots for the MNR consisted, for the most part, of LAB personnel, five pilots and all of the co-pilots of the line, plus some ex-FAB officers who had been 'retired' for yet earlier revolutionary activities – including that of December 1943, noted earlier. The rebel forces depended on the fuel stores seized in Santa Cruz and Cochabamba, as well as the rather extensive maintenance shops at the latter city, as their source of supply and basic, day-to-day maintenance. Enormous confusion prevailed during the first day of the revolution and, for the time being, little air activity took place.

On Sunday, 29 August 1949, three FAB C-47s, employed as ad hoc bombers, dropped 130kg (about 250lb) bombs on the airfield at Cochabamba. Crews had installed a wooden chute over the lip of the port-side main cargo door, removed the doors entirely, and then greased the chutes. An intrepid 'kicker' in the rear of the aircraft, with a rope tied around his waist, then shoved the bombs down the chute on signal from the cockpit. Surprisingly, accuracy was fair, in that they actually hit the airport, but of approximately eighty bombs used during the entire operation, it was estimated that about 50 per cent were duds, the ordnance apparently having survived from the Chaco War period! An estimated 20,000 gallons of fuel was destroyed at Cochabamba, however, and the LAB maintenance shops there were also damaged, as was the administrative building. Several LAB aircraft that had the misfortune of being at Cochabamba at the time also sustained some shrapnel damage.

TAM-17 entered service sometime between 1964 and 1965 and was a MAP-supplied C-47D. She is seen here at Oshkosh, Wisconsin, after having been acquired by Basler as N46BF and, after conversion to BT-67, saw further service with the Air Force of Mali as TZ-390. *J.M.G. Gradidge*

Another view of TAM-17 at Oshkosh, Wisconsin, wearing definitive TAM colours and markings, including the rarely seen unit badge on the port nose. Also note that 'TAM-17' was worn on at least the starboard lower wing. *via Jonathan Olguin*

TAM-25 in happier times in nearly perfect TAM colours and markings, seen here around November 1985 after having been in service by then for twenty-one years. *George G.J. Kamp*

By the time the FAB took delivery of TAM-25 under MAP in mid-March 1964, the standard TAM colour scheme had been adopted – but readers can understand from the photo selection presented here that no two Bolivian C-47s were configured the same. Pictured withdrawn from use at Cochabamba with both engines missing in this April 1991 image, she was resurrected once again and sold to civil marks as CP-2290 by September 1997! *George G.J. Kamp*

Similar bombing attacks were also carried out against Sucre and Santa Cruz, using the same C-47s, but with negligible results, other than striking the fear of God into those sprinting for cover at the sound of an aircraft, although some damage was, miraculously, done to the runways.

The greatest blow to the FAB came on Monday, the 29th, however, when, after a maximum-effort C-47 bombing raid on Santa Cruz with all five aircraft, they flew on to land at Camiri, where they had been ordered to pick up loyal troops. When they had departed, Camiri had been reliably reported to be in the hands of forces loyal to the government but, upon arrival, a Coronel Covarrubias had assumed command for the rebels and immediately seized all five aircraft, and in one fell swoop gave the rebel forces a preponderance of effective airpower. The FAB flew a crew to Trinidad and picked up a LAB C-47 which had been captured there on landing by loyal troops, but this one has remained unidentified. On the 29th, the count for the 'rebel air force' was thus thirteen airworthy transport types, while the loyal FAB held a total of just four.

During the same period, the rebel AT-6Cs and AT-6Ds seized at Santa Cruz had been engaged only for reconnaissance and the distribution of leaflets over loyalist held towns and installations. Incredibly, however, an air-to-air combat between two opposing C-47s

carrying troops equipped with automatic weapons resulted in damage to one of the rebel-held C-47s, causing it to make a forced landing in inaccessible territory. Armed FAB AT-6Ds also attempted to intercept and engage rebel held transports but found that the limitations of the aircraft at altitudes up to 17,000ft prevented them from overtaking the transports, which had nearly identical maximum speeds at full power.

On 30 August, a loyal FAB crew crash landed the seized Aramayo Mines C-47, resulting in major damage to the aircraft. It was found that it had been caused by the failure of the crew to switch tanks, an elementary error, suggesting that the crews assigned to the aircraft did not possess much C-47 time. The FAB was, in fact, critically short of pilots, necessitating the recall of their few retired and reserve pilots to man the remaining aircraft.

With the capture of Cochabamba on the 31st, the FAB gained one former LAB C-47, which had been damaged by their own bombing, but which was found to be relatively simple to repair and, in the process, liberated several loyal pilots who had been arrested there by the rebels for duty in La Paz. The seizure also gave the FAB access to the spares and some spare engines that the rebels had, in their hasty retreat, left at the LAB depot there. The loss of Cochabamba thus deprived the rebels of their only genuine maintenance base, as well as the spares there and their largest source of aviation fuel, although they did have some 1,600 drums at Santa Cruz owned, for what little it was worth at the time, by Panagra. With the evacuation of Cochabamba, the rebels took with them a few high-value spares and nearly all of the maintenance personnel, but, from this time on, they were limited in their ability to man the considerable number of aircraft in their command. Even some time after the revolt ended, the FAB continued operating the seized LAB aircraft, including those eventually recovered from the rebels, and thus these must, in some fashion, be regarded as FAB assets during the period, although they did return one of the CBF C-46Ds to that operator.

Rebel forces, during their rampage at the Sucre aircraft, completely demolished one LAB Lockheed Model 18-10 Lodestar, probably CB-27, which had actually been a C-56D. The FAB and loyal Army ground forces, in the meantime, centred their attentions on Sucre and Santa Cruz, and did not bomb Camiri for fear of sustaining damage to Bolivia's main oil resources there.

On 1 and 2 September, rebel aircraft made several attempts to bomb El Alto, using captured mortar rounds and artillery shells, but, aside from the psychological impact, hit nothing of value. They bombed from an altitude of approximately 20,000ft and the enthusiastic and energetic Bolivian Army anti-aircraft crews, while putting on quite a pyrotechnics show for the local citizens, had no

One of the aircraft donated to Bolivia by Argentina in June 1969, TAM-32 was formerly FAA T-26. Here, she wears no TAM titles on her fuselage and is missing a number of parts but was refurbished and sold to civil marks as CP-1470 after February 1979. *ALPS*

Another MAP-supplied aircraft, TAM-35 entered the service around 29 February 1964, which seems chronologically challenged by earlier serials that had not been taken up until later! The aircraft is also unusual, in this operational image taken prior to July 1979, in having her distinctive TAM logo on her vertical fin oriented so it can be read 'level' when on the ground! The titles on the fuselage also present yet another variation on the theme. *MAP*

effect whatsoever on the attacking aircraft. Two of the rounds dropped actually exploded: one on the football field at the Colegio Militar at Calacoto and the other nearly a mile from the field. One of their C-47s also made at least six flights into Yacuiba carrying munitions, although exactly when cannot be determined from existing records. On one of these flights, the crew went into the town and dynamited the bank vault there, making off with about $45,000 in local currency.

After the fall of Sucre to loyal forces, the rebels attempted bombing the advancing Army forces with dud bombs they had retrieved from FAB raids earlier, certainly an intrepid exercise. Miraculously, of six that they dropped, three actually exploded, but caused only minor damage to the main runway at Sucre. Rebel aircraft also attempted to interfere with FAB-flown aircraft coming into Sucre with armed C-47s – in effect attempting to use them as interceptors – but caused no damage to the FAB aircraft, although, as one USAF observer reported at the time, 'it shook the FAB crews' morale'.

On 5 September, the FAB introduced a game-changer into the air equation when it purchased a Lockheed P-38L Lightning, the former 44-53059 and NX-69800, from the PANAGRA station manager in Lima, Peru.[20] Hastily rearmed with a pair of Chaco War-vintage Colt 7.65mm machine guns firing metal-linked rounds, bomb racks were also adapted to the aircraft, apparently taken from AT-6s. This aircraft, thus armed, carried out three raids on Santa Cruz, causing little damage from her guns, which jammed continuously, but causing widespread panic among the rebels and, with perhaps a lucky hit by a relatively small-calibre bomb, totally destroying one of the rebel-seized LAB C-47s (CB-33) there with a direct hit. Although subsequent P-38 missions specifically targeted the remaining rebel transport aircraft, their luck held, and none were seriously damaged. The P-38, for its part, sustained eight rifle-calibre bullet holes.

Throughout the entire period, the rebel forces used their considerable transport fleet to very good effect in the movement of troops from, mainly, the Beni region, to bolster the garrisons at Santa Cruz and Camiri. The FAB did some support work for the Army by transporting ammunition, food and troops, but their main effort was in their numerous bombing attacks against Cochabamba, Santa Cruz and Sucre.

With the sudden collapse of the rebellion, the rebel leadership, in traditional fashion, escaped to neighbouring Argentina aboard four of the transports, all of which were eventually returned to Bolivia.

The final score consisted of two aircraft totally destroyed (one C-47 and the Lockheed C-56D), another C-47 that was essentially lost, as it had crash landed in totally inaccessible territory and from

which, at best, some spares might be recovered, and one that crash landed at El Alto that was ruled damaged beyond economic repair, the four transports in Argentina (one of which was the former CBF C-46D, CB-41), which eventually returned, as well as one AT-6D there as well.

Although Bolivia has suffered a large number of revolutions over the course of its existence, this one was different than most in its scope, use of air power, and its violence. It was well-organised but, ultimately, it failed because the plot was discovered by key government officers, who took unusually quick and effective action at both La Paz and Oruro. The Chief of the National Police Force, the Carabineros, Coronel Vincenti was central to all of this, completely foiling the revolutionary attempt in the capitol itself while the Army commander in the Oruro area was responsible for breaking up the revolutionary elements there. During the first few days, the outcome was very much in doubt, but loyal Army and US-trained FAB crews seized the day at Cochabamba.

But the FAB C-47 situation just before the revolutionary exertions of September 1949 requires care in review as, even though the known acceptances, as shown in the following table, aid our understanding, they require adjustment, as suggested in a 1 June 1949 'Air Estimate of the Situation' assembled by the USAF in Periodic Aviation Report No. 582121. It stated that, 'during the last quarter, the FAB has lost through operations three more planes, including a C-47 which is at Todos Santos, but regarded as repairable'. Exactly which aircraft this was, and if it was actually recovered and repaired or not, is unknown. The picture was further complicated by 'in-the-pipeline' administrative changes. For example, Bolivia was slated to receive at least one C-47 under the provisions of the American Republics Projects (ARP), on Project ARP72017. This was to have been C-47A-25-DK 42-93793 (MSN 13744) but, as of 22 June 1948, the FAB was unable to come up with the money. To further muddy the water, when this aircraft had arrived for temporary, open storage in the Panama Canal Zone, it had been earmarked for Peru under ARP 72015 around 7 April 1948, but this, too, was changed, and it was offered to Mexico instead. The FAM was overextended at the time as well, and the aircraft ended up going to Uruguay instead as FAU 508 (q.v.) – but did not arrive until 21 November 1949!

Here, then, is a summary of what is known of those first eight nearly legendary FAB C-47s and at least five others that arrived in the very midst of the revolution and very shortly after it ended.

FAB Serial	Previous Identity	Built As	MSN	Assignments and Notes
E.T.A.I	42-23345	C-47A-1-DL	9207	Made ready at the SAAD and flown to Albrook Field, CZ, on 28 Jan 45, the very first Latin American-owned C-47, and attached to the 20th TCS, USAAF. When handed over, had a total time of 2,651hrs. Suffered an accident on 28 Feb 46 and was apparently repaired sufficiently to be flown back to the US around 17 Feb 48 for further work and to escort E.T.A. IX, X, and XI back home from Kelly Field, Texas (see below). Apparently rebuilt at some point and later became TAM-24 (q.v.). This aircraft apparently survived the 1949 revolution and was still on the AOB as such on 2 Mar 50. Indeed, the USAF Mission reported on 5 Feb 50 that it had taken an active part in repairing this aircraft, 'which had been damaged at Santa Cruz during the recent revolution'. This aircraft is known to have operated with this marking as late as 2 Mar 50 and 'considerable progress' had been made by the USAF Mission to her repair by 3 Apr 50. The aircraft was not reported after 1952.
E.T.A.II	42-23790	C-47A-35-DL	9652	Departed the SAAD on 5 Apr 45. At time of acceptance had a total of 1,838hrs flight time. Some USAAF documents show, for some reason, the actual handover date as 18 or 29 Jan 46 at Kelly Field, TX, and that she departed Kelly for Bolivia on 4 Feb 46. Last reported in 1952. Sold to LAB between 1949 and 1950 to finance the acquisition of the first F-47D and F-51Ds.
E.T.A.III	43-30688	C-47A-DL	13839	Inexplicably, this aircraft was invariably cited in Lend-Lease and MAB (Air) documents as 42-30688 (which was a B-17F). Departed the SAAD on 5 Apr 45. Total time at handover 1,923hrs. Apparently survived to become TAM-03 (q.v.).
E.T.A.IV	43-48060	C-47A-30-DK	13876/25321	Had been flown to Kelly Field, TX, after selection for Lend-Lease offset to Bolivia on 29 Jan 45. Departed the SAAD on 5 Apr 45. At time of acceptance, total time was 606hrs, thus the 'newest' of the first four FAB Lend-Lease C-47s. Oddly, the 'official' handover date for this aircraft is shown in some USAAF documents as 4 Feb 46. This was very probably the FAB aircraft that forced-landed in inaccessible territory during the September 1949 revolution, as she was officially reclaimed on 2 Mar 50, although one source suggests she survived until 1956.
E.T.A.??	BuA4695 NC-41075	R4D-1	4302	This aircraft was issued US State Department Clearance to depart Kelly Field, TX, bound for the FAB between 10 and 15 Mar 47, and was positively identified as 'R4D-1 serial number 4695' at the time. The problem is, there was no such Navy BuA number for an R4D-1 and MSN 4695 was a USAAF C-47-DL. It had served exclusively within the CONUS during the Second World War and was sold via the RFC on 3 Oct 45, and is known to have gone to Canada as CF-BXZ. CF-BXZ was registered 5 Oct 45 and was known written off on 22 Mar 52, so this seems to eliminate this as a concrete connection. There is no known E.T.A. number associated with this aircraft. In a subsequent document found in RG59 at NARA, dated 11 Mar 47, the aircraft was identified as MSN 4302 and 'marked as 4695', and was again noted as due to depart for Bolivia between 10 and 15 Mar 47.
E.T.A.V	(41-38694) BuA37662 NC-67809	(C-47-DL) R4D-1	6153	Delivered on 6 Feb 48 after purchase from The Charles Babb Co. This may have been the C-47 that was lost in Sep 49 during the civil war.
E.T.A.VI	43-15775 NC-54090	C-47A-90-DL	20241	Delivered on 6 Feb 48. This aircraft received US State Department Clearance to depart Kelly Field, TX, fully marked with FAB markings as '6' this date. Apparently became TAM-06.

TAM's fleet was discretely but rather intensively engaged in supporting the war against narco-traffickers. Here, one of its aircraft, which has had her national roundels and TAM codes scrubbed off, receives attention from maintainers at Trinidad airport in 1986. The 'T' antenna over the cockpit roof is non-standard, but the small TAM unit badges can still just be seen on either side of her nose. *Dave Schad*

E.T.A.VII	*42-23524*	*C-47A-20-DL*	*9386*	Most sources have this former Twelfth Air Force aircraft as having been salvaged in Italy in late Oct 44. However, several USAF documents make note of this MSN in relation to the FAB. Delivered on 6 Feb 48. This aircraft received US State Department Clearance to depart Kelly Field, TX, fully marked with FAB markings as '7' this date. This aircraft crashed at 1510hrs on 26 Mar 1951, shortly after take-off from Cochabamba. Her pilot, 1ºTte Manuel Isidoro Belzu Muñoz, was killed when pieces of the prop from the port engine shattered on impact with the ground and came through the cockpit. Dr Luis Ponce Caballero, who was for some reason seated at the radio operator's position, sustained fatal wounds from the same cause. He had been the contract surgeon at BAM 1 El Alto. The aircraft had a load of about twenty-seven passengers at the time – an overload for a C-47 operating at 8,500ft above sea level.
E.T.A.VIII	–	–	–	Delivered on 6 Feb 48. This aircraft received US State Department Clearance to depart Kelly Field, TX, fully marked with FAB markings as '8' this date. However, the aircraft with the MSN usually cited in most sources (9996) has always been reported to have been diverted to Czechoslovakia after the war as OK-WCO with CSA. The aircraft marked as E.T.A.VIII is known to have been written off on 26 Mar 51 in any event.
E.T.A.IX (or 9)	42-100773	C-47A-70-DL	19236	A Second World War Eighth Air Force veteran, this aircraft has often been linked with Aerovias Q in Cuba as CU-T5 post-war, but this must be in error, as USAF documents and State Department Clearances for Bolivia are quite explicit. This aircraft received US State Department Clearance to depart Kelly Field, TX, fully marked with FAB markings as '9' on 6 Feb 48 but is once again cited on 12 Sep 49. It later became CB-65 with the Corporación Minera de Bolivia as CB-65 around September 1953, which seems to confirm the Bolivian connection, as the Bolivian DGAC lists CB-65 as having formerly been CU-T5. The USAF Mission was engaged in repairs to this aircraft at Trinidad by 3 Apr 50. She was not reported after 1952 and was apparently sold to COMIBOL that year as CB-65, later CP-565 with BOA.
E.T.A.X (or 10)	42-23315 BuA12405	(C-47A-1-DL) R4D-5	9177	Delivered on 16 Sep 49, US State Department Clearance granted on 19 Sep 49. Had served during the Second World War with the US Marines. Reported lost on 21 Jan 50 en route Vallegrande to CBB with four crew and twenty-eight troops on board. Fatal to one of the troopers.
E.T.A.XI (or 11)	42-24415	C-47-DL	13786	A Second World War Fifth Air Force veteran, this aircraft has always been reported as salvaged in Australia on 24 Feb 45. However, the RG59 records at NARA clearly report her as 'Serial 13786'. Delivered on 26 Sep 49 and US State Department Clearance granted on 28 Sep 49.
E.T.A.XII (or 12)	42-24266 NC-54450	C-47A-40-DL DC-3C-S4C4G	10128	A veteran of the North African campaign during the Second World War, this aircraft was sold surplus via the RFC on 29 Oct 45 and then apparently acquired by the Bolivian Army Purchasing Commission from a US dealer, AAXICO at Miami (along with two others)m *c.*October 1949 (see candidates TAM-10 and TAM-11 above). Delivered *c.*11 Oct 49 and US State Department Clearance granted the day before. This aircraft, by 17 Jan 52, had been marked as E.T.A.12 and served as escort aircraft to twelve refurbished North American T-6Gs being ferried to Bolivia, piloted during the trip by LTC M. Quick and Capt. E. Fox, members of the USAF Mission to Bolivia at the time.

Following the 1949 revolution, the surviving FAB C-47 fleet clearly entered into a period when the originally assigned E.T.A. serials were either converted to Arabic numerals or were shuffled and reassigned, surviving records leaving this unclear. By 6 November 1949, FAB agents in the US had located three C-47s in 'as is' condition and these were hastily acquired and rushed to Bolivia, momentarily bringing the total FAB C-47 fleet back to a total of eleven, three of which were reported as 'badly damaged but flyable, due to the recent revolution'. Having witnessed the impact of a solitary P-38L on the rebels during the revolution, the FAB leadership was actively considering selling four of their C-47s to LAB to acquire a surplus F-47D and two or three F-51s in the US, as well as one properly reconditioned C-47 from the same source. Coincident with this proposed deal, the actual qualified

pilot strength of the E.T.A. had fallen by three, when two pilots transferred to LAB and another resigned his commission outright. By 6 December 1949, the US Air Attaché reported that the FAB was on the verge of the LAB sale and, perhaps to no one's surprise, this was to have comprised the 'four oldest' aircraft, probably the surviving Lend-Lease aircraft and one of the first privately acquired examples. As existing Bolivian civil registry and LAB records do not corroborate that this sale ever took place, cooler heads apparently prevailed, and LAB probably concluded that, in spite of local political pressures, it really didn't need worn out, bullet-riddled aircraft when it could acquire fairly well kitted out passenger aircraft on the US second-hand market instead. By 6 January 1950, the US Air Attaché reported that the proposed sale had still not taken place and 'was in doubt'.

Taken the same day as the preceding image at Trinidad in 1986, the C-47 at left was being operated on anti-drug trafficking operations by a mixed DEA and FAB crew sans markings other than the rather colourful trim. A DEA Sikorsky UH-60 runs up in the foreground. Note the crowd of locals being entertained by the activity in the background. *Dave Schad*

In the aftermath of the 1949 revolution, at least 200 former Ejército and FAB officers, including some of its best-trained airmen, were still confined and many had been summarily discharged from the Bolivian military establishment. However, this only added to the substantial group of malcontents in the country, and after its surprising showing during the revolution, the FAB had rapidly deteriorated to what a US intelligence report (IR-48-49) described as a 'very low point'. Morale was described as universally bad, and many officers and pilots were not even reporting to their assigned duty stations. The only bright spot was at BAM Santa Cruz, where the considerable number of assorted training aircraft, many recovered with damage from the rebels, under the command of Coronel Alarcón, had resumed cadet training. Some thirty-eight bewildered cadets had been transferred there from the Colegio Militar and had been enrolled in primary training. The faculty was contending with a shortage of fuel, serviceable aircraft and spare parts in the face of all of this, and the barracks provided for the cadets was described as 'extremely bad'. Patterned after USAF primary training, at the urging of the USAF Mission, which had been striving to remain neutral through all of this, it had failed to meet the standards that had been set down and eight of the thirty-eight were washed out in short order. The 'New' C-47 that had been acquired along with at least one additional example of the P-38 and the F-47D, and the much-anticipated F-51Ds, were all out of commission for parts.

The next known substantive report was Periodic Aviation Report (PAR) No. 648976 for 7 January 1950, which showed the FAB with a total of nine C-47s, of which two were inoperable. This appears to agree with the foregoing table, and suggests that, besides E.T.A.IV, at least two others had been lost to unknown causes. It should be noted that, for weeks at a time during this tumultuous period, every single C-47 was grounded for one reason or another. Then, around 2 May 1950, possibly as a direct consequence, the USAF suddenly assigned three C-47D aircraft (43-15688, 43-48301 and 43-48402) to its Mission in Bolivia. Clearly intended for transfer to the FAB, the crisis demands of the first months of the Korean War intervened instead and by 15 October 1950, 43-48301 was in Japan and the other two had returned to the US. PAR No. 692654, dated 1 July 1950, reflected a total of nine C-47s, confirming that these transfers never occurred, but noted that by then that of that total, three were inoperable due to required engine changes but that one other that had crash landed (undoubtedly E.T.A.I) was 'being repaired'.

Between 21 August and the end of November 1951, with the assistance of the USAF Mission, the FAB attempted to get its inventory into shape, and submitted a detailed request for military assistance under OSD/OMA Case Number Bolivia-6. This was a very ambitious request and included justification for the supply of no fewer than ten C-47s, as well as for a lengthy list of spares for the seven aircraft then on hand. It also included justification for fifteen Boeing-Stearman PT-17s, twenty-five more T-6Gs (plus spares for a mixed bag of twenty-five Lend-Lease-supplied AT-6s then still on hand). The Office of Military Assistance replied that no PT-17s, T-6Gs or C-47s were available at the time, probably because of the demands of the Korean conflict.

All of this was exacerbated by the reorganisation of the FAB transport element sometime between 15 February and 15 November 1952, when the Escuadrón de Transportes Aéreos became the Transportes Aéreos Militares (TAM). By 15 February, the E.T.A. could count a total of seven C-47s on its strength, indicating that significant attrition had occurred since 1950. By the time the unit had become TAM on 15 November, it still had seven C-47s, all assigned to what had by then been designated as BAM No. 1 El Alto, but, of these, only four were rated as 'combat ready'. What is not clear, unfortunately, is what happened with the former E.T.A. serials between I and XII at this point. While logic would dictate a simple adaptation to the 'new' TAM serials, one for one, the losses that had taken place to this point, reducing the total received from at least twelve to seven, mitigated against this.

The TAM inventory fluctuated rather drastically from one period to the next, and attrition, in the rugged operating conditions prevailing at the time in Bolivia, took a higher than average toll. By 30 June 1954, a total of seven aircraft were reported in the inventory. The service did acquire a reconditioned C-47 around 11 October 1954, from the American Aeronautics Corporation (Gordon D. Strube) in California, as noted, along with three F-51Ds. The total FAB Air Order of Battle for the period 12 July to 31 December 1954, however, shows a total of only six, indicating that one had been lost to some cause, probably the unidentified TAM aircraft that had crashed and burned on take-off from Santa Cruz in December. Of these, however, the US report stated that only four were 'combat ready' by USAF standards.

The FAB Air Order of Battle for 1 January 11955, reflected a total of just six C-47s, of which four were rated 'combat ready', all assigned to El Alto along with a single Beech C-45 and two converted AT-11s that may well have worn TAM numbers at the time, and which may account for some of the 'missing' codes. USAF Intelligence Report IR-23-55, dated 18 April 1955, however, provided a detailed 'snapshot' of the fleet as of that date. It reported a decrease of two and an increase of one (one had been lost due to a crash in the preceding three-month period and a second had been cannibalised for parts). It also observed that 'the FAB was able to purchase a plush DC-3 from PANAGRA, which gives the President two plush "VIP" aircraft, both of which are kept in immaculate condition. It has been rumoured that the President holds both aircraft

This Basler BT-67/PT-6, still bearing US registration N387T, is shown preparing for a test flight at Oshkosh, Wisconsin, in August 1991, although most sources claim she was delivered to Bolivia on 3 July. She became TAM-38 and was formally described on her FAA registration as type DC-3-G202A, MSN 20507. The Vietnam-era camouflage is unique on a Bolivian C-47-series aircraft. *Larry Wilson*

TAM-38 in country after delivery, by which time the tropical operating environment had already taken a toll on her pristine camouflage seen in the previous image. She experienced some form of accident between November 1994 and September 1997 and was noted derelict at Santa Cruz. Note the unusual placement of small-size roundels on both the fuselage and under-wing extremities. *George G.J. Kamp*

in readiness at any given moment, in the event of any sudden rupture within the government that might require his departure from the country. It is doubtful that this is really the case, however, as the airport is relatively inaccessible from the city and its single road access would preclude a forceful escape attempt.' Between 1 July and 31 December 1955, however, the total on hand had risen to nine. By the end of 1955, TAM and the by then nationalised LAB were, for all intents and purposes, both conducting commercial operations on behalf of the government. Besides its tacit mission of support to the Army, TAM was charged with providing what amounted to commercial service to locations where regular air lines did not operate. The relationship between the two was described by one observer at the time as 'exceptionally close' and, in fact, the Director General of Civil Aviation in the country at the time was a serving FAB officer, Coronel Edmundo Vaca. The Commanding Officer of TAM at the same time was Mayor Walter Coronel C.

A similar report for the first six months of 1956 reflected a total of seven but noted that TAM-09 had suffered a serious accident in January 1956 and that TAM-03 had sustained extensive damage at Cochabamba in May. TAM purchased an unidentified C-47 in October 1956, possibly under the provisions of Military Sales Case OPC/Bolivia-15 dated 31 July 1956 (which had actually requested two aircraft), probably as an attrition replacement using insurance proceeds, so that by the end of the year strength had risen once again to a total of eight – six in pure cargo configuration and two outfitted for passengers. By 30 June 1957, the total on hand had dropped once again to seven, while by the end of June 1958, the total was six, suggesting at least two additional losses.

The difficulties in researching Bolivian use of assorted DC-3s and C-47s, especially during the turbulent decade of the 1950s, may best be illustrated by the little-known adventures of one Sr Bernandini, commencing, as it were, with a Boeing B-17F, CP-633.

CP-633 was the subject of scrutiny by the US State Department and, as of 10 June 1957 was located at Limatambo Field in Lima, Peru, just north of the CORPAC terminal there with one engine missing.

The USAF Attaché in Lima had learned that this aircraft had somehow been acquired by Bernandini in connection with his RAPSA enterprise, which had essentially gone broke during 1956. Somehow, the Bolivian Government had been convinced to advance some $500,000 to Sr Bernandini for the purchase of this aircraft – sight unseen – as well as some spare parts. Those parts, cited by the Attaché as 'a bunch of junk', had been purchased in the US and

diverted to Bolivia after the bankruptcy of RAPSA. Bernandini alleged to have secured contracts in Lima with two men, one a pilot and the other a mechanic, to whom he advanced $1,000 each, and who were to deliver and operate the B-17F in Bolivia. Bernandini forwarded copies of these contracts to the Bolivian Government with the request that he be advanced an additional $100,000 to 'put the aircraft in condition'. Incredibly, the Government complied, with the understanding that this final sum was all that was required to finally complete delivery and ownership of the B-17F.

Unfortunately, unbeknownst to the Bolivians, Bernandini had quite a few judgments against the aircraft (including claims from the Peruvian Customs authorities, CORPAC, various former employees and the shipper of the spares), the sum total of which exceeded the value of the aircraft!

In the midst of all of this, and finally getting to our story, upon learning of these realities, the Bolivian Government immediately seized an unidentified C-47 ostensibly owned by Bernandini, which he was using in connection with the IXIMAS colonisation project in Bolivia, but which has escaped identification. The aircraft was immediately pressed into service with TAM – but was promptly wrecked. Because associated insurance matters remained open, the insurer, incredibly, was ready to compensate Bernandini for his loss, but the Government learned of the manoeuvre – and that Bernandini also owned an interest in a Fairchild C-82 that was idle at Limatambo, and the Government eyed this as a potential asset worth seizing. It, too, had sat idle for some months, had been unable to obtain a Peruvian registration or flight permit, and was subject to Customs duties, and charges from CORPAC and others. By the end of June, perhaps to no one's surprise, Bernandini was reported 'jailed in the North'.

Thus, after all of this, we have yet another C-47 that was clearly operated by TAM but for which no identity can be suggested. It is unknown whether the aircraft was operated with her civil identity or a TAM serial and titles.

After this and similar subterfuges, probably the low point in Bolivian C-47 strength came around 29 July 1958, when only six C-47s and DC-3s were reported on strength and active. However, that same year, the first post-Second World War group of FAB officers departed for the newly reconstituted USAF School of the Americas at Albrook AFB, CZ, and the results proved to be a boon to the service in the years that followed and more attended. An unidentified C-47 was acquired by 30 November 1961 from Fraibert and Firm, Inc., Douglas, Arizona.

A USAF Statistical Digest for Fiscal year 1962 reported that the FAB acquired two C-47s under MDAP as of 30 September 1961 under Grant Aid provisions but, and that these had been received by 31 March 1962, these apparently having become TAM-15 and TAM-16, as reflected in the table that follows.

By 31 December 1963, the USAF was describing TAM, for some reason, as the Escuadrón de Transporte, and stated that the unit had ten 'C-47Ds', although this is probably a simplification of a much more diverse fleet. It stated that no fewer than fourteen C-47s had been programmed for the FAB under the provisions of MAP but that only four of these had actually been delivered as of December 1963, one of the four having arrived on 11 July 1963. These had joined the operating unit, alongside six that had been acquired by the service independently.

The US made good on part of its promised MAP deliveries in April 1964, when four more C-47Ds were delivered.[21] Between July and September 1964, intelligence data showed the FAB with a total of thirteen C-47s programmed for supply under MAP, all of which had been received by that date, and that the service also possessed five others that it had acquired independently and that the total number of flight hours for the fleet during that period was a quite respectable average of 1,201:35 hours. The operating unit had twenty-two crews assigned, certainly one of its highest ratios ever, and was fully rated as 'C-1' (Combat Ready) by the USAF Mission, a rarely awarded rating in Latin America, and the solitary FAB unit at the time so rated. The hard-working Mission had arranged the overhaul of six spare engines for the C-47s at the San Antonio Air Materiel Area (SAAMA) in San Antonio, Texas, and additional spare engines procured had started to arrive from commercial sources. The Mission also rated the unit's maintenance at the time as 'excellent'. It also reported an extraordinary achievement: on 5 August 1964, 154 paratroopers (including six women) were dropped from nine of the unit's aircraft at El Alto without injury. This was believed to have been the largest Latin American paratroop drop ever made to that time. These achievements were blemished between October and December 1964 when Bolivia once again succumbed to an internal revolution, although the C-47 unit was used effectively by the government to transport troops throughout the country to 'hotspots'. The USAF Mission reported that, subsequently, between January and March 1965, C-47 operations had increased 'noticeably' after the hostilities ended and the unit amassed some 990:15 hours of flight time as a result during that quarter. Then, by the third quarter of Fiscal Year 1966 (which would have actually have been in 1965), two more examples were added as Military Assistance Sales procured.

Between July and December 1967, the FAB attained what was probably its peak C-47 strength, when a total of seventeen had been received, but of which only nine were actually still in service, one having been lost through attrition and the other eight 'in the inventory' but inactive. Of these, remarkably, at least thirteen had been MAP supported for parts. By the end of 1967, however, the total had increased to eighteen, reflecting that an additional machine had arrived from somewhere. However, by 30 September 1968, while seventeen C-47s (with thirty rated crews) were still on strength, the unit's combat rating had dropped to C-3 due to the low in-commission rate.

The 8 January 1969 AOB showed a total of eighteen C-47s having been received, of which seventeen were still possessed, and one lost, probably TAM-14, which had been reported written off on 26 April 1969 and was a non-MAP supported aircraft. Of these, twelve were MAP supplied or supported, alongside five acquired independently by Bolivia. It noted that, while these provided a modest payload in lowland areas of the country, in the mountains their capability was 'very limited', but that the FAB was still investing in the aircraft, having purchased some $10,000 worth of spares for their non-MAP supported aircraft. The AOB for 30 June 1969 showed sixteen 'C-47Ds' but also noted that, of these, no more than ten were ever operable at any one time, and that many were often without both engines. This was because the extreme operating altitude of most of the FAB C-47 fleet necessitated engine changes every 800 flying hours, instead of the normal 1,400 hours that was routine nearly everywhere else. The FAB engine shop could only overhaul two engines per month and, as a direct consequence, simply could not keep up with the demand. As a direct consequence of this, the USAF Mission commenced urging the FAB to reduce the number of C-47s in its inventory, reasoning that a total of ten would meet any conceivable demand on the service.

By 31 December 1969, the USAF reported that the FAB to that date had been programmed to receive twelve C-47Ds but had, by some means of accounting, concluded that Bolivia had actually acquired a total of twenty-one assorted C-47s to that point, of which nineteen were still in the inventory. Of these, sixteen were active, three others inactive for various reasons, two had been lost, and ten were MAP-supported. It also noted that, of the MAP-supported aircraft, three were not economically repairable and that the USAF Mission was waiting for disposition instructions. These were subsequently disposed of in country, probably as hulks for spares as noted in the accompanying table.

Then, due to the political situation in Bolivia, US MAP assistance was suspended between January and March 1970, bringing spares

Right: Her solitary concession to operator identity of Basler BT-67/PT-6 TAM-38 is evidenced by this unidentified unit logo on either side of her nose. *George G.J. Kamp*

Below: Another view of TAM-38 showing her round fuselage windows and the rear aspect of the PT-6 engine exhausts. *George G.J. Kamp*

and parts that had been requisitioned to support the C-47 fleet to a screeching halt. This resulted in an almost immediate crisis for R-1830 engine parts and the engine shop had no fewer than twenty-five engines awaiting work, with no parts to support the work and, within days, the number of airworthy C-47s had plummeted to just two aircraft. The FAB took a more expeditious alternative and ordered ten 'new' R-1830 engines from a commercial firm in California, and then audaciously requested that the USAF arrange to transport them to Bolivia via MATS aircraft! By 30 June 1970, the USAF reported that TAM had fifteen 'C-47Ds', but only nine trained crews for them, as well as two Curtiss C-46Ds, but that the in-commission rate of the C-47s at any one time was low, with only an average of a rather dismal three aircraft. In the midst of all of this, a former USAF 24th Special Operations Wing C-47D, 43-48912, was apparently delivered to Bolivia under MAP around 2 November 1970.

The period between 1971 and 1975 is poorly documented, but MAP documents reported that the FAB possessed at least nineteen C-47s during this period, although serviceability was not described. In late July 1974, however, the FAB toyed with the idea of purchasing the one and only Conroy Turbo-Three DC-3, N4700C (MSN 4903) and at least one enthusiast publication has claimed that it was in fact purchased to become 'Air Force One' for the service around that date, but this has completely eluded verification.

At least one scholarly publication suggested that Bolivia acquired six surplus C-47s from Taiwan, of all places, in 1979, but this has also reportedly been confused with Curtiss C-46s, and the report does not appear to be credible.

By August 1987, the FAB transport element had all been consolidated under Brigada Aérea 1 as the Grupo Aéreo de Transporte 71 although it continued to operate under the TAM logo and, besides seven rather weary assorted C-47s, the unit by then had added a Lockheed C-130H, an L-100-30, six Fokker F-27s, four Convair CV-440s, four IAI-201 Aravas and a number of Pilatus PC-6 Turbo Porters.

We thus arrive at the point where an accounting of the known TAM numbers and associated deliveries is in order. The following table reflects known, confirmed links but also a few assumptions based on circumstantial data, and these are italicised for emphasis.

TAM Number	Previous Identity	Built As	MSN	Assignments and Notes
'TAM-00'				A C-47 empennage with this obviously fictitious serial code was noted being used as a gate guard at El Alto by 22 Sep 94.
TAM-01	NC-17319 42-57512 NC-17319	DC-3B-202 C-84 DC-3B-202	1934	Clearly a retrospective serial, this aircraft did not join the FAB until around March 1954 and, if the same aircraft, was last noted at El Alto on 14 Apr 72. It appears likely that she served as the escort aircraft for the first F-51D Mustangs acquired by the FAB in California in 1954. She was also the first Bolivian Presidential aircraft and apparently had a VIP interior at first. The remains of this aircraft were noted at El Alto in May 82 after the failure of her undercarriage on take-off, and only the wings remained by 21 Sep 97. This should not be confused with a similarly marked aircraft placed on semi-permanent display at El Alto by 22 Sep 94, the actual identity of which is unknown. Aviation historian John M. Davis has suggested she was in fact MSN 11774, formerly Panagra NC-30091. One source claims that this was the Presidential aircraft, with a VIP interior at one point.
TAM-02	*42-24186 N2883D*	C-47A-50-DL	*10048*	FAA records suggest that this aircraft may have gone to TAM sometime after 1 Nov 47. However, Second World War Ninth Air Force veterans USAAF records seem to suggest she was salvaged in Europe after the war. Other reports strongly suggest that this serial was not issued until the mid-1950s and she was reported in service possibly by 1956 and certainly by 24 Jan 58. In any event, an aircraft with this marking (TAM-02) was noted partially dismantled and derelict at El Alto in January 1981 in very poor condition. While often speculated to have formerly been E.T.A.II, this has not been concretely established.
TAM-03	43-30688 (43-15614) (NC-60819) (NC-50034)	C-47A-DL (C-47A-85-DL)	20080	FAA records definitely indicate that this aircraft was sold to TAM, however, insurance data also strongly suggests that it was in fact the former E.T.A.III, a Lend-Lease aircraft as shown above. The first report for the aircraft as TAM-03 is in Air-Britain, which gives Jun 48. This aircraft suffered extensive damage in a belly landing at Cochabamba in May 56 and is reported to have sustained yet another undocumented accident on 9 Sep 57. However, an aircraft with this serial (TAM-03) was reported missing while being flown by Capitán Luis Perdriel Peña, somewhere en route from Bermejo to Tarija, north of Villa Montes on 15 Oct 58 around 1730hrs, suggesting that either the accident at Cochabamba was recoverable or that the serial was reissued to another aircraft. The remains of the aircraft were found on 23 Oct 58 north of Villa Montes.
TAM-04	'42-9386'	–	–	This aircraft reportedly disappeared on a twenty-five-minute flight between Tipurni and El Alto on 20 Jan 58 (also reported as 2 Jan 58) with a crew of four, headed by Capitán Luis H. Pinto and six passengers. The previous USAAF identity cited is a non-starter, even though Lloyd's of London show this as the serial as given and cited by the FAB in its claim – but it is also the same MSN they quoted for TAM-11! The aircraft was found around 15 Jun 58 by another TAM C-47 that was inbound to La Paz in the mountains at Huayna Potosí. It was at an altitude of some 16,000ft on the peak of 'El Centinela', partially buried in the snow, and the remains indicated that it had burned after impact. A party was dispatched to recover the remains on 16 Jun 58.
TAM-05	–	–	–	This aircraft went missing on a flight between San Borja and El Alto on 8 Nov 58. It had departed San Borja for El Alto that date with a load of 2,000kg of beef plus a three-man crew and three passengers. Overcast and low ceiling in the area hampered the extensive search and rescue efforts. The crew consisted of 1ºTte Carlos Milton Morales, co-pilot 2ºTte Luis Robles and radio operator Sgto Luis Burgos. This was the third TAM C-47 lost during 1958.

TAM-06	43-15775 NC-54090 E.T.A.VI	C-47A-90-DL	20241	Written off on Tuesday, 26 Aug 52 after an aborted take-off from El Alto with a crew of three and twenty passengers, all of whom miraculously survived without injury. The starboard main tyre had blown out just as the aircraft became airborne, which somehow resulted in the starboard engine being sheared completely off the aircraft. After departing the aircraft, it then was seen to cartwheel alongside the aircraft as it crossed over, then hitting the port propeller and finally cutting a deep gash in the skin of the aircraft just forward of the empennage. A fire in the port engine was extinguished, or the result may have been catastrophic. However, Jonathan Olguin reports that an aircraft with serial TAM-06 was still in the inventory as late as 4 Feb 63, having been taken up in 1956, raising the possibility that this serial was used twice.
TAM-07	–	–	*13371*	Apparently taken up in 1956. Written off on 4 Jul 66 at Rio Orton while en route from Riberalta to Cobija, thirteen killed.
TAM-08	*42-93457* *KG612* *PP-JAD* *PP-YPW*	*C-47A-25-DK* *Dakota III*	*13371*	This aircraft appears to have been acquired by TAM from REAL in Brazil sometime after August 1949. The former PP-YPW was registered in Bolivia as CP-680 15 Jan 60, however.
TAM-09	42-32804 NC-50041	C-47-DL	9030	Nosed up on landing at Madrid in January 1956 and was thought at the time to be a possible write-off but was apparently recovered and repaired. Crashed 15 miles from Tipuani on 1 Aug 60 while being flown by Capitanes Hugo Sanzatena and Juan Lampo with Crew Chief Sub.Ofc. Mario Arnez Camacho, all fatal.
TAM-10	*42-23314* *NC-79033*	*C-47A-1-DL* *DC-3C-S4C4G*	*9176*	Purchased from AAXICO on 29 Nov 49, the type was also cited on some CAA documents as 'DC-3C-R1830-90D'.
TAM-11	*42-93786* *NC-57673*	*C-47A-25-DK* *DC-3C-S4C4G*	*13736*	It has been suggested that this was an ex-Força Aérea Brasileira (FAB) aircraft, but this seems most unlikely. It appears it was, instead, one of three aircraft acquired by the FAB from AAXICO on 29 Nov 49. She was granted a Permission to Overfly Brazilian territory in September 1959, however. She crashed near Laja, Bolivia, about 10km from La Paz on either 2 or 12 Feb 70 and was destroyed by fire. The crew of four and one passenger survived.
TAM-12	43-48186 KG770 0-348186	C-47A-30-DK Dakota III C-47D	14002/25447	Apparently, a MAP delivery 17 Mar 64. This aircraft was written off on 23 Sep 64 although Jonathan Olguin cites 1 Sep 75 at La Paz.
(TAM-13)	–	–	–	Although this serial has been cited in several enthusiast publications, there is no evidence whatsoever that it was actually used and Jonathan Olguin states it was definitely not used due to reasons of superstition.
TAM-14	41-18477 NC-88772 PP-YPL	C-47-DL	4569	Reportedly acquired after this aircraft had suffered an accident at Londrina, Paraná, Brazil on 15 Apr 58 and was reported as damaged beyond repair. The USAF Mission reported that this aircraft was written off on 26 Apr 69 north-east of Huayna Potosi while being flown by Mayor Carlos Carrasco, Capt. Gastón Quiroga, Tte Porfirio Salazar and Sub.Ofc. Aroldo Belar with fourteen passengers, fatal to all on board. However, an aircraft with this serial was noted in service at El Alto on 21 Nov 73 and she was reportedly still in service as late as 1976, suggesting that the serial was reissued to a second unknown aircraft
TAM-15	43-49543 3-49543 0-49543	C-47B-15-DK C-47D	15359/26804	MAP supplied on 2 Oct 61. This aircraft was reported derelict at El Alto as of September 1975 and as late as October 1977, when she was noted all-natural metal but with blue cheatlines. She is also reported to have gone to civil marks CP-1417 with Aerolíneas La Paz by 1 May 78, yet another instance of the resilience of Bolivian aircraft.
TAM-16	43-49405 0-49405	C-47B-15-DK C-47D	15221/26666	MAP supplied on 2 Oct 61 and was still active by Nov 74. She was derelict and being cannibalised by January 1981 and has been suggested as the source for the gate guard marked as 'TAM-01' (q.v.).
TAM-17	42-100710 0-00710 0-21710 0-2100710 N86458	C-47A-70-DL C-47D	19173	This aircraft had entered service by 1964–65 and was one of five TAM C-47s engaged in flying beef from Bolivia to Porto Velho, Rondônia, Brazil, during that time frame, but had been withdrawn from use and was engineless at El Alto by January 1981 as the result of an accident on 14 Jul 70, when she had been described as damaged beyond repair. Curiously, she was also reported as wrecked at El Alto in May 1982, suggesting she had been resurrected. Finally, she is reported to have been sold to Basler by 1993 for conversion as N46BF on behalf of the Air Force of Mali as TZ-390.
TAM-18	*44-76656* *0-76656*	*C-47B-30-DK* *C-47D*	*16240/32988*	The aircraft shown at left as a candidate was apparently acquired by the FAB/TAM via FMS via the Miami LOG AINMF on 21 June 1963, but has not been positively linked to TAM-18 or, indeed, TAM. An aircraft coded TAM-18 had entered service by 1964–65 and was one of the five TAM C-47s engaged in flying beef from Bolivia to Porto Velho, Rondônia, Brazil, during that time frame, and was reported still active at Ñancahuazú in 1967, at El Alto on 27 Nov 72 and as late as 1976. If this was in fact MSN 16240/32988, she became CP-1419 by Jan 81.
TAM-19	44-76657 0-76657	C-47B-30-DK C-47D	16241/32989	MAP supplied on 8 Jun 73, strongly suggesting this as the second use of this serial. There are no spotting reports for this serial, and the USAAF serial has also been reported, believed erroneously, as '44-77657', but that was a Curtiss C-46D.
TAM-20	43-48412 0-48412	C-47B-1-DK C-47D	14228/25673	MAP supplied on 6 Feb 64. Noted derelict (fuselage only) at El Alto by November 1974 and still there by 22 Sep 94. However, in October 1994 the remains were sold, reportedly to Capitán Dicky Chávez. However, her remains were still noted at El Alto in basic TAM colours by 8 Dec 94, suggesting she was acquired for parts only. Stricken from the inventory on 1 Jan 97.

Above: The end of a long road for this former TAM DC-3, the identity of which is unknown, reveals that she had been adorned on her vertical fin with the insignia of some unknown Bolivian unit by the time of this December 1994 photograph. *George G.J. Kamp*

Above right: Also out to pasture was TAM-20, a MAP-supplied C-47D that had been taken up in early February 1964. Devoid by the time of this December 1994 photo of many parts, she was not officially stricken from the inventory until 1 January 1997! *George G.J. Kamp*

Right: A sad line-up for DC-3 and C-47 enthusiasts, this December 1994 view reveals the last resting place for at least seven former TAM aircraft. The only ones that can be positively identified are TAM-20 and TAM-35. *George G.J. Kamp*

TAM-21	–	–	–	The remains of this aircraft were noted as dismantled by January 1981 at El Alto.
TAM-22	–	–	–	This aircraft was reported in service as early as 1 Jan 64 and was one of five TAM C-47s flying beef from Bolivia to Porto Velho, Rondônia, Brazil, around that time. She is also reported as having been written off after take-off from El Alto on 4 May 71, crashing on gravel at Río Seco, about one mile from the field with two crew and one passenger.
TAM-23	–	–	–	This aircraft was reported wrecked near El Alto on 28 Sep 72 and was noted dismantled there by Jan 81.
TAM-24	42-23345 E.T.A.I	C-47A-1-DL	9207	If this identity is correct, this was the first C-47 acquired by the FAB in January 1945, although Air-Britain gives her delivery or acquisition date as 28 Feb 46. She was one of five TAM C-47s engaged in flying beef from Bolivia to Porto Velho, Rondônia, Brazil, in 1964–65. She was reportedly named 'Lobito' at some point, possibly during 1964, and was written off at Caranavi on 25 Sep 72 with a crew of two on board, both of whom survived, although her fuselage was noted at El Alto in Jan 81.
TAM-25	44-76294 0-76294	C-47B-28-DK VC-47B C-47B VC-47B VC-47D VC-47B C-47B	15878/32626	MAP supplied on 19 Mar 64, having been reconditioned by Air International around 16 Mar 64 at Miami. She was noted at Campo Grande, Mato Grosso do Sul, Brazil, on 24 Apr 79. She was noted withdrawn from use by Jan 81 and May 1982. However, an aircraft with this serial was noted withdrawn from use with no engines at Cochabamba on 18 Apr 91. Thus, she may have been returned to service after May 82 and subsequently withdrawn a second time. She was reportedly sold to Capitán Dicky Chávez but was noted still in basic TAM colours at El Alto on 8 Dec 94, so was probably sold for parts. However, she was resurrected once again and became CP-2290 in Sep 97!
TAM-26	–	–	–	Reported in service by 1964–65 and one of the five TAM C-47s engaged in flying beef from Bolivia to Porto Velho, Rondônia, Brazil, during that time frame. She was noted withdrawn from service at Trinidad by 12 Dec 90 although Jonathan Olguin gives her strike date as 4 Jul 66, having been written off that date en route from Riberalta to Puerto Rico while under the command of Capt. Pastor Castro (fatal), Tte Carlos Jaldin and Sub.Ofcs. Juan Paco and Emilio Salazar, also fatal and ten troops (of whom six survived).
TAM-27	–	–	–	Reported active *c.*1975 and Sep 76.

Latin American military DC-3s and C-47s rarely flew in formation, but these three immaculate TAM aircraft over La Paz reveal markings variations. The two nearest aircraft both have the national roundel on the upper port wing, with 'FAB' on the upper starboard wing, while the farthest aircraft has no markings on her wings whatsoever! *FAB*

A statement of both the geographic grandeur and hazards of their operating environment, this TAM C-47 poses over the wilds of the Andes in complete service markings. *FAB*

TAM-28	44-77294 0-77294	C-47B-35-DK C-47D	16878/33626	MAP supplied on 17 Mar 64. Noted withdrawn from use and dismantled possibly as early as 3 Jun 78 but certainly by Jan 81 at El Alto.
TAM-29	–	–	–	Although reported by several enthusiast publications, no confirmed spotting reports have surfaced.
TAM-30	42-92151 FL599 LV-ACP T-12 (*FAA*)	C-47A-1-DK Dakota III DC-3C	11920	Donated to the FAB by Argentina on 12 Jul 69. Reportedly belly landed at Laja on 19 Jan 74 after departure from El Alto and its remains scrapped. She was apparently recovered, however, as she was noted at El Alto in Nov 74.
TAM-31	42-100881 LV-XFW T-48 (*FAA*) T-02 (*FAA*)	C-47A-75-DL DC-3C	19344	Donated to the FAB by Argentina on 12 Jun 69. Sold by Oct 94 (one source cites 1981) and became CP-1418 with Aerolíneas La Paz.
TAM-32	42-100932 LV-XFX T-26 (*FAA*)	C-47A-75-DL DC-3C	19395	Donated to the FAB by Argentina on 12 Jun 69. Was sold after 9 Feb 79, and was based at El Alto at the time, as CP-1470.
TAM-33	*42-100505*	*C-47A-65-DL*	*18968*	This aircraft has often been linked to Argentina as former FAA T-49 and T-02, but this has been found to be incorrect. First reported on 1 Aug 70 and still in service as late as 9 Feb 79 at El Alto. She was noted dismantled there by 21 May 82.
TAM-34	–	–	–	This aircraft reportedly crashed on a mountain at Sorata on 11 Nov 74 and suffered extensive damage while being flown by Capts Raúl Estrada and Jonás Olmos and Sub.Ofcs Julián Erquicia and Alfredo Llerna, all fatalities.
TAM-35	*43-48489*	*C-47B-1-DK*	*14305/25750*	If MSN is correct, was MAP supplied on 29 Feb 64 via AIIMF Miami. This serial was first reported on 7 Feb 79 at Santa Cruz and was active at Cochabamba the same month, but had been withdrawn from use by May 82, last noted at La Paz in Feb 85.
TAM-36	–	–	–	This aircraft was reported in service on 9 Feb 79 but noted withdrawn from use at Trinidad by 12 Dec 90.
TAM-37	–	–	–	First reported on 12 Dec 90, by 18 Apr 91 she was noted withdrawn from service at Trinidad.
TAM-38	43-16041 0-16041 N387T	(C-47A-90-DL) DC-3-G202 Basler BT-67/PT-6	20507 (Basler #8)	The last FAB aircraft in the C-47/DC-3 family acquired, this aircraft was delivered on 3 Jul 91 and was noted in service as late as 3 Nov 94. Her fuselage was noted at Santa Cruz by 19 Sep 97, however.
TAM-102	–	–	–	This aircraft has been repeatedly reported, as early as 1972 when she was said to be with the Grupo Aéreo de Transporte. Exactly why she was issued such an out of sequence serial remains a mystery. Her remains were sold to Capitán Dicky Chávez around 8 Dec 94, probably for parts.
(CP-583)	42-23806 PP-XAZ PP-LPE CB-83 CP-583	C-47A-35-DL	9668	This aircraft was last operated by Transportes Aéreos San Miguel as CP-583 around 1990 but was impounded at Trinidad, Bolivia, in December that year as a drug smuggler and stored in the FAB compound there. Thus, strictly speaking, she became FAB property, and may have been scavenged for certain items of equipment.

CHAPTER FOUR

Brazil

B Y FAR THE LARGEST and most geographically challenging of all Latin American nations, in retrospect it appears that the Douglas C-47 series was precisely the right aircraft at the right time for Brazil.

With a legitimate claim to being at the very forefront of the evolution of practical aeronautics, via her native son, Alberto Santos-Dumont, the huge and endlessly diverse country embraced aviation, civil and military, near the very beginning, and forward-thinking entrepreneurs and adventurers were quick to recognise that the 'aeroplane', at last, offered a means of exploring and serving the Portuguese-speaking reaches of an interior that had hitherto swallowed land and water-borne expeditions.

During the first two full decades of practical aviation in Brazil, the 1920s and '30s, most flying enterprises, whether civil, military or naval, were largely confined, however, to the two regions near the two major population centres, São Paulo and Rio de Janeiro, with a few others scattered among the lessor cities along her long coastline. Both the Army and Navy, however, acquired aircraft specifically for light transport, especially for the carriage of air mail, in which Brazil was a pioneer.

An excellent study of the pristine C-47 2009, the first C-47B for the FAB, after her factory-applied USAAF style camouflage had been removed. The Brazilian aircraft were distinctive in having two RDF 'bullets' atop their forward fuselages through most of the first two waves of Lend-Lease and ARP supplied aircraft. Although taxiing under power, her forward cargo door is cracked to aid ventilation when photographed at hot and humid Miami! *Harold G. Martin*

The primary influences between the wars came from France and Great Britain but, after the civil war of 1932, US and German interests arrived in force, and the former dalliance with French aeronautical equipment and philosophy came to a rather abrupt end, other than in the form of French and Italian-backed airline services, Aeropostale and LATI.

As what would become the Second World War loomed, the Brazil of dictator Getulio Vargas became adept at 'walking the fence' between the Fascist influences of Germany and Italy, and the growing regional influence of the post-depression United States, which viewed Brazil's large and influential German and Italian colonies with extreme suspicion, especially in the most powerful Brazilian state, São Paulo. After the fall of France, and feared German acquisition of former French assets in West Africa, the War Plans Division of the US War Department General Staff was consumed with the notion of a co-operative German and Italian leap across the relatively narrow South Atlantic to the 'hump' of Brazil, and thence through the virtually undefended reaches of the far north-eastern area of the mainland South American land mass to the vital Panama Canal itself. Vargas was acutely aware of this concern, and played it for all it was worth, both diplomatically and from a military standpoint. Had Germany, in particular, not been absorbed with other ambitions in Europe, and exercised a gambit in Brazil instead, the course of the war that followed and world history might well have been very different.

As a direct result of this, Brazil became one of the few Latin American nations to acquire relatively modern aircraft from the US under the terms of the brief predecessor of Lend-Lease, the Defence Aid Program. The few second-hand Curtiss P-36A fighters and Douglas B-18 bombers, drawn from USAAC units in Panama and the Caribbean, even though obsolescent by world standards at the time, were still superior to just about anything else Brazil had, aside from a number of nearly brand new Vultee V-11-GB and North American NA-72 (NA-44) attack aircraft. Although these were supplemented by ground forces and naval equipment as well, they appear to have turned Vargas at precisely the right moment, and although tenuous, brought Brazil into the Allied fold. Until the advent of war, the FAB's only twin-engine transport experience with modern, retractable gear land monoplane twins had been eight Lockheed Model 12-A Electra Juniors acquired in small increments between September 1937 and April 1941 and, ironically, a substantial number of Focke-Wulf Fw 58B-2s and Fw 58V-9s that were essentially useless as cargo and meaningful personnel transports.

At almost precisely the same moment, Brazil became one of the first world powers to consolidate its naval and army aviation elements into a single air force. Initially dubbed the Forças Aéreas Nacionais upon amalgamation on 20 January 1941, this was changed to the definitive Força Aérea Brasileira (FAB) in May 1941, and so remains to this day. This combined force, stretched very thinly indeed along the Brazilian coastline, comprised a total of only 214 aircraft of all types, more than 135 of which were assorted US-built and British biplanes. Following the sinking of a number of Brazilian merchant ships by German submarines – in retrospect, a huge mistake – Brazil finally declared war on Germany and Italy on 31 August 1942, and immediately put coastal facilities at the disposal of the US armed forces.

The FAB then became the primary beneficiary of the US Lend-Lease programme in Latin America and commenced dispatching an almost endless series of requisitions to the Munitions Assignment Board (Air), once its staff had gained an understanding of the rather cumbersome process. Although a much greater number had been requested, by the end of the Second World War, the FAB had been totally modernised and transformed, receiving some 946 aircraft of all types, and having fielded to the Mediterranean Theatre the nearly legendary Republic P-47D Thunderbolt-equipped 1°GAvC.

Given its geographic challenges and, by 1944, the justification that its forces had truly become international in reach, the FAB staff included Requisition B-849, intended to cover five C-47s, among its very first shopping lists submitted. The MAB (Air) disapproved this one, on the grounds that, as of the date of submission, there simply were not yet enough disposable C-47s being produced to meet warfront demands, and that Brazil had yet to train the unit that would

become the 1°GAvC. This was followed, after a rather stinging disapproval of the first one, by a 1944 requisition, B-54320, for eleven brand-new aircraft and, perhaps to the surprise of one and all, it was approved, as evidenced in the table at the end of this chapter. Apparently emboldened by this action, the FAB then organised two additional C-47 requests, B-54447 for thirteen aircraft (justified on the grounds that they were needed to support the Brazilian Expeditionary Force headed for Italy), which was cancelled, and a radically revised B-54447-A1, covering an astonishing thirty-three C-47s, with a refined justification for the support of the Brazilian forces afield – which was also cancelled for undocumented reasons.

As noted in Chapter 3, although Brazil was, administratively, the first Latin American air arm to be approved for brand-new C-47s, and these were scheduled for delivery in September 1944 (four), October 1944 (four), January 1945 (2) and March 1945 (1), in fact Bolivia had taken delivery of her first one in January 1945 while Brazil, for various reasons, although approved for deliveries as early as September 1944–January 1945, did not in fact officially take legal possession of its first aircraft until 9 February 1945.

The reasons for the delay can be found in the very equipment bounty that the air arm was being afforded. In May 1942, President Vargas had received the one-and-only Lockheed C-66, a plushly outfitted Lodestar, and this was followed between February and June 1943 by eight new Lockheed C-60As for the FAB itself, its first genuinely modern and capable transports. At nearly the same time and through precisely the same period in which its eleven factory-fresh C-47Bs were approved, the FAB's very limited ability to train multi-engine crews and actually man these aircraft was exacerbated by the Lend-Lease delivery of sufficient Lockheed A-28As, B-34s and PV-2s, Douglas A-20Ks, the first North American B-25, Beech UC-45s, AT-7s and AT-11s to equip squadron-size units.

In fact, the first C-47 crews were seconded from a relatively low-time Lockheed PV-2-equipped unit, while others were selected, vetted and transferred to Kelly Field, Texas, to undergo an intensive On the Job Training (OJT) programme. Thus, even though Brazil 'owned' its new C-47s on paper, it was in no position to actually take delivery of them and place them in active service until nearly the end of the first quarter of 1945.

As with the Bolivian aircraft, those for Brazil were disbursed via the San Antonio Air Depot (SAAD) at Kelly Field and, like the Bolivian machines, were for the most part were eventually flown home by Brazilian crews – the training of whom, as noted, accounted for the delay in heading south. The November 1944 and subsequent approval dates may, in fact, have been accurate, in order to give the USAAF time to train the delivery crews before flying the long route to Brazil. One Brazilian historian has written that the first one, in fact, had departed for Rio on 12 September 1944 – ahead of even the

Apparently, the Lend-Lease C-47Bs supplied to Brazil were delivered initially with Second World War-era USAAF olive drab over light grey colour schemes. This side view of FAB 2009, the first aircraft, also reveals that full service titles were applied and, unusually, that the national insignia was worn on the fuselage sides. *Aparecido Camazano*

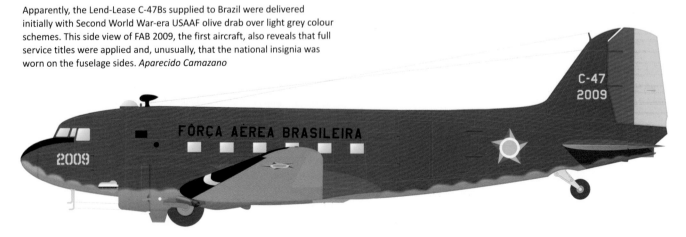

Above: FAB C-47 2009 was initially marked as simply FAB 01, and following a lengthy career is unique in being the only 'first' example of a Latin American military C-47 to be preserved in her home country, at the Museu Aerospacial de FAB. She is pictured here in 1959 in her fifteenth year of service. *ATP#3001477*

Right: Gradually, the FAB C-47 fleet gained a more or less standard colour scheme, although slight variations and exceptions abounded. Here, C-47 2011, the third Lend-Lease aircraft, wears the diminutive version of the badge of the 6º Esquadrão de Transporte Aéreo based at Rio, with the last two digits of her serial repeated on her nose. *Capt. Carlos Dufriche*

most optimistic schedule for handover of the first four – and that the aircraft arrived at Rio six days later. If this is correct, then administratively the aircraft was still USAAF property, as the 'official' MAB (Air) handover date was set down as 9 February 1945.

In anticipation of the arrival of its first truly modern cargo aircraft, the FAB created two dedicated transport units on 5 October 1944. These were the 1º Grupo de Transporte and 2º Grupo de Transporte, both co-located at Rio de Janeiro, with the 1º Grupo at the primarily civil Santos-Dumont Airport and the 2º Grupo at the military Campo dos Afonsos. As the 1º GT was already equipped with eight Lend-Lease supplied Lockheed C-60A Lodestars received between February and June 1943, only the initial Lend-lease C-47 was allocated to it, the remaining 'first wave' of ten going directly to the 2º GT. It is significant that the USAAF serials painted on these aircraft at the factory were retained as late as March 1945, again probably due to legal niceties associated with the official handover but, from that month on, these were scrubbed off and replaced with the then current FAB practice of marking the aircraft of a type sequentially as simply FAB 01 to FAB 11.

Above right: Showing the relative positions of the distinctive Brazilian national insignia on her outer wing panels, C-47 2013 has, by the time of this spring 1961 view at Miami, Florida, also had the rear section of her cargo door sealed and the hinges removed. *via Dr Gary Kuhn*

Right: Another view of C-47 2013 following the adoption of generous Day-Glo by many FAB transport types during the 1960s to aid visibility over the vast reaches of the Amazon. Note the similarly marked UC-45F in the background. She was reportedly lost to an accident on 1 July 1969, although the circumstances have eluded verification. *Dr Jean Magendie*

C-47 2015 was photographed here at the Rio-Galeao airport in 1971. Another Lend-Lease survivor, note the slight variation in the size of the lettering and numerals in her serial code compared to other aircraft. The FAB C-47 fleet was very well maintained. *Mario Roberto vaz Carneiro*

The earliest known photo of one of the Lend-Lease C-47Bs, C-47 2017 clearly wears Second World War-era USAAF camouflage but with the Brazilian rudder stripes. It is not clear if she also had the national insignia on her fuselage sides. *via Aparecido Camazano*

The utilisation of these new aircraft for the balance of the war was relatively intense. It is not known if any were, in fact, used to reach its overseas units in Italy, as had been postulated in the original Lend-Lease requisition, but at least a few travelled as far as the Panama Canal-based Sixth Air Force, where some Brazilian personnel were still undergoing training at what would eventually become the USAF Inter-American Air Force Academy at Albrook Field, CZ.

Brazil was a major beneficiary of the post-war American Republics Projects (ARP) and, possibly as a bone thrown to the FAB as a consolation prize for the denial of Project B-54447-A1 for thirty-three aircraft, no fewer than twenty-nine[22] ex-USAAF C-47s were handed over to the Brazilians, some of the first examples at Natal during the course of 1946 that, doing the maths, and added to the actual wartime deliveries, came to a tidy total of more than the thirty-three originally requested under Lend-lease![23] Of these, seven were issued to the 1º GT and the remainder to the 2º GT. The ARP-supplied aircraft, when combined with the factory-fresh, initial Lend-Lease aircraft, provided the FAB with a substantial fleet

of fairly low-time, fairly well-maintained aircraft that were, as of the time of transfer, processed through the San Antonio Air Depot (SAAD) for the most part, and were thus up to the latest Technical Order (TO) compliance. Needless to say, this provided the service with an across-the-board standard of maintenance and equipment that considerably eased serviceability and availability.

Meanwhile, in August 1945, the FAB had introduced a new serialing and designation system for its vastly larger inventory, and the existing C-47 fleet (the first eleven Lend-Lease aircraft) were issued C-47 2009 to C-47 2019, the 'C-47' prefix being regarded as part of the serial on the vertical fins of the aircraft. The ARP and subsequent C-47 acquisitions continued this series, the final and highest 'official' serial issued having been C-47 2092. However, muddying the waters in arriving at a total based on these issues, it must be noted that serials 2054, 2057 and 2058 were issued to other types. Serial 2054 was the one-and-only four-engine aircraft supplied to any Latin American nation under Lend-Lease, a Consolidated C-87 (initially serialed 2823), but which was, in the event, ostensibly used only as an 'instructional airframe', while 2057 and 2058 were both Curtiss C-46s.

Right: The official, full version of the 1º ETA shown on the colour image of C-47 2018. *Helio Higuchi*

Below: Prior to adopting her final serial codes, C-47 2018, this 12 January 1945 Lend-Lease delivery had worn a mix of codes, including FAB 61, a contraction of her original USAAF serial, and FAB-09. The badge on her upper fin is the diminutive of that of the 1ºEsquadrão de Transporte Aéreo – Esquadrão Tracajá home based at the time at Belém-Pará. She survived to be transferred to the Fuerza Aérea Paraguaya as FAP-2034. *MAP1984-102 #043*

Below: The first post-war C-47 acquisition by the FAB, C-47 2020 was captured here at distant Howard AFB, Canal Zone, on 20 February 1967 in her twentieth year of continuous service. She was declared surplus in October 1978 and was acquired by VOTEC as PT-KZE. *Hagedorn*

Built as a C-47B-45-DK, 45-1035, C-47 2022 was acquired surplus at Natal from among the huge post-war accumulation that had been stored there. Pictured here in Uruguay fairly early in her career, the aircraft at right is a C-47 of the ALA – Aerotransportes Litoral Argentino S.A. C-47 2022 also survived to be sold surplus to RICO as PT-KUW in September 1976. *Nery Mendiburu via Dr Gary Kuhn*

Following the initial ARP offsets, twelve more C-47s were delivered to the FAB via USAF stocks[24] and all of these were allocated to the 1º GT, but of these, two had been specially kitted out for the use of the President (C-47 2051, for Maj. General Enrico Casper Dutre, president at the time) and the Air Ministry (C-47 2052). These two special aircraft had been delivered from the Aviation Maintenance Corporation by 18 July 1947, and the special cabins were said to have cost about $30,000 each. Each had a forward compartment equipped with a davenport sofa and two lounge chairs and a centre compartment with twelve reclining seats and two tables.

In 1948 and afterwards, smaller increments of C-47s entered the inventory, and of these, one came from the USAF and two were former Brazilian commercial aircraft. Of these, two went to the 1º GT. In 1950, six more arrived via the first wave of post-war MAP offsets, and these were split evenly between the two operating units. TEMCO received a contract around November 1949 to completely rehabilitate and overhaul six C-47s. Valued at some $140,000, it included the requirement that TEMCO crews pick up the six aircraft at Davis-Monthan AFB, AZ, and fly them to Dallas for the work.

In 1952, the FAB created the Seção de Aviões de Comando and, together with other types, was issued four C-47s. This unusual unit had the mission of what we would today describe as a 'special duties' organisation, mainly consisting of providing communications and semi-VIP transport of officers and personnel. By 1 July 1952, the total strength of C-47s, service-wide, had grown to forty-nine, but serviceability was a problem because, of this total, only twenty-nine were in commission. Of these, eleven were then assigned to the 1º GT while the 2ºGT, Zona Aérea 3 had a mix of eight C-47As and C-47Bs plus the single C-46A. The remainder were all assigned to diverse organisations.

In January 1953, the 1º GT was reorganised to consist of two subordinate Esquadrões, of which the 1º/1º GT retained an all-C-47 inventory. The 2º GT was reorganised in the same manner and was also initially fully equipped with C-47s. In 1954, both Grupos were transferred to the Galeão airbase, also in Rio. By 30 June 1954, despite a few losses, the service could count a total of forty-six C-47s of all variants in the inventory that, while large by Latin American standards, were stretched very thinly indeed across the breadth of this huge nation. By 1 January 1955, the FAB C-47 strength remained unchanged, although a USAF intelligence note commented that, of the forty-six on hand, forty-one were 'combat ready' and all were by this time assigned to the 2º GT, which also held a single C-46A.

A most unusual markings anomaly for a Brazilian C-47. Here, C-47 2023 wears the national insignia on the fuselage side aft of the cargo doors, one of the very few such instances noted over a service period of more than thirty years. Her nose ventral loop antenna and absence of RDF loops atop her fuselage mark her as a very late C-47B, 45-1095. *Peter M. Bowers*

Built as a C-47A-30-DK, this aircraft was actually the first C-47 acquired by Brazil under the terms of the American Republics Projects (ARP) in October 1946. Photographed here at Rio-Galeao airport, not only does she wear Day-Glo on her nose, aft fuselage and wing tips, but on her engine cowlings as well. The badge on her vertical fin is that of the 2º/1º Grupo de Transporte. Although the cheatline on the FAB C-47s looked black, it was in fact a deep blue. She also had a lengthy service career and was sold surplus to the Club Nautico Agua Limpa as PT-KVI in December 1976. *via Dr Gary Kuhn*

For the most part, and in contrast to many of her neighbours, Brazil's C-47 fleet did not become embroiled in revolutionary or counter-insurgency actions. However, in 1956, the so-called 'Jacareacanga Incident' flared briefly. Two serving FAB officers, Mayor's Veloso and Paulo Vitor, decided to act in defiance of the sitting President, Juscelino Kubitschek. They seized a C-47 (serial 2059) and a Beech AT-11, and, somehow loading them with light bombs and cohorts to assist them, fled to Jacareacanga, deep in the midst of the Amazon. Loyal Brazilian Army forces took days to reach there and, meanwhile, an FAB Consolidated PBY-5A Catalina and a Boeing SB-17G made an attempt to destroy the two 'rebel' aircraft with machine gun fire – certainly the only known instance when any of the Flying Fortresses fired their guns in anger – or even had guns mounted, for that matter. The FAB crews of the PBY and B-17 were, however, very reluctant to fire on 'one of their own', and while they followed orders and fired in the general vicinity, their marksmanship was noticeably poor. The two officers were subsequently arrested but President Kubitschek decided to neutralise the incident and sooth the concerns of the military by granting the officers amnesty instead of retribution.

By 1957, the newly created Grupo de Transporte Especial (GTE) was formed from the nucleus of the former Seção de Aviões de Comando, retaining some passenger-configured C-47s in the process.

The same year, in August, the 2º/1º GT was formed and, by December, all C-47s from the 2º GT were transferred to both Esquadrões of the 1º GT, bringing its effective strength to a quite respectable thirty-nine aircraft. By 1 June 1958, the total FAB C-47 fleet comprised fifty-four aircraft.

In 1958, after a brief hiatus, another C-47 was acquired, this time a specially equipped aircraft that had been supplied under MAP specifically to check radio aids and airways within the vast airspace of Brazil. It was designated as an EC-47D by the FAB. It was also during 1958 that the only other incident involving FAB C-47s and revolutionary activity occurred. One of the same officers who had revolted in 1956 (see above), Mayor Veloso, organised a second attempted coup, having arranged the seizure of a number of civil as well as military aircraft at Aragarças. At the end of this hopeless incursion, one of the C-47s that had been seized (C-47 2060) was destroyed on the ground while attempting to land there – the solitary FAB C-47 'lost in action'. Following this affair, the next major increment of DC-3s and C-47s were an astonishing mix of variants acquired from several long-serving civil airlines. A total of fifteen were acquired at quite reasonable prices from a consortium comprising REAL, Aerovias Nacional and Aeronorte between 1958 and 1960, as well as two others from VASP and five more from Cruzeiro do Sul between 1960 and 1962.

Another markings variation, noted only rarely, was worn on C-47 2027, an ARP-supplied C-47A-90-DL photographed at Bolling Field, DC on 12 July 1960. Not only was her four-digit code repeated on either side of the nose but she also had a diamond-shaped scallop on her extreme nose with the numeral '1' in its centre, probably denoting the 1º GT. Unfortunately, the colour of the outline is unknown. Note the USAF Boeing C-97 in the distant background. The white upper decking and blue cheatlines had not yet been adopted by this time. *Carson Seely via Dr Gary Kuhn*

By the time of this image, the white upper decking and cheatline had appeared, dating it after the early 1960s, but the four-digit repeat of the individual serial has been retained on the nose. When photographed, the enthusiast who took the picture described her as a 'VC-47A' and she does indeed have curtains in the windows. An ARP acquisition, this aircraft also survived to pass to RICO in August 1979 as PT-KYX. *via Dr Gary Kuhn*

In March 1964, a second EC-47D was received via the USAF, followed by another in 1965, and a total of nine assorted C-47s of all variants were acquired via MAP between January and March 1964. In 1968, a C-47 was donated to the FAB by the Territorial Government of Acre, and two more were taken up in 1971 and 1974, one from Panair do Brasil and the other a former VASP aircraft. The first EC-47D, by 1 July 1964, was being used rather casually to check flight navigation facilities in the entire country in conjunction with the US FAA. Unfortunately, the USAF had not supplied technical publications for the actual operation and maintenance of the rather complex electronic equipment installed. Some of the equipment was found to be inoperative and could not be repaired locally. The aircraft thus flew only 19:20 hours during its first six months in Brazil.

Starting around 1958, C-47s started being assigned to individual FAB bases, Zonas Aéreas and sundry headquarters and support units and gradually, the once robust C-47 strength of the 1° GT was reduced to an even sixteen aircraft in each of its two Esquadrões. In 1965, the 1°/1° GT reequipped with the first of a long line of Lockheed C-130Es and its veteran C-47s were distributed amongst a plethora of other units, including the 2°/1° Grupo de Aviação at Belem, the 2°/6° GAv at Recife, the Headquarters of the 4th Air Zone at São Paulo and the new airbase at Brasilia.

Although the FAB fleet made frequent excursions to neighbouring countries, to USAF installations in the former Panama Canal Zone and even to the US, the farthest afield any of her C-47 crews ever sojourned was with United Nations forces in the Congo around 8 September 1961, when at least three experienced crews flew as part of the so-called 'C-47 Squadron' there, alongside crews from other nations, including Argentina, using seconded USAF, former AVIANCA and other aircraft.

A significant change in FAB organisation took effect in May 1969 when six new Esquadrões de Transporte Aéreo (ETAs) were formed, the objective having been a general decentralisation of existing transport units, in order to service an expanding air arm. The 1° ETA replaced the 2°/1° GAv at Belem, while the 2° ETA replaced the 2°/6° GAv at Recife. Likewise, the 3° ETA replaced the 2°/1° GT at Rio and the 4° ETA was established from the ground up at São Paulo as well as the 5° ETA at Porto Alegre and the 6° ETA in Brasilia. Each of the ETAs had a statutory strength of between six and eight C-47s, except the 3° ETA at Rio-Galeão, which hovered around fifteen examples, the last large concentration of the type in Brazilian service. At about the same juncture, the GTE finally relinquished its VIP C-47s, and these were dispersed to delighted station commanders throughout the country. By 30 September 1969, the FAB had also received two specially equipped EC-47s under MAP. However, even though supplied in that manner, they were not MAP-supported for spares, etc.

From 1974 onward, C-47s were gradually replaced in the existing ETAs by the indigenously designed and built EMBRAER EMB-110 Bandeirante and, starting in 1976, a number started being sold[25] off to civil ownership. Only fifteen remained in service by December 1976 and one, which has remained unidentified, was used as a target in manoeuvres around that time. Nine more were offered for sale on 10 May 1977.[26] Nine more were put on the auction block on 10 August 1978, along with some eighty C-47 main tyres.[27] By February 1979, the only FAB unit still retaining C-47s in any numbers was the 1° ETA at Belem, flying them alongside their equally venerable Consolidated PBY-5A Catalina fleet on duties into the Amazon interior. Apparently, three of the last aircraft in service were offered for sale on 5 September 1980.

This immaculate C-47A-80-DL was acquired under ARP at Kelly Field, TX, in December 1946 and also survived to be surplused in October 1978 as PT-KZV. Seen here at Rio on 28 May 1984, she wears the unit badge of the 4º ETA, based in São Paulo on her nose. *Mario Roberto vaz Carneiro via Brian R. Baker*

Trips to the US were gruelling but highly sought after by crews, such as those who flew C-47 2044 to Bolling Field, DC, around 12 July 1960, in company with a C-54G just visible in the background. She also has the diamond scallop on her nose as seen earlier on C-47 2027. *via Carson Seely via Dr Gary Kuhn*

Oddly, several DC-3s and C-47s were operated by the FAB in a rather curious quasi-military status. These aircraft usually retained most, or part of, their Brazilian civil registrations, but wore full FAB national insignia at the same time. Such was the instance with PT-BUQ and PT-BUR, which later became PP-FBO and PP-FBR. Other examples of this phenomenon were PP-CCY, PP-EDL, and PT-BQX.

The exploits of the C-47 series in Brazilian military service are legion. Besides the continuation of pioneering work developing the nationwide Correio Aéreo Nacional (CAN) first started with Waco biplanes in the 1930s, FAB C-47s also provided a unique service in nation-building, when they were used extensively to help with the start-up work associated with building a brand-new capital city, Brasilia, where no roads or railroads had yet penetrated.

FAB Serial	Previous Identity	Built As	MSN	Assignments and Notes
FAB 01 C-47 2009	43-48418	C-47B-1-DK	14234/25679	All of the first eleven Lend-Lease C-47Bs for Brazil were built at the Douglas-Oklahoma City, Oklahoma, plant. This aircraft was accepted on 13 Aug 44, picked up by a Brazilian crew at Kelly Field, TX, and departed the US for home 12 Sep 1944 but was still marked as 43-4(8418) when at Miami, FL, 14 Oct 44 and 1 Jul 45. On the actual Individual Aircraft History Card, the FAB crews were referred to as 'beneficiary pilots'. The new seral code C-47 2009 was applied around 30 Jul 45. This aircraft visited Miami, FL, as '01' on 11 Sep 45 and again 4 Jan 46, this time as C-47 2009. This aircraft enjoyed a lengthy service career, going as far afield as Bolling AFB, DC, in 1960 and was last noted in service after a highly successful career in May 1972 with the 6° ETA. She survived to be preserved, appropriately, in the Museu Aeroespacial da FAB.
FAB 02 C-47 2010	43-48419	C-47B-1-DK	14235/25680	Accepted by the USAAF on 16 Aug 44, this aircraft also went to Kelly Field, TX, and departed there with a Brazilian crew for home on 12 Sep 44. This aircraft also enjoyed a lengthy service career, being noted in service at Rio as late as 26 Jan 69. She was badly damaged in Jun 72 at Porto Alegre, however.
FAB 03 C-47 2011	43-48420	C-47B-1-DK	14236/25681	Accepted by the USAAF on 14 Aug 44, this aircraft moved by an ATC crew to Kelly Field, TX, where a Brazilian crew departed the US for home on 9 Oct 44. This aircraft was noted at Miami, FL, 1 Oct 45 as '03' and at the Reconstruction Finance Corporation (RFC) Surplus Centre at Miami, FL, in November 1945, still as FAB 03, probably there in connection with the FAB's interest in acquiring yet further surplus C-47s held there. She visited Miami as C-47 2011 on 8 Jul 47 and 25 Jan 48. This was also a long-serving aircraft, being last reported on 20 Jun 75, after which she was withdrawn from use and probably scrapped.
FAB 04 C-47 2012	43-48421	C-47B-1-DK	14237/25682	Accepted by the USAAF on 14 Aug 44, this aircraft was also moved by an ATC crew to Kelly Field, TX, where a Brazilian crew departed the US for Rio on 14 Sep 44. She visited Miami, FL, on 9 Feb 46 and 21 Jul 47 marked as C-47 2012. She was last reported in service on 6 Jun 73 and was probably withdrawn from use and scrapped shortly thereafter.
FAB 05 C-47 2013	43-48422	C-47B-1-DK	14238/25683	Accepted by the USAAF on 13 Aug 44, this aircraft was flown to Kelly Field, TX, by an ATC crew on 17 Aug 44 and departed there for Brazil with a Brazilian crew on 30 Sep 44. She was noted at Miami, FL, as '05' on 10 Jan 46. This aircraft was noted transiting Howard AFB, CZ, probably coincident with the refurbishing of FAB Douglas B-26s, between 10 Oct 68 and 4 Nov 68 but was reported written off on 1 Jul 69.
FAB 06 C-47 2014	43-48423	C-47B-1-DK	14239/25684	Accepted by the USAAF on 13 Aug 44, she was flown to Kelly Field, TX, by an ATC crew 17 Aug 44 and departed there for Brazil with a Brazilian crew on 30 Sep 44. She visited Miami, FL, 8 Jan 46, 10 May 46, 20 Mar 48 and 24 Jun 48 marked as C-47 2014. By April 1972 she is known to have been assigned to the 3° ETA and survived to be sold surplus as PT-KVM with Conagra on 20 Sep 76.

FAB 24 FAB 07 C-47 2015	43-48424	C-47B-1-DK	14240/25685	Accepted by the USAAF on 13 Aug 44, she was flown to Kelly Field, TX, by an ATC crew on 17 Aug 44 and departed there for Brazil with a Brazilian crew on 9 Oct 44. She was noted at Miami, FL, marked simply as FAB 24 (obviously a corruption of her full USAAF serial, the remainder apparently having been painted over) and was still marked a bit differently, as 43-4(8424), by 21 Sep 45. By 26 Apr 46 she was seen at Miami again, this time marked as C-47 2015 and was there again on 29 Jun 47, 28 Jul 47 and 14 Jan 48. Another long-serving aircraft, she was designated as a monument aircraft around 20 Nov 80 and had been mounted on a plinth by 12 Jun 81 at the entrance of the GAPAF Officers Club at Campo dos Afonsos. She has been held in trust by the Museu Aerospacial since Oct 01.
FAB 08 (C-47 2016)	43-48425	C-47B-1-DK	14241/25686	Accepted by the USAAF on 14 Aug 44, she was flown to Kelly Field, TX, by an ATC crew on 29 Aug 44. She apparently departed there with a USAAF crew for Brazil on 13 Sep 44. She holds the distinction of becoming the first FAB C-47 lost (but see C-47 2019 below) and crashed on either 31 Mar 45 or 31 May 45 (sources differ) at Barreiras, Bahia, still marked as FAB 08. The subsequent marks FAB 2016 were thus never worn but were assigned retrospectively.
FAB 60 FAB 11 C-47 2017	43-49660	C-47B-20-DK	15476/26921	Accepted by the USAAF on 12 Dec 44, this aircraft was flown to Kelly Field, TX, where she underwent unspecified modifications after 20 Dec 44. She departed the US for Brazil with a USAAF crew on 3 Mar 45, apparently arriving on 7 Mar 45. She transited Miami, FL, 25 Jun 45 marked as FAB 60 (another instance of an obvious corruption of her USAAF serial, the remainder probably simply painted over). Some sources have her initially being marked as FAB 09, in sequence, but for some reason, she apparently received FAB 11 instead. She was seen at Miami, FL, as '11' on 13 Oct 45 and again 29 Mar 46, this time as C-47 2017, returning again on 14 Jul 47 and 8 Oct 47. She was noted still active at Rio-Galeão on 4 Jul 73 but by then was in the twilight of her service, being sold on 10 Oct 78 to VOTEC, becoming PT-KZG. However, the water has been rather muddied on this aircraft, as a C-47 marked as 2017 was noted at one point preserved at the 20° Batalhao Logistico, at Deodoro, Rio.
FAB 61 FAB 09 C-47 2018	43-49661	C-47B-20-DK	15477/26922	Accepted by the USAAF on 12 Dec 44, this aircraft was flown to Kelly Field, TX, by an ATC crew on 14 Dec 44. She departed the US for Brazil with a USAAF crew on 12 Jan 45, arriving on 15 Jan 45, which probably accounts for her 'out-of-sequence' initial serial FAB 09. However, she transited Miami, FL, 26 Jun 45 as FAB 61, another instance of a simple corruption of her previous USAAF identity. She was noted as FAB 09 at Miami, FL on 3 Nov 45, however. She was noted assigned to the 1° ETA by 1981 after having been overhauled at Rio-Jacarepagua in March 1980. Brazil donated this aircraft to the Fuerza Aérea Paraguaya as FAP-2034 (q.v.).
FAB 10 (C-47 2019)	43-49662	C-47B-20-DK	15478/26923	Oddly, the Individual Aircraft History Card for this aircraft is missing, and this may be incident to the fact that, although known to have arrived at Rio under an ATC crew on 15 Jan 45, she was reportedly lost on 14 Apr 45 and, if the extant records are to be believed, also at Barreiras, Bahia, the exact same place as C-47 2016 above. She consequently never assumed the marks C-47 2019.
C-47 2020	45-1000	C-47B-45-DK	17003/34266	The first post-war FAB C-47 acquisition, this was one of the well-worn South Atlantic Wing, Air Transport Command, aircraft that Brazil acquired for a pittance at Natal on either 17 Dec 45 or 23 Jul 45, depending on which source is reliable. She visited Miami, FL, 20 Oct 46 marked as C-47 2020 and again on 22 Jan 47 and 28 May 47. Another long-serving aircraft, she was noted at Howard AFB, CZ, in Jan 67 and was sold surplus as PT-KZE to VOTEC on 10 Oct 78.
C-47 2021	45-1001	C-47B-45-DK	17004/34267	Also acquired surplus at Natal either on 17 Dec 45 or 23 Jul 45, this aircraft also served for at least thirty-three years until sold to VOTEC as PT-KYW on 10 Jul 78. She visited Miami, FL, on 19 Sep 47.
C-47 51035 C-47 2022	45-1035	C-47B-45-DK	17038/34303	This aircraft may also have been acquired surplus at Natal around 28 Nov 45 although 23 Jul 46 has also been found in some records. She visited Miami, FL, 4 Sep 46 still marked as '51035'. She was at Miami again 8 Oct 46, this time as C-47 2022, and again on 22 Jan 47, 7 Jan 48 and 4 Feb 48. She was noted in service at Rio on 8 Sep 67 and was sold surplus on 20 Sep 76 as PT-KUW to RICO.
C-47 51095 C-47 2023	45-1095	C-47B-45-DK	17098/34365	Another probable former South Atlantic Wing, ATC acquisition at Natal, this aircraft had been acquired by the FAB by 17 Dec 45, although again, some records state 23 Jul 46. She visited Miami, FL, marked as '51095' 11 Aug 46 and again on 24 Oct 46, this time as C-47 2023. She was lost on 6 Jun 49 at Cambirck, Catarina.
C-47 2024	43-16089	C-47A-90-DL	20555	This is probably one of the aircraft the FAB acquired via the RFC Surplus Centre in Miami, having served in the CONUS with the USAAF after acceptance in mid-June 1944. Two dates are found in records: 22 Sep 46 and 10 Dec 46. She was noted in service at Rio 26 Jan 69 and was assigned to the 1° ETA as of 27 Jul 81. Her provenance was confused for a time as she was displayed at the Museu Aerospacial from about 27 Mar 98 painted in full Aerovias Brasil colours as PP-AVJ (which was actually MSN 7333), that marking having been historically significant as having been the first Brazilian aircraft to fly in the US Her sale to the US firm All American Aviation as N4946F in May 1984, and subsequent movements as noted in the massive two-volume Air-Britain DC-3 monograph, seem very questionable.

Another ARP-supplied C-47A-50-DL, this is the former 42-24310, received by the FAB on or about 22 May 1947 at Kelly Field, here wearing the badge of the 1º GT. Also serving until surplused in October 1978, she became RICO's PT-KZH. *via Dr Gary Kuhn*

C-47 2025	43-48136	C-47A-30-DK	13952/25397	The first Brazilian ARP-supplied C-47, she was received on 4 Oct 46, having departed the US on delivery on 1 Oct 46. She visited Miami, FL, on 16 Jan 48. She was sold on 12 Dec 76 to the Club Nautico Agua Limpa, becoming PT-KVI.
C-47 2026	43-15993	C-47A-90-DL	20459	Another ARP-supplied aircraft, the delivery dates are given in different records as either via Kelly Field, TX, on 22 Sep 46 or 10 Dec 46. She visited Miami, FL, on 6 Jan 48. She was noted in service at Rio 8 Sep 67 but was stricken off charge in 1969.
C-47 2027	43-16000	C-47A-90-DL	20466	Also an ARP-supplied aircraft, delivery was also cited for two different dates – probably the date the aircraft arrived in Brazil and the actual formal handover date. She had been designated for ARP at Kelly Field, TX, by 25 Aug 46 but probably did not depart until 22 Sep 46 although a second date, 10 Dec 46, is also cited. She visited Miami, FL, on 28 Jan 48 and 12 May 48. She was reported in service at São Paulo on 22 Mar 69 but was written off on 17 Mar 74 at Xingu, Amazonas.
C-47 2028	42-92082	C-47A-DK	11843	Another ARP aircraft, her formal handover date is given as 10 Dec 46. However, FLC documents show her to Brazil ex-Kelly Field, TX, on 25 Feb 46! She visited Miami, FL, on 24 Sep 47. The Air-Britain monograph states that this aircraft was written off at Jacarepagua on 7 Aug 51 but noted Brazilian aviation historian, the late Capt. Carlos Dufriche, reported she was lost on 27 Aug 57 at Rio!
C-47 2029	42-23384	C-47A-5-DL	9246	ARP. A rather weary aircraft originally delivered to the USAAF on 18 Mar 43 and used in CONUS during the war. Delivered to the FAB 8 Oct 46 but officially handed over on 10 Dec 46. Most sources give this aircraft as lost on 1 Dec 58, but USAF Intelligence Report IR-156-57 reported that she in fact crashed on take-off from the airfield named Augusto Servero at Natal on or about 28 Sep 57. She was engaged in a routine cargo flight and all five crew members were killed. She was assigned to the 1ºGT at Rio-Galeão at the time.
C-47 2030	42-24123	C-47A-45-DL	9985	Long believed to have been the last of the ARP batch, this aircraft was reported at Kelly Field, TX, designated for Brazil as early as 11 Aug 46 but not delivered until 10 Dec 46 but apparently not formally handed over, for some reason, until 10 Nov 47 and then via the FLC, suggesting that the FAB apparently decided to purchase it via surplus outright. She was long-serving, being sold surplus around 12 Nov 76 to a private citizen as PT-KVR.
C-47 2031 VC-47 2031	43-15740	C-47A-90-DL VC-47	20206	Another ARP aircraft, this aircraft was apparently specially outfitted as noted in the text for the exclusive use of the President, at FAB expense and delivered on 8 Dec 46, and formally handed over on 1 Jan 47 after the VIP interior was installed. She was noted in service at Santa Cruz on 22 Apr 70 and at Rio-Galeão by 13 Nov 73 but, by Sep 80 was being stored at Campo dos Afonsos for the Museu Aeroespacial. She has more recently been reported as on permanent display somewhere in Brasilia from about 1995.

The solitary FAB aircraft to officially wear the designation VC-47, serial 2053 had been specially converted and outfitted at Glendale, California, for the exclusive, VIP use of the President of the country. Note her highly polished empennage when photographed at Rio on 28 April 1968. This aircraft also survived to be surplused, as PT-KVL, and was the last of the ARP-supplied examples. *Bud Joyce*

C-47 2032	43-15948	C-47A-90-DL	20414	Another ARP aircraft, she was delivered on 8 Dec 46 and formally handed over on 1 Jan 47. Noted at Miami on 31 Aug 47 and 20 Oct 47, she apparently did not depart there for home until 13 Nov 47, however, apparently having had some work done in the area. Although often reported as having been lost in an accident in 1975, an aircraft with this serial has been on display at the Museu Belem since at least Feb 01.
C-47 2033	43-48155	C-47A-30-DK	13971/25416	Another ARP-supplied aircraft, she departed the US on 10 Dec 46 and was noted in service at Rio as late as 20 Dec 69. One report has her undergoing work at Jacarepaguá around Mar 80. She was unusual in being sold back into the US to All American Aviation, Miami, as N49472 around Jul 84.
C-47 2034	43-30672	C-47A-DL	13823	Another ARP-supplied aircraft, she departed Kelly Field, TX, on 10 Dec 46 and was formally handed over on 1 Jan 47. She visited Miami, FL, 17 Feb 48. She was substantially damaged in an accident on 3 Sep 67 at Urubupunga, São Paulo, but had somehow returned to Rio-Galeao by 4 Jul 73, where she was noted semi-derelict.
C-47 2035 VC-47A	43-30670	C-47A-DL	13821	ARP, departed Kelly Field, TX, on 10 Dec 46, handed over on 1 Jan 47. She visited Miami, FL on 28 Sep 47. Noted in service at Rio 26 Jan 69. Sold surplus to RICO Taxi Aéreo, Ltda, around 6 Aug 79 as PT-KYX.
C-47 2036	43-48157	C-47A-30-DK	13973/25418	ARP, departed the US on 10 Dec 46, handed over on 1 Jan 47 but visited Miami, FL, on 2 Nov 47 and again on 4 Jun 48. Known to have been assigned to the 1º ETA by Feb 79, she was also noted being overhauled between Mar and Sep 80 at Jacarepagua and was sold around Mar 84 to All American Aviation, Miami as N4948J.
C-47 2037	43-48165	C-47A-30-DK	13981/25426	ARP, departed the US on 10 Dec 46 and formally handed over on 1 Jan 47. She was lost to an accident 27 Aug 66 at Altamira, Pará.
C-47 2038	42-92077	C-47A-DK	11837	ARP, departed the US on 10 Dec 46, and formally handed over on 1 Jan 47. Sold surplus to RICO around 10 Jul 78 as PT-KYZ.
C-47 2039	43-15309	C-47A-80-DL	19775	ARP, departed Kelly Field, TX, on 10 Dec 46, and formally handed over on 1 Jan 47. Noted active at Rio 18 May 74 with the 4º ETA. Was stored at Campo dos Afonsos for a time before being sold surplus around Oct 78 to a private citizen as PT-KZV.
C-47 2040	43-15582	C-47A-85-DL	20048	ARP, departed Kelly Field, TX, on 10 Dec 46, and formally handed over on 1 Jan 47. She visited Miami, FL, 3 Dec 47. Written off at Arnajas (also cited as 'Anavas'), Pará, on 27 Feb 48.
C-47 2041 VC-47 VC-47	43-15985	C-47A-90-DL	20451	Designated for ARP on 21 Nov 46 and departed Kelly Field, TX, on 10 Dec 46, and formally handed over on 1 Jan 47. She visited Miami, FL, 3 Aug 47. This was apparently the aircraft converted to VIP configuration at FAB expense for the Minister of Aeronautics. Last known with the 5º ETA and sold surplus around 12 Dec 76 (although also reported as late as September 1980) to Clube Nautico Agua Limpa as PT-KVH.

Yet another survivor, this C-47A-90-DL, formerly 43-15744 was received between November 1949 and March 1950 and later became PT-KVX with an engineering firm. Pictured here prior to November 1974, she displays the insignia of the 3º ETA on her port nose. *ATP*

Several FAB C-47s were locally designated as EC-47s, including 2065 but was not acquired until July 1956, having seen US and Mexican civil identities. Note the Viewmaster window on the forward fuselage and the plethora of antennas. She was photographed at Rio on 28 July 1968 but was lost when she ditched at sea off Itaparica, Bahia, on 13 September 1975 after experiencing a double engine failure. *Bud Joyce*

A busy apron scene with C-47 2077, former RAF Dakota III FZ592, preparing to start up sometime in the 1960s, having joined the force ex-REAL as PP-AXF on 13 July 1960. She reverted to civil marks PT-KVT in November 1976 with RICO. *via Dr Gary Kuhn*

C-47 2042	43-30693	C-47A-DL	13844	ARP, departed Kelly Field, TX, 22 Apr 47, and formally handed over 22 May 47. She was noted at Miami, FL, 27 Nov 47. Last reported in service at Rio 20 Dec 69 and believed stricken in May 72.
C-47 2043	42-108969	C-47A-25-DK	13538	Designated for ARP and to Kelly Field, TX, on 4 Mar 47. Departed the US on 22 Apr 47, and formally handed over on 22 May 47. She visited Miami, FL, on 29 Jul 47 and again on 19 Feb 48 and 7 Apr 48. Noted active at Howard AFB, CZ, in Jan 67. Stored at Campo dos Afonsos by Feb 79 and sold surplus around 31 Dec 78 to a private citizen as PT-KZJ.
C-47 2044	42-24070	C-47A-40-DL	9932	ARP, departed the US on 9 Feb 47, and formally handed over on 22 May 47. She visited Miami, FL, on 29 Oct 47 and travelled to Bolling AFB, DC, on 12 Jul 60. Last reported at Rio on 26 Jan 79. Sold surplus *c.*Nov 76 to a private citizen as PT-KUR.
C-47 2045	42-24315	C-47A-50-DL	10177	ARP, departed the US on 4 Feb 47 and was formally handed over on 22 May 47 via the FLC. She is known to have visited Miami, FL, 4 Oct 47. Known to have been assigned to the 1° ETA. Sold in May 84 to All American Aviation, Miami, as N49454.
C-47 2046	42-24310	C-47A-50-DL	10172	ARP, departed the US via Kelly Field, TX, and formally handed over on 22 May 47 via FLC. She visited Miami, FL, 3 Aug 47. Was one of thirty airworthy FAB C-47s in service as of 1966. Sold surplus *c.*10 Oct 78 to RICO as PT-KZH.
C-47 2047	43-30690	C-47A-DL	13841	ARP, departed Kelly Field, TX, on 9 Feb 47, formally handed over 22 May 47. She visited Miami, FL, 10 Jan 48. Reported active at Rio on 5 Jun 69. Written off on 4 Mar 75 on take-off at Peixe, Goiás, one passenger being killed.
C-47 2048	42-23915	C-47A-35-DL	9777	ARP, departed Kelly Field, TX, on 19 Dec 46, formally handed over on 22 May 47. She departed Miami en route to Brazil on 10 Nov 47, apparently having undergone some modifications there. Lost on 11 Jul 52 when she ditched offshore Salvador, Brazil.
C-47 2049	43-30711	C-47A-DL	13862	ARP, departed Kelly Field, TX, on 25 Dec 46, formally handed over on 2 Jun 47, although Air-Britain reported 6 Feb 47. She visited Miami, FL, 26 Aug 47 and again 4 Jun 48. Lost on 2 Sep 53 at Rio, some reports stating 9 Sep 54.
VC-47 2050	42-92053	C-47A-DK	11811	ARP, departed Kelly Field, TX, on 10 Feb 47, formally handed over on 23 May 47. She visited Miami, FL, 9 Sep 47 and again 14 Feb 48. This aircraft was modified by Pacific Airmotive at Glendale, CA, as a VIP aircraft for President Vargas, replacing his VC-66, and her delivery was thus delayed. Reported still active at Rio-Manguinhas on 17 Jan 70. Crashed on 13 Nov 74 at Tomé-Açu, Brazil, seven killed.
C-47 2051	42-93221	C-47A-20-DK	13109	ARP Project 94539-S departed Kelly Field, TX, on 10 Feb 47, formally handed over on 29 May 47 but another report stated 24 Mar 48. Reported lost on 17 Oct 56.
C-47 2052	42-100530	C-47A-65-DL	18993	ARP Project 94539-S departed Kelly Field, TX, on 10 Feb 47, formally handed over on 29 May 47 but another report stated 24 Mar 48. Active at Rio on 16 Nov 70 and noted in service as late as 20 Jun 75. Sold surplus *c.*12 Nov 76 to a construction firm as PT-KVN.
C-47 2053 VC-47A VC-47	42-100842	C-47A-75-DL	19305	ARP departed Kelly Field, TX, on 27 Oct 47 and formally handed over on 20 Apr 48, although one report states 10 Dec 48. Sold surplus on 20 Sep 76, to CONAGRO as PT-KVL. This was the last of the ARP-supplied C-47s.
(IS-C-87 2054)	(44-52985)	Consolidated C-87	–	–
C-47 2055	41-18411 PP-FVA	C-47-DL	4473	Actually acquired for a Brazilian governmental agency, the Ministerio da Viação e Obras Públicas, in the governmental registration series as PP-FVA, it was transferred to the Fabrica Nacional de Motores on 9 Nov 47. Held only briefly, she passed to the FAB on 2 Feb 48. She was lost in an accident at Natal on 25 Mar 61.

Although marked as the former REAL aircraft PP-ANR, C-47 2079, which joined the FAB on 27 September 1960, the aircraft pictured here is actually a curious imposter. In actuality, she is N259DC, which was acquired by the Museo Aerospacial by October 1988 and displayed as such. Note her Viewmaster-style forward windows and the unusual outline around the cabin door. Exactly why the museum went to the trouble, when it already possessed the far more historic C-47 2011 and at least one other, remains unclear. *Ron Mak*

C-47 2056	42-100592 NC-68221 PP-ETE	C-47A-65-DL	19055	An Eighth Air Force Second World War veteran aircraft, and initially acquired for use by the Gobierno do Estado do Acre at Rio Bronco, this aircraft was transferred to the FAB on 24 Sep 47. She was reported active at Rio on 12 Aug 70 but was sold surplus on 13 Apr 77 to a private citizen as PT-KXR.
(C-46 2057)	(43-46973)	Curtiss C-46A-5-CK	–	–
(C-46 2058)	(43-47084)	Curtiss C-46A-55-CK	–	–
C-47 2059	43-15589	C-47A-85-DL	20055	A late ARP delivery, this aircraft was drawn via surplus stocks at Davis-Monthan AFB on either 10 Dec 49 or 30 Mar 50, according to separate official documents. She was implicated in the so-called 'Jacareacanga Incident' in 1956, as mentioned in the main text. She last served with the 1º ETA and was reported active at Rio on 26 Jan 69. She was sold surplus to RICO rather later than other examples, on 21 Nov 80, becoming PT-LBL.
C-47 2060	43-15608	C-47A-85-DL	20074	Another ARP-supplied aircraft, this aircraft was also acquired via surplus stocks at Davis-Monthan AFB on 17 Nov 49 or 30 Mar 50, depending on which of two official documents are accurate. Although cited as having been lost on 1 Mar 59 at Aragarças, Mato Grosso, by Air-Britain, another source states she was in fact lost 4 Dec 59 at Goiás. In reality, she was destroyed in action on the ground in 1958 during an attempted coup, as noted in the main text.
C-47 2061	43-15744	C-47A-90-DL	20210	Another ARP delivery, she was also drawn from surplus at Davis-Monthan AFB either on 10 Nov 49 or 30 Mar 50, depending on differing official documents but was, according to her IAHC handed over on 17 Nov 49. She survived to be sold surplus on 13 Apr 76 to an engineering firm as PT-KVX.
C-47 2062	43-15750	C-47A-90-DL	20216	ARP, this aircraft was drawn from surplus on 17 Nov 49 or 10 Apr 50, depending on two different official sources. She was written off on take-off on 9 Jul 56 at Rio Branco, Acre, while assigned to the 2º GT at the time. The pilot and three members of the crew were killed, and two other airmen and three civilians were seriously injured. This was a regularly scheduled flight on the Correio Aéreo Nacional route system.
C-47 2063	43-15944	C-47A-90-DL	20410	ARP, drawn from surplus at Davis-Monthan AFB, AZ, on 17 Nov 49 and handed over officially on 10 Apr 50. This aircraft was reported written off in an undocumented accident at São Luiz in Jan 62.
C-47 2064 VC-47 2064 VC-47A	43-15962	C-47A-90-DL	20428	ARP, designated for Brazil as early as 10 Nov 49, drawn from surplus at Davis-Monthan AFB, AZ, on 8 Dec 49 and officially handed over on 30 Mar 50. Converted to VC-47A status by TEMCO around 14 Nov 49 and substituted for 43-15548. Known to have been assigned to the 3º ETA as of May 1972. Sold surplus on 16 Feb 77 to RICO as PT-KVS.
EC 47 2065	42-100754 NC-1369N XA-FIX XC-ABW N1369N	C-47A-70-DL EC-47A	19217	A very well-travelled aircraft, exactly when she was converted to EC-47A status is not clear. She was the first aircraft acquired by the FAB after a lapse of almost six years since the last ARP aircraft, around 13 Jul 56. She was noted in service at Rio-Santos Dumont between 21 Oct 67 and 25 Jan 75 but was lost to an accident either on 9 Sep 75 or 13 Sep 75 off Itaparica, Bahia. She ditched at sea after both engines failed and all on board were rescued. The aircraft sank.
C-47 2066	42-93696 NC-54215 PP-XDU PP-AXK	C-47A-25-DK	13636	The first of a number of well-worn former Brazilian commercial transports acquired ex-REAL, this aircraft joined the FAB sometime after 20 Mar 58, most sources cite 16 Apr 58. She was lost to an accident at Brasilia on 13 or 14 Mar 61.

C-47 2067	43-49808 N4892V PP-ANW	TC-47B-20-DK TC-47D C-47D TC-47D	15624/27069	Another former REAL aircraft, this aircraft joined the FAB on 23 May 58. The identity of this aircraft, however, has been confused for years with that for C-47 2071 (q.v.). It is not clear which is correct from existing records. C-47 2067 was reported written off at Rio in Dec 61, however.
C-47 2068	–	–	–	Another aircraft for which the provenance is hopelessly corrupted. Known to have formerly been PP-AXY with REAL, her MSN was cited as '45117' in most official documents, which, of course, is a non-starter. She is known to have joined the FAB on 8 Aug 58. Speculated to have been 45-1017 (MSN 17020/34284), this aircraft has since been determined to have gone to Mexico on 13 Dec 45 where she was salvaged. In any event, C-47 2068 was written off on 16 Jun 67 in the Amazon.
C-47 2069	43-15778 N5900V PP-AXZ PP-NBL	C-47A-90-DL	20244	A former REAL aircraft, she was taken up by the FAB on either 15 Sep 58 or 24 Jul 59. She was sold surplus on 10 Oct 78 to VOTEC as PT-KZF.
C-47 2070	43-30671 NC-79045 NC-58775 XA-HIN N58775 PP-ANZ	C-47A-DL	13822	An exceptionally well-travelled aircraft, this former REAL aircraft joined the FAB on 6 Oct 58 or 24 Jul 59. She was lost to an accident on 4 Dec 59 at Cumuruxatiba, Bahia, although the date has also been suggested as 1 Mar 59 or 1 Mar 60!
C-47 2071	43-49808 N4893V PP-AOC PP-AKC	C-47B-20-DK	15624/27069	As noted in C-47 2067 above, the true identity of this aircraft is in doubt, although that shown is believed to be the most likely for C-47 2071. She was acquired from REAL, joined the FAB on 13 Jul 59 and was noted in service as late as 10 Dec 69. She was sold surplus around 20 Sep 76 to a private citizen and became PT-KVJ.
C-47 2072	43-15670 NC-54337 PP-AOD PP-AKD	C-47A-90-DL	20136	Another former REAL aircraft, taken up by the FAB on 13 Jul 59 (although 13 Jul 58 has also been quoted). She was noted in service as late as 23 Dec 72. Sold surplus on 20 Sep 76 to Clube Nautico Agua Limpa as PT-KVB.
C-47 2073	BuA 05064 NC-69010 XA-XYZ-1(2) XA-GUM N4673V PP-ANY	R4D-1	4756	One of the oldest aircraft acquired from REAL, this tired aircraft joined the FAB on 31 Aug 59 and was sold surplus to RICO on 5 Nov 76, becoming PT-KVA.
C-47 2074	44-77241 KP271 N4731V PP-AOB PP-AKB	C-47B-40-DK Dakota IV	16825/33573	Another former REAL aircraft, this one joined the FAB on 24 Mar 61. Her provenance is regarded as suspect. She was reportedly written off at Florianopolis, SC, in May 65.
C-47 2075	43-16053 NC-79038 (PP-ATT) PP-SDE PP-ANQ	C-47A-90-DL	20519	A former Transportes Aéreos Nacional, Ltda aircraft, this one joined the FAB either on 27 Nov 58 or 31 Aug 59. Oddly, not a single subsequent spotting report has surfaced, and her fate remains an open question.

Another former Brazilian airliner, where she served Linhas Aéreas Brasileiras as PP-BRD and Nacional as PP-ANE, she joined the FAB on 11 January 1961 and is unusual in having returned to the US in May 1979 as N9049Y. She is pictured here at Rio-Galeao on 21 April 1969. She wears the unusual code 'QG4', denoting her assignment at the time to the Seção de Aviões do Quartel General de 4ª Zona Aérea, under her port wing and, in yellow script, a name on her nose under the cockpit window. What appears to be a new window on the rear cargo door is in fact some sort of placard. *Mario Roberto vaz Carneiro*

Taken at Rio on 28 April 1968, C-47 2082 was built as a C-47-DL, 41-18529, and was an Eighth Air Force veteran of the war. She was modified post-war as a DC-3C-S1C3G and, in addition to her Day-Glo panels, also features curtains in her cabin windows. Formerly with VASP as PP-SQM, she joined the FAB on 11 January 1961, passing again to civil marks as PT-KZM in December 1978. *Bud Joyce*

Another of the FAB aircraft coded as an EC-47, serial 2088 was actually supplied to the service under MAP as a USAF EC-47D in late May 1964 and was photographed here at Rio four years later, in April 1968. She does not, however, have the antenna array as noted earlier on EC-47 2065, but does have the radar nose. Serial 2089 was similarly configured. The aircraft was apparently scrapped after February 1979. *Bud Joyce*

C-47 2076	42-92544 KG349 PP-ACB PP-AXE	C-47A-5-DK Dakota III	12356	A former REAL aircraft, this one joined the FAB on 13 May 60 and was last reported active in 1971. She was sold surplus on 12 Nov 76 to RICO as PT-KVU.
C-47 2077	42-92356 FZ592 PP-ACC PP-AXF	C-47A-1-DK Dakota III	12147	Frequently reported in error previously as MSN 12140, this was another former REAL aircraft, and joined the FAB on 13 Jul 60, although Air-Britain cites 13 May 60. She was noted active at Rio on 5 Jun 69. Sold surplus on 12 Nov 76 to RICO as PT-KVT.
C-47 2078	BuA05063 NC-1086M PP-YPN	R4D-1 DC-3C-S1C3G	4755	Another former REAL aircraft, this one joined the FAB on 31 May 60. She has been positively linked with post-war conversion to DC-3C-S1C3G configuration, and it is probable that most, if not all, of the former Brazilian civil C-47s acquired in the 1950s and 1960 had been similarly reconfigured, or to a similar configuration. Last reported active on 13 Nov 73, she is believed to have been scrapped.
C-47 2079	41-18579 NC-41169 NC-56969 (PP-KAC) (PP-BRF) PP-IBA PP-ANR	C-47-DL	4704	Formerly with REAL, this aircraft was added to the FAB inventory on 27 Sep 60. At one point was assigned to the 1° ETA. Last reported on 4 Jul 80, when she was noted withdrawn from use at Campo dos Afonsos. An aircraft marked with the serial was put on display as early as 22 Oct 88 in the Museu Aerospacial but is in fact MSN 14506/25951 and formerly N259DC, an R4D-8, and in fact never served a day with the FAB! It was acquired via the Brazilian Aeronautical Commission specifically for display at the museum 26 Aug 88 and had one side inscribed 'Museo Aeroespacial' still with its last US civil registration, N259DC, while the other was marked as FAB C-47 2079 in full FAB colours.
C-47 2080	45-1031 PP-BRD PP-ANE	C-47B-45-DK	17034/34299	This aircraft was first identified with Brazil on 25 Nov 45 and was taken up by Linhas Aéreas Brasileiras (LAB) as PP-BRD on 15 Apr 46, and thus was destined to spend essentially her entire service life, aside from a brief period after being accepted by the USAAF, in Brazil. She joined the FAB ex-Nacional on 11 Jan 61 and was, unusually, sold back into the US around 22 May 79 as N9049Y.
C-47 2081	45-1028 PP-SPN	C-47B-45-DK	17031/34296	This aircraft also arrived in Brazil around 25 Nov 45 for VASP. She joined the FAB on 23 Jun 60 and was last reported active on 2 Mar 75. She was sold surplus around 20 Sep 76 as PT-KVK to CONAGRO.
C-47 2082	41-18529 NC-62253 PP-SQM	C-47-DL DC-3C-S1C3G	4621	An Eighth Air Force Second World War veteran, this former and long-serving VASP aircraft passed to the FAB on 11 Jan 61. She was noted active at Rio as late as 13 May 68 and was being offered for sale as early as 1976. Sold around 11 Dec 78 to a private citizen as PT-KZM.
C-47 2083	45-1096 PP-BRE PP-CCW	C-47B-50-DK	17099/34366	Another long-serving aircraft, this one arrived in Brazil around 27 Nov 45 and last served with Cruzeiro do Sul before joining the FAB on either 4 or 26 Jul 60. Last reported active in 1972, she was apparently scrapped.
C-47 2084	42-100545 NC-79035 PP-CDB	C-47A-65-DL	19008	Also a former Cruzeiro do Sul aircraft, this one joined the FAB on 27 Sep 60 and was noted still active at Rio as late as 26 Jan 69. She was sold surplus around 20 Sep 76 to RICO as PT-KUY.
C-47 2085	42-93264 KG564 LV-ACI PP-XEU PP-CDN	C-47A-20-DK Dakota III DC-3C-S1C3G	13156	Yet another former Cruzeiro do Sul aircraft, this one passed to the FAB on 27 Sep 60 and at one point served with the 2° ETA. She was sold surplus on 30 Dec 80 and became PT-LBK with RICO, although her registration date was 21 Nov 80.

The solitary FAB C-47 to be coded with a suffix, C-47A 2090 was also a former RAF Dakota IV, KN230. She was acquired from the Brazilian state government of Acre as PP-ENB in September 1069. She was destined to be one of the last operational FAB C-47s, not being transferred to Paraguay as FAP-2032 until after 14 May 1984. Note the barely visible 1º ETA codes under her port wing. *MAP*

C-47 2086	43-16120 NC-62387 PP-DLM PP-CEB	C-47A-90-DL	20586	Also formerly with Cruzeiro do Sul, this aircraft joined the FAB either on 20 Sep 60 or 5 Oct 60, depending on two sources. She was last known assigned to the 6º ETA and was sold surplus on 21 Nov 80 or 30 Dec 80 to RICO as PT-LBM.
C-47 2087	41-18578 NC-44782 PP-PCC PP-CCT PP-FVI PP-CCT	C-47-DL	4703	A Fifth Air Force Second World War veteran, this was a very well-travelled aircraft and she joined the FAB from Cruzeiro do Sul on 31 Dec 61 or 30 Jan 62. Her fate is uncertain, although it appears she was scrapped.
EC-47 2088	45-1002	C-47B-45-DK C-47D AC-47D EC-47D	17005/34268	MAP supplied on 18 Mar 64 but not delivered until further modified on 25 May 64. She was last known assigned to the GEIV. She was sold surplus to a private citizen around 10 Oct 78 and may have become PT-KZW, but it is not clear if this was actually taken up.
EC-47 2089	45-985	C-47B-45-DK C-47D AC-47D EC-47D	16988/34249	At one point earmarked for Russia under Lend-Lease, this aircraft went to MAP after lengthy USAF service on 29 Aug 65, but by then had actually been handed over to the FAB on 23 Jul 65. She was noted in service at Rio on 12 Aug 70 and was still in the inventory as late as Feb 79. She was apparently scrapped.
C-47A 2090	43-49837 KN230 NC-4724V YV-C-ARC PP-ASN PT-AYC PP-ENB	C-47B-20-DK Dakota IV	15653/27098	This aircraft was acquired by the FAB from the Gobierno do Acre on 9 Sep 69 and is last known having been assigned to the 1º ETA. She was stricken on 14 May 84, one of the very last FAB C-47s, and donated to Paraguay as FAP-2032 (q.v.).
C-47 2091	NC-21718 PP-PCP PP-NAY PP-PED	DC-3-279	2134	Unquestionably the oldest DC-3 series aircraft to see service with the FAB, this one passed from Cruzeiro do Sul by 7 Sep 70 and was noted still with the FAB at São Paulo-Congonhas on 28 May 73. She survived to be sold surplus around 10 Jul 78 and became PT-KZB with RICO.
C-47 2092	NC-34984 PP-NAM	DC-3D	42980	The solitary purpose-built DC-3D known to have served with a Latin American air arm, this one passed to the FAB from the government organisation Projeto Rondon sometime after September 1970. She was sold surplus to Clube Nautico Agua Limpa around 20 Sep 76, becoming PT-KVC.
C-47 BUQ	42-92778 PP-CCO PP-FBJ PT-BUQ	C-47A-15-DK	12616	Formerly operated by the government entity Fundaçao Brasil Central from around 17 Sep 62, this aircraft wore this abbreviated civil registration with partial FAB national insignia and titles Convenio F.B.C. Comara by 1966 and as late as 6 Nov 67. She then reverted once again to government marks PP-FBO on 14 Feb 68.
PT-BQX	44-76400 KN364 VMYBE PP-VBC	C-47B-25-DK Dakota IV	1598432732	For some reason, this aircraft served with these marks with the FAB between about 19 Oct 61 and April 1977.

Probably the least standardised of any FAB colour scheme, C-47 2091 was in fact a DC-3-279 and the oldest aircraft of the genre to serve with the air force there. Formerly with Cruzeiro do Sul as PP-PED, she still retains most of her former colour scheme here. She was stricken on 10 July 1978 and became PT-KZB with RICO. *Ronaldo Carvalho*

C-47 BUR (PT-KTV)	41-18654 NC-65358 NC-65387 LV-ABE PP-XET PP-FBK PT-BUR	C-47-DL	6015	As with C-47 BUQ above, this aircraft followed essentially the same trajectory, but passed to PP-FBR where, according to one report, she was operated jointly with marks PP-FBR by the Convenio Sudeco and FAB and, after passing to PT-KTV, continued to operate in full FAB colour scheme with these marks as well by May 72.
PP-CCY	(43-15660) PP-CCY	(C-47A-90-DL)	(20126)	This aircraft is known to have worn FAB national insignia briefly, but still in Cruzeiro do Sul colours for some reason but had become PT-FAG by 9 Jan 91. This may have been in connection with her work after 21 Dec 71 in cloud-seeding experiments. Her provenance is suspect, as the aircraft with this identity was lost with the Ninth Air Force in Europe on 25 Dec 44!
C-47 EDL	42-6458 TI-71 PP-AVK PP-EDL	C-53-DO	4910	If her provenance is accurate, this was a veteran of the Fourteenth Air Force in China. She was operated by the FAB with these odd, abbreviated marks between 4 May 60 and 16 Jun 69. She passed to PT-KVP with the Clube Nautico Agua Limpa around 12 Nov 76.

Late in its C-47 experience, the FAB operated a number of unusual aircraft in non-standard markings, including C-47 BUQ seen here at Rio-Galeao on 6 November 1967 wearing Convenio F.B.C. Comara titles. Formerly marked as PP-FBJ, she returned to civil governmental marks as PP-FBO on 14 February 1968. Interestingly, her elevators are painted red! *U. Neumann*

Yet another non-standard aircraft, C-47 EDL was one of the very few C-53s operated by any air arm in Latin America, a fact apparently not appreciate by the FAB's logistics folks, who invariably referred to her as a C-47. Although her provenance is tenuous, it appears she was a Second World War veteran of the Fourteenth Air Force in the CBI. She also was sold surplus as PT-KVP in mid-November 1976. She appears to have had two small transparent panels cut into her upper rear fuselage and wears 'FAB' under her starboard wing along with the national insignia. *Mario Roberto vaz Carneiro*

In addition to the foregoing, there are some anomalies that should be mentioned. For instance, C-47B-11-DK 43-49082 (MSN 14898/26343) was set aside for Brazil under ARP on 20 August 1946 and annotated as such in the Division of Military Intelligence on 5 May 1946. However, she is not known to have gone to the FAB but, rather, to VASP as PP-SPS on 17 July 1946, suggesting that the FAB either declined the aircraft or almost immediately sold her to a civil operator, which would have been a violation of the ARP tenets. The FAB also became the 'owner' of an impounded aircraft, C-47A-65-DL MSN 19046, by 28 June 2004, by which time she was noted derelict in very faded Aviopacifico colours, apparently at Tabatinga, Amazonas. This aircraft had survived an amazing trek in Latin

American skies after being acquired by TACA as surplus in late 1945 as TI-62, subsequently being registered in Honduras, Nicaragua, and Ecuador. She apparently ended her days as a smuggler.

Exercito do Brasil

The Brazilian Army (Exercito do Brasil) did in fact acquire a single former civil C-47A for use as an instructional airframe at the Escola do Paracaidistas. Donated by VARIG, the former PP-AKA (built as C-47A-90-DL MSN 20193, and ex-43-15727 and N4908V) never flew with the Army, and was in fact delivered by road from São Paulo to the parachute training facility near Rio in January 1971.

Although not apparent from her markings, C-47B-25-DK and former Dakota IV KN364 was operated, for some reason, by the FAB briefly, as seen, sometime between October 1961 and April 1977 – possibly on clandestine duties. The abbreviated registration 'BQX' is repeated on her upper starboard wing. *via Steve Kraus*

CHAPTER FIVE

Chile

WHILE IT MAY be fairly said that all of the mainland South American nations each possess unique geographic challenges that made use of DC-3 and C-47 variants exceptionally welcome, Chile must certainly rate at the very top. Stretching from Cape Horn in the extreme south near latitude 55° to Arica at the north-westernmost point, some 4,329km apart, most readers may be surprised to learn that, even at that, Chile is smaller in actual land area than all of the other major nations save Ecuador, Paraguay and Uruguay in actual land area.

Her nearly unique configuration, a ribbon of land lying between the mighty Andes and the Pacific Ocean averages only about 180km east-to-west. Of this width, the Andes and a coastal range of highlands take up from a third to a half of her total area. Her extraordinary length includes an exceptionally wide variation of soil and astonishing differences in climate.

The evolution of practical aviation in Chile has, as a consequence, been dictated by her configuration. There are, generally speaking, eight distinct inhabited areas: the far north, south of Antofagasta to Illapel, the very heartland – including Santiago – south through the Central Valley, forested Chile (Temuco to Puerto Montt), the Chiloé region, archipelagic Chile and the Chilean Patagonia. Strictly speaking, a ninth zone should be added: the Antarctic airbase Teniente Marsh, which operates all year long.

Like Brazil and Argentina, the other two of the so-called 'A-B-C' powers, Chile has benefited over the years by a diverse immigrant population, including major German and Italian colonies, and these unquestionably played a part in the evolution of aeronautics, mixed with a generous infusion of British philosophy as well in the 1920s and '30s. French influences, unlike elsewhere, were virtually negligible.

Because of its natural resources and strategic position on the length of the mainland South American land mass, Chile was one of the three major Latin American beneficiaries of Lend-Lease during the Second World War. Surprisingly, although it did submit a requisition for five Lockheed C-60A Lodestars – all of which were in fact immediately passed to the military-run Línea Aérea Nacional (LAN) organisation between June 1943 and February 1945 – Chile for some reason did not register any known demand for C-47s during the war that, in retrospect, is rather surprising. She did receive some combat aircraft, including Douglas A-24Bs, Consolidated PBY-5s and PBY-5As and some Vought-Sikorsky OS2U-3s, but the majority of the aircraft received were the traditional mix of variants of the North American AT-6, Vultee BT-13 and Fairchild PT-19.

The American Republics Projects (ARP), however, focused on making each Latin American recipient national air arm a 'well-rounded' force, and C-47s were always included. Five were delivered between September 1946 and 2 January 1947 under ARP Project 94555-S from Albrook Field, Canal Zone,[28] and these augmented the Fuerza Aérea de Chile's (FACh) existing rather mixed transport fleet, which included the final surviving examples of pre-war Junkers Ju-86s. Chile had initially indicated that it wanted a total of six C-47s under ARP but, by 15 October 1947 notified the USAAF ARP Cadre at Quintero that, instead, it desired only five. This meant that the elusive sixth aircraft, which was in fact 42-23398 and was actually in place at Quintero at that date, was to have been diverted, initially, to the Cadre in Cuba.[29] However, this was changed to Venezuela on the grounds that this was closer. In fact, the aircraft ended up returning to CONUS and then on to the Pacific, despite her wanderings throughout South America.

Often reported by spotters as a Chilean military aircraft, this C-47A-25-DK, modified at some point to DC-3 configuration, wore both A4 214 and simply '214' while assigned to the DGAC, although she was in fact operated and maintained by the air force. *Mario Magliochetti*

As noted in the text, US intelligence documents reported a C-47 in service with the Fuerza Aérea de Chile as early as 15 January 1946 – well ahead of ARP deliveries much later that year. It has been speculated that the aircraft in question may have been CC-CLL-0010, seen here wearing Servicio Experimental – Santiago-Punta Arenas titles. MSN 16993/34255, this aircraft was not formally registered to LAN until July 1946 and may have been operating with a joint DGAC and military crew on this route-proving flight in January. *FACh*

Purchased from TEMCO in May 1947, this DC-3C became 'El Canela', the Chilean Presidential aircraft, first as serial 901 and later as 950 after 1957. *Mario Magliochetti*

The change from a desired total of six to five was probably due to the fact that Chile elected to commercially acquire a specially modified aircraft reconfigured into a VIP transport for the President and even though acquiring the 'lowest' serial number, her actual entry into service did not occur until 28 May 1947, after undergoing VIP transformation by TEMCO in Texas. Reports that this was an ARP-supplied aircraft are incorrect. Indeed, like ARP-supplied aircraft elsewhere in Latin America, the date of arrival 'in country' differed substantially from their formal handover dates. The six C-47s, for instance, had arrived starting in September 1946, but were not paid for and turned over until 29 September 1947, even though they had been operating, for all intents and purposes, as Chilean aircraft for a little over a year while the small USAF cadre trained indigenous crews. With these aircraft, the FACh finally enjoyed an air transport and cargo capability it had never experienced before and by 1 January 1949, these new assets had been consolidated as the nucleus of the Grupo de Transporte, which had been formed on 29 December 1945 and, unlike other FACh units, reported directly to the Comando en Jefe of the service. On 21 July 1948, however, the unit had been redesignated in the existing Chilean system as the Grupo de Aviación N.º10, de Transporte. Besides the five ARP-supplied C-47s, the unit also included five Vultee BT-13s, six assorted North American AT-6s and eight Beech AT-11s, all initially working out of the so-called Brest hangar at Base Aérea de Los Cerrillos.

Those first five or six aircraft, however, and contrary to most accounts, were initially issued Chilean serials between 901 and 906, with 902, 903, 905 and 906 definitely confirmed. It appears that at

least one of these may have been the former ARP Cadre training aircraft 43-49043. These serials were retained only briefly, however, apparently between 1948 and 1949, when the conversion to the more familiar 950, 951, etc, took place.

By 1 April 1949, however, the special Presidential C-47 had been added to the unit inventory, for a total of six, and the number of BT-13s and AT-6s had increased to eight and eleven respectively. The AT-11s had been transferred to other units and had been replaced by a single Beech UC-45F shortly thereafter, however. Of the C-47s, two were non-operative as of that date, awaiting various parts.

The six C-47s remained on hand well into April 1950 but, by this time, four were inoperative awaiting parts, as the FACh logistics system attempted to cope with the intricacies of the USAF supply system, and put behind them the remnants of pre-war procedures and a rather casual attitude regarding periodic and scheduled maintenance that had been preached religiously by the USAF ARP cadre. The USAF Mission apparently stepped up, however, because by 12 July 1950, all six were once again airworthy. By 24 September 1951, the unit had lost its BT-13s and AT-6s and retained only the six C-47s and single Beech UC-45F. Besides routine personnel movement and cargo duties, the unit also had a small parachute squad of just ten officers and men.

Commencing around 1952, the C-47 fleet had all received the colour scheme with which they came to be identified, comprising white upper decking, an ample blue cheatline and, of course, the distinctive Chilean national insignia and rudder marking, plus their individual aircraft serials, in generous numerals, on the rear fuselages. The unit diversified further, adding brand-new de Havilland Canada DHC-2 Beavers and two ARP-supplied Consolidated OA-10 Catalinas. During the first six months of 1952, the so-called Bostick Survey Team visited Chile to assess the state of the aircraft supplied to that time under ARP and, as a result, and in concert with the USAF Mission Chief in place at that time, recommended highly that the FACh be immediately approved for grant aid support for its existing fleet of six C-47s.

By late 1952, the FACh had gained a keen appreciation for the utility of the C-47s and sent a delegation to the US to seek six more assorted surplus aircraft, with a view to bringing the unit up to a full squadron strength. By the end of 1953, this had been increased to a total of fifteen of all variants and, besides far-ranging internal missions on nearly a daily basis, were also being used on the important weekly diplomatic exchange flight to distant Arica in the far north.

One of the first DC-3 series aircraft specifically acquired and dedicated to Presidential duty, 901 had been built as a C-47B-1-DL but was completely refurbished into a VIP configuration by TEMCO in May 1947 as 901. Named 'El Canela', she wore three different colour schemes and two different serials during her lengthy service career. *Samuel Matamala Fuentes*

Although the first five ARP-supplied C-47s were initially coded 902 to 906, these were soon changed to the 950s, including 954, which had served previously in the Caribbean Air Command (CAC) in Panama. During the 1950s, the USAF started the use of Day-Glo paint on many aircraft, and Latin American operators were quick to copy. This aircraft was being cannibalised for parts by December 1969. *Georg von Roitberg*

Readers will note that, by March 1953, the FACh had somehow arrived at an arrangement with the Witbeck Corporation (sometimes, for some reason, also cited as Widbeck), which, itself, was a subsidiary of TEMCO, to overhaul a total of five DC-3s or C-47s for Chile, one of which was to be the highly unusual aircraft outfitted as an ambulance or 'flying hospital'. As part of its contract, Witbeck was also providing Chilean ground crews with training in major overhauls under the instruction of its own licensed CAA crews.

The first of these Witbeck-supplied aircraft arrived on 4 March 1953. Described as a 'zero-hour' aircraft, the FACh reportedly paid $110,000 for the aircraft that, after reading the details in the following table, must certainly be regarded as most handsome profit for the Texas firm. She was flown home by a Chilean crew, taking a rather leisurely seven days to make the trip, being piloted by Capitán de Bandada Germán Díaz Visconti. Witbeck had apparently loaded the aircraft with 'bells and whistles', including VHF, liaison and command radio sets, a galley, airline-type seats as, by all accounts, a VIP aircraft – but not the Presidential aircraft (serial 901), which had been acquired more than six years earlier. Two more of the Witbeck overhauls were due to be received in April and May. The USAF intelligence officer who described this delivery went on to record that 'the three new C-47s will supplement the needy transport group, who are having increasing maintenance problems on a daily-increasing basis. At present, two of their assigned C-47s are sitting AOCP (aircraft out-of-commission for parts) at Balmaceda and Iquique.' Interestingly, this report went on to say that the FACh was also engaged in negotiations with Witbeck at the time to rebuild five of the six Chilean C-47s before August 1953. Thus, some of the aircraft shown on the following list may, in fact, have had prior Chilean antecedents. The only aircraft not being discussed with Witbeck was the Presidential aircraft, named 'El Canela' due to the colour of its interior, which had been overhauled somewhere else. The report, however, went on to say that, besides the possibility of overhauling five existing Chilean aircraft, the negotiators were also discussing the procurement from Witbeck of 'three more similar C-47 aircraft for the same unit price, as well as the offer to overhaul to zero-hours the five Chilean C-47s'. The truth of all of this appears to have been somewhere in the middle.

Sometime prior to 8 March 1954, a Grupo 10 C-47 sustained extensive damage at distant Puerto Montt as the result of a bad ground loop while landing long and hot in foul weather, and was reported under repair. This may well be one of the ARP aircraft, and the serial of this aircraft has not been identified.

A little more than a month later, on 12 April 1954, tragedy struck the Chilean C-47 operating fleet and, indeed, the entire service. An unidentified Grupo 10 C-47, crewed by pilot Capt. Fernando Rojas Mercado, co-pilot Capt. Alfonso Mueller Rivera, two engineers (one of them a trainee) and a radio operator, plus nine passengers, crashed and burned shortly after take-off from Los Cerrillos bound for Iquique. The accident occurred about ten minutes after take-off some 30km north of Santiago near the small village of Batuco. According to observers, the port engine had failed and caught fire. The crew commenced circling, and were apparently looking for a spot to make a forced landing. However, the fire in the port engine was so intense that the engine tore free of the aircraft, and the aircraft immediately entered into a tight spiral and crashed. As this loss cannot be linked to any of the known C-47s or DC-3s in our accompanying list, it is assumed that this is yet another instance of a serial that was used twice.

As of 30 June 1954, the FACh was in possession of a total of eleven C-47s of all versions, suggesting that the five ARP aircraft, joined by the six commercially acquired aircraft in 1953, were all still extant. Of these, ten were assigned to the dedicated Grupo 10 at Santiago, but of these, only six were regarded as 'combat ready', while the VIP-configured aircraft was assigned to the Escuadrón de Comando en Jefe, also at Los Cerrillos, but was also regarded as 'combat ready'. The report also noted that a twelfth aircraft had crashed during the first half of 1954, with fatalities, probably referring to serial 956. However, an undocumented loss of a Grupo 10 C-47 occurred on 8 November 1954 when a runaway Piper PA-22-135 Tri-Pacer ran into it on the military parking ramp at Los Cerrillos. The Piper, which was owned by the Club Aéreo de Talca, had been parked near the C-47 on the military side of the field. The accident occurred when the Piper's pilot attempted to start the aircraft by himself. When he 'propped' the engine, the engine suddenly engaged and the aircraft simply took off on its own and ran directly into the port engine nacelle and main landing gear of the stationary C-47. Damage to the C-47 consisted chiefly of a lacerated tyre, destroyed oil cooler, crushed engine nacelle and other minor abrasions and contusions. Fortunately, the engine and prop were not damaged. The C-47 was apparently back in service in several weeks. Air Orders of Battle for 1 January 1955 still reflected a total of eleven C-47s, of which six were combat ready, assigned alongside four de Havilland Canada DHC-2s and a single Ryan Navion 260 (serial 902), but also listed the VIP Escuadrón de Comando en Jefe with the customised C-47, two Beech C-45s, three DHC-2s and, surprisingly, the first three de Havilland Vampires.

By 15 April 1956, ten C-47s were still assigned to Grupo 10, which also still had four DHC-2s, the Ryan Navion 260, and three helicopters. Only five of the C-47s were 'combat ready', however, and the reporting officer noted that 'C-47 utilisation has dropped off appreciably in the last few months. In fact, at one point, all of them were grounded for lack of various vital spares.'

Chilean C-47 strength remained static between 1 January 1957 and 1 June 1958 at a total of eleven aircraft. A little earlier, as of 3 April 1958, Grupo 10 still was routinely operating ten C-47s, but by this time also had two DHC-2s, two Beech C-45s, one Beech AT-11, a Cessna 182, three Bell 47D-1ss and four new Sikorsky S-55s – certainly a highly specialised transport unit! The unit had a total of twenty qualified crews, of whom fifteen were rated by the USAF as 'combat ready', which was a highly coveted designation at the time. The VIP aircraft assigned to the Escuadrón de Comando en Jefe (which the AOB said was 'often referred to locally as the Presidential Squadron') served alongside a single DHC-2 and two Beech C-45s. The AOB added that 'in addition to the four hand-picked and fully Combat Ready crews assigned to this unit, various staff officers from the Chilean Air Force Headquarters also fly these aircraft', apparently to qualify for their monthly flying pay. Later that year, on 1 October 1958, the VIP unit had apparently been consolidated into Grupo 10 as the unit by then had eleven C-47s as well as three de Havilland Canada DHC-3 Otters, two DHC-2s, five C-45s, one North American T-6G Standard, two Cessna 182s, three Bell 47D-1s, one Sikorsky S-55 and a new Beech C50 Twin Bonanza. Of the C-47s, eight were rated 'combat ready' and the unit boasted a total of twenty-four complete crews, of whom nineteen held 'combat rated' credentials.

Grupo 10 dispatched two of its best C-47s to support FACh Lockheed F-80Cs from Grupo 7 taking part in Operation Banyan Tree III in the Panama Canal Zone in March 1960, where for the first time they exercised with similar units from the USAF, Brazil, Colombia, Panama and Peru.

Around 1962, the first dedicated MAP supplied aircraft started to arrive, and as of 31 March two of these had been supplied via the Grant Aid provisions of MAP. These included at least one configured

as an EC-47 and one as a dedicated medical/ambulance aircraft. The MAP V-12 report for December 1963 thus reported that, to that date, the FACh had acquired a total of sixteen DC-3s and C-47s of all variants, of which fifteen were still possessed, although two were not active and one had been lost through attrition. These were all still assigned to Grupo 10, which, oddly, also had two Douglas B-26 Invaders on strength by that time. Another MAP-supplied C-47 arrived during September 1964, apparently in company with two of the first Chilean Cessna T-37Bs.

The MAP continued to support a total of fourteen C-47s as late as December 1966 for spares and technical updates, and this total included ten C-47As, two C-47Bs and two EC-47s. However, the report for the period July to December 1967 reflected a total of fifteen C-47As having been received (of which ten were still possessed and active and five lost through attrition), two C-47Bs (both still on hand) and three EC-47s, of which two were active and one was lost through attrition. This apparently included serial 971. By 31 December 1968, while Grupo 10 still retained a total of twelve C-47 and EC-47 aircraft (with sixteen complete crews for them), the unit had also added three Douglas DC-6Bs and three Bell UH-1D helicopters, further defining its universal approach to providing transport service.

By September 1969, Chilean use of C-47s was on the decline. The country had been allocated a total of seven MAP-supplied C-47s, and actually had, according to the USAF count at the time, acquired a total of fifteen from all sources, of which ten were active. They had flown a total of 325:20 hours during the preceding three months. The report also showed Chile as having received two C-47Bs (which flew a combined 195:55 during the previous quarter) and the three, elusive EC-47s, two of which were still on the AOB, but not-MAP supported. Between them, they had flown 48:20.

Late in their Chilean service lives, the surviving C-47s were dispersed to smaller support units throughout the country. Some went to the Escuadrilla de Enlace, an element of Ala 1 at Cerro Moreno, Antofagasta, where they operated in co-operation with Lama helicopters, while others went to the Escuadrilla de Enlace of Ala 4 'Los Cóndores' at Iquique, also operating with Lamas.

One of the aircraft acquired from the rather dubious Witbeck Aircraft, Inc. of Gainesville, Texas, in 1953, code 955 was actually a C-53D. Pictured here at Love Field, Dallas, on 13 February 1953, and has not as yet had her white Fuerza Aérea de Chile titles added to her forward cheatline. Cannibalised for parts by September 1965, she apparently had serviceability issues throughout her service life. *Pete Bulban via Dr Gary Kuhn*

FACh Serial	Previous Identity	Built As	MSN	Assignments and Notes
A4 214 CC-CBJ	42-93390 CA39 (CATC) XT-T31 N8326C N4660V CC-CBJ	C-47A-25-DK DC-3	13296	Operated for the DGAC by the FACh as A4 214, this aircraft arrived in Chile in Feb 54 for LAN as their Fleet Number '214'/CC-CBJ, but it only served with the DGAC as an airways check aircraft for a relatively brief period. To LAN as CC-CLDT by 1 Mar 54 and CC-CBX in Dec 62, from whence much confusion has arisen. It returned to DGAC control again around Apr 72 and was sold to Aerotal in Jul 75 but not taken up. It then passed to Aeroservicios Parragué. She is displayed today at the Museo Nacional Aeronáutico y del Espacio as LAN CC-CBX.
901	43-16162 NC-81388	C-47B-1-DL DC-3C	20628	Although purchased as early as 13 May 47 from TEMCO, this aircraft was not actually delivered after being outfitted by TEMCO for Presidential duties until 28 May 47 on Export CofA E-12494. She was delivered by a US crew on 11 Jun 47. Named 'El Canela', she was long-lived. She was flown back to the US between 8 and 10 Jun 51 for overhaul at Bolling AFB, DC and was reserialed as 950(2) in 1957.
902 (?) 950 (1)	42-93281	C-47A-20-DK	13175	ARP supplied, arrived in country on 3 Sep 46 but not formally handed over until 29 Sep 47. A former Sixth Air Force aircraft. When the former 901 was reserialed as 950 in 1957, this aircraft was reserialed as 961 (q.v.).
950 (2)	43-16162 NC-81388 901	C-47B-1-DL DC-3C	20628	The Presidential aircraft. Received this new serial in 1957 and the aircraft that had worn it before, above, was reserialed as 961. Reported on 8 Jul 73 at La Serena-Florida and then that she was stored at Los Cerrillos by Apr 1977.
903 (?) 951 (1)	42-101002	C-47A-75-DL	19465	ARP on 3 Sep 46, handed over on 29 Sep 47.
951 (2)	45-995 CC-CLM-011 CC-CLDI-203	C-47B-45-DK DC-3C	16998/34260	Transferred from LAN by 17 Oct 60. Also reported as CC-CBO in Dec 62 however! Reported in service at La Serena on 15 Jan 74.
904 (?) 952 (1)	42-93102	C-47A-20-DK	12976	ARP on 15 Oct 47. Written off at Osorno on 28 Jan 59.
952 (2)	43-48004	C-47A-30-DK	13820/25265	Issued permission to transit the Panama Canal Zone on 1 Sep 53 flying from Gainesville, Texas (home of Witbeck Aircraft, Inc., source of other Chilean C-47s around this time.) An FACh C-47 with this serial was also granted permission to transit the Canal Zone on 21 Jan 53 while escorting home a batch of new Beech T-34s (serials 101 to 112). By 13 Nov 53, a C-47 with this serial was at Gainesville, TX, being overhauled, presumably by Witbeck. Crashed on 28 Jan 59 at Osorno Volcano.
905 (?) 953	42-100998	C-47A-75-DL	19461	ARP on 3 Oct 46. Written off on 16 Jun 63 42km from Aysén with twenty on board.
906 (?) 954	43-48002	C-47A-30-DK	13818/25263	A former CAC aircraft, ARP to Chile c.15 Oct 47. This aircraft was used to provide escort to a batch of reconditioned North American T-6G Standard aircraft between 10 and 15 Jan 50. By 31 Dec 69 this aircraft had been removed from the inventory and was being cannibalised. This aircraft or one marked with this serial was noted on a pedestal on display at Viña del Mar, Chile, by Nov 76. Later acquired by private interests and configured as the 'C-47 Café' but to San Gregorio as 'Discotheque C-47' by Feb 78. Highly respected Chilean aero-historian Dr Sergio Barriga Kreft has cast doubt upon the actual identification of this aircraft.
955	42-68775 NC-49549	C-53D-DO	11702	Probably acquired commercially on 2 Feb 53 from Witbeck Aircraft, Inc., Gainesville, TX, but actually delivered somewhat earlier, as Chile requested US permission to transit the Canal Zone with a C-47 marked as 955, flying from Gainesville, TX, on 21 Jan 53. This aircraft has also been reported in some sources as MSN 11709. The MAP V-12 Report for 30 Sep 65 reported that this aircraft had not flown since 6 Apr 61 and that she was being cannibalised for parts as of Sep 65. The fuselage of what is believed to be this aircraft had been on display at the La Cisterna Municipal Stadium (formerly known as Estadio del Palestino) in Santiago c.Sep 77.

Also wearing rather weathered Day-Glo on her rear fuselage, nose and underside of her wing tips, code 962 was a September 1965 MAP-supplied aircraft, C-47A-20-DK – possibly the second use of this code. She is seen here visiting the Aeroparque at Buenos Aires, Argentina. *via Dr Gary Kuhn*

956	41-18408 NC-361	C-47-DL	4470	Direct purchase from Witbeck Aircraft, Inc., Gainesville, TX, on 27 Apr 53. This aircraft had a most bizarre provenance. Initially used by the US CAA's Region 5 as NC-361 as early as 20 Nov 45, this was cancelled 12 Dec 46 and she was sold to Clarence E. Page of Page Aviation Service, Oklahoma City, OK, when she was described as a 'used aluminum DC-3 fuselage' for a mere $126! Page then sold the aircraft to Gordon B. Hamilton of Tucson, AZ, on 20 Apr 51, who was doing business as Aircraft Conversion & Maintenance Company. It then went to International Airports, Inc., on 24 Apr 51 of Burbank, CA, which reported it was going to rebuild the aircraft using the fuselage of former Navy R4D-4 BuA33820 – that, coincidentally, had been NC-226 with the CAA. The rebuild was accomplished as N-361 around 30 Oct 51. Witbeck then acquired this hybrid on 25 Oct 52, and it is virtually certain that it was sold at a bargain price to the totally unknowing Chileans on 20 Oct 52 on Export Certificate of Airworthiness E-27550. Reported involved in an accident on 13 Apr 54 at Batuco, Chile. However, also reported as lost on 12 May 67 at El Plumerillo, suggesting that this serial may have been used a second time.
957 (1)	*N6200C*	*DC-3A-S1C3G*	*'25445'*	Apparently yet another 'Witbeck Special', the hulk of this aircraft had been purchased as a 'fuselage, repairable', from Headquarters, III US Army Corps, Fort MacArthur, CA, on 23 May 52 by none other than Lee Mansdorf & Company of Los Angeles, CA, for $757. Mansdorf then built up an aircraft using the fuselage and claimed that Douglas had issued him this MSN for the resulting aircraft. The III US Army Corps had identified the aircraft only as '6NSVC', which appears to be without significant meaning. Commencing on 23 Apr 53, the aircraft was cited repeatedly as type 'DC-3A-S1C3G'. At this point, Witbeck acquired the result on 20 Apr 53 and sold it to the Chileans quickly, on 29 Apr 53, the aircraft receiving Export Certificate of Airworthiness E-18649. There were apparently two aircraft with this serial. The first was noted at Gainesville, TX, presumed at Witbeck Aviation, as of 11–14 May 53.
957 (2)	42-92101 0-92101	C-47A-1-DK	11864	MAP on 24 Nov 60. This aircraft was reported on the MAP V-12 report for 30 Sep 65 as previously 42-92101, and as being unserviceable for lack of certain engine parts as of that date. It was an aircraft that had spent most of its post-war service life with the USAF in Europe.
958	NC-1943 N1943	DC-3-362 DC-3-G202A	3268	Direct purchase from Witbeck Aircraft, Inc., Gainesville, TX, on 27 Apr 53. TEMCO apparently overhauled this aircraft around 25 Oct 61. Chile had apparently requested that the aircraft be converted from passenger to cargo configuration but, when confronted with the cost of the work, at least $55,000, it elected not to proceed. Reported salvaged on 1 Jul 65 but cited on the MAP V-12 report, with this MSN, as a 'C-47A'. Withdrawn from service in Jul 65.
959	41-38692 CNAC-67 XT-87 NC-8357C N75097	C-47-DL DC-3C-S1C3G	6151	Direct purchase from Witbeck Aircraft, Inc., Gainesville, TX, on 28 Sep 53 on Export CoA E-27551. This aircraft was initially outfitted as a flying 'ambulance'/medical care aircraft, but later reverted to conventional transport configuration. Last reported in service on 27 Apr 62 but also reported destroyed by fire on 7 Mar 74, location unknown.
960	43-16284 YV-AZP YV-C-AZP N1848M	C-47B-1-DL	20750 (or 20744?)	Direct purchase from the Madon Corporation, Las Vegas, NV, on 3 Nov 53 (although the Air-Britain monograph initially suggested Oct 47) but not reported delivered to Chile until 25 Sep 63, which seems most unlikely. This notion is reinforced by the fact that a C-47 coded 960 was used to escort brand-new Beech T-34s (serials 113 to 125) on the long journey home around 23 Apr 54. Reportedly crashed on 18 Jan 74 20km south of Chaitén, Los Lagos, and her remains subsequently used as a house. An aircraft wearing this serial has been preserved since Jul 80 near the Santiago International Airport but is clearly not the same aircraft.
961	42-93067	C-47A-20-DK	12937	MAP on 24 Nov 60. The 30 Sep 65 MAP V-12 report gives serial 961 with this identity, and stated that she was inactive as of that date for lack of certain engine parts. This aircraft was still inoperative due to lack of certain parts by 10 Apr 67. Preserved as such at the Museo Nacional de Aeronáutica y del Espacio – MNAE.
962	42-93094	C-47A-20-DK	12967	MAP supplied by 30 Sep 65, as of which date she was inactive due to lack of certain engine parts, probably ex-USAFSO. Reported in service at on 19 Nov 73. Reported withdrawn from use on 7 Mar 74.
963	43-48854	C-47B-5-DK	14670/26115	MAP supplied by 25 Nov 60. The MAP V-12 Report for 30 Sep 65 cites serial 963 as '14670' and reported her inactive due to lack of certain engine parts. This conflicts with the Air-Britain account for this aircraft, which describes her as a Dakota III, KJ941 which went to the South African Air Force as SAAF-6847 and which crashed 8 Jul 45 at Zwartkop. In service by 22 Apr 72 and Mar 84. This was one of only a few FACh C-47s that was camouflaged in rather unusual two-tone desert colours. This aircraft is now preserved at the MNAE.
964	44-77083 KN699 RNAF X-8/ZU-8 44-77083	C-47B-35-DK Dakota IV	16667/33415	MAP redistribution from the Netherlands to Chile on 31 Aug 62. This aircraft was employed as the VIP-configured aircraft for the use of the Commander in Chief of the FACh. Reported in service as of 19 Nov 73. Donated to Paraguay as FAP-2028 10 Dec 81.

965	42-92832	C-47A-15-DK	12676	MAP redistribution to Chile on 21 Jun 62, an exceptionally storied aircraft. Reported crashed on 12 May 65 at Guaymallén, Mendoza, Argentina, and damaged beyond repair. Retired from service and converted to a nightclub at Las Condes, Santiago.
966	42-23301	C-47A-1-DL	9163	MAP on 25 Apr 62 to Chile. Utilised as an aerophotogrammetric platform. Known to have been assigned to Grupo 6 as of 1965 and as late as 9 Oct 74. Withdrawn from service on 30 Jan 78.
967	42-23839	C-47A-30-DL	9701	MAP to Chile after 17 Feb 62. Withdrawn from use and cannibalised by 31 Dec 69.
968	43-48843 KJ932 RNAF X-16/ZU-16	C-47B-5-DK Dakota III	14659/26104	MAP redistribution from the Netherlands to Chile after 8 Mar 61. This aircraft was reported active at La Serena-Florida 7 Sep 73. To N2782G, All American Aviation, Inc. (or Atlas Aircraft Corp.), Miami, FL, on 8 Oct 82.
969	42-92725	C-47A-10-DK	12557	MAP to Chile on 24 Apr 62 but apparently either returned for conversion to ambulance aircraft or delivery delayed until 1964. This is believed to have been the so-called 'Medical-Dental' C-47. However, while the aircraft arrived in Sep 64, the portable medical equipment intended to be installed aboard did not arrive for some time afterwards. Donated to Paraguay as FAP-2030 10 Dec 81.
970	43-15264	C-47A-80-DL EC-47A JC-47A C-47A EC-47A	19730	MAP to Chile on 25 Aug 64. Reported in service at La Serena on 7 Dec 73. Crashed on 31 Jul 75 at Colina, north of Santiago, after the parachute lines of a paratrooper training on the aircraft got tangled in the ailerons as he exited the aircraft, ten killed.
971 A1-971	41-7684 NC-84 N24	DC-3A-368 C-48A-DO	4148	Purchased direct in 1964. The MAP V-12 report for July–December 1967 referred to this aircraft as '41-4148', an obvious attempt to make sense of her purely civil MSN. To A1-971 with the DGAC as a radio aid check aircraft as early as 1968 and on 26 Aug 70 was noted in an FAA-style high-visibility colour scheme by that date with Chilean national insignia. Some years later, still being operated by the DGAC, the serial was changed to simply A1 and the '971' dropped. Sold after 10 Feb 80 to N2782S, All American Aviation, Inc., Miami, FL.
972	43-16381 0-16381	C-47B-1-DL C-47D	20847	Former USAF Mission to Chile aircraft from at least 11 Aug 53 until passed to Chile under MAP on 13 Nov 70. Sold to All American Aviation, Inc. (also cited as the Atlas Aircraft Corp.), Miami, FL, as N2782N on 5 Oct 82.

C-47B-5-DK 43-48854 as she appears presently in the open-air park of the MNAE at Los Cerrillos. A close examination of the airframe revealed no trace of the two-tone camouflage shown in the three-view. The abbreviated Day-Glo band around the rear fuselage is noteworthy. The service titles on the forward fuselage were often slanted in service, however. *via Mario Overall*

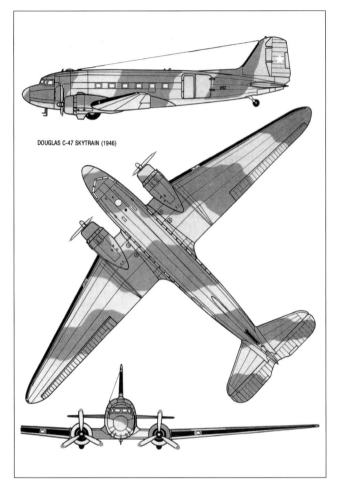

DOUGLAS C-47 SKYTRAIN (1946)

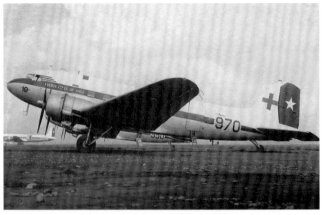

Above: Code 970, an August 1964 MAP acquisition, last served in the USAF as an EC-47A. The red cross on the vertical fin suggests that this may in fact have been the aircraft modified as a flying clinic. Note the open cabin door on code 950 in the background, the Presidential DC-3C, 'El Canela', and the Grupo 10 unit insignia on the nose of 970. *Mario Magliochetti*

Left: Only a few Chilean C-47s were camouflaged during their service, but included code 963 shown here, which was painted with highly unusual desert colours – obviously for use in the north of the country in the Atacama region. Her solitary concessions to markings were the white star on either side of the rudder and her serial in small black numerals on the rear fuselage. Supplied under MAP by November 1960, an aircraft with this serial, as shown in another illustration, survives in the collections of the MNAE. *FACh*

Below: Certainly a candidate for one of the most attractive Latin American military Douglas twin, code 971 was built as a DC-3A-368 and then became a rare C-48A. Purchased in 1964, she had been A1-971 with the DGAC as a radio aid check aircraft, and in fact retains the DGAC emblem on her nose in this 26 August 1970 image at Howard AFB, CZ. *Jimmy Stark*

Above: This view of C-48A code 971 reveals that her special markings were not confined to the fuselage. Photographed at Howard AFB, CZ, on 13 August 1966, she clearly wears the Chilean national insignia on her upper starboard wing. *Hagedorn*

Right: Noted in the open-air display area of the MNAE at Los Cerrillos in the 1970s, this C-47 is rather mysterious, as there was no evidence of a serial code on the aircraft. Although speculated to have been 963, the antenna array and lack of an astrodome on the forward fuselage do not agree, not to mention the camouflage, which appears closer to that worn on the Chilean Hawker Hunter fleet! *Pedro Turina*

Chilean Navy

In keeping with its long tradition as a Latin American naval power, Chile had actually created the nucleus of a naval air arm when the Navy detailed several junior officers to attend flight training at the Army school in 1916. However, it was not until 16 March 1923 that the Servicio de Aviación Naval de la Armada de Chile was officially formed, although the Navy had acquired, via the British donation of 1918, a number of aircraft and operated them independently of the separate Army establishment prior to that time.

In March 1930, however, in one of the earliest such actions anywhere, Chile decided to merge the separate Army and Naval aviation services into a single service, then known as the Fuerza Aérea Nacional (FAN).

This situation persisted until around January 1952, and although a number of attempts were made to reactivate a dedicated naval aviation service when Lend-Lease equipment started to arrive, specifically to operate the decidedly maritime aircraft received such as the Consolidated PBY-5s and PBY-5As, as well as Vought-Sikorsky OS2U-3s, the FAN successfully opposed encroachment attempts on its rather jealously guarded success as establishing itself as a separate branch of service. However, it was an open secret that a substantial percentage of the members of the serving officer corps of the FAN and FACh when it was renamed were graduates of the Naval Academy, and had accumulated, as a direct result, extensive at-sea service. Indeed, practically all of the qualified 'mission' pilots, that is, those in the middle age group, which by 1952, comprised some 20 per cent of the officer corps of the FACh, were graduates of the US Navy training curriculum completed at Corpus Christi NAS, Texas, during the war. While post-war emergence of the USAF Mission had a marked influence on all of this, the Naval tradition within the FACh remained significant. What is more, the primary – and practically only – combat mission of the FACh by that time was naval support and anti-submarine work. One USAF Mission officer, Col William E. Ross, went to far as to describe Chile as 'a long, narrow, geographically fixed "aircraft carrier"'.

Then, in 1953, what was to become the Servicio de Aviación was reborn, and its first aircraft started arriving between September and November 1954, comprising three Bell 47G helicopters and three Beech D18S transports. After training, they entered into formal service around 15 December. The D18s were at the time located at El Belloto, Quilpué, and, while the helicopters were assembled there by Bell crews, two of them were intended for service aboard the cruisers ARC *Capitán Prat* and *Bernardo O'Higgins*, while the third was to be stationed at El Belloto. The service had still not received the official blessing of the government at the time, however, and the officer in charge, Capitán de Fragata Calixto Pereira, was described as 'the Officer in Charge of Aviation Matters'. The new establishment had a total of eleven pilots at the time, all of whom were qualified on the D18Ss, and six of whom were cross-trained and qualified on the Bell 47Gs as well. They had all been trained by the US Navy, while enlisted ratings had been trained at Bell and Beech. According to the USAF Assistant Air Attaché at the time, LTC Robert F. Kolstad, the FACh 'was unhappy and quite apprehensive about the Chilean Navy receiving aircraft'.

The US Navy Mission, on the other hand, was encouraging a broader view and, not unexpectedly, cited the separate roles and professionalism of the USAF and US Naval Aviation as a model for Chile. Not surprisingly, additional aircraft followed, including Sikorsky SH-34J antisubmarine helicopters and, between January 1969 and July 1970, perhaps to no one's surprise, five former US Navy R4D/C-47 transports. These provided the Navy, for the first time, with a modest cargo and personnel transport capability that the Beech D18s simply could not support and, given the scope of Chile's extremely long seaboard and the distances between naval anchorages, these were most welcome. The C-47s apparently only served for about ten years before being replaced by more modern types and the last one is believed to have been sold around January 1981. It should be noted that previously published spotting reports citing a Chilean Naval C-47 marked as NAVAL 127 *c*.1977 appear to have been erroneous, probably an error for 121.

The first of five Chilean Navy aircraft, code 121 last served in the US Navy as a C-47H and was a MAS acquisition in January 1969, the former BuA17198. She was last reported in April 2000. *via Carlos Planas*

ARC Code	Previous Identity	Built As	MSN	Assignments and Notes
NAVAL 121	(42-93131) BuA17198	C-47A-20-DK R4D-5 C-47H	13009	Acquired via MAS from storage on 27 Jan 69. Noted on the line at El Belloto on 15 Mar 74. After withdrawal was exhibited first at Quelpie by Apr 78, then to the Chilean Naval aviation facility at Viña del Mar by Nov 97, and finally last reported at Torquemada by Apr 00.
NAVAL 122	(43-49327) BuA50794	C-47B-15-DK R4D-6 C-47J C-47M	15143/26588	Acquired via MAS from Davis-Monthan AFB in Feb 69. In service at La Serena-Florida, Coquimbo, on 12 Jul 73 along with NAVAL 123 and at El Belloto on 15 Mar 74. Last reported in service in 1977.
NAVAL 123	(44-76458) BuA50839	C-47B-25-DK R4D-6 C-47J	16042/32790	Acquired via MAS from storage after 18 Feb 69. Noted at Howard AFB, CZ, on 8 Mar 69. Last reported in service on 12 Jul 73.
NAVAL 124	(43-49697) BuA50827 N79961	C-47B-20-DK R4D-6 C-47J C-47L C-47M	15513/26958	Acquired via MAS from storage on 23 Jul 69. Noted in service at La Serena-Florida, Coquimbo, on 4 Dec 73 and at El Belloto on 15 Mar 74. Sold surplus by 1980 to CC-CJL.
NAVAL 125	(43-48687) BuA17283	C-47B-5-DK R4D-6 C-47J C-47M	14503/25948	Reported in error in some sources as MSN 14501/25946. Acquired via MAS from storage on 30 Jul 70. Oddly, no known spotting reports whatsoever. Thus, this may be the aircraft that was lost on 17 Sep 75.

You have to hunt for the serial code on this Chilean Navy C-47J, 123, just visible on her extreme nose. Compare the locations of the codes and national markings on this aircraft compared to 121, acquired within a month of each other. She was last reported in July 1973 and her fate is unknown. She was photographed at Howard AFB, CZ, in March 1969. *Hagedorn*

CHAPTER SIX

Colombia

O F ALL LATIN AMERICAN military operators of DC-3 and C-47 variants, Colombia may be fairly said to have entered into that relationship with in-depth experience in operating multi-engine transports throughout its extremely challenging territory.

With that, it must also be said that a study of Colombian use of the Douglas twin series has presented what are arguably the most challenging obstacles to documentation. The story of the aircraft in Colombia is fraught with contradictions, misinformation that has gained a life of its own over the years, and, in more recent years, the added complication of aircraft that have had their 'true' and original identities obscured intentionally by the harsh realities of the rise of the *narcotráfico*.

As noted earlier, Colombia shared the distinction of being only one of three Latin American nations to acquire C-47s under the provisions of the Lend-Lease programme during the actual Second World War years. The country's proximity to the Panama Canal unquestionably influenced the Munitions Assignment Board (Air) in the decision to approve the offset of a single aircraft, which quickly became the pride of the service.

The Fuerza Aérea Colombiana (FAC) also holds the distinction of having engaged its long-serving and extensive C-47 fleet in combat operations from nearly the beginning of their service. What has amounted to a seemingly endless insurrection in the country, which is usually dated as having commenced around 1946, and which has been inadequately described as *La Violencia,* dominated Colombian military aeronautics for twelve years between 1946 and

1958 but, in the midst of this, Colombia managed to find the wherewithal to support the United Nations in Korea as well – at the very height of its own internal problems. From the early stages of the so-called 'Korean Police Action', Colombia maintained a 1,000-man reinforced Army battalion in the brutal conflict, where it served with exemplary distinction. It must be said that the experience also provided at least 4,000 members of the Army, who rotated through the Korean crucible, with incomparable front-line experience, however, with which to deal with its problems at home.

When Colombia committed to the Korean War contingent, the FAC at home was organised as an Air Regiment with three primary groups, each of which was, in theory, comprised of three subordinate squadrons. Although the FAC itself did not take part in the Korean deployment, its participation undoubtedly qualified it for further US aid, which, with occasional hesitation, has continued to this writing.

Over the years leading up to the acquisition of its first C-47 in 1944, the FAC had not only evolved its own appreciation for air mobility, a lesson learned during the 1930s adventure known as the Leticia Incident, but also by cross-pollination with the pioneering aircraft, crews and management of the former SCADTA, which evolved into AVIANCA, the world's oldest, continuously operating airline. As a direct result of the war with Peru, by the end of the 1930s, the FAC had already operated more than fifteen multi-engine, land transports, consisting of five assorted Ford 5-AT Tri-Motors, six Junkers Ju 52/3m bomber/transports and four Curtiss-Wright T-32 Condor bomber/transports, not to mention other multi-engine types such as water-based Dornier Do J Wals and Consolidated P2Y-1C flying boats. No other Latin American nation came even close to this achievement.

The first FAC C-47? This aircraft has always been assumed to have been that first Lend-Lease C-47A-30-DK, 43-48240, which entered service around October 1944 – marking her as the very first genuine Latin American C-47. However, this may actually be a second aircraft with the same serial, as this image was taken in 1979 and the aircraft was written off in February 1983. *MAP1981-70 #269*

The earliest known image of a Colombian military C-47, this is clearly a late-block C-47B based on the distinctive nose ventral RDF loop. The troops being loaded, with both doors open, unfortunately obscure her serial, but she was probably FAC-652 or 662, as the details of the last digit can just be discerned. Aside from the rudder stripes in the national colours, she had no other fuselage markings. *via Ing. Gustavo Arias de Greiff*

A find study of FAC-651 on final approach, showing one of the earlier, standard schemes worn by most FAC C-47s for most of the 1950s and early '60s. Note the repetition of the individual code under the port wing, repeated on the upper starboard wing. *FAC via John M. Davis*

As its need for an ever-larger transport element became obvious from 1946 on, Colombia eventually amassed one of the largest – and most diverse – fleets of DC-3s and C-47s in Latin America, although it must be observed that only a fraction of those eventually acquired were ever operational at any one given time. It also created a virtually unique method of identifying aircraft within its serial numbering system that represented aircraft that were either rebuilt, or which represented the second use of a particular serial, by appending the alpha charter 'A'. This convention has led to no end of confusion over the years, but this data, where known, has been included in our table showing all known FAC aircraft.

That first Lend-Lease C-47 was requisitioned under Project CM-109. The Munitions Sub-Committee (Air) had actually received this request on 22 March 1944, and recommended approval to the senior MAB on 5 April 1944 and, following flight delivery by a Colombian crew from Kelly Field, Texas, and intensive crew training in the Panama Canal Zone, was in service by 5 October 1944, qualifying Colombia as the first Latin American military recipient of the type, remaining the solitary example as of 11 September 1946, when she was assigned to the Escuadrón de Transporte at Palanquero (Germán Olano), although the service was eagerly awaiting the delivery of three 'new' C-47Ds under the auspices of the ARP at the time. Perhaps emboldened by the unexpected MAB (Air) approval, the Colombians almost immediately submitted another requisition on 8 February 1945 for a mix of three C-47s and four sturdy Noorduyn UC-64s, and the (by then) Munitions Assignment Committee (MAC) (Air) noted that this request 'should be submitted for current consideration' although, in the event, it was not acted upon. Disappointed but at the same time encouraged by the language, Colombia then submitted CM-120 dated 2 May 1945, for no fewer than ten C-47s, although they obviously softened this request by including the caveat that the service would be more than happy to secure 'used' examples (with a one-year supply of spares), if necessary. Surprisingly, the MAC (Air) did not deny this request out of hand, but actually placed it on to the 'pending' file, although, in the event, the successful ending of the war precluded further action on the request.

When the Second World War ended and the outline of General Arnold's post-war ARP Projects became known throughout military circles in Latin America, the FAC had by then become enchanted with the capabilities of its single Lend-Lease C-47 and was eager to acquire more. Spurred on by some chance comments by a USAAF pilot who had taken part in the aborted USAAF project to mount a C-47 on giant Edo floats (the solitary XC-47C), on 25 June 1945, the FAC dispatched a formal request for information on this conversion

and, at the same time, a request that at least a few of its anticipated ARP C-47s be so equipped upon delivery. Since the 1930s war with Peru over the Leticia region, the FAC had gradually become one of the world's leading amphibious air arms, and, allied with the experiences amassed by SCADTA with float-equipped aircraft, found that aircraft so configured met the peculiar geographical demands of their operating environment. The FAC had hopes of acquiring a number of Consolidated OA-10 Catalinas under ARP (which it did), and had observed that this type was the closest any extant aircraft came to their requirements – but the OA-10 was, by no means, a 'cargo' aircraft. As a direct consequence, the FAC made not just one, but repeated requests to the USAAF and USAF for information on float-equipped C-47s. The FAC advised that it eventually received conflicting information on the practicality of the notion, some US advisors promoting the idea, while others, quoting from documents received from Wright Field about the limitations of the XC-47C, finally resulted in the discouragement of the idea.

With the eruption of the internal strife in 1946, coincident with the activities of what was, in its initial form, termed the Interim Program of the American Republics Projects (ARP), USAAF planners were watching the situation carefully – as were the senior leadership of the US State Department. By 18 May 1946, the first increment of C-47s for the FAC under the provisions of the ARP programme under Project No. 94484-S[30] were in country and, together with the USAAF training cadre that accompanied them, the service was eagerly assimilating the training delivered. However, at about the same time, the Chief of the US Military Mission, Col Henry A. Barber, Jr, was approached by Tte Cnel Luis F. Pinto, Commander of the FAC, demanding to know when the FAC would gain clear title to the three ARP C-47s then in the country.[31] When Col Barber reminded Pinto of the provisions of the transition, and asked him about the urgency, Pinto confessed that the aircraft were 'urgently needed to move FAC personnel and supplies'. Col Barber then volunteered to modify the established training programme to aid the FAC in carrying out these movements with mixed crews. Pinto then reported up his chain of command that the US Mission had denied his request, and then no less than Gen. Germán Campo, Chief of the Colombian General Staff in the Ministry of War, attempted to 'lean' on Col Barber to secure unfettered use of the aircraft. Barber then determined, through his own resources, that the real reason the FAC needed use of the aircraft 'urgently' was to ferry Colombian Army troops to a number of cities and towns in the country to quell riots that were expected to break out during the looming presidential elections. Col Barber then explained patiently to these two Colombian officers that the aircraft were still very much US property,

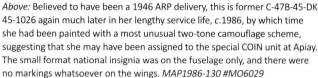

Above: Believed to have been a 1946 ARP delivery, this is former C-47B-45-DK 45-1026 again much later in her lengthy service life, *c.*1986, by which time she had been painted with a most unusual two-tone camouflage scheme, suggesting that she may have been assigned to the special COIN unit at Apiay. The small format national insignia was on the fuselage only, and there were no markings whatsoever on the wings. *MAP1986-130 #MO6029*

Above right: By the late 1970s, the *FAC* had adopted a rather handsome tropical scheme for most of its C-47s, and this new acquisition, C-47D FAC-653A, indicating a second use of that serial, has been prepped for delivery at Marana Air Park, Arizona, as of 14 March 1978. *ALPS*

Right: Compare this 1967 image of FAC-654 with the preceding view of FAC-653A. The service titles are noticeably smaller in size, as is the individual serial on her nose, and the distinctive 'lightning bolt' cheatline aligns with the top of the cabin windows in this image taken at Howard AFB, CZ. *Tom Surlak*

and that they could not be seen to be engaged in such activities. Barber did grant that the Mission had, by this, trained a sufficient number of FAC crews so that they were essentially ready to take over the operation of the aircraft, but until the formal title had been executed (and payment made[32]) the aircraft remained US property. Inevitably, this all-but-forgotten minor diplomatic skirmish was duly investigated by senior officers dispatched for that reason from the Caribbean Defence Command in Panama, all of whom exonerated Col Barber, concluding that he acted properly under the circumstances. Possibly as a result of this episode, in addition to further ARP deliveries, in fits and starts, it appears that the FAC acquired at least seven additional C-47s via the expanded ARP programme, although commercial acquisitions at almost exactly the same time have rather clouded the matter. From then on, the service added aircraft from a multitude of sources, including the various conditions of MAS and MAP. Although some sources have attempted to put a definitive number on the total of C-47s and DC-3s operated by the FAC, usually coming in at around as high as eighty-seven, the actual number was substantially different, as will be seen in the accompanying table.

But before the dust had even settled on the issue of the FAC making use of ARP C-47s still in US custody to transport troops, but probably as a US State Department initiative to sooth Colombian feelings, after the actual elections, the President-elect Mariano Ospina was formally invited to make a State Visit to the US, to arrive around 6 June 1946, to be accompanied by ten to twelve prominent Colombian politicians and businessmen as well as none other than the US Ambassador to Colombia, John C. Wiley. The solitary transport owned by Colombia at the time capable of making the trip, the C-47 (FAC-650) acquired via Lend-Lease, was in the US being reconditioned. Thus, to his astonishment, Col Barber was instructed to make one of the US Mission's ARP C-47s available to the party and, what is more, to remove the US insignia and replace it with full

Colombian military national markings! To make matters worse, he was directed to make available his 'most experienced' C-47 pilot, a serving USAAF officer, to make the trip as pilot-in-command. The entire sojourn that followed occupied nearly four weeks and included housing the entire party at the prestigious Blair House in Washington. It is not clear whether this aircraft acquired an FAC serial or not, but it appears that the US serial number was retained, which must certainly have raised some eyebrows when the aircraft landed at Bolling Field, District of Colombia!

Such was the need of the FAC as insurgency actions exploded throughout the country that, on 14 April 1948, a C-47 owned by the Compañía Expreso Aéreo Ltda. crashed 3km south of Palanquero and, while there were no injuries, the aircraft had been commandeered at the time by the Colombian Army. The airline had suspended operations in late 1947 and was, in fact, negotiating the sale of the aircraft at the time, even though it is not clear if the intended buyer was the FAC. Thus, although never being formally accessioned by the FAC, this aircraft necessarily must be included in this narrative. This operator is known to have operated C-900 (MSN 4363) and C-901 (MSN 4727) but, since both of these aircraft are known to have returned subsequently to the US, the aircraft lost must have been an otherwise unidentified registration.

By 25 October 1948, despite vigorous opposition to the Interim Program of ARP from the US State Department, the overall project had matured significantly, and continued apace through 1949, with the FAC counting a total of three C-47s on its Order of Battle by 1 January 1949. This total was undoubtedly the three provided under the terms of the initial Interim Program, but did not account for the single example acquired under Lend-Lease, suggesting that one aircraft had been lost by that date.[33] By 1 March 1949, the FAC had been placed on full alert due to reported insurgency on its southern border and, probably as a direct result, the Command of the FAC publicly announced that it was his intention to purchase eight C-47s, twelve Republic F-47Ds and two Consolidated PBY-5As from the US and that they were to be overhauled there by TEMCO under a $300,000 contract prior to delivery. The FAC, in the first stages of what few could realise at the time would be a counter-insurgency effort spanning decades, was scheduled to receive fifty-two additional surplus USAF aircraft, of which at least twelve were identified as C-47s, probably an amended total noted by the CinC earlier. By 1 September 1949, the FAC had direct-purchased four C-47s in the US (as well as two Consolidated PBY-5As and six Republic F-47Ds) and was reporting that, by the end of that month, these would be augmented by a further ten C-47s and six more F-47Ds.

The FAC Air Order of Battle for 1 January 1950 reflected a total of eleven C-47As, these including both the aircraft supplied under the Interim Program and the mature ARP of 1949, but with two more 'on order'. By 1 May 1950, the service possessed a total of ten C-47s, of which four were non-operable at the time. One had been written off on 6 February 1950 and another had crashed on 21 February 1950 but was deemed repairable. Nine of the C-47s were assigned to the Escuadrón de Transporte at Base Aérea Madrid (serving alongside two Lockheed C-60As, five Consolidated PBY-5As and OA-10As, two Beech AT-7s and seven assorted North American AT-6s), while one was assigned to the Maintenance and Supply depot at Palanquero, alongside a single Beech AT-11, twelve assorted North American AT-6s, seven Fairchild PT-19s, two North American B-25Js, fifteen Republic F-47Ds and three Vultee BT-15s.

On 16 April 1951, the FAC filed a lengthy request (which eventually received the formal nature of OSD/OMA Case Colombia-8) for aircraft it wished to acquire with the assistance of the USAF Mission and, perhaps a case of wishful thinking, included on the list a 'requirement' for no fewer than six brand-new Douglas Super DC-3s, six additional Consolidated PBY-5As, three de Havilland Canada L-20s, thirty North American T-6Gs, three Beech D18Ss and nine Douglas A-26Bs! The USAF, quite properly, commented that these were not within its normal supply chain, but suggested that such an acquisition could eventually be arranged if the FAC would supply one complete C-47 airframe for each

Super DC-3 requested!

In the meantime, besides C-47s being acquired from the US via military channels, between 1 January and 31 December 1952, the FAC is known to have received US State Department Export Licences for at least two commercially acquired C-47s. Thus, by 1 July 1952, the disposition of known FAC C-47s showed six at Madrid alongside a single DHC-2, four Beech AT-7s and a single AT-11, five PBY-5As and two Lockheed C-60As), one at Tres Esquinas (alongside two venerable Consolidated PT-11Cs, one ancient Junkers W34 and four North American AT-6s) and two at Apiay (alongside a single DHC-2 and seven AT-6s).

Between 20 April and 30 August 1954, the FAC, undoubtedly with the administrative assistance of the USAF Mission, submitted yet another Military Assistance request, this time for six Curtiss C-46s, three additional C-47s and ten Beech T-34s, which was assigned OSD/OMA Case No. Colombia-26. Surprisingly, the USAF responded that no C-47s were available at that time but that six C-46Fs were in storage and available, having just returned from commercial lease. The FAC decided, instead, to stick with the C-47 and not introduce yet another type into its maintenance nightmares.

By 30 June 1954, the FAC possessed a mix of nine C-47s and one DC-3, and all were assigned to Base Aérea Madrid. The USAF Mission judged all of them to be 'combat ready', including the DC-3. Since available data suggests that the service should have received a total of at least sixteen assorted aircraft by this time, the losses noted in the accompanying table prior to this date should be considered. By 1 January 1955, the FAC AOB showed a total of nine C-47s and one DC-3, of which all but one C-47 were rated 'combat ready', all based at Madrid, operating alongside a single Lockheed C-60A, seven assorted PBY-5As and OA-10s, seven DHC-2s, a single VIP-configured DC-4, an unidentified Cessna, two Beech AT-7s, a single AT-11 and five Beech D18s. The AOB noted that the FAC would 'undoubtedly acquire several more C-47s in the near future'. Subsequent Air Order of Battle data provides a glimpse of the ebb and flow of C-47s in the FAC: that for the period between 1 July and 31 December 1956 reflected a total of twelve, as did that for the period 1 January to 31 June 1957.

Photographed at Marana Air Park at the same time as FAC-653A, number 654A is marked identically in this March 1978 image, by which time she had been configured as a C-47D. She survived to be rebuilt as a Basler BT-67 as FAC-1654. *ALPS*

By January 1958, the FAC's depot at BA Madrid was routinely performing Inspect and Repair as Necessary (IRAN) periodic overhauls of the FAC C-47 fleet (as well as its fleet of AT-6s and PBY-5A/OA-10 aircraft), and on some of its earliest Bell 47 helicopters and R-1830 series engines. By 16 October 1958, the FAC had established a specialised unit at Techo airport and equipped it with five C-47s (three of which had been acquired in 1953 and two in 1954), alongside six Consolidated PBY-5A and OA-10s, nine mixed Beech twins, three C-54s and a single Lockheed C-60A.

Organisationally, by the 1960s, the FAC's transport elements had been broken into three separate commands. The Comando Aéreo de Transporte Militar (CATAM) consisted of two Grupos and a special organisation, known as the SATENA (Servicio Aéreo a Territorios Nacionales) airline. Of these, the Grupo de Transportes Aéreos Militares generally was responsible for heavy cargo for both the air force and the Army, while the Grupo de Helicópteros comprised, for the most part, rotary-wing assets – although there is some evidence that C-47s were assigned to support them from time to time. By 1961, the growing insurgency internally had almost completely preoccupied the established armed force of Colombia, and the realisation within the US aid community had finally recognised that, while the FAC was coping with very well-worn equipment, urgent reinforcement was needed. On 10 November 1961, Headquarters, USAF advised the Commander in Chief, US Caribbean Command, that it was taking the most unusual step of redirecting four C-47s that had actually been programmeed for Chile on Project MAP1C-31, to Colombia instead. These four aircraft, 44-76325, -76920, -76957 and -77079, were at the time being overhauled by OGMA in Portugal and were due to be completed by 30 December. The HQS, USAF directed CinC CARIB that 'it is mandatory that delivery of these four aircraft to Columbia be completed before February 1, 1962. Slippage will not be accepted.' Headquarters did, however, promise to replace the four aircraft intended for Chile as soon

as it could. They were apparently provided under the FMS provisions of MAP at a total cost of $163,800, not including certain support equipment. The CinC, CARIB commented that it was his understanding that the FAC needed these aircraft urgently to 'assist their inability to move sufficient numbers of troops into the remote Amazon river watershed area'. In addition to the C-47s, the Chief of Staff of the Colombian Army, Ruiz, had included in the FAC's 'wish list' three additional Douglas C-54s and information on the possible availability of Grumman SA-16 Albatross series aircraft as well.

By December 1963, the total number of C-47s listed as having been acquired by the service to that time was cited as sixteen, of which fourteen were still on hand, two having been lost through attrition. These were all assigned to what was described at the time as the 1º Escuadrón de Transporte based at BA Madrid. Of these, one C-47 had been delivered on 3 September 1963. During US Fiscal year 1964, the FAC also acquired three C-47s (and two C-54) via a most unusual source, the US Agency for International Development (USAID). Together with limited additional support for overhaul and rehabilitation, these all came from US surplus and at no cost to USAID or MAP. USAID promised that if the FAC demonstrated effective use of the aircraft supplied via this means, it would provide an equal number in FY65. With the internal situation entering into its third decade by the 1970s, the FAC commenced camouflaging some of its C-47s for the first time. Six more surplus USAF C-47s were acquired via MAS on 11 May 1965 and, sometime between January and June 1966, five C-47s were MAP-redeployed to the FAC that had previously served with the Royal Netherlands Air Force.

Right: A much earlier photograph, FAC-655 was also a 1949 ARP delivery, most likely the former C-47A-40-DL 42-24061. By 1990 she had been camouflaged and was noted on the dump at El Dorado. *MAP*

Below: Yet another slight variation on the 1950–60s colour scheme, FAC-656 has a matt black rectangle under her forward fuselage. Seen here at Howard AFB, CZ, on 9 July 1967, she was returning recent graduates of the Inter-American Air Forces Academy home. *Hagedorn*

The same aircraft ten years later in January 1977. Her upper white decking is gone and her service titles are in much larger format letters. She has also had a blade antenna added atop the mid fuselage. *PFI*

A starboard rear view of FAC-656 once again, this time as seen in July 1975, showing yet another form of blade antenna atop her mid fuselage! *Denis Hughes*

By December 1967, the USAF credited the FAC as having acquired a total of twenty-two C-47s from all sources, of which eighteen were possessed and active, four having been lost to 'other' unspecified causes. Other acquisitions during the period include one between July and 30 September 1968, which had previously been operated by the Colombian Ministerio de Obras Públicas, almost certainly HK-1109G, MSN 9809 and formerly 42-23947, a C-47A-35-DL. By 11 July 1969, the so-called Escuadrón de Transporte (Ligero) at Base Aérea El Dorado possessed fifteen C-47s. SATENA, formed by Presidential Decree No. 940, dated 12 April 1962 (with actual operations commencing 31 July 1962) by this time was routinely operating semi-scheduled services into frontier areas of the country where Colombia's otherwise prolific airline infrastructure, accustomed to less than ideal operating environments, could not or would not operate. While crews and maintenance were provided by the FAC, its aircraft were in fact 'owned' by SATENA, a separate chartered entity. By the end of 1964, SATENA possessed two C-54s, six C-47s, three PBY-5As and two DHC-2s.

By October 1969, the Douglas B-26Cs that the FAC had operated for a number of years had at last been withdrawn from service and their ARC-44 radios removed. Two had been installed in FAC Consolidated PBY-5As operating coastal patrol and were being used to communicate with Colombian Army units in the northern coastal areas. Four others were installed aboard FAC C-47s stationed with the so-called Special Air Warfare (Fixed Wing) Squadron, sometimes also cited as the '1st COIN Squadron' in MAP-support V-12 reports,

at Apiay, Melgar, where they operated alongside six DHC-2s, and were being used in direct support of Colombian Army paratroopers. With the four C-47s acquired in 1962, the service by 30 June 1969 had a total of nineteen C-47s of all variants on strength, and these had accumulated a total of 1,952 flying hours between April and June 1969. Four additional C-47s were programmed for MAP delivery some time in 1969.

By 30 September 1969, the USAF was showing that the FAC was programmeed to receive an additional four C-47s, and that it by that date had received a total of nineteen, of which fifteen were actually possessed and active, and these had accumulated 1,574 hours of total flight time during the preceding quarters. Of the total, fifteen were MAP-supported, and four of them were assigned to the Special Air Warfare (Fixed Wing) Squadron at Apiay, Melgar, with seven fully qualified crews, the unit also possessing six DHC-2s. This unit had previously also operated the FAC's B-26Cs. The Escuadrón de Transporte at El Dorado had fifteen C-47s and seventeen crews, and was rated fully combat ready.

By the autumn of 1976, the FAC had taken the decision to reserial most – but not all – of its surviving C-47s and C-54s operated by SATENA, in most instances by changing the serials into the 1100 range, which has led to no end of confusion and apparently erroneous speculation about the relationships between these and previous serials in the 'old' 600-range. By October 1976, C-47s FAC-1120, 1122 and 1124 had been sighted, these also wearing smart SATENA titles and new broad-chord black and blue cheatlines. These may have been among the six ex-USAF C-47s acquired by the FAC under MAS in April 1976. It is interesting to note that nearly all of the SATENA aircraft in the 1100 serials range had the titles 'Equipado con Radar' painted on at the forward upper white fuselage decking area just behind the cockpit.

This fine study of FAC-658, probably one of the last ARP aircraft received in May 1949, shows the configuration of the wing-top markings on both port and starboard sides. Note the two unusual circular-shaped structures on top of the fuselage, probably vents to circulate air in the fuselage in the stifling tropical environment. Noted here at El Dorado in 1969, she had been withdrawn from service by November 1980 and replaced by FAC-658A. *MAP1983-98 #123*

FAC-659 displays a very standard scheme as of 25 January 1977 at El Dorado. Note that the interior was painted a matt light blue. *PFI*

Above: Photographed at Marana Air Park, Arizona, in March 1978, there is some question as to whether this is the same aircraft as shown in the preceding image or possibly a second use of the same serial. The aircraft is highly polished and now sports a 'lightning bolt' cheatline as well as a small added window on her rear fuselage, possibly to admit light to the lavatory. *Capt. George G. Farinas*

Right: The original painting of FAC-659, depicted as camouflaged, now hangs in the FAC Museum and is assumed to be reliable. *FAC*

With the growth of the most unfortunate *narcotráfico* from the 1960s onward, the FAC found itself being obliged to take responsibility for aircraft engaged by the smugglers and which had been captured by various military and police agencies. By the 1980s, most of these had been concentrated at the Base Aérea Barroblanco at Madrid, some 25 miles west of Bogotá, amounting to no fewer than twenty assorted DC-3s and C-47s. Of these, at least seven had genuine or fictitious US civil registrations, while at least two others had been registered on the Brazilian civil aircraft register. These provide a bit of irony, as if indeed former PT-xxx series aircraft, they are almost certainly ex-Força Aérea Brasileira (FAB) aircraft. Some had been completely sanitised and their true provenance may never be known. Since they were, arguably, FAC property by this point, these have been appended to the end of the FAC summary table to hopefully aid further investigation.

However, the actual disposition of FAC assets by 1991 was rather different. The special mission Escuadrón de Operaciones Especiales, based at Apiay, possessed a number of locally produced AC-47 'gun ships', operating alongside the surviving Argentine-built DINFIA IA-58A Pucarás. The Grupo de Transporte, Escuadrón de Transporte at El Dorado operated with an eclectic fleet of mixed C-47s, C-130s, IAI-201s, Cessna 550s, Beech C90 King Airs, NAR 980s and 1000s, while the CAMAN/Escuadrón de CAMAN at Madrid had a mix of C-47s and at least one C-117. Often forgotten in the mix, however, was the Grupo Aéreo del Sur, Escuadrón de Transporte at distant BA Tres Esquinas, which operated C-47s as well as DHC-2 Beavers and a few Piper PA-28s.

Throughout the course of their service in Colombia, a significant number of C-47 series aircraft have been lost that have eluded identification. The earliest of these was on or about 7 June 1951, when an FAC C-47 lost an engine on take-off from Tres Esquinas and crashed, killing pilot Tte Gustavo Enrique Garzón, co-pilot Tte Leonidas González Plata and Sub.Ofc. Emilio Lobo Silva. These have included one as recently as 30 August 1988 at Villavicencio.

The study and analysis of Colombian military DC-3 and C-47 series aircraft has been complicated by the realisation that the serial numbering system that has been employed since 1944 commenced with what can only be described as a bizarre anomaly.

There is evidence that this aircraft, FAC-660, photographed in 1946, may in fact have been the 'first' FAC Lend-Lease C-47A delivered in October 1944. In this image, she depicts a typical late 1940s and early '50s scheme and serial arrangement, but additionally has red engine cowlings – most unusual for an FAC C-47 at any time. The 'T' antenna atop the forward fuselage was not known to have been standard on C-47As as of 1944, however. *Coombs via Dr Gary Kuhn*

Nothing is ever simple in the study of Latin American military aviation! Here, clearly marked as FAC-660, this aircraft was photographed at Los Angeles in 1955 and, with the curtains in the windows and many national flags on the upper forward fuselage – as well as the earliest known 'white upper decking,' was almost certainly the Presidential VIP conversion. However, she is clearly a DC-3A or C-53, as evidenced by the cabin door! Note also the RDF 'bullet' atop the forward fuselage. Unusually, she also wears the Colombian national insignia under the port wing, as well as her serial. *Doug Olson via Dr Gary Kuhn*

Readers will note in the accompanying images that FAC-650 is the 'lowest' known FAC serial, unless FAC-611, which remains tentative, is taken into account. Reason has always suggested that this, then, must have been the serial assigned to that first, Lend-Lease aircraft, 43-48240.

However, more recently, a photo of FAC-660 has been located, also reproduced in these pages, and there is circumstantial evidence that this, in fact, may have been the 'first' and, at the time, 'lowest' C-47 serial. This notion is supported by the fact that the earliest known photo showing at least five FAC C-47s arrayed on the apron at BA Madrid shows FAC-665 nearest – and this image was published in a 1948 Colombian aviation periodical. Thus, if FAC-650 had actually been the first serial, and with known acquisitions in mind, there is no conceivable way that FAC-665 could have been reached by 1948. If the first serial was, in fact, FAC-660, the presence of five aircraft as of 1948 rather neatly suggests these may have been FAC-660, 661, 662, 663, 664 and 665. Furthermore, the manner in which the serial is painted on FAC-660 is more consistent with known FAC practices as of the late 1940s than that adopted in the 1950s, as represented by FAC-650.

If this was in fact the case, it raises the inevitable question of exactly why the service 'reverted' serial assignments – and inadvertently confused the matter – to include the known, 'lower' serial 650 to 659 – and when.

With these issues in mind, the following listing represents the concerted efforts of a number of aero-historians, including Dr Gustavo Arias deGreiff, Douglas Hernández, John M. Davis and Dr Gary Kuhn. In the interest of full disclosure, we must unfortunately record that, despite repeated attempts, we are obliged to report that the FAC and its several agencies, including the FAC's own museum, have been either unable or unwilling to assist an accurate compilation of the C-47 aircraft operated by the service.

Entries in the table in normal typeface represent confirmed information from more than one source. Data in italics represents information that appears to be associated with a known FAC serial, but which is not confirmed by either physical inspection or official documents. It will quickly be noted that there are at least twenty-six serials between FAC-611 and 689A for which no confirmed identity can be nominated. Some of these are almost certainly rebuilt aircraft – possibly involving the remains of more than one aircraft – which subsequently received a serial with the 'A' suffix. However, some of the 'A' suffixed aircraft were arbitrarily issued to entirely 'new' acquisitions as well, and thus caution must be exercised in the understanding of the actual definition of this convention.

As if the foregoing were not enough, FAC-660A, pictured here in May 1978, was an FMS-procured C-47D accepted around 1 December 1977. Her fate is unknown. *ALPS*

The 'Antichrist?' FAC-666 apparently held no special significance for the FAC as of 15 May 1968 when she visited Howard AFB, CZ. She displays standard colours and markings for the period, but in this instance her interior is painted zinc chromate, rather than the matt light blue usually seen. Note she has no astrodome and the blade antenna is rather far forward on her upper fuselage. *Hagedorn*

FAC-667 as marked in July 1975 at El Dorado. She has curtained windows, suggesting a passenger interior, an astrodome and her blade antenna, in this case, is much farther aft on her upper fuselage. She was last reported in August 1985. *Denis Hughes*

Among the purely SATENA serials in the range FAC-1120 to at least FAC-1132 and FAC-1635 to FAC-1686, many of these appear to have been reserialed C-47s from the '600' ranges. However, they also include 'new' aircraft as well, thus additionally cluttering a solution. Now, between November 1961 and 1978, the FAC received at least twenty-five assorted C-47s via the MAP/FMS process. Of these, only six have been positively linked to known FAC serials, a mix of '600' series numbers (both with and without the 'A' suffix) and two purely SATENA aircraft in the 1100s. A separate table denotes these aircraft and their identities, in the hope that, in the fullness of time, researchers may at last be able to definitively link them with known FAC aircraft.

Several conclusions suggest themselves. First, the FAC apparently acquired as many as ten C-47 series aircraft in the US between 1949 and

1954, quite apart from the (at least) four reconditioned aircraft purchased via TEMCO. Second, besides the redeployment of a Colombian Government C-47 to the FAC, there must certainly have been other 'local' acquisitions, apart from impounded drug smugglers, especially during the decade of the 1950s, which have eluded verification.

Finally, from a historical perspective, Colombia ranks as the first Latin American military air arm to have operated C-47s and will almost certainly be the last. What is more, it is the solitary air arm, worldwide, still operating C-47 variants operationally and in squadron strength. The Escuadrón de Combate Táctico 113, an element of the GRUPO 11, CACOM 1 at BAM#2, Palanquero presently holds a fleet of at least seven Basler BT-67/AC-47T Fantasma gunships, operating alongside Cessna 208s, CASA ECN-235s and IAI-201 Aravas, and will almost certainly continue to do so for the immediate future.

A rather handsomely turned out FAC-667 photographed around December 1977, she has clearly been converted from C-47 to DC-3C configuration but now had a 'lightning bolt' cheatline. *Capt. George G. Farinas*

Known FAC Aircraft

FAC Serial	Previous Identity	Built As	MSN	Assignments and Notes
FAC-611				Normally associated with the first FAC C-54, a C-47 bearing this serial was issued authorisation as a C-47 by the US State Department to land at Miami on 24 Aug 50. It is possible this was the ARP C-47 loaned to the President-elect of Colombia to make a state visit to the US.
FAC-645	–	C-47	–	One source believes this may, in fact, have been the first, Lend-Lease C-47A usually cited as FAC-650 (see below). Written off 6 Feb 50.
FAC-650	43-48240	C-47A-30-DK	14056/25501	An Oklahoma City-built aircraft, she was accepted at the factory 27 Jul 44. Lend-Lease Project CM-109. Delivered via SAAD on 20 Sep 44 by a Colombian crew, and apparently went to the Canal Zone, where intensive crew training was conducted, possibly with the 20th Troop Carrier Squadron, Sixth Air Force, as was done with the Bolivians. Finally officially delivered to Colombia in Oct 44. There is, however, evidence that this aircraft may, in fact, have been marked as FAC-660 initially. However, an aircraft marked FAC-650 was reported as late as 16 Dec 81, and persistent reports claim it was converted into an AC-47 but this may, in fact, have been a second aircraft with the same serial. Believed written off on 21 Feb 83 at Valle or Caldas, four killed. However, also reported to FAC-1650 (q.v.).
FAC-651	*44-77258*	*C-47B-40-DK*	*16842/33590*	Believed ARP Project 94484-S at a cost of $105,000 on 29 Jan 46 and officially handed over on 1 Jan 47 or 27 Mar 47. However, while still with the US Mission prior to handover, this aircraft had suffered an accident on 11 Oct 46 while being flown by Lt Joel C. Lee. It was apparently repaired. Reported at Bogotá as late as 23 Oct 77. Also reported as written off 21 Feb 83 and wreckage noted at Cerro el Pinto in 2015.
FAC-651A	–	C-47	–	Became FAC-1651.
FAC-652	*45-1026*	*C-47B-45-DK* AC-47	*17029/34294*	Believed ARP Project 94484-S ex-Kelly Field, TX, Jan 46 and officially handed over on 1 Jan 47 or 27 Mar 47. Camouflaged by Apr 80 and as late as 1986 in an odd two-tone olive drab and light grey scheme. Reportedly reserialed as FAC-1652.
FAC-653 (1)	*45-1034*	*C-47B-45-DK*	*17037/34302*	Believed ARP Project 94484-S ex-Kelly Field, TX, on 29 Jan 46 and officially handed over on 27 Mar 47.
FAC-653A	43-48928 0-48928	C-47B-10-DK C-47D	14744/26189	FMS from Davis-Monthan AFB after 1 Dec 77. Reportedly converted to a Basler BT-67 but unconfirmed, as she was also reported as written off 21 Jan 71 8km east-north-east of Floridablanca with four killed.
FAC-654 (1)	*42-24031*	*C-47A-40-DL*	*9893*	ARP delivered on 11 May 49. First reported on 1 Jan 50 but this serial has also been reported used on an FAC Lockheed C-60A. Active as a C-47, however, by Jan 68 and noted at Howard AFB, CZ, as such. Reported written off on 26 Jul 75 at Sierra del Cocuy, near Pisba, Boyacá, with ten killed.
FAC-654A	43-49031 0-49031	C-47B-10-DK C-47D Basler BT-67	14847/26292	A Second World War Ninth Air Force veteran, the FAC acquired this aircraft under FMS at Davis-Monthan on 5 Dec 77. She was reserialed as FAC-1654 (q.v.).
FAC-655	*42-24061*	*C-47A-40-DL*	*9923*	ARP delivered on 11 May 49. First reported on 1 Jan 50 and active at Bogotá on 22 Mar 71. Noted on the dump at El Dorado by Oct 90, camouflaged.
FAC-656	*42-24072*	*C-47A-40-DL*	*9934*	ARP delivered on 11 May 49. First reported on 1 Jan 50 and active at Howard AFB, CZ, on 7 Jul 67. At Bogotá on 22 Mar 71 and still in service as late as 23 Jan 77. However, nose only noted at Madrid AB by Oct 88.
FAC-657 (1)	*'42-100521'*	*C-47A-65-DL*	*18984*	Although a number of documents cite this as USAAF serial as an ARP delivery to the FAC on 11 May 49, this aircraft has been positively shown to have gone to NC-65384 with Executive Transport Corp. in Texas and then to other commercial operators until sold to the French Navy in March 1963. To date, no other viable candidate has been identified. First reported at Bogotá on 22 Mar 71 and again on 23 Jan 77.
FAC-657A	42-6480 N69032 N48CG N489G CF-WGO CF-WGO-X CF-WGO C-FWGO 8P-WGO C-FWGO	XC-53A C-53-DO	4932	It is not clear when the FAC operated this apparently impounded aircraft, but it was probably after Oct 82. It went to N603MC Jul 96, so the period of use was probably between those two dates.
FAC-658 (1)	*42-100524 (also reported as '04240'*	*C-47A-65-DL*	*18987*	ARP delivered on 11 May 49, a Second World War Eighth Air Force veteran. The original aircraft with this serial is reported to have been written off on 28 Jan 64 at Ibagué, although another report gives the date as 28 Jun 64. However, a C-47 with this serial was reported at Bogotá on 23 Jan 77! A C-47 with this serial was reported withdrawn from use at Bogotá by 17 Nov 80.

FAC-658A	41-7753 NC-41757 XA-KAD YV-C-EVO HK-793	C-47-DL	4240	Noted at Bogotá on 22 Mar 71 but reported withdrawn from use by 17 Nov 80. A spotting report dated 25 Dec 82 has been interpreted to suggest she was back in service by that date, but this is believed to have been a hulk instead. Believed last operated by SATENA.
FAC-659 (1)	*42-100548*	*C-47A-65-DL*	*19011*	ARP delivered on 11 May 49 ex-Davis-Monthan AFB. Crashed on 1 Feb 70 and deemed not economically repairable. The known loss date and the delivery date of her replacement cannot be reconciled but the USAAF serial for the first use is documented. A painting of this aircraft in Vietnam-era camouflage is at the FAC Museum.
FAC-659 (2)	44-76652 0-76652	TC-47B-30-DK TC-47D	16236/32984	MAS on 15 Apr 65 ex-Davis-Monthan. Why this aircraft did not receive an 'A' suffix to its serial in second use is unknown. First reported on 19 Jan 74 at Bogotá and again on 6 Aug 86. For some reason, this aircraft was noted at the USA Airpark at Marana, Arizona, on 14 Mar 78, possibly acquiring spare parts. Reported to have been reserialed as FAC-1659 (q.v.).
FAC-660 (1)	*42-100584*	*C-47A-65-DL*	*19047*	An aircraft with this serial was noted at Bolling Field, DC, in 1946 and may have been the aircraft loaned to the FAC for the President-elect to make his state visit as noted in the text. ARP on 11 May 49 ex-Davis-Monthan AFB. However a second (?) aircraft with this serial, appearing only on her nose but otherwise in full FAC colours, was clearly equipped with a DC-3 or C-53 port-side entry door and was reported to have been written off on 20 Oct 69! However, FAC-660 was at Marana Air Park, AZ, on 14 Mar 78 suggesting a third aircraft with this root serial.
FAC-660A	43-49090 0-49090	C-47B-10-DK C-47D	14906/26351	Another Second World War Ninth Air Force veteran, this aircraft was acquired via FMS at Davis-Monthan on 1 Dec 77. To FAC-1660 by Jul 78.
FAC-661	*42-100589*	*C-47A-65-DL*	*19052*	Known to have been an ARP delivery on 11 May 49 ex-Davis-Monthan AFB. However, a report cites a C-47 with this serial as having been written off 30 May 47 5km from Base Aérea Germán Olano. This may have been a typographical error, but no other candidates suggest themselves.
FAC-661A	–	–	–	Reported written off while operating with SATENA on 21 Jan 72 on a mountain near Betania during an electrical storm and six passengers and three crew were lost.
FAC-662	*42-100655*	*C-47A-90-DL*	*19118*	ARP on 11 Sep 49. However, a separate reports states that a C-47 with serial FAC-662 was written off on 24 May 48 at Base Aérea Madrid, four killed but an FAC C-47 with this serial was reported at Bogotá on 23 Jan 77!
FAC-662A	–	C-47	–	Noted WFU in Scramble database.
FAC-663	*41-20070* *VHCDV(?)* *VHCWA* *PI-C151* *N73422*	*C-53-DO*	*4840*	Acquired via the Master Equipment Co., Cheyenne, Wyoming on 26 Jan 53 on Export Certificate of Airworthiness E-25646. While operating for SATENA, written off 3 May 75 near La Cuchilla, north of Santander in north-western Colombia near the border with Venezuela on the inaugural flight from Ocaña to Cúcuta, fatal to nine passengers and three crew.
FAC-664 (1)	–	–	–	Severely damaged on 21 Feb 50 near Campo Alegre. Reported withdrawn from use at Bogotá by 17 Nov 80.
FAC-664A	42-68774 NC-13437 N84B N902 N503 N80B	C-53D-DO	11701	First reported Nov 80. WFU at Madrid, wings only, by Jun 90.
FAC-665 (1)	–	–	–	Lost near Cali on 6 Feb 50 with four fatalities.
FAC-665A	–	–	–	Unconfirmed, but reported lost on 29 Aug 65 near Cali.
FAC-666	–	–	–	The Memoria del Ministerio de Guerra 1963 & 1965 noted that this aircraft suffered an accident on 2 Apr 63 at El Refugio. Noted at Howard AFB, CZ, on 15 May 68. This aircraft was reported again at Bogotá on 23 Jan 77. A C-47 with this identity is reported preserved at Bogota.
FAC-667 (1)	*42-100589*	*C-47A-65-DL* *DC-3C*	*19052*	Apparently a late ARP delivery on 11 May 49. She had apparently become FAC-1667 by February 1997 (q.v.). Reportedly suffered an accident on 30 Jul 64 at Hato Barreto, Casanare, and again on 15 Sep 64 at Puerto Rico, Colombia, while operating with SATENA. However, noted at Bogotá on 23 Jan 77, at Neiva on 2 May 84 and at Bogotá again on 16 Aug 85. A C-47 with this identity is reportedly preserved at the Museo Aerospacial Parque Jaime Duque.
FAC-667A	–	–	–	A C-47 wearing this serial is exhibited near the entrance to Base Aérea CATAM.
FAC-668	–	–	–	The US State Department issued authorisation for an FAC C-47 with this serial to land at Miami on 13 Oct 50, establishing the earliest known date for this aircraft. Noted at Bogotá on 23 Jan 77. The Scramble Database reports this aircraft written off 21 Feb 78.
FAC-669 (1)	–	–	–	The US State Department authored an FAC C-47 with this serial approval to land at Miami on 21 Feb 50, establishing the earliest known date for this aircraft. Noted at Howard AFB, CZ, in November 1969. Reportedly written off on 31 Jul 70 at Eldorado. The Scramble Database reports this aircraft as written off.

Above: A rather weary-looking FAC-668, which in fact may have been in service since February 1950 when photographed here in 1969. She was written off on 31 July 1970 at El Dorado. *MAP via Leif Hëllstrom*

Above right: Special markings have been rarely noted on *FAC* C-47 series aircraft. However, here, FAC-668, which had apparently been in service since October 1950, is seen around January 1977 at Bogota bearing the coat of arms of the FAC under her cockpit. She was probably on one of the experimental SATENA services at the time, in view of the distinctive SATENA portable boarding apron rolled up to her waiting cargo doors. *MAP*

Right: To this time, the service acronym and serials worn on the vertical fins on FAC C-47s had usually been illustrated without a 'dash' and sometimes with 'FAC' atop the serial and, at other times, in front of the serial – with and without spacing but, on FAC-669 shown here and FAC-666 earlier, the protocol observed in this 18 July 1967 view at Howard AFB, CZ, clearly shows the use of a 'dash'. She also sports a unit insignia on her nose, outlined in white lettering, but which has escaped verification. *Hagedorn*

FAC-669 once again, showing that the earlier 'FAC-669' arrangement has been superseded by the time of this November 1969 photograph at Howard AFB during a visit. The former serial appeared to have been burned off with a torch! The small unit insignia remained low on the nose, however. *Hagedorn*

FAC-669A	45-993	C-47B-45-DK	16996/34258	Apparently acquired by the FAC under MAS from Davis-Monthan AFB after 5 Dec 77. Stored at the Base Aérea Barroblanco, Madrid, by 1990.
	C-47D			
	45993 (French AF)			
	50993 (SVAF)			
FAC-670	*41-20054*	*C-53-DO*	*4824*	Purchased by the FAC on 19 Sep 52 from the Master Equipment Co., Cheyenne, Wyoming, via the good offices of Pan American on Export Certificate of Airworthiness No. E-11885. Cited initially as type 'C-53A' but changed in most subsequent documents before the sale to DC-3A-S1C3G. Believed to SATENA as FAC-1128 (q.v.). However, also reported written off 30km from Cravo Norte on 23 Aug 50! However, a C-47 with this serial was noted at Bogotá on 19 Jan 74 and again on 23 Jan 77!
	VHCCC	*'C-53A'*		
	PI-C150	*DC-3A-S1C3G*		
	N73421			

This photo clearly shows what appears to be a standard C-47A or C-47B, FAC-670, being readied for painted for SATENA. However, the only known candidate for this serial was a C-53/DC-3A-S1C3G, suggesting that either the serial was used twice, or the candidate is not correct for this aircraft, a September 1952 acquisition. *MAP via Leif Hëllstrom*

FAC-671	–	–	–	The US State Department issued authorisation for an FAC C-47 with this serial to land at Miami on 5 Jul 50, the earliest known date for this aircraft. Reportedly destroyed on 21 Apr 51 at Base Aérea Tres Esquinas with three killed.
FAC-672	–	–	–	The US State Department issued an FAC C-47 with this serial authorisation to land at Miami during the week of 13 Dec 50, the earliest known report for this aircraft.
FAC-673	–	–	–	Reportedly written off near Apiay on 6 Apr 62, thirty-one killed.
FAC-674	–	–	–	Reportedly written off near Apiay on 31 Jan 54, three killed.
FAC-675	–	–	–	Suffered an accident on 14 Jan 65 at Hato Corozal and reportedly written off on 9 Jan 66 near Chipaque, eleven killed.
FAC-676 (1)	42-32882 RCAF 652 A.509 (RCAF) N45F CF-ITQ 6Y-JJQ	C-47-DL AC-47	9108	Noted in standard configuration at Howard AFB, CZ, by author Hagedorn on 16 Dec 66. However, various sources report her in service with Viewmaster windows and Millardair-style cheatline c.Aug 1986, suggesting two completely different aircraft. To FAC-1676. However, also reported as written off in a lake on 2 Apr 76 near Puerto Asis while on approach to land at Puerto Leguizamo en route between Florencia and Puerto Asis, about 500km south of Bogotá, while flying for SATENA, five killed.
FAC-676A	–	–	–	Cited by the Scramble Database as possessing most of the service history of FAC-676(1) above.
FAC-677 (1)	44-77238 KP268 4715 (Pakistan AF) N4723V	C-47B-40-DK Dakota IV	'32550' (but believed actually 33570)	Sold to the FAC by Harry Mansdorf Inc., on 14 Sep 53 with what is suspected as having been a 'convenient' MSN on Export Certificate of Airworthiness No. E-22008. In his letter to the CAA requesting N4723V for this aircraft, which he cited as MSN '33550', he stated that 'the component parts for aircraft serial number 33550 were supplied from Lee Mansdorf & Co. spare parts stock'. While assigned to the 1° Grupo de Transporte at Techo, this aircraft crashed on 29 Dec 57 at Girardot when it overran the runway and into a riverbank. The pilot, Tte Marco A. Posada, suffered a broken back but the aircraft was deemed repairable.
FAC-677A	–	–	–	Noted at Bogotá on 16 Aug 85.
FAC-678	–	–	–	Reportedly written off on 2 Jul 63 at the Tauramena airport, six victims.
FAC-679	–	–	–	Reported at Bogotá on 23 Jan 77, camouflaged.
FAC-680 (1)	–	–	–	The Memoria del Ministerio de Guerra 1963 & 1965 reported this aircraft having suffered an accident on 1 Sep 62 at the Melgar airfield. She was camouflaged by 31 Oct 74 and not reported again until seen in an all-metallic colour scheme at Bogotá on 5 Dec 77. Reportedly written off on 16 Jul 78 near Cerro Kennedy, eight killed.
FAC-680A	41-18427 NC-75431 N75431	C-47-DL	4489	Apparently acquired from a US private owner around June 1979 and noted at BA Madrid in June 1990 and February 1993, the latter date as a wreck, still with 'N75431' visible on one wing.
FAC-681	44-76916 KN605 VMYCO X-12/ZU-12 44-76916	C-47B-35-DK Dakota IV	16500/33248	Reported at Bogotá on 23 Jan 77 and again Jun 78 with her cabin windows missing, suggesting possibly experimental gunship trials, camouflaged. Reported reserialed as FAC-1681 (q.v.).

Photographed at Howard AFB, CZ, on the distant western taxiway – usually reserved for aircraft awaiting 'sensitive loads', FAC-676, a rather well-travelled C-47-DL, was in actuality being loaded with Christmas consumer goods acquired by an enthusiastic FAC crew at the Howard AFB Base Exchange in this 12 December 1966 image. Sometime reported with Viewmaster-type forward windows, that is clearly not evident on this incarnation. *Hagedorn*

Another view of FAC-676, this time with a small unit insignia on her lower nose. *MAP*

Although not obvious, this is FAC-680 wearing exceptionally weathered camouflage as of 31 October 1974 – and clearly, a rudder from yet another aircraft. Another camouflaged FAC C-47 can just be seen to her left, in a completely different random scheme. In this case, the small-size national insignia on the fuselage is repeated atop at least her port wing. When next reported, in December 1977, she had shed her camouflage. *via Nick J. Waters III*

Her very worn camouflage in MAP-supplied SEA colours compromised by a full-colour rudder, FAC-681 was photographed at El Dorado in June 1978 and has eluded identification. Her cabin windows appear to be missing entirely, leading to speculation that she may have been an experimental gunship. *MAP*

A more-or-less stock FAC-682, which has not been positively identified, at Howard AFB, CZ, on 2 April 1967. Note here again that her interior is the matt light blue and that her service titles are smaller than usual. *Hagedorn*

The same aircraft in 1969 at El Dorado, but this time bearing an unknown unit emblem in subdued form on her nose. Note the C-54s and two C-47s near the hangar line in the background. *MAP 1983-99*

FAC-682	–	–	–	This aircraft suffered an accident on 24 Dec 64 at the Neiva airfield but photographed at Howard AFB, CZ, by author Hagedorn on 2 Apr 67 in an overall doped aluminium colour scheme. Reported at Bogotá on 23 Jan 77, camouflaged. Reported WFU Jan 79.
FAC-683	*43-15880* *N8327C* *N1796B*	*C-47A-90-DL*	*20346*	One of the four TEMCO refurbished aircraft acquired between Mar and Sep 54. Reported lost on 7 Jan 67 but not definitely linked to FAC-683. Noted with white upper decking but her fuselage windows sealed off by 1972. Reported WFU by Jun 90.
FAC-684 (1)	43-49790 HK-1331?	TC-47B-20-DK TC-47D C-47D	15606/27051	Reported written off 30 Jul 79, no details.
FAC-684A	–	–	–	Noted stored at Base Aérea Barroblanco, Madrid, by 1990.
FAC-685 (1)	*43-49404* *0-49404*	*C-47B-15-DK* *C-47D*	*15220/26665*	MAP on 28 Jan 70 after extensive use from 1949 in CAC and USAFSO Panama. Reported written off 20 Sep 64.
FAC-685A	–	–	–	Reported written off on 8 Sep 69 on a SATENA flight on a mountain near Chocó, 30 miles from its destination, after becoming disoriented in a storm. Twenty-nine passengers and three crew died.
FAC-686	(43-48182) BuA17245 N1561M N54V	(C-47A-30-DK) R4D-5	13998/25443	Apparently acquired commercially from The Aviation Corporation, Miami, FL, first reported on 23 Jan 77 and as late as August 1986. To FAC-1686 as a Basler conversion (q.v.).
FAC-687	42-92625 KG411 42-92625 N73853	C-47A-10-DK Dakota III	12446	Believed acquired by direct purchase from Charlotte Aircraft Corp. in 1962 as a C-47 with this serial suffered damage on 14 Sep 64 while operating with SATENA at Puerto Rico Caquetá and as written off on 17 Mar 67 near Subachoque while operating with SATENA but reported in service again by 22 Mar 71. However, when photographed on 30 Aug 69, she had standard FAC titles and colour scheme, but noted once again at Bogotá with SATENA by 6 Mar 72. Reported damaged again on landing on or about 22 Aug 73 at Guapi while operating with SATENA. To FAC-1120 by Jan 77. This aircraft was at one time also reported as MSN 9759 but this has been disproven.

FAC-683 is unusual in having an unidentified unit insignia on her forward fuselage and her cabin windows have either been painted over from inside or covered for some reason in this 1972 photo. She was probably one of the TEMCO-refurbished aircraft acquired in 1954. She has not been subsequently reported. *Paul Hayes*

Acquired from The Aviation Corporation in Miami in 1962, here FAC-686 is pictured, for some reason, at Opa Locka, Florida, with nothing but her rudder stripes and serial. The cabin air stair just visible beneath the fuselage suggests conversion to DC-3C. Note the nose ventral RDF bullet and two blade antennas atop her fuselage. *via Dr Gary Kuhn*

Although clearly marked as FAC-686, this is an entirely different aircraft than that in the previous image and has a full C-47A or C-47B cargo door arrangement in this excellent December 1977 image at El Dorado. *Capt. George G. Farinas*

Another 1962 Miami purchase, FAC-687 was formerly RAF Dakota III KG411 during the war. Once again, she wears only her serial and rudder markings but, this time, white tropical upper decking. She was destined for SATENA use. *via Dr Gary Kuhn*

Although wearing full FAC titles at the time of this 30 August 1965 image, FAC-687 was operating at the time for SATENA, as evidenced by one of their unique portable boarding aprons. This aircraft also had a small insignia on her nose, but it cannot be defined. *Paul Hayes*

FAC-687 once again but this time with full, early SATENA all lower-case titles. The acronym is repeated under the serial on her nose, but she is otherwise very much still an FAC aircraft. She was only two numbers away from the 'highest' known three-digit FAC serial, 689A. *MAP via Leif Hëllstrom*

With the remains of her former Illinois Air National Guard titles still visible, C-47A-80-DL 43-15140 has been crudely marked for ferry home from Davis-Monthan AFB, AZ, in this April 1976 image, bound for SATENA. *MAP1985-118 #39*

FAC-688 (1)	43-15497 0-15497	C-47A-85-DL C-47D	19963	MAP on 29 Jan 70 ex-USAFSO Panama. While with SATENA, this aircraft reportedly crashed in the Amazonian jungle near Docello, 312 air miles south of Bogotá, on 8 Jan 75 with thirty casualties.
FAC-688A	–	–	–	–
FAC-689 (1)	43-15556	C-47A-85-DL	20022	Apparently originally earmarked for the Philippine AF under MAP *c.*1 Mar 63 as '315556' but noted with SATENA by 6 Mar 72 at Bogotá. Reserialed as FAC-1121 by Jan 77.
FAC-689A	43-15566 0-15566	C-47A-85-DL	20032	MAP to FAC on either 20 Jun 64 or 25 Jul 65 according to two different sources. Noted on the dump at Madrid AB by Feb 95.
FAC-1120	42-92625 KG411 42-92625 N73853 FAC-687	C-47A-10-DK Dakota III	12446	To SATENA by Oct 76. Reported crashed on 20 Nov 77 at Llanos del Yari and noted derelict at Madrid AB between Jun 90 and Sep 97.
FAC-1121 (1)	43-15556 0-15556 FAC-689	C-47A-85-DL	20022	SATENA first reported as such January 1977 and as late as 25 Dec 82. Fuselage noted at Madrid-Barroblanco by Jun 90.
FAC-1122	43-15140 0-15140	C-47A-80-DL	19606	MAS ex-Davis-Monthan AFB on 26 Apr 76. A Ninth Air Force Second World War veteran, this aircraft saw considerable service with various US Air National Guard units before going to SATENA under MAS. Last reported on 22 Sep 78. To HK-3176X by 1986.
FAC-1123	43-48783 0-48783	C-47B-5-DK C-47D EC-47D	14599/26044	MAS ex-Davis-Monthan AFB on 16 Feb 76 to SATENA. Reported withdrawn from service by Jan 77 and noted minus engines at Bogotá by December 1977 but reported airworthy again by 25 Dec 82 and last noted at Bogotá on 16 Aug 85. To HK-3199.
FAC-1124	43-49514 0-49514	C-47B-15-DK C-47D	15330/26775	MAS ex-Davis-Monthan AFB SATENA 26 Apr 76. First noted in service in Oct 76. Accident on 19 Nov 76 at El Yopal and severely damaged but apparently repaired and still active in 1982. Full SATENA colours by 1979. To HK-3177 by Jan 87. Often reported as MSN 14599/26044 but this is believed to be FAC-1123 (q.v.).

SATENA adopted a decidedly attractive mix of airline-style markings and military root identity, such as shown on FAC-1122 the year after she was acquired, on 27 January 1977. Although more or less standard throughout the fleet, there were curious variations, as seen in the series of photos that follow. FAC-1122 proudly proclaims in red script Spanish just behind the cockpit that she was '*Equipado con Radar*', which was actually questionable. Note there is no national insignia under the starboard wing. *PFI*

Acquired for the service direct from Davis-Monthan AFB, AZ, under FMS in February 1976, this SATENA aircraft, formerly a USAF EC-47D, awaits new engines at the unit's compound on 23 January 1977. FAC-1123 does not have the red script aft of the cockpit advising she was equipped with radar, and has a discoloured section under the aft cheatline, suggesting sheet metal work to the fuselage at some point. It is interesting to note the vertical fins of Fairchild C-82A HK-426 in the background. *Stephen Piercey*

Another April 1976 FMS acquisition, by 1979 C-47D FAC-1124 was wearing a substantially revised SATENA colour scheme. The line's new logo is displayed on the vertical fin and the serial has been moved down to the rear fuselage, just above a much smaller national insignia. The SATENA titles have also undergone a radical stylisation. She survived to pass to airline service as HK-3177 by January 1987. *MAP*

FAC-1125	43-48715 0-48715	C-47B-5-DK C-47D	14531/25976	MAS 76117 ex-Davis-Monthan AFB for SATENA on 26 Apr 76. Reported written off on 17 Feb 77 Camanaos, Mitu, when she crashed into trees on take-off.
FAC-1126	44-77276 0-77276	C-47B-40-DK C-47D	16860/33608	MAS ex-Davis-Monthan AFB for SATENA on 26 Apr 76. Suffered damage on 29 Mar 78 at Condoto, and was extensively damaged, but apparently recovered and repaired, as she was written off on 3 May 83 near Palmaseca, Cali, no fatalities.
FAC-1127	44-76706 KN506 0-76706	C-47B-30-DK Dakota IV C-47D	16290/33038	MAS ex-Davis-Monthan AFB on 26 Apr 76. A veteran of both the Second World War and the Vietnam War, this was a MAS delivery specifically for SATENA on 27 Apr 75. She was written off on 20 Nov 77.
FAC-1128 (1)	*41-20054* *VHCCC* *PI-C150* *N73421* *FAC-670*	*C-53-DO*	*4824*	First reported on 17 Nov 80 at Bogotá. Last reported on 25 Dec 82. One source suggests there is a 90 per cent chance that this aircraft was actually the former DC-3A-408 MSN 4809, ex-NC-30000, 43-36600 and N33649, impounded some time after 21 Feb 79.
FAC-1129	–	C-47	–	First noted Nov 80. Reported written off 25 Jun 81 and noted on the dump at Villavicencio by Nov 97.
FAC-1130	43-30698 N4682T	C-47A-DL	13849	SATENA noted at Villavicencio on 15 Nov 80 and as late as Feb 82. WFU at Madrid by Jun 90.
FAC-1131	45-1022 CU-T2 N2027A N49DE N49DF	C-47B-45-DK DC-3C?	17025/34289	Reportedly written off 13 Nov 80 at Subachoque while operating with SATENA, no casualties.

Also an April 1976 FMS acquisition, this former USAF C-47D did not survive long, and was written off on 17 February 1977 at Camanaos, Mitu, one of the obscure small communities that the hard-working fleet serviced. Note that the national insignia was the original size and a rather odd structure of some sort is on top of the upper forward fuselage. *S.A.P.*

Another former USAF C-47D, FAC-1126 was also bought via FMS in April 1976 and wears the second iteration of the SATENA colour scheme in this March 1978 pose. She too fell victim to the primitive airstrips into which these aircraft routinely operated, being lost on 3 May 1983 near Palmaseca, Cali, although there were no fatalities. *C.A.F.*

FAC-1127 was among the batch of former USAF C-47Ds acquired at Davis-Monthan AFB, AZ, in April 1976 and is seen here around February 1977 in standard colours and markings. She, too, was written off in small field operations, on 20 November that year, having served less than twenty months. *Capt. George G. Farinas*

The provenance of FAC-1130 is unknown, although she has all of the characteristics of a former USAF C-47D. First noted in November 1980, this image was taken after being painted in the second colour scheme, in February 1982. Her fate is unknown. *IAGI Schaefer PG-4-166*

FAC-1132 (1)	(43-48518) BuA17276 41-7276 N48159	(C-47B-1-DK) R4D-5 C-47J	14334/25779	First noted at Bogotá Feb 82 in non-standard SATENA colours and markings. WFU at Bogota by Aug 85.
FAC-1132 (2)	BuA39070 N4458H N34AH	R4D-8 C-117D	(10020) 43360	At Madrid-Barro Blanco on 29 Sep 94 and as late as 1999, an impounded drug runner. Subsequently returned to the US.
FAC-1635	43-15161 N87644 C-GNOA N171MV	C-47A-80-DL	19627	First reported Jun 99. Hulk only noted stored at Manita by Feb 2009.
FAC-1636	–	–	–	An aircraft with this serial is reportedly on display at Base Aérea Apiay.
FAC-1639	–	C-47	–	First noted Oct 94 WFU at Bogota.
FAC-1650	43-48240 FAC-650?	C-47A-30-DK AC-47A-30-DK	14056/25501	Noted at Howard AFB, CZ, in Jul 87. Reportedly lost 30 Aug 88 while on a SATENA flight between Villavicencio and Neiva with eight lost. However, this aircraft has also been nominated as the first (and possibly only) 'straight' C-47 gunship converted to Fantasma-like configuration. If so, it would not have been on a SATENA flight!
FAC-1651	FAC-651A?	C-47	–	First reported Dec 1980. SATENA. Last reported as an instructional airframe at Madrid Nov 97.
FAC-1652	*45-1026* *FAC-652?*	*C-47B-45-DK* *AC-47*	*17029/34294*	First reported March 1990 with SATENA. Noted on the dump at Madrid-Barroblanco by 29 Sep 94 and as late as Mar 14.
FAC-1653	–	–	–	SATENA.

Wearing the third and final SATENA titles and colour scheme *c.*1986, FAC-1132 also has her serial repeated, unusually, in small white characters on her nose. She is also unusual in having had her wings and engine cowlings painted white, although the top engine cover on the starboard engine appears to be a replacement! The first of two aircraft to wear this serial, her provenance is unfortunately unknown. *MAP1986-129 #MO5911*

Although of marginal quality, this is nonetheless a fascinating image of FAC-1650 taxiing at Howard AFB, CZ, in July 1987 wearing a nearly overall grey colour scheme almost completely devoid of any national markings or titles. Reportedly lost on 30 August 1988 while operating a SATENA flight, she has also been nominated as one of the first FAC gunships. Given her configuration in this image, that appears more likely. *Carlos Planas*

FAC-1654	43-49031 FAC-654A	C-47B-10-DK C-47D Basler BT-67	14847/26292 Basler #26	This aircraft was converted to BT-67 configuration on 12 Aug 96. Reportedly crashed near Villavicencio with twenty-eight fatalities, but date not cited. However, this aircraft has also been reported as currently active with the Escuadrón de Combate Táctico 113, GRUPO 11 at BAM#2 Palanquero.
FAC-1655	–	–	–	SATENA.
FAC-1656	*43-48162 NC-17645*	*C-47A-30-DK Basler BT-67*	*25423 Basler #??*	The aircraft with this MSN cited was reportedly written off on 5 May 48 while owned by the Superior Oil Company, however.
FAC-1658	44-76209 KN292 476209/76209 (French AF) 709 (French Navy) N91BF	C-47B-25-DK Dakota IV C-47D Basler BT-67 AC-47T Fantasma	15793/32541 Basler #37	Acquired Nov 87. Noted withdrawn from use at BA Madrid-Barroblanco as FAC-1658 on 29 Sep 94. Converted to BT-67 *c.*Jan 01. While with Escuadrón 613, this aircraft was badly damaged on 5 Jan 16 when it veered off the side of the runway while landing at the Comando Aéreo de Combate No. 6 (CACOM 6) at Base Aérea Tres Esquinas Ernesto Esguerra Cubudes, Caquetá. It came to rest in a ditch. No injuries were reported to the two-man crew, consisting of Mayor Forero and Cpt. Puentes. However, an independent report states that this aircraft is still in service.
FAC-1659	44-76652 0-76652 FAC-659	TC-47B-30-DK TC-47D AC-47 Basler BT-67(A)	16236/32984 Basler #29	Noted in full FAC colours and markings, natural metal by Jan 95 as a standard C-47. Converted to Basler BT-67 by Aug 97 and camouflaged dark grey overall. Displayed as such at Oshkosh in 1998. Reportedly crashed into Mount Montezuma on 2 Feb 00 with seven victims.

Harking back to 1970s colours and markings, this former USAF AC-47, FAC-1659, was photographed around January 1995. She had been converted to Basler BT-67 configuration by August 1997. *George G.J. Kamp*

Hard to believe, this is the same basic airframe as the previous image, FAC-1659, following conversion to BT-67 at Oshkosh, Wisconsin, in 1998. She was lost on operations on 2 February 2000 on Mount Montezuma with the loss of all seven crew. *David W. Ostrowski*

Another very late acquisition, this former USAF C-47D had joined the force by September 1982 and, although withdrawn from service by September 1994, was recalled as she is pictured here in September 1998 fully airworthy. She too was destined for Basler conversion. *George G.J. Kamp*

FAC-1660	43-49090 FAC-660A	C-47B-10-DK C-47D	14906/26351	First reported with SATENA Jul 78. Noted on the dump at Madrid-Barroblanco by Nov 1997.
FAC-1661	–	–	–	SATENA.
FAC-1662	–	–	–	SATENA.
FAC-1663	–	–	–	SATENA.
FAC-1664	–	–	–	SATENA.
FAC-1667	42-100589 FAC-667?	C-47A-65-DL Basler BT-67	19052 (Basler #38)	Noted on the dump as Madrid AB as FAC-1667 in Feb 97 but apparently resurrected and shipped to Basler for conversion and in service as such by 15 Jan 02. Also reported as MSN 19125, however. Reportedly still in service again by Nov 17 and at this writing.
FAC-1670	42-100662 N40359	C-47A-70-DL C-47B C-47A C-47D EC-47D JC-47D C-47D Basler BT-67A	19125 (Basler #36 & #41)	Exactly why the FAC selected the use of this serial for an aircraft that had no prior FAC service is not clear. She was first noted in service in standard C-47 configuration and colour scheme in Sep 82 but had been withdrawn from use at BA Madrid-Barroblanco by 29 Sep 94. After Basler's conversion, she was redelivered to the FAC on 30 Jun 00 and, after an undocumented accident, was reworked once again as Basler #41. She crashed again on 18 Feb 09 at Purnio and was returned to Basler once again for rebuild. She reportedly crashed once again at Base Aérea Germán Olano with five victims, but the date has not been noted. Remarkably, components of this aircraft were once again shipped to Basler and she was rebuilt as PNC-214 (q.v.).
FAC-1674	–	–	–	Noted on the dump at BA Madrid-Barroblanco by 29 Sep 94.
FAC-1676	42-32882 RCAF 652 A.509 (RCAF) N45F CF-ITQ 6Y-JJQ FAC-676	C-47-DL AC-47	9108	Reported in service as such Jan 90. Noted derelict at BA Gómez, Colombia, by Feb 97.
FAC-1677	–	–	–	–
FAC-1681	44-76916 KN605 VMYCO X-12/ZU-16 (RNLAF) 44-76916 FAC-681	C-47B-35-DK Dakota IV AC-47T Basler BT-67	16500/33248 (Basler #23)	MAP Colombia on 31 Aug 62 and thus probably had an earlier serial in the 600s. Had become an AC-47 by Nov 87 and the Basler conversion was completed around 17 Sep 94. Still in service as of 2017 and at this writing.
FAC-1683	–	Basler BT-67 AC-47T	–	Still in service 2017 and at this writing.
FAC-1685	BuA39072 N5584R N5597V	R4D-8 R4D-8T TC-117D	(10092) 43382	Former drug smuggler. Noted at Madrid between June 1990 and February 1993. Fuselage only at Villavicencio from February 1997.
FAC-1686	(43-48182) BuA17245 N1561M N54V FAC-686	(C-47A-30-DK) R4D-5 Basler BT-67	13998/25443 (Basler #24)	Converted to BT-67 c.17 Sep 94. Still in service 2017 and at this writing.

Above: Seldom pictured, the subdued version of the FAC national insignia is evident in this view of FAC-1683, as well as her two miniguns and a flare dispenser. The FAC is the last air arm in the world to operate C-47 variants in squadron strength, not to mention very operationally. *Douglas Hernandez*

Above top: FAC-1683 in current colours and markings, a genuine gunship, and locally cited as type AC-47T. Note the airflow deflector panels on the fuselage side ahead of the forward entry cargo door. *Douglas Hernandez*

Middle right: The weapons operator's station on the forward starboard side of the AC-47T FAC-1683. The aircraft is very well maintained. *Douglas Hernandez*

Right: The 'office' of FAC-1683, barely recognisable to veteran C-47 crews. *Douglas Hernandez*

(N777X)	NC-18102 42-56098 NC-18102 N912F? N612F N777X	DST-A-207 C-48B DC-3A	1960	Seized as a drug smuggler and impounded by the FAC at Base Aérea Barroblanco, Madrid, by Jun 90.
(N49FN)	NC-30010 YV-C-AVE N88752 N49FN	DC-3A-414	4179	Seized as a drug smuggler and impounded by the FAC at Base Aérea Barroblanco, Madrid, by Jun 90 and as late as Sep 97.
(N2111M)	41-7820 TC-ALA N53F N2111M	C-47-DL	4319	Seized as a drug smuggler and impounded by the FAC at Base Aérea Barroblanco, Madrid by Jun 90 and as late as Feb 93. However, refurbished and sold at auction to Sadelca as HK-3994.
(N75T)	42-92867 TTD-6007 or 6008 (FAM) XB-VUT N47F N75T	C-47A-15-DK DC-3C/Viewmaster	12715	An aircraft with the data plate for this C-47A was located at a high school in Bogotá, Colombia, around Apr 08, having been converted for executive use by Remmert-Werner, Inc. on 25 Jun 56. School officials stated that the aircraft was 'on loan' to them from the FAC, and was almost certainly a seized drug runner. Of course, N47F has always been associated with MSN 12726 from about 1956, but this was impossible as MSN 12726 was still in service at the time with the USAF.
(N98H)	43-15595 NC-65121 N98H	C-47A-85-DL	20061	This aircraft is known to have been forced down by FAC aircraft near Villavicencio on 2 Oct 77. Last registered to one Jack Lenhardt of Hubbard, Texas, it was engaged at the time in drug smuggling. As it has not resurfaced elsewhere, it is assumed to have been confiscated and incorporated into the FAC inventory.
(N151D)	43-15705 NC-79055 N151D	C-47A-90-DL	20171	This aircraft was impounded by the FAC at Bogotá from 1976 on suspected drug smuggling charges. It was sold at auction, however, and had become HK-2820X with Vías Aéreas Colombianas by Aug 83.
(N872A)	42-15886 NC-49556 N67SA\ N872A N212NW N872A	C-53-DO	7403	Seized as a drug smuggler and impounded by the FAC at Base Aérea Barroblanco, Madrid, by Jun 90 but apparently returned to the US by 1994.
(N239GB)	(42-108796) BuA17094 N39 N39AH N239GB	(C-47A-DK) R4D-5	11808	Seized by the Colombian Government at Barranquilla on 2 Oct 84. Had apparently been auctioned to HK-3220 by 22 Oct 85.
(N5597V)	BuA39072 N5584R N5597V	R4D-8 R4D-8T TC-117D	(10092) 43382	Seized as a drug smuggler and impounded by the FAC at Base Aérea Barroblanco, Madrid. Apparently refurbished and became FAC-1685 (q.v.).
(N374)	(unknown)	(unknown)	(unknown)	Seized as a drug smuggler and impounded by the FAC at Base Aérea Barroblanco, Madrid, an obviously bogus or prostituted US registration.
(N25689)	NC25689 42-38329 NC25689 N25689	DC-3-313C C-49H DC-3A	4099	Noted impounded and stored at Barranquilla.

A mystery aircraft. Pictured here in July 1975, this FAC C-47 was one of the first to be camouflaged but had no indication of her individual serial number anywhere on the aircraft! *Denis Hughes*

Similarly obscure, this aircraft wears yet another random camouflage scheme but full colour FAC rudder stripes. At least two aircraft were similarly marked. Interestingly, a Canadian Forces Boeing 707 can just be seen at right rear. *MAP via Leif Hëllstrom*

Yet another camouflaged *FAC* C-47, this one at least wears a small format national insignia on her fuselage, and what appears to be either FAC-675 or 676 on her vertical fin. Her ailerons appear to have been borrowed from an uncamouflaged aircraft, and she has had recent repair work done to her upper rudder! *via Ken F. Measures*

(HK-556)	NC34947 YV-C-AVC HK-556	DC-3A-438	4958	Although reported to have been on lost 10 Apr 77 operating with Taxi Aéreo El Venado south-west of Villavicencio it appears that this aircraft may have been impounded by the FAC prior to being leased by El Venado.
(HK-500P)	43-15171 NC66025 C-500 HK-500 HK-500P	C-47A-80-DL	19637	Found abandoned in a field at Sabanalarga, Urena, Venezuela, as HK-500 20 Apr 77 and dismantled and moved to Cucuta, Colombia, and then on to Villavicencio and noted impounded and derelict as HK-500P from Dec 90 till at least Sep 97.
(N25669)	NC25669	DC-3-314A	2242	First reported as seized by the FAC Aug 83. Fate unknown but probably assumed an FAC serial.
(PT-KZJ)	42-108969 FAB C-47 2043 PT-KZJ	C-47A-25-DK	13538	Reported impounded and stored somewhere in Colombia.
FAC–	43-15910 N1796B	C-47A-90-DL	20376	Apparently acquired by the FAC prior to 7 Jan 67 when it was reported written off.

Known MAP or FMS Acquisitions – 1961–72 Not Linked

USAAF/ USAF Serial	Serial Worn Acquisition at and Previous Identity	Built as and Last Designation	MSN	Notes
44-76325	44-76325 KN342 VMYAW X-6 (Royal Netherlands AF) ZU-6 (Royal Netherlands AF) 44-76325	C-47B-28-DK Dakota IV	15909/32657	MAP redeployed from the Netherlands *c.*10 Nov 61. As a consequence, she almost certainly received a '600' series FAC serial initially.
44-76920	44-76920 KN608 VMCYX X-7 (Royal Netherlands Air Force) ZU-7 (Royal Netherlands Air Force) 44-76920	C-47B-35-DK Dakota IV	16504/33252	MAP redeployed from the Netherlands between 10 Nov 61 and Aug 62. As a consequence, she almost certainly received a '600' series FAC serial initially.
44-76957	44-76957 KN632 VMYDB X-14 (Royal Netherlands AF) ZU-14 (Royal Netherlands AF) 44-76957	C-47B-35-DK Dakota IV	16541/33289	MAP redeployed from the Netherlands between 10 Nov 61 and 31 Aug 62. As a consequence, she almost certainly received a '600' series FAC serial initially.
42-108911	0-108911	C-47A-20-DK	12958	MAP/FMS ex-Davis-Monthan AFB, AZ, between 20 Jun and 24 Jul 64.
43-15501	0-15501	C-47A-85-DL	19967	MAP/MAS ex-Davis-Monthan AFB, AZ, between 29 Oct 64 and 10 May 65.
43-15672	0-15672	C-47A-90-DL	20138	MAP/MAS ex-Davis-Monthan AFB, AZ, between 15 Apr and 10 May 65.

43-16068	0-16068	C-47A-90-DL	20534	MAP/MAS ex-Davis-Monthan AFB, AZ, between 15 Apr and 19 May 65.
43-48090	0-48090	C-47A-30-DK VC-47A	13906/25351	MAP/MAS on 15 Apr 65.
43-49348	0-49348	TC-47B-15-DK TC-47D	15164/26609	MAS ex-Davis-Monthan AFB, AZ, between 1 Mar and 10 May 65.
43-48799	0-48799	C-47B-5-DK C-47D VC-47D	14615/26060	Another long-serving CAC and USAFSO aircraft, from as early as Jul 45, to MAP on 1 Feb 70.
44-76455	0-76455	C-47B-25-DK C-47D	16039/32787	Yet another ex-CAC an USAFSO aircraft, having served in Latin America between Sep 47 and MAP offset on 29 Jan 70.
43-49205	0-49205	C-47B-10-DK C-47D	15021/26466	Another ex-USAFO aircraft to MAP on 28 Jan 70.
44-76385	44-76385 KN354 VMYBZ 44-76385 0-76385	C-47B-25-DK Dakota IV C-47D	15969/32717	Also a long-serving CAC and USAFSO aircraft, this aircraft had been based in Latin America with the USAF since Feb 61. To MAP on 28 Jan 70.
43-49404	0-49404	C-47B-15-DK C-47D	15220/26665	This aircraft had also served extensively with the USAF in Latin America from Jun 49 and went to MAP on 28 Jan 70.
43-15497	0-15497	C-47A-85-DL	19963	This is also a former USAFO aircraft, but had only joined the 24th ACW a Howard AFB, CZ, in Jun 68. It was a Second World War Ninth Air Force veteran and went to MAP on 29 Jan 1970.

Policía Nacional de Colombia

A truly veteran force originally established in 1891, by 1962 the various departmental police forces in the country, which had hitherto existed as independent or semi-independent entities nominally subordinated to the Ministerio de la Defensa Nacional – and hence institutionally endowed with a long tradition of paramilitary character – were combined to form a homogeneous national police force with the responsibility of maintaining public order in the entire national territory.

Nevertheless, some of Colombia's larger cities continued to maintain independent police forces with functions that were effectively limited to the direction of traffic and enforcement of parking regulations.

Given the seemingly endless insurrection, which gradually came to be known as *La Violencia*, and accompanying chronic internal instability, it was probably inevitable that the Policía Nacional de Colombia (PNC) functions would be extended to embrace a paramilitary internal security role. As a direct result, special units trained in counter-insurgency were formed and given the title Carabineros, with their own distinctive uniforms. With total staff somewhere in excess of 50,000, of whom about 5,000 are Carabineros, the force by the 1980s was organised into twenty-four sections – one with responsibility for each of the administrative departments of the republic and one for the national capital. These sections were, in turn, divided into districts, stations and sub-stations/posts. Recognising early on the necessity of possessing its own organic aviation assets, by 1984 a significant number of helicopters had been acquired, and the service commenced its own serialing system for its aircraft, quite distinctly different from the FAC.

Besides helicopters, the PNC has gradually expanded its supporting air arm to include no fewer than thirty-seven assorted fixed-wing and rotary-wing types – including at least seven Basler-converted BT-67s, which are described below.

PNC Serial	Previous Identity	Configured as	MSN	Assignments and Notes
PNC-211 PNC-0211	43-48406 D-18 (Czech AF) 8406 (Czech AF) OK-WZA D-CABE 4X-AOA 48406 (French Navy) N95BF	Basler BT-67	14222/25667 Basler #14	An aircraft with what must certainly have been one of the most exotic service histories of any Latin American military DC-3 series aircraft, this one was converted around 2 Nov 92 and delivered to the PNC on 12 Feb 93. This aircraft was destroyed by the accidental explosion of a tear gas grenade aboard the aircraft while being boarded by twenty-five PNC officers en route to El Caraño, Quibdó, at the Medellín airport on 18 Feb 09. Miraculously, there were only eight injuries.
PNC-212 PNC-0212	42-93222 N145Z N145ZA	Basler BT-67	13110 Basler #9	Converted around 9 Aug 90. Sold to the PNC on 10 Sep 91. Why this aircraft had a PNC number higher than the above is unknown. This aircraft was written off on 30 Apr 03 when it overran the runway at Aguas Claras, Ocaña, although one source gives the date alternatively as 30 Aug 03.
PNC-213 PNC-0213	43-16409 316409 (French AF) F-BTDG CF-POX N8059P N607W N8059P HK-3576 HK-3576X N8059P	C-47B-1-DL Basler BT-67	20875 Basler #2	Another extraordinarily well-travelled aircraft, this one had actually been impounded by the US Drug Enforcement Administration (DEA) and turned over to the Asset Seizure & Forfeiture programme around 13 Dec 94. The US Department of State then made her available to the PNC sometime after 22 Jun 98. She was noted withdrawn from use with the PNC by Feb 01 but had returned to service by Oct 01. She was reported sold on 3 Nov 04.

A very attractively turned out Basler BT-67 conversion for the Policia Nacional, PNC-0256 was delivered on 22 December 2004 although she was photographed here in July. She was formerly C-47D FAC-1670. *David W. Ostrowski*

PNC-214 PNC-0214	42-100662 N40359 FAC-1670	C-47A-65-DL C-47B C-47A C-47D EC-47D JC-47D C-47D Basler BT-67 (#36)	19125 Basler #41	This aircraft was a second Basler conversion of most of the same airframe and was delivered to the PNC sometime after Jun 00.
PNC-0256	43-15219 N93042 N845MB	C-47A-80-DL Basler BT-67	19685 Basler #43	Delivered to the PNC on 22 Dec 04 but noted at Basler in Oshkosh, WI, in full PNC colours as early as Jul 04.
PNC-0257	42-23808 N840M N840MB	C-47A-35-DL Basler BT-67A	9670 Basler #45	Delivered after 3 Mar 01.
PNC-0258	–	C-47 Basler BT-67A		

Colombia is unique in having been the solitary Latin American operator of C-117 variants, having impounded at least three former drug runners and placed them into limited service. Pictured here in January 1997, FAC-1632 has reportedly since returned to the US. *George G.J. Kamp*

CHAPTER SEVEN

Costa Rica

THE MILITARY USE of the Douglas DC-3 and C-47 variants in Costa Rica is surrounded by mystery and presents quite a challenge for the aero-historian. Both the government and the rebels flew the aircraft during a revolt that took place in 1948, not only as transports, but also as improvised bombers, and it would not be bold to say that the role they played influenced considerably the turn of events. Despite their importance, the official narrative has reduced their participation to a mere footnote; there are virtually no records of their identities and we only have a vague idea of their provenance. Hence, what follows is perhaps the most honest attempt to shed some light into the military utilisation of the Douglas twin series in that Central American nation.

First though, we need to set the stage. So, bear with us. It won't take long.

Described for years on end as a beacon of democracy and social progress in the generally backward and politically turbulent Central America, Costa Rica began showing signs of a deep social polarisation right after the outbreak of the Second World War. The government of Rafael Ángel Calderón Guardia declared war on Japan on 8 December 1941, followed by declarations against Germany and Italy shortly after. Even though this was a symbolic act, since the small Costa Rican Army could not contribute directly to the fighting, it implied that the nation had to take in the consequences of being an ally. Therefore, the government ordered the internment of all German, Italian and Japanese nationals, as well as the expropriation of their lands and businesses.

The situation turned for the worse on 2 July 1942, when the German submarine *U-161* sank the freighter SS *San Pablo*, owned by the United Fruit Company, at Puerto Limón, killing twenty-four Costa Ricans. Two days later, when the news reached San José, the country's capital, a large demonstration against Germany took place, but it

quickly got out of hand and more than 120 German-owned businesses were looted. It was not until very late that night that the police finally intervened, dispersing the protesters within a few minutes. Shortly after, no fewer than 100 German residents were detained.

The German community was extremely well integrated into the Costa Rican society, however, and many of those who ended up in the country's sole concentration camp were, in fact, *Ticos* of German descent. The upper classes were outraged, to say the least, and among the malcontents was a wealthy landowner named José Figueres, who bought radio air time to chastise Calderón Guardia for thrusting the country into a war it was not prepared for, and condemned the seizure of the German properties as an illegal act. The police promptly captured Figueres, and days later, he was bound for Mexico as an exile.

The only known photo of TACA de Costa Rica's C-47-DL TI-1000 after being captured by the rebel forces on 12 March 1948. Allegedly taken at San Isidro del General, the image shows the aircraft surrounded by Figueres' guerrillas right after landing. Later on, she was used to transport arms and ammunition from Guatemala, and also took part in the 'tactical' operations that the rebel forces launched across the country.

On the other hand, the war complicated the economic situation of the country and the Communist Party, led by Manuel Mora Valverde, did not lose any time in bringing the 'social question' to the public's attention. The extent of poverty and inequality in the country rapidly became a political issue, resulting in widespread unrest. Thus, in order to quell an imminent uprising that would endanger his government, Calderón Guardia set out to introduce a series of unprecedented social reforms.

The enactment of these laws, albeit slow and convoluted, earned him not only the lower classes' support, but that of the Communist Party. In fact, in June 1943, that political organisation changed its name to Vanguardia Popular in order to make it more palatable, and began helping the government with the implementation of the reforms.

Inevitably, the shift in the status quo was taken rather badly by the upper and middle classes, since many of the newly enacted laws affected them directly. Therefore, it did not take long for them to accuse the President, as well as his National Republican Party, of corruption and inefficiency. Shortly after, Costa Rica entered a downward spiral of violence that intensified dramatically during the electoral campaign for the 1944 elections.

Teodoro Picado, the candidate of the newly formed coalition comprised by the National Republican Party and Vanguardia Popular, was elected President on 3 February 1944, amid serious accusations of fraud. It did not take long for the average Costa Rican to realise that Picado's presidency was just a stand-in for Calderón Guardia. Also, it became evident that Guardia pretended to run for President in the 1948 elections, and for all intents and purposes, the entire government apparatus would be placed at his disposal in order for him to reach this goal.

José Figueres returned from exile on 23 May 1944, already transformed into a symbol of resistance to the 'tyrannical ambitions' of Calderón Guardia. His local collaborators organised a rally to welcome him back and from the balcony of the *Diario de Costa Rica* newspaper, Figueres called the *Ticos* to arms, stating that the only way of getting rid of Calderón Guardia, and establish the 'Second Republic', was through a revolution.

Far from being spontaneous, Figueres' call to arms was just the initial step of a major plan aimed at creating the appropriate conditions for launching an armed insurrection. Part of this first phase was also the consolidation of the opposition parties under only one organisation, called the Social Democratic Party, which was established on 11 May 1945. Its mission was to maintain a solid political presence, capable of counterbalancing – or even neutralising – any government initiative.

The second phase, which consisted of exerting maximum pressure upon the government by means of acts of terrorism and sabotage, required the creation of a select group of individuals who, under Figueres' direct command, would launch the attacks. Despite their best efforts, such actions did not become serious until late in 1946 when the group managed to partially destroy Mora Valverde's home with dynamite. Shortly after, the attacks were redirected against public services, waterlines, electrical installations, and railways, all of which were aimed at disrupting the normal activities of the population. Furthermore, groups of young men, organised in neighbourhood brigades, went out to the streets of San José generating chaos, usually clashing with the police or beating members of Vanguardia Popular.

The third phase of the plan, which comprised the acquisition of enough arms and ammunition to equip a small army, proved to be a slow and complicated process. Through the efforts of Rosendo Argüello and Edelberto Torres, two Nicaraguan exiles who lived in Mexico, Figueres had been purchasing whatever rifles, machine guns or grenades that could be found and, in early August 1947, the Nicaraguans were ready to ship to Costa Rica what was thought to be a sufficient stock to launch the revolution. The Mexican authorities got wind of their intentions though, and in a surprisingly quick operation, the police raided the warehouse where the arms were stored and seized them all. Argüello and Torres, on the other hand, managed to escape to Guatemala.

After this major setback, Figueres' plan was on the brink of disaster. Furthermore, his terrorist group had not been able to destabilise the government and all efforts to incite a general strike had failed miserably. His last great hope remained with his international connections, though. The failure of Dominican exiles led by General Juan Rodríguez García to launch an invasion on their homeland from Cayo Confites, in Cuba, had resulted in the transfer of their arsenal to Guatemala, where it came under the control of President Juan José Arévalo and the Chief of the Armed Forces, Col Francisco Arana. Figueres and his Nicaraguan allies formed one of several groups struggling for access to the arsenal, which nominally still belonged to Rodríguez García.

President Arévalo planned to see the arms employed to achieve a Central American Union under a democratic government and to overthrow dictatorships in the Caribbean. Figueres and his agents in Guatemala, Argüello and later Argüello's Costa Rican brother-in-law, Fernando Figuls, convinced Arévalo of their Unionism and of their willingness to fight in the larger battle of the Caribbean. In the context of the fight against tyranny, Figueres persuaded Arévalo that the battle should begin in Costa Rica, as it was the weakest nation in the region. In addition, as soon as Figueres seized power, the Nicaraguan exiles would be in an excellent position for launching an attack against Somoza's Nicaragua over a long land frontier, difficult to control.

On 16 December 1947, President Arévalo, Figueres and the Dominican and Nicaraguan leaders signed the so-called Pact of Alliance, pledging themselves to battle to free Central American and the Caribbean of dictatorships. Even though Figueres returned to Costa Rica shortly after the pact was signed, it was not until late in January 1948 that he retreated to his farm, named La Lucha Sin Fin, to start organising what would be known as the 'National Liberation Army.' By 4 February, the first recruits – mostly inexperienced students and sons of farm owners – began arriving for accelerated military training. Within days, the number of recruits grew to 600 men. The only problem was that the arms needed to equip them were still in Guatemala.

The Rebel Aircraft

Even though Figueres did not have enough arms for his ragtag army, beyond a few rifles and shotguns that farmers and other supporters had contributed, he decided to set 12 March as the D-Day for his revolution. Early on that day, a group of armed men departed La Lucha and set up defensive positions at a place known as La Sierra, effectively blocking the Inter-American Highway – then still under construction – as well as the access road to Figueres' farm. This action also allowed them to isolate San Isidro del General, a town situated 75km south of San José, which was also taken by a group of Figueres' men, supported by at least eighty locals. San Isidro had a small airstrip that was serviced regularly by TACA airlines, which was promptly secured. The idea behind this was to wait for the first aeroplane to land and seize it, so it could be flown to Guatemala and bring some of the arms. Conveniently, among Figueres' men who assaulted the town were two aviators: Guillermo 'Macho' Núñez and Otto Escalante, the latter being a co-pilot-in-training with a local small airline.

Around 6.30am, a TACA C-47 – presumably civilian registration TI-1000 – landed at San Isidro as usual. What followed was narrated by Núñez in Guillermo Villegas Hoffmeister's book, *La Hora del Fin*: 'When the first plane arrived, we allowed it to park, and when the pilot shut down the engines, we came out of our hiding and surrounded it. We all were carrying guns. The pilot, a North American – and a friend of mine – only stared at us with suppressed fury. The co-pilot was a Costa Rican. I opened the door of the plane and informed the passengers that the revolution had begun, but that they didn't need to be afraid, because the old ladies of San Isidro would shelter and feed the female passengers, while the men were invited to join the revolution. Almost every male passenger accepted.'

The North American pilot did not join the revolution, though, and reported to have been 'visibly upset', was taken to Villa Mills, where the company that was building the Inter-American Highway has set up a camp, and was kept there until the end of the revolution.

After securing the aircraft, one of Figueres' men named Edmond Woodbridge, who had captured the airfield's radio transmitter, radioed a message to TACA headquarters saying that the morning aircraft had blown a tyre during the landing, and that a spare should be sent in the following flight, set to arrive at 9am. TACA headquarters, allegedly unaware that one of its aircraft had been captured, replied that they would send the spare tyre immediately, along with tools and mechanics to perform the replacement, using for this a DC-3 that was about to depart San José's airport on a test flight.

The second TACA aircraft, a DC-3 civilian registration TI-161, arrived in San Isidro around 8.30am and was seized immediately by Figueres' men. On board were two mechanics, who promptly joined the revolution and played a rather important role during the following days, not only by maintaining the captured aircraft, but by manufacturing 'fake' anti-aircraft guns that kept the government 'air force' at bay for a while. By all indications, the pilots, who remain anonymous to this day, also joined the rebels.

With the second aircraft already secured, Woodbridge set to work again, and, incredibly, requested TACA Headquarters to dispatch yet a third aircraft, arguing that the last one had suffered unrepairable damage during the landing and that spares were needed. A that point it is not clear how TACA Headquarters managed to send the third DC-3, civilian registration TI-165, to San Isidro, since by then the government was fully aware of the situation and had prohibited any aircraft from leaving the capital's airport. It is not clear either why only TI-161 and TI-165 departed for Guatemala around midday on that day, with the aim of bringing the first load of arms. In fact, the majority of official accounts mention only those two aircraft as the ones that the rebels captured, ignoring completely the fact that there is photographic proof that TI-1000 was the first aircraft to be seized, and that it arrived in San Isidro in good condition.

The rebel aircraft managed to complete fourteen flights to Guatemala during the following two weeks, bringing a large quantity of the arms needed to equip Figueres' army properly, something that allowed him to extend his defensive operations. Along with the arms came a group of General García Rodríguez's men led by the Dominican exile Horacio Ornes, who were incorporated into Figueres's forces almost immediately.

On 22 March, while the three TACA aircraft were completing the first leg of yet another flight to Guatemala City, President Arévalo ordered their capture and their crews imprisoned. Such change of heart on the part of the Guatemalan President had been influenced by the pressure exerted mainly by the Costa Rican ambassador and some serious doubts that he had about Figueres' intentions. During the following days there was considerable back-and-forth between the rebel representatives and the Guatemalan government, but the negotiations soon came to naught. Meanwhile, Figueres' men were running dangerously short of ammunition, allowing the government forces to increase their offensive operations.

Six days later, on the 28th, Manuel 'Pillique' Guerra, a renowned *Tico* pilot and friend of Figueres, decided to mount a 'rescue operation' aimed to retrieve the rebel aircraft and crews, and restart the supply

flights. First, he departed Costa Rica hiding in the radio compartment of one of the TACA DC-3s that were being repositioned to El Salvador due to the civil war. Then, from San Salvador he took a commercial flight bound to Miami, where he contacted his business partner C.N. Shelton and asked him for an aircraft that he could use to reach Guatemala incognito. Shelton lent Guerra a C-47 – most probably US registration NC66176 – and without losing any time took off for Guatemala City. Upon reaching La Aurora Airport, Guerra got rid of the aircraft's US registration and replaced it with a fake Salvadoran one in order to disguise its origin. Next, he set out to convince Coronel Arana, Chief of the Guatemalan armed forces, to release the *Tico* pilots and their aircraft, and allow them to take the last load of arms and ammunition to Costa Rica. According to Guerra's own account, Arana was convinced that Figueres' revolution had failed and the Guatemalan government's involvement was becoming extremely inconvenient, especially before the eyes of the US and the neighbouring nations.

It was not until the next day that Arana relented and allowed the crews and their aircraft to leave Guatemala under the promise of not coming back again. Thus, Guerra and the pilots loaded the four aircraft to their limits and departed for San Isidro. From that day onwards, Guerra and 'his' C-47, which carried the Salvadoran fake registration 'YS-18', were incorporated into the rebel air force.

On 31 March, Figueres decided to give the government a psychological blow by bombing the Presidential residence. Accordingly, Guillermo Núñez, a mechanic flying as his co-pilot and six rebel soldiers loaded TI-161 with a handful of French-made 25lb bombs and departed San Isidro for San José. Approaching the capital at low altitude, Núñez soon found his way towards the building and once he was over it, he gave the soldiers the signal to roll one of the bombs out of the cargo hatch. The explosive device missed the target completely, so Núñez turned around and tried again. In the second attempt, the bomb fell in the residence's garden, causing little damage. The explosion was loud enough for the Presidential Guard to order the evacuation of the building, however. Next, the pilot headed towards La Sabana Airport, which was his secondary target. The intention was to bomb the government's aircraft that had been causing serious damage to the rebel forces. Núñez's crew rolled the rest of the bombs out of the hatch as soon as the DC-3 was over the airport, but none of them hit any of the aircraft on the ground.

A single-engine aircraft, presumably an AT-6, took off immediately from La Sabana and went after Núñez's DC-3. According to the rebel pilot, a 'gunner' riding in the Texan's back cockpit tried desperately to fire at them with a Thompson submachine gun, but did not hit them. In the end, as soon as Núñez began descending into the El General Valley through thick fog, the Texan desisted from chasing the DC-3 and departed in the direction of San José.

The problems for Núñez were far from over though, since upon touching down at San Isidro, the DC-3's right main landing gear retracted, causing the wing and propeller to impact the ground. Upon being evaluated by the rebel mechanics, TI-161 was deemed unrepairable on the field and, days later, Figueres' men torched her before leaving San Isidro, so the government could not repair her and use her for attacking them (other unconfirmed sources claim that the aircraft was destroyed by government troops, though.)

Despite the ineptitude of the Costa Rican Army, Figueres' forces had been on the defensive since the beginning of the revolution. However, on 8 April, the rebel leader decided to turn the tables and launched two simultaneous operations, the first aimed to take the city of Cartago, located 20km south of the capital, using for this a compact force of some of their best men who were transported by two of the DC-3s. Then, two of the rebel aircraft, carrying a total of sixty-five men commanded by Horacio Ornes and Ludwig 'Vico' Starke, took off from San Isidro bound for Altamira, far to the north on the San Carlos Plains, in order to replace the force commanded by 'Chico' Orlich. In turn, Orlich's men were flown to San Isidro, from where they would also march towards Cartago, and eventually towards San José. After carrying out this often-overlooked series of flights, the pair of aircraft returned to Altamira and continued with the Ornes-Starke force for the second operation that was aimed to attack Port Limón. Figueres needed that port in order to open a more capable sea route for supplies, as he claimed that a vessel was already under sail there from Cuba, bringing even more arms and equipment.

By then, the government had realised the importance of the rebel 'air force' and sent virtually all of its aircraft searching for Figueres' DC-3s. In fact, on 10 April, two of the government DC-3s, flown by Sherman Wilson and Jerry Delarm, and a solitary North American AT-6, located the rebel aircraft at Altamira and attacked them with bombs and machine gun fire with poor results. The rebels returned the fire and managed to hit Wilson's DC-3, which caught fire and crashed. Delarm, discouraged by the fierce ground fire, made two more bombing runs at a higher altitude and then returned to La Sabana, escorted by the AT-6.

The next day, two of the rebel DC-3s took off from Altamira carrying the Ornes-Starke force towards Port Limón. During the flight, a government AT-6 intercepted them and tried to shoot them down. However, the DC-3s climbed to a safe altitude and continued to their objective under the cover of thick clouds. Less than half an hour later, the two aircraft landed safely at Limon's airfield.

After rushing out of the aircraft, the rebel group split in two columns and launched a fierce attack on the port, but did not meet considerable resistance, beyond a couple of air attacks from a pair of government DC-3s. For this airborne assault, considered a first in Central America, Ornes' group was bestowed with the name Legión del Caribe (Caribbean Legion) by none other than Figueres himself, who used to honour his columns with some grandiose name or designation. The name stuck and, indeed, General Rodríguez adopted the title informally at first, feeling that it suggested an invincible force that would have great impact in what was to follow for the Dominican exiles.

Following a series of setbacks, Figueres' forces finally entered Cartago on 12 April, meeting only mild resistance, while a second column occupied Alto de Ochomogo, from whence the insurgents commanded the entire stretch of the highway leading into the capital itself. On the 13th, Costa Rican Army troops broke through a third rebel column at Cangrejal, but the insurgents were able to defeat them at El Tejar after a twelve-hour battle that was the single fiercest action of the civil war. That same day, President Picado authorised a delegation to negotiate a ceasefire with Núñez, on behalf of Figueres. But San José itself, the main prize, was effectively in the hands of the Communist militia that defended it, and Mora Valverde refused to order his troops to abandon their fairly well-established positions until the rebels had agreed to certain conditions respecting their safety.

After endless negotiations, it was not until 19 April that President Picado and Núñez finally signed an agreement at the Mexican Embassy, which effectively brought the hostilities to an end, while also enabling the conditional surrender of the Government.

Regarding the rebel DC-3/C-47 fleet, the following table lists what little is known about it:

Registration	Previous Identity	Built As	MSN	Notes
TI-161		DC-3?		Captured by the rebel forces on 12 Mar 48. Previously operated by TACA de Costa Rica. No known records exist about this aircraft, beyond what is mentioned in official accounts. It was destroyed by fire at San Isidro, presumably on 11 Apr 48, when the rebel forces abandoned the town during the offensive against Cartago.
TI-165	42-100583 TI-62 XH-TAZ	C-47A-65-DL		Transferred from TACA Airlines to TACA de Costa Rica in 1947. Captured by the rebel forces on 12 Mar 48. Reverted to XH-TAZ on 5 Feb 50. Re-registered TI-1003 in 1952 with LACSA, and TI-1003C in 1959. To LANICA as AN-AOK in 1962.
TI-1000	41-19495	C-47-DL	6138	Captured by the rebel forces on 12 Mar 48. Previously operated by TACA de Costa Rica. Acquired by LACSA in 1952. Then sold as HK-1511W in 1954.
'YS-18'	41-38759 NC66176	C-47-DL	6218	In service with the rebels since 29 Mar 48, when his pilot Guillermo Guerra joined the revolution, as noted in the text. Registered as TI-109 with Transportes Aéreos Nacionales in 1947, but the date may be wrong or false. Fate unknown.

The Government Aircraft

At the time of the outbreak of the revolution, the Costa Rican Army did not have an air arm, only a unit called División Aérea (Air Division), intended for airfield security rather than flight operations. Its ten officers were based at San José Airport supplemented by four others deployed at the airfields at Alajuela, Cartago and Heredia. Of these men, at least one received training as either a pilot or engineering officer during the Second World War. Therefore, when the first news of the revolt reached San José on 12 March, the government rushed to issue a decree to essentially impress every airworthy aircraft in the country for possible military service. These included three LACSA airlines DC-3s, another C-47 owned by Transportes Aéreos Nacionales -TAN, two Boeing 247Ds owned by Aerovías Occidentales (AVO) and virtually all the flyable, privately owned aircraft, including at least one AT-6 and a BT-13. The decree also called for all private and commercial pilots, as well as aviation mechanics, to be drafted as part of a newly formed 'air force'. In addition, a handful of foreign aviators, among them the North Americans Jerry Delarm and Clarence Martin, and the Canadian Sherman 'Snark' Wilson, volunteered their services to the government. In fact, Wilson was immediately appointed as the commanding officer of the air unit, with the rank of colonel.

Since all aircraft requisitioned by the government were civilian, the first order of business was to provide them with some sort of offensive capability. Delarm related that the DC-3s were converted to makeshift 'attack-bombers', with .50 calibre machine guns installed on their cabin windows and another in a hole cut on the side of the toilet compartment. For the bombing role, the mechanics, led by a Spaniard named Julio López Masegosa, made some bombs out of oxygen cylinders and milk cans filled with dynamite, as well as nuts and bolts. According to Delarm, upon a signal from the pilot, a match string fuse would be lit with a cigar, then the 'bomb' would be slid out the cargo hatch of the aircraft by two men. In the case of the AT-6 and BT-13, a 'gunner' armed with a handheld machine gun, flew in the back cockpit of the aircraft that –invariably – were used for escorting the DC-3s.

The first combat sortie of a loyalist DC-3 was launched during the early morning of 13 March, when one of the aircraft, piloted by Sherman Wilson, bombed the rebel troops that had blocked the

Inter-American highway at La Sierra. This attack, which consisted of four bomb runs over the enemy positions, was made in support of the renowned Unidad Móvil (Mobile Unit), comprised of the only US-trained troops of the Costa Rican Army. Even though the air bombardment was far from accurate, it was good enough to allow the troops of the Unidad to break the blockade and force a retreat of the rebels. Incredibly, once the highway was freed, the Army troops did not continue their advance, electing to regroup 5 or 6km from La Sierra. In that way, the Army missed an excellent opportunity to launch an assault on San Isidro and capture the rebel's logistics centre, which at that time was poorly defended.

Two days later, on 15 March, two DC-3s were launched in two separate missions. The first was aimed at stopping the rebels' retreat from Santa María de Dota after being defeated by the Army. During this mission, a DC-3 armed with a pair of .50 calibre machine guns established a circular pattern over Figueres' troops and strafed them for no less than an hour, managing to disperse them. The other aircraft, also armed with machine guns, supported the Army troops that launched an assault on La Lucha, which at that time had been abandoned by the rebels.

On that same day, three anonymous Nicaragua C-47s – with their registrations and titles covered by splotches of black paint[34] – arrived in San José as part of unsolicited assistance provided by President Anastasio Somoza. It turns out that the Nicaraguan dictator had been informed that among Figueres' men there were Nicaraguan exiles who were planning to launch an invasion of Nicaragua once Figueres had seized power. Thus, he did not hesitate in getting involved, even though President Picado had begged him not to do so. In fact, by then Nicaraguan Guardia Nacional troops had already crossed the border and were marching towards the town of Los Chiles, in the Alajuela province, with the intention of setting up a forward operating base from where they could launch attacks against the rebels' northern front.

Unable to get rid of the Nicaraguan C-47s, the Costa Rican government decided to hide their presence by covering the markings of all its DC-3s, thus introducing a great deal of confusion about their registrations and the operations in which they participated. In any case, during the following days the three loyalist DC-3s conducted several attacks against the rebels, always with mixed results, while the Nicaraguan C-47s were utilised for evacuating casualties and move troops around the country. By the end of March, a seventh

aircraft, a TACA DC-3 carrying Salvadoran registration YS-34, was requisitioned by the government and promptly impressed into service. This aircraft was also employed in combat duties, undergoing the 'attack-bomber' conversion described above.

On 10 April, after the rebels had moved their aircraft to Altamira in preparation for the airborne assault on Port Limón, the government launched all its aircraft in search of them. As noted in the previous section, a pair of loyalist DC-3s, escorted by a solitary AT-6, located two of the rebel DC-3s at the Altamira airfield and attempted to destroy them. During the attack one of the loyalist DC-3 was hit by ground fire and crashed shortly after, killing all on board. Flying this aircraft was Sherman Wilson, while his co-pilot was a TACA mechanic named Alejo Poveda. Riding as gunners/bombers were Arquímides Álvarez, Antonio Carmona, Alfredo Chamorro, Jorge Suárez, Ramón Muñóz, Juan Montero and Victor Chacón.

There is considerable confusion about the circumstances of this crash. According to witnesses, after being hit by machine gun fire at Altamira, the DC-3 turned around and headed towards the south, probably trying to return to San José. However, after a couple of minutes, the aircraft lost altitude and slammed against a hill near the small village of Palmira. People who saw the aircraft shortly before the crash state that fire was visible through the cabin windows, as well as smoke spilling from the cargo hatch. This is consistent with rebel accounts that mention a small explosion inside the aircraft after being hit. On the other hand, in some rebel literature it is mentioned that Wilson was hit by bullets that killed him instantly, and with no one onboard who could fly the aircraft, it continued its flight until striking high terrain. A third version, told by Robert Darmsted, the owner of an aircraft repair company in San José, states that he saw Wilson drinking whisky at a cantina near the airport, shortly before departing for the mission. In Darmsted's opinion, Wilson must have been very drunk due to the whisky and the altitude when the aircraft reached Altamira, and that would explain why he bombed the rebels so low and then crashed when trying to return to his base. Last, but not least, the government's official version, published in *La Tribuna* newspaper the next day, says that the aircraft crashed due to bad weather. The press release does not even mention that the aircraft was involved in a combat mission.

Regarding the identity of Wilson's aircraft, there is also considerable confusion. The US Ambassador to Costa Rica, in a note to the Department of State dated 11 April, reports it as 'a LACSA DC-3' that crashed on a 'Bombing mission, killing Wilson, a Canadian pilot, and several others'. This affirmation clearly conflicts with LACSA's fleet history, since the only two aircraft that the government requisitioned from that airline were returned once the civil war was over. Another unconfirmed source states that the aircraft belonged to the small airline Empresa Nacional de Transportes Aéreos (ENTA) but this company had been absorbed by TACA de Costa Rica almost nine years earlier. Lastly, it has been mentioned that this aircraft was in fact the C-47 that the government requisitioned from TAN airlines, which makes much more sense, but would be almost impossible to prove since that company's fleet history is full of holes at best!

The three surviving aircraft, all LACSA assets as shown in the accompanying table, following the signature of a 'peace pact' on 19 April that amounted to the complete surrender of the

An undated photo of TACA de Costa Rica's DC-3 fleet. Judging by their liveries, the image must have been taken before the outbreak of the revolution. The aircraft at the centre is Honduran-registered and surely was undergoing maintenance at the TACA workshops in La Sabana; she definitively wasn't involved in the air operations, since the company flew out of the country most of its foreign-registered aircraft during the first forty-eight hours of the revolution. Of interest is the DC-3 on the right, as it seems to carry some sort of official titles, which are partially visible.

Government forces to the revolutionary group, were then used to transport high officials and supporters of the deposed government to Managua, Nicaragua, on 24 April – initially aboard two of the DC-3s – a third having been forced to land somewhere in Nicaraguan territory, probably with additional refugees aboard. All three were promptly impounded by the Nicaraguans and became bargaining chips in a complex legal and diplomatic squabble that persisted, incredibly, until July 1951, when they were eventually returned to LACSA control. As noted in Chapter 16, the adventures of these three aircraft continued, however, and they did not sit idle at Managua!

What follows is what is known so far about the Costa Rican government-controlled DC-3/C-47 fleet during the civil war.

According to the rebels' narrative, the aircraft shown in this photograph is one of the C-47s that were captured at San Isidro del General on 12 March. However, she does not seem to be painted in the colour scheme applied to the TACA aircraft. Of interest is that its registration has been covered with black paint.

Registration	Previous Identity	Built As	MSN	Notes
TI-17	NC34925	DC-3A-345	4957	Transferred from Pan American to LACSA in 1946. Requisitioned by the government on 12 Mar 48 and converted to 'attack-bomber'. Impounded in Nicaragua 24 Apr 48 and became either GN 53, 54 or 55. Returned to LACSA control July 1951. Sold to Aerovías Brasil as PP-AXW in November 1951. Then re-registered as PP-NBJ. Sold to Argentine Air Force in 1962 as T-37.
TI-18	41-18381 NC51182	C-47-DL	4419	Transferred from Pan American to LACSA in 1946. Requisitioned by the government on 12 Mar 48 and converted to 'attack-bomber'. Impounded in Nicaragua 24 Apr 48 and became either GN 53, 54 or 55. Returned to LACSA July 1951. Sold to Aerovías Brasil as PP-AXV in Nov 51. Then re-registered as PP-NBK on 5 May 53 with Aeronorte. Then to PP-ABE in Feb 58 with Suprimentos Aeronáuticos do Brasil, N6893C on 12 Aug 58 with Stewart Davis, XA-NAA in Sep 59 with Aerolíneas Vega. Noted derelict at Oaxaca, MX, in 1976.
TI-108	41-38699 NC66147 C-60 C-407	C-47-DL	6158	Acquired by TAN from Vías Aéreas Colombianas in Feb 47. Requisitioned by the government on 12 Mar 48 and converted to 'attack-bomber'. Most likely to be the aircraft that crashed at Palmira on 10 Apr 48 after bombing the rebels in Altamira.
YS-34	42-92279 FL635 YS-34 C-209	C-47A-15-DK	12062	Transferred from TACA Airlines to TACA de Costa Rica in May 47. Requisitioned by the government on 28 March and converted to 'attack-bomber'. Almost certainly the third government aircraft impounded in Nicaragua 24 Apr 48 and became either GN 53, 54 or 55 – probably the latter (see Chapter 16).

Virtually the entire LACSA DC-3 fleet photographed at La Sabana sometime before the outbreak of the revolution. These aircraft were promptly requisitioned by the government and flown as 'attack-bombers' during the hostilities.

CHAPTER EIGHT

Cuba

A S BY FAR THE LARGEST of the long Antilles chain of islands, Cuba had first proposed the creation of a military air arm as early as 1915 – and had in fact gone so far as to very nearly field a squadron of aircraft in support of the Allied war effort in the First World War.

It was not until May 1919, however, that the first elements of what was labelled at the time as the Cuerpo de Aviación was activated. But that early investment slowly matured during the inter-war period and Cuba benefited rather handsomely from the Second World War-era Lend-Lease programme, both in terms of equipment and the training of both pilots and maintenance personnel.

By 1946, styled as the Cuerpo de Aviación, Ejército de Cuba (CAEC) the service became eligible for modest deliveries of Second World War-era aircraft under the provisions of the post-war American Republics Projects (ARP) and, as elsewhere, the selected 'mix' of equipment included four C-47s that, joined by small numbers of Beech AT-7, AT-11 and C-45 twins, became the first multi-engined aircraft to be operated by the Army. The first of the ARP aircraft had entered the inventory by 9 December1946.The resulting compact multi-engine fleet, for the first time, gave the Cuban Army the capability to at last link its widely dispersed garrisons the length of the island, and in a very real sense, the C-47s proved nearly ideal for the Cuban operating environment. They ranged not only up and down the length of the country, but also to the United States. Although less than 100 miles distant, until the advent of the C-47 in Cuban military service, it may as well have been thousands.

In fact, the initial increment of four ARP C-47s was reduced to just three when the CAEC surrendered one of the four, 43-48962 (msn 14778/26223) back to the USAF around 1 July 1948, apparently in favour of additional Consolidated OA-10s instead. It was thus the 'first' CAEC-203 and wore these marks for only two years before they were retroactively assigned to one of the seized Cayo Confites aircraft. Oddly, while these aircraft are invariably cited in most documents as having been provided under the provisions of the ARP, other sources show that the three aircraft – all C-47Bs – had been acquired from the Foreign Liquidation Commission (FLC) and were all ex-European Theatre of Operations Second World War veteran aircraft. This does not seem to agree with known acquisitions, however.

Cuba was also at the centre of the post-Second World War explosion of pro-democracy activists and elements within the sitting government gave rather more than tacit support to the most robust of these, aimed at the overthrow of totalitarian regimes in, first and foremost, the Dominican Republic, but also in Nicaragua and elsewhere. Ironically,

A former RAF Dakota IV, KN358, FAEC-201 here wears the definitive Batista-era service markings and national insignia as of 3 January 1957 when photographed. *Harold G. Martin*

Long a matter of controversy, this image of the remains of Cuban C-47B serial 200 should put the issue to rest once and for all. Having been repaired in Alabama following an earlier accident, she succumbed to Hurricane Fox, which devastated the (then) Fuerza Aérea – Ejercito de Cuba at its main operating base, Campo Columbia, on 5 October 1949. *via Rod Simpson, Air-Britain*

The earliest known photo of an FAEC C-47, although of low quality, serial 201 here displays the markings used in the period 1919–52, with the national insignia that at the time consisted of a blue disc with a red triangle and white star superimposed worn on the four wing positions only. An ARP delivery on 11 December 1946, she survived to pass to the Castro-era FAR and subsequently to civil marks as CU-T810. *via Georg von Roitberg*

it was via this very movement that the CAEC quite suddenly came into possession of its next two C-47s, seized from the so-called Cayo Confites 'air force' in August and September 1947. Suddenly, the service had five C-47s, although the official USAF Air Orders of Battle for 31 January 1948 and 1 January 1949, reported only four. In 1947, the hard-working CAEC C-47 trio flew some 323,386 air miles, carrying 4,040 passengers. By 7 July 1950, with the addition of the Cayo Confites pair, bringing the total on hand to four (of which one was non-operative by that date) this had skyrocketed to 384,439 air miles and 4,960 passengers. But with the addition of yet more C-47s via commercial purchases and the Grant Aid provisions of MAP, by 1952 the totals had reached an astonishing 779,307 air miles and 9,980 passengers – including, of course, troop movements. The USAF Mission had arranged with the Air Materiel Command (AMC) to supply the CAEC with a special shipment of C-47 spares between January and June 1952, 'sufficient to support five C-47s'. The FY52 budget for MDAP Title IV recipients also included $177,900 for the rehabilitation of certain CAEC C-47 and B-25 aircraft for Cuba under what was described as Project 931.

Between 13 July 1951 and 24 March 1953, Cuba submitted what amounted to a running series of Military Assistance requests to the US and these were all consolidated by the OSD/OMA into what came to be known as Case No. Cuba-21. These exceptionally ambitious requests included demands for twelve Lockheed F-80C fighter-bombers, six T-33As and five North American T-28As. The CAEC, apparently in an attempt to appear reasonable, admitted that, if the F-80Cs were not available, it would accept North American F-51Ds instead and, failing that, either Vought F4U, Grumman F8F, F9F or McDonnell F2H series aircraft! The service also requested either nine North American B-25Js or Douglas B-26Cs, four Consolidated PBY-5As, and either twelve Fairchild C-82As, Curtiss C-46Ds or Douglas C-47Bs! Displaying admirable restraint, the USAF replied by September 1951 that F-80Cs, B-25Js, F-51Ds and C-82As were 'simply not available (undoubtedly because of the demands of the expanding Korean conflict) but did offer four PBY-5As in lieu of B-25Js by March 1952. Had any of these requests been honoured at that particular juncture, in whole or in part, it does not require unusual powers of deduction to conclude that the subsequent success of the Castro insurgency may have turned out very differently and, with it, the history of the Caribbean and Cuba.

Apparently unhappy with the reticence exhibited by the USAF, the CAEC turned to the export firm of Smith-Kirkpatrick and Company of New York, with whom the Cuban Army had concluded a deal by 12 May 1952 for some 500,000 rounds of .30-06 calibre of Mexican manufacture. Additionally, Smith-Kirkpatrick expressed confidence that it could supply the CAEC with a mix of seventeen refurbished DC-3 and C-47 aircraft, all via contacts also in Mexico. However, apparently the New York firm was getting a bit ahead of itself as, when the USAF Attaché in Cuba, Col William J. Hovde, queried USAF Intelligence about this possibility, they reported that nothing approaching this total of DC-3s or C-47s were available in Mexico for sale at the time, but that the Fuerza Aérea Mexicana (FAM) had offered to sell two or three of their highest-time aircraft – if the price were right. All of this came to nothing, however, although the small arms ammunition was shipped.

By 30 June 1953, the service counted a total of five C-47s on hand, one of which had been added to the inventory by utilising two damaged aircraft and Grant Aid spares to build one complete aircraft (probably the aircraft covered by Project 931 noted above), although the total was increased to six in July when two Grant Aid C-47s arrived. These two aircraft (42-100850 and 42-100989), covered by Project MDA604, arrived on 22 July 1953 and had exceptionally colourful service careers to this point. Both had latterly been used by CIA proprietaries in Central America and, at least notionally, passed through the Mobile, Alabama, AMA at Brookley AFB en route to Cuba. This may well have been the mechanism via which the solution to the confusion over CAEC-203 (1) and CAEC-206 could be resolved once and for all (See table). By March 1953, work on this unique project was described as 'progressing satisfactorily', the two aircraft involved having been previously damaged in a hurricane, and the work was expected to be completed by July 1953. One other CAEC C-47 was at the San Bernardino Air Materiel Area depot in California, being completely rehabilitated under MDAP. By 30 June 1954, the Air Order of Battle reflected a total of seven C-47s, all assigned to the Escuadrón de Transporte at Campo Columbia, all of which were judged by the USAF as 'combat ready' at the time, and all of which were, curiously, MDAP-supported at the time, which, given the nature of the acquisition of at least one and possibly two of them, is quite extraordinary. The USAF also noted on this report that the service was scheduled and approved for three additional aircraft in the FY54 MDA Programme and, by December 1957, all five of the Grant Aid aircraft had been received.

A fine study of another former RAF Dakota IV, KP212, FAEC-202 was also an ARP delivery on 11 December 1946. By the time of this photo, however, the service titles atop the fuselage had changed to those of the operating unit, the Escuadron de Transporte, and in fact the unit's distinctive Indian head emblem can just be seen behind the cockpit. This aircraft was used by Batista and his top aides to escape to the Dominican Republic in 1958 and was then absorbed into the FAD C-47 fleet. *Harold G. Martin*

This close-up of FAEC-202 was taken early in her service career, and shows the damage sustained during Hurricane Fox in October 1949, and the early position of her serial number. *Rod Simpson, Air-Britain*

The aftermath of Hurricane Fox at Campo Columbia in October 1949 shows FAEC-203 (second use) and the wing placement of the then current national insignia and serial on her starboard wing. Note that the white star point is facing *aft*. Besides the impounded former Cayo Confites Lockheed P-38M visible, in the middle are the remains of the USAF Attaché's C-47 and, nearest, a former Cayo Confites C-46. *Rod Simpson, Air-Britain*

Although wearing serial 203, initial Castro-era national insignia and titles II Frente Frank Pais, and FAR on her upper starboard wing, this is clearly a Hi-Per DC-3C conversion and thus almost certainly not the original FAEC-203, which is believed to have been one of the aircraft that escaped to the Dominican Republic in 1958. She is seen here at Miami in February 1961. *Ralph Brown via Brian R. Baker*

Another seized Cayo Confites aircraft, C-47-DL MSN 4528 was in good condition when she joined the FAEC and probably survived into the Castro era. *via Dr Gary Kuhn*

Displaying service titles as worn early in her service career, FAEC-205 was also seized from the Cayo Confites conspirators. Shown her during the aftermath of Hurricane Fox in 1949, she was repaired and subsequently flown to American Airmotive Corp. in Miami for conversion into VIP configuration. She survived to become CU-T808. *Rod Simpson, Air-Britain*

A measure of the experience that had been gained by the CAEC Escuadrón de Transporte crews by 30 September 1953 may be gained from the fact that the service actually stepped up to air-deliver some 100,000lb of MDAP Grant Aid material back home from Brookley AFB, AL, during the course of no fewer than thirty round-trip flights. Using CAEC-201, 202 and 204 through 207, the route taken was either Havana to Mobile avoiding the Eglin AFB, FL, danger area or, alternatively, the civil Tampa Airway.

By July 1956, the Escuadrón de Transporte was being lauded in the local Cuban press, having to date carried an average of some 24,312 passengers annually and a very impressive 757,620lb of mail and cargo. The passengers were, in fact, actually a mix of service personnel and their extended families, which in itself must have been an invaluable benefit of service at the time.

By 1 January 1958 the USAF reported that the 'C-47-equipped Transport Squadron has continued its exceptionally active passenger and flight operations. Despite its unusually high utilisation rate, the unit's shortage of equipment prevents it from being rated "fully combat ready", as the 10 aircraft on hand represent only a portion of the 16 that would constitute a UE unit.' Between 31 December 1956 and 30 June 1958, the by then FAEC was shown with a total of ten C-47s (and one 'VC-53') on hand, its peak strength. Of these, five had been acquired via MAP Grant Aid between FY1950 and FY1955, these having been almost certainly serials 207, 208, 211 and 212. Six of these were used to shuttle arms and ammunition from Ciudad Trujillo, Dominican Republic, back home to Cuba around 2–3 April 1958 to attempt to reinforce the beleaguered Army forces who were crumbling to the Castro insurgency across the breadth of the island. Starting in March 1958, by 22 July 1958, the US delivered what amounted to a series of knockout blows to the Batista regime when it suspended arms shipments to Cuba. Significantly, one of the most 'urgent' line items were what were euphemistically referred to as 'non-combat' spares for C-47-type aircraft.

At least a few words must be recorded herein regarding the rather tenuous use of C-47s by Castro and his insurgents while at large in the hinterland prior to their 1958 triumph over demoralised government forces. A C-47 with the titles Motilón Corporación apparently acquired via Admiral Wolfgang Larrazabal, the erstwhile leader of the Venezuelan liberal-oriented junta *c*.1958, is known to have made several intrepid excursions into the Sierra Maestra carrying arms and supplies.

The CAEC/FAEC enjoyed a rather accident-free existence with its C-47 fleet, although one is known to have suffered a forced landing in Nicaragua on 6 June 1949 while en route to Costa Rica, the damage from which has escaped verification. Another is known to have been lost to an undocumented accident in February 1960, by which time it was probably serialed in the FAR series. An unidentified FAR C-47 was shot down by 'friendly fire' on 21 January 1964 at San Antonio de los Baños, however, one of the few Cuban C-47s 'lost in action', after a fashion.

The final known report, dated in March 1959, and before the political situation in Cuba had crystalised, still showed the Escuadrón de Transporte at Campo Columbia with a total of ten C-47s on hand, and with eight qualified crews with the notation that 'five of the 10 had been provided under Grant Aid'. Average monthly utilisation, however, had fallen to only ninety-three hours, but the total flown during calendar year 1958 had been a very impressive 5,551 hours.

While the CAEC eventually enjoyed the services of at least fourteen and possibly fifteen assorted C-47s and DC-3s, the service was also destined to operate the type for a far briefer period than anywhere else in Latin American military service. With the advent of the Communist regime of Fidel Castro, and the subsequent destruction of a number of the surviving former CAEC aircraft during the so-called Bay of Pigs invasion – by which time the few airworthy survivors had been remarked with 'FAR' titles – spares support and the on-hand advice of the very active USAF Mission to Cuba ended abruptly and even though at least eleven were still nominally in existence by May 1958, by the early 1960s they had been almost completely discarded in favour of Soviet equipment.

After the Batista regime fell, what was left of the FAEC was quickly absorbed into the restyled Fuerza Aérea Revolucionaria (FAR) and the Western intelligence community was impressed when, on the first anniversary of the success of the revolution, 26 July 1959, the FAR managed to get eight Hawker Sea Furys, nine Douglas B-26Cs, four Lockheed T-33As, two venerable Republic F-47Ds, single examples of the Douglas C-54 and Curtiss C-46 – and no fewer than four C-47s – into the air for the victory parade. Although aided by a number of 'civilian' pilots, this report at least indicates that of the total number of C-47s once operated by the pre-Castro regime, at least four survived the ensuing debacle.

After the Castro regime had settled in, however, a number of highly unusual C-47 sightings started being recorded. For example, on the morning of 5 November 1961, a C-47 landed at Los Caños airfield, Cuba, not far from the US Navy installations at Guantanamo Bay, having been forced down by bad weather. The aircraft was noted by US agents at the time as having been manned by a 'European crew' and, even more unusually, had been obviously modified for aerial photography. The observer noted that the aircraft bore the obviously bogus identification marks 'CU-CZOZ'. The origins and fate of this intriguing aircraft remain unknown, but that it might have been a Lisunov Li-2 cannot be ruled out.

CAEC Serial	Previous Identity	Built as	MSN	Assignments and Notes
200	42-76392 KN359 '359'	C-47B-25-DK	15976/32724	Although many historians have openly questioned the existence of this aircraft, as can be seen by the accompanying photos, she was definitely acquired via ARP by 1 Oct 46. She was a frequent visitor to Miami, FL, her first visit after delivery having been on 2 Nov 46 and then again on 24 Mar 47, 2 Jun 47, 12 Sep 47 and 11 Nov 47. At some point, she suffered unspecified damage and was a candidate for rebuild under Grant Aid at the Mobile Air Depot, Alabama. She had arrived under her own power at Miami on 11 Nov 47 en route to Mobile, however, so whatever the extent of the damage, it was apparently at least flyable. She was subsequently significantly damaged by Hurricane Fox on 5 Oct 49, and this may have been her end, based on photos of the damage.
201	44-76391 KN358 VMYBR '358'	C-47B-25-DK Dakota IV	15975/32723	ARP on 11 Dec 46. She was actually flight delivered, however, on 4 Feb 47 from the US. She is known to have visited Miami on at least twelve occasions between 15 Mar 47 and 25 Jun 48. This aircraft enjoyed a lengthy service career as late as 3 Aug 59 and eventually became CU-T810 on the Cuban civil register.
202	44-77093 KP212 VMYDT	C-47B-35-DK Dakota IV	16677/33425	ARP on 11 Dec 46. Following delivery, she was a frequent visitor to Miami, FL, arriving there at least fourteen times between 2 Jun 47 and 9 Jun 48. This aircraft travelled to Guatemala City on 20 Jul 49 with Eufemio Fernández as passenger. This aircraft was destined to become a Fuerza Aérea Dominicana (FAD) aircraft in 1958 when she was used by escaping Batista officials to flee to the sanctuary offered by Rafael Trujillo, and thus served only twelve years in Cuba. She made her last flight to Miami as a Cuban aircraft on 5 Feb 58.
203 (1)	41-18535 NC-56001	C-47-DL	4627	One of the two Cayo Confites 'air force' C-47s, and a Second World War Eighth Air Force veteran, this one had actually escaped to Managua, Province of La Habana (not Nicaragua, as has often been reported), with some of the conspirators and small arms, where it experienced engine problems, but was seized there and returned to Campo Columbia to join the CAEC. However, she crashed on 27 Aug 47 under unknown circumstances but may have been eventually rebuilt and returned to service.
203 (2) FAR-203	44-76392	C-47B-25-DK	15976/32724	ARP on 11 Dec 46. This aircraft was authorised to be flight-delivered to Cuba on 3 Mar 47 and is identified in US State Department documents with this MSN, hopefully putting to rest any confusion as to her identity. She was a frequent visitor to Miami, FL, also, making the journey at least thirteen times between 5 Jul 47 and 30 Jun 48. A Hi-Per DC-3 with serial FAR 203 was at Miami in Feb 61 with 'II Frente Frank Pais' titles and may have in fact been yet a third aircraft. This may support reports that this aircraft was later CP-691 in Bolivia by Apr 61, via a post-Castro sale.
204	41-38579 NC-57650 NC-66113	C-47-DL	4528	The second of the Cayo Confites aircraft seized, this one at Santiago de Cuba on 5 Sep 47, this aircraft continued in service as late as 13 Oct 58.
205	41-18359 NC-69354	C-47-DL	4397	Apparently, a commercial acquisition, this aircraft was first reported with the CAEC by Oct 49, when she was moderately damaged during Hurricane Fox. She was made airworthy and then flown to American Airmotive Corp. of Miami for conversion to VIP configuration. This comprised an office with two circular lounges and seats for six. She survived as late as 8 Apr 59. She reportedly passed to CU-T808. This may have, in fact, been the 'first' Cuban 'Air Force One' in a VIP configuration, named El Mambí, which the 'Boletín del Ejército' for Sep–Oct 51 noted as being in service by that time.
206	43-48962	C-47B-10-DK	14778/26223	Although known to have been an ARP offset on 10 Dec 47, this aircraft had a rather convoluted subsequent history, including a reported period with the French Air Force after 15 Jun 50 as '38962'. She was definitely with Cuba as of 13 Jan 55 as she visited Miami on that date. This casts considerable doubt on the actual identity of this aircraft as CAEC-206. However, an aircraft with serial 206 was one of two that fled to the Dominican Republic around 1 Jan 59 with Batista's party on board, and which was subsequently incorporated into the FAD.

A very rare colour image of an FAEC C-47, here serial 206, a C-47B-10-DK, is pictured after arrival at Ciudad Trujillo, Dominican Republic, in 1958, with the nose of FAEC-202 just visible in the background. She was incorporated into the FAD. *via Leif Hëllstrom*

207	42-100850 CNAC 89 XT-T48 N8348C N4884V	C-47A-75-DL	19313	Almost certainly a 22 Jul 53 MAP Grant Aid delivery. Reported as early as Jul 53 and as late as 29 Jul 59.
208	42-100989 CNAC 91 XT-T54 N8352C N4883V 42-100989	C-47A-75-DL DC-3C-S1C3G	19452	Almost certainly a 22 Jul 53 MAP Grant Aid delivery. Reported as early as Jul 53 and as late as 5 May 58.
209	42-68716 NC-59410 VC-53	C-53D-DO Hi-Per DC-3	11643	Acquired on 20 Dec 54 with the assistance of Pan Am in VIP configuration and initially named 'Caballo de Batalla', but later renamed 'Guaimaró'. Last reported on 13 Mar 58. This is almost certainly the aircraft with a Cuban Presidential seal on the fuselage side aft of the door that was modified to this configuration by Pan Am at its Brownsville, Texas, depot. After Castro came to power, the aircraft was reserialed as FAR-209 and once again renamed, this time as 'Sierra Maestra'. A CIA report dated 30 Mar 61 stated that the 'Sierra Maestra' had been lost by that date and replaced by one named 'El Pico Turquino' (possibly FAR-1212, q.v.).
210	*42-100927*	*C-47A-75-DL*	*19390*	MDAP 27 May 55. Serial 210 first reported on 15 Nov 55 and as late as 10 May 58. This aircraft was reported at Fort Worth, Texas, on 12 Jul 56 and at Miami on 16 Jul 59. Noted Cuban aviation historian Capt. George G. Farinas reported that this serial was allocated to MSN 11647, USAAF 42-68720, a C-53D converted to DC-3A configuration. However, that aircraft was condemned in North Africa on 8 Jul 44! He also reports that FAEC-210 survived to pass to Cubana with civil marks CU-T836 in 1961.

Right: Although of marginal quality, this is the only known image of Fidel Castro's Hi-Per DC-3C FAR-209 marked as 'Sierra Maestra'. Ironically, the aircraft had been plushed up for his predecessor, Fulgencio Batista, by Pan Am in December 1954. Note the unusual window arrangement. *via Javier Quintero*

Below: Believed to have been one of three late MAP deliveries, FAEC-210 was first reported in service in November 1955 and survived into the Castro FAR. She was captured in this image at distant Meacham Field, Fort Worth, Texas. *Ev Haney via Dave Lucabaugh*

211	42-93600	C-47A-25-DK	13530	MDA 18 Feb 57. Serial 211 first reported on 28 Apr 57. Last reported on 18 May 59.
212 'FAR-1212'	–	–	–	Last reported on 27 Mar 58. A much later serial, FAR-1212, may be associated with this aircraft. A CIA report dated 30 Mar 61 stated that Castro's replacement aircraft for the 'lost' 'Sierra Maestra', was named 'El Pico Turquino', after a peak in the Sierra Maestra mountain range, and that it was equipped with special auxiliary fuel tanks and stationed in a very restricted area at the intersections of Runways #3 and the north–south runway at San Antonio de los Baños near a tower fortified with numerous machine guns. Clearly a 'bolt' aircraft if the balloon went up.

Among the aircraft damaged in the October 1949 hurricane at Campo Columbia near Havana was C-47A-1-DL, 42-23346, the aircraft of the USAF Air Attaché to Haiti and the Dominican Republic named 'The Brass Hat'. Although appearing to be the subject of the amorous intentions of a Cayo Confites C-46 in this image, the aircraft was salvaged and sold to Haiti, which used the hulk to rebuild one of its C-47s. Note the crushed FAEC B-25 also mounted by the C-46. *via Leif Hëllstrom*

CHAPTER NINE

Dominican Republic

A LTHOUGH FUNDING to create an indigenous air arm in this relatively small island nation sharing the land area of the island of Hispaniola with Haiti to its west was set aside as early as 1928, it was not until five years later that the small Compañía de Aviación was finally formed.

Essentially the private air force of dictator Rafael Leonidas Trujillo, the service remained quite small, and even with the addition of modest Lend-Lease deliveries of modern equipment during the Second World War, did not become a regional power until Trujillo, alarmed by pro-democracy movements with the avowed objective of toppling his regime, surfaced with a vengeance in 1946 and 1947.

With the assistance of a number of agents acting on his direct behalf, by 1950 the recrafted Cuerpo de Aviación Militar Dominicana had grown into a force to be reckoned with, and frankly out of all proportion to the actual needs of the country. By 1952, the Cuerpo was the largest in all of Central America and the Caribbean and, at least on paper, was very nearly on a par with the major Latin American powers. Former Swedish de Havilland Vampire jets were introduced, as well as a substantial number of North American F-51Ds, while at nearly the same time, the United States provided twenty-five Republic F-47D Thunderbolts.

Although vast distances were not a problem in handling logistics in the Dominican Republic, the road and rail infrastructure as of the 1950s was still very poor, and although Trujillo focused most of his energy on acquiring an astonishing array of purely tactical and armament-capable aircraft, the absolute dictator recognised that an organic transport capability would also be necessary to link his garrisons and centres of power, deploy loyal troops rapidly to hotspots, and move equipment and supplies between the island and foreign sources. As a direct result, the air arm acquired a number of Curtiss C-46 and Beech C-45 series aircraft commencing in 1949, as well as at least one Lockheed L-18 Lodestar.

Thus, unlike virtually every other Latin American air arm, the Dominican Republic apparently did not acquire its first DC-3/C-47 series aircraft until much later than anywhere else, the earliest report dating from 30 June 1954, although a Dominican request for authorisation to export two C-47s and two C-45s from the US was dated 5 February 1946 and suggests that these aircraft were either for the AMD or the government-sponsored flag carrier airline, CDA, which, in an emergency, could be called upon by Trujillo, who essentially controlled it as well . At least one of these aircraft wore the rather grandiose titles, nearly the entire length of her upper fuselage decking, reading Escuadrón de Transporte Aéreo AMD, the latter being the initials for Aviación Militar Dominicana. It is believed that these aircraft may, in fact, have worn serials 3401 and 3402.

The AMD submitted a Foreign Military Sales (FMS) request, identified as Case OPC/DR-21, on 23 October 1956 covering two C-47s, a Douglas C-54 and a Douglas TB-26 to be used as a target tug. The TB-26 was, the USAF advised, available, but they had no C-47s or C-54s to offer. The AMD apparently gave up and signalled that it was withdrawing the request on 10 April 1957.

The earliest known image showing an AMD C-47, probably either 3401 or 3402, sometime after December 1955, as a line-up of ex-Swedish de Havilland Vampires can be seen in the background. She is in company with two of the other three transport types in service at the time, a Beech C-45 and Douglas C-54, and her rather generous titles proclaim she is with the Escuadron de Transporte Aéreo A.M.D. *Lennart Engerby via Leif Hëllstrom*

Then, when the two ex-Cuban C-47s, FAEC-202 and 206, arrived unexpectedly with Batista and his entourage in 1958, these, too, were enlisted into the service, bringing the total on hand to three, suggesting that one had either been lost or, more likely, transferred to CDA.

By 1964, the 'flying medical dispensary' provided under MAP, always assumed to have been FAD-3405, comprised the entire Dominican participation in the so-called Civic Action Programme then being promoted by the US To November of that year. The aircraft had been provided with a five-man medical team trained with MAP funds and a second was then in training at the USAF School for Latin America (later the IAAFA). The supporting materiel package was, unfortunately, suspended when the Dominican Republic temporarily broke diplomatic relations with the US, and was only 60 per cent complete.

By June 1966, the USAF reported that the FAD had, to that time, operated a total of four C-47s, which agrees with known data. This remained essentially unchanged through 4 November 1969, with the Escuadrón de Transporte also operating four C-46s as well by that time.

As odd as it may seem to readers unfamiliar with the politics of the Caribbean, besides the paranoia of Trujillo, Dominican foreign policy has always been shaped by a rather curious fear of invasion by neighbouring Haiti. Although the population of Haiti is, indeed, much greater than that of the DR and is constrained into an area little more than half the area of the Dominican Republic, and despite a history of Haitian invasion and conquest of her eastern neighbours, the military strength of the Dominican Republic – even though much less by the 1960s than in its heyday under Trujillo – meant that the reality was that a military threat from Haiti was patently ridiculous. Trujillo had

used the supposed threat from Haiti as a partial justification for the maintenance of his huge military establishment as, indeed, did subsequent governments. Even though there has been some chronic, low-level guerrilla activity in the mountainous regions of the interior of the Republic, these have been easily contained – although they did help justify renewed US military aid and, as it happened, the next infusion of C-47s for what had become, by this time, the Fuerza Aérea Dominicana (FAD). This resulted in two being supplied in late 1965 and two more in 1970, as can be gleaned from the accompanying table. Utilisation was rather low, however, as the four C-47s on strength as of 17 April 1969 – all but one of them MAP-supported – had flown only a total of seventy-six hours during the preceding three-month period. By October 1969, one of the C-47s was out of service for more than two weeks due to the fact that a replacement oil cooler that had been shipped for it was being held up by Dominican Customs, while another was down for a 100-hour inspection.

By January 1970, with MAP support, one of the FADs C-47s had been placed in a 'special' IRAN programme, possibly incident to its conversion to a gunship, and had also been repainted (assumed to have been Vietnam-era camouflage) and, between 1972 and 1974, at least four had been camouflaged in wildly varying schemes using – mostly – SEA paints. The USAF V-12 Report went on to say that 'it is the intent to do this to all of the C-47s if money can be located for paint. In-commission rate is 65 per cent and total hours flown during the quarter was 90.'

Frequently cited use of serials '3110' (usually around May 1965 but more likely a C-46) and '3412' on FAD C-47s appear to be completely without foundation.

After 1972 most, if not all, of the surviving FAD C-47s were repainted in assorted camouflage schemes, no two being alike. This is FAD-3404 at San Isidro on 17 November 1974, wearing what is believed to be the unit insignia of the Escuadron de Transporte on both her nose and vertical fine. The significance of the yellow stripe high on the fin is unknown and what appears to be an insignia on the fuselage just behind the national insignia is damage to the surface from having the rear cargo door impact it! *via Nick J. Waters III*

Taken after the service was restyled as the Fuerza Aérea Dominicana (FAD) after 1958, FAD-3402 appears to be in very good condition. It is one of the former Cuban aircraft and appears to be in full USAF T.O. compliance for the period. *via Dax Roman*

FAD C-47s were fairly regular visitors to Miami, and FAD-3403, another of the ex-Cuban aircraft, is seen here after 1958 without rudder markings but still retaining Escuadron de Transporte titles. She appears to be very well maintained. *Harold G. Martin*

FAD Serial	Previous Identity	Built as	MSN	Assignments and Notes
3401	*41-38590* *HI-7*	*C-47-DL*	*4539*	Believed to have been handed back and forth to CDA at least twice, although tentative, this appears to hold a high degree of probability as the identity of FAD-3401. First reported on 30 Jun 54 and as late as 1968.
3402	*44-77093* *KP212* *VMYDT* *FAEC-202*	*C-47B-35-DK* *Dakota IV*	*16677/33425*	One of the two Cuban aircraft that fled to the Dominican Republic with Batista's entourage on 1 Jan 59. It was subsequently incorporated into the FAD and was last reported in Dec 67. The FAD had submitted a MAP requisition for spares for this aircraft in Dec 67.
3403	*43-48962* *FAEC-206*	*C-47B-10-DK* *C-47D*	*14778/26223*	The other Cuban aircraft that fled to the Dominican Republic on 1 Jan 59, although it is possible that the order of their FAD serials may in fact be reversed. This aircraft was last reported active by Sep 69, was noted derelict by Jul 88 and still on the dump at San Isidro by May 96.
3404	43-48269 0-48269	C-47B-1-DK C-47D	14085/25530	MAP on 3 Dec 65 via the Miami AIIMF. Last reported in service on 17 Nov 74, by which time she had been camouflaged. She was derelict by Jul 88 and still on the dump at San Isidro by May 96.
3405	*43-48766* *0-48766*	*C-47B-5-DK* *C-47D*	*43-48766*	This aircraft had actually been identified for MAP via the LOG Miami as early as 2 May 63, although the intended recipient is not known. She apparently suffered an accident either before or during her delivery flight on 23 Jul 63 but was subsequently repaired and MAP supplied to the FAD in Jan 70. This may have been the C-47 equipped as an ambulance aircraft via MAP.
3406	*44-76566* *0-76566*	*TC-47B-30-DK* *TC-47D* *C-47D* *AC-47D*	*16150/32898*	Like 3405 above, this aircraft had been identified for MAP as early as 25 Jul 63 via the Miami AINMF but was either not delivered or was redeployed, as the FAD did not receive her until January 1970. This aircraft appears to have been converted locally, with the assistance of MAP and the USAF Mission, to a quasi-AC-47D. She was still in service, camouflaged, by 1990 but was noted wrecked at Santiago-Cibao by 8 May 91 following an accident there.
3407	43-16379 0-16379	C-47B-1-DL C-47D AC-47D	20845	MAP on 27 Aug 70, although on 23 Sep 70 seems to have been the official handover date. This aircraft was also converted to AC-47D configuration but it is not clear if this was accomplished 'in country', like 3406 above, or by the SAAMA in Texas. This aircraft had served in USAFSO with the 605th Air Commando Squadron. She was camouflaged but withdrawn from use by 5 May 98 and scrapped in May 00.

Two examples of the widely varying camouflage schemes employed, this 1983 view is believed to show FAD-3407 nearest and -3405 in the background. Note that 3407 appears to have the engine cowlings from a different aircraft, as the light grey underside does not match the paint on the accessory covers. *Jeff Ethel*

FAD-3406 at the principal FAD base at San Isidro as of 29 November 1972 before being camouflaged and in excellent condition, no doubt due to the MAP support she received. *Rafael Power*

Arguably the most curious of the at least four FAD C-47s to be camouflaged, the colours used on FAD-3406 in this 1990 view are completely different from any other. Note that she is missing her extreme tail cone and has a small, subdued Dominican national insignia above the service acronym and serial on the vertical fin. *Peter Steinemann*

The port nose of AC-47D FAD-3407 reveals that the previous USAF data block was retained and that she was indeed 43-16379, received on 27 August 1970. Note also the special antennas on the port side of her nose and the whip antenna atop her forward fuselage. *via Nick J. Waters III*

Possibly the first Latin American C-47 to be converted to gunship status, the three .50 calibre M2 machine gun barrels can be seen in the two aft port-side windows. Exactly what threat the AC-47 was intended to counter remains unknown. *via Nick J. Waters III*

The breeches of the three .50 calibre guns on the port side of FAD-3407. Note the canvas or leather covers inserted into the windows to help shield the interior from both blast at night as well as smoke and draft. *Nick J. Waters III*

The gunsight and associated controls at the pilot-in-command station on the port side of the cockpit of FAD-3407. *Nick J. Waters III*

FAD-3407, still equipped as a gunship, after being camouflaged by 29 November 1972 at San Isidro. *Rafael Power*

Although a marginal image, this is AC-47D FAD-3407, again at San Isidro, on 31 October 1974, by which time her camouflage was rather faded. The unit insignia had been added to nose and vertical fin but her guns and whip antenna removed. *via Nick J. Waters III*

Above: *FAD* C-47 prepares to mount up a squad of Dominican commandos at San Isidro in 1982. Her serial is unknown, and her camouflage pattern does not match any other known aircraft. *Jeff Ethel*

Left: This aerial view shows the FAD cantonment area at San Isidro as of the 1965 Dominican Crisis. Visible under close scrutiny are one C-46D, four Douglas B-26Bs, one North American B-25, one C-54 (missing her rudder), two C-45s or AT-11s, seven de Havilland Vampires, two C-47s (one minus engines and rudder and the other airworthy) and, oddly, four Cessna 188s, as well as USAF C-130Es and one US Army Bell H-13. *NARA 342-KE-23070*

Below: The end of the road for what was believed to have been FAD-3403 with a Cessna T-41D in the foreground at San Isidro in December 1998. The C-47 had some sort of unit insignia on her nose, which has escaped identification. *Henrico A. Angerman*

CHAPTER TEN

Ecuador

E CUADOR'S DEFENCE structure is, and nearly always has been, dominated by its relations with Peru, the somewhat forlorn aspiration of regaining the territory lost in the 1941 conflict with the same antagonist, and the resolve to prevent further losses of territory.

When co-author Hagedorn was last in Ecuador in April 1969, the lofty capital city, Quito, seemed to be alive with uniforms of every conceivable description and, for the purposes of this narrative, the advent of the DC-3 and C-47 for military purposes following the Second World War must have seemed a Godsend to Ecuadorian strategists, as at long last it provided what was very nearly the ideal platform with which to link the principal military centres of the country and the thin line of remote aerodromes that had been carved out of the jungle to defend national interests in those same years.

Although the Fuerza Aérea Ecuatoriana (FAE) did not become fully independent of the Army until 1944, it had benefited modestly during the war years from Lend-Lease and in the immediate post-war years from the ARP. By the 1950s the air arm was enjoying the greatest concentration of the annual defence budget – the distant Galápagos Islands, Ecuadorian property, having played no small part in this largesse and, it can be reasonably argued, a key element in the FAE's strategy to expand its own, organic transport capability.

Indeed, FAE interest in acquiring C-47s under the provisions of Lend-Lease first manifested itself on 23 August 1944, when the service submitted a requisition for a single C-47A and no fewer than six Beech AT-7s to the Munitions Assignment Board (Air) in Washington, DC. The MAB (Air) in fact gave the Ecuadorian request

considerable weight, as it had the support of the Caribbean Defence Command in Panama, where the Sixth Air Force operated a key defence installation on Seymour Island in the Galápagos, the CDC taking the position that delivery of a C-47 to Ecuador would ease demands on its own limited transport capability to the islands, where a small Ecuadorian garrison was, for the purposes of pride and practical politics, maintained throughout the war years. Oddly, however, action on the request was shelved at the express request of the State Department, which invoked 'Jurisdiction' over this particular transaction and thus the FAE transport element, which ironically included a seized SEDTA Junkers Ju 52/3m, had to wait until after the war to acquire her first C-47s.

Thus, it came to pass that the first four C-47s acquired by the FAE came via the region-wide ARP programme, these being officially handed over from the US cadre between 29 September 1947 and 1 January 1948, all having been reconditioned and flown down via Panama from Kelly Field, Texas. Oddly, however, an early report stated that the service was anticipating its first ARP delivery in November 1946, but this may have been an instance of the ARP cadre having arrived with the first aircraft but formal handover being delayed until the host nation crews had completed their training and associated transfer documentation finalised.[35] This is borne out by a 12 December 1946 report that included mention of a 'plea from the Ecuadorians for expeditious delivery of the aircraft purchased via ARP Interim Program in the US, which included one C-47, six Republic P-47Ds and a mix of three C-45/AT-7/AT-11 series aircraft.

Well and truly a write-off in spectacular fashion, FAE-902 was almost certainly the first Ecuadorian C-47, but her previous identity has remained a mystery. She met her end at the remote Shell Mera airstrip in the interior in June 1948, as noted in the narrative. *via Henk C. Kavelaars*

Besides shedding both engines in the accident at Shell Mera, FAE-902 lost portions of both wings, and her nose was crushed. Traces of her previous USAAF identity have clearly been painted over. Note the engineless Shell Budd RB-1 in the background. *via Henk C. Kavelaars*

The earliest known image of an Ecuadorian C-47 bearing a 500 series serial. FAE-503 is pictured here at Quito delivering some dignitary before reviewing troops. This was an ARP-supplied aircraft. *via Capt. Jorge Delgado*

Above: By the time this view of FAE-506 had been taken, white upper decking had been applied, but without benefit of a separating cheatline. At this point, the national insignia roundels were worn on all four wing positions but not on the fuselage. *via Alfredo Jurado*

Right: With FAE-505 in the background, the nose of FAE-506 in the foreground reveals vestiges of her previous USAAF existence as the 'Donald Duck' nose art applied by some unknown US crew was apparently a subject of curiosity to the Ecuadorian crews. *Guido Chavez via Capt. Jorge Delgado*

When FAE-506 was returned to TEMCO in Greenville, Texas, for conversion to VIP executive configuration after November 1952, she was completely refurbished – but already had a special emblem on her nose not seen on any other *FAE* C-47. *via Dr Gary Kuhn*

Below: Photos showing FAE C-47s with TAME titles are rare. FAE-1969, built originally as a DC-3-209, was later converted back to C-47A-like configuration – the opposite of most such conversions. All aircraft used on TAME services wore dual FAE serials and civil registrations, in this case HC-AUV. *via George G.J. Kamp*

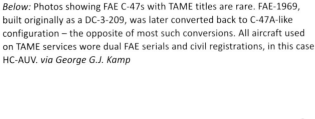

FAE-11747 was a C-53D acquired commercially in October 1967 in Brazil and here wears typical FAE transport colours of the 1970s. *ATP via Capt. George G. Farinas*

FAE officers are threatening to resign their commissions if something is not done immediately.' It appears, however, that the aircraft content of this first wave of ARP aircraft was changed, however, as US State Department files contained a copy of the final contract, dated 7 May 1947, which covered one C-47A, twelve P-47Ds and only one Beech AT-7 or AT-11. For a brief period, once finally in country, these aircraft apparently retained their US serials – or corruptions of these – until the FAE decided to assign transport types three-digit serials, initially in the 900s for some reason, and then changed by 1949 to the 500s. This was not as straightforward as it might appear, however, as for instance FAE-501 was retrospectively assigned to the former SEDTA Junkers Ju-52/3m, which had been seized in 1941, while FAE-504 was assigned to the first of the ARP-supplied Beech AT-7s. It is not clear if FAE-502 was used on the first ARP C-47 or not and thus the first known Ecuadorian C-47 serial was FAE-503. This

serialing scheme continued as late as September 1961 when, for some reason, the service decided upon the convention of using either the particular aircraft's original manufacturer's serial number or a contraction of the former US serial number as the FAE serial. Some of these also employed what appeared to be Ecuadorian versions of 'Buzz Numbers' while, much later, some of the aircraft assigned to the military-run Transportes Aéreos Militares Ecuatorianos (TAME) also wore quasi-civil registrations as well.

By 8 January 1949, the FAE Order of Battle finally reflected a total of four C-47s on strength. However, by 1 July 1952, the total number was cited as just three, and these were all assigned to what was at the time identified as Base Aérea Quito Zona I alongside the ubiquitous Beech AT-7, seven Vultee BT-13As and BT-13Bs, the venerable Junkers Ju 52/3m, the solitary remaining Seversky P-35 and ten Republic F-47Ds, a 'force within a force'.

The same aircraft, FAE-11747 coded CA-747, revealing the location of her starboard lower wing roundel on display as a gate guard in very good condition at BA Cotapaxi, Latacunga, at the paratrooper school there in November 1996. She had been placed there by September 1994 sans markings of any kind but was very nicely restored by troop labour. *LCDR Kolin Campbell*

A rarity, FAE-15222 coded CA-222 on her nose, displays the national insignia roundel on her rear fuselage. A July 1961 MAP delivery, she had suffered an accident some time prior to July 1967 but was completely rebuilt in country with the aid of the USAF Mission. *Guido Chavez via Capt. Jorge Delgado*

The FAE adopted a system of codes for their aircraft similar to USAF 'buzz numbers.' Sometimes, these were separated by a hyphen (i.e., 'CA-677') while in others, they were simply painted on as CA 677 as seen here. This was actually FAE-15677, which also wore HC-AUR, an August 1961 MAP-supplied C-47D. Although wearing full service titles, she was unquestionably also flown on TAME duties, a violation of her MAP status. She was derelict at Quito by January 1977. *LCDR Kolin Campbell*

Left: Although she later gained joint civil marks HC-AUW, FAE-20120 was acquired commercially in May 1968 (although some sources cite September 1963!) and had previously flown with LANICA in Nicaragua at one point. She was not reported after 1972 and is assumed to have been one of the aircraft noted in the narrative lost to an undocumented accident. *via George G.J. Kamp*

Below: Seen from the observation deck at Quito on 8 May 1969, co-author Hagedorn watched purely civilian passengers deplaning from FAE-20179, coded as CA-179 – but not as yet having gained her TAME joint markings HC-AUK. The passengers took turns deplaning alongside large boxes and other assorted cargo. The aircraft was clearly on a TAME service. *Hagedorn*

CA 677 was FAE-15677, later also HC-AUR, an August 1961 MAP C-47D delivery. She is pictured here at the remote FAE station at Salinas with service personnel playing football in the foreground. *LCDR Kolin Campbell*

CA 677 once again after having gained joint military and civil marks, HC-AUR, near the end of her days at Quito by January 1977. Note the rather curious curvature of the nose codes to conform to the antiglare panel. *MAP172 via Ken F. Measures*

Like other Latin American operators, after receipt of the ARP aircraft, the FAE had gained a proper appreciation for the utility of the type, and set about acquiring an assortment of other aircraft on the second- and third-hand market, one being overhauled for them by TEMCO in Greenville, Texas, in November 1952. It is not clear from available records which aircraft this was. An 'urgent' Airgram, dated 1 July 1953, advised US intelligence offices at Albrook Field, Canal Zone, that the FAE had placed orders via the US Department of Defence for 'three C-47s … to replace those destroyed in the recent airlift operation in Ecuador', this referring to two FAE C-47s that had been lost while ferrying supplies to a flooded area of the country between 8 and 10 April 1953. The three C-47s were acquired from Witbeck Aircraft, Inc., under RAP Case No. OMA/Ecuador-4 on a USAF contract at a total cost of $317,400. Although actually purchased on 28 April 1953, these had been delivered after extensive rebuild nearly a year later, in May 1954, and were MSNs 1969, 2016 and 2028.

By 30 June 1954, taking known losses into account, the FAE had a total of five C-47s in its inventory and these were all assigned to what was known at the time as the 1º Escuadrón de Transporte alongside a single Beech C-45 or AT-7. This strength remained unchanged through 30 June 1955, although the unit also had an Aero Commander 520 by then as well. The British Air Attaché in Quito, however, reported on 31 December 1955, that the FAE possessed six C-47s, and that of these, five were in Quito and one at Guayaquil.

An FAE C-47 is known to have been lost on a flight from Guayaquil to La Toma Loja on 21 March 1956 and was destroyed by fire, killing the pilot, Coronel Ernesto Delgado and co-pilot Capt. Galo Torres Moreno, but unfortunately the serial of this aircraft has not been discovered. By 31 December 1956, however, the total number of C-47s on hand had increased to six, indicating that another aircraft had been acquired during the interim period. The FAE is known to have purchased and taken delivery of three C-47s under the provisions of the Reimbursable Aid Program (RAP) sometime prior to the second half of 1957, although the identities of these have not been matched. However, by 1 June 1958, the total number on strength with the operating unit had once again dropped to just five, the unit also possessing one Beech C-45/AT-7 and two Consolidated OA-10s or PBY-5As at Quito. However, the USAF rated all five C-47 as 'combat ready', a coveted accolade among MAP-supported C-47 units in Latin America.

The FAE received three C-47s on MAP Project MAP1C-250 from USAF surplus stocks held at Davis-Monthan AFB, AZ, at a base excess value of $286,398, although repair and rehabilitation prior to delivery added another $253,533 to the final bill. These aircraft were originally to have been drawn from Royal Netherlands Air Force redeployed aircraft but these were apparently diverted to Colombia instead. Delivery was slated for late August 1961. One of these is identified in the accompanying table, but the other two can only be deduced.

The ground crewman who applied the serial and registration to FAE-49785/HC-AUP, a MAP Grant Aid C-47D received in March 1970, apparently did not appreciate at the time that his handiwork would be running 'nose down' in flight! The aircraft has significant port wingtip damage in this view. *Alfredo Jurado*

The FAE organised the Transportes Aéreos Militares Ecuatorianos (TAME) around 2 December 1962 to provide regularly scheduled air freight and passenger services within the country. The initial, rather ambitious schedule, called for TAME aircraft to make fifty-seven flights per week. Three destinations, relatively close to Quito and with acceptable surface transportation facilities, were soon dropped from the service. A DC-6 augmented both capacity and quality of services and commenced making regular flights to the Galápagos Islandt. An FAE-rebuilt DC-3 was added to the fleet by late December 1962. Rates were low compared to commercial air carriers, but competition was not a problem as TAME flew mainly to destinations that were not commercially viable, although the service also flew five routes that were not duplicated by commercial carriers at all. While the crews and maintenance personnel were military, the clerks, stewardesses and ticket agents were civilians. The line averaged between 300 to 350 flight hours per month, and the effort enjoyed very good public acceptance. In some instances, friction was generated when TAME overlapped routes flown by some struggling Ecuadorian commercial carriers. AREA, which as of 1962 was the largest in the country, was obliged, they claimed, to have to cancel a total of eight scheduled flights per week due to TAME's 'unfair' competition. Perhaps to compensate, TAME opened a new route to Santa Rosa not covered by AREA. The FAE had promised the US MAAG that it would not use the two most recently MAP-delivered C-47s if they were found to be competitive to commercial carriers, which would have clearly placed the US in an awkward position. However, the MAAG noted that the FAE had broken this promise in many instances, with at least one of the aircraft, cited as FAE-164 (undoubtedly FAE-77164), seen to have been used for several full days on the primary Quito–Guayaquil route.

By December 1963, the FAE had formalised the designation of the C-47 operating unit, and it had become the 1111º Escuadrón de Transporte based at Quito. It possessed a total of ten C-47s, probably representing peak strength. Of these, nine were active. Of the total of eight MAP/RAP aircraft acquired, all were overhauled by TEMCO, and four of these were delivered on 17 April 1961, the other four following on 29 June 1961. During this same period, one of the existing C-47s was completely rebuilt with the assistance of the USAF Mission, although exactly which one is not clear.

The USAF Mission assisted the FAE in conducting inspections of two of its oldest aircraft between July and December 1963, and FAE-43-2016 and FAE-43-2028 and -2028 was found to have substantial corrosion. Although the USAF Mission pressed to have this aircraft stricken, they apparently were unable to get the FAE to move on this recommendation, although both remained grounded from August. The Mission also reported that two FAE C-47s had been lost to that time, one of them MAP provided and the other acquired commercially. By 2 April 1964, the FAE component of the Preventive Medicine Civic Action Program, which was all the rage with US policy makers by that time, was, in addition to a purpose-delivered Cessna 185, to have included a C-47 'flying laboratory', but this portion of the project was cancelled. Two additional C-47s had been due for delivery in early January 1964, but these aircraft were cancelled because of the apparent lack of enthusiasm and support for the Civic Action medical programme evidenced by the FAE leadership, which apparently had difficulty understanding how such a mission was their job. To add fuel to the fire, the FAE's central maintenance organisation at the time was apparently producing mediocre results with overhauling C-47 engines, and, on top of this, TAME aircraft got 'first dibs' on the best of these.

By 20 October 1964, the operating unit, the 1111º Escuadrón de Transporte, had lost a C-47 in a fatal accident on 30 August, although the aircraft involved has not been identified. While engaged in a Civic Action flight, the aircraft lost an engine about five minutes after take-off from a remote airstrip in Oriente, and the pilot apparently failed to negotiate a successful landing on the return to the airstrip. Two officers and two airmen were killed in the resulting crash, which rendered the aircraft damaged in situ beyond repair. The otherwise near-perfect safety record of the unit was further marred by two more serious accidents within thirty days of the fatal accident. On 11 September 1964, the main landing gear on a unit C-47 was inadvertently retracted on the runway, much to the chagrin of the co-pilot, causing an unprogrammed double engine change as well as other damage. On 26 September, a double engine failure while a C-47 was turning on to final approach resulted in a crash landing and major damage to the aircraft, but the serial number of this aircraft remains unclear.

By 1965, the FAE was also operating one VIP-configured C-47 or DC-3, although exactly which one this was, as indicated on the accompanying table, is a matter of deduction. In January 1965, the FAE maintenance organisation accomplished yet another complete rebuild of one of the aircraft, this one being FAE-1969 (but cited by the USAF as FAE-969), completing a nearly eighteen-month effort. The aircraft was described as having been 'completely' rebuilt. As of 15 April 1965, the 1111º Escuadrón de Transporte C-47 fleet had flown a total of 1,194 hours during the preceding quarter, versus 1,325 in the quarter prior to that, for an average utilisation of between forty-two and fifty hours per aircraft. The decrease was reportedly due to the delivery of two four-engine Douglas DC-6s to the unit, combined with adverse 'winter' weather during the three-month

Although a number of FAE C-47s are known to have been camouflaged late in their service careers, the scheme worn here by FAE-76448/HC-AUQ certainly rates as one of the most unusual worn by any Latin American C-47. Semi-derelict here, she may have been photographed at an Army base near Guayaquil.
Capt. Jorge Delgado

FAE-77164/CA-164/HC-AUT was an April 1963 MAP-supplied C-47D but is seen here on display at the FAE cantonment at Quito around October 1977. She had been noted last in service in January that year wearing only FAE-77164, so the other markings were probably added after she was placed on display.
George G.J. Kamp

period. These observations, taken together, seem to corroborate the observations of 7 May 1969, when co-author Hagedorn conducted a close inspection of FAE operations at Quito. A total of nine military C-47s was noted, although one of them was clearly derelict. This appears to support the data shown in the accompanying tables. The FAE also took the unusual step of buying three very high-time ex-Brazilian civil C-47s in 1968, as apparently TAME needed the extra capacity pending delivery of newer aircraft then on order.

On 6 September 1969, TAME aircraft and crews experienced what can only be described as a nearly unique and tragic series of incidents. Two C-47s, FAE-4341 and FAE-1969, were commandeered in an exceptionally well-co-ordinated operation by Communist terrorist hijackers. Serial 4341 had taken off from Guayaquil at 0700 en route to Manta under the command of pilot Mayor Fausto Sevilla with co-pilot Sub.Tte José E. Báez and Flight Engineer Sgto Gerardo Amaguaña with a young stewardess, either Nelly Checa or Betty Aguilar, in the cabin, while 1969 had departed Quito at precisely the same hour en route to Esmeraldas under the command of Tte.Cnel Pazmiño with co-pilot Tte Rodrigo Jacome, also with one of the two stewardesses named in the cabin. Not long after departure, a total of five terrorists aboard the two aircraft announced that this was 'Operación Ho-Chi-Minh' and that they were taking the two aircraft to Cuba. They brandished pistols and dynamite sticks with short fuses inserted. They ordered the two aircraft to land at Manta in order to secure sufficient fuel for the flight to Cuba. Aboard serial 4341, Sub.Tte Báez and Sgto Amaguaña heroically confronted the hijackers, and the young lieutenant was shot dead on the spot through the heart, while the sergeant was wounded. After landing at Manta, officials on the ground refused to accede to the terrorists' demands for fuel, whereupon the terrorists somehow shoved Sub.Tte Báez's dead body through the cockpit starboard window to intimidate the officials on the ground to co-operate with their demands. A fuel truck was then produced and refuelled both aircraft but, by then, serial 1969 went inoperative due to unspecified engine problems (possibly induced by the crew) and the frustrated and angry conspirators were forced to wait for another aircraft to be flown to Manta from Quito with spares and a mechanic qualified to repair the aircraft, the third aircraft having been FAE-49789. After repairs were affected, and crews and passengers

transferred to the third aircraft, they took off for Cuba and, transiting unmolested through Tocumen Airport, Panama and Kingston, Jamaica, they completed the journey. Two days later, the survivors and the two aircraft returned safely to Quito, much to the relief of family and friends of those aboard. This was the only known instance of military operated C-47 series aircraft being hijacked in Latin America.

So far as can be determined, the last three C-47s acquired by the FAE were delivered under MAP Grant Aid in 1970. However, the MAP Plan for Ecuador for FY71 to FY75, which covered the all-important spares and technical support only for these aircraft, reveal that the US fully intended to continue to nurture the fleet. The narrative included interesting language. The numbers to be supported apparently considered anticipated attrition, as they reflected twelve in FY71, eleven in FY72, ten in FY77 and FY74 and nine by FY75. Comments also acknowledged the three that had been acquired from Brazil, as well as an unidentified aircraft 'acquired from a Miami firm', but which together brought the total inventory as of 28 April 1969 to twelve. One had crashed, however, reducing this to eleven, 'but does not include the Presidential DC-3'. It also noted that two of the remaining eleven were 'corroded beyond repair'.

TAME suffered a tragic loss on 12 September 1971 when FAE-20179/CA-179, under the command of Mayor César Alfredo Egas Mena with co-pilot Tte Galo Molina Hidalgo and two other crew members, carrying four passengers, crashed into a mountain near Celica, Pichincha.

Although of marginal quality, this is an exceptionally intrepid image of TAME C-47-DL FAE-4342 taken by a passenger from the cockpit of the other C-47 hijacked in September 1969 as noted in the text. The circled figure was one of the hijackers. *'VISTAZO' via Capt. Jorge Delgado*

First Serial Series – The 500s

FAE Serial	Previous Identity	Built As	MSN	Assignments and Notes
902	–	C-47A	–	This is the aircraft written off at Shell Mera in Jun 48 and the only C-47 series aircraft definitely known to have worn a 900 series serial. Curiously, there are no known ARP candidates for the identity of this aircraft, and it may possibly have been a commercial acquisition.
502 or 503	42-23926	C-47A-35-DL	9788	Probably ARP project 72011, although the Individual Aircraft history Card is not definitive. Last known at Kelly Field, TX, on 18 Jun 47. However, as FAE-93926/HC-AVF (q.v.) is well established, this may well have in fact been the first ARP aircraft for Ecuador. The FAE was granted authority to fly a C-47 marked as 503 via the Panama Canal (Albrook Field) and Dallas, Texas, on 20 Jun 49, for the purpose of overhaul.
(503?)	42-23390	C-47A-5-DL	9252	ARP Project No. 72011 via Kelly Field, TX, on 22 Aug 47 delivered via Mexico on 30 Sep 47. Reported on 10 Mar 48 when an aircraft with this serial visited Bogotá, Colombia, on 20 Jun 49 and still current as late as May 1951. Curiously, the same identity is cited for FAM E.T.A. 6011 by August 1993. While not inconceivable, this would constitute a most unusual transfer. The possibility that this aircraft may have been diverted to Mexico en route to Ecuador and replaced by another aircraft cannot be ruled out as the aircraft does not show up in any subsequent incarnation in FAE service. Unfortunately, no alternate aircraft has been identified, yet Ecuador did in fact receive four C-47s under ARP!
505	42-92066	C-47A-DK	11825	ARP Project 72011 via Kelly Field, TX, on 29 Sep 47 but did not depart Kelly for Ecuador until 25 Jan 48. First reported in Apr 48, when she was granted permission to transit the Panama Canal Zone, and again on 11 Sep 50. She was noted 'in country' as late as May 51. This was a very long-serving aircraft, eventually being assigned serial FAE-92066 (q.v.).
506	42-100557	C-47A-65-DL	19020	ARP Project 72011 via Kelly Field, TX, on 29 Sep 47 but did not depart Kelly for Ecuador until 25 Mar 48. When delivered, she apparently had Donald Duck nose art left over from her last USAAF operator, and this persisted in FAE service for a time – one of a very few Latin American C-47s to ever been so adorned. First reported in April 1948 when she was granted permission to transit the Panama Canal Zone, again in May 1951 and on 15 Aug 50 (when she was granted permission to transit the Canal Zone again en route to Bolling Field, DC) and as late as 21 Sep 61. This aircraft was apparently returned to TEMCO under Contract 822-120 for conversion to 'executive type', and is thus almost certainly the Presidential aircraft noted in the text. The TEMCO work included a comprehensive overhaul and was the second C-47 overhauled by TEMCO at Greenville, TX, the first having been delivered in Nov 52. However a C-47 cited with a completely out-of-sequence serial, FAE-902, which could be a corruption of this aircraft's MSN, was reported written off in Jun 48 in a landing accident at the Shell Mera jungle airfield.
507	42-92909	C-47A-15-DK	12762	ARP Project 72011 via Kelly Field, TX, on 1 Oct 47. First reported in Apr 48 when she was granted permission to transit the Panama Canal Zone.
508	NC-18954 TWA Fleet Number 359 42-56623 N18954	DC-3B-202 DC-3-202 (SDT) DC-3B-G202A C-49E G-202A C-49F DC-3A-S1C3G C-47A	2028	Acquired commercially from Union Steel & Wrecking Co., which had acquired the aircraft on 23 Dec 52. It sold her to Witbeck Aircraft Corp., Gainesville, TX, on 16 Jun 53. Sold to the USAF on behalf of Ecuador on 18 Jun 53. Sold to Ecuador on MAP Grant Aid on 3 Jul 53 and cited on Bill of Sale (ACA-1911-1) as type 'C-47 (DC-3)/DC-3A-S1C3G'. First reported on 15 Jul 53, when permission was requested for this aircraft to overfly the Panama Canal Zone en route home to Ecuador from Gainesville, Texas, evidently on her actual delivery flight. Reserialed as FAE43-2028 (q.v.).
509	NC-17323 TWA Fleet Number 373 N17323	DC-3-209 DC-3-G102 DC-3-G202A DC-3A-S1C3G C-47A	1969	Acquired commercially from Union Steel & Wrecking Co., which had acquired the aircraft on 16 Jan 53 with 14,872:54 hours on the airframe. Sold to Witbeck Aircraft Corp., Gainesville, TX, on 16 Jun 53. Sold to the USAF acting on behalf of Ecuador on 18 Jun 53. Sold to Ecuador on MAP Grant Aid on 13 Aug 53 and, interestingly, cited on the Bill of Sale as type 'C-47A (DC-3)/DC-3A-S1C3G'! Had already been delivered, however, ahead of the actual Bill of Sale as, by 5 Aug 53, permission was requested for the aircraft to transit the Panama Canal Zone en route to Miami, Florida. First reported 'in country' on 15 Aug 53. Survived to pass to FAE-31969/1969/HC-AUV (q.v.).
510	NC-18952 TWA Fleet Number 378 N18952	DC-3-G102 DC-3-209 DC-3B-G102 DC-3B-G202A DC-3A-S1C3G C-47A	2016	Acquired commercially from Union Steel & Wrecking Co., which had acquired the aircraft on 23 Dec 52. Sold to Witbeck Aircraft Corp., Gainesville, TX, on 16 Jun 53. Sold to the USAF on behalf of Ecuador on 18 Jun 53. Sold to Ecuador on 3 Aug 53 and described on the Bill of Sale as type 'C-47A (DC-3)/DC-3A-S1C3G'. Permission for this aircraft to overfly the Panama Canal Zone en route to La Guardia Airport, New York, was requested on 16 Jul 54. Survived to pass to FAE-32016 (q.v.).

Second Serial Series

FAE Serial	Previous Identity	Built as	MSN	Assignments and Notes
1969 31969/ HC-AUV	NC-17323 N17323 *FAE-509*	DC-3-209 DC-3-G102 DC-3A-S1C3G C-47A	1969	Noted as such (1969) as early as 16 Mar 1972 and as late as 17 Dec 81 as 31969/HC-AUV. Had been withdrawn from service by 18 May 82 last with TAME.
32016	NC-18952 *FAE-510*	DC-3-G102 DC-3-209 DC-3B-G202A C-47A DC-3A-S1C3G	2016	Grounded due to severe corrosion between Jul and Dec 63. Noted as such Aug 67 withdrawn from service.
43-2028	NC-18954 42-56623 NC-18954 *FAE-508*	DC-3B-202A C-49F DC-3A	2028	Noted withdrawn from service as such by Aug 67.
2066 92066/ HC-AVC	42-92066 *FAE-505*	C-47A-DK	11825	Noted at Guayaquil on 15 Mar 72 marked as 92066/HC-AVC with TAME. This aircraft was noted preserved at Guayaquil marked as such by 17 Sep 85.
23926/ HC-AVF ('32926/ CA-926')	42-23926 *FAE-502 or 503?*	C-47A-35-DL	9788	This aircraft was salvaged by the FAE *c*.30 Jun 65, apparently following a forced landing there and was noted derelict at Quito by co-author Hagedorn in May 69. Oddly however, a photo taken following the crash landing clearly shows the aircraft marked as FAE-32926/CA-926, which must have been corrupted at some point.
4341 CA4341/ HC-AUZ	41-7842 NC-41061 NC-56968 PP-IBB PP-ANP	C-47-DL	4341	Said to have been acquired by Ecuador in Mar 58, it is more likely that the acquisition date was closer to 1962, when the aircraft was last noted withdrawn from use by VARIG in Brazil. Noted at Guayaquil on 27 Jan 77 marked as 4341, she was last reported on 28 Oct 77 and is almost certainly the same aircraft as the oft-reported CA4341/HC-AUZ, usually cited as MSN 10203, which is most unlikely. She was last in service with TAME.
11775/HC-AVD	42-68848 NC-30092 PP-PCO PP-NAX N9321R	C-53D-DO DC-3BD	11775	Acquired in 1960 commercially, although sometimes cited in error as Jul 73. Noted at Guayaquil as simply 11775 on 27 Jan 77. Last with TAME and noted withdrawn from use at Guayaquil by May 1982, going to display by Sep 85. This aircraft is said to have been resurrected and sold to APEL in Colombia as HK-3348X together with two other unidentified ex-FAE C-47s, which became HK-3349X and HK-3350X with the same operator by 1987 however.
15677/CA-677 HC-AUR	43-15677	C-47A-90-DL C-47D	20143	MAP Project MAP1C-250 to Ecuador on 8 Aug 61. The USAF Mission reported that this aircraft (which they cited as FAE-677) had suffered an accident some time prior to June 1967 and, although substantially repaired, was still awaiting engines at that time. Obviously repaired and returned to service, this aircraft visited Howard AFB, CZ, on 24 Feb 68 marked as 15677/CA677. She was noted at Quito on 26 Mar 71 and 16 Mar 72. Noted derelict at Quito by 28 Jan 77 marked as 15677/HC-AUR.

A nearly pristine view of FAE-76448/HC-AUQ, the last MAP C-47D acquired by the service in August 1970. Usually overlooked is the fact that her lower fuselage and wings are actually painted light grey in this 28 January 1977 image, reflecting her last service days with the USAF in Panama. She was almost certainly the last operational FAE C-47. *PFI*

During the drama surrounding the hijacking of two TAME C-47s in September 1969, the FAE and armed forces were necessarily deeply involved in addressing the incident. Here, at centre, Ecuadorian Gen. Rohn and other officers are seen approaching a camouflaged FAE C-47 at Guayaquil to fly to scene of the crisis. *Reportaje via Andrea Garcia Saeteros/Capt. Jorge Delgado*

This FAE C-47, in poor condition, with a spurious serial, was placed on display near Quito and clearly has a DC-3C-style air stair deployed, so is probably the former FAE-11747. *Guido Chavez via Capt. Jorge Delgado*

15685/CA-685	43-15685	C-47A-90-DL	20151	MAP to Ecuador from Miami 15 Aug 61. While with TAME executed a forced landing around 1245hrs 17 Apr 63 en route from Quito to Guayaquil on a highway due to engine failure. Not subsequently reported.
77164/ CA-164/ HC-AUT C-47D	44-77164	C-47B-35-DK	16748/33496	MAP to Ecuador on 30 Apr 63. Noted operational as 77164/HC-AUT with TAME at Guayaquil on 15 Mar 72. Noted at Guayaquil as simply 77164 on 27 Jan 77. Last reported in service with TAME but to display at Quito by 28 Oct 77.
15222/CA222	43-15222	C-47A-80-DL	19688	MAP to Ecuador on 21 Jul 61. Although reported independently by two different sources as current on 10 Jul 67, there have been no other reported sightings of this aircraft, suggesting that she may have been lost to an accident. One of these sources was none other than the USAF Mission, which noted that an aircraft with this serial had crashed, but with the assistance of the Mission repairs had been completed by 10 Jul 67. This aircraft was unusual in wearing the Ecuadorian national roundel on her fuselage at one point, only one of two FAE C-47s known to have done so, the other being 32926.
11747/ CA-747/ HC-AUY	42-68820 PP-PBS PP-AKI	C-53D-DO	11747	Acquired commercially in October 1967. Noted as simply 11747 at Quito on 26 Mar 71 and 16 Mar 72. Noted as such at Guayaquil on 25 Apr 73. Was operating for TAME by 1 Oct 75 and last reported in service on 28 Oct 77. Reported preserved and on display at Latacunga at the Paratrooper Brigada Patria there by 15 Sep 94 but without any identifying serials.

This anonymous FAE C-47, showing obvious damage to her nose, windscreen and missing her mail compartment door, was semi-derelict at Guayaquil in September 1996 when photographed. This may be the former FAE-49785/HC-AUP. *LCDR Kolin Campbell*

20179/CA-179/ HC-AUK	43-15713 NC-49745 PP-YPJ	C-47A-90-DL	20179	Acquired commercially in October 1967, although on 10 Jan 68 has also been suggested. Written off on 12 Sep 71 en route from Quito to Portoviejo when she hit a mountain in bad weather.
20120/ HC-AUW	43-15654 NC-66006 AN-ACR N16774	C-47A-90-DL	20120	Acquired commercially around 29 May 68, although 3 Sep 63 has also been suggested. Last reported in 1972.
49789/ HC-AUS	43-49789 0-49789	C-47B-20-DK C-47D	15605/27050	MAP on 17 Jan 69. This is probably the MAP-funded C-47 acquired from 'a firm in Miami' noted in the text. Noted as 49789 at Quito on 26 Mar 71 and 16 Mar 72. Noted at Guayaquil on 29 Jan 77 as simply 49789. Last reported on 14 Dec 81.
49785/HC-AUP	43-49785 0-49785	C-47B-20-DK C-47D	15601/27046	MAP Grant Aid on 23 Mar 70 at a cost of $77,000. A former long-serving CAC and USAFSO aircraft, the official handover date was apparently 21 Aug 70. Noted at Guayaquil on 29 Jul 71 and at Quito on 16 Mar 72 marked as 49785/HC-AUP on 16 Mar 72. Noted at Guayaquil as 49785 on 27 Jan 77 and reported withdrawn from use there by 18 May 82. She is still there, but completely devoid of identifying markings at this writing.
76448/CA-448 HC-AUQ	44-76448 0-76448	C-47B-25-DK C-47D	16032/32780	MAP on 21 Aug 70. Noted marked as 76448/HC-AUQ with TAME at Guayaquil on 15 Mar 72 and at Quito on 28 Jan 77. Noted in service at an Army base near Guayaquil on 15 Sep 85, but placed on display at the same installation by 30 Oct 94, very possibly the last operational FAE C-47.

Although the Ecuadorian Navy never operated any C-47s, the service developed its own small air arm, and in the process benefited from the considerable contributions of the US Naval Mission to Ecuador, and their C-47J, BuA50794 is pictured here, curiously, undergoing significant work at Lima, Peru, in 1963. Note the unusual presentation of the national insignia under her starboard wing. *via Dr Gary Kuhn*

CHAPTER ELEVEN

El Salvador

THE MILITARY UTILISATION of the Douglas twin series in the smallest country of Latin America is fascinating, to say the least. The Fuerza Aérea Salvadoreña (FAS) or Salvadoran Air Force – took the fullest advantage of the versatility and ruggedness of the type, and its crews flew the C-47 in every imaginable role, most of the time with surprising results. In fact, their exploits with the type across two wars and innumerable national emergencies could fill a couple of volumes. Therefore, the reader can imagine how difficult it is to condense its history into just one chapter.

The FAS acquired its first C-47 in late-1948, during the government of General Salvador Castañeda Castro, and contrary to what one may think, the aircraft was purchased from a civilian source: the Hughes Aircraft Company. She was intended to become the Salvadoran 'Air Force One', replacing a Beech AT-11 that had been acquired through the US Mission in May 1948, which FAS and US mechanics had converted to a combination of light bomber and VIP transport. However, by the time she arrived at Ilopango Airbase – the FAS headquarters located west of the Capital San Salvador – in April 1949, General Castañeda had been deposed in a coup that young officers organised in December of the previous year. In any case, the aircraft was incorporated into the air force inventory with the serial FAS-101.

FAS-101 was followed by a second C-47 that was also purchased from the Hughes Aircraft Company and delivered in the first quarter of 1949. Assigned the serial FAS-102, this example came configured as a troop and cargo transport; however, sometime in 1952, she was converted to VIP configuration and, from then on, she became the presidential aircraft. Unfortunately, on 24 August 1962, she made an emergency landing in a swamp at the Asino village, approximately 3km south-east of Ilopango Airbase, while conducting a training flight. Upon recovering her, the FAS mechanics determined that she was beyond repair. Hence, she was stripped of all of her usable parts and her remains were dumped at the airbase scrapyard. Years later, her fuselage was transferred to the Parachute Corps – also located at the Ilopango Airbase – to be used as a training aid. In fact, at the time of this writing, her fuselage still is there, although sporting a 'fantasy' camouflage scheme.

During the second half of 1962, the US Central Intelligence Agency (CIA) published an estimate about Fidel Castro's subversive capabilities in Latin America. The document stated that the Cuban dictator, along with the Soviet Union, were taking advantage of the dangerously unstable political and economic situation prevailing throughout the continent, mainly by expanding the Marxist influence and exporting the so-called Cuban Revolution. In fact, El Salvador's neighbour, Guatemala, was already battling a growing rebel movement that was receiving training, funds and equipment from Castro, thanks to the mediation of local Marxist organisations. Hence, the CIA estimate urged the US government to take the appropriate steps to mitigate the contagion that could affect El Salvador and Honduras in the short term, and assist the countries in dealing with armed revolutions. Not wasting any time, the US Army's Caribbean Command was ordered to organise an unprecedented counter-insurgency exercise in the Central American region with the participation of combat units from Honduras – the host nation – Colombia, Peru, Guatemala, Nicaragua and El Salvador. Named Operación Fraternidad (Operation Fraternity), the exercise also served to evaluate the needs of the participating nations' armed forces, which were gradually included in the US Military Assistance Program – commonly known as MAP – that had been created a year earlier under the Foreign Assistance Act.

FAS-101 at Ilopango, sporting the elegant white over aluminium finish colour scheme that the C-47s had from 1960 to 1968, which included the stylised wing behind the cockpit and two light-blue cheatlines along the fuselage. *Brigadier General Hal Ahrens via David W. Ostrowski*

Above: FAS-101 photographed shortly after her arrival in Ilopango in late 1948. The Beech AT-11 that she replaced (the only example ever operated by the FAS) as an ad hoc VIP transport can be seen behind her. At the time, the aircraft had a natural metal finish, with the national colours painted on the rudder. *via Hélio Higuchi*

Above right: FAS-101 at Ilopango, right after returning from a bombing mission over the Nueva Ocotepeque area in Honduras during the 100-Hour War, in which she was intercepted and machine-gunned by a Honduran F4U Corsair. Posing before her are Sgt Muñoz, Capt. Adrian Panameño (co-pilot), Maj. Sigfredo Velasco (pilot) and Lt Daniel Cañas. Battle damage can be seen on the upper part of the fuselage, right behind the cockpit. *Salvadoran Air Force Museum, via Douglas Cornejo*

Right: FAS-102 at Ilopango, photographed while she was the Salvadoran 'Air Force One'. Of interest is the variance of the 'early' colour scheme of this bird, in which the white colour extends to the nose, while in other aircraft it ended right behind the cockpit window. Also, the flags of the countries she had visited are visible, as well as the FAS 'service badge'. *via Douglas Cornejo*

After Fraternidad, it became evident that the participating armies needed to invest in tactical air mobility in order to fight the guerrilla movements effectively, therefore the US began assisting them in the creation of parachute units and providing them with transport aircraft. In the case of El Salvador, the MAP planners provisioned the delivery of additional C-47s and the appropriate equipment for the creation of a Parachute Battalion. The first of the MAP-provided Douglas transports arrived in May 1963, and was assigned the serial FAS-103. Accordingly, the 1st Parachute Battalion was established two months later. However, no other MAP C-47 deliveries were completed that year, nor the following, allegedly due to the complicated US political scene after President John F. Kennedy's assassination and the escalation of the Vietnam War. Unfortunately, the limited troop air mobility that the FAS had gained almost disappeared on 10 September 1965, when FAS-103 ditched in the Ilopango Lake following an in-flight emergency. From then on, the FAS was left – once again – with only one C-47.

Even though by 1965 Communist groups in El Salvador were short of funds and without sizable financial assistance from Castro, there were at least 115 Salvadorans studying guerrilla warfare in Cuba and other Communist countries. Along with the mounting insurgency problem in Guatemala, that was enough for the US Southern Command – SOUTHCOM – to organise a second joint counter-insurgency exercise that also took place in Honduras, with the participation of troops from the host nation and from Guatemala,

The sad end of FAS-102 at a swamp near Asino village in August 1962, as documented by a local newspaper. Upon recovering her, the FAS mechanics determined that she was beyond repair and she was written off. *El Diario de Hoy, via Mario Alfaro*

Despite its disastrous quality, this image documents the delivery of FAS-103(I) in April 1963, as a donation of the US government. As it can be seen, she arrived at Ilopango already sporting the 'early' colour scheme of white over aluminium, with light-blue cheatlines along the fuselage, the only variance being that horrendous black nose.
El Diario de Hoy, Via Mario Alfaro

On 10 September 1965, FAS-103(I) had an emergency after taking off from Ilopango and ditched in the lake near the airport. Fortunately, the crew of three survived. The aircraft, on the other hand, sunk to the bottom of the lake, where it remains to this day. *via Mario Alfaro*

Perhaps one of the few photos of FAS-103(I) while she was operational.
via Marco Lavagnino

Nicaragua and El Salvador. Additionally, the US government finally arranged for the transfer of three additional Douglas transports through MAP for the FAS, the first of which arrived in Ilopango in August 1966 and was assigned the serial FAS-104. Due to bureaucracy, the transfer of the other C-47 took almost a year, being delivered on 12 May 1967. This aircraft was assigned the serial FAS-103, effectively turning her into the replacement of the one that had crashed at the Ilopango Lake two years earlier.

Despite the impending Communist threat looming over the region, the government of El Salvador was more preoccupied with the events taking place in Honduras by then: There had been sporadic acts of violence against Salvadorans living in that country, mainly at the hands of clandestine armed groups that had tacit government support. On the other hand, the Honduran President, General Oswaldo Lopez Arellano, was considering the expulsion of no fewer than 300,000 Salvadorans, claiming that they were a burden on the country's economy. The problem was that if such expulsions materialised, El Salvador's economy would go down the drain, since the country did not have enough resources to feed the returnees nor could the country provide them with housing and jobs.

Below: Beautiful study of FAS-104 sporting the 'early' colour scheme. The photo was taken at Howard AFB, Panama Canal Zone, on 18 November 1966. By then, this aircraft was VIP configured. *Dan Hagedorn*

During 1968, all the FAS C-47s received a new colour scheme, much simpler than the previous one. In this photo, taken at Howard AFB, Panama Canal Zone, in October 1969, FAS-104 can be seen sporting those new colours. *Dan Hagedorn*

Even though the two governments had initiated negotiations aimed at solving the immigration problem, the Salvadoran President, Col Julio Adalberto Rivera Carballo, began considering a military solution aimed at 'reclaiming' Honduran territories close to the border, which were considered 'vital space' for El Salvador. Thus, the Salvadoran Army's high command started to work on a highly secret plan that comprised troop movements distributed around multiple theatres of operations, with the objective of taking Honduran territory and capturing border towns long enough to force a negotiated solution under the auspices of an international body like the Organisation of American States (OAS), the United Nations, or even the US government.

Right from the beginning, it was clear to the Salvadoran high command that the invasion plan's success would depend entirely on establishing an efficient logistics chain for supplying the troops in the different theatres of operations. Therefore, the Salvadoran government launched into a shopping spree and, by mid-May 1967, two C-47s had been acquired from civilian sources. According to official records, these aircraft were assigned the serials FAS-105 and FAS-106, and arrived in Ilopango on 15 May that year. For reasons that have never been established, however, the arrival dates recorded in MAP documents for these aircraft are given as 20 November 1964 for FAS-105, and 4 September 1970, for FAS-106. The latter is of interest since by that date, as we will see, the MAP for El Salvador had been suspended, therefore making any aircraft delivery or inclusion into the programme virtually impossible. In the case of FAS-105, the date seems to correspond to a projected MAP transfer that never took place or the aircraft that was transferred – much later – was assigned a different FAS serial upon its arrival.

A couple of days after the arrival of the C-47s, the war almost began when members of the Salvadoran Guardia Nacional (National Guard) crossed into Honduras near the Lajitas River, in the La Paz department, and stormed a farm called Hacienda Dolores, clashing with Honduran troops and taking some civilian prisoners. Then, four days later, Salvadoran guards crossed into Honduras once again, and after a heavy firefight with Honduran troops, stormed Hacienda Dolores for a second time and burned it to the ground. However, thanks to the quick intervention of the US and the OAS, the extremely complicated situation was defused.

It was not until July 1967, right after the inauguration of the newly elected President, Col Fidel Sánchez Hernández, that the Salvadoran Army finally set out to implement the plan for invading Honduras. During the following months, the Salvadoran Army conducted a nationwide recruiting campaign, followed by the activation of the reserves and the creation of a paramilitary organisation for supporting the war effort. In addition, an exhaustive training programme was established, which included conducting tactical exercises across the country. The surprising part was that all this was done with utmost secrecy, denoting a high degree of organisation and efficiency on the part of the Salvadoran military. Not even the US embassy was aware of what was taking place, despite the fact that two high-ranking members of the US Military Group were secretly assisting the Salvadoran high command with the planning of the combat operations against Honduras.

By then, the FAS had five Douglas transports, of which three were MAP-supported, this being FAS-101, which had been added to the assistance programme in 1963, as well as FAS-103 and FAS-104. The other two, FAS-105 and FAS-106, which were acquired from civilian sources, were included in the MAP almost eight years later.

In May 1968, the US Ambassador to El Salvador presented to President Sánchez a report detailing the results of a thorough analysis of the Salvadoran armed forces that the US Military Assistance Advisory Group (MAAG) had conducted during the second half of 1967. The document recommended the implementation of a 'modernisation programme' for the armed forces in order to improve their capabilities against potential Communist threats in the region. The timing could not have been more appropriate, because the Ministry of Defence, following the implementation of the invasion plan, was looking forward to acquiring critical assets such as combat and utility vehicles, uniforms, communication equipment and enough infantry weapons and munitions to equip no fewer than three new battalions.

Not wasting any time, the Salvadoran government made the Military Group's recommendation its own and, through the US Military Sales Program (MSP) acquired the weapons and equipment that the report suggested. Far from the eyes of the North Americans, however, the government went on yet another shopping spree aimed at acquiring additional armament that could not be obtained through the MSP.

Incredibly, the Ministry of Defence left the FAS out of the so-called modernisation programme. In fact, the officers at the high command were undecided about whether they should equip three additional infantry battalions or yield to the repeated requests of the FAS Commander, Maj. Salvador Adalberto Henríquez, for fuel, spare parts and additional combat aircraft. At the time, the Salvadoran Air Force was equipped with the last five airworthy Goodyear FG-1D Corsairs of the twenty acquired in 1957 under the US Military Assistance Sales (MAS) programme, and a motley array of barely flyable aircraft that included a North American SNJ-5 Texan armed trainer, five Cessna U-17A utility light aircraft, six Cessna T-41 primary trainers, the six C-47 transports and a Canadair DC-4M that had been acquired from a civilian source in December 1967.

Regarding its personnel, there were 1,000 men serving with the FAS, of which only thirty-four were pilots. In a report by Lt Col Edward Griemsmann, Chief of the Air Force Section of the Military Group, the Salvadoran aviators were described as 'good, eager, and extremely familiar with their country's terrain'. However, they restricted their flying to daylight, fair weather exclusively, and the only IFR experience they had was in the right seat of the USAF Mission's C-47 on its flights to the Panama Canal Zone. Moreover, not all were permanently available because, to make ends meet, the FAS had some of them assigned to local airline TACA and to a couple of aerial crop-dusting companies, while a dedicated crew periodically flew the DC-4M transport to Miami, carrying lobsters on behalf of local export firms. Other officers had to attend the Army's Command and General Staff Course in order to be promoted, and once they had started this course, they were not allowed to fly until they were done with it.

The reason behind the sorry state of the FAS was that, at the time, the Salvadoran armed forces' leadership was comprised entirely of infantry officers, who had a serious problem grasping the concept of airpower and did not quite understand the importance of having an air force. According to them, the FAS' only acceptable roles were to provide tactical transport and close air support for the ground troops. For the former role, they had authorised the purchase of the additional C-47s a year earlier, and for the latter, they believed that the handful of battered Goodyear FG-1D fighters were more than enough.

In the end, and thanks to the Military Group's and Maj. Henríquez's insistence, the high command authorised the purchase of five Trans Florida Aviation F-51D Mustang II fighter-bombers and a single dual-control Cavalier-refurbished TF-51D, under special provisions of the MSP, which were delivered in September 1968. This, however, was a far cry from the full fighter squadron that the FAS required to go to war.

In April 1969, after considerable diplomatic back and forth, serious mutual provocations and failed mediation attempts on the part of the OAS, the Salvadoran Army began the implementation of the final phase of the invasion plan; it consisted of moving troops, combat equipment and supplies to the four theatres of operations that had been established along the border with Honduras. For their part, the few FAS pilots available began conducting air-to-air and air-to-ground combat training in their FG-1Ds and Mustang IIs. The FAS' reserves were also called upon and its members began training as co-pilots in the five C-47s as well as in the handful of Cessna U-17As and T-41s the FAS had, which were going to be used as improvised attack aircraft.

In June, the qualifying rounds for football's 1970 World Cup began, and the national teams of El Salvador and Honduras were drawn to face each other. At the same time as the game was taking place, the violence against Salvadoran immigrants in Honduras increased, causing strong protests from the Salvadoran Government. Shortly after, the expelling of thousands of Salvadorans began, complicating El Salvador's economy and causing a humanitarian crisis. In fact, it did not take long for the Salvadoran society to begin clamouring for some sort of military response against Honduras. On the 26th, the Salvadoran government notified its Honduran counterpart that they were officially breaking diplomatic relations and requesting the OAS to conduct a thorough investigation of the attacks and violent expulsions of the Salvadorans in Honduras. Additional border incidents followed, the most serious one being the strafing of a Honduran airliner while it was taking off from the city of Nueva Ocotepeque on 3 July.

The colour scheme applied to all FAS C-47s in 1968 consisted of a white over aluminium finish, with a thick dark-blue cheatline that ended behind the cockpit window. FAS-103(II), shown in this excellent photo taken in April 1969, was delivered – via MAP – already sporting these colours. Incredibly, during the 100-Hour War, FAS-103 carried out a daring bombing mission over the Honduran capital, Tegucigalpa. *via Rich Dann*

FAS-105 during a short visit to Howard AFB, Panama Canal Zone, in October 1969, along with FAS-104, whose wing can be seen in the upper part of the image. *Dan Hagedorn*

FAS-106 being loaded at Howard AFB, Panama Canal Zone, in April 1968. *Dan Hagedorn*

By the mid-1970s, the surviving C-47s had been camouflaged. In this image, a very weathered FAS-106 can be seen at the 'Pista de Comando' airfield, loading up paratroopers. Although not dated, the photo must have been taken in the early 1980s. *Ricardo Palomo, via Mario Alfaro*

Taken at Ilopango in March 1999, the image shows a well-travelled FAS-106 sporting the 'gunship grey' colour scheme applied to the surviving Salvadoran C-47s in the mid-1980s. *API*

FAS-107 was part of a batch of four C-47s delivered via MAP to El Salvador in May 1974. Interesting to note is that the colour scheme in which these aircraft were delivered was slightly different from the one applied to the fleet in 1968. First, the aluminium finish on the wings and undersides gave way to a nice light grey, while the thick dark-blue cheatline that ended behind the cockpit window was less rounded. This photo was taken on 25 May 1974, while the aircraft was still in the US. *George G. Farinas*

Another member of the batch of four C-47s delivered via MAP to El Salvador in May 1974, FAS-108 is seen here somewhere in the US while on her way to Central America, already sporting the white over light-grey colour scheme, with the thick dark-blue cheatline ending behind the cockpit window being straighter than the curved one seen in the colour scheme applied to all the C-47s in 1968. The photo was taken on 25 May 1974. *George G. Farinas*

FAS-109, the third member of the batch of four C-47s delivered via MAP to El Salvador in May 1974, is seen here still in the US sporting the catchy white over light-grey colour scheme, although the cargo doors seem to be unfinished. *APB*

Although VIP configured, FAS-110 is seen here a bit weathered and with traces of her old identity still visible. This aircraft was delivered in May 1974 via MAP to El Salvador. The photo was taken at Ilopango in October of that same year. *Nick J. Waters III*

The sorry sight of what was left of FAS-110, being used as training aid at the counter-terrorism unit's headquarters in Ilopango. She was written off on 27 January 1982, during the so-called raid on Ilopango Airbase. The photo was taken in September 2007. *via Mario Alfaro*

By then, the FAS was already conducting tactical manoeuvres, beginning with preparation of the runways located at Madresal Island, San Miguel, Santa Ana, San Andrés and Usulután, which were to be used as dispersion airfields. Shortly after, all the Salvadoran civilian pilots were called upon to join the Air Force in order to supplement the lack of military aircrews. At the strategic level, the FAS Commander, Maj. Henríquez, was trying to get authorisation from the Army's high command to launch a pre-emptive bombing strike aimed at destroying the Fuerza Aérea Hondureña's (FAH) (Honduran Air Force) aircraft on the ground in order to achieve air superiority as quickly as possible, but the toxic infantry mindset at the high command prevailed, and instead of allowing him to bomb the FAH airbases, he was ordered to plan a 'massive' air attack on military facilities where, according to the available intelligence, the Honduran troops would probably concentrate once the invasion had started. According to the Salvadoran ground commanders, such action would clear the path to their targets of any potential opposition.

What no one at the high command understood was that the FAS, under the current circumstances, would not be capable of accomplishing such a task, first because the air arm did not have dedicated bomber aircraft and then, due to the sorry state of its fleet. Even the recently acquired Mustang IIs were showing some signs of mishandling and attrition, and not all of them had their reflex gunsights working, while some others lacked armour plates in the cockpit to protect the pilot. The situation with the older FG-1D Corsairs was even worse; they had turned into maintenance nightmares and keeping them on the flight line was a testimonial to the Salvadoran line ground crews' perseverance. In contrast, the MAP-supported aircraft, that is, three C-47s and five U-17As, were fully operational, the only problem being that there were not enough crews to man them.

Things began to look grim for the FAS on 5 July, when the US government – fearing that El Salvador was serious about invading Honduras – decided to suspend indefinitely the Military Assistance Program. It meant that the continuous flow of spare parts and components for the C-47s and U-17As was discontinued. Three days later, Maj. Henríquez had managed to requisition fourteen civilian aircraft, mostly light Cessna and Piper types, which the FAS mechanics began readying for combat, mainly by removing their left-hand side doors so 60mm and 81mm mortar rounds – strapped to the seats – could be lobbed out by the pilot while banking steeply. In the case of the Pipers, sections of the cabin floor were removed to allow the dropping of the mortar rounds by a member of the crew.

Also, on 8 July, the FAS mechanics began installing railings on the cargo hold floors of the five C-47s in order to facilitate the dropping of bombs through their side doors, effectively converting them into improvised bombers. Each C-47, manned by a crew of four, would be carrying eighteen AN-M30 100lb general-purpose bombs into combat. By then, the Army high command had finally decided to follow Maj. Henríquez's suggestion about hitting the FAH airbases at Tegucigalpa and San Pedro Sula at least once in order to destroy the Honduran aircraft on the ground. Thus, a C-47 and a pair of Mustang IIs had been assigned to bomb the Honduran capital's airport, while San Pedro Sula's would be attacked by a flight of three FG-1Ds. For their part, the civilian Cessnas and Pipers would be attacking Honduran defensive positions at El Amatillo and Nueva Ocotepeque, which were the main targets for the ground forces. Here it is worth noting that, with the exception of the C-47 pilots, the majority of these aviators had little or no experience in air navigation, much less in long-distance flights. Thus, the aspect of the mission they were preoccupied with was precisely finding their way towards their targets and then returning safely to their dispersal airfields amidst a complete blackout of the country's air navigation aids.

Finally, on 14 July, the FAS launched the much-anticipated air strike against Honduras. Near 1600hrs, the slower Cessnas and Pipers, packed full of mortar rounds, departed Ilopango, followed ten minutes later by the C-47 serial FAS-104, flown by Majors Jorge Domínguez and Fidel Fernández, supported by Sergeants Miguel Túnchez and Miguel Jiménez. Then it was the turn of three Mustang IIs and the three FG-1Ds. By 1750hrs, thirty-one Salvadoran aircraft – certainly one of the most bizarre attack forces in aviation history – were winging their way to their assigned targets.

At 1820hrs, the Honduran Army's high command received the first indications that the Salvadoran invasion had begun. Several reports sent from El Poy and El Amatillo border posts said that they were under heavy artillery and machine gun attack. Minutes later, more alarming reports began pouring in, this time of air attacks at Nacaome, Choluteca and Amapala, the latter on El Tigre Island. To everyone's surprise, it was the pilots flying the Cessnas and Pipers, who had managed to beat the complicated weather conditions over the Goascorán–Aramecina area and were attacking their assigned targets. Another group, also flying civilian aircraft, had reached their assigned targets at Nueva Ocotepeque and Santa Rosa de Copán, and were attacking them too. However, due to the type of ordnance the aircraft were carrying, these air strikes were generating more noise than damage.

FAS-113 was part of a batch of four C-47s delivered via MAP to El Salvador in July 1974. Even though these aircraft arrived in the familiar white over light-grey colour scheme, by the end of 1977 all had been camouflaged. *Stephen Piercey*

FAES-115 was part of the first batch of AC-47s delivered to the Salvadoran Air Force in late 1984. She can be seen landing at Ilopango, sometime in 1985, after a close support mission. Notice that the aircraft did not have the AN/ALE-47 chaff and flare dispensers installed yet. *Estudio Canessa via Marco Lavagnino*

A very rare image showing the .50 calibre machine guns installed in the AC-47 FAES-116. Interesting to note are the replacement machine guns on the floor, in case one of the mounted ones got jammed or overheated. *via Mario Alfaro*

Around the same time, FAS-104 arrived over Tegucigalpa and immediately established a circular pattern over Toncontín Airport at 8,000ft. Within seconds, one of the sergeants began sliding the AN-M30 bombs along the railing fixed to the floor of the aircraft towards the cargo door, while the other pushed them out. Inevitably, when the first bombs exploded on the ground, the lights in Tegucigalpa went out, leaving Maj. Domínguez without a much-needed visual reference. Shortly after, a .50 callibre machine gun emplaced on the outskirts of Toncontín Airport opened fire, trying to shoot down the C-47. Luckily for the Salvadoran crew, the gunner was having a hard time trying to locate the improvised bomber, and upon running out of ordnance, FAS-104 climbed away from the area and headed back to El Salvador. For the record, it was not until a couple of days later that the Salvadorans realised that all eighteen bombs dropped by FAS-104 had missed their target completely, some falling on an unpopulated mountain south of the airport, while others fell on the San José subdivision near Comayagüela, and a few kilometres west on the 15 de Septiembre subdivision, without causing any damage.

Additionally, the two Mustang IIs that had been assigned to escort FAS-104 and also attack the Honduran main airport failed to rendezvous with the transport and, for reasons that have never been established, did not make it to Tegucigalpa. It has been assumed that both aircraft got lost along the way and were the ones that bombed the small towns of Jalteva, El Suyatal, Guaimaca and Catacamas, none of which had any tactical or strategic value.

San Pedro Sula's airbase was also spared from being bombed because the three FG-1Ds failed to arrive over the target. As in the case of the Mustang IIs, it seems that these pilots got lost along the way and opted to drop their bombs near the town of Santa Rosa de Copán before returning to their dispersal airfield in El Salvador.

Even though the air attacks in general had more of a psychological than strategic value, they generated considerable chaos in the Nacaome–El Amatillo region and in the Nueva Ocotepeque area. In both places, the air strikes conducted by the Salvadoran Cessnas and Pipers were followed by heavy artillery and machine gun attacks against the border posts and military facilities nearby, which caught the Honduran troops completely by surprise, as some of them still were setting up defensive positions or in the process of being reinforced and resupplied.

FAES-117, another AC-47, was delivered in March 1985 under the assistance programme called 'Elsa'. This excellent image was most probably taken during the late 1980s, since the aircraft does not have the AN/ALE-47 chaff and flare dispensers. *via Marco Lavagnino*

During the following days, the Salvadoran ground forces conducted a fairly effective campaign that allowed them to capture the towns of El Amatillo, Aramecina, Goascorán and Alianza on the north-eastern front, and Nueva Ocotepeque in the north-western theatre of operations. In the case of the FAS, despite being incapable of stopping air strikes launched by the FAH during the early hours of the 15th against the Ilopango Airbase and the ports of Cutuco and Acajutla, its aircraft began conducting – rather successfully – a series of close support missions on all the fronts, particularly the C-47 'bombers', which were sent to attack Honduran positions in the Nueva Ocotepeque area. It was during one of those dangerous sorties that FAS-101 was intercepted by a Honduran F4U-4, which scored various hits on the C-47's fuselage and on one of its engines. Piloted by Maj. Sigfredo Velasco and Capt. Adrian Panameño, FAS-101 was able to escape into Salvadoran airspace and – trailing smoke – barely made it back to Ilopango, where she made an emergency landing that put her out of commission for the duration of the war.

By 16 July, things began going downhill for the FAS. To this day, it is not known why the Salvadoran Air Force did not carry out any offensive actions, despite the counter-attacks that the Honduran Army launched. Something catastrophic must have happened that obliged the FAS Commander to cancel every single combat sortie planned for that day and to resort to asking for volunteers for the missions that were planned for the 17th. In any case, the situation went from bad to worse the next day, since FAH F4U Corsairs managed to shoot down a Salvadoran Mustang II and two FG-1Ds while conducting close support missions over the El Amatillo area. That same day, another FG-1D was shot down by Salvadoran anti-aircraft batteries emplaced near the port of Cutuco, during a friendly fire incident. From then on, incredibly, the FAS ceased all flight operations and did not provide any air support during the 'maximum efforts' that the Salvadoran Army launched on the 18th on all the battle fronts that, perhaps significantly, were being successfully stopped by the Honduran Air Force.

Still on the 18th, near 1700hrs, while the dust was still settling after the 'maximum efforts' launched by the Salvadoran Army, President Sánchez Hernández notified the OAS that the government of El Salvador had agreed on and accepted a Honduran ceasefire proposal. Seizing the opportunity, the OAS notified Honduran President López Arellano that the proposal had been accepted by his counterpart, and that the ceasefire would be enforced at 2200hrs.

The next day, 19 July, the Salvadoran high command was informed that it was necessary to resupply the troops operating at the Nueva Ocotepeque front, especially after the heavy fighting they had taken part in the day before. Thus, Maj. Henríquez was ordered to disregard the ceasefire's mandate that prohibited any military flights in both countries, and immediately send the FAS C-47s to parachute food and medical supplies over the combat posts that the Salvadorans still held. These were the last missions the Douglas transports flew during the so-called 100-Hour War.

The rapid neutralisation that the FAS suffered during the conflict forced the Salvadoran high command to redefine the air arm's doctrine and objectives. This contributed in large measure to helping the FAS to revive soon after, and commence the process of being transformed into a very professional air arm, with relatively better equipment. In fact, during the second week of August, the service acquired its very first dedicated bomber from a civilian source, this being a Douglas TB-26B Invader, which was followed by a second one a couple of days later.

But difficulties for El Salvador – as a nation – were far from over. In the months following the war, social unrest became an acute problem and by April 1970, a small group of Salvadoran Communists formed the Fuerzas Populares de Liberación (Popular Liberation Forces) or FPL. Its members were heavily influenced by the war in Vietnam, and believed that Communism could only come to power through a prolonged war of national liberation. Two years later, another group, the Ejército Revolucionario del Pueblo (Popular Revolutionary Army) or ERP, broke off from the FPL. Inspired by the success of the Tupamaros in Uruguay and the Montoneros in Argentina, this guerrilla group proclaimed that, instead of victory by prolonged rural war, winning power was only possible through urban terrorism.

By then, the Salvadoran Guardia Nacional and Police were in charge of fighting the guerrilla groups across the country, which were still considered bands of outlaws. However, the Salvadoran Army was already preparing to assume a more important role in what seemed to be the beginning of armed insurrection. In fact, the high command had embraced the concept of 'vertical insertion' in the planning of their military operations, mainly in the form of parachute troops and helicopter mobility. Hence, the FAS was ordered to come up with the appropriate equipment to fulfill this 'new' type of mission and, in May 1974, the air arm acquired six Sud Aviation SA315B Lama and five SA316B Alouette helicopters. Additionally, the US supplied the first four of eight C-47s, which arrived at Ilopango on 30 May, and were assigned the serials FAS-107, FAS-108, FAS-109 and FAS-110; the other three were delivered on 7 July of that same year, their serials being FAS-111, FAS-112, FAS-113 and FAS-114.

In May 1975, yet another guerrilla group emerged. Called Resistencia Nacional (National Resistance) or RN, it was made up of dissidents of the ERP, who broke away when two predominant figures of said clandestine organisation were assassinated by their own comrades. At this point, the Salvadoran armed forces were still trying to come to terms with a complicated situation: On one hand it was necessary to keep a close watch on Honduras, since there was a possibility of crossing sabres again over the border and immigration problem that the war did not fully resolve; on the other, the growing insurgence mandated the adoption of a counter-insurgency doctrine and tactics by all the branches of the armed forces.

In the case of the FAS, the contradictory proposition was reflected in the type of aircraft purchases the air arm had made until then: First, it acquired eighteen ex-Israeli Dassault MD.450 Ouragan fighter-bombers, which were part of an arms package negotiated with Israel that also included five Fouga CM-170 Magister attack-trainers. These acquisitions were complemented by four Israeli Aircraft Industries IAI-201 Arava medium transport aircraft, which could be easily converted for close air support missions, making them a superb counter-insurgency platform.

In January of the following year, a third guerrilla group began to form. Known as the Partido Revolucionario de los Trabajadores Centroamericanos (Central American Workers Party) or PRTC it was made up of radical university students who had visions of a pan-Central American socialist revolution, not just in El Salvador. By then, the three guerrilla organisations were carrying out 'petty terrorism' across the country, which included kidnappings, murder, extortion, bombing and even bank robberies. However, the Salvadoran government was not perceiving these as an armed insurrection just yet. In fact, the spark that escalated the growth of the Salvadoran guerrilla organisations – and changed the government's perception for good – occurred in neighbouring Nicaragua, when the Frente Sandinista de Liberación Nacional (Sandinista National Liberation Front) or FSLN toppled the dictator Anastasio Somoza on 19 July 1979. The Salvadoran guerrillas, as well as other guerrilla groups all over the continent, had provided men, training, weapons, and money to the Sandinistas. Because of this, the Sandinistas would allow them to use Nicaragua as a base for spreading revolution throughout the hemisphere.

A very weathered FAES-118 can be seen at Ilopango, sometime in the late 1980s. This aircraft was delivered in May 1985 and was converted to a BT-67 in the early 1990s. *via Marco Lavagnino*

Things turned for the worse in December 1979, when a fourth guerrilla organisation surfaced in El Salvador. Called Fuerzas Armadas de Liberación (Armed Forces of Liberation) or FAL, this group was founded by members of the Salvadoran Communist Party who had decided to abandon Soviet guidelines about limiting the struggle to the political arena and adopt armed revolution. Exploiting its excellent international connections, the FAL began negotiations with Cuba and Nicaragua in order to secure armament and training. Fidel Castro had other ideas, however, and his vision was not limited to help just one of the Salvadoran guerrilla groups. Hence, the Cuban Dirección General de Inteligencia (General Directorate of Intelligence) or DGI representative for El Salvador called for a meeting with the Salvadoran guerrilla factions in Managua, Nicaragua, in which he told them – rather bluntly – that the Cubans and Nicaraguans were willing to provide funds, weapons and training only on the condition that they would form a single, co-ordinated opposition front. Even though the guerrilla groups hated each other, their leaders agreed to the Cuban proposal and, in May 1980, the Frente Farabundo Martí para la Liberación Nacional (Farabundo Martí Front for National Liberation) or FMLN was officially born.

The debut of the FMLN's initial efforts was the so-called 'Final Offensive' that was launched on 10 January 1981, which turned out to be anything but 'final', since it marked the beginning of the fiercest civil war in Latin America. For the Salvadoran military, this was the last push towards transitioning into a counter-insurgency force. In fact, by the end of that same month, the Salvadoran Army had already conducted five air assaults: three with helicopters, one with an IAI-201 and another with a C-47, which transported thirty-five paratroopers to a place called Hacienda La Carrera, in Usulután, from where they launched a successful attack against a small guerrilla group. In the process, a CM-170 scored the first 'kill' in the history of the FAS when the small jet managed to shoot down a Piper PA-23-250 Aztec that was trying to escape after delivering armament and supplies for the guerrillas. This took place at a farm called Hacienda La Sabana on 24 January.

By the end of 1981, the Salvadoran Army had conducted three additional large-scale airmobile operations, many of them using the FAS' newly acquired Bell UH-1H helicopters. In fact, the implementation of the 'vertical insertion' concept was so successful that the FMLN leadership decided to create an elite group with the specific mission of attacking the FAS airbases and develop efficient anti-aircraft tactics. Hence, twelve men – provided by the ERP – were sent to Cuba to receive sapper and commando training.

Upon the return of the special group from Cuba, the FMLN organised an attack against the Ilopango airbase, aimed to destroy the entire FAS fleet on the ground. The operation began around 0100hrs on 27 January 1982, when eight members of the special group infiltrated the airbase and began placing explosive charges close to the aircraft parked on the main ramp. Once the guerrillas had exited the airport safely, the charges were detonated, destroying five MD.450s, six UH-1H helicopters and four C-47s, the latter being FAS-101, FAS-107, FAS-108 and FAS-110.

Nice in-flight shot of AC-47s FAES-124 and FAES-117, most probably taken during the late 1980s. FAES-124 was the only gunship that was not converted to a BT-67. *Estudio Canessa via Marco Lavagnino*

At this juncture, it is worth noting that the Ilopango raid left the FAS with only five operational C-47s, since FAS-103, FAS-104, FAS-105 and FAS-111 had been retired between 1977 and 1978 due to attrition. Hence, the Transport Squadron only had four IAI-201s and five C-47s, the survivors being FAS-106, FAS-109, FAS-112, FAS-113 and FAS-114. Obviously, this situation diminished dramatically the FAS' capability to conduct large-scale airmobile operations, but it also opened the door for a substantial increase of US military assistance. In fact, that year the FAS received its first twenty Cessna O-2 light strike aircraft, as well as its first eight Cessna OA-37B COIN jets. These were followed by three much-needed Fairchild C-123Ks for the Transport Squadron.

During the period from 1981 to 1984, the war reached its peak, both in the number of combat operations and brutality. In general, the FMLN forces had the initiative and, despite a widespread bombing campaign started by the FAS against rebel-held villages, which brought the FMLN under some pressure, the rebel organisation managed to decimate several Army companies, capturing their weapons and ammunition in the process.

It was precisely in 1984 that things began to change. First of all, the US military assistance and training began paying off, increasing the Salvadoran armed forces effectiveness. The FMLN also failed to increase the number of its combatants that, by then, had reached about 10,000 across the country. The FMLN's overrunning and capture of the headquarters of an Army brigade at El Paraiso on the New Year's Eve reflected how the tables had turned, since the FAS' firepower played a key role in recovering the base. In fact, from then on, the air force increased its number of strike and close air support missions across the country, conducted mainly by the OA-37Bs, the O-2s and the UH-1 helicopters.

By the end of 1984, the close air support/strike capabilities of the FAS were greatly increased when the first two of seven US-supplied AC-47s were delivered on 24 December. Serialed FAS-115 and FAS-116, these aircraft were fitted with three .50 calibre machine guns on the port side, firing through two rear windows. The following year, in March, a third AC-47 was delivered. Similarly equipped, this example was assigned the serial FAES-117, the newly implemented FAES acronym meaning Fuerza Aérea El Salvador (Air Force of El Salvador.) In fact, that same year, all of the operational aircraft in the air force inventory were reserialed using that acronym, in order to distinguish them from the aircraft in neighbouring Nicaragua, which had started to use the prefix FAS for Fuerza Aérea Sandinista or

AC-47 FAES-124 at Ilopango, probably in the late-1980s. *Estudio Canessa via Marco Lavagnino*

Sandinista Air Force. Two more AC-47s were delivered in May 1985, being assigned the serials FAES-118 and FAES-119. These were followed by the last two in July, which received the serials FAES-124 and FAES-125.

Without any doubt, the arrival of the AC-47s played a major role in further turning the initiative over to the government. In fact, with the combined use of the newly acquired gunships and the light strike/COIN aircraft, the rebels were no longer able to operate freely, much less in large formations. Hence, the FMLN was forced to transition from a semi-conventional force to a fully guerrilla organisation, comprised mainly of smaller columns. However, the FAS had already learned to insert company-sized units to deal with the FMLN wherever its members were discovered, while the Army had created a number of well-trained and highly mobile units that could be inserted by helicopter to search out the enemy and establish remote posts from where they could launch quick search and destroy operations, usually supported by FAS aircraft.

By the end of 1985, the US Military Mission for El Salvador rated the FAS operations as 'particularly effective', especially those missions carried out by the AC-47s, which by then were considered essential for operations where long loiter time and heavy firepower was required, even at night.

AC-47s FAES-117 and FAES-119 photographed in August 1992, at Basler headquarters in Oshkosh, WI, right before being converted to BT-67. *Nick Veronico*

In the case of the 'old' C-47s, attrition had settled in and, during the following three years, FAS-112, FAS-113 and FAS-114 were retired, the latter due to corrosion. Also, acquiring new engines for the Douglas transports became a nightmare, while the ones on hand were practically unserviceable after having been overhauled too many times. By early 1988, FAS-106 and FAS-109 were the last two aircraft operational of the US-supplied batch that had arrived in 1974.

Inevitably, the scarcity of engines and other components was a looming threat over the AC-47s, too. Hence, beginning in mid-1988, under the auspices of the US government, the FAS sent its first three aircraft, FAES-116, FAES-118 and FAES-125 to Oshkosh, Wisconsin, for a complete modernisation at Basler Turbo Conversions. Such modernisation included the installation of Pratt & Whitney PT-6A-67R turbines and Hartzell five-bladed propellers, as well as a semi-digital cockpit. It also included the strengthening of their entire airframe and the enlargement of their forward fuselage section.

By 1989, with only two C-47s on hand, the FAS had to eventually use its four AC-47s for troop transport and logistical missions. Such was the case on 12 December, when FAES-115 was returning to Ilopango from a resupplying mission and overran the runway. After a thorough evaluation, it was determined that the aircraft was beyond repair and – sadly – was retired from active service.

In August 1990, FAES-116, FAES-118 and FAES-125 – by then converted to Basler BT-67s – finally returned to El Salvador. Two months later, it was the turn for FAES-117 and FAES-119 to undergo their turbo conversion and, accordingly, the two aircraft were flown to Oshkosh. In the case of FAES-124, Basler technicians deemed her unfit for the BT-67 conversion and she was left behind. In fact, she was retired in 1992 due to attrition.

By the end of 1990, the FMLN managed to acquire man-portable surface-to-air missiles from Nicaragua, mainly soviet-made 9K32 Strela-2s and 9K34 Strela-3s, as well as US-made FIM-43C Redeyes that the Sandinistas had seized from the Contras. Their debut took place on 23 November of that year, when OA-37B FAES-423 was shot down while conducting a close air support mission in Usulután. Then, on 4 December, BT-67 FAES-125 was brought down over Chalatenango, while also conducting a close air support sortie, killing

seven of a crew of eight. Miraculously, Airman Carlos Arturo García Zaldaña was able to bail out from the flaming aircraft.

The introduction of the surface-to-air missiles by the FMLN forced the FAS to change its tactics immediately, beginning with the norm of employing two or more aircraft simultaneously during a sortie. The idea was that each aircraft would watch out for the other. By then, the Salvadoran pilots had realised that the guerrillas needed to fire two or three missiles in order to shoot down a single aircraft or helicopter. This gave them a good chance to spot the location from where the missile had been fired and neutralise the shooter. The US also came to the rescue and lent ECM and anti-missile equipment that included the AN/ALQ-123 infrared jammer for the OA-37Bs, the AN/ALQ-144 infrared countermeasure device as well as heat suppressors for the UH-1H/M helicopters. In the case of the AC-47 and BT-67 gunships, AN/ALE-47 chaff and flare dispensers were installed in the upper part of their mid-fuselages. Despite the quick adoption of the jamming equipment and the new tactics, the FMLN managed to shoot down an UH-1M on 12 March 1991. This turned out to be the last FAS aircraft destroyed by a surface-to-air missile.

On 31 December of that same year, the government and the FMLN agreed on a preliminary peace agreement under the auspices of the UN, and less than month later, a ceasefire took effect, bringing the civil war to an end.

Regarding the last two AC-47s that had been sent to Oshkosh for turbo conversion at Basler, these arrived in Ilopango in October 1994, almost two years too late to participate in the war. From then on, the FAS' C-47/BT-67 fleet began suffering the inevitable post-war attrition. Of these, FAS-106, the oldest flyable C-47 in the inventory, was retired in 2002, while considerable efforts were made between 2007 and 2008 to get FAS-124 airworthy again. In the case of the BT-67s, the last flyable aircraft, serialed FAS-116, was damaged beyond repair in October 2019, after an emergency landing at Ilopango. In fact, with the accident involving this BT-67, the military history of the magnificent Douglas twin in El Salvador came to an end.

What follows is the complete list of the Salvadoran Douglas C-47/AC-47/BT-67 aircraft, including their previous identities and their final fates, where known.

FAES-118 photographed at Kelly AFB, TX, in August 1990, during her ferry flight to El Salvador after being converted to a BT-67. *Manuel Delgado*

FAS Serial	Previous Identity	Type as Built	MSN	Assignments and Notes
FAS-101	42-23594 NC5606V YS-34C	C-47A-25-DL	9456	Acquired in 1948 as a VIP aircraft from civilian sources. MAP supported since FY63. Carried out offensive missions during the 100-Hour War and was machine-gunned by FAH Corsairs. Damaged beyond repair at Ilopango Airbase on 27 Jan 82 during a guerrilla raid. On Ilopango dump in 2002.
FAS-102	42-23394 YS-26C(?)	C-47A-15-DL	9256	Acquired in 1949 from civilian sources. Converted to VIP aircraft in 1952. Damaged beyond repair on 24 Aug 62 during emergency landing at Asino. As parachuting training aid at Ilopango Airbase, without wings.
FAS-103	42-24295 0-24295	C-47A-50-DL	10157	Donated by the US Government on 7 May 63. MAP supported. Ditched at Ilopango Lake on 10 Sep 65.
FAS-103(2)	43-49096 0-49096	C-47B-10-DK	14912/26357	Acquired via MAP in 1966 and delivered on 12 May 67. Carried out a bombing mission over Tegucigalpa, Honduras, on 14 Jul 69, during the 100-Hour War. WFU on 20 Oct 77. As parachuting training aid at Ilopango Airbase.
FAS-104	43-49772A 0-49772A	C-47B-20-DK	15588/27033	Acquired via MAP and delivered in Aug 66. Carried out offensive missions during the 100-Hour War. WFU on 20 Oct 77, used for spares.
FAS-105	43-49498 0-49498	C-47B-15-DK C-47D	15314/26759	Acquired from civilian sources on 15 May 67, although MAP documents give 20 Nov 64 as the acquisition date. Carried out offensive missions during the 100-Hour War. WFU in Jul 78. At dump in Ilopango Airbase.
FAS-106	42-92104 0-92104	C-47A-1-DK C-47D	11867	Acquired from civilian sources on 15 May 67, although MAP documents give 4 Sep 70 as acquisition date, which is practically impossible, as noted in the text. Carried out offensive missions during the 100-Hour War. WFU in 2002 as the FAS' last operative C-47. On dump in Ilopango Airbase.
FAS-107	44-77204 0-77204 N49249	C-47B-40-DK C-47D VC-47D	16788/33536	Acquired via MAP on 30 May 74. Destroyed on 27 Jan 82 during a guerrilla raid on Ilopango Airbase.
FAS-108	43-49505A 0-49505 N49250	C-47B-15-DK C-47D	15321/26766	Acquired on 30 May 74. Destroyed on 27Jan 82 during a guerrilla raid on Ilopango Airbase.
FAS-109	44-76378 0-476378	TC-47B-25-DK TC-47D C-47D TC-47D	15962/32710	Acquired on 30 May 74. Sustained minor damage during rough landing at Santa Ana. WFU in 1990. On display at El Zapote Military Museum since 2017.
AS-110	44-77214 KP244 44-77214 0-77214	C-47B-40-DK Dakota IV C-47D VC-47D	16798/33546	Acquired on 30 May 74. Damaged beyond repair on 27 Jan 82 during a guerrilla raid on Ilopango Airbase. As training aid with the counter-terrorism unit CEAT.

FAES-116 photographed at Kelly AFB, TX, in August 1990, during her ferry flight to El Salvador after being converted to a BT-67. *Manuel Delgado*

In this excellent image, taken in January 1996, BT-67 FAES-118 can be seen with the AN/ALE-47 chaff and flare dispensers already installed in her mid-fuselage. *Julio A. Montes*

Delivered in October 1994, BT-67 FAES-117 arrived in El Salvador too late to take part in the war. In fact, Basler delivered her in this elegant 'white-blue' colour scheme. Notice also that she does not have the chaff and flare dispensers installed. *Eric Wagner*

FAS-111	44-76711 0-76711	TC-47B-30-DK TC-47D C-47D TC-47D	16295/33043	Acquired via MAP on 07 Jul 74. WFU in Jul 78. As parachuting training aid at Ilopango Airbase.
FAS-112	43-48451 0-48451	C-47B-1-DK C-47D		Acquired via MAP on 7 Jul 74. WFU.
FAS-113	44-76265 0-76265	TC-47B-25-DK TC-47D C-47D	15849/32597	Acquired via MAP on 7 Jul 74. WFU. Forward section displayed at the FAS Museum in Ilopango Airbase.
FAS-114	43-16269 0-16269	C-47B-1-DL C-47D	20745	Always assumed to have been salvaged after an accident in November 1944, this aircraft was apparently resurrected. Acquired via MAP on 7 Jul 74. WFU due to corrosion in 1988. As monument in front of Ilopango Airbase since 1990.
FAS-115	43-48157 FAB-2036 N4948J	C-47A-30-DK AC-47	13973/25418	Acquired on 24 Dec 84 in AC-47 gunship configuration. Written off on 12 Dec 89 at Ilopango Airbase.
FAES-116	44-76950 KN628 G-AOGZ N4849 F-OGDZ N4957W	C-47B-40-DK Dakota IV AC-47 Basler BT-67	16534/33282 Basler #3	Acquired on 24 Dec 84 in AC-47 gunship configuration. Converted to BT-67 in Aug 90. Delivered by Basler in 'Gunship Grey' colour scheme. Written off during landing on 22 Oct 19 at Ilopango Airbase.
FAES-117	43-48148 N405E N1499V N40CE N50CE N200ZZ N104CA	C-47A-30-DK AC-47 Basler BT-67	13964/25409 Basler #16	Acquired on 29 Mar 85 in AC-47 gunship configuration. Converted to BT-67 in Oct 94. Delivered by Basler with 'white-blue' colour scheme. Written off 23 Jul 04 at El Jagüey, La Unión. Forward section on display at the First Air Brigade, Ilopango, as 'FAS-125'.

Although Basler delivered FAES-116 painted in the 'Gunship Grey' scheme, after the war she was repainted in the more patriotic white-blue colour scheme. Here she can be seen landing at Ilopango in January 2011. *Layo Leiva*

FAES-118	44-76906 KN597 44-76906 GA+102 AS+587 GR+111 ND+106 CA+014 N10801	C-47B-35-DK Dakota IV AC-47 Basler BT-67	16490/33238 Basler #4	Acquired on 29 May 85 in AC-47 gunship configuration. Converted to BT-67 in Aug 90. Delivered by Basler in 'Gunship Grey' colour scheme. Damaged on 23 Apr 05 at Ilopango Airbase. Currently repairable but lacking spare parts.
FAES-119	41-38745 NC-75406 N721A	C-47A-1-DL AC-47 Basler BT-67	6204 Basler #17	Acquired on 29 May 85 in AC-47 gunship configuration. Converted to BT-67 in Oct 94. Delivered by Basler with 'Gunship Grey' colour scheme. Written off at Los Comandos Airfield, Morazán, on 11 Nov 00.
FAES-124	42-23706 NC44585 N44585	C-47A-1-DL AC-47	9568	Acquired on 20 Jul 85 in AC-47 gunship configuration. WFU in Dec 92. From 2007 to 2008 considerable efforts were made to bring her back to the flight line, but in the end, she was placed in open storage at Ilopango Airbase, where she remains at the time of writing.
FAES-125	42-93451 PI-C91 N1280N	C-47A-25-DK AC-47 Basler BT-67	13364 Basler #?	Acquired on 20 Jul 85 in AC-47 gunship configuration. Converted to BT-67 in Aug 90. Delivered by Basler with 'Gunship Grey' colour scheme. Shot down by an SA-14 missile on 4 Dec 90, at La Laguna, Chalatenango. One survivor.

On 22 January 2019, FAES-116 sustained irreparable damage after suffering a runway excursion at Ilopango while returning from a parachute drop mission. She was the last flyable Salvadoran C-47/BT-67.
La Prensa Gráfica via Mario Overall

CHAPTER TWELVE

Guatemala

Notwithstanding that for over seventy years the Douglas C-47 was a familiar sight in the Guatemalan skies, very little is known about its military service in that nation. Therefore, it could come as a surprise to know that the adoption of these aircraft contributed decisively to transforming the doctrine and tactics of the Guatemalan armed forces, to the point of allowing them – for the very first time – to project power beyond the country's borders by means of airborne operations.

Since its creation in 1871, the Ejército de Guatemala (Guatemalan Army) had limited itself to enforcing the will of the ruling dictators and making sure that no one would try to depose them. In fact, its troops rarely conducted combat exercises and when they did it was usually in the outskirts of Guatemala City, at locations that could be easily reached by train or truck. Similarly, the Cuerpo de Aeronáutica Militar (Military Aeronautics Corps) or CAM, created on 12 March 1921, had focused entirely on acquiring attack and pursuit aircraft that could be employed as psychological deterrents to any potential enemy of the ruling dictator. This mentality persisted during much of the Second World War when the CAM acquired – under US Lend-Lease – three armed North American AT-6Cs and seven Boeing P-26As for its fighter-attack component, the latter being among the few fighters delivered to any Latin American country – Mexico and Brazil, much larger, being the only others. Additional wartime acquisitions comprised the inevitable trainer aircraft in the form of two Vultee BT-15s and two Boeing-Stearman PT-17s, but not a single tactical transport aircraft.

After the unexpected resignation of the ruthless dictator General Jorge Ubico in July 1944, and the overthrowing of his successor General Federico Ponce three months later, the Revolutionary Junta that took power set out to reorganise the armed forces, beginning with the drafting of a new constitutive law, as well as laying the foundations for their professionalisation by means of training programmes for both officers and enlisted men, and most important of all, the acquisition of modern military equipment. To achieve these ambitious objectives, the Junta requested the assistance of the US Government, which quickly established a military mission to help with the creation of the training programmes and to co-ordinate the transfer of military equipment through the unobligated funds still available from the Lend-Lease programme.

Formally established on 21 February 1945, the US Military Mission also included an Air Section, led by Col Frank J. Puerta, which would oversee the disbandment of the CAM and its reorganisation into the Fuerza Aérea de Guatemala (Guatemala's Air Force) or FAG; the Air Section would also evaluate the requirements of the newly created air arm and determine the most expedient manner by which to meet them. However, the most immediate action taken was to start training a handful of Guatemalan aviators as co-pilots in the USAAF Missions C-47A, serial 43-15580, which had been assigned for support of these assorted activities. For all intents and purposes, that was the first time Guatemalan military pilots had the opportunity to fly the venerable Douglas transport.

One of the earliest images of any of the AVIATECA C-47s, this one most probably being LG-AHA (ex 41-38669, and ex FAG T-2) photographed at La Aurora, in late 1946. *LAAHS Collection*

Excellent colour study of the C-47A-90-DL FAG serial T-1 (C/N 20469, ex 43-16003), photographed at La Aurora Airbase in early 1947. Of interest is the long fairing that can be seen over the engine nacelle, denoting that the aircraft's powerplants are equipped with Ram-Nonram Air Induction Systems, typical of the 'late' versions of the C-47As and early C-47Bs.
Peter C. Boisseau, via Gary Kuhn

The fast-paced changes continued during the first half of 1945, starting with the enactment of a new constitution and the inauguration of Dr Juan José Arévalo as the first democratically elected president in almost forty years. The Congress, for its part, approved even more reforms that included a new labour code, a considerable increase in the minimum wage, the creation of an unprecedented social security system, as well as the new constitutive law for the armed forces which formalised – once and for all – the disbandment of the CAM and the creation of the FAG.

On 9 May, officers of the US Army and Navy, led by Lt Gen. George H. Brett, began a series of meetings with the Guatemalan Defence Minister, Lt Col Jacobo Arbenz, and members of his staff, during which the latter presented the progress achieved so far in the transformation of the armed forces and, incidentally, requested the acquisition of military equipment through the still functioning Lend-Lease programme. The idea was to equip a full infantry division, a mechanised cavalry squadron, a field artillery battalion and a coastal artillery battalion. For equipping the FAG, the Guatemalan officers requested twelve BT-13 basic trainers, twelve AT-6 armed trainers, three C-45 light transports, one C-47 and twelve P-36 or P-51 fighters. The wish list provided by Minister Arbenz made it all the way up to the Secretary of State, Edward Stettinius Jr, who did not hesitate in rejecting it, stating that the goal of the US across Latin America was to reduce the size of the armed forces both in terms of men and equipment. However, Stettinius offered to replace any equipment deemed obsolete, as well as any non-American equipment.

There was a considerable back and forth between the two governments during the following weeks, with the Guatemalans submitting increasingly ambitious requests, trying to take full advantage of the remaining credit that the country had with the Lend-Lease programme, only to be rejected by the US government every time. In the middle was the Military Mission, trying to mediate between the two parties, making more modest proposals in terms of quantity and type of equipment, which simply went ignored by Arbenz and his staff.

To further strain the relations between the two governments, President Arévalo had just finished the expropriation of Aerovías de Guatemala, an airline owned jointly by Alfred Denby – a US citizen – and none other than Pan American Airways! Not surprisingly, the Department of State had been following the expropriation process closely, making sure that no US interests were harmed. Unfortunately, the Guatemalan government had repeatedly failed to reach an agreement with Denby and Pan American regarding the airline's share price, so an all-out legal battle seemed inevitable.

Meanwhile, the expropriated airline – now officially renamed Compañía Guatemalteca de Aviación (Guatemalan Aviation Company) or AVIATECA, had been unable to resume operations because shortly before the expropriation process began, Pan American had flown all the company's aircraft out of the country. Predictably, when the Guatemalan Ministry of Communications attempted to acquire a pair of surplus C-47s for the crippled airline, the US Government immediately intervened, stating that no aircraft would be sold to AVIATECA until its former owners had been paid in full.

On 20 October, President Arévalo ordered the creation of an ambitious programme aimed at distributing the lands of the remote and jungle-covered northern region of the country among poor campesinos from the highlands. The plan was to establish no fewer than ten agricultural colonies throughout El Petén department, which would be linked with the nation's ports and the capital by a network of roads to be built during the following five years, or so Arévalo stated. The first of these colonies was going to be established at the town of Poptún, located 230km north-east of Guatemala City and 111km north-west of the nearest port, Puerto Barrios.

Seldom photographed, C-47B-50-DK (C/N 34406/17139, ex 45-1136), FAG serial T-2, can be seen in this image while parked on La Aurora Airbase's northern apron, sometime in 1947. The long fairing that can be seen over the engine nacelle indicates that the aircraft's powerplants are equipped with Ram-Nonram Air Induction Systems, typical of the early C-47Bs.
Peter C. Boisseau, via Gary Kuhn

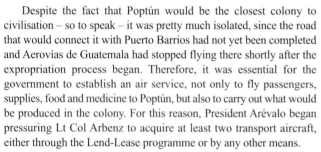

The Guatemalan Air Force mechanics learned quickly to keep their aircraft airworthy most of the time. In this image, the C-47 T-1 (ex 43-16003) is undergoing a revision of its engines at La Aurora Airbase, sometime in 1948. *Guatemalan Air Force Photo Archives via LAAHS*

C-47s 0961 (ex 43-16003, ex T-1) and 0749 (ex 43-15580, ex T-3) parked on La Aurora Airbase's northern apron shortly after receiving their new serial numbers in late July 1949. By then, all three aircraft had gone through modifications that included the installation of new radios and navigation equipment. *Guatemalan Air Force Photo Archives via LAAHS*

Despite the fact that Poptún would be the closest colony to civilisation – so to speak – it was pretty much isolated, since the road that would connect it with Puerto Barrios had not yet been completed and Aerovías de Guatemala had stopped flying there shortly after the expropriation process began. Therefore, it was essential for the government to establish an air service, not only to fly passengers, supplies, food and medicine to Poptún, but also to carry out what would be produced in the colony. For this reason, President Arévalo began pressuring Lt Col Arbenz to acquire at least two transport aircraft, either through the Lend-Lease programme or by any other means.

By then, negotiations between the Defence Minister and the US State Department regarding the transfer of military equipment had virtually stalled. In addition, the majority of the high-ranking officers who had been assigned to the Military Mission had already departed the country, being replaced by majors and captains. The Air Section was no exception, as Col Puerta had been replaced by Maj. Merle S. Else. Hence, with no other option for acquiring the transports, Lt Col Arbenz decided to fork out US$40,000 of the Army budget for purchasing two surplus C-47-DLs from the US Foreign Liquidation Commission (FLC). These aircraft, USAAF serials 41-19499 (C/N 6142) and 41-38669 (C/N 6052), arrived at La Aurora Airbase on 18 December, where they were assigned the FAG numbers T-1 and T-2 respectively, the 'T' prefix meaning Transporte or transport.

Much to dismay of the military pilots, however, within hours of the arrival of the aircraft, President Arévalo ordered that both be turned over to AVIATECA, alleging that the FAG did not have competent aviators to fly them and that it was extremely urgent for said aircraft to start flying the airline's regular routes. For Arévalo it was also extremely urgent that those C-47s began flying to Poptún, carrying construction materials and machinery, since the most important project of his administration was well behind schedule, and was drawing considerable criticism from the press. Thus, by the end of December, AVIATECA crews began flying the two C-47s – both still carrying FAG markings – to all the destinations that Aerovías had covered in the past and to Poptún. The military pilots, on their part, had to settle for continuing their training in the C-47A of the US Military Mission.

In January 1946, right after the US Department of State had issued the export licences for the two C-47s acquired by the FAG, the US Embassy in Guatemala found out that both aircraft were being flown by AVIATECA on commercial routes. Hence, on the

28th, the Department of State formally asked the Guatemalan government to withdraw them from the airline and return them to the air force as soon as possible. On his part, the Guatemalan Ambassador in Washington, Col Oscar Morales López, replied that the aircraft were involved in an important government-sponsored project and that only AVIATECA had competent crews for flying them, hence complying with such a request was impracticable. Predictably, there was an intense exchange of diplomatic notes during the following months, yet the Guatemalan government stubbornly kept up its position.

On 1 February, Lt Col Stephen D. McElroy was appointed as the new chief of the US Military Mission in Guatemala and was immediately given the mission to resume negotiations for the transfer of military equipment under the Lend-Lease programme. Fortunately, McElroy found a better disposition on the part of the Guatemalan government, and in a matter of a few weeks he had reached a consensus with the Defence Ministry on a list of military equipment to be transferred in the coming months. In the case of the FAG, the list included six AT-6D armed trainers, four AT-11 light bombers, two C-45 light transports and two C-47 medium transports besides the two that had been delivered the previous year and that were being flown by AVIATECA.

By 25 February, in a move aimed at complying with the legal requirements imposed by the US government regarding the two C-47s that had been turned over to AVIATECA, the Guatemalan government decided to withdraw the aircraft from the airline and formally assign them to the Ministry of Communications. Much to the US Ambassador's dismay, however, both transports kept flying commercially for the airline, with the difference that they were now maintained by FAG mechanics at La Aurora Airbase. Not surprisingly, the US Embassy asked once more that the aircraft be returned to the FAG, since the air arm was their legitimate owner. This time however, the Guatemalan government abandoned all kinds of formalities and, by 9 July, decided to assign civilian registrations to both aircraft, thus ending their rather short military service in the country. Consequently, both were registered to AVIATECA, with 41-19499 becoming LG-AGA and 41-38669 being registered as LG-AHA. Less than two weeks later, the Guatemalan government finally reached an agreement with the former owners of AVIATECA. Then, on 20 July, the airline was finally absorbed by the Ministry of Communications, thus becoming a state-owned company from then on.

C-47 0653 (ex 43-1136, ex T-2) parked on La Aurora Airbase's northern apron, after receiving her new four-digit serial number, in late July 1949. By then, the three FAG C-47s had gone through modifications that included the installation of new radios and navigation equipment.
Guatemalan Air Force Photo Archives via LAAHS

Once the Arévalo administration had settled the dispute with the former owners of AVIATECA, there was a substantial change in the attitude of the US Department of State regarding the military assistance programme. In the case of the FAG, the first aircraft deliveries under the Interim Allocation Program of the American Republics Project (ARP) commenced by mid-October when six AT-6D armed trainers arrived in La Aurora Airbase and were assigned to the air arm's fighter-attack squadron.

The six Texans were followed by the US Military Mission's own C-47A-85-DL, C/N 20046, ex 43-15580, which was formally handed over to the FAG on 21 October. This aircraft was not assigned a FAG serial number immediately though, as she continued operating with her USAAF identity for more than three years, eventually gaining – at least on paper – the serial T-3. Shortly after, the US Department of State authorised the export of a pair of Douglas transports intended to replace the ones that had been transferred to AVIATECA. In fact, these new C-47s were given the same FAG serial numbers of the aircraft that they replaced, something that has puzzled aero-historians for decades. The first was a C-47A-90-DL, C/N 20469, ex 43-16003, which was delivered under the ARP on 26 November, and was assigned the FAG serial T-1. The second, also delivered under the ARP, was a C-47B-50-DK, C/N 34406/17139, ex 45-1136, which arrived in La Aurora Airbase on 10 December and was assigned the FAG serial T-2.

It is worth mentioning that both T-1 and T-2 had carburettors equipped with Ram-Nonram Electrical Air Induction Systems, easily recognisable by the long fairings the aircraft had over each engine nacelle, which were typical of the late versions of the C-47As and early C-47Bs. In contrast, the aircraft that the Military Mission handed over to the FAG had carburettors equipped with much simpler ram air induction systems, which had just a small intake placed atop each engine nacelle, right behind the cowling. This system was commonly used in the C-47s and early C-47As.

Although there are several reports suggesting a fourth C-47 was delivered to the FAG during 1947, this is simply not true, as there is no documentary evidence to support such a claim. In fact, the FAG Transport Squadron, already equipped with the three C-47s, was expanded on 3 March of that year when five Beech AT-11B light bombers were delivered under the Lend-Lease programme. Why these aircraft were assigned to the transport component of the

Guatemalan air arm is beyond any explanation. The truth is that the versatile Kansans were operated interchangeably as bombers and as transports, as well as being used as twin-engine trainers for the new pilots of the squadron.

By May 1947, the first C-47 crews who had been checked out began flying the aircraft beyond Guatemalan borders, initially to the neighbouring Central American nations and then to the Panama Canal Zone. However, the degree of proficiency reached by the crews was demonstrated two months later when one of the C-47s conducted a flight to Argentina, carrying a group of university students who were attending a congress at Buenos Aires. During that flight, which made refuelling stops in the Panama Canal Zone, Peru, Ecuador and Chile, the aircraft crossed the Aconcagua pass, thus becoming the first Guatemalan aircraft to fly over the Andes.

The C-47's capability to carry out long-range flights and the outstanding performance shown by the FAG crews during those missions did not escape the notice of President Arévalo, who immediately set out to employ them as instruments of diplomacy as he was determined to influence the establishment of democracy across Central America, as well as ending any form of imperialism in the region. It was also around this time that the FAG transports began flying clandestine missions ordered by Arévalo himself, with the first taking place in mid-October, when the C-47s T-1 and T-2 were rushed to Campo Columbia, in Cuba, to pick up a group of Dominican revolutionaries who had been expelled by the government of that island nation, as well as their armament and combat equipment. Thus, during the following two weeks, the FAG transports, along with a Douglas B-18 owned by the rebels and a couple of aircraft apparently leased from a Cuban airline, completed no fewer than fifteen flights that had as their final destination the Los Cipresales Airbase, located a few miles north of Guatemala City's downtown.

The history behind the Dominican rebel organisation, which at some point adopted the name Ejército de Liberación del Caribe (Caribbean Liberation Army) or ELC, is long and convoluted, and beyond the scope of this study; suffice it to say that the group was led by a wealthy rancher named Juan Rodríguez, who had escaped from the Dominican Republic in February 1946 and had settled in Havana, Cuba, where he set out to organise an armed group aimed at overthrowing the Dominican Republic's fearsome dictator, Generalissimo Rafael Leónidas Trujillo.

Above: C-47 0653 (ex 43-1136, ex T-2) photographed during one of the relief missions that the FAG transports conducted over the Guatemalan Pacific coast in October 1949. *Guatemalan Air Force Photo Archives via LAAHS*

Right: This photo was taken aboard the C-47 serialed 0749 (ex 43-15580, ex T-3) during one of the relief missions that the FAG transports conducted over the Guatemalan Pacific coast in October 1949. The bundles containing food and medicines can be seen already strapped to their respective parachutes. *Guatemalan Air Force Photo Archives via LAAHS*

After arriving in Havana, Rodríguez – now calling himself General – secured the moral and financial support of President Arévalo, who promptly provided him with 1,000 Mauser rifles that his government had purchased in Argentina for the Guatemalan Army, as well as enough ammunition to start a small war. The Cuban President, Ramón Grau, also sympathised with Rodríguez's cause and allowed him to operate freely across the island. Hence, by May 1947, Rodríguez had already assembled a fairly well-equipped force of 1,200 men, composed of Cubans, Dominicans, Hondurans, Nicaraguans, Venezuelans and a few Spaniards. In addition, the old general had also acquired small numbers of fighter, bomber and transport aircraft, as well as a handful of cargo and assault ships. Less than a month later, and without much fanfare, Rodríguez's staff decided that the invasion should be launched no later than mid-August.

By the end of July, however, diplomatic pressure exerted by the US Department of State and the Dominican Republic forced President Grau to ask Gen. Rodríguez to relocate his troops from the Polytechnic School at Holguín, where they had been training, to the less conspicuous Cayo Confites, which was an island roughly 800 yards long and 200 yards wide, described by some members of Rodríguez's outfit as the most inhospitable place on the Cuban coast. Not surprisingly, the troops' morale plummeted within days due to the harsh conditions in which they were living and due to the uncertainty about when the invasion would be launched, as D-Day was being constantly postponed by Gen. Rodríguez's staff.

By mid-September, following a pitched gun battle between President Grau's police and members of the military establishment, the Cuban Army Chief of Staff, General Genovevo Pérez Dámera, set out to restore order and rounded up all illegal arms in the country, including all the armament, aircraft and ships of Rodríguez's organisation. A true patriot, Pérez Dámera had fumed over what he viewed as the prostitution of the Cuban Army's authority by Grau in letting an armed force organise and train at will in the country.

Sensing that the apprehension of his personnel was imminent, General Rodríguez ordered his force to abandon Cayo Confites on 22 September in the few ships that they had there. However, after mounting difficulties and sailing aimlessly around the island for a couple of days, the Cuban Navy captured and disarmed them on the 29th and took them to Campo Columbia where, on 3 October, a judge ordered their release stating that they had posed no threat to the nation. Shortly after, the Cuban Army returned Rodríguez the 1,000 Mauser rifles, as well as other weapons and ammunition that had been captured, and ordered him to leave the island as soon as possible, along with his staff. That is when the FAG C-47s had come to pick them up. Ironically, as will be seen, this would not be the only time that the Guatemalan pilots had to go to the rescue of the Dominican rebels.

The last international flight made by a FAG C-47 that year occurred on 16 November when the aircraft T-1 was sent to NAS Miami carrying a crew that would ferry a Grumman JRF-6B Goose that the Ministry of Defence had acquired for the use of President Arévalo. The VIP-configured seaplane arrived in La Aurora Airbase the following day, accompanied by T-1, whose crew had provided navigation services during the return flight. From then on, Arévalo's Goose became a familiar sight at Lake Amatitlán, some 15 miles south of the capital, as the Presidential chalet was situated there. In fact, it was in that luxurious residence that Arévalo took the extraordinary step of committing his support to Juan Rodríguez's organisation, now going by the name of Ejército de Liberación de América (American Liberation Army) or ELA, in a written document, the so-called Pacto de Alianza (Pact of Alliance), which was signed by himself and the revolutionaries on 16 December 1947. In that document, they jointly

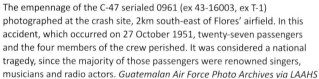

The empennage of the C-47 serialed 0961 (ex 43-16003, ex T-1) photographed at the crash site, 2km south-east of Flores' airfield. In this accident, which occurred on 27 October 1951, twenty-seven passengers and the four members of the crew perished. It was considered a national tragedy, since the majority of those passengers were renowned singers, musicians and radio actors. *Guatemalan Air Force Photo Archives via LAAHS*

Above: What was left of the nose section of 0961 after the transport crashed after the starboard engine caught fire during its take-off roll at Flores' on 27 October 1951. *Guatemalan Air Force Photo Archives via LAAHS*

Top: According to eyewitnesses, 0961 crashed after its right engine caught fire during the take-off roll at Flores on 27 October 1951. Here parts of the right-wing fuel tank and nacelle can be seen.
Guatemalan Air Force Photo Archives via LAAHS

laid down the framework through which they would carry out the liberation of the Dominican Republic, Costa Rica and Nicaragua from the tyrannical regimes that they then suffered under. It is worth noting that the Pacto actually named Nicaragua as the first target, but a wealthy Costa Rican landowner named José 'Pépe' Figueres convinced the ELA leadership to go after his country's president first. What occurred in Costa Rica was discussed at length in Chapter 7, since both parties, Figueres' rebels and the government, widely utilised variants of the Douglas DC-3 and C-47 during that conflict.

Meanwhile, in January 1948, relations between the United Kingdom and Guatemala became tense once again due to the centuries-long territorial dispute over British Honduras, known to the Guatemalans as Belice. Encouraged by a widespread anti-imperialist sentiment on the continent, President Arévalo decided to try – for the first time – a military solution to end the dispute. Hence, around 15 January, the three FAG C-47s, as well as two from AVIATECA, began transporting troops from Guatemala City to the Army garrison at Flores, in El Petén, from whence the soldiers deployed to the towns of Melchor de Mencos and El Arenal, both situated very close to the demarcation line that served as border with the British colony. The scarce available documentation indicates that the plan was to land the three FAG C-47s at Belize City Airport carrying 190 soldiers, who would capture it along with the British Army garrison and other key buildings in the capital. Simultaneously, the troops deployed at Melchor de Mencos and El Arenal would seize the town of Benque

Viejo del Carmen and advance towards Belize City with the aim of aiding in its capture. In both cases, FAG AT-6s would provide close air support to the ground troops, while the AT-11s would bomb the port of Belize City in order to discourage any potential British attempts of disembarking troops.

Even though the plan seemed far-fetched, considering that the Guatemalan Army was risking being completely annihilated by one of the world's great powers, the truth is that the timing could not have been more appropriate, since the few British troops that were stationed in the colony at that time, wouldn't have been capable of withstanding an attack of that magnitude. In fact, if executed correctly, the operation would have given the Guatemalan government enough time to seek the mediation of the Organisation of American States, or even the United Nations, and then negotiate with the British from a better position.

Much to President Arevalo's regret, however, the US Military Mission got wind of what was occurring and rushed to inform the US Embassy, which, in turn, alerted the British Legation. Predictably, three Royal Navy cruisers were rushed to British Honduras immediately, with the first arriving on 27 February and the other two on 1 March. Four days later, more than 1,000 British troops had already secured Belize City, as well as the majority of the towns close to the border with Guatemala.

The mysterious 0515 seen here at La Aurora Airbase, sometime after being incorporated in the FAG inventory. *Dan Hagedorn Collection*

Even though the British military presence in Belize made any Guatemalan attack virtually impossible, during the following weeks the FAG C-47s kept flying troops to Flores, where the Guatemalan Army had established the headquarters of the newly created Fuerzas Expedicionarias de El Petén (El Petén Expeditionary Forces) or FEP, which – at least on paper – would have the mission of safeguarding the national sovereignty in that region. Curiously, by May, the FEP had established forward operating bases in the towns of Melchor de Mencos, Santa Cruz Frontera and in the small inland port of Modesto Méndez, as well as a second garrison near the airfield at Poptún, all very close to the demarcation line with the British colony.

For its part, the FAG AT-6s and AT-11s began flying a series of armed patrols along the border with Belize, while the C-47s were employed – for the very first time in the history of the Guatemalan air arm – for conducting paratroop drops. In fact, by October, Lts Plinio Grazioso and René Cuellar, both military pilots, had established the FAG's pararescue unit, which they intended to expand – eventually – to a full parachute battalion.

The last notable event of 1948 in which the FAG C-47s were involved occurred during the evening of 27 November when 300 rebels, led by Col (ret.) Marciano Casado, attacked with machine guns and hand grenades the Army garrison and the port facilities at Puerto Barrios. Even though the few policemen and Army soldiers guarding those buildings were caught by surprise, they were able to hold out until the break of dawn on the 28th, when a pair of AT-6s arrived in the area and began strafing the rebel positions. Then, around midday, the three FAG C-47s landed at the town's airfield carrying 100 troops, who immediately went after the insurgents, managing to round up the majority of them on the outskirts of the town as they were trying to escape. By midday, one of the C-47s – escorted by an AT-6 – returned to Guatemala City carrying twenty-six prisoners on board, including Col Casado.

C-47 serial 0749 at Malden AFB in November 1955. By then, the colour scheme of the FAG C-47s had changed considerably, with the addition of the white upper side of the fuselage and the black lettering. *Mitch Mayborn via AAHS*

Around the third week of April 1949, Gen. Juan Rodríguez needed to ferry back to Guatemala the Mauser rifles and other combat equipment that his organisation had loaned to José Figueres for his revolution in Costa Rica the previous year. President Arévalo, always happy to lend a hand, arranged for two of the FAG C-47s to help in the process. Hence, on the 22nd, the aircraft T-1 and T-2, along with a Costa Rican-registered B-18B, began flying the arms from the Costa Rican capital to the La Aurora Airbase in Guatemala City. Even though there is not much documentation about the highly secret operation, it seems that the FAG transports completed no fewer than six flights during that week, all conducted by the same four aviators: Lt Col Eduardo Wayman and Maj. Carlos Sarti in T-1, and Lt Col Julio Archila and Maj. Luis Urrutia de León in T-2.

It turned out that the transfer of the arms to Guatemala was actually part of the final phase of yet another clandestine operation of Gen. Rodríguez's organisation, which by then had adopted the grandiose name of Legión del Caribe, or Caribbean Legion. As in the previous adventure, which had ended in the Cayo Confites fiasco, this new operation was aimed at invading the Dominican Republic and deposing Trujillo. However, instead of involving a large force, the plan was actually much simpler: initially, Legion operatives would smuggle arms and combat equipment into the island nation and create what they rather optimistically called the Internal Front. Then, a relatively small cadre of veterans and leaders would be airlifted, along with as many weapons as could be carried, to designated locations, and once there, inflame the local population, train and arm them on the spot, and then launch an all-out attack against Ciudad Trujillo.

It may never be known how General Rodríguez managed to convince President Arévalo to support him in his new plan. The truth is that by the end of April, besides the substantial aid that he had provided to the Legion thus far, Arévalo also had arranged access to something that the organisation had never enjoyed: an actual base of operations.

Located 77km south of Guatemala City, San José Airbase had been built by the US Army in 1942 as part of a regional network of airfields from which patrol flights could be launched in order to protect the approaches to the vital Panama Canal. However, on 19 April 1949, the US government transferred it formally to its Guatemalan counterpart. Since the FAG was not prepared to take over such a first-class air station, at least not at the time, President Arévalo decided to lend it temporarily to Rodríguez's organisation. Hence, by 23 May, the Legion had already based at least six aircraft there, including a relatively exotic Douglas DST-144/C-49E bearing the Mexican civil registration XA-HOS, a Curtiss C-46 also registered in Mexico as XB-HUV, a Consolidated PBY-5A/OA-10 Catalina seaplane carrying the US registration N1096M, a C-47 that remains unidentified to this day, an Avro Anson Mk V and a diminutive Cessna Model T-50 Bobcat. Additionally, the Legion had a second PBY-5A/OA-10 docked at the former Pan American Airways seaplane terminal at Puerto Barrios, on the Caribbean coast, which right after its arrival in the country had been painted in full FAG markings!

For manning the ragtag air force, the Legion had hired a group of pilots, among which a US Department of State report listed the North Americans Herbert Maroot, John Chewing, George Scruggs, Ralph Wells and Robert Hosford, as well as the Mexican nationals Pablo Herrera and Arturo Camacho, and the Nicaraguan Alejandro Selva. However, it seems that these aviators were not fully aware of what they were getting into, since shortly before dawn on the operation's D-Day, 18 June, as the Legion leadership briefed the aircrews on the details of the plan, the pilots Wells, Hosford, Herrera and Camacho promptly deserted the San José Airbase with the unidentified C-47 and one of the PBY-5As and headed for Mexico, while the crews of the C-46 and the C-49E, all Mexicans, were forced to stay at gunpoint. Minutes later, Gen. Juan Rodríguez, now lacking two important transport aircraft, contacted President Arévalo for help. Thus, without losing any time, Arévalo ordered the FAG commander, Lt Col Francisco Cosenza, to lend two of the FAG C-47s to the expedition in order to fill the gap as shuttle aircraft to fly at least some percentage of the arms to a halfway refuelling point in Cozumel, Mexico. This was an exceptional action on the part of an established hemispheric nation and, either because the action was directed at such short notice or because no orders were issued to the contrary, C-47s T-1 and T-2 embarked on this escapade in full FAG markings, crewed by Guatemalan aviators. In fact, a US Department of State document indicates that the pilots manning those aircraft were Capts Gerardín Mazariegos Sanabria and Ángel René Valenzuela, as well as Lts Factor Méndez and Manuel de Jesús Girón.

In the end, Gen. Rodríguez mustered his Legionnaires at the San José Airbase, and following a brief series of exhortations, the men loaded the C-49E and C-46, as well as the two FAG C-47s, and headed for Puerto Barrios, where a much smaller force was finishing loading the remaining PBY-5A/OA-10 Catalina. Around midday, the four land-planes flew over Puerto Barrios twice, signalling the men there to get on with the operation. Thus, the crew of the Catalina duly fired up the two engines and attempted to take off, only to find that the amphibian would not get off the water as she was overloaded. Five repeated attempts to take off failed.

Unaware that the Catalina had not been able to get airborne, the four transports headed for the refuelling rendezvous on Cozumel, Mexico, shortly after midday. Even though the C-49E and C-46 had been described by several of the Legion leaders as 'of the first quality' and 'ideal' for the expedition, the truth was that both aircraft were lacking important instruments, especially the C-46, which had a primary altimeter that refused to operate properly. In fact, this aircraft soon got separated from the other three in the middle of a rainstorm and never arrived in Cozumel. In any case, for reasons that remain unclear to this day, the expedition ended abruptly when the C-49E and the two FAG C-47s were seized immediately upon landing at Cozumel by Mexican authorities.

As for the Catalina, it was not until the next day, 19 July, that she was able to depart Puerto Barrios, with her crew totally unaware of what had transpired with the rest of the fleet. In fact, this amphibian became the solitary element of the entire force to reach its intended target, but was destroyed by two Dominican P-51 Mustangs that strafed her shortly after landing at Luperón Bay.

Even though the Mexican government tried to play down the whole incident and rushed to release the two FAG C-47s and their crews, the Dominican regime made a great deal out of it, accusing the Guatemalan government of blatant aggression. Hence, by 24 June, the Arévalo administration was already in damage control mode, denying any involvement in the expedition, claiming that from 17 to 23 June, T-1 never left Guatemala and that T-2 had been in Houston, Texas. However, the US Department of State was quick to conduct its own investigation and determined that neither of the two transports had been at La Aurora nor at Houston during those days.

The international scandal was the proverbial straw that broke the camel's back, since it convinced a good part of the extremely conservative Guatemalan society, as well as members of the right-wing political parties, that Arévalo was a Communist who had to be deposed. In fact, not even the Army escaped the country's polarisation, since much of the 'old guard', who consisted of officers who had gone through their military lives without professional studies and had earned their ranks through hard work or simply by being loyal to the dictator in turn, considered Arévalo a progressive who favoured 'career' officers, as they called those officers who had attended the Escuela Politécnica – the Guatemalan Army's Military Academy – and had achieved their ranks by rigorous promotions every four years. Due to their academic background, the career officers tended to look down on the line officers, even if the latter held higher ranks, and considered them uncouth remnants of dictatorial times. The resulting division was more than evident in the strained relationship between Lt Cols Jacobo Arbenz and Francisco Javier Arana, Arevalo's Defence Minister and the Chief of the Armed Forces respectively, since Arana was a line officer, while Arbenz had graduated, with the highest honours, from the Escuela Politécnica.

In any case, a couple of days after the news of the failed invasion had reached Guatemala, Lt Col Arana set out to seize all the armament the Caribbean Legion still had in the country, especially 400 of the Mauser rifles that had been left behind at Puerto Barrios when they could not be loaded on to the Catalina. Reacting much faster, Arbenz ordered Lt Col Cosenza to send the C-47s T-1 and T-2 to pick them up and transport them to La Aurora Airbase. From there, the arms were secretly trucked to El Morlón, the presidential retreat located on the shores of Lake Amatitlán.

Virtually the entire FAG C-47 fleet can be seen in this image, taken at La Aurora Airbase. Note the differences in the antenna configuration as well as the engine nacelles of the three aircraft. *Guatemalan Air Force Photo Archives via LAAHS*

On his part, Arana spent almost two weeks vainly looking for the rifles across the Guatemalan capital at first, and then at Puerto Barrios and at the San José Airbase. It was not until 18 July, though, that President Arévalo himself told him where Cosenza had hidden the arms. Furious, Arana fired Cosenza immediately and appointed Lt Col Arturo Altolaguirre Ubico as the new FAG Commander. He then headed to El Morlón in order to seize the cache of arms. However, a couple of hours later, Lt Col Arana was ambushed and killed on the outskirts of the town of Amatitlán, while returning to the capital after having confiscated the weapons. To this date, there are many conflicting versions of what really happened, but friends and acquaintances of the deceased lieutenant colonel soon learned that Arbenz's bodyguards as well as members of a leftist political party, and even a congressman, had been involved in the assassination. Some accounts even placed Arbenz on a hill nearby, watching the ambush unfold.

Predictably, a large group of Army officers, supported by leaders of right-leaning political parties and sympathisers of Arana, staged a revolt at the Guardia de honour garrison. Arbenz, on the other hand, summoned labour union members and peasants with whom he organised civilian battalions that joined the few loyal Army troops in the defence of the government. What followed was, in fact, the bloodiest rebellion that Arevalo's administration had to face during its tenure.

Initially, the FAG had sided with the rebels, as Altolaguirre was a good friend of Arana, but during the evening of the 19th, Lt Col Cosenza and a group of pilots, supported by loyal troops and armed civilians, assaulted La Aurora Airbase and captured Altolaguirre and other rebel aviators. Shortly after, at least three AT-6s took off and went to strafe and bomb the Guardia de Honor, as well as other positions held by the rebels across the capital. The air arm's participation was short, though, since by the next day, it had lost two of the Texans and had run out of 25lb bombs. In the afternoon of the 20th, the rebels finally surrendered and the government troops regained control of the Guardia de Honor. By then, the confrontation had left a death toll of 150 and more than 200 wounded. Incredibly, the bloodiest coup attempt that Arévalo's administration had to face during its period ended in a rather anticlimactic way: On 21 July, the government issued a stark press release stating that the assassins of Lt Col Arana seemed to be 'mysterious outlaws, friends of his', who had killed him after having an argument, and that the incident was under investigation.

Once the dust had settled, Col Carlos Paz Tejada, Head of the Defence Council, arranged the substitution of the unit commanders who had been involved in the failed revolt with officers considered neutral, meaning that they were not sympathisers of Arbenz or Arana. In the case of the FAG, Col Cosenza was replaced by Col Luis Antonio Girón Cartagena, who was an experienced aviator with a degree in aircraft engineering. In fact, shortly after Girón took over the air force, the service's three C-47s underwent a thorough inspection and maintenance procedure, which also included updating their avionics, radios and navigation equipment. Externally, those changes were reflected in the installation of a tall antenna mast atop the forward fuselage and the removal of the distinctive astrodome that was installed in nearly all the C-47s during the Second World War.

By early August, Col Girón had ordered a full reorganisation of the FAG, which entailed the creation of nine composite squadrons, each of them to be equipped with trainer, fighter, bomber, transport and utility aircraft. The idea was that each squadron could function as a self-sufficient unit, regardless of where they were based. The reorganisation also included the introduction of a new serialing system that consisted of a two-digit prefix that identified the squadron and a two-digit suffix for identifying the aircraft within the squadron. This new system, which has been the source of endless confusion among aero-historians for decades, presented a complication: while the prefix followed a logical numerical progression, the suffix was assigned randomly. Thus, in the case of the C-47s, they ended up in three different squadrons, with T-1 receiving the serial 0961, T-2 becoming 0653, and T-3 being reserialed as 0749, besides receiving full FAG colours for the first time since she was handed over by the US Military Mission almost three years earlier.

Not all the squadrons were fully equipped by then, though. For example, 0961 was the only aircraft in the 9th squadron, while 0653 joined a Boeing P-26A and an AT-6D in the 6th squadron. In the case of 0749, her stablemates in the 7th squadron were an AT-6D and an AT-11. Col Girón's idea was to acquire more aircraft in the coming months in order to equip all the squadrons. Accordingly, on 12 October, the Guatemalan Ambassador in Washington approached the Department of State with an informal request for purchase, among other aircraft types, eighteen North American P-51s for the purpose of 'strengthening the Guatemalan Air Force'. The request was rejected by the Bureau of Inter-American Affairs, however, stating that the aircraft could not be exported in view of prevailing unsettled conditions in the Caribbean area, in an obvious reference to the failed invasion of the Dominican Republic that Arévalo's government had supported. In fact, it took years for the FAG to acquire enough aircraft to fully equip just one of the composite squadrons before the concept was abandoned.

The C-47 serialed 525 seen in a rather embarrassing position at Teculután airfield on 25 May 1956, during the operation for retrieving the bodies of the victims who died in the crash of TG-AHA at mount Raxón. *Guatemalan Air Force Photo Archives via LAAHS*

Excellent view of the C-47 serial 515 over the Motagua Valley during a parachuting mission sometime in 1956. *Guatemalan Air Force Photo Archives via LAAHS*

Members of the 1st Parachute Platoon posing before the C-47 serialed 520 at La Aurora Airbase, before their graduation jump on 30 June 1961 over Campo de Marte. *Guatemalan Air Force Photo Archives via LAAHS*

Along with the prohibition of exporting military aircraft to Guatemala, the US government imposed a spare parts and ammunition embargo that did not impact the FAG operations immediately, but did it in the medium term. As a matter of fact, in mid-October, the three C-47s were involved in a relief operation, the first of its kind carried out by the FAG, which required the C-47s 0653 and 0749 to be deployed to the San José Airbase, from where they flew no fewer than 170 missions parachuting food and medicine over towns and villages that had been affected by floods after heavy rains had hit the highlands and the Pacific coast of the country. For its part, aircraft 0961 was tasked with flying supplies from the capital to said airbase, supported by the last three remaining AT-11s and a recently acquired C-45. Also, around that time, 0961 conducted a search mission over Escuintla, looking for the AT-6D FAG serial 52 that went missing while en route from Guatemala City to the San José Airbase, transporting a medic who was required at said airbase. In fact, within hours the crew of the C-47 was able to locate the wreckage of the Texan on a hill at the Terranova ranch, near San Vicente Pacaya. Unfortunately, the pilot. Lt Factor Méndez Álvarez, and the passenger, Doctor Carlos Martínez Palma, were killed upon impact in what was regarded as a controlled flight into terrain. Last but not least, two of the C-47s, most probably 0653 and 0961, conducted a long-range search mission along the Caribbean coast of the country, looking for a USAF OA-10B Catalina seaplane that went missing after departing France AFB, in the Panama Canal Zone, for Guatemala, where she was to have rescued a group of North American tourists that were trapped in the small village of Panajachel, on the shores of Lake Atitlán. In the end, it was determined that the Catalina, serial 45-57840, had crashed at sea near the Escudo de Veraguas Island, in Panama.

By December, the FAG was flying its aircraft to exhaustion, since the US was no longer providing any spare parts. In fact, an intelligence report of that time stated that all three FAG C-47s were operational but were fast wearing out due to poor maintenance. The report added that the FAG pilots did not consider these aircraft safe for flying. Instead, the FAG signed an agreement with AVIATECA under which the military pilots – to stay current – were incorporated into the airline as co-pilots at first, and later on as pilots and even as instructors. In fact, when the US Military Mission's C-47, serial 45-1113, crashed after taking off from La Tinta airfield, in Alta Verapaz on 31 January 1950, it was an AVIATECA C-47 – flown by a military crew – that was sent to rescue the North American aviators.

The year 1950 was an extremely complicated one for Arévalo's government, which barely made it to the next elections due to numerous coup attempts that occurred almost on a weekly basis. In fact, many controversial laws that left-wing parties wanted enacted were shelved and never sent to Congress through fear of enraging the opposition. One of those laws was the so-called 'Tenancy Law' that would mandate the expropriation of idle private lands and their redistribution among poor peasants and Indians.

Regarding the FAG C-47s, a report by the US Air Attaché dated on 30 June stated that the three aircraft still were operational, but were seldom flown. Similarly, another intelligence report from the US Military Mission's Air Section dated 1 September , mentioned that the FAG had three C-47s in service, their serials being T-1, T-2 and T-3, which was an error obviously, since by that date, the aircraft had already been assigned the four-digit serials.

In November, Col Jacobo Arbenz, former Defence Minister, was declared the winner of the presidential elections, even when there were several allegations of fraud at many polling centres. After his inauguration on 15 March 1951, Arbenz began implementing a government plan almost entirely based on the recommendations that a joint US–Canadian commission had drafted after a thorough study of the country's social and economic problems during Arevalo's administration. Such recommendations included the construction of at least one hydroelectric power generation plant, a new seaport on the Caribbean coast and a road to link said port with the capital. The commission's document also listed twenty-four additional recommendations, mainly related to agriculture, mining, education, labour and social issues. Regarding the armed forces, Arbenz immediately began negotiations with the US government in order to acquire new equipment, including aircraft, but as before, the requests were turned down.

C-47s 515, 520 and 525 dropping paratroopers somewhere over Honduras, during Operación Fraternidad in September 1962. *Guatemalan Air Force Photo Archives via Dan Hagedorn*

C-47s 515, 520, 525 and 530 dropping paratroopers somewhere over Retalhuleu in November 1962. *Guatemalan Air Force Photo Archives via LAAHS*

In April, Col Richard C. Hutchinson was appointed as the head of the USAF Mission and through his mediation the embargo imposed on the FAG was relaxed somewhat, so the flow of spare parts resumed enough to get the service's five AT-6s, three AT-11s, and three C-47s back on the flight line. In fact, by mid-May, the C-47s began conducting flights carrying renowned Guatemalan singers, musicians and radio actors, who performed widely acclaimed shows at remote towns and small villages as part of a civic projection programme called La Hora Cultural del Ejército, or The Army's Cultural Hour, which was also broadcast nationwide by the government's radio station.

Sadly, it was during one of those civic projection missions that the C-47 serialed 0961 crashed, killing twenty-seven passengers and the five members of the crew. This accident, considered a national tragedy since the majority of the passengers were beloved artists, occurred in the late afternoon of 27 October, at Flores' airfield, in El Petén. According to eyewitnesses, during the take-off roll a fire broke out in the starboard engine. Since the unpaved runway was a bit short, the pilot, Maj. Enrique Pérez Guisasola, decided to continue the take-off and climb to a safe altitude in order to deal with the emergency. However, ninety seconds after leaving the ground, the C-47 plunged into a wooded area 2km south-east of the airfield, in a slightly right-bank, nose-down attitude. Incredibly, five passengers were rescued alive from the burning wreckage and were taken to the hospital at San Benito,

where three of them died. Besides Maj. Pérez Guisasola, the crew comprised the co-pilot, Lt José Escobar Mendieta, and the mechanics Casiano Castañeda, Miguel De León and Enrique Meléndez.

During the following months, the Communists, now with considerable influence over the Congress and with individuals occupying key positions in the cabinet, set out to implement the reforms that the US–Canadian commission had recommended. They also brought back the infamous 'Tenancy Law' proposal and transformed it into a full-fledged agrarian reform, which was announced as the panacea that would end poverty and inequality in the country. Known as Decree No. 900, this controversial law was enacted on 18 June 1952 and marked the beginning of a series of expropriations of ranches and large farms that had been classified as 'idle land' by the Agriculture Ministry. Predictably, these confiscations outraged landowners and a large part of Guatemalan society, since they were considered a direct attack on private property. Furthermore, a North American firm called United Fruit Company (UFCO) which owned enormous banana plantations on both coasts of the country (besides the railway company, the telegraph service, and the country's two seaports) became a natural target of the land expropriations. Initially, the UFCO tried to negotiate with the government in order to be left out of them, but soon realised that the old methods of bribing and manipulating its way out were now futile, such was the discipline, determination and ruthlessness of the Communists conducting the agrarian reform.

By then, it was more than evident that the Communists' intentions were directed towards establishing a Marxist regime in Guatemala. Thus, businessmen, landowners and members of right-wing political parties decided to join forces and form an anti-Communist front, which staged numerous demonstrations in the country's capital, and at the same time, began plotting how to get rid of Arbenz. For its part, the UFCO's Public Relations office in Boston launched an extensive discrediting campaign, publishing in renowned media outlets a series of articles that presented damning evidence of a deep Communist penetration in Guatemala. The campaign went to such extremes that a full-length film about the country's precarious situation was produced and then screened across the US. Shortly after, UFCO representatives began lobbying the US Department of State, attempting to obtain a reaction from the Truman administration, which in turn, began taking timid steps towards fixing the situation, like providing funds, arms and combat equipment to a couple of Guatemalan exile groups in Honduras and El Salvador through a Central Intelligence Agency (CIA) overt programme code-named PBFortune. However, this did not take off due to insurmountable difficulties in shipping the arms and equipment while maintaining

C-47 serial 530 (C/N 20031, ex 43-15565) during a visit to Howard AFB, in the Panama Canal Zone, in December 1966. *Dan Hagedorn*

plausible deniability. It was not until January 1953, when the Eisenhower administration was inaugurated, that the idea of a covert military intervention gained enough traction. However, it took almost a year for the CIA to come up with a plan for getting rid of Arbenz. Code-named PBSuccess, the covert operation was approved by the CIA Director on 9 December of that year.

PBSuccess entailed a very sophisticated psychological warfare operation whose main components were a clandestine radio station and a tactical air force comprised of transport and fighter-bomber aircraft, both of which would support a small but well-equipped army of Guatemalan exiles that would simulate a major invasion of the country, led by a heroic caudillo who would replace Arbenz. The ultimate goal was to spread terror and uncertainty among the population, but especially in the Army, and induce them to depose Arbenz before facing total annihilation by a superior force.

Even though the CIA's premise was to maintain plausible deniability by disguising the operation as an indigenous rebel movement, the apparatus behind it was impressive. The project had its headquarters at a nearly abandoned naval air station located at Opa-Locka airport, some 19km north of Miami, Florida, while troop and radio-operator training sites were established on the outskirts of Managua, the capital of Nicaragua, along with an airbase at Las Mercedes airport. In addition, PBSuccess had its logistical centre at France AFB in the Panama Canal Zone and, later on, 'staging points' from where the simulated invasion was to be launched were established in Honduras and El Salvador. On its part, the broadcasting equipment of the clandestine radio-station was installed in an inconspicuous hut in the small village of Santa Fe, in Ocotepeque, Honduras, less than 6km from the border with Guatemala.

Regarding the heroic caudillo required for the operation, the CIA, disguised as an 'anonymous group of persons dedicated to the cause of free men and opposed to the dangers of Communism', approached many of the Guatemalan exiles in El Salvador and Honduras in order to evaluate them, but in the end the agency picked Lt Col Carlos Castillo Armas since he already had his own anti-Communist organisation in Honduras, or so he claimed, which could be turned into the small rebel army that the project needed. Castillo Armas also assured them that there was a clandestine organisation inside Guatemala that was willing to support him by conducting acts of sabotage and espionage.

Perhaps the most impressive component of the operation was the so-called rebel air force, which besides supporting the simulated invasion, would also conduct psychological operations, mostly leaflet-dropping missions, over the capital and other major towns. At first, the CIA authorised the project to acquire three C-47s and two Cessnas as its only air assets, but later on, the programme was allowed to procure tactical aircraft in the form of six Republic F-47N from the Puerto Rico Air National Guard and a solitary P-38M from the Nicaraguan Air Force. The C-47s and the F-47Ns were based initially at France AFB, but when the psychological warfare operations began in late May 1954, the aircraft were moved permanently to the forward operating airbase that the Agency established at Las Mercedes airport, in Managua, Nicaragua.

In any case, the initial phase of the covert operation was conducted in such a careless manner that by April, the Guatemalan government already had a pretty good idea of how the rebel organisation was composed, what their tactical plans were, and who their contacts were inside Guatemala. In fact, Arbenz, who did not completely trust the Army by then, rushed to organise the civil defence brigades, officially called Reserva de la Guardia Civil (Civil Guard Reserves), in order to establish the first line of defence against the upcoming invasion. Furthermore, earlier that year, Arbenz had sent a couple of his aides to Czechoslovakia to purchase an important load of arms and ammunition for these militias, even though it clearly was unconstitutional, since only the Army was allowed to have combat equipment in the country.

The arrival of the arms at Puerto Barrios aboard the Swedish ship SS *Alfhem* on 16 May, further strained the already tense relationship between Arbenz and the military, since the majority of officers considered that the President had ceded too much control to the Communists in his cabinet. In addition, they thought that the creation of the militias, besides being illegal, was insulting and extremely dangerous. Hence, when news of the *Alfhem*'s imminent arrival transpired, many senior Army officers, up to and including the Minister of Defense, Col Ángel Sánchez, took it upon themselves to seize the arms shipment.

Consequently, by midday, the two FAG C-47s, in their first mission during the crisis, landed at the airfield of Puerto Barrios, carrying the Minister of Defence and Col José Barzanallana, the Guardia de Honor Commanding Officer, along with 100 soldiers who promptly took control of the port. This action nearly ended in a confrontation with Maj. Alfonso Martínez Estevez, the man in charge of organising the civil defence brigades and Chief of the National Agrarian Department, who showed up at the port with a handful of trucks and a bunch of poorly organised 'agraristas', determined to retrieve the arms.

C-47 serial 535 (C/N 20732, ex 43-16266) during a visit to Howard AFB, in the Panama Canal Zone, in August 1966. *Dan Hagedorn*

The arrival of the arms also hastened the start of the tactical phase of PBSuccess, which consisted of the launch of the fake invasion. Thus, by 10 June, the CIA C-47s, as well as one provided by the Honduran Air Force, began flying supplies to the different staging points from where the invasion would be launched, which were established in Honduras, close to the border with Guatemala and, four days later, two of the Agency's C-47s entered Guatemalan airspace while conducting the first two supply-dropping missions along the routes that Castillo Armas' troops would follow towards the predefined locations from where they would launch harassment attacks against the towns of Jalapa, Chiquimula, Zacapa and Puerto Barrios. That same day, the CIA ordered that all the resident radio operators be infiltrated into Guatemala, so they could take up their respective positions and start sending vital information about the Army movements.

By then, the Guatemalan Army had got wind of what was brewing across the border and immediately set in motion a defence plan that consisted of setting up a protective barrier along the border with Honduras and El Salvador, with troops from the Puerto Barrios, Zacapa, Chiquimula and Jalapa garrisons, reinforced by companies from the 1st and 2nd Infantry Regiments from the Guardia de honour and the La Aurora garrisons respectively. This force took up the name of Ejército de Operaciones (Operations Army) and was led by Col Víctor M. León, who established the campaign headquarters at Zacapa, and two advance command posts at the towns of Chiquimula and Jalapa. Incredibly, the remote and rather vulnerable airfield at Puerto Barrios became the logistical centre for the campaign.

On 11 June, while the bulk of the 1st and 2nd Infantry Regiments was being transported by rail and trucks to the theatre of operations, the two FAG C-47s, along with two from AVIATECA, began airlifting men, equipment, and supplies to Puerto Barrios, Zacapa and Jalapa, in a sustained effort that lasted until the end of the campaign. These highly critical missions, flown while the CIA fighters were constantly violating Guatemalan airspace with impunity, were conducted without any escorts since Col Girón Cartagena had grounded all the FAG's combat aircraft after a couple of them had deserted to El Salvador. Fortunately, the cumbersome Douglas transports never encountered the Agency's fearsome F-47Ns!

The events that occurred during the following days, especially the air operations, are thoroughly documented in the book titled *PBSuccess: The CIA's covert operation to overthrow Guatemalan president Jacobo Arbenz in June-July 1954*, published by the authors, and will not be discussed here. Suffice it to say that Arbenz resigned on the evening of 27 June, just as the CIA was about to call off the entire operation due to a series of defeats sustained by Castillo Armas' forces. Subsequently, after endless negotiations in El Salvador, Castillo Armas became part of a temporary governing junta comprised of officers of the Guatemalan Army, which lasted less than a month, since CIA operatives assigned to the Guatemalan station convinced the other members of the junta to resign so Castillo Armas could become president. In the end, Castillo Armas' presidency was formally inaugurated on 1 September, and was reconfirmed by a plebiscite that took place on 10 October.

The FAG benefited greatly after PBSuccess, since US military assistance was resumed almost immediately under the Reimbursable Aid Program (RAP), allowing the air arm to receive – at last – its first three North American F-51D Mustangs in early July, along with an F-47N from the fleet the CIA had acquired for the covert operation. The Agency also handed over to the FAG one of the C-47s that had been originally provided to Castillo Armas' organisation, which was incorporated into the air arm with the serial number 0515. Unfortunately, the true identity of this aircraft remains unknown as she was thoroughly sanitised before being acquired for the clandestine project, with all identification plates, even those on the engines, removed in order to preclude any attempt of determining her origin. In any case, the declassified PBSuccess documentation gives some clues of its probable origin, stating that the 'very battered' aircraft was purchased in the Washington DC area from a civilian vendor around 14 May of that year. On the other hand, available photographic evidence indicates that she was an early C-47A equipped with simple ram air induction systems for her carburettors, as the small intakes atop the engine nacelles attest. She also had the characteristic astrodome and an array of antennas that definitively were not present in the other two FAG C-47s.

In December, the FAG received three additional F-51Ds for its fighter-bomber squadron, which thereafter became the government's 'weapon of choice' for projecting military power, both locally and beyond the country's borders, displacing the C-47s from the important role that the transports had played since 1946. In contrast, the C-47s began to perform rather mundane missions such as transporting supplies to the different Army garrisons across the country, conducting patrol flights over Guatemalan territorial waters looking for illegal fishing boats, and the habitual civic projection flights carrying high school students to the Mayan ruins of Tikal or transporting agricultural supplies to remote villages. Perhaps the most daring flights conducted during those days took place on 1 November 1955, when C-47 serial 0653 flew a group of pilots and mechanics to Malden AFB, in Dunklin County, Missouri, where they picked up a batch of twelve North American T-6G trainers that the FAG had acquired through the Mutual Defence Aid Program (MDAP). Then, on 28 November, C-47 serial 0749 accompanied those T-6Gs on their delivery flight from Malden to Guatemala.

During the first half of 1956, the FAG, now under the command of Lt Col Luis Urrutia De León, went through yet another reorganisation that included the disbanding of the composite squadrons that had been created seven years earlier, and the introduction of nine dedicated or 'specialised' squadrons. As before, such reorganisation entailed the introduction of a new serialing system for identifying the aircraft, which consisted of three-digit serials, with the first single-digit indicating the squadron number and the following two digits identifying the aircraft within the squadron. The two-digit suffix started invariably at 00 and progressed in multiples of the single-digit prefix. In the case of the Transport Squadron, which was equipped with two of the four surviving AT-11s, a C-45, as well as the three C-47s, its single-digit prefix was 5, therefore their assigned serials were 500 for the C-45, 505 and 510 for the AT-11s, while the C-47s were renumbered as follows: 0515 became 515, 0653 was reserialed as 520 and 0749 was assigned the new serial 525. Similarly, when the squadron was supplemented with three additional C-45s in August, such aircraft received the serials 530, 535 and 540. Regarding the other air units, the AT-6s and T-6Gs of the Training Squadron were serialed in the 2XX range, while the F-51Ds of the Fighter-bomber Squadron had their serials in the 3XX range. Likewise, the two AT-11s that had been assigned to an incipient Bomber Squadron received the serial 400 and 404, while the little Cessnas of the Liaisons Squadron were reserialed in the 6XX range.

Right: C-47s serials 500 (C/N 19687, ex 43-15221) and 505 (C/N 25249, ex 43-47988) photographed at La Aurora Airbase, in December 1967. *Tom Surlak via Dan Hagedorn*

Below: C-47 serial 540 (C/N 13980/25425, ex 43-48164) undergoing repairs at La Aurora Airbase, in November 1967. *Guatemalan Air Force Photo Archives via LAAHS*

On 24 May, one of the C-47s acquired by the FAG in 1945, but that had been transferred to AVIATECA shortly after its arrival, went missing during a scheduled flight from Puerto Barrios to Guatemala City, with thirty-two passengers on board and a crew of three. The aircraft, civil registration TG-AHA (ex 41-38669, ex T-1 and ex LG-AHA), disappeared in marginal weather conditions while approaching La Tinta airfield in Baja Verapaz for a planned stop. As soon as the news of the missing transport reached the capital, the FAG launched an unprecedented air search operation that involved its three C-47s, as well as a USAF Grumman HU-16 amphibian and a US Army Sikorsky UH-19B helicopter. In fact, it was this helicopter that located the wreck of TG-AHA early the following day, approximately 11km south-east of La Tinta, on the northern slopes of Mount Raxón, where she had crashed. The helicopter crew also discovered a badly wounded survivor among the aircraft's wreckage, prompting the immediate insertion of two FAG pararescue men who, carrying first aid kits, conducted a low-altitude jump from the UH-19B.

That same day, the C-47 520 transported an infantry platoon to La Tinta airfield, from where the soldiers continued on foot towards the crash site in order to help with the retrieval of the bodies of the victims, which would be taken to a morgue that had been set up at the airfield in the town of Teculután, some 32km south of Mount Raxón. In addition, the C-47 serial 525 transported another infantry platoon to Teculután, which would also be sent to Mount Raxón to support the extraction operation. Near midday, President Castillo Armas, his Minister of Defence and the Director of Civil Aeronautics arrived in Teculután aboard the C-47 515 in order to personally supervise the entire operation. Much to the FAG crew's dismay, while the President was at the airfield, the C-47 525 suffered a nose-over upon landing while carrying medical personnel that would perform the autopsies on the bodies of the victims. Fortunately, the aircraft did not sustain any damage and after a thorough on-site check, she was declared flyable again. In fact, the C-47 525 along with 515 began transporting the first bodies to the capital during that same afternoon.

After the assassination of President Castillo Armas on 26 July 1957, the country entered a tumultuous period that saw three short-lived de facto governments and the beginning of a left-leaning movement that sought to reinstate the political, social and economic achievements that the 1944 revolution had brought, many of which had been reversed after the CIA-sponsored counter-revolution ten years later. In fact, the temporary government led by Gen. Guillermo Flores Avendaño prohibited any of the left-leaning political parties to present candidates for the upcoming general elections, tacitly favouring the coalition of political organisations led by Gen. (Ret.) Miguel Ydígoras Fuentes, a conservative who had served under the dictator Ubico and that the CIA had considered for leading the fake invasion that deposed Arbenz. In the end, Ydígoras was not picked because the CIA deemed him too authoritarian and corrupt for the job!

To no one's surprise, Gen. Ydígoras was inaugurated on 2 March 1958, and as predicted, it did not take long for the press to begin reporting acts of corruption and mismanagement in his administration. Resourceful as he was, every time that a scandal was reported, Ydígoras orchestrated fake or even real incidents to draw away the attention of the press and the public in general, usually appealing to national pride and disregarding any caution. As a matter of fact, one such event almost sparked a war with neighbouring Mexico late in December of that year. It all started when the three FAG C-47s began flying periodic patrols over the Pacific coast of the country, looking for foreign ships fishing illegally inside Guatemalan territorial waters. During one such flight, conducted on 28 December, a C-47 located a group of thirteen Mexican shrimp boats fishing just off the coast of the port of Champerico, in Retalhuleu. The next day, a pair of AT-6s were sent to investigate and upon confirming that the ships were not Guatemalan, the FAG Commander, Col Luis Urrutia de León, was ordered to organise an operation aimed to either capture or destroy the illegal boats.

Named officially Operación Drake (Operation Drake), the punitive action was launched on 31 December, when the C-47 serialed 525 arrived over the area where the Mexican boats were still fishing and visually confirmed their nationality. Then, the transport established a circular pattern at 5,000ft over the area and assumed the role of a command and communication platform for the operation. Also aboard the aircraft were journalists and photographers of virtually every local newspaper, who would document everything that was about to take place. Next, a FAG Cessna 182 – equipped with a loudspeaker – was sent to make several low-altitude passes over the boats, warning them that they were in Guatemalan waters and that they had to proceed towards Champerico for questioning. When the crews of the boats blatantly ignored the orders, three F-51D Mustangs were brought into the area and began firing warning shots ahead and behind the boats repeatedly. Predictably, the ships changed course, trying to flee towards Mexico at full speed. Then, the Cessna was brought in again, and made a couple of passes ordering the boats to head towards the Guatemalan port immediately, but once more the crews ignored the orders. In the end, the F-51D pilots strafed the boats, seriously damaging three of them, as well as wounding fourteen crew members and killing three, including the captain of one of the vessels. For its part, the C-47 serial 525 sustained some damage to the left windshield after hitting a vulture while trying to land on a beach near Ocós, where one of the damaged boats had run aground. As expected, the situation escalated rather quickly during the following hours, since the Mexican government broke diplomatic relations with its Guatemalan counterpart and, shortly after, both nations mobilised troops towards the border, showing no qualms about going to war. Fortunately, the embarrassing incident was left behind after eight tense months, when both governments agreed to re-establish diplomatic relations.

In the meantime, however, the discontent among the population due to the rampant corruption in the government gave way to a couple of revolts launched by ill-trained and poorly equipped left-leaning groups, which the Army crushed in short order. There were also a series of demonstrations clamouring for Ydígoras' resignation, which the National Police subdued with ease. What no one noticed by then was a large group of disgruntled junior Army officers who not only resented the government's corruption scandals, which had reached even the highest ranks of the armed forces, but also that Ydígoras had allowed the CIA to build an airbase and a training camp at Retalhuleu, where Cuban exiles were training for the ill-fated Bay of Pigs Invasion. The group of malcontents, which had adopted secretly the name of Asociación del Niño Dios (God Child Association), considered that the presence of foreign troops on Guatemalan soil was a serious affront not only to the constitution, but to the Army and the nation as whole. In addition, the members of the Asociación wanted to purge the Army of corrupt elements and punish those senior officers who had betrayed Arbenz during the CIA-sponsored invasion of 1954.

C-47 serial 550 (C/N 26286/14841, ex 43-49025) on 17 January 1970, at the Tocumen International Airport, in Panama City, while accompanying the FAG's T-33 aerobatic team. *Dan Hagedorn*

On 13 November 1960, some 120 junior officers and 3,000 enlisted soldiers, led by a group of colonels who were members of the Asociación, launched a more-or-less co-ordinated attack against Fort Matamoros –the Army headquarters located in the capital – and the Zacapa garrison, as well as the Puerto Barrios Airbase. The objective was to acquire enough weapons and ammunition in order to equip a credible force that could capture the rest of the Army garrisons in the city, but especially the National Palace, and then force President Ydígoras to resign. However, the rebel group that was tasked with capturing Matamoros met a vastly superior and better-equipped force and had to escape in trucks and jeeps towards Zacapa, where rebel troops, led by Lt Luis Trejo Esquivel, had already captured the garrison in that city. By then, Col Eduardo Llerena Müller, leading a large group of rebel soldiers, had also managed to capture the Puerto Barrios Airbase, practically without firing a single shot.

Furious, President Ydígoras ordered the FAG commander, Col Miguel Angel Ponciano to send the F-51D fighters and recently acquired Douglas B-26 attack aircraft to destroy the rebel convoy, but Col Ponciano refused, stating emphatically that the air force would remain neutral! Ironically, it was the CIA B-26s based at Retalhuleu that went after the rebels and bombed the Zacapa garrison and the Puerto Barrios Airbase, effectively suppressing the coup once and for all. In fact, the loyal Army troops that were rushed to capture the Army installations held by the rebels had to be transported in a couple of Curtiss C-46 transports that were provided by the Agency, which were also based at Retalhuleu. In the end, a considerable number of rebel officers escaped capture, among them Lts Marco Antonio Yon Sosa, Luis Augusto Turcios Lima and Luis Trejo Esquivel, who had recently returned from counter-insurgency training at Fort Benning in Georgia and Fort Gulick in the Panama Canal Zone.

In August 1961, Yon Sosa, Turcios Lima and Trejo Esquivel announced the formation of a guerrilla group named Movimiento Revolucionario 13 de Noviembre (Revolutionary Movement 13 of November), which was based on nationalistic principles and, through armed rebellion, sought to instate social justice and a just redistribution of the national wealth. It was not until early 1962, however, that the MR-13 began operations by launching a series of hit-and-run attacks against installations of the United Fruit Company in Izabal, as well as against offices of the National Police in Zacapa and Chiquimula. Shortly after, the insurgents began ambushing regular Army units patrolling the Atlantic highway, usually while transiting from Zacapa to Izabal.

At first, the Army was able to cope with the sporadic attacks launched by the MR-13, managing to keep the insurgent organisation in constant movement and denying them the chance to establish a social base in the areas where they were operating. However, the spectacular nature of the guerrilla attacks sparked solidarity demonstrations and student walkouts in the capital, which despite being violently dispersed by the police, encouraged Marxist organisations and left-wing student groups to establish contact with the MR-13 and offer them not only funds, manpower and eventually armament, but also political direction. By that time, in fact, these organisations were already sending young students to Cuba to receive guerrilla warfare training. Shortly after, the MR-13 leadership and the Marxist organisations began talks in order to form a coalition aimed at instating a Communist regime in Guatemala by means of armed rebellion.

By then, the Guatemalan armed forces' leadership had realised that they were no longer facing a band of outlaws but a well-organised guerrilla force and that it was necessary to implement counter-insurgency tactics as soon as possible, as well as stepping up the training of officers and enlisted men in irregular warfare techniques. In the case of the FAG, two measures were taken: The first was the formation of 'hunter-killer' flights comprised of two or

C-47 serial 555 (C/N 16820/33499, ex 44-77167) taking off from La Aurora Airbase in July 1969. This aircraft, along with the one serialed 550, were delivered in VIP configuration. However, by 1972 both aircraft had been converted to troop carriers. *Guatemalan Air Force Photo Archives via LAAHS*

three F-51Ds and a single B-26, which were permanently on alert at La Aurora Airbase and were scrambled as soon as a guerrilla column was spotted or close air support was required; the other was that the newly created 1st Parachute Platoon – led by Lt Benedicto Lucas García – began conducting jumps from the FAG C-47s in areas where it was known that the guerrillas had established camps or training centres, and then launching search and destroy operations in said areas. So effective were those 'vertical insertions' that the FAG leadership requested the help of the US Military Mission in acquiring two additional C-47s in order to increase the air arms' capability for such type of airborne counter-insurgency operations.

Paperwork for the transfer of the two C-47s began in May 1962, under the newly created Military Aid Program – commonly known as MAP – and materialised on 25 August, when the first aircraft arrived in La Aurora Airbase. She was a C-47A-85-DL (C/N 20031, ex USAF 43-15565) that was assigned the FAG serial 530, effectively replacing a C-45 that had been retired due to attrition. Meanwhile, the delivery of the second C-47s was scheduled for late November, since the selected airframe still had to undergo a full overhaul before being transferred.

This aircraft, FAG serial 560 (C/N 17131/34398, ex 45-1128), turned out to be the last MAP-supplied C-47. She was delivered on 20 August 1970 and survived to be converted to a BT-67 in 1992.
Alberto Fortner via George G. Farinas

Above: The Transport Squadron's mechanics posing before C-47 serial 540 in December 1971. Of interest is the 'invasion' camouflage scheme of the aircraft, which was sported by the majority of the FAG C-47s from 1970 to 1973. A truly nightmare for scale modellers who value historical realism, this scheme seems to be comprised of three different tones of green.
Guatemalan Air Force Photo Archives via LAAHS

Left: C-47 serial 535, sporting the 'invasion' camouflage scheme, is seen here taking off from La Aurora Airbase in December 1971.
Guatemalan Air Force Photo Archives via LAAHS

Around this time, the CIA published an estimate stating that the growing rebel movement in Guatemala was in fact the first attempt of Fidel Castro at exporting the so-called 'Cuban Revolution' to Central America. In the document, the Agency urged the US government to take the appropriate steps to mitigate the possibility of a Communist contagion that could affect the entire region in the short term, and assist the rest of the Latin American countries in dealing with Marxist uprisings. Accordingly, in September, the US Army's Caribbean Command organised an unprecedented counter-insurgency exercise in Honduras, with the participation of combat units from the host nation, Colombia, Peru, Guatemala, Nicaragua and El Salvador. Named Operación Fraternidad (Operation Fraternity), the exercise also served to evaluate the needs of the participating nations' armed forces, which were gradually included in the now widespread Military Aid Program.

During Fraternidad, the four Guatemalan C-47s, along with those from the Honduran and Salvadoran air forces, provided tactical transportation for the parachute units of the participating countries, including the Guatemalan Army's 1st Parachute Platoon, which conducted its first deployment outside the country on that occasion. Of interest was also that at least two of the FAG transports sported updated versions of old squadron badges on their fuselages during the exercise. Even though this practice has not been documented beyond the existing photos, it appears to have become widespread during the period when Col José Lemus Ramis was in command of the FAG, since many of the air arm's aircraft had painted on their fuselages the squadron insignias from the late 1930s and early '40s.

In November, the delivery of the second MAP-supplied C-47 to the FAG had to be postponed, along with the transfer of four

Lockheed T-33A jets, because the political scene in the country became extremely turbulent. It all began on the 25th with a badly planned and poorly executed revolt against President Ydígoras, led by Col Lemus Ramis and a group of aviators, which failed to secure the support of the ground forces. On that day, the presidential residence and the main Army garrisons in the capital were machine-gunned by a couple of B-26s, which were captured when their pilots, unaware that the La Aurora Airbase had been taken by loyal forces, landed to refuel and reload. Predictably, the failed coup unleashed a purge of the air arm, which lost most of its experienced pilots and mechanics, including Col Lemus Ramis, who was dishonourably discharged. Then, on 31 March 1963, it was the Army that launched its own revolt against Ydígoras. Led by none other than the Defence Minister, Col Enrique Peralta Azurdia, the rebel Army units were able to capture the National Palace as well as the presidential residence, and made Ydígoras their prisoner. Shortly after, Col Peralta Azurdia assumed executive powers as Chief of State, and ordered the expelling of the deposed president and his family from the country.

Beginning in May, Peralta Azurdia's regime had to step up the counter-insurgency campaign when the guerrillas began launching daring attacks on banana plantations located near the towns of Entre Ríos and Tenedores, in the Izabal department. By then, the 1st Parachute Platoon had fallen short as it did not have enough manpower for conducting all the search and destroy operations that were required. Therefore, it was the FAG F-51Ds and B-26s that had to go after the insurgents, usually followed by infantry units – transported in trucks and jeeps – that secured the affected areas and conducted patrols around them. Predictably, it became of utmost importance for the Army to increase the mobility of its troops in order to fight the guerrillas wherever they emerged. In such regard, on 30 June, the Army created the 1st Parachute Company, which was placed in the capable hands of Lts Arturo de la Cruz and Alfredo Matta Gálvez, both former members of the now disbanded 1st Parachute Platoon. Officially named as the

Above: C-47 serial 535, at McGuire AFB, in New Jersey, on 19 May 1973, still sporting the 'invasion' camouflage scheme. *via Dan Hagedorn*

Right: C-47 serial 570, sporting the olive drab overall scheme that was applied to some of the aircraft in the squadron during the first half of 1977. *via Ken, F. Measures*

'Quetzales' (Quetzals), the 1st Parachute Company was comprised of 150 paratroopers who began training at the San José Airbase during the first week of July. The following month, however, the unit was transferred to the Retalhuleu Airbase, so the paratroopers could conduct tactical jumps over the highlands situated north of the department. It was during one of those missions that the C-47 serialed 515 sustained irreparable damage after an extremely rough landing at the 'El Cedro' Army Reserve Base, where she was about to pick up a group of paratroopers who had just completed a tactical jump.

After the mishap of C-47 515, the FAG Transport Squadron was left with two C-45s (serials 500 and 505), two AT-11s (numbered 510 and 540), a VIP-configured Aero Commander 680 acquired during Ydígoras' presidency (serial 545), and three C-47s, serialed 520, 525 and 530, which were the squadron's only aircraft capable of conducting parachuting missions. Hence, the new FAG commander, Col Manuel Zea Carrascosa, resumed negotiations with the USAF Mission in order to acquire two more C-47 transports through the MAP programme. Despite the best efforts of the newly appointed Commander of the USAF Mission, Col Gene L. Douglas, it was not until 17 January 1964 that the first of the two transports arrived in La Aurora Airbase. She was a C-47B-1-DL (C/N 20732, ex USAF 43-16266) that earned the serial 535, which was the second occurrence of said number as it had been carried previously by an AT-11 that had been retired due to attrition earlier that year. The second MAP-supplied transport arrived in La Aurora almost five months later. She was a C-47A-80-DL (C/N 19687, ex USAF 43-15221) that was assigned the serial 500, replacing a C-45 that was retired due to attrition. A third transport, also transferred under the MAP programme, arrived at La Aurora in November of that year. This example was a C-47A-30-DK (C/N 25249, ex USAF 43-47988) that took up the serial 505, which was precisely the number that had been assigned to the last C-45 of the squadron and that had been retired two months earlier.

Early in 1965, the different guerrilla columns that had popped up during the preceding five years, decided to group into a larger organisation named Fuerzas Armadas Revolucionarias (FAR). This new insurgent organisation came up with new tactics that included the reduction in size of their operational units to the point of creating very small, fast-moving columns composed of five to ten individuals that launched simultaneous hit and run attacks, usually where they were least expected. Such change of tactics demanded much more effectiveness from the Army, who could barely keep up with the pace of the war. In response, the FAG leadership began considering using helicopters as a viable solution for improving the troops' mobility.

Hence, Col Zea Carrascosa asked the Air Section of the newly created US Military Group for Guatemala to lend a hand in getting two or three helicopters, preferably Bell UH-1 Hueys, through the MAP programme. After a bit of back and forth between the two governments, however, the US finally decided to transfer two Sikorsky UH-19B Chickasaw helicopters, which arrived in La Aurora on 17 June, and were assigned the serials 110 and 120. These slow birds proved to be so effective in air assault duties that the FAG leadership requested two more while waiting for the availability of the much-needed UH-1s. In addition, the air arm solicited the US government for the transfer of another C-47 to reinforce the transport squadron, since that unit still was supporting the majority of the Army's airborne operations.

The new MAP aircraft deliveries began with the first UH-19B of the second batch, which was delivered on 10 December 1966, just in time to replace the one carrying the serial 120 that sustained damage beyond repair during a COIN mission in Zacapa; this helicopter was assigned the serial 130. The other UH-19B arrived in La Aurora on 9 January 1967, and received the serial number 140. Finally, on 10 July, C-47A-30-DK, (C/N 13980/25425, ex USAF 43-48164), was delivered to the FAG, being assigned the serial 540.

In October 1967, the Army leadership decided to transition to airmobile operations completely. Accordingly, on 1 November, the 2nd Parachute Company was renamed as the Special Forces Company and was transferred to a new unit called Grupo Táctico Mixto (Tactical Composite Group) or GTM, which would be equipped with the three surviving UH-19Bs and the three newly acquired Bell UH-1Ds (serials 150, 160, and 170), as well as a handful of M113 armoured personnel carriers. During the first week of January 1968, while still undergoing training, the GTM conducted its first air assaults against well-formed guerrilla columns at Los Amates and Río Hondo, with relative success. During these sorties, the UH-1Ds were flown with rocket pods and door-mounted .30 calibre Machine guns, while the UH-19s were employed as troop carriers. These missions marked the beginning of the C-47s' withdrawal from combat operations and their relegation to more mundane duties as tactical transports.

By the end of June, the GTM had conducted no fewer than seventeen air assaults on its own and had participated in a similar number of operations supporting the regular infantry units. This offensive resulted in a considerable decrease of guerrilla activity in the theatre of operations. In fact, on 25 June, the few guerrilla groups operating in the Izabal area gathered for one last attempt to 'liberate'

C-47s 540 and 555 sporting the olive drab overall scheme applied to some of the aircraft in 1977, and 550 with the traditional white-blue colour scheme. Photo taken in 1978 at La Aurora Airbase.
Guatemalan Air Force Photo Archives via LAAHS

Close-up of C-47 555, sporting the olive drab overall scheme at La Aurora Airbase in 1978. *Guatemalan Air Force Photo Archives via LAAHS*

the eastern regions of Guatemala by means of co-ordinated attacks against the towns of Morales and El Choco in order to establish their command posts there, and then advance towards Puerto Barrios and Zacapa. The Army was quick to anticipate the desperate effort, however, and a reinforced infantry battalion was dispatched immediately from Puerto Barrios to face the guerrillas while the GTM's helicopters, carrying several fire squads, were sent to the area in order to locate and attack the enemy columns, supported by the FAG F-51Ds and B-26s. The ensuing campaign lasted almost thirty-five days and, after the dust settled, the guerrilla movement had ceased to exist operationally, leaving behind only a handful of very small and disorganised groups that retreated into the capital and other urban centres, while others escaped to Mexico. It would take the Marxist leaders almost four years to rebuild the rebel movement and resurface in the Western Highlands of the country.

The radical change of mission of the FAG Transport Squadron became evident in June 1969, when a pair of MAP-supplied, VIP-configured, VC-47Ds arrived at La Aurora. The first one, C/N 26286/14841, ex USAF 43-49025, was assigned the serial 550, while the other, C/N 16820/33499, ex USAF 44-77167, received the serial 555. These transports did not retain their luxurious interior for too long, however, since less than two years later both had been converted to troop carriers, and in the specific case of 555, she had received a rather aggressive-looking camouflage colour scheme!

In September of that same year, Hurricane Fracelia made landfall near Punta Gorda, Belize, and the accompanying rainstorms caused landslides and flash floods all over the Guatemalan Pacific coast and the Western Highlands, leaving a path of destruction and more than 10,000 people homeless. Accordingly, the FAG rushed to establish air bridges to the San José Airbase and the Quetzaltenango and Huehuetenango airfields with the C-47s, which carried clothing, food and medicines that were distributed to the affected towns and villages by the UH-19Bs and UH-1Ds. In the end, it turned out to be the largest relief operation ever conducted by the FAG, during which an UH-1D sustained unrepairable damage after a hard landing at Santa Cruz, in El Quiché, and the C-47 serialed 500 suffered a runway excursion while taking off from the Huehuetenango airfield. Fortunately, the Douglas transport was repaired and returned to active service shortly after.

During the first quarter of 1970, the Army's high command began preparing a highly secret campaign aimed at invading British Honduras. This decision was made in anticipation of a round of negotiations that the Guatemalan government, led by the newly elected Gen. Carlos Arana Osorio, considered pointless and a waste of time. As part of the preparations, the 2nd Parachute Company was created in July, taking up the name of 'Pentágonos' (Pentagons), and conducted its graduation jump on the 30th of that month at Melchor de Mencos, close to the border with the British colony. By then, half of the C-47 squadron had been painted in a three-tone camouflage pattern, very similar to the one used by the USAF in Southeast Asia. Such a scheme had also been applied to the surviving F-51Ds and to a handful of Cessna 180 and 182 light aircraft. In August, a couple of Lockheed T-33As, equipped with cameras, began flying reconnaissance missions over Belize City and Punta Gorda, in the Toledo District, which would be the prime targets of the invasion. Even though there is scarce documentation about this new attempt at reclaiming Belize, it all indicated that the campaign would consist of parachuting troops into Belize City and Punta Gorda with the aim of seizing them, and then the bulk of the 1st and 2nd Infantry Brigade's would cross the border in order to advance towards the two towns and reinforce the paratroopers. Like before, the main objective was to capture some territories in order to have a better negotiating position at the OAS or the UN.

Unaware of what was transpiring, the US government transferred to the FAG yet another C-47 through the MAP programme. This aircraft was a C-47B-50-DK, C/N 17131/34398, ex USAF 45-1128, which arrived in La Aurora Airbase on 20 August, just in time to participate, along with the rest of the C-47 fleet, in the inaugural jump of the 1st Parachute Battalion that took place at the San José Airbase on 5 September. This example was assigned the serial 560. Two weeks later, a pair of F-51Ds conducted a series of low-altitude reconnaissance missions over Punta Gorda and other towns in the Toledo district. In fact, British intelligence documents stated rather alarmingly that the old fighters had 'buzzed repeatedly' the district capital and the villages along the shores of the Sarstoon River, obviously in a blatant show of force. On 1 October, however, the British thought that the invasion had begun when half of the 1st Parachute Battalion conducted a tactical jump from six C-47s over Melchor de Mencos. This massive jump was repeated on 6 November over Poptún, also close to the border with Belize. Then, on 31 December, the Special Forces Company was disbanded and its personnel transferred to the newly created 3rd Parachute Company, which took up the name of 'Flechas' or Arrows. After the addition of this company to the 1st Parachute Battalion, it was more than evident that the FAG would need more C-47s, since the Army's high command intended that the entire battalion could conduct tactical jumps at once. Hence, the FAG Commander, Col Federico Fuentes Corado, began negotiations with the Air Section of the US Military Group in order to acquire at least eleven more of the venerable transports through the MAP programme.

The tensions between Guatemala and the United Kingdom over Belize continued for much of 1971. In fact, in January, the Guatemalan Army deployed a considerable number of troops to the border, while the air force based its F-51Ds at the Tikal airfield, where a 'forward operating base' was established, and from where numerous 'harassment' sorties were launched, usually against the Belizean towns and small villages located close to the border. Simultaneously, the C-47s conducted several parachute missions near Melchor de Mencos, after which the transports usually violated Belizean airspace, albeit briefly.

In any case, the conflict reached its climax a year later, when the Guatemalan Army pulled out all of the stops and was on the brink of finally invading the British colony. Not wasting any time, the United Kingdom deployed the aircraft carrier HMS *Ark Royal*, which docked in Belize on 30 January. A day earlier however, while the aircraft carrier still was near the Bahamas, a pair of Blackburn Buccaneer attack jets were launched for a long-range mission in order to overfly

C-47 serial 575 (C/N 19674, ex 43-15208) parked at Santa Elena Airbase in January 1987. *Jan Koppen*

Belize City 'showing the flag' and letting the Guatemalans know that powerful reinforcements were coming. Predictably, the Guatemalan government abandoned the idea of invading Belize immediately and withdrew its troops from the border, also discontinuing the 'harassment' flights. Much to the Army leadership's dismay, nonetheless, this episode also precluded the FAG from acquiring additional C-47s through the MAP programme, since the US government imposed a ban expressly prohibiting it in order to prevent the British colony from being threatened again. In the end, the Guatemalans turned to Israel for acquiring the much-needed transport aircraft, these being ten Israel Aircraft Industries IAI 201 Arava STOL turboprops, capable of transporting twenty soldiers or bulky payloads like a Jeep, besides being armed with two cheek-mounted .50 calibre machine guns and two rocket pods installed under the fuselage. The delivery of these aircraft commenced in January 1975, and a year later, they were conducting extremely important missions, transporting relief aid for the victims of the earthquake that struck the country on 4 February 1976.

During the first half of 1977, incredibly, the Guatemalan Army was getting ready to invade Belize yet again. This time, the idea was to launch co-ordinated air attacks against the British Army garrisons at Belize City and Punta Gorda, which would be followed by an airborne assault aimed at capturing the entire Toledo district. Accordingly, the FAG set out to acquire additional aircraft in order to be able to transport two parachute battalions at the least. The first

C-47 580 over the beaches of San José, in Escuintla, in December 1978. *Diego Molina via LAAHS*

By 1988, all the C-47s in the squadron went through a wing spar and general structure inspection, during which some of the aircraft received a new camouflage scheme. Aircraft 555 can be seen sporting the new colours in November 1989. *Guatemalan Air Force Photo Archives via LAAHS*

The crew and mechanics of the first two Basler BT-67s that arrived at La Aurora Airbase, in November 1992. The aircraft in the back is in fact the one that was originally assigned the serial 580, but was delivered sporting erroneously the number 575. However, the error was corrected by the Guatemalan mechanics a couple of days later. The aircraft in the forefront is 590. *Guatemalan Air Force Photo Archives via LAAHS*

two new C-47s arrived in La Aurora in April of that year, being assigned the serials 510 and 515, the latter being the second use of that number. Those two aircraft were followed by two more in May, which received the serials 570 and 575. Then, in June, the last aircraft arrived, being assigned the serial 580. Of these, only 510 and 575 have been fully identified, the first being a C-47D, C/N 12196, ex USAF 42-92400 and N755VM, and the other being a C-47A-DL, C/N 19674, ex USAF 43-15208, ex N62102. In all instances, however, it has been impossible to establish the origin of the aircraft and, as it can be seen in the table at the end of this chapter, the final fates of some of them remains a mystery.

During the preparation of the invasion, one of the C-47s was lost while returning from a parachute drop mission at the San José Airbase. It occurred on 3 June, when the aircraft carrying the serial 505 slammed against the slopes of the Agua Volcano in harsh weather conditions. The pilot, Lt Edgar Guillermo, the co-pilot Lt Ramón Prado and Airman Jesús Salvador Herrera, were killed upon impact. Weeks later, on 9 July, President Kjell Laugerud ordered the mobilisation of troops to the border with Belize, while the FAG was placed on alert. Fortunately, the potentially volatile situation was defused forty-eight hours later, thus becoming the very last time that the Guatemalan government tried to invade the British colony. According to a US intelligence report, at that time, the FAG had the following C-47s operational: 500, 510, 515, 520, 530, 535, 540, 550, 555, 560, 570, 575 and 580.

Less than three years later, on 28 February 1980, the C-47 carrying the serial 535 crashed after taking off from the Poptún airfield, killing thirty-one civilian passengers and the crew composed of Col Otto Martínez (pilot), Lt Carlos Morales (co-pilot) and Airman Asbel Calderón. Then, on 21 November 1982, the C-47 serial 500, crashed shortly after taking off from the Huehuetenango airfield, killing the pilot Col Julio Contreras, the co-pilot Capt. Otto René Rivas and Airman José Arenas. Seven passengers miraculously survived, although with some injuries. Three months later, on 25 February 1983, the aircraft serialed 540 was withdrawn from use after corrosion was discovered in her wing spar and fuselage; On 4 December of that same year, the aircraft number 580 was destroyed when a Pilatus PC-7,

practising low-altitude aerobatics, collided with her while she was parked at the main ramp of the Santa Elena Airbase in El Petén. The pilot of the PC-7, Lt Carlos Moreira, died on impact.

On 4 July 1985, the C-47 number 550 was damaged beyond repair after a runway excursion at Santa Elena Airbase. The pilot, Capt. Jaime Santiesteban, the co-pilot Lt Carlos Morales and mechanic Airman Luis Cruz Méndez did not suffer any injuries. During the following weeks the aircraft was cannibalised and then abandoned close to the officers' housing complex. Two years later, on 28 May 1987, the C-47 carrying the serial 520 crashed while trying to return to Santa Elena Airbase, killing nineteen passengers and the pilot Lt Víctor Contreras, the co-pilot Lt Víctor Aguirre, the mechanic Sgt Efrán Sandoval and the loadmaster Sgt Carlos Gómez.

During the first half of 1992, a USAF maintenance team arrived in La Aurora Airbase to evaluate the status of the surviving C-47s and pick the best in order to convert at least five to Basler Turbo BT-67s. This project, funded by the US government, was the result of lengthy negotiations conducted by the Guatemalan President, Jorge Serrano Elías, and the Department of State. In any case, the aircraft selected to undergo conversion were: 530, 555, 560 and 575; two more, which have not been identified, were used for spare parts, and Basler offered to replace them with two aircraft already converted. Hence, starting in June, the aircraft were flown to Oshkosh, Wisconsin, by Guatemalan crews in their last mission before retirement. In contrast, young pilots would be sent to receive training on the BT-67s, and then ferry them home to Guatemala.

The first to be sent for conversion was the C-47 serialed 575, which departed La Aurora on 7 June; On 6 September , the BT-67 C/N 9100, ex USAF 44-77210, which Basler had traded for one of the C-47s that had been cannibalised, arrived in La Aurora airbase carrying the serial 575. However, within hours of her arrival, her serial was changed to 580, which was the second occurrence of that number in the Transport Squadron. On 28 September, it was the C-47 serialed 560 that departed for Oshkosh. Nine days later, the BT-67 C/N 16794/33542, which Basler had traded for one of the C-47s that had been cannibalised, arrived in La Aurora, carrying the serial 590. On 19 November, it was the C-47 serialed 555 that departed for Oshkosh.

Unfortunately, the BT-67 proved to be too much for the young pilots who, accustomed to a tricycle undercarriage, had serious problems handling the aircraft's conventional landing gears during landings and while taxiing. On 7 February 1994, for example, the crew of Col Federico Monzón, Maj. Guido Santiesteban and Airman Marco Contreras were involved in a mishap at the Playa Grande airfield, during which the aircraft serialed 575 sustained heavy damage to the main undercarriage, both engines and fuselage, after an extremely hard landing. In fact, this BT-67, which had arrived in the country less than a year earlier, was declared unrepairable and was abandoned there. Then, on 7 May, it was aircraft 560 that suffered propeller strikes at the San José Airbase while being flown by the pilot Maj. Mario Reyes Toledo, assisted by co-pilot Lt Edwin Pérez Pineda and Airman Cruz Méndez. The result was that both engines sustained unrepairable damage and the FAG had to borrow a couple of turbines from Basler in order to ferry it back to La Aurora.

In March 1998, the BT-67 serialed 555 was grounded after sustaining heavy damage during a runway excursion at Santa Elena Airbase, while being flown by Lt Col Bertín Salguero, Capt. Mario Castañeda and Airman Fajardo Pérez. A similar fate befell serial 580, which sustained damage to both propellers and engines during a rough landing at Santa Elena Airbase while being flown by Maj. Jorge Ruiz Serovic, Lt Carlos Espinoza and Airman Humberto González.

At the time of this writing, the five surviving BT-67s are still grounded but all are considered repairable. In fact, the serials 590 and 560 were waiting to be flown to Oshkosh for a major repair, but the effort was blocked by left-leaning politicians in Congress. To make things even worse, the FAG is under extreme budgetary restrictions that preclude any attempt at maintaining or even repairing its fleet.

The following is the complete list of the Guatemalan Douglas C-47 and BT-67 aircraft, including their previous identities and their final fates, where known.

FAG Serial	Previous Identity	Type as Built	MSN	Assignments and Notes
T-1(I)	41-19499	C-47-DL	6142	Acquired from the Foreign Liquidation Commission (FLC) and delivered to the Fuerza Aérea de Guatemala on 18 Dec 45. Transferred to AVIATECA as LG-AGA in Jul 46, then to TG-AGA on 29 Oct 49.
T-2(I)	41-38669	C-47-DL	6052	Acquired from the Foreign Liquidation Commission (FLC) and delivered to the Fuerza Aérea de Guatemala on 18 Dec 45. Transferred to AVIATECA as LG-AHA in Jul 46, then to TG-AHA on 29 Oct 49.
T-1 (II)	43-16003	C-47A-90-DL	20469	Acquired through the American Republics Project (ARP) and delivered on 26 Nov 46. To 0961 after the creation of the composite squadrons' in 1950. Added to MAP support on 24 Oct 50.
T-2 (II)	43-1136	C-47B-50-DK	34406	Acquired through the American Republics Project (ARP) and delivered on 10 Dec 46. To 0653 after the creation of the composite squadrons in 1950. Added to MAP support on 24 Oct 50.
T-3	43-15580	C-47A-85-DL	20046	Transferred from the US Air Mission to the Guatemalan Air Force on 22 Oct 46, under the American Republics Project (ARP), although export declaration date is 23 Jan 47. To 0749 after the creation of the composite squadrons in 1950. Added to MAP support on 24 Oct 50.
0515		C-47A		Transferred from CIA project PBSuccess to the Guatemalan Air Force on 2 Jul 54. To 515 after the squadrons' general reorganisation of 1956–57.
0653	43-1136 T-2 (II)	C-47B-50-DK	34406	To 520 after the transport squadron's general reorganisation of 1956–57.
0749	43-15580 T-3	C-47A-85-DL	20046	To 525 after the transport squadron's general reorganisation of 1956–57.
0961	43-16003 T-1 (II)	C-47A-90-DL	20469	Written off 27 Oct 51 at Flores, El Petén.
FAG-500	43-15221	C-47A-80-DL	19687	Delivered in May 64 via MAP. Written off 21 Nov 81 at Huehuetenango.
FAG-505	43-47988	C-47A-30-DK	25249	Delivered in Nov 64 via MAP. Written off 3 Jun 77 at the Agua Volcano.

Basler BT-67 serial 530 at La Aurora Airbase in November 1996. *via George J. Kamp*

Basler BT-67 serial 590 at La Aurora Airbase in April 2020. *Mario Ávila*

FAG-510	42-92400 FZ639 CF-GJZ N510Z N755VM	C-47A-1-DK	12196	Most probably acquired on 11 Apr 77 from civilian sources. WFU on 18 Mar 92. Cannibalised and abandoned at La Aurora AB, Guatemala City.
FAG-515	0515	C-47A		Written off on 1 Sep 63 at 'El Cedro' Army Reserve Base in Retalhuleu, after sustaining heavy damage during a rough landing.
FAG-515 (II)		C-47?		Most probably acquired from civilian sources in Apr 1977. Last noted Oct 82. Fate unknown.
FAG-520	45-1136 NC67796 XH-TAF XH-SAF T-2 (II) 0653	C-47B-50-DK	17139/ 34406	Written off 28 May 87 at El Petén.
FAG-525	43-15580 T-3 0749	C-47A-85-DL	20046	Last noted Feb 87. Fate unknown.
FAG-530	43-15565 BT-67	C-47A-85-DL	20031 Basler #25	Delivered on 25 Aug 62 via MAP. Converted to BT-67 and delivered back on 4 Aug 96. In line for change of both engines by Basler as of Mar 2020.
FAG-535	43-16266	C-47B-1-DL C-47D	20732	Delivered on 17 Jan 64 via MAP. Written off on 28 Feb 80 at Poptún Airfield.

Mechanics removing the engines of BT-67 serial 575, which suffered a mishap while landing at the Playa Grande airfield, in El Quiché, on 6 February 1994. Sadly, the aircraft was deemed beyond repair and was abandoned there. *Guatemalan Air Force Photo Archives via LAAHS*

BT-67 serial 530 landing at the Playa Grande airfield in El Quiché, in April 1994. An engineless 575 can be seen in the background.
Guatemalan Air Force Photo Archives via LAAHS

BT-67s 580 and 555 stored at Santa Elena AB, in El Petén. Both aircraft sustained damage while landing at the airbase, but due to budgetary constraints it is improbable that the air force will repair them.
Juan C. García via LAAHS

FAG-540	43-48164 0-348164	C-47A-30-DK	13980/ 25425	Delivered on 10 Jul 67 via MAP. WFU since 25 Feb 83. Stored at La Aurora AB, Guatemala City.
FAG-550	43-49025 0-349025 0-49025	C-47B-10-DK C-47D VC-47D	14841/ 26286	Delivered on 21 Jun 69 via MAP. Written off at Santa Elena AB on 4 Jul 85. Fuselage abandoned near the end of the runway, close to the officers' housing complex.
FAG-555	44-77167	C-47B-35-DK C-47D VC-47D BT-67	16751/ 33499 Basler #20	Delivered on 21 Jun 69 via MAP. Converted to BT-67 between 19 Nov 92 and 26 Jun 94. Damaged during hard landing at Santa Elena AB on 11 Mar 98. Stored without engines.
FAG-560	45-1128	C-47B-50-DK C-47D VC-47D BT-67	17131/ 34398 Basler #19	Delivered on 20 Aug 70 via MAP. Converted to BT-67 between 28 Sep 92 and 8 Mar 94. Damaged during hard landing at San José airfield, in Escuintla, on 7 May 94. Recovered and placed in storage without engines at La Aurora AB, Guatemala City.
FAG-570		C-47?		Most probably acquired from civilian sources between Apr and May 1977. Last noted 20 Sep 80. Fate unknown.
FAG-575	43-15208 315208 (RNorAF) N62102	C-47A-80-DL BT-67	19674 Basler #15	Delivered on 29 May 77. Converted to BT-67 between 7 Jul 92 and 18 Feb 93. Damaged during rough landing at Playa Grande airfield, in El Quiché, on 6 Feb 94. Cannibalised and abandoned there.
FAG-580(I)		C-47?		Most probably acquired in Jun 77. Damaged beyond repair by PC-7 that crashed into her while practising low-altitude aerobatics at Santa Elena AB on 4 Dec 83.
FAG-580(II)	42-32874 NC-61989 N5109 N51091 N510NR	C-47A-80-DL BT-67	9100 Basler #12	Arrived on 9 Jun 92 already converted from Basler. Damaged during rough landing at Santa Elena AB on 17 Apr 03. Stored without engines.
FAG-590	44-77210 KP240 G-AMSO VP-KKH(?) N2702A N29DR	C-47B-40-DK BT-67	16794/ 33542 Basler #13	Arrived on 7 Nov 92 already converted from Basler. Identified in GAF official documents as '33568' and '47-33568'. Waiting to be sent to Basler for IRAN as of Mar 2020.

BT-67s 590 and 530 parked at La Aurora Airbase in May 2020. Aircraft 590 was scheduled to fly to Oshkosh for maintenance, and would carry on board the engines of 530 to be overhauled. In the end, the Guatemalan Congress did not approve the necessary funds and it appears that both aircraft will be retired from service. *Mario Ávila*

CHAPTER THIRTEEN

Haiti

O F ALL OF THE 'TRADITIONAL' national military aviation organisations in the Americas, that of Haiti is the youngest, if one dates the creation of a Panamanian air arm from faltering starts in the 1930s.

Occupying the western third of the island of Hispaniola with the much larger Dominican Republic to the east, Haiti is extremely mountainous and, until 1934, was effectively administered by the United States Marine Corps who, although essentially an occupying power, gave the extremely poor country what is often described as its one true period of peace. The Marines, among other things, introduced modern sanitation to what was previously a squalid nightmare in the capital, Port-au-Prince, and improved the general level of public health. The US occupation also, however, fostered the return of mulatto dominance, with two successive mulatto Presidents holding office between 1934 and 1946. A succession of coups led to the accession of 'Papa Doc' Duvalier, who declared himself president for life in 1964.

The dominant power in Haiti throughout the earlier period was the Garde d'Haiti, another creation of the USMC, organised in 1916 as the Gendarmerie D'Haiti. Then, in December 1942, despite all odds, the poor nation decided to foster the creation of a small air arm, known as the Corps d'Aviation de l'Armée d'Haiti, and a solitary serving USAAF major, Dean H. Eshelman, was detailed to this extraordinary task – not a USMC mission, as has so frequently been recorded.

The challenges facing this process were exceptionally daunting. Of the young Haitian cadets selected, not a single one had ever even driven a car, let alone an aircraft, although one solitary Haitian native

pilot (Maj. Edouard Roy), a pioneer, aided the nascent period enormously. Eventually, seven pilots qualified, and these became the stalwarts of the service for years to come. Supplied initially with four Taylorcraft L-2Bs as ab initio trainers in the very finest definition of the term, these were followed by Lend-Lease deliveries of six venerable Douglas O-38Es – the very first tactical aircraft – a Luscombe 8A that had somehow made its way to Haiti via private means, three Vultee BT-13As in April 1943, a single Cessna UC-78 (the first Haitian multi-engine aircraft) in July 1943 (with three more acquired surplus in January 1945), two North American AT-6Cs in September 1943, and finally three Fairchild PT-19As in March 1944. With this modest array of aircraft, the hard-working US instructor forged a brand new air force that, by 1944, was mounting regularly scheduled anti-submarine patrols with its aged O-38Es, dragging a 325lb depth charge under their lower starboard wings. This was, by any measure, a remarkable achievement.

The power represented by an armed air force was not lost upon the several post-war regimes, however, nor was the flexibility in rapid deployment of troops represented by even a modest transport element.

Rarely photographed wearing full COHATA titles, serial 4262 also displays the unusual line logo atop her vertical fin and appears very well maintained circa September 1949 at Miami. *Harold G. Martin*

As a direct result, in the heady post-war surplus bonanza period, Haiti elected to acquire transport types, leading to the creation of a dedicated air mobility element. This was led by the three Cessna UC-78s noted above, plus at least one Lockheed C-60A, two Beech twins (one a C-45B and the other an AT-11 modified with a 'solid' nose) – and three C-47s. The first of these was apparently acquired in 1948 and was almost certainly the former USAF Attaché to Cuba, Haiti and the Dominican Republic aircraft that had been damaged in a hurricane at Campo Columbia near Havana, Cuba, on 5 October 1948. The USAF had ordered the aircraft to be reclaimed (salvaged) and sold locally. The Haitian government entered a bid at $1,500 and won it, and somehow had the aircraft returned to airworthiness by 2 June 1949, possibly in Miami. The service was reported as having two C-47s as of 7 October 1949, of which one was undergoing repair, and total qualified pilots in the air arm numbered just twelve. Two more C-47s or DC-3s were acquired commercially in 1950 and these probably were the pair noted at American Airmotive in Miami undergoing modifications as of 7 April 1950. Oddly, the two operable aircraft were noted on the 7 July 1950 Air Order of Battle as type C-47E and C-47D, respectively 5878 and 4262.

Haiti was originally scheduled to have received eighteen aircraft under the American Republics Projects (ARP), comprising five additional Fairchild PT-19As or PT-19Bs, depending on availability, six more North American AT-6Ds, two more Beech C-45s and five exotic Stinson L-9 Voyagers, these to have been commercially produced Stinson 108-3s acquired by the USAF specifically for offset to Haiti. However, for political reasons, the country was excluded from ARP allocations at the direct request of the US State Department and thus became one of only four nations to receive nothing via that programme, the others having been Argentina, Costa Rica and Panama.

By the end of 1950, a USAF Mission had arrived to aid the Corps d'Aviation and assisted the force to acquire six surplus North American F-51Ds, as well as a rather weary Boeing 307, which was retrofitted as a Presidential aircraft befitting Papa Doc, and, by 15 November 1951, C-47 strength remained at three. Between its creation in 1942 and December 1951, aircraft of the small service transported 57,964 passengers, 33,206kg of mail and 13,033kg of cargo without a serious accident. The service operated its own internal meteorological and maintenance sections – the only ones in the country and the latter, under the direction of the only engineering officer in the country, Capt. Yvon Boyer, managed to overhaul its own engines. By 30 June 1954, however, the Haitian Air Order of Battle still reflected a total of three C-47s in the inventory, although one other aircraft appears to have come and gone by that date, for a total of four.

Although Haiti is known to have acquired at least four C-47 variants as early as 1 November 1948, by 1969 a new serialing system was adopted that suggests at least seven may have eventually been operated. However, while an impressive number for a service with such daunting day-to-day challenges, at no time were more than two of them operational. By 24 August 1954, the total number of C-47s on hand was still three, and the USAF had rated them all, remarkably, as 'combat ready'. The officer strength of the service had grown modestly, however, now at twenty-six officers, of whom eleven were rated pilots, and besides the C-47s, the entire inventory comprised only fourteen other aircraft: four F-51Ds, one C-45B, one AT-11, three

AT-6Cs, two BT-13As and three PT-19As. These figures remained essentially unchanged through at least 1 June 1958, although a Boeing 307 was added as noted.

By May 1961, the paucity and inadequacy of surface communications within the challenging national territory had only been slightly remediated and, besides commerce, this meant that the sitting regime was also unable to move any significant portion of its rather numerous armed organisations – except by air. By then, six airfields had been carved out capable of taking C-47s, and, not surprisingly, these were located in strategic areas. Thus, the sole means of tactical transport for combat troops rested with the (then) trio of C-47s on strength, and the US MAAG was rather forcefully lobbying USCARIB Command for at least one more, and two beyond this, for a total of six, being optimum. By way of justification, they pointed out that, at the time, there was a complete lack of motor transport at the Military District and Sub-District Headquarters level throughout rural Haiti. While the road network was deemed totally inadequate for any large-scale transport, there was a pronounced requirement for some means to transport a limited number of security personnel. The MAAG also rather pointedly reported that the armed forces, should Duvalier somehow be overthrown, constituted the solitary barrier against complete and utter anarchy in the poor nation.

From the very beginning of the service, apparently having noted the financial benefits being reaped by other Latin American military-operated quasi-airline operations, the Haitian government enabled the Corps d'Aviation to eventually form what was known as the Compagnie Haitienne de Transports Aeriens (COHATA), granting it authority to operate not only all of the C-47s on hand, but the two Beech twins as well. Intended to provide airline service to remote areas of the country, it certainly did so, but at the same time the crews are known to have modified the fares on a rather selective basis, apparently based on how prosperous the prospective passenger appeared! In fact, the air transport activities of the service had commenced when it acquired the first of four Cessna UC-78 noted above. At first carrying mail only, with intermittent flights from Bowen Field just on the north side of the capital to cities on the north coast and others on the south coast, these eventually included Jacmel, Auc Cayes, Jeremie, Gonaives, Mole St Nicolas, Minche, Port de Paix and Cap Haitien. As the service matured, a regular schedule of three trips weekly to each of these points was flown but, at the complete discretion of the pilot tasked with each flight, if he determined a profitable payload was not on hand, he could cancel the flight!

Although details are sparse, it is known that one Haitian C-47 had already been lost in flight operations before 22 January 1966, when an aircraft identified as serial 4662 (but more likely 4262), operating on a regularly scheduled COHATA flight, came down in the vicinity of Duchity after having taken off from Les Cayes at about 1145hrs. Lt Roger Maignan, six other crew and twenty-three of the twenty-eight passengers aboard were killed, the remainder being seriously injured.

Wearing two forms of her serial, 3681 on the fin and simply '681' on the fuselage ahead of the distinctive Haitian three-colour national insignia (black, red and white), she is seen visiting Mexico City, with an Aviateca Guatemala DC-3 in the left background. She was one of the first two aircraft, and with curtains in the windows, was probably being flown in VIP passenger configuration at the time. *Ing. Jose Villela*

As mentioned above, by 1969, the Corps d'Aviation had modernised its serialing system. Where before they had used either a contraction of an aircraft's former US serial number or the Manufacturer's Serial Number, the new system appears to have been a rather straight-forward numeric system issued to aircraft arbitrarily as they either entered the inventory, or retrospectively in an apparently random order. The surviving C-47s were issued serials in the 1200s.

Probably the final act for the small cadre of Haitian C-47s, co-author Hagedorn noted two derelict fuselages without serials at Bowen Field in May 1979, although a third aircraft, serial 1235, appeared in good condition on the flight line, but was missing both engines. There have been no subsequent reports of Haitian C-47s beyond that date.

Haitian Serial	Previous Identity	Built As	MSN	Assignments and Notes
–	42-23346	C-47A-1-DL	9208	The former US Air Attaché to Haiti and the Dominican Republic's aircraft, named The Brass Hat, this aircraft had sustained damage in a hurricane at Campo Columbia, Havana, Cuba, on 5 Oct 48 when a C-46 had been deposited atop her fuselage and starboard wing. Having been assigned to the Sixth Air Force since 18 Dec 46, she was to have been salvaged and the remains sold locally to the highest bidder. Haiti entered a bid of an incredibly low $1,500 and won. To have been used only as a 'spares source', the remains at Campo Columbia had been dismantled by 7 Oct 49 and a very nearly complete aircraft was then, according to one source, somehow transported to Miami and rebuilt or, far less likely, shipped to Haiti where these parts were used to complete the second Haitian C-47.
4262	41-7775 NC-54327	C-47-DL DC-3A or DC-3C	4262	Apparently acquired from US Airlines, Inc. of St Petersburg, FL, by 1 Nov 48 via some form of governmental aid, she eventually served with COHATA as late as 1971. Noted derelict by 1995 at Bowen Field. Although serial '4265' has also been reported in some sources, this is believed to have been a mis-sighting or corruption of 4262, as there have been no other reports. Similarly, a Haitian C-47 with serial '4662' is reported to have suffered an accident on 22 Jan 66 but is believed to have actually been 4262.
3681 681	42-93736 NC-62568 CU-T100	C-47A-25-DK	13681	Although usually cited as having been acquired via Aerovias Q in Cuba in 1954, this aircraft was actually in service with the Haitians by 24 Nov 52, as she was granted clearance to make a flight via Miami to New York City and return on 5–6 Dec 1952, and is more likely to have been acquired from Aerovias Q in 1950. She visited Miami, FL, on 24 Jan 55. She was noted stored in rough condition at Bowen Field by 1976 and derelict by May 91.

Marked similarly to 3681, with the last three digits of her serial repeated on the fuselage, this aircraft is clearly a late series C-47B that had been acquired via the WAA at Miami on 3 December 1949. She had curtained windows when seen at Newark, New Jersey in 1950, and the entire top of her vertical fin and rudder had been painted black as well. *A.L. Bachman via Brian R. Baker*

Very rarely ever illustrated, the surviving Haitian Air Corps C-47s and DC-3s were reserialed in the 1200s by May 1969, and CAH-1235, a C-47A, sans titles of any sort, is seen here on finals at Miami on 18 April 1972. *Harold G. Martin*

5878 878	45-878	C-47B-45-DK C-47E	16881/34137	Acquired via the War Assets Administration (WAA) on 3 Dec 49, she was in service by 27 Jul 50 and is known to have operated with COHATA as 5878. She visited Miami, FL, on 27 Jan 55, certainly one of her most distant excursions. Crashed at Bowen Field, Port-au-Prince on 31 Mar 59. As a direct result of this accident, the Corps d'Aviation lost two of its most experienced aviators: the co-pilot (probably Capt. Albert Maignar) was killed and LTC Edouard Roy was summarily retired by the ruling President for destroying one of his prized aircraft, although he survived.
9175	42-23313 NC-68390 N91227 N147A	C-47A-1-DL DC-3C-S1C3G	9175	Acquired by 14 Jul 60 and with COHATA by 1972. Apparently abandoned by May 82 and noted derelict by May 91.
1233	–	–	–	First reported in 1969 and with COHATA by 1972. In service as late as 1 Sep 85 and noted at, of all places, the Middleton Airport, Middleton, Delaware, but abandoned by 11 May 91.
1235	–	C-47A	–	First reported on 18 Apr 72 with COHATA and in service as late as Dec 83, possibly the one sighted by co-author Hagedorn at Bowen Field in May 79. Abandoned by 11 May 91.
1238	–	–	–	Although reported in several DC-3 enthusiast publications as in service in 1986, there have been no actual sightings of this aircraft reported.
1275	–	–	–	Although reported in several DC-3 enthusiast publications as in service in 1986, there have been no actual sightings of this aircraft reported.
1278	–	–	–	First reported in December 1983 and still in service by May 91, making her almost certainly the last Haitian military C-47.
1281	–	–	–	Listed by a couple of sources as in service with the Corps d'Aviation, but without dates or any additional information.
1282	–	–	–	Listed by a couple of sources as in service with the Corps d'Aviation, but without dates or any additional information.
HH-1294	–	–	–	Reported on 1 Sep 85, also at Middleton Airport, Middleton, Delaware, although it is unclear if the civil 'HH-' prefix was actually worn or just assumed.

CHAPTER FOURTEEN

Honduras

D UE TO ITS TOPOGRAPHY, the second largest country in Central America has relied almost entirely upon air transportation for its economic and social development. In fact, it was in Honduras that the one and only TACA airline was born, and within a few years, transformed itself into a monster with which only Pan American Airways was able to contend. Predictably, the Catracho military learned the lesson well and in 1936, their air arm was among the first in the isthmus to acquire transport aircraft, including three Boeing Model 95s, eight Boeing Model 40Bs and a single Curtiss-Wright T-32C Condor, the latter being the only multi-engine aircraft in service with a Central American air arm at the time. Surprisingly, these aircraft were used interchangeably as transports and as bombers, the T-32C being fitted with racks for six 100lb bombs along with locally fabricated bomb doors. Unfortunately, the Condor was lost on 27 February 1942, during a flight from the port of La Ceiba in the Caribbean coast of the country, to Tegucigalpa, the Honduran capital. This aircraft went missing for more than fifty years, and it was not until November 1998 that the wreckage was found in the mountains near the town of La Masica, in the Atlántida Department, some 25km south-east of La Ceiba.

After the end of the Second World War the Fuerza Aérea Hondureña (Honduran Air Force) or FAH finally had access to relatively modern aircraft, which included, besides a handful of the inevitable North American AT-6 Texan trainers, the service's very first Douglas transport. Acquired through the US War Assets Administration, this aircraft was a C-47A-20-DK, MSN 12786, ex USAAF serial 42-92931, which arrived in the Toncontín Airbase, the FAH headquarters at Tegucigalpa, on 21 December 1947, piloted by Maj. Hernán Acosta Mejía and Capt. Alberto Alvarado. Shortly after her arrival, this example was assigned the FAH serial 300.

The second FAH Douglas transport was acquired from the Nicaraguan Air Force in September 1951 for US$60,000. She was a C-47A-DL, C/N 6096, ex USAF 41-18690, ex NC-54075 and ex AN-ADP, which up to that point had been President Anastasio Somoza's personal aircraft (the rather peculiar background of this C-47 is discussed at length in Chapter 16). Upon her arrival at

Toncontín, this aircraft was assigned the FAH serial 301, and contrary to what has been reported for years, she was ferried from Managua to Tegucigalpa by a Honduran crew, as noted by the Nicaraguan aero-historian Ricardo Boza in his book *La Aviación en Nicaragua – 1922–1976*.

In June 1954, a CIA-backed rebel army was about to launch an invasion against Guatemala from Honduran soil, with the aim of deposing the president of said country, Col. Jacobo Arbenz. Even though the covert project operated three C-47s for hauling troops and supplies, they were not sufficient to accomplish all the required missions during the last stage of the operation. Hence, the US Ambassador to Honduras, Withing Willauer, convinced Lt Col Hernán Acosta Mejía,

C-47 serial 301 sporting the colour scheme that was applied to the C-47s in the late 1960s. This aircraft was purchased from the Nicaraguan Air Force in 1951. *Honduran Aviation Museum, via LAAHS*

The mythical C-47A serial 300, seen here at Toncontín Airbase. Note the overall aluminium finish. *Carlos Planas, via Dan Hagedorn*

Partial view of C-53D serial 302, which served as the Honduran 'Air Force One' during the presidency of Ramón Villeda. This aircraft was reserialed as 321 in the early 1970s. *via Amado Aguiluz*

the FAH commander at the time, to lend one of the service's C-47s in order to move a large quantity of rifles, ammunition and supplies from Tegucigalpa to Nueva Ocotepeque, from where they would be trucked to the different 'staging points' situated along the border. Therefore, on 9 June, the C-47 serial 300 accomplished no fewer than three flights, and four more on the 10th. In total, the aircraft flew more than 5 tons of arms and supplies before being grounded by what was termed as an act of sabotage, since on the morning of the 11th, the C-47 was found without batteries and other critical components. (To learn more about the aerial operations during the CIA-backed invasion to Guatemala, see Chapter 12 as well as the book entitled *PBSuccess: The CIA's covert operation to overthrow Guatemalan president Jacobo Arbenz in June–July 1954*, published by the authors.)

Three years later, in 1957, Honduras almost went to war with Nicaragua over a territorial dispute. In February of that year, the Honduran government created the Gracias a Dios department, which included some territories that had been under de facto Nicaraguan control for years. Predictably, on 18 April, the Nicaraguan government strengthened its military presence by ordering troops of the Guardia Nacional (National Guard) or GN to cross the Coco River and occupy the area known as Mocorón. In response, the Honduran government began flying troops to the town of Guagüina, situated some 50km north-west of Mocorón, from where an offensive aimed at recapturing the occupied territory would be launched. For this, the FAH employed the C-47 serial 300 and four others borrowed from the SAHSA Airline. However, it was not until May 2nd that the Honduran troops were able to launch a heavy attack on Mocorón, supported by four Lockheed P-38L and four Bell P-63E fighters, which also conducted bombing missions against bridges along the Coco River. By the end of the day, the Hondurans had routed the Nicaraguan troops and had recaptured Mocorón, prompting President Luis Somoza to call for a general mobilisation, while sporadic skirmishes continued during the next seven days.

Amid this tense situation, the FAH suffered the loss of its first C-47 transport. It occurred on 5 May, when the aircraft serial 300 was returning to Tegucigalpa, after having resupplied the troops deployed at Mocorón. Upon arriving over Toncontín, the crew realised that the marginal weather conditions would prevent them from landing, thus the pilot, Lt Héctor López Urquía, decided to continue the flight and land at the Ilopango Airport, in San Salvador,

El Salvador. Unfortunately, marginal weather conditions prevailed at the Salvadoran capital also, making it impossible for them to attempt a landing. Running low on fuel and with darkness closing in, Lt López finally decided to ditch the aircraft off the coast of port La Libertad. Lt López survived the impact and was able to reach the shore after a couple of minutes; however, the co-pilot, 2nd Lt Mario Moya Muñóz, and the mechanic, Sgt Gustavo Andino Valladares, drowned while attempting to reach the shore, as none of them knew how to swim.

The Mocorón crisis continued for four more days, and it was not until 9 May that a ceasefire was agreed by both nations, as well as a plan for the withdrawal of their troops. An OAS-sponsored Observer Group was also accepted by the two countries, while the dispute was submitted to the International Court of Justice which, in November 1960, ruled in favour of Honduras.

After the loss of the C-47 serial 300, the aircraft serialed 301, which had been acquired for VIP duties, was reconfigured locally for transporting troops and cargo. In the meantime, however, Col Armando Escalón, the FAH commander at the time, set out to acquire another Douglas transport that could fulfill the role of presidential aircraft. In the end, the Honduran government struck a deal with Trans International Airlines for a C-53D-DO, C/N 11696, ex 42-68769, ex NC86593 and ex N99C, which arrived in Toncontín Airbase on 2 April 1958. Regarding the FAH serial assigned to this aircraft, there is quite a debate on whether it was assigned the number 302 after her arrival or not. On one hand, the Honduran aero-historian Ramiro Mondragón, in a 1984 unpublished paper, claims that the aircraft was assigned the serial 321 upon arrival, and something similar is affirmed by Capt. Carlos Gamundi, who flew the aircraft for President Ramón Villeda Morales. On the other hand, however, the accepted version by the aero-history community is that this aircraft was assigned the serial 302 initially and was reserialed as 321 after the war with El Salvador in July 1969. Adding to the confusion, a period photograph exists showing the aft section of an aircraft that clearly was a C-53, which has a diminutive serial '302' painted near the right-hand air stair door. In any case, and for the purposes of this chapter, we'll go with the aero-historian community's accepted version: This C-53 was serialed 302 upon arrival. We stand to be corrected and would welcome constructive confirmation, either way.

C-53D serial 321, shortly after the 100-Hour War of 1969. *FAH, via Jaime Güell*

By mid-1962, it was more than evident that the Cuban dictator, Fidel Castro, supported by the Soviet Union, was taking advantage of the unstable political and economic conditions that prevailed across the continent in order to export the so-called Cuban Revolution. In fact, by that time, the Guatemalan government was already battling a Marxist guerrilla force that was receiving training, funds and equipment from Castro, and was inspiring similar movements in neighbouring countries, namely El Salvador and Honduras.

The CIA was quick to anticipate Castro's intentions, however, and in May, the agency published an estimate in which it urged the US government to take appropriate steps to mitigate the expansion of the Marxist movement in Latin America as soon as possible, mainly by including its nations in the Military Assistance Program (MAP) that had been created a year earlier, and train their armed forces for dealing with insurgent groups. For its part, the US Army's Caribbean Command set out to organise a major counter-insurgency exercise in Honduras, with the participation of combat units from the host nation and from Colombia, Peru, Guatemala, Nicaragua and El Salvador. Named Operación Fraternidad (Operation Fraternity), the exercise began on 3 September and lasted three days, during which the troops of the participating nations made several parachute jumps from the

C-47s of the Guatemalan, Salvadoran, Peruvian and Colombian air forces, while the Vought F4U-5s of the FAH provided close air support and conducted numerous low-level bombing missions.

Originally, the FAH was scheduled to receive three MAP-supplied C-47s that would take part in Fraternidad, but due to delays in the paperwork, the aircraft arrived in Honduras too late. The first two were ferried to Honduras on 18 October, these being a C-47A-20-DK, MSN 12962, ex USAF 42-93089, which was assigned the serial FAH serial 304, and a C-47A-75-DL, MSN 19426, ex USAF 42-100963, which received the FAH serial 305. The reason why the serial 303 was not assigned to any of these aircraft has eluded aero-historians for years, and has been the source of numerous myths and legends. In fact, it was not until the 1980s that this serial number was assigned to a FAH C-47, as we'll see. In any case, the third MAP-supplied aircraft, which took up the FAH serial 306, arrived in Tegucigalpa on 10 June 1963, she being a C-47A-25-DK, MSN 13642, ex USAF 42-93701.

On 1 August 1967, the C-47B-15-DK, MSN 15320/26765, ex USAF 43-49504, assigned to the US Military Mission in Honduras, sustained heavy damage to her undercarriage while landing at the Santa Rosa de Copán airfield. Upon a thorough evaluation, the USAF mechanics determined that the repairs were too expensive and recommended that the aircraft should be abandoned there. Therefore, the US Southern Command made the decision to donate the aircraft to the FAH, so she could be used as a source of spare parts for the rest of the Honduran fleet. In the end, however, the FAH mechanics set out to repair her and on 17 June 1968, she was incorporated to the air force inventory with the serial 307. Something was not quite right with that aircraft, though, since according to accounts from pilots who flew her, she needed constant trim adjustments in order to fly straight.

During the first half of 1969, the relations between the governments of El Salvador and Honduras deteriorated considerably due to an immigration dispute that had its roots back in the early twentieth century, when more than 300,000 Salvadorans settled in Honduras, so they could work for the North American companies United Fruit and its rival, Standard Fruit. This arrival of Salvadoran peasants, which had been tacitly approved by the Honduran government, occurred when the North American companies realised that the Honduran workers were not sufficient in numbers to maintain the banana production.

C-47A serial 304, at Howard AFB, in the Panama Canal Zone, on 2 December 1969. Note the Day-Glo identification marks applied after the 100-Hour War. *Dan Hagedorn*

Things began to change in the early 1960s, though, when political changes and the liberalisation of the region's commerce through the Common Market Treaty made it painfully evident that the country that benefited the most from it was El Salvador, while Honduras was to be destined to carry a heavy economic burden. Inevitably, that realisation chilled the relations between the two countries and had a direct bearing on the treatment from the Hondurans towards the Salvadoran immigrants.

During the mid-1960s, amidst sporadic violence against the Salvadorans living in Honduras, the two governments began negotiations aimed at solving the problem and signed three agreements. However, while the negotiations were taking place, clandestine armed groups were organised in Honduras with the purpose of harassing and controlling the Salvadoran people living in that country. This situation was worsened by a coup d'etat that brought to the presidency the Honduran General Oswaldo López Arellano, who had a very different point of view than his predecessor regarding the immigrants' situation. Shortly after, the expelling of thousands of Salvadorans began.

Predictably, the return of the peasants to El Salvador introduced a series of problems for that country, since all were returning unemployed and needing food, clothing and some kind of shelter – all of this in the midst of an economic crisis that not even the advantages obtained through the Common Market Treaty had been able to alleviate. Thus, it did not take long for the Salvadoran society to begin clamouring for some sort of military response against Honduras.

With this delicate political background, the qualifying rounds for the 1970 football World Cup (to be held in Mexico the following year) began – and El Salvador and Honduras were drawn to face each other. At the same time as the game, the violence against Salvadoran immigrants in Honduras increased and caused strong protests from the Salvadoran government, which ended in the rupturing of diplomatic relations, followed by additional border incidents that included the strafing of a Honduran airliner while it was taking off from Nueva Ocotepeque.

As noted in Chapter 11, the Salvadoran armed forces had spent quite some time planning a military operation aimed at occupying Honduran towns and villages along the border, in order to increase the size of the country's territory and distribute those lands among the peasants who had been expelled from Honduras. Such an operation was launched on 14 July, when troops of the Army and the National Guard crossed the border with Honduras and occupied key locations in the southern departments of Valle, La Paz, Intibucá, Lempira and Ocotepeque, giving way to 'the 100-hour War' as the Hondurans knew it, or 'The War of Legitimate Defence' as the Salvadorans called it. This initial offensive also included a series of air strikes against targets deep inside Honduras, of which very few had a strategic impact.

As unbelievable as it may seem, it took some time for the Honduran government to realise what was happening. President López Arellano himself thought that the air strikes and the incursions of the Salvadoran troops into Honduran territory were not yet worthy of a military response. In contrast, the FAH's Commander, Col Enrique Soto Cano, suggested launching a series of air attacks against strategic targets in El Salvador, including its main airbase at Ilopango. However, the infantry officers of the Army's high command quickly dismissed the idea, stating that such missions could compromise the air arm's resources, which in any case should be used to support the troops on the combat fronts. The Honduran Foreign Minister, Dr Tiburcio Carías, was also opposed to aerial attacks against targets in El Salvador, proposing instead that the armed forces should limit themselves to repel the invasion in Honduran territory, all with the purpose of requesting a cessation of hostilities via diplomatic channels and to seek having the OAS declare El Salvador as the aggressor.

At that time, the FAH's order of battle listed six Vought F4U-5N and five F4U-4 Corsair fighter-bombers, six Douglas C-47 transports (serials 301, 302, 304, 305, 306 and 307), a Douglas C-54 medium transport, a Beech C-45 light transport, three Cessna 185B (U-17A and U-17C) light utility aircraft, five North American T-28A Trojan armed trainers and six North American AT-6 Texans, also capable of carrying armament. All these aircraft were organised into a Grupo de Combate (Combat Group) composed of three squadrons, namely the Escuadrón de Caza-Bombardeo (Fighter-Bomber Squadron) equipped with the Corsairs, the Escuadrón de Transporte (Transport Squadron), equipped with the C-47s, the C-45 and C-54, and the Escuadrón de Reconocimiento (Reconnaissance Squadron) that had assigned the Trojans, the Texans and the Cessna 185Bs.

C-47A serial 305, at Toncontín Airbase in April 1986. The aircraft in the squadron still sported the white-blue scheme applied during the 1970s.
R.E.G. Davies, via Dan Hagedorn

C-47B USAF serial 43-49504, seen at the Santa Rosa de Copán airfield in October 1967 after having suffered a rough landing. The US donated her to the FAH as a source of spare parts, but the Honduran mechanics repaired her. She was assigned the FAH serial 307 in June 1968. *5700th Air Base Wing, Howard AFB*

Due to the lack of proper maintenance facilities, almost the entire FAH strength was based at the Toncontín Airbase, with three or four Corsairs deploying periodically to the La Mesa airfield, in San Pedro Sula, for border and coastal patrol duties as well as combat training. Regarding its personnel, the FAH had twenty pilots and a well-established in-country flight training programme. In addition, there were 730 men assigned to the maintenance, armament, security and base services elements. In contrast to its Salvadoran counterpart, the FAH had achieved a certain degree of operational efficiency and its transport element had enough capacity to deploy important units of ground forces and to successfully resupply those contingents when necessary.

Despite overwhelming opposition from the President and the Army's high command, Col Soto Cano kept trying to convince them of the need to return the blow, striking far inland, to the very heart of El Salvador. From Soto Cano's standpoint, it was of vital importance to heavily attack the Salvadoran airbases and destroy their aircraft on the ground in order to attain aerial superiority. He also considered that the Salvadoran fuel depots should be attacked and destroyed, thus limiting the Salvadoran Army's actions. At one point, the situation was so tense that Col Soto Cano went to the extreme of arguing in a loud voice with the President and the high command's officers about the importance of effecting these strategic attacks. It was not until 11pm on the 14th that a still reticent López Arellano authorised Col Soto Cano to launch an air strike. Minutes later, the FAH's commander rushed back to Toncontín in order to brief his pilots and get the aircraft ready.

During the first few minutes of 15 July, the strategic bombing that Col Soto Cano wished so much to inflict upon the Salvadorans finally began taking shape. Just as their Salvadoran counterparts had done, a group of FAH mechanics installed rails along the cargo hold floor of the C-47 transport marked with the serial 304, and began loading the aircraft with eighteen AN-M30 bombs. Meanwhile, in the cockpit, the crew led by Capt. Rodolfo Figueroa was already going through the before engines start checklist. Their mission would be to bomb the Ilopango airport, so long as they could negotiate the marginal weather conditions along the way.

At 1.50am, the C-47 304 finally took off from Toncontín, and in complete darkness, headed towards El Salvador. Minutes later, however, a warning light on the instrument panel forced the crew to abort the mission and return to Tegucigalpa. Upon landing, the FAH mechanics rushed to remove the bombs and cargo railings and transferred them to another C-47, in this case the one bearing the serial 306.

It was not until 3.20am that the second C-47 was able to take off from Toncontín. Along the way, Capt. Figueroa noted that none of the Salvadoran navigation aids were operating, so he had to rely on his time and distance calculations in order to reach the target. If he made any mistakes in his navigation, the C-47 could end up anywhere but over the place it was intended to be. To further complicate the flight, the night was pitch black and almost no lights could be seen in the ground.

Around 4.10am, Capt. Figueroa considered that he was over the target. He was not sure, however, because due to the weather conditions and the generalised blackout in the Salvadoran capital, he had not been able to visually locate Ilopango. With nothing left to do but trust his calculations, he ordered the cargo master to roll out the bombs while establishing a tight circular pattern at 10,000ft above the area where he thought the airbase was. In less than five minutes, the eighteen bombs were gone and the old bird climbed away, heading back to its base.

As soon as the C-47 was back in Honduran airspace, Figueroa radioed Col Soto Cano informing him that the results of the mission were inconclusive. The crew had been able to hear the bombs exploding, but no one could obtain a visual confirmation of where they had fallen. Sensing that this mission would not be enough to deter the Salvadorans, the FAH Commander decided to contravene President López Arellano's order about launching only one air strike, and without delay ordered two additional bombing missions, which were carried out by the F4U-5s based at Toncontín and the F4U-4s that had been deployed to La Mesa, their targets being the Ilopango Airbase and the port of Cutuco, in the La Unión department for the F4U-5s, and the fuel storage tanks at the port of Acajutla for the F4U-4s.

That same day the Salvadoran ground forces managed to capture the towns of Nueva Ocotepeque and Goascorán, delivering a heavy psychological blow to the Honduran military. Hence, in a desperate attempt, the high command proposed a plan that comprised two phases: the first of which was to launch an all-out counteroffensive in the El Amatillo–Nacaome area, aimed at deflecting the attention of the Salvadorans from the Nueva Ocotepeque front, which hopefully would delay their advance towards Santa Rosa de Copán and other towns in the north. The second phase, to be executed simultaneously, would involve reinforcing the defences around Santa Rosa de Copán with troops from the Guardia de Honor Battalion (Honour Guard Battalion) and the Guardia Presidencial (Presidential Guard). With that, the Hondurans hoped, the Salvadoran invasion would stall, allowing the government enough time to seek the OAS' intervention.

Deploying the Guardia de Honor and the Guardia Presidencial to Santa Rosa de Copán was a highly controversial operation, however, because it meant that Tegucigalpa would be left defenseless, and if the counter-attack on the El Amatillo–Nacaome front failed, the Salvadorans would be free to advance towards the capital virtually unopposed. Its execution would also be very difficult, because on the one hand, the units deployed on both fronts were running short of ammunition and were having persistent problems with the batteries of their tactical radios; and on the other, the entire Guardia de honour Battalion and the Guardia Presidencial would have to be airlifted – as soon as possible – to Santa Rosa de Copán.

C-47D serial 308, at Toncontín airbase in April 1986, still sporting the white-blue scheme. *R.E.G. Davies, via Dan Hagedorn*

It was not until 3am that President López Arellano finally made the decision about launching the operation, and shortly after, the respective orders were issued to all combat units in the El Amatillo–Nacaome area. On his part, Col Soto Cano was ordered to prepare the FAH's six C-47 transports for airlifting the Guardia de honour Battalion and the Guardia Presidencial to Santa Rosa de Copán. Sensing that the handful of FAH transports would not be enough for carrying out the mission, the indefatigable Air Force Commander enlisted the help of the SAHSA airline, which promptly supplied a pair of its own C-47s for transporting the troops.

Incredibly, the Honduran C-47 squadron was able to accomplish the mission of transporting more than to 1,000 soldiers within forty-eight hours, its crews demonstrating a high degree of proficiency. Then, the aircraft began to fly resupply missions to all the fronts where the Army had deployed combat units, most of the time doing so unescorted, since the Corsair crews had their hands full conducting close air support and air superiority missions around the clock.

Last, but not least, on 17 July, the C-47s serialed 304 and 306 conducted no fewer than three bombing missions in support of the counter-attack in the El Amatillo–Nacaome area, along with the

F4U-5s based at Toncontín, which proved to be decisive. That same day, Capt. Fernando Soto, flying the F4U-5 serial 609, managed to shoot down three Salvadoran fighters. Then, during the evening of 18 July, and thanks to the mediation of the OAS and the Nicaraguan Chancellor, Guillermo Sevilla Sacasa, a ceasefire was agreed between the two nations, which was finally enforced at 10pm. (For a complete account of the aerial operations during this conflict, see the book *The 100-Hour War: The Conflict Between Honduras and El Salvador in July 1969*, published by the authors.)

The US feared that an arms race would follow the war between El Salvador and Honduras, hence it was decided to suspend the Military Assistance Program for the two nations. In the case of Honduras, the suspension prevented the transfer of a handful of C-47s that were scheduled to arrive in Tegucigalpa between July and September of that year. Incredibly, the paperwork for the transfer of one of those aircraft was so advanced that she was delivered from the lot that the USAF kept at Howard AFB in the Panama Canal Zone. This aircraft was an AC-47D gunship that had the MSN 17035/34300, and the USAF serial 45-1032, which according to the MAP papers arrived at Toncontín Airbase on 19 August 1970, right in the middle of the arms embargo!

C-47B serial 309 at Davis-Monthan AFB in early October 1974, before her ferry flight to Honduras. *Brian R. Baker, via Dan Hagedorn*

Nice view of the C-47B serial 309, already sporting the white-blue colour scheme applied to all the C-47s in the 1970s. *LTC Basset via Ed Furler*

C-47B serial 310 at Davis-Monthan AFB in early October 1974, before her ferry flight to Honduras. *Brian R. Baker, via Dan Hagedorn*

C-47 serial 310 at Toncontín Airbase in April 1986. *R.E.G. Davies, via Dan Hagedorn.*

C-47 serial 311 at Davis-Monthan AFB in early October 1974, before her ferry flight to Honduras. *Brian R. Baker, via Dan Hagedorn*

C-47 serial 312 at Davis-Monthan AFB in early October 1974, before her ferry flight to Honduras. *Brian R. Baker, via Dan Hagedorn*

C-47B serial 314 in 1978 at the main ramp of the Toncontín International airport. *Military Aircraft Photographs No.19782-85#AO7683*

Excellent in-flight image of C-47A serial 305, taken sometime in the late 1970s. *Honduran Aviation Museum, via LAAHS*

In any case, the MAP programme for Honduras and El Salvador resumed in July 1974, but it was not until 17 October that the FAH received four C-47s, which were used initially to transport relief aid for the victims of Hurricane Fifi that had hit the country two weeks earlier. Of these aircraft, which were assigned the serials 308, 309, 310 and 311, only two have been fully identified, as can be noted in the table at the end of the chapter. Ten days later, on 27 October, four more MAP-supplied C-47s were delivered to the FAH, taking up the serials 312, 313, 314 and 315. Of these, only the one marked with the serial 312 remains unidentified. The last aircraft supplied by the MAP, a VC-47D, MSN 15096/26541, ex USAF 43-49280, arrived in Toncontín on 24 December 1975, and was assigned the FAH serial 319.

On 25 July 1977, the oldest C-47 in the FAH fleet, serial 301, was lost when she slammed against the Siriano hill after taking off from the airfield in Yoro, killing twenty-two passengers and the three members of the crew. According to witnesses, one of the aircraft's engines malfunctioned during the take-off roll but the pilot, Capt. Rafael Salgado, decided to continue in order to deal with the emergency in flight. However, the fully loaded aircraft failed to climb to a safe altitude and crashed against the hill. Besides Capt. Salgado, the crew included 2nd Lt Edwin Serrano and Sgt Julio Midence. This was just the second C-47 mishap in more than thirty years of faithful service. Then, on 25 July 1979, another C-47 loss occurred, this time at Puerto Lempira. Apparently, the pilot lost control of the aircraft, FAH serial 313, during the take-off run, due to a malfunction in the left engine. Within seconds, the aircraft exited the runway and hit the airport terminal with one of its wings, catching fire almost immediately. Miraculously, of the twenty-six passengers onboard, only two were killed, along with the three members of the crew, Capt. Alexis Maldonado, 2nd Lt José Espinoza and Sgt Roberto Aguilar.

During the early 1980s, the government of Honduras found itself in a worrying situation: on one hand, neighbouring Nicaragua was ruled by the Sandinistas who, with the support of Cuba, the Soviet Union and other Communist countries, had launched an unprecedented military build-up that threatened the stability of the region. On the other, the Salvadoran government seemed to be losing the war against the FMLN guerrillas, which were being supported morally and logistically by the Sandinista regime. Something similar was happening in Guatemala, where the different guerrilla groups were launching increasingly daring offensives against that nation's Army, while negotiating their unification under a single organisation that could consolidate the financial and military assistance that Cuba and Nicaragua were providing.

The extremely delicate situation in Central America did not escape the recently inaugurated Reagan administration, which set out to increase the military assistance to Honduras with two clear objectives: the first was to give the Honduran armed forces the necessary combat equipment and training for stopping the flow of arms and supplies that the Sandinistas were providing to the Salvadoran guerrillas, which usually went through Honduran roads, waterways and even airspace. The other objective was to obtain the approval of the Honduran government for establishing bases in its territory for a clandestine guerrilla force that would launch an asymmetric war against the Sandinistas. Such a guerrilla force, nicknamed 'Contras', as in counterrevolutionaries, was populated primarily by ex-Nicaraguan National Guard members who had escaped to the US or the neighbouring Central American countries right after the overthrowing of the Nicaraguan President Anastasio Somoza Debayle, in July 1979. The deal also included establishing a US airbase at Palmerola, in Comayagua, where the FAH's José Enrique Soto Cano Airbase was situated.

C-47B serial 315, at an undetermined location, sometime in the early 1980s. *via Dan Hagedorn*

Beautiful in-flight photo of the C-47s 310 and 311 during acceptance flights at Davis-Monthan AFB, in October 1974, just before their delivery to Honduras. *Honduran Aviation Museum, via LAAHS*

C-47 serial 319 at Toncontín Airbase, in April 1986. *R.E.G. Davies, via Dan Hagedorn*

Starting in late 1979, the FAH C-47s were gradually painted in a Southeast Asia-type camouflage schemes, and only the aircraft marked with the number 305 received a 'civilian' colour scheme that consisted in an overall silver finish, with blue cheatlines. The following year, the aircraft carrying the serials 308 and 314, which were originally AC-47Ds, were fitted with three .50 calibre machine guns each, and conducted diurnal and nocturnal live fire exercises at the firing range of the 1st Infantry Battalion, located outside Tegucigalpa. Interestingly, none of them were used during the campaign against the Marxist guerrilla group led by Dr José María Reyes Mata, launched during the second half of 1983.

By the second half of 1985, a small war had developed in the south-west of Olancho, close to the border with Nicaragua, since units of the Sandinista Army constantly crossed into Honduras in hot pursuit of Contra elements. These incursions were supported by Soviet-built Mil Mi-8 and Mi-24 helicopters of the Fuerza Aérea Sandinista (Sandinista Air Force) or FAS, which proved to be very effective in providing close air support for the Nicaraguan troops. The FAH set out to reclaim air superiority, however, and on 13 September, two Dassault SMB-2s and two Cessna A-37Bs scrambled from the Héctor Caraccioli Moncada Airbase, at La Ceiba, arrived in the area and immediately went after the Nicaraguans, with the A-37Bs attacking the Sandinista troops while the SMB-2s pursued the helicopters, shooting down a Mi-8 and damaging a Mi-24.

It was around this time that an embarrassing episode involving a FAH C-47 took place. The aircraft marked with the serial 309 departed the Armando Escalón Airbase, at La Mesa, in San Pedro Sula, for Puerto Lempira on an undetermined date. Due to marginal weather conditions along the route, the crew got lost and only realised it when they descended from cruise altitude and did not see Puerto Lempira's airport. In fact, by then they were flying over an unfamiliar valley, not far from the Caribbean coast. After a couple of minutes, the pilot saw a small airfield close to a lagoon, and decided to land there and ask where they were. After landing, the pilot got down and saw a group of soldiers running towards the aircraft, but the weapons they were carrying were not of the type used by the Honduran Army, nor their uniforms. Sure that they had landed somewhere in Nicaragua, the pilot got back on the plane and ordered the co-pilot to take off immediately. In the end, the aircraft made it to Puerto Lempira in one piece. Later on, it was determined that the 309 had landed at the airstrip of Bismuna Tara, a small village located in Nicaragua, some 30km south of the border with Honduras. But the story does not end there, though, since upon returning to La Mesa, the airbase commander ordered that the aircraft's serial number be changed to avoid an international incident. It was in this way that C-47 serialed 309 was reserialed as 303. To further complicate things for aero-historians, days later, the serial 309 was painted on the vertical stabiliser of what was left of a DC-3A (MSN 1961, ex N17336) that had been captured with contraband at La Ceiba airfield in 1969, in a futile attempt to hide the disappearance of the C-47 that was assigned such a serial initially.

Unidentified FAH C-47 parked at the Héctor Caraccioli Moncada Airbase in La Ceiba, in 1988. Of note is the badge that the aircraft has painted on the left side of the nose, as well as the Northrop F-5s in the background. *Carlos Planas, via Dan Hagedorn*

Above: C-47A serial 305 at Toncontín Airbase. By the mid-1980s, this aircraft was painted in an elegant variation of the white-blue colour scheme, while the rest of the C-47 fleet was camouflaged. *via George J. Kamp*

Right: C-47A serial 304 at Toncontín Airbase, sporting the camouflage scheme that was applied to almost all the aircraft in the squadron during the early 1980s. *Honduran Aviation Museum, via LAAHS*

In 1999, the FAH C-47s were withdrawn from active service, since their maintenance had become a nightmare. Even though the majority of the aircraft ended up at the scrapyard at Toncontín airport, three had been transferred to the Honduran Aviation Museum for preservation.

What follows is the complete list of the Honduran Douglas C-47/AC-47/C-53 aircraft, including their previous identities and their final fates, where known.

Below: C-47B serial 313 at Toncontín Airbase in 1979. *R.E.G. Davies, via Dan Hagedorn*

C-47B serial 309, shortly after receiving the camouflage scheme in the early 1980s. *Aircraft Photo News APN130, via Ken F. Measures*

Originally assigned the serial 309, this C-47B was reserialed as 303 to hide its involvement in a little-known incident that took place in the early 1980s in Nicaragua. Even though the veracity of the event has been confirmed by official sources, a few local aero-historians refuse to acknowledge it, and list 309 as 'missing'. In any case, just compare the camouflage pattern of the aircraft serialed 309 and the one that appears in this photo. Both are identical! *Carlos Planas via Dan Hagedorn*

This DC-3A, ex N17336, was impounded at La Ceiba in 1969 and then flown to Tegucigalpa. After that the aircraft was left to rot at the Toncontín Airbase's scrapyard. However, shortly after the original 309 was reserialed as 303, it was decided to paint the '309' serial on the vertical stabiliser of what was left of this aircraft, in a futile attempt to hide the disappearance of the C-47 that was assigned this serial initially. The image was taken in January 1982. *Carlos Planas via Dan Hagedorn*

FAH Serial	Previous Identity	Type as Built	MSN	Assignments and Notes
FAH-300	42-92931	C-47A-20-DK	12786	Purchased from the US War Assets Administration. Delivered on 21 Dec 47. Crashed off the coast of La Libertad, El Salvador, on 5 May 57.
FAH-301	41-18690 NC-54075 AN-ADP	C-47-DL	6096	Purchased from the Nicaraguan Air Force. Delivered on 4 Sep 51. Crashed against a mountain at Yoro on 25 Jul 77.
FAH-302	42-68769 NC86593 N99C	C-53D-DO	11696	Purchased from Trans International Airlines. Delivered on 2 Apr 58. Reserialed as FAH-321 after July 1969.
FAH-303	43-48485 309	C-47B-1-DK	14301/25746	This aircraft was reserialed as such after an international incident that occurred in Nicaragua in the early 1980s, as noted in the text. Stored at the Hernán Acosta Airbase, in Tegucigalpa.
FAH-304	42-93089	C-47A-20-DK	12962	Delivered on 18 Oct 62 via MAP. WFU in 2003. At the scrapyard of the Hernán Acosta Airbase, in Tegucigalpa.
FAH-305	42-100963	C-47A-75-DL	19426	Delivered on 18 Oct 62 via MAP. WFU in 1999. At the scrapyard of the Hernán Acosta Airbase, in Tegucigalpa.

A handful of C-47s at Toncontín in 2003. By then, the aircraft had been retired and were in different stages of decay. *Honduran Aviation Museum via LAAHS*

FAH-306	42-93701	C-47A-25-DK C-47D	13642	Delivered on 10 Jun 63 via MAP. WFU in 1986. Preserved at the Honduran Air Museum, Tegucigalpa, since 2001.
FAH-307	43-49504 0-49504	C-47B-15-DK	15320/26765	Former US Mission aircraft, which had a mishap at Santa Rosa de Copán on 16 Oct 67. Donated to the FAH and repaired. Entered active service on 17 Jun 68. WFU in 1982. At the scrapyard of the Hernán Acosta Airbase, in Tegucigalpa.
FAH-308	45-1032 0-51032	C-47D-45-DK AC-47D	17035/34300	Delivered on 19 Aug 70 via MAP, already converted to AC-47D. WFU in 1999. At the scrapyard of the Hernán Acosta Airbase, in Tegucigalpa.
FAH-309 (I)	NC17336 N17336	C-48B DC-3-208 DC-3A	1961	Impounded sometime in the late 1970s while on a smuggling flight. Even though she was already abandoned at the Toncontín scrapyard, she received a FAH serial in the early 1980s, in connection with an international incident in Nicaragua, as noted in the text. Last seen at the Támara parachute training range.
FAH-309 (II)	43-48485	C-47B-1-DK	14301/25746	Delivered on 17 Oct 74 via MAP. Reserialed as 303 in the early 1980s after an international incident in Nicaragua, as noted in the text.
FAH-310		C-47?		Delivered on 17 Oct 74 via MAP. WFU in 1992. At the scrapyard of the Héctor Caraccioli Airbase, in La Ceiba.
FAH-311		C-47?		Delivered on 17 Oct 74 via MAP. WFU in 1987. At the scrapyard of the Hernán Acosta Airbase, in Tegucigalpa.
FAH-312		C-47?		Delivered on 27 Oct 74 via MAP. WFU after sustaining damage during take-off on an undetermined date. As training aid at La Venta.
FAH-313	43-16373	C-47B-1-DL	20839	Delivered on 2 Oct 74 via MAP. Crashed shortly after taking off from Puerto Lempira airport on 27 Dec 79.
FAH-314	43-16165	C-47B-1-DL AC-47D	20631	Delivered on 27 Oct 74 via MAP already converted to AC-47D. WFU in 1999. Waiting to be transferred to the Honduran Aviation Museum, as of Nov 20.
FAH-315	43-48917 0-48917	C-47B-10-DK	14733/26178	Delivered on 27 Oct 74 via MAP. WFU in 1999. Preserved at the Honduran Air Museum, Tegucigalpa, since 2003 with the fake registration XH-TAZ and TACA livery.
FAH-319	43-49280	C-47B-15-DK VC-47D	15096/26541	Delivered on 24 Dec 75 via MAP. WFU in 1999. At the scrapyard of the Hernán Acosta Airbase, in Tegucigalpa.
FAH-321	42-68769 NC86593 N99CFAH-302	C-53D-DO	11696	Reserialed as 321 after the war with El Salvador in Jul 69. Sold as HR-AIF in Oct 80, then to YV-389CP.

By the mid-2000s, the C-47s were being scrapped. In this photo, the remains of at least five of them can be seen. *Honduran Aviation Museum via LAAHS*

CHAPTER FIFTEEN

Mexico

IT MAY BE FAIRLY SAID that, had Donald Douglas and his design team set out from the beginning to design an aircraft series destined to evolve into the DC-3 and C-47 that was practically tailor-made for a specific geographic environment, Mexico would certainly qualify close to the top of such a listing.

The study of the use of C-47 series aircraft in Mexican military and naval service, however, has proven to be among the most challenging of all chapters in this book. To a large extent, this is due to the fact that, despite the best efforts of a dedicated group of Mexican aero-historians and friends in the US and elsewhere, the two operating organisations, the Fuerza Aérea Mexicana (FAM) and the Navy's Servicio de Aviación de la Armada Mexicana rank among the most secretive and steadfastly security-conscious organisations in the Western Hemisphere. As a direct consequence, while the same group of Mexican aero-historians have managed to arrange access to some isolated documents of a general nature, nothing approaching the degree of transparency of operational records enjoyed by US or European historians has ever been realised.

All of this has been exacerbated by a series of historical anomalies, the first of which revolves around the fact that, at the very beginning of the FAM's rather modest affiliation with the C-47, a hitherto virtually unknown serialing system was briefly employed, and what is known of this system is described in the first of our tables below. While the relationships between the known FAM serials and the prior USAAF serials are not linked concretely in a single instance, they have been deduced based on the known date of transfer, assuming of course that the FAM may have then assigned their own serials to these aircraft as they entered service. However, the impact of these initial serials on the second, larger series, and the several specialised serials and quasi-governmental civil registrations assigned to the surprising number of DC-3s and C-47s detailed to the exclusive Presidential operating unit is largely unknown.

While the FAM eventually gained the distinction of having been the second largest operator of DC-3 and C-47 series aircraft in all of Latin America, until the 1970s this had not yet been achieved. Until then, at no time did the FAM possess as many as a dozen airworthy examples, not including those assigned to VIP use – a number that was far less than adequate for a national area of responsibility as vast as that of Mexico. It was not until the several major Mexican commercial airlines – Cia. Mexicana de Aviación (more commonly known as simply Mexicana) and Aeronaves de México – started to divest themselves of their substantial DC-3 and C-47 fleets, at bargain prices, together with a plethora of other, smaller operators, that the numbers of DC-3s and C-47s in the FAM inventory started to climb substantially, eventually reaching a total of more than fifty-six known airframes. Similarly, the FAM also was given 'hand-me-downs' from other governmental operating agencies. Finally, the FAM also was gifted an unknown number of seized drug and contraband smuggler aircraft, nearly all of which had been 'sanitised', making tracing their actual provenance all but impossible.

Built as a C-47B, F.A.M.6007 was modified somewhere along the line to include an air stair in place of her former twin cargo doors. She wears four-star placards under both her cockpit and under her serial on the vertical fin, and is named 'Galeana'. She is seen at either Meacham Field, Fort Worth or Love Field, Dallas, Texas, in December 1967. Her appearance is pristine, in keeping with her obvious use as a VIP transport at the time. *Pete Bulban via Jay Miller*

Above: C-47A TE102, otherwise devoid of any markings whatsoever, and almost certainly one of the JUSMDC aircraft, flying in formation with a fully marked aircraft, which appears to have been either the elusive TTD 6005 or 6006. Note also the distinctive black paint on the lower rear fuselage, which is not a shadow. TE102 has an RDF 'bullet' rather far aft under her forward fuselage that, for this circa 1947–48 image, is very unusual. *Dr Esnarriaga via Santiago Flores*

Right: Another of the previously unreported *FAM* C-47s, TE107, almost certainly one of the ARP-supplied aircraft. The unusual black area under the rear fuselage was seen on a number of FAM aircraft over the years and, in this instance, has apparently been crudely modified to accommodate the application of the national insignia. Her identity is a matter of deduction. *Dr Esnarriaga via Santiago Flores*

Right: Three of the nearly anonymous early FAM C-47s, probably all ARP-supplied examples, with TE118, the highest number known, circa September 1949. Just visible at left is the extreme nose of the single FAM Budd RB-1. *Dr Esnarriaga via Santiago Flores*

Below: The serial prefix seen here on veteran C-47 6006, 'T.E.D.', dates this photo as from the early 1970s, by which time she had been in more or less continuous service for more than twenty years. Her cursive name, 'Plan de Ayala', was worn during most of that time, and can just be seen on the upper forward fuselage. Note also the non-standard small skylight window in the lavatory at the upper right corner of the fuselage national insignia and her unit insignia of the Escuadron Aéreo de Transportes on her nose. Her blue cheatline is trimmed with gold paint, which wraps around the horizontal tail root. *ATP No.4615*

Here is T.E.D.6006 again very late in her service life at Mexico City on 8 January 1978, next to a completely stripped FAM C-47. She soldiered on, however, into September 1993, when she was, incredibly, undergoing extensive overhaul after nearly forty-three years of faithful service at BAM#1, nominally assigned to Escuadrón 311. *Dr Gary Kuhn*

Another view of F.A.M.6007, this one from 1970, reveals that the leading edges of her engine cowlings had also been painted blue by this time, to match her cheatline, which was trimmed in gold paint. Her starboard engine has been removed. Note the specially deployed air stair installation. *MAP1980-59 #200*

But at the beginning, what may be fairly described as the first three FAM C-47s arrived under very unusual circumstances. Unusually, while a thorough study of the records of the Munitions Assignment Board (Air) held by the National Archives was conducted some years ago, not a solitary Mexican Lend-Lease requisition for C-47-series aircraft was located in the very detailed minutes of that organisation. Instead, the Board reluctantly approved the allocation of six Lockheed C-60A Lodestars, although, in the event, only four were actually delivered between August 1943 and February 1944. Perhaps encouraged by this, and the fact that the country had mounted a dedicated fighter unit to fly alongside the Allies in the Pacific, the FAM submitted a follow-up requisition in January 1944 for no fewer than thirty C-60As. But not a word about C-47s, which has remained a puzzle.

While the quartet of C-60As had their virtues, especially as VIP transports, a tasking to which nearly all of them were almost immediately diverted, their utility as actual troop transports and cargo haulers was very modest indeed, and while the ranking

Her nose ventral RDF bullet and antenna array strongly suggest that F.A.M.6007 'Galeana' was a late-production C-47B, marking her almost certainly as one of the Lend-Lease aircraft. Note the non-standard circular porthole on the upper fuselage and the titles under her four-star placard that read 'Secretaria Defensa Nacional, Secretario'.
Pete Bulban via Jay Miller

Mexican political and military personalities dashed about the country in the Lodestars, the FAM's tactical leaders realised that there had to be C-47s in their future if they were to be regarded among the front-runners in Latin American military aeronautics.

The wartime Commander of the US Army Air Forces, General Henry H. 'Hap' Arnold, felt exactly the same way, as it happened. He held a special vision for a truly hemispheric defensive air force, in which each national air arm, based on their unique circumstances and resources, would contribute – with USAAF assistance – a 'Tab Force' crafted to operate co-operatively as a sort of 'Monroe Doctrine of the Air'. His vision, which had started taking shape as the successor to the highly successful Lend-Lease programme, became known as the American Republics Projects (ARP), and was guided by a strictly USAAF creation, the so-called Joint Advisory Board for American Republics (JABAR), which he allowed would include token representatives from the US Navy and state Department, this having been regularly constituted by June 1947.

But even before JABAR and the ARP, Arnold had accorded to Mexico a unique organisation, known as the Demonstration Flight Project – and by 1950 as the US Air Liaison Unit. Mexican pride and sensitivity to what was perceived as an overpowering US presence dictated that the training and guidance that the FAM very much needed from the United States could not be moulded in the same shape and description as it was nearly everywhere else in the Americas. In every other instance, the conveyance of training and equipment standardisation envisioned by Arnold was conveyed by means of what was, under formal government-to-government protocols, known universally as a 'USAAF Mission, USAF Mission, US Mission' or 'US Military Assistance Advisory Group (MAAG)' – except Mexico. The British Air Attaché with responsibility for Mexico who was, oddly, headquartered in Caracas, Venezuela, at the time, observed the true nature of this aberration in December 1950 when he said, 'the US Mission to Mexico's true title is US Air Liaison Unit, as the FAM had no wish to be put in the same category as all those other Latin American countries with USAF Missions'.

Arnold acted unilaterally with regard to his plans for Mexico, however, and essentially circumvented the advice or consent of the usual State Department trump. He detailed a tidy number of multi-lingual, experienced USAAF aviators to the Mexican Demonstration Flight Project, as well as three brand-new North American B-25Js, six North American AT-6Cs – and three Douglas C-47Bs, all of which arrived at the Central Airfield near Mexico City on 13 December 1945.

This starboard view of 6007, which had 'T.E.D.' prefix characters at the time, reveal the dual port holes over the lavatory in the rear cabin roof and that she was wearing the insignia of the Escuadron Aéreo de Transportes. Additionally, her engine cowlings and accessory covers have been painted blue. FAM-operated DC-3s and C-47s nearly all experienced colour and markings changes during their service lives. *via George G.J. Kamp*

While these aircraft initially retained their USAAF markings and serials, this soon manifested itself as a sensitive issue with the Mexicans, and, on his own authority, Arnold verbally authorised the officer in charge of the Project to mark them with Mexican national insignia while for a time retaining their USAAF serial numbers, before they were 'loaned' to the FAM, again totally on Arnold's own considerable authority. The language of a US Intelligence report describing this arrival left little doubt about their eventual intended disposition, saying that they had arrived 'for eventual handing over to the FAM'. Not surprisingly, the US Embassy in Mexico City soon became aware of this 'unconventional' arrangement, taking a very dim view of the fact that they had been completely blind-sided, and Arnold was put on the spot to explain on what authority he had 'loaned' ten virtually brand new aircraft to a foreign power. The voluminous administrative and legal wrangling that ensued are beyond the remit of this volume but Arnold, ever the consummate mover and shaker, contrived to declare the aircraft 'excess', directed they be 'reclaimed' and sold to the highest bidder as merely surplus property – for essentially $1 each. The buyer, of course, was the FAM, and all of the ten aircraft, which by then had been passed to the custody of the Joint US/Mexico Defence Commission (JUSMDC), are believed to have simply been handed over in airworthy condition 'as is/where is'. The ten included two C-47s, five T-6Cs, two B-25Js and one UC-45F. This was once and for all tidied up with what was termed Project MEX253, which, although not a properly coded MDAP project, made USAF accountants happy, and finally closed this rather curious affair.

This may account for the fact that the US Military Intelligence Division, in its Air Orders of Battle for Mexico dated 24 May and 7 August 1946, listed the service as possessing three C-47s as first-line equipment, and all were assigned to the Escuadrón de Transporte at Mexico City, operating alongside three Lockheed C-60As and one Beech AT-7. Since none of the projected ARP deliveries were even in the 'pipeline' at this point, these had to be the C-47s 'owned' by the USAAF's DFP. A similar report for 31 January 1947, showed only two, both assigned as before, alongside the C-60As.

Mexico was, however, a designated recipient for at least seven C-47s under the provisions of the Interim ARP Project No. 72014 in 1947 and 1948,[36] although the JABAR had recommended that a minimum of thirteen, to completely equip one squadron, was the optimum number. These were unquestionably the aircraft that populated the relatively short-lived first serial system between TE-101 and TE-118 noted in the second table below. The 'TE-' prefix is assumed to denote Transporte Ejército, although Mexican aero-historian Santiago Flores has suggested it denoted Transporte Entrenador instead, as the FAM remained very much subordinated to the Army. The fact that the serials have significant gaps (104 to 106, 109 and 112 to 117 are notably 'missing') may have been a simple ploy on the part of the FAM to deceive prying eyes to their actual strength, as the service certainly did not acquire eighteen C-47 aircraft during that early period, the ARP offsets and one apparent commercial or seizure acquisition having been the only known sources at the time. However, a FAM C-47 is known to have crashed and been written off on 2 October 1946 at Hermosillo, and the identity of this aircraft has not been established. It may thus have well been one of the 'missing' serials.

A very early image of TTD-6010 shot at Clover Field, California, on 23 June 1948. Note the distinctive black lower rear fuselage, assumed to have been applied to protect the lower rear fuselage from debris thrown up when landing. She is in very much stock configuration. *William T. Larkins*

This view of TTD-6010 shows her wearing both the unit insignia, barely visible on her extreme nose, and the apparently abbreviated titles of the Escuadron de Transportes. *Santiago Flores*

This is actually a highly significant image. Serial 6011 is clearly visible in the near foreground, with the unit insignia of the Escuadron de Transportes but also with a most unusual RDF bullet just aft of her astrodome. The next aircraft, devoid of any obvious markings, is a late model C-47B but, next in line, are two North American B-25Js of three received. Based on the crowd assembled, something important was about to happen.
José Quevado via Mario Overall

Serial 6010 once again seen much later in her service life, with the unit insignia prominent on her nose but now with full Fuerza Aerea Mexicana titles. White upper decking on the fuselage had been added, as well as yet another variation on the cheatlines utilised. *Capt. Rich Dann, USNR (Ret)*

A much later view of TTD-6011, revealing that she too has been modified by the installation of an air stair, and that she also wears a three-star placard over her serial on the vertical fin and under the cockpit window with the abbreviated titles 'Jefe F.A.M'. The presence of a modified Douglas B-18A sitting next to her, minus props, is of interest as well.
Dr Gary Kuhn

The first serial sequences apparently only lasted until around February 1948, however, as by that time the current series, in the 6000s, commencing with TTD-6005, are known to have been adopted and so the 'TE-' prefixes and serials were only used about one year at best, some probably 'grandfathered' to be changed to the definitive series as they came up for depot maintenance to ease tasking on the limited number of qualified maintainers. It should be noted, however, that the final series did not commence with 6001 as might be reasonably assumed: serials 6001 to 6004 had been assigned to the four Lend-Lease Lockheed C-60As, and thus the 'lowest' FAM C-47 serial was 6005 and of those that followed, the first four aircraft are assumed to have been a mix of former ARP and DFP aircraft. Serial 6009 was not assigned to a C-47, however, being used on the Siperstein y Maldonado Model 5 post-war light twin indigenous design. Initially, these were prefixed by another post-war FAM convention, the letters 'TTD-' denoting Transporte de Tropas Douglas. This system persisted for some years but was gradually supplemented in a few instances by the acronym prefix 'TED-', which translated to Transporte Ejecutivo Douglas. More recently, however, most of the surviving aircraft appear to have had their serials prefixed by 'ETM-', which defined Escuadrón Transporte Mediano. Although a generalisation, these prefixes can aid in establishing the relative chronological time frame of individual aircraft.

Reliable information on the status of the FAM C-47 inventory in the years immediately following their entry into service is, at best, confusing. A US Air Order of Battle for 5 May 1948 showed the service with a total of seven that, taking known losses into account and ARP gains, is probably accurate. That for 1 January 1949 reflected a total of nine, and this remained constant until 1 April 1950, when it increased to eleven.

By 1 December 1948, a US document entitled 'Status of Foreign Military Aid' reported that, cumulatively to that date, Mexico had received eight C-47s, which would seem to cover the surviving Lend-Lease aircraft and the seven ARP machines. In a letter dated 24 May 1950, however, Mexico formally requested, on the basis of having been a signatory to the MDA agreements of 1949, that it be sold ten C-47s – as well as twenty-five North American F-51Ds, no fewer than ninety-nine North American T-6Ds,[37] ten Vultee BT-13As, twenty Beech AT-11s and ten North American B-25Js. Of the aircraft on this 'wish list', the US approved only a portion of the T-6Ds and AT-11s, replying that the other types were either no longer available due to the onset of the Korean conflict, or no longer in the USAF supply chain.

Then, around 26 May 1949, the rather staid and somewhat complacent FAM was shaken when orders were issued to shuffle all existing units and commands. Existing squadrons (escuadrones) were to be subordinated to four grupos headquartered at Balbuena Field,

Mexico City (Grupo 1/°); Ixtepec, Oaxaca (Grupo 2/°); Ensenada, Baja California (Grupo 3/°); and Cozumel, Quintana Roo (Grupo 4/°). This reorganisation, according to the Secretary of Defence, had the objective of aiding stringent economy measures then in effect, centralisation of command, control and a very limited strike power at strategically located airbases and unification of unit doctrine and training, as well as simplification of supply and transport. To have been completed within the month, fuel and funding for same at certain points en route delayed the actual implementation. Escuadrón 203's ground echelon, for example, took nine days to travel from Mazatlán to Mexicali via rail and truck, and special orders had to be issued by none other than the Secretariat of National Defence himself to permit the purchase of local petrol to complete the journey to Ensenada, following a two-day delay in Mexicali. Perhaps not unexpectedly, the impact of all of this on FAM morale was universally bad, at a time when, in the view of the USAF Air Attaché at the time, Maj. LeRoy Nigra, 'it had already been stretched pretty thin'. What was worse was that movement of wives and families was not expected to be completed for two months, not just because of transportation shortages, but exacerbated by a nearly complete lack of appropriate housing at the new stations. When complaints inevitably started working their way up the Chain of Command, the FAM Deputy Chiefs of Staff appealed to President Alemán himself to allow the Escuadrón de Transporte to help ease the situation. At the time, the Escuadrón de Transporte was not permitted to fly any of its C-47 fleet without the express authorisation of the Presidencia. In fact, while the reorganisation was decried by the rank and file at the time, it actually resulted in a sounder tactical and strategic structure – much better than the overlapping, helter-skelter structure that had existed previously. Grupo 1/° and 4/° had previously been garrisoned essentially side by side at Balbuena Field, Mexico City, while the Grupo 2/° had been at Veracruz and the Grupo 3/° at Ensenada. This set-up had been, in effect, a heterogeneous paper empire, the scattered subordinate escuadrones operating essentially independently and, in many instances, on municipal airfields with totally inadequate military facilities available.

The British Air Attaché reported the FAM with seven C-47s serviceable as of 31 December 1950, but also noted four others unserviceable and one destroyed by that date, for a total of twelve. He also noted that the Escuadrón de Transporte had flown a total of 1,076:50 hours between 1 January and 31 December 1950 – a very modest achievement, and that the unit was commanded at the time by Tte.Cnel Héctor Berthier Aguiluz. USAF Report, IR-133-51 dated 23 November 1951, noted the FAM with a total of twelve C-47s, with the footnote that '11 of them are rated as 'USAF supportable'.

Compare this 15 September 1986 view of recoded E.T.M.6011 with the previous view. The RDF bullet and antennas are gone, she has a much later stylised cheatline and matching blue engine cowlings at BAM#1 Santa Lucia. *via George G.J. Kamp*

Apparently not discouraged by the MDA request of May 1950 noted above, Mexico once again submitted another request around 17 December 1951, via the USAF Attaché at the time, Col William K. Skaer. This time, the 'wish list' included forty North American T-6Ds or T-6Gs, twenty more Beech AT-11s, which the FAM seemed to regard as nearly ideal for their operating conditions, twenty-four North American F-51Ds,[38] five unspecified 'jet fighters' and ten C-47s. Col Skaer noted that the FAM desired only 'reconditioned' aircraft at 'bargain prices' but, once again, the requisite funding was not forthcoming.

The US Air Order of Battle report for Mexico dated 1 July 1952, reflected a total of twelve C-47s on strength, of which nine were with the Escuadrón de Transporte at Balbuena Field, the other three undoubtedly by this time having been detailed to Presidential duty, although one had been loaned to the Mexican Navy by 20 August 1952. This had altered slightly by 30 June 1954, when the total number of C-47s on strength had changed to eight, one having been known to have been lost in an undocumented accident in October 1953, but the USAF observer who wrote the report rather wryly noted that 'the air force can put only two of them in the air at the same time.' By 1 January 1955, the situation had remained essentially static, with a total of ten C-47s reported on the Air Order of Battle for that date, all with the Escuadrón de Transporte at Balbuena Field, of which seven were rated 'combat ready'. This remained unchanged by February 1956 at ten, seven of which were still assigned to the same unit, all 'combat ready'.

Displaying yet another variation on cheatline colour and design, T.T.D.6012 was a May 1947 commercial acquisition and, by the time of this 3 October 1968 view at BAM#1, was still well maintained in her nineteenth year of service. Note the unit insignia of the Escuadron Aéreo de Transportes on her nose. *Guido E. Bühlmann*

To this point, the FAM operating unit had amassed some nine years of experience with the C-47, and the aircraft, with its civilian cohorts, had become all but ubiquitous across the length and breadth of the Republic. On 19 June 1954, however, an added dimension to day-to-day operations requires recounting. TTD-6014 was en route that day to Balbuena Field, Mexico City, on what, by all appearances, was a routine freight run, the flight having originated at El Ciprés, Baja California, which had been a FAM station since the Second World War. Unfortunately, the aircraft crashed under unknown circumstances north-west of Mexico City in the mountains known as Cerro Pelón and, almost immediately, rumours started circulating of articles and merchandise found among the debris at the crash site that the rather strident news media of the day almost immediately suggested could have been regarded as contraband. There were nineteen passengers aboard and all perished, among whom was Tte.Gen. Leobardo Tellechea, one of the most notable figures of the nearly legendary revolution of 1910. The aircraft had departed Mazatlán at 1515hrs bound for Mexico City. At around 1600 hrs, the aircraft's radio operator made contact with Guadalajara, and at 1900hrs a position report was made to Querétaro. At 1920hrs, the aircraft communicated with Balbuena Field tower, asking for local weather conditions – and that was the last heard. Weather was unquestionably the deciding factor in the crash that followed. The location of the crash site made retrieval of the victims exceptionally difficult. The FAM even dropped some paratroopers near the scene to attempt to recover the bodies, while motorised equipment had proceeded as close to the scene as possible. The US Air Attaché offered the services of the Air Rescue Service to help recover the bodies, but this was declined. In one of the newspapers, a reporter who had claimed to have actually visited the scene, which,

Although modified several times over the years, the basic design of the primary C-47 operating unit for most of the 1950–70 era, the Escuadron Aéreo de Transportes remained the same. Interestingly, this image was taken of a C-47 with Day-Glo on her nose – none of which have been documented! *via Santiago Flores*

under the circumstances seems exceptionally unlikely, recorded nonetheless that 'in an area of some 100 meters, we found the lifeless, mutilated bodies of the passengers. Surrounding the bodies were more than 1,000 fine cigarette lighters, boxes of women's stockings of North American brand, and other large boxes containing North American made merchandise. Also, all of the passengers had in their luggage North American women's clothing, underclothing, costume jewelry and cameras amounting to an approximate value of one million Pesos. The supposition has to be that this material was being brought in for contraband purposes. At long last, the last of our great honorable institutions has been infested with dishonor. The Mexican Army, long the most honorable and loyal of our services, has fallen prey to past governmental traditions.'

Needless to say, the FAM and other government agencies immediately denied the report, but the US Assistant Air Attaché at the time, Maj. Sigurd L. Jensen, Jr, commented that 'it is the writer's opinion that the practice of carrying goods of the above nature is fairly common practice in the Mexican Air Force. This is not to be construed to mean the FAM is conducting contraband activities but, on the whole, the personnel were probably carrying only what they intended to use personally or for the use of their relatives. It was a misfortune for the FAM that the aircraft which crashed carried such items, but it is believed the amount and value as voiced in the quoted article was exaggerated.' There was no further comment on this report, and Maj. Jensen probably summed it all up very well, as the Mexican military had few friends in the press at the time. This reduced the total number of C-47s in the inventory at the time to just ten.

An excellent study of C-47A TTD-6016, with the distinctive black lower rear fuselage, next to the two surviving B-25Js and the obscure FAM Budd RB-1. *Ing. Jose Villela*

By 30 January 1957, the FAM still possessed only five C-47s assigned to the Escuadrón de Transporte, all of which were rated 'combat ready', although two others, for a total of seven, were assigned to Grupo Aéreo 1, also at Balbuena, of which one was combat ready. By 1 July, the stats had remained unchanged, but the FAM was hopeful that it could use at least $500,000 of a $2 million credit from the US towards acquiring additional surplus aircraft, preferably more C-47s. By 28 October 1958, the total at hand had increased to eight, indicating one had been acquired in the interim, possibly by using a portion of the credit noted, while the same report noted that the 'Mexican Presidency Special Air Section', an anglicisation of the proper operating name of this unit, had two 'VIP' DC-3s at the same time, for a total of ten.

Between 1959 and 1964, the leading Mexican airlines were starting to dispose of their long-serving DC-3s, and of these, Aeronaves de México is known to have sold one DC-3 (and two C-54s) to the FAM for 6,383,178.72 pesos between those years. By February 1964, a declassified CIA document showed the FAM with a total of only eight C-47s.

There have been at least eight undocumented accidents and losses to the FAM C-47 inventory over the years. One was on 13 June 1972, followed by another on 14 May 1977 at Mexicali, BC. These were followed by four in the 1980s: 29 April 1985 at Zapopán, Jalisco; 31 December 1985 at BAM#1 Santa Lucía; 9 February 1989 at the same station, and 6 December 1989 at Tepic, Nayarit. Two of the most recent occurred on 8 December 1991 when an unidentified aircraft came down on the Sangangüey volcano, 20km south-east of Tepic, Nayarit, and was fatal to all five on board. The last was on 13 November 1992, again at BAM#1, Santa Lucía.

By 16 June 1993, C-47s and DC-3s were entering the twilight period of their service with the FAM, although the 9° Grupo Aéreo at BAM#1, Santa Lucía, was still shown as operating a total of five C-47s and one DC-3 in two different E.A.T.M.s, numbers 311 and 312. These were TTD-6006, 6011, 6025, 6040, 6042 and 6043.

No discussion of the Mexican military and Presidential use of DC-3s and C-47s would be complete without at least passing mention of a most unusual and little-known convention employed by the Mexican Dirección General de Aviación Civil during the late 1940s and most of the '50s. Mexico has, since the inception of its modern civil aircraft register, used registration prefixes XA-, XB-, and XC- to denote commercial, general aviation and governmental aircraft, each prefix then being followed, in alphabetical order, by three letters. For example, XA-AAA to AAZ, XA-ABA o XA-ABZ etc. Around February 1949, however, a curious anomaly was first noted. Aircraft that had been procured on behalf of the Presidencia in nearly every known instance were reserved for registration sequences ending in the letter 'X'. For example, XB-DOX, one of the first

This view of the nose of TTD-6016 shows not only her unit insignia, but the presence of at least nineteen other Latin American nations, suggesting she may have been the FAM aircraft detailed to the annual Posta Aérea Latinoamericana joint international exercise. The aircraft just visible in the background appears to be the elusive TTD-6013. *via Dr Gary Kuhn*

known, was for a Convair 240-8 acquired by the agent for the President, Ing. Jorge Pasquel, on 7 February 1949, or Lic. Miguel Alemán V. himself, and so on. There have been at least an astonishing fifty-two possible combinations between XB-DOX and XB-TAX, which may possibly have been reserved for aircraft intended for the President, his staff, or his principal ministerial agencies. However, of these, only twenty-three are known to have actually been assigned. Of these, no fewer than seven are known to have been worn by C-47 or DC-3 aircraft: XB-FAX, XB-JEX, XB-JIX, XB-JOX, XB-JUX, XB-LAX, and XB-MEX. That some of these were, in fact, assigned to the Presidential flight unit is unquestionable, and some in fact are known to have worn quasi-military style serials as well. That more of them may have at some point passed to the FAM for day-to-day use cannot be therefore discounted, and these may well figure prominently in the serials in the accompany tables that are otherwise not matched with known aircraft.

And then, of course, there are the substantial number of DC-3s and C-47s that were operated during the 1950s and into the '70s by various Mexican Government agencies other than the Presidencia with 'XC-' prefixes, many of which are suspected of passing to FAM marks when their several operators moved on to more modern types, as the eventual fates of most of them are not known. These have included candidates XC-ABF, XC-BCE, XC-BNO, XC-CFE, XC-CIC, XC-CIY, XC-CNI, XC-DAK, XC-DOE, XC-OPS.

TTD-6016 again, now with white upper decking, a cheatline and service titles much later in her service career circa 1978, the last known sighting. This may be one of the aircraft lost to one of the undocumented accidents described in the narrative. *Dr Gary Kuhn*

A fine study of what is believed to be a former Aeronaves de Mexico aircraft, T.T.D.6021, affording a view of the standard underside markings. This aircraft is unusual in having two ventral RDF bullets under the forward fuselage and a ram-air ventilation intake on the forward starboard fuselage. She wears the unit insignia of the Escuadron Aéreo de Transportes, rather faded, on her nose. *via Will Blount*

Finally, some readers will quickly note, in reviewing the tables that follow, that in the 6000 series alone, between the known serial issues of 6005 and 6056, there are a total of twelve serials in that series for which not a solitary sighting report has been located, namely 6013, 6017 and 6018, 6026 and 6027, 6030, 6034, 6039, 6041 and 6050 to 6052. Considering that C-47 aircraft have been in more-or-less continuous service with the FAM since 1946, the complete absence of any reports whatsoever on these 'missing' aircraft stretch the realm of credulity. The small but energetic Mexican aviation history community, joined by the occasional visiting 'spotter' or enthusiast, most of whom have been physically located in the vicinity of the principal FAM C-47 operating stations – Balbuena Field, DF and BAM#1 Santa Lucía – can hardly have completely missed twelve aircraft over the intervening seventy-plus years. Some observers have speculated that these serials were reserved against C-47s operated by other Federal government agencies (see above), which just happens to be exactly twelve aircraft, in the event they were required in a national emergency, while others have suggested that they represent a mix of unreported losses and aircraft that may have been lost during the poorly reported counter-insurgency operations in the hinterland during the 1970s and '80s. That they must have been issued, if not actually assigned, in light of the fact that serials on either side of the 'missing' numbers have in fact been noted, seems beyond doubt. It is the profound hope of your scribes that additional research may at last put this perplexing anomaly to rest.

This view of the same aircraft, T.T.D.6021, shows her wearing the much later standard blue 'lightning bolt'-style cheatline outlined in gold paint as of this 1970 photo, and she has shed the two ventral RDF bullets, apparently replacing them a pair of streamlined nodes, now on the top of the forward fuselage. Believed to have been built as a C-47A, she has had her cargo doors modified to a single air stair design. *MAP 1980-59 #196*

Above: Although initially built as a C-47A-20-DK, FAM 6023 was converted to DC-3C-S1C3G, as evidenced by her passenger door as seen here in 1972. She has also been named 'Gral. De División Antonio Cardenas R.' and displays yet another form of cheatline. Her lower fuselage and wings have been painted light grey. *MAP1981-68 #C265*

Above: DC-3C-S1C3G 6023 again, on 8 January 1978, still named as before on her upper forward fuselage, but with her serial now prefixed with 'T.E.D.' and the unit insignia on her nose. Her cheatline has by now been outlined, rather heavily, with gold paint, which has been carried up and over the root of the horizontal tailplanes. Note also that her starboard wing root fillet is completely missing. *Dr Gary Kuhn*

Right: Another former airline aircraft, probably converted at some point to DC-3 configuration, T.T.D.6024 appears to have been a late-model C-47B, although she was built as a C-47A-25-DK! The thin, light blue cheatline and unit insignia on her nose was standard prior to November 1974, as was the total wrap-around red propeller warning band on the forward fuselage. *Wings of Progress #4616*

Below: An excellent study of TTD 6029, a C-53, at BAM#1 on 6 August 1974 displaying an unusual array of radio antenna masts. Although her 'lightning bolt'-style cheatline appears black, it is actually very dark blue and is outlined in white with a very thin strip of gold. *Guido E. Bühlmann*

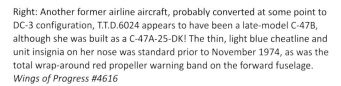

Below: An exceptionally rare aircraft, experienced aircraft spotters will have noted immediately that TTD 6032 lacks any sort of access door on her port rear fuselage. Outfitted with curtains in her windows, this is because she was built as a Douglas DST-217A and saw service during the Second World War as a C-49E. A former CMA aircraft, she also, very unusually, has the legend under her cockpit window reading 'Mayor APA Gustavo Vallejo R., Commandante'. Far from home, she was visiting Shaw AFB, South Carolina, on 1 June 1973. *Norm Taylor*

Wearing the titles of the Secretaria de Obras Publicas (SOP), XC-DOE served with that agency from at least 1971 until passing to, initially, TTD-6040 by June 1982. However, there is evidence to suggest that this was the second aircraft to wear serial 6040, as an aircraft with that code was in service with the FAM from 1967 until September 1983! *Wings of Progress #4586*

The aircraft that became ETM 6043 as XC-OPS while serving with the Mexican government oil monopoly PEMEX. She had been registered as such on 21 January 1969. *Eddy Gual*

The end of the line for a storied aircraft, ETM 6043 at BAM#1, stripped of all useful equipment. She had at one time been the solitary XCG-17 glider! Another former governmental aircraft, she was acquired by the FAM sometime after September 1980, the former XC-OPS. *Eddy Gual #70640*

Built as a C-47B and almost certainly an impounded drug runner, ETM 6048 was first reported ex-N512AC on 20 August 1993 with Escuadrón 312. *via George G.J. Kamp*

The first FAM C-47s – the Demonstration Flight Project Aircraft

Serial As Worn	Previous Identity	Built As	MSN	Assignments and Notes
4-77255	44-77255	C-47B-40-DK	16839/33587	Delivered to the USAAF on 2 Jul 45 and via San Bernardino to Kelly Field, TX on 16 Jul 45. Arrived at the DFP in Mexico City on 13 Dec 45. Still nominally owned by the USAF by 31 Mar 50 and assigned to the Project but 'on loan' to the FAM and counted on the strength of the Escuadrón de Transporte at Balbuena Field, DF, alongside one other Project C-47 on loan (45-1017), nine C-47s 'owned' by the FAM, two C-60As, and one each Beech AT-7 and UC-45F. She almost certainly received a FAM serial in the first series noted in the next table, but it can only be speculated as to which this may have been. From available evidence, however, she may in fact have become one of the first Presidential aircraft as none of the known first series tactical serials otherwise fit her circumstances.
5-968	45-968	C-47B-45-DK	16971/34231	Delivered to the USAAF on 8 Oct 45 and to Kelly Field, TX. Arrived at the DFP in Mexico City on 13 Dec 45. Reports that this aircraft was subsequently with USAAF ATC in the Pacific by 30 Apr 47 are incorrect, as she never left Mexico. She was lost in an accident on 2 Oct 46 at Hermosillo, Sonora, while being flown by Ramón Pardo Atristain, although for some reason, other reports give this loss as having occurred on 26 Oct 46.
5-1017	45-1017	C-47B-45-DK	17020/34283	Delivered to the USAAF by 1 Aug 45 and to the DFP in Mexico City on 13 Dec 45. Although recorded elsewhere as being 'salvaged' on 22 Dec 50 as a C-47D, she was in fact passed to the FAM for $1, as noted in the text, and to sooth administrative feathers was subsequently included in the MDA programme for Mexico and 'formally' transferred in Jan 51. She was also on strength with the Escuadrón de Transporte as noted in the description for 44-77255 above 'on loan' as late as 31 Mar 50. She almost certainly also received a FAM serial in the first series noted in the next table, but it can only be speculated as to which this may have been.

ETM 6040 is just one of what are believed to have been a number of former Mexican governmental aircraft passed to the FAM, in this case DC-3C MSN 43076, the former XC-DOE. Note the Vistavision-style window, the insignia of E.A.T.M.-312 atop her forward fuselage and the two swept-blade antenna atop her fuselage. *via Aldo Ciarini #FO2532*

A candidate for the last semi-stock operational military C-47A in all of Latin America, this specially marked aircraft, bearing the non-standard identity 'FAM-UNO', was the former TTD-6042, and experienced several commemorative repaints prior to December 2001, when it is seen here. The small titles on the nose show an arc spelling out 'Fuerza Aérea Mexicana' over the name 'Presidente Madero'. *PFI*

American Republics Project Deliveries and the First FAM Serial Series

FAM Serial	Previous Identity	Built As	MSN	Assignments and Notes
TE101	*42-100634*	*C-47A-65-DL*	*19047*	ARP Mexico on 14 or 19 Sep 47 ex-Kelly Field and actually delivered on 30 Sep 47. However, it appears that this aircraft may have been diverted to the CAC in Panama instead, and then on to Colombia on 11 May 49.
TE102	*42-100913*	*C-47A-75-DL:*	*19376*	ARP Mexico on 8 Sep 47 but actually delivered on 14 Sep 47 ex-Kelly Field. A Second World War Eighth Air Force veteran.
TE103	*42-92867*	*C-47A-15-DK*	*12715*	ARP Mexico on 19 Sep 47 apparently actually delivered ex-Kelly Field on 21 Sep 47. Another Second World War Eighth Air Force veteran. This aircraft passed to marks TTD-6008.
TE107	*42-93816*	*C-47A-25-DK*	*13770*	ARP Mexico on 30 Sep 47. Originally intended for Ecuador, she was diverted instead to Mexico. A Second World War Ninth Air Force veteran. Known to have been in service as such by 9 Dec 47.
TE108	*42-100526*	*C-47A-65-DL*	*18989*	ARP Mexico and allotted as such on 19 Sep 47 but not delivered until 5 Oct 47. Eighth Air Force veteran.
TE110	*42-24292*	*C-47A-50-DL*	*10154*	ARP Mexico on 10 Sep 47 but not delivered until 5 Oct 47 ex-Kelly Field.
TE111	*41-18354* *NC-58492* *XA-FUH* *N4618V*	*C-47-DL*	*4392*	The circumstances of this acquisition are unknown, and she may have been a seized aircraft but, in any event, she had joined the inventory by 13 Sep 49.
TE-???	*42-100552*	*C-47A-65-DL*	*19015*	Although the Individual Aircraft Record card for this Eighth Air Force veteran aircraft indicates she had been earmarked for ARP to Mexico on 12 Apr 48 ex-Kelly Field and actually delivered on 3 Aug 48, she may have been diverted to Secretaría de Agricultura y Ganadería instead and, if used by the FAM at all, it may have only been long enough to satisfy ARP contractual requirements, as she is known to have gone to XB-KEK. As of 2 Apr 48, she was being offered to the FAM for $120,000, and had originally been earmarked for Peru under ARP Project No. 72015 and then Cuba under ARP Project No. 72016, along with 42-93793. However, she is also reliably reported to have become TTD-6019, which seems far more likely.
TE118	*45-1017*	*C-47B-45-DK*	*17020/34284*	One of the former DFP aircraft, this aircraft was formally handed over to the FAM in Jan 51, but had in fact been operated by the Mexicans from Dec 45.

By the time of this 8 January 1978 photo, FAM use of the stalwart C-47 was in rapid decline, and these four aircraft had apparently been sitting idle at Mexico City for some time. They all bear late standard markings, but only the first three have the unit insignia on their noses. All have blue engine cowlings. *Dr Gary Kuhn*

The number of DC-3s and C-47s that served the Mexican presidency in some manner is the subject of debate. This, however, is believed to have been the very first and was apparently devoid of any serial or registration, wearing only the word 'Mexico' under her starboard wing, the national flag on her nose, and the titles 'El Mexicano' – but with FAM rudder stripes and small national insignia under her extreme outer starboard wing. *José Antonio Quevedo*

The Definitive and Current FAM Serial System – the 6000s

FAM Serial	Previous Identity	Built As	MSN	Assignments and Notes
ETM-2118	–	C-47?	–	This out-of-sequence serial was noted by a spotter on 6 Oct 79 at Mexico City and cannot be reconciled with any known serials. It may in fact have been a simple, elementary spotting error, as the ETM-2xxx serials were used on IAI-201 Aravas, Douglas A-24Bs, Pilatus PC-7s and (presently) Beech King Airs.
ETM-5011	–	C-47	–	Veteran aero-historian the late George G.J. Kamp reported this serial some years ago, but it may well have been a spotting error for ETM-6011 (q.v.).
TTD-6005	–	–	–	This, the first FAM C-47 to receive a prefixed serial in the definitive series, it is believed to have worn the same for the first time after 1947. She is known to have visited Brownsville, Texas, on 28 Jan 50. Oddly, however, no known photos have been located relating to this historic aircraft.
TTD-6006 T.E.D.6006 ETM-6006	–	–	–	First reported in Sep 50 as TTD-6006. Noted in service at Mexico City between 19 and 21 Sep 76. By 8 Jan 78 she was noted at Mexico City completely stripped of all paint except her serial number but noted active there again on 8 Jan 78 and again 6 Oct 79 as T.E.D. 6006. At one point, possibly as early as Sep 50, named Plan de Ayala (or, according to one source, Ayutla). This aircraft is last known having been assigned to Escuadrón 311 *c.*10 Sep 93 when she was noted undergoing extensive overhaul with her wings removed. Withdrawn from service at BAM#1, Santa Lucía.
TTD-6007 T.E.D.6007 F.A.M. 6007 TP-6007	–	C-47B	–	First reported on 26 May 57 when she was cleared to fly to San Antonio, Texas, but still in service at Mexico City between Oct 71 and as late as 6 Oct 79 as T.E.D. 6007. As of Dec 67 she was named Galeana and serialed F.A.M. 6007 with a four-star placard, thus probably operating as either the FAM Commander's personal barge or the Secretario de Defensa Nacional. She was last noted in Dec 80.
TTD-6008	42-92867 TE-103	C-47A-15-DK	12715	Originally one of the ARP aircraft, the aircraft was first reported with this serial in Nov 53. It is believed to have passed to civil owner as XB-VUT at some point.
TTD-610 TTD-6010	–	–	–	First reported 23 Jun 48 when visiting Clover Field, California, some sources claim she had at one point been serialed as TTD-610, although this has escaped verification. By Oct 48, she was noted again at Clover Field, California. This was one of the aircraft used to fly Organisation of American States (OAS) observers along the Costa Rica/Nicaragua border conflict area around 20 Jan 55. She was written off on 15 Nov 63 in a landing accident, with four killed and three injured at BAM#2, Pie de la Cuesta.
TTD-6011 ETM-6011	42-23390 FAE-503?	C-7A-10-DL	9252	First noted wearing a three-star placard on her vertical fin and nose as TTD-6011, probably indicating use by a high-ranking officer. If this aircraft was in fact a former FAE aircraft, exactly how and why she ended up with the FAM is a mystery. She was reported airworthy at BAM#1 Santa Lucía on 15 Sep 86 as ETM-6011, and noted undergoing extensive overhaul with her wings removed as of 20 Aug 93 but was airworthy again as of *c.*Mar 94 and 95, by which time she was assigned to Escuadrón 311. A beautifully marked C-47 with this serial is now on display.
T.T.D.6012	FAM-6012 VHCGT NC-1605M	42-23657 C-47A-30-DL	9519	MSN 9519 was acquired via the WAA by Earl Douglas Aircraft Sales Co. of San Francisco, CA, on 19 May 47 for $10,151.13 as NC-1605M. This registration was cancelled by this owner as exported to an unreported destination on 15 Oct 47. She was seen at BAM#1 Santa Lucía on 3 Oct 68 with her serial prefix punctuated as 'T.T.D.', a rare use of this convention. As the aircraft has been otherwise reported, it is a candidate, chronologically, for the FAM. TTD-6012 is known to have been named Anahuac, this aircraft went missing on 13 or 14 Jun 72 in the vicinity of Sierra de Vallejo, Compostela, Nayarit, with officials of Plan Hulcot and members of the news media aboard.

It is not clear when F.A.M. AP-0201 first adopted this special VIP colour scheme, but this is the earliest known photo, dated 11 April 1960 at, of all places, Baltimore, Maryland – suggesting that her VIP accoutrements may have been fashioned there. This may have been the aircraft that was formerly marked simply as 'El Mexicano'. Note the great seal of the Estados Unidos de Mexicanas on the cabin DC-3C-style air stair door and her name, 'Revolucionario', on her lower nose. There were no national insignia on her wings at this point. *Carson Seely via Brian R. Baker*

Four years later, on 10 February 1964, F.A.M. AP-0201's spectacular colour scheme had been modified to include a blue and gold 'arrow' at the base of the vertical fin, as seen here at Love Field, Dallas, Texas. *Pete Bulban via Jay Miller*

TTD-6013 FAM-6013	–	C-47B	–	–
TTD-6014	–	DC-3	–	First reported 7 Feb 50 at Brownsville, Texas. Written off on 19 Jun 54, at La Petaca, Estado de Mexico, twenty killed. See details in the main text.
TTD-6015	–	–	–	First reported on 8 Jun 50.
TTD-6016	42-93816 TE-107	C-47A-25-DK	13770	First reported February 1948 when she was granted permission to overfly Brazilian territory, probably the farthest that any FAM C-47 had been from home to this point. Exactly why she was that far south is unknown, although she wore the flags on her nose of nearly every Latin American nation, and Escuadrón de Transporte titles on her upper fuselage decking, suggesting she was on a region-wide goodwill flight at the time and, again, as late as 8 Nov 51 when she landed without prior authorisation at El Paso, Texas. The MSN has not been confirmed.
TTD-6017 TP-6017	–	–	–	–
TTD-6018	–	C-47	–	Photograph evidence confirms the use of this serial.
TTD-6019	42-100552 TE-???	C-47A-65-DL	19015	Known to have been on strength and noted at Brownsville, Texas, on 7 May 50 and on four subsequent occasions through to 19 Feb 51, all under the command of Capt. Jorge Martínez de Hijar. This aircraft was named Sierra Hermosa, as was registered as XB-KUX. Since we know that Lopez Mateos, President of Mexico in 1952–58, was born 47km from the town of that name, and later owned substantial property near Sierra Hermosa, the aircraft could have been named after him. Although the connections are tenuous, they may be pertinent.
TTD-6020	–	–	–	First reported in Jun 54. This was one of the aircraft used to carry OAS observers along the Costa Rica/Nicaragua border conflict area around 20 Jan 55. The 4° Escalón de Mantenimiento completed an IRAN overhaul of this aircraft sometime between 1959 and 1964 at a cost of 350,000 Pesos, and she had approximately 8,000hrs total time at that point. Reported written off on 7 Nov 70 at Matamoros, Tamaulipas, four killed.
T.T.D.6021	43-15336 NC-53219 XA-HUF	C-47A-80-DL	19802	If the identity suggested is correct, this was a former Aeronaves de México aircraft last reported in 1954. As T.T.D. 6021, she was first reported in 1963 and as late as Feb 71. Another source suggests she may have been MSN 10069.

TTD-6022	*42-93025* *NC-50788* *XA-HUE*	*C-47A-20-DK*	*12891*	In 1962 or 1963, three former Trans Mar de Cortez aircraft passed to the FAM, probably via Aeronaves de México. Chronologically, TTD-6022, 6023 and 6024 are candidates. A C-47 with these markings, and camouflaged, was preserved at the Colegio Militar in Mexico City as early as Feb 02 and was apparently designated as an Entrenador de Paracaidistas with Escuadrón 301.
TTD-6023 T.E.D.6023 TP-6023	FAM-6023 *XA-JEL*	*42-93114* *C-47A-20-DK* *DC-3C-S1C3G*	*12990*	See the notes for TTD-6022 above. First reported on 31 Oct 71 and in service at Mexico City between 19 and 21 Sep 76. She was noted at Mexico City as T.E.D.6023 on 8 Jan 78 and as late as Aug 85, by which time she was marked TED-6023. Named Gral. De División Antonio Cárdenas R. at one point. Her remains were noted at Balbuena, DF. One source claims she was camouflaged during the 1980s.
TTD-6024 T.E.D.6024	*42-93755* *XB-FIR* *XA-FIR*	*C-47A-25-DK*	*13702*	See the notes for TTD-6022 above. Reportedly suffered an accident on 13 Apr 70 at BAM#1 Santa Lucia but perhaps repaired as reported again on 31 Oct 71. She was active at Mexico City between 19 and 21 Sep 76 and 6 Oct 79 (as T.E.D.6024 but without engines) and then derelict at Mexico City by 9 Sep 80. However, a C-47 with marks T.E.D.6024 was reported preserved at Campo No. 1. This aircraft has also been reported as having been camouflaged at one point.
TTD-6025 TED-6025 ETM-6025	41-18345 NC-75413 XA-GUX XC-CIJ XC-DOJ	C-47-DL	4383	A veteran of Operation Bolero in the Second World War, this was a very well-travelled aircraft, first reported with the FAM in July 1978 and as having been broken up by 10 Sep 93. She was at that last date with E.A.T.M.-312.
TTD-6026 TP-6026	–	–	–	–

Marked almost identically to AP-0201, a second Presidential barge, F.A.M. TP-0202, had emerged by 19 November 1969, when she was noted at San Antonio, Texas, named 'Mexicano'. Note her twin-blade antenna array, however. *Hagedorn*

The same aircraft as seen as previously, here is F.A.M. TP-0202 again in a completely different colour scheme nine years later in July 1978, again at San Antonio, but still named 'Mexicano'. *Hagedorn*

As described in the narrative, an extraordinary number of aircraft acquired and operated on behalf of the Mexican Presidency have populated the XB-XXX series of the civil register. XB-JOX, built as C-47-DL MSN 4218 but converted to DC-3A configuration and registered to Jorge Pasquel Casanova as early as 1952, was but one example. She became XC-BEX in July 1962. These aircraft afforded the President and his entourage a modicum of anonymity but were operated by hand-picked crews with security detachments. *Hagedorn*

6027	NC-25617 XA-FUV XB-JBR	DC-3A-197D	3261	Had been impounded by the FAM at Toluca as early as Sep 95.
TTD-6028	–	C-53	–	First reported in Jul 76.
TTD-6029 ETM-6029	42-15566 NC-33320 XA-HEP	C-53-DO	7361	Assigned to E.A.T.M.-312 at one point.
6030	–	–	–	–
TTD-6031 ETM-6031	NC-25613 XA-JUT	DC-3A-197D	3257	The last civil registration was cancelled in 1976, suggesting that it passed to the FAM from Aeronaves Alimentadoras sometime after Jan 70.
TTD-6032 ETM-6032	NC-21769 42-43621 NC-19921 XA-GUQ	DST-217A C-49E	2149	Last known with Aeroméxico, first reported with the FAM in Jun 72. Assigned to E.A.T.M.-312 by 1982 at BAM#1 Santa Lucía.
TTD-6033 ETM-6033	NC-25618 XA-FUJ	DC-3A-197D	3262	Last known with Aeroméxico noted being offered for sale by the FAM in Feb 95 and listed as 'EIM'-6033, almost certainly a typographical error for 'ETM'.
6034	–	–	–	–
TTD-6035 TED-6035	–	DC-3	–	Noted in service as early as Jun 72 and active at Mexico City between 19 and 21 Sep 76, and as late as 6 Oct 79 (as TED-6035). Engineless by 6 Oct 79, last noted Apr 82.
TED-6036	–	C-53 DC-3	–	First noted between 19 and 21 Sep 76 active at Mexico City and as late as 1981, at one point with the E.M.A.T.E.
TED-6037	–	C-47	–	First reported 1967 and as late as 19–21 Sep 76 active at Mexico City. Noted at Mexico City again on 6 Oct 79 and Aug 83. At one point assigned to the E.M.A.T.E.
ETM-6038	NC-33610 XA-GOC	DC-3A-228F	4101	–
ETM-6039	–	–	–	Photo evidence exists confirming use of ETM-6039.
TTD-6040 TED-6040	NC-34915 NC-24H	DC-3C	43076	First reported in 1967 and as late as 10 Sep 83. However, an official Mexican document shows XC-DOE being formally transferred from the S.A.H.O.P. to the FAM on 2 Jun 82!

As noted in the narrative, a surprising number of DC-3s and C-47s were registered on the Mexican governmental series civil register in the 'XC-' series, including XC-ABF noted anonymous here at San Antonio, Texas, on 1 September 1969. As a number of these aircraft are known to have passed to FAM service as early as the mid-1970s, this and several other images are presented here as candidates for FAM service. XC-ABF, initially registered in December 1954 to the Secretaria de Hacienda and is thought to have become F.A.M. AP-0201 at some point. However, she has also been reported to have become XC-BCE in November 1967 – which, as evidenced by this image, did not happen. *Hagedorn*

Immaculate in Banco Nacional de Obras y Servicios Publicos S.A. titles here as XC-BNO, DC-3A-228F MSN 4104 was registered with these marks in June 1969. However, she has not been reported since 1971 and is a strong candidate to have passed to the FAM. Note the distinctive double Vistavision windows. *APB*

ETM-6040	N124H N355MJ XB-ZAT XC-DOE	–	–	Assigned to E.A.T.M.-312 as of 10 Sep 93, operational. Last reported 1995.
TED-6041	–	–	–	Photographic evidence confirms the use of this serial.
TTD-6042 ETM-6042 FAM-UNO XC-UNO	42-23414 TC-AFA N58U XC-BUR XC-SAG	C-47A-5-DL	9276	Reported taken up after Jul 68 the first time, apparently with Escuadrón 312, and passed to CMA/Mexicana temporarily for 50th anniversary ceremonial purposes as 'XA-CMA' between Aug 93 and 96 but returned to ETM-6042 by Aug 1996. Had been restored by the FAM to immaculate condition and marked as 'FAM-UNO/Presidente Madero' by Apr 99 and as late as Dec 01, but also noted as wearing marks 'XC-UNO' beneath both wings at the same time, apparently being operated by Escuadrón 305, and reportedly then sold to Líneas Aéreas Canedo as XB-UNO in VIP configuration. While still as FAM-UNO, the aircraft reportedly made an emergency landing on a football field in the suburbs of Mexico City. However, Dr Alfonso Flores has also nominated this aircraft as having been MSN 12736, formerly XC-CNI, which is known to have passed to the FAM on 9 Feb 80. MSN 9276, on the other hand, is known to have passed to the FAM on 29 Jan 80 and is thus more likely to have been ETM-6042. The aircraft was at one point, probably around Dec 93, operated by E.A.T.M.-312.
TTD-6043 TED-6043 ETM-6043	41-18496 N69030 XA-JID XC-OPS XCG-17	C-47-DL C-47-DL	4588	Taken up some time after Sep 80 and as late as 10 Sep 93. Noted on the dump at BAM#1 as early as 20 Aug 93 and as late as Dec 93, last assigned to E.A.T.M.-311.
TED-6044 ETM-6044	–	–	–	Noted withdrawn from service by 20 Aug 93 and to scrap at BAM#1 by Dec 93.
TED-6045 ETM-6045	NC-28379 N95C N2818D N144D N6M N144D N19LR	DC-3-343A	3283	First reported on 27 Nov 91 and as late as 20 Aug 93 at BAM#1 awaiting new engines. She was assigned to E.A.T.M.-311 by Dec 93.
ETM-6046	42-92806 VHCKG VHCJW G-AJTO VH-INF VH-AKR VH-MAN P2-MAN P2-ANY N55892	C-47A-15-DK	12647	An exceptionally high-time aircraft, she was awaiting new engines as of 20 Aug 93 and was probably an impounded drug runner or smuggler. She was assigned to E.A.T.M.-311 by Dec 93. She has since been cosmetically restored and placed on external display at BAM#1, Santa Lucía, in good condition from 2001.

With her registration painted on vertically on her fin, XC-CIY was a DC-3A-228D, MSN 3293 and was registered when seen here to the Centro Internacional de Aviación Civil (CIACC) with whom she had served from around 1962. However, she has not been reported since being cancelled in June 1970 and almost certainly went to the FAM. *Wings of Progress #4545*

Devoid of titles, but wearing the name in script 'Presidente Madero' just aft of the cockpit, XC-CNI was almost certainly used twice, which has confused the issue. Seen here at San Antonio, Texas, in April 1978 with a Vistavision window far aft, she has not been reported since 1980. Note the DC-3-style air stair deployed on the port side. *Hagedorn*

Believed to be a spurious registration, XC-MEX is the former F.A.M. TP-0202, her basic colour scheme and twin antenna blades a sure tip-off. The emblem on the nose may be that of the Estados Unidos de Mexicanas. In good condition when seen on a plinth at the *E.U.M.* in January 1983, her current condition is unknown. *Dr Gary Kuhn*

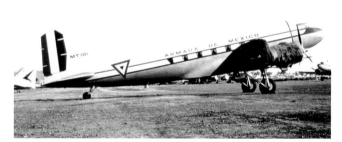

With full Navy titles, MT 101, if indeed the aircraft 'loaned' from the FAM in August 1952, is in remarkably good condition here some time prior to November 1974. She is clearly an executive transport, indicated by the nicely deployed curtains, but has eluded identification. She is suspected of having been the 'missing' TTD 6005. *Wings of Progress #4607*

While nicely turned out on display, the titles on MT-104 are very non-standard, and what is more, this serial has never actually been reported in service. Note the two swept antenna blades atop her fuselage, then see the image of MT-202 in the following series. All but the most forward cabin window have been blocked out or painted over as well. *API*

A line-up of Navy MT-201, MT-202 and MT-204, which reveals that, sometime prior to November 1974, at least the first two are DC-3s or DC-3 conversions, and that MT-202 has a rear Vistavision window arrangement identical to that of XC-CNI pictured earlier. *Wings of Progress #4610*

Another view of MT-202 with just about everything hanging open. Note the absence of any national or service insignia under her port wing. *via Ken F. Measures*

[TE-6047] [ETM-6047]	–	–	–	First reported in Sep 84, this was in fact another Curtiss C-46. She was at the 4° Escalón de Mantenimiento, Escuela de Mantenimiento by Dec 93.
ETM-6048	43-48273 0-48273 N87652 N512AC	C-47B-1-DK	14089/25534	First reported 20 Aug 93 with Escuadrón 312 and as withdrawn from use by Dec 1993 and derelict at BAM#1 with severe corrosion. Offered for sale in Feb 95 and listed as 'EIM'-6048, almost certainly a typographical error for 'ETM'.
[TEC-6049] [ETM-6049]	–	–	–	Another aircraft always assumed to have been a C-47 or DC-3, this was in fact a Curtiss C-46, last reported in Dec 93 with Escuadrón 312.
[TEC-6050]	–	–	–	Often nominated as a 'missing' C-47 series serial, this was in fact a Curtiss C-46 on the dump at BAM#1 by 1993.
[TEC-6051]	–	–	–	Also nominated as a 'missing' C-47 serial, this was in fact a Curtiss C-46, also noted on the dump at BAM#1 in 1993.
[TEC-6052]	–	–	–	Another impounded Curtiss C-46, erroneously reported as a C-47.
ETM-6053	44-77014 KN652 G-AMYB SN-AAK ST-AAK G-AZDF G-AMYB 5N-AJE N6CA	C-47B-35-DK Dakota IV	16598/33346	First reported after 8 Jun 84 and withdrawn from use by Jan 93. At BAM#1 by 20 Aug 93 awaiting new engines. By Dec 93 she was assigned to E.A.T.M.-311.
ETM-6054 FAM-6054	(43-48696) BuA50740 N8666	(C-47B-5-DK) R4D-6 C-47J	14512/25957	First reported in Jul 78. Although there is no way they could have known it at the time, this aircraft was assigned to the US Navy Attaché in Mexico City on 1 Sep 54. Due to severe corrosion, it was dispatched to the scrapyard at BAM#1 by 20 Aug 93. It was assigned to Escuadrón 312 by Dec 93. Offered for sale in Feb 95.
ETM-6055	42-100775 NC-65378 PP-ANB PP-BAD N9897F HK-595	C-47A-70-DL	19238	The identity of this aircraft is subject to verification. She may have been an impounded drug runner or smuggler. She was written off 6 Dec 89 at Sangangüey volcano, Nayarit, and five were killed in the accident. One of the last – if not the last – operational loss of a FAM C-47.
ETM-6056	43-16232 N6430 N83FA N101CA N301SF	C-47B-1-DL C-47D VC-47D	20698	Impounded drug runner as early as Jul 78, although most sources cite Aug 93. She was noted at BAM#1 Santa Lucía on 20 Aug 93 still bearing most of her former civil colour scheme, including marks N301SF but was otherwise operational. She was assigned to the E.A.T.M.-312 by Dec 93. Offered for sale in Feb 95.
FAM 6203	NC-25617 XA-FUV XB-JBR	DC-3A-197D	3261	As no other aircraft seems to 'fit' the circumstances, this aircraft is known to have been impounded at Toluca, Mexico, by Sep 95 and cannot otherwise be accounted for. This irregular serial was reported 5 Aug 03 at Campo Militar #1, D.F. by a reliable spotter but requires verification.

Awaiting her fate, here is another view of MT-202, her only visible identity being the serial code on her upper starboard wing. She was photographed at Mexico City on 8 January 1978 and had been withdrawn from active service for some time. *Dr Gary Kuhn*

Presidential and VIP Transport Series

Special Marks	Previous Identity	Built As	MSN	Assignments and Notes
'El Mexicano'				This aircraft apparently initially operated with no other markings, and is generally regarded by leading Mexican aero-historians as the first Presidential aircraft.
XC-DOE	NC-34915 NC-24H N124H N355MJ XB-ZAT	DC-3C	43076	Reportedly operated within the Presidential flight, or SDP between 1976 and about February 1980 and then passed to regular FAM markings as TED-6040 (q.v.).
XB-FUX	42-92930 NC-88783	C-47A-20-DK	12785	Substantial information suggesting this aircraft was intended for assignment to the Presidential flight. However, she crashed on 4 Feb 48 at Loma de Campo Viejo, Chihuahua, and may not have thus been reflected in Order of Battle data of the period. The crew had been issued verbal orders to take delivery of this aircraft in California on 26 Jan. The Pilot in Command, Leopoldo Meza Rodríguez, who was lost in the accident, had gained notoriety in 1942 when he was one of the FAM pilots who had claimed to have attacked a German submarine off the coast of Mazatlán, Sinaloa, while assigned to what was then the 1/° Regimiento Aéreo. His co-pilot, Tte.Mec. Alberto Alvarado Islas, was also a casualty.
XB-JEX	42-100986 NC-19136 CU-T???	C-47A-75-DL	19449	Apparently acquired from EAI in Cuba in 1948 expressly for Presidential duty.
F.A.M. AP-0201	42-100946 NC-88801 XB-JUX	C-47A-75-DL	19409	Apparently assumed these marks sometime after 1950, this may have been the aircraft noted above named 'El Mexicano'. However, it has also been reported as named Revolucionario at Baltimore, MD, on 11 Apr 60 and again at Love Field, Dallas, TX, on 10 Feb 64 and to have passed to governmental markings or call-sign XC-PAA by 25 Mar 59, although one report also suggests call-sign XC-PAZ. She was reported in service on 15 Apr 60 when she visited Friendship Airport at Baltimore, Maryland, and on 10 Feb 64. It must be noted that AP-0201 has also been reliably reported as MSN 7377 and 43083, leading to the possibility that this Presidential serial was used on more than one aircraft.

Right: Formerly XC-DAK, the twin Vistavision windows aft on MT-203 are evidence, as are the wheel covers, of a Hi-Per DC-3 conversion, just visible on the starboard side. This image dates from the early 1970s. *Wings of Progress #4608*

Below: Although marked as MT-203 for display purposes at the Museo Tecnológico, CFE, the identity of this aircraft was suspect when seen in February 1995, as the preceding photo is the actual aircraft. She also displays a form of national insignia not seen on any operational Navy C-47s or DC-3s, and which did not come into use until much later. Additionally, the national insignia under her starboard wing is far too inboard and too close to the leading edge. *George G.J. Kamp*

XC-FAB? XC-PAB AP-0202 FAM TP-0202 XC-UPE	XB-FAB XC-PAB	DC-3C	43083	There is evidence that this aircraft may well have operated for the Presidencia as both XC-FAB and XC-PAB, as she was registered in the first instance to Sr Jorge Pasquel on 14 Jun 47, a known agent functioning on behalf of the procurement of aircraft for the Presidency. At one point named Mexicano, she was noted at San Antonio, Texas, by co-author Hagedorn in Nov 69 (as FAM AP-0202) and again in Jul 1978 marked as FAM TP-0202! As TP-0202 she is known to have been named Mexicano as of 1972. She subsequently passed to TP-302/XC-MEX (see below) and then the FAM quasi-governmental series as XC-UPE. However, an aircraft marked as TP-0202 has been preserved in the vicinity of Mexico City at the FAM Museum, but this may be merely a vanity mark.
TP-0203	–	C-47	–	Noted at San Antonio, Texas, 13 Aug 74.
TP-302 XC-MEX	XB-FAB XC-PAB AP-0202 TP-0202	DC-3C	43083	Named El Mexicano the authenticity of these marks may be in question, as she was noted as a monument/display aircraft at Mexico City International Airport at some point.
AP-0304 TP-304 XC-UPD	–	C-47	–	Reported with the UTAPEF as early as 6 Oct 79 as TP-304/XC-UPD.

Left: A good study of MT 204 prior to November 1974, clearly a DC-3 VIP conversion. *Wings of Progress #4609*

Bottom: The port side of MT 204 as she sat, minus her cabin door, rudder and the skin of her port aileron at Mexico City on the same day. Her fate is unknown. *Dr Gary Kuhn*

Below: Although missing her starboard ailerons and rudder – possibly in the workshop for recovering – MT 204, photographed at Mexico City on 8 January 1978 is otherwise completely intact, although her starboard main tyre is nearly flat! She was last reported in October 1979 and not since. *Dr Gary Kuhn*

Mexican Navy

One of the oldest and most respected of all Mexican institutions, the modest Navy establishment of the Republic, besides having the daunting task of being obliged to be a 'two-ocean' fleet covering coastal frontiers facing the Caribbean/Gulf of Mexico and the vast Pacific approaches, has in more recent years emerged as the 'go-to' military branch in combating the extremely serious national crisis of narcotics traffickers, which have eroded the domestic fabric.

Essentially a coastal defence and patrol organisation, with widely separated operating bases and command and control installations, the Navy recognised the utility of aviation in supporting its bases as early as the 1930s. It was not until 1940 however, that the Servicio de Aviación de la Armada Mexicana emerged as a formal organisation. For most of the Second World War years and well into the 1960s, the air arm consisted entirely of transport, training and communications types, although a small number of Vought-Sikorsky OS2U-3 Kingfishers, augmented in 1950 by several Grumman J2F-6 Ducks, did provide its first modestly armed tactical equipment.

But the most pressing need of the service, in terms of aviation, was in connecting its stations with headquarters elements, redeployment of crews and supplies and the occasional search-and-rescue operation in conjunction with surface units. For this, the service turned to a mix of Beech AT-7, AT-11 and C-45 aircraft procured between November 1944 (seconded from the FAM) and June 1961, when six surplus USAF C-45Hs were acquired. While these aircraft provided good service, they possessed only limited airlift potential, and were basically useless in moving large naval parts and spares rapidly, and thus the Navy appealed directly to the central government, around August 1952, for the offset of at least one C-47 from the FAM's small and jealously guarded inventory, for Navy use. The FAM thus, very grudgingly, 'loaned' a C-47 to the Navy on 20 August 1952, and this is assumed to have acquired the earliest known marks for a Navy C-47, MT-101.

Since then, the Navy appears to have operated a possible total of six C-47s but, of these, only three have been positively identified, and as a number of the aircraft are known to have been reserialed over the years, the actual number may actually have been only four.

Mexican Navy Serial	Previous Identity	Built As	MSN	Assignments and Notes
MT 101	–	–	–	Suggested as possibly the former TTD-6005 or 6006, which seem to have disappeared at about the same time, this aircraft was on loan to the Navy from the FAM by 20 Aug 52 and, at the time, was the solitary Navy C-47. An aircraft with this serial was noted at Balbuena Field, DF, Mexico City on 31 Oct 71 and if the same aircraft, then the FAM 'loan' must have matured into an actual transfer. It has been said to have been assigned to the 1/° Escuadrón Aeronaval.
MT-104	–	–	–	A C-47 with this serial has been photographed on external display, but the location is unknown.
MT-201	–	C-53/DC-3	–	It has been suggested that this aircraft is a reserialed MT-101 and that she was assigned to the 2/° Escuadrón Aeronaval. However, photo evidence shows her to have a C-53/DC-3 type port-side passenger door, and MT-101 is believed to have been a C-47 with a standard cargo door.
MT-202	42-92057 NC-65331 N502T N502V N125V N502V N766X XC-DOS	C-47A-DK DC-3C-S1C3G	11815	This aircraft passed to the Navy from the Secretaria de Recursos Hidráulicos sometime after 1971 but was noted as stored by 19 Sep 76 and in very poor condition and missing her rudder at Balbuena Field, Mexico City, by 8 Jan 78, although she appeared to be undergoing renovation, with her serial visible on the upper starboard wing only. She was last reported at Mexico City on 6 Oct 79 although her status was not noted. Reportedly assigned in her prime to the 2/o Escuadrón Aeronaval, she was finally scrapped in Jun 81. A photo of this aircraft in a line-up shows her with 'Viewmaster' passenger windows.
MT-203	42-10073 NC-88776 XB-COC XA-LEX XC-DAK	C-47A-70-DL Hi-Per DC-3	19201	The identity cited for this aircraft may be suspect as XC-DAK, last known with the Secretaría de Comunicaciones y Transportes was noted at Mexico City operational on 21 Sep 76 but derelict as such at Mexico City by Jan 79. However, an aircraft marked as MT-203 is now on display at the Museo Tecnológico, CFE, and it has been suggested that this is actually MSN 4282, a former R4D-1 (BuA3141 and NC-41046, XC-CTM) which seems to be more likely. It is not clear if either of these aircraft actually served with the Navy as MT-203, or if they are merely painted to represent an aircraft that did. The actual MT-203 is known to have had 'Viewmaster' style cabin windows, which would have made her a DC-3 conversion. The aircraft on display at the Museo does not have such windows, and was noted there as late as Feb 95, although she did have a DC-3-type port-side passenger door.
MT 204	–	C-47 DC-3	–	First reported prior to Nov 74 at Mexico City, apparently operational, and as late as 6 Oct 79, this aircraft was apparently assigned to the 2/o Escuadrón Aeronaval while operational. She was noted with a DC-3 style port-side entry door and missing her rudder at Balbuena Field, DF, Mexico City, on 8 Jan 78 but otherwise in fair condition. She was noted there again on 6 Oct 79, although her status was not noted.
MT-330	–	C-47A	–	This aircraft was noted withdrawn from use at Veracruz by Jan 95.

CHAPTER SIXTEEN

Nicaragua

F EW C-47 MILITARY operators have suffered anything approaching the tortured relationship experienced starting in 1948 by the Nicaraguan military in Central America.

Complicated by the post-Second World War struggle between democratic forces and the well-entrenched fiefdoms that held on to power and dominance that was nearly total, in the case of Nicaragua, and proper understanding of the acquisition and use of these aircraft there must begin with the proper understanding that the Somoza regime owned or controlled every significant facet of public life in the country.

Indeed, although the Guardia Nacional, created in the beginning by the US Marine Corps as a nation-building force, and which inherited many of the traditions, discipline and sense of loyalty universally ascribed to the Marines, was in one sense the national Army of the country, it in fact became the very pillar on which the perpetuation and dominance of the dictators rested. For all intents and purposes, it was, by Central American standards, a proficiently trained and fiercely nationalistic private army.

With all of that, Somoza and his Guardia got a rather late start in military aviation. Although sporadic attempts to establish an aviation branch had commenced as early as the 1920s, it was not until the late 1930s that the organisation was finally constituted to be essentially on a par with its Central American neighbours.

Although formally known as the Fuerza Aérea de la Guardia Nacional, the service was generally cited both domestically as well as by foreign military observers as the rather less cumbersome Fuerza Aérea Nicaragüense (FAN) and, for the purposes of this account readers will note that we cite appropriate serials issued, in turn, by the organisation as it evolved as having been prefixed by either GN or FAN.

By the time that the FAN first gained its first examples of the DC-3/C-47 family that it could actually call its own via a series of Central American political upheavals, and its character as a two-station force, firmly subordinate to the GN and ruling Caudillo's whims, it comprised a total personnel strength of a scant 130 officers and men, of whom twenty-five were commissioned officers. Even the usually staid and conservation periodic comments of a USAF Air Intelligence Report of the time characterised the service as 'used as both a military and a political tool in Central American affairs'. Although Nicaragua benefited modestly from Lend-Lease during the war years, and took full advantage of the immediate post-war glut of inexpensive surplus military aircraft, by April 1948, when the first DC-3/C-47 aircraft suddenly arrived, the force had operated since inception a grand total of less than fifty-three aircraft of all types, sixteen of which had arrived via Lend-Lease. Of these, only two were transports: a single Fairchild 24-C8E and a Cessna UC-78 of questionable provenance – and not a solitary DC-3 or C-47, alone among the Central American air arms by this time and conspicuous by their absence.

Arguably the first Nicaraguan-owned C-47 to be flown by GN and FAN crew regularly – and thus of significant training value – C-47-DL AN-ACN (MSN 6090) had gained her marks by 1947 but, as can be seen, flew for an unknown initial period without any LaNICA or other titles whatsoever. She was seen here in Florida during one of many unscheduled flights. *Harold G. Martin*

A singularly historic image, taken at San José, Costa Rica, showing at least two of the three LACSA aircraft – TI-17 and TI-18 – impounded by Nicaragua on 24 April 1948 and, essentially utilised free of charge for nearly four years by a combination of FAN, FANSA and LaNICA crews as GN 53 and GN 55. At least initially, they operated in Nicaragua with their LACSA colour schemes (minus titles and Costa Rican registrations) with only small GN serials on their vertical fins. *via Mario Overall*

Seen at Panama's Tocumen International Airport sometime prior to her demise in January 1962, FAN-208 was one of the three Costa Rican aircraft impounded in April 1948, having previously been TI-18 and GN 55. She was one of the first – if not the first – C-47 to actually wear full FAN markings, including, here, the pre-1960s' national roundel on the fuselage. Her rudder markings are irregular, however, having just four (instead of the prescribed five) horizontal stripes. At one time, this aircraft sported five rocket rails under each wing and was engaged on at least one occasion in a strafing attack on an insurgent aircraft. *Harold G. Martin*

Any Port in a Storm...

As described in Chapter 7 (Costa Rica), however, during the closing stages of the Costa Rican civil war of early 1948, Nicaraguan forces, at Somoza's behest, attempted to intervene in force – including the use of what have been described, in numerous published accounts, as a trio of 'Nicaraguan Air Force' – including a previous report by co-author Hagedorn in an Air-Britain monograph.

However, as subsequent research and primary documentation have revealed, this was a non-starter, as the GN/FAN of March and April 1948 possessed no such organic aircraft.

While we did record properly that the aircraft had 'their national markings covered by splotches of black paint' the aircraft, in fact, were owned by either LaNICA[39] or FANSA – or a combination of both, while their crew composition may have been equally cosmopolitan. If indeed anything was overpainted, it was probably Nicaraguan – or US – registrations and possibly the titles of these two carriers. We may never know exactly which of the aircraft described in these paragraphs were actually involved.[40]

The Guardia's relationship with the rather nebulous FANSA was described more bluntly in a 19 June 1948 US State Department Dispatch, which noted that 'FANSA operated two C-46s and two C-47s with the full co-operation of the Nicaraguan Air Force. One of the C-46's was XH-014. This registration was reported cancelled the day after the aircraft left Honduras. The other has "provisional" Nicaraguan registry.

The two C-47s were obtained through Charles Mathews of Miami, and were NC-53192 and NC-17079 leased from AAXICO.'

In fact, this semi-covert use of what were clearly Nicaraguan-originated aircraft was a manifestation of Somoza's total control of all aspects of national life. LaNICA (Líneas Aéreas de Nicaragua, sometimes printed at the time as La NICA) had been created as a local affiliate by Pan Am on 17 November 1944 but did not commence operations until 1946 – initially with two elderly Boeing 247Ds – as a direct counterstroke to TACA de Nicaragua. In 1948, it effectively ran the later out of the country when Somoza abruptly cancelled TACA's contract.

The contract between the Nicaraguan government (e.g., Somoza) and the founders of the line was signed on 25 July 1945, and stipulated, to no one's surprise, that at least 55 per cent of the stock of the new airline had to be owned by Nicaraguan citizens 'or foreigners who have resided in Nicaragua for more than 10 years'. Excluding, significantly, the General Manager, pilots and mechanics – at least 75 per cent of all other staff had to be Nicaraguans. Originally, PAA held only 40 per cent of the stock, the remaining 60 per cent being held by Nicaraguans, nearly all of whom were controlled by Somoza. Initially, the line conducted only charter operations, and did not commence anything resembling scheduled services until 1946. Soon, with the assistance of PAA, four assorted DC-3s were added to the fleet.

The very first C-47 acquired by Nicaragua via MAP was FAN-410, delivered in November 1962. Initially, she served as 'Air Force One' for Somoza with a five-star placard but, by the time of this February 1978 view, was in normal cargo configuration. She survived to pass to the Sandinista air arm after the fall of the regime. *Capt. George G. Farinas*

The second MAP-supplied C-47 for Nicaragua was C-47D FAN-411, which arrived on 14 December 1962, seen here at Howard AFB, CZ, on 17 February 1968 loading treasures from the USAF Base Exchange to take home. She was lost on 4 December 1970 when she crashed into a volcano. *Dan Hagedorn*

For all intents and purposes, as will be seen, La NICA became essentially the overt transport operational training unit of the FAN, and both captains and first officers on all of its aircraft during this period were predominantly serving GN officers, trained initially by contracted US crews. Somoza had clearly reasoned that there was no need to purchase expensive C-47s for the FAN at this juncture, as the terms by which Pan Am seconded aircraft to the affiliate provided him with the best of both worlds: he could make money with the aircraft on a day-to-day basis, yet was able to transfer them literally on a single word to military control if and when the need arose. This curious relationship persisted from, effectively, 1946 until 1951, by which time La NICA had acquired at least seven assorted DC-3s and C-47s. There is evidence that, during approximately the same period, the aircraft bore both Nicaraguan civil registrations (see the accompanying Table) as well as small, two-digit GN serials on most vertical fins.

In the midst of all of this, the three Costa Rican aircraft noted in Chapter 7 landed at Managua (LACSA TI-17 and TI-18) and elsewhere in Nicaraguan territory (TACA de Costa Rica YS-34)[41] carrying high Costa Rican officials of the Teodoro Picado regime, lately deposed and their families, and other political refugees where, on 14 April 1948, they were promptly impounded by the Guardia Nacional.

Suddenly, the GN/FAN was in possession of, for a time, three well-maintained passenger-configured aircraft, all bearing the registrations of foreign nations, and the legal status of which was highly questionable. Somoza did not miss a stroke. He immediately ordered their registrations and titles removed, and the FAN issued them serials GN 53, 54 and 55 – the first purely military DC-3/C-47 aircraft 'owned' by the service, although that term may be going a bit too far.

Then, perhaps not coincidentally, less than three months later, in June 1948, Somoza apparently became enchanted with the idea of having an all-cargo airline in Nicaragua in addition to the mostly passenger activities of La NICA. Most published sources define the creature that shortly emerged with the acronym FANSA as translating to Flota Aérea Nicaragüense S.A. However, upon investigation, not a solitary primary document could be located to substantiate this operating name, while a US State Department Dispatch dated 30 June 1950, appears to have come much closer to the mark when it defined FANSA as standing for Fuerza Aérea Nacional, S.A. The 'airline' was, in fact, the covert transport element of the FAN, the dispatch going on to describe its activities as having been 'operated on an irregular basis, using principally Curtiss C-46 planes, hauling cargo to the mining and lumbering centres in the central and eastern parts of the country.

Another view of FAN-411 taken at San José, Costa Rica, on 18 January 1968 when she, in company with two other FAN C-47s, was being loaded with sterile fruit flies for dispersal over Nicaraguan territory as part of 'Project Savage Fly', an effort to eradicate the Mediterranean Fruit Fly in Central America. The aircraft were apparently fitted with ventral gates for this work. *USAF 109408*

Towards the close of the year, this airline began to operate as far west as Managua on an irregular basis and to carry passengers from time to time. Finally, the airline sometimes runs flights to Miami and return, and in such cases attempts to combine necessary overhaul operations with cargo carrying for the mining centres.' FANSA is known to have at one time or another to have operated two C-46Ds (AN-ADF and AN-FAA), two C-46As (AN-ADG, but actually operated for about one day – as noted above – with Honduran marks XH-014 for some reason, and AN-FAX), a Lockheed C-60 Lodestar (probably AN-ADI) and, pertinent to this account, at least two or three and possibly four C-47s and DC-3s (NC-53192 and NC-17079, confirmed and both leased as such *c.*June 1948, as well as AN-ADJ)[42] – and, somewhere in the mix, the three impounded Costa Rican aircraft. It must be noted, however, that not a solitary photograph of any aircraft bearing FANSA titles has ever surfaced. Again, Somoza had devised a means of not only creating a cargo capability for his regime, which in a sense was able to support its own activities, and at the same time train aircrew, while actually 'owning' less than 50 per cent of the fleet – the others either on short-term leases or acquired through impoundment.

By 9 June 1950, the status of the three impounded Costa Rican DC-3s just would not go away, and an unnamed 'government official' advised the US Embassy that the decision had been made 'for FANSA to pay Costa Rican government for DC-3 airplanes formerly belonging to LACSA of Costa Rica which were seized by the Nicaraguan Government at the time of Figueres revolution, and which are now being operated by FANSA. Apparently, the Nicaraguan Government will assist FANSA in the purchase.'

Then, possibly as an effort to tidy things up a bit more, and make sense of the fates of the three aircraft impounded on 24 April 1948 noted above, on 4 October 1950, the US Embassy in Managua submitted an even more extraordinary report regarding all of this. Significantly, the Assistant Attaché of the Embassy, J. Phillip Rourk, wrote that 'the local manager of La NICA told me that a deal had just been completed whereby La NICA purchased FANSA – or perhaps it would be better to say that a merger took place'. The long and short of the deal was that Somoza, personally, became the majority stockholder of La NICA with PAA's interest reduced to just 20 per cent, while 'all others' amounted to a scant 10 per cent! As part of the deal, La NICA acquired two C-46s, a single C-47 and the C-60. 'Two other planes, formerly the property of LACSA (Costa Rica) and which had been "loaned" to FANSA by the FAN, by whom they had been taken over during the 1948 Costa Rican revolution, will be returned to the FAN.'

But this was not the final act of this extraordinary episode.

On 19 May 1951, a serving GN officer finally informed the US Embassy in Managua that 'the three Costa Rican planes which were impounded in Managua at the close of the 1948 revolution in that country are now being readied for return in accordance with the agreement reached between Costa Rican Minister Mario Echandi and President Somoza during the inauguration of the latter. It is understood that two of the planes are in a serviceable state now, and that the third will be in condition to fly shortly. The same source states that the planes will be flown to San José by pilots of the FAN.'[43] Thus, for all intents and purposes, the first three Nicaraguan 'military' DC-3/C-47 aircraft had been utilised heavily and flown, in turn, by the FAN, FANSA and La Nica at absolutely no cost whatsoever to Nicaragua for more than four years!

Throughout all of this, the US Air Attaché for Central America had, by 1 January 1949, finally concluded – correctly – that two of the three 'impounded' Costa Rican DC-3/C-47 aircraft were, in fact, being operated with GN/FAN colours and markings, while the third had apparently been seconded for a time to La NICA. By 17 January 1950, however, he reported that the GN/FAN in fact held all three (a single DC-3 and two C-47s), but was obliged to modify this observation in his report of 3 July 1950 by inserting a footnote that stated 'the DC-3 and one of the C-47s listed on a previous report have actually belonged to FANSA' although they had been operating with the military. These were unquestionably GN 53, 54 and 55.

Use of these aircraft was more than coincidental. Following the devastating earthquake in Ecuador on 5 August 1950, President Somoza directed (then) Capitan Carlos Vanegas, in what was almost certainly one of the first FAN long-distance flights ever, to journey there with GN 55 bearing medical supplies and equipment to aid in the relief. Apparently his work was commendable, as he was shortly promoted to mayor and designated as the Commander of the FAN.

And Then There Was One

It is not clear from existing records exactly what happened between July 1950 and the end of the year, but the official USAF Air Order of Battle (AOB) for the FAN as of December reflected only one organic C-47 on strength. An official Nicaraguan request, submitted through USAF channels in March 1951, a scant three months later, stated that the FAN desired spares support for its solitary C-47 – which was listed as former USAAF 41-18381 and established her as the former LACSA TI-18 (MSN 4419). Needless to say, the Nicaraguans did not happen to mention that the legal ownership status of this aircraft, for which official spares support was being requested, was very much in doubt!

As noted, Somoza finally relented and, a month later, authorised the return of the three Costa Rican aircraft that, it has always been assumed, were the same three that had been impounded. However, it appears that Somoza in fact perpetrated a switch for at least one of them. The story goes that, just before the repatriation, Somoza transferred his own 'personal' DC-3 to the FAN, Nicaraguan registration AN-ADP, ex 41-18690, ex NC-54075, and ordered Coronel Vanegas (the service Commander) to see to it that all 'the good parts' were stripped from the Tico aircraft, and to replace them with old or damaged components, the basic idea being, apparently, to thus secure enough 'good' parts to keep airworthy the single C-47 that the FAN would then have. Although, as noted, three aircraft were in fact flown to San José, LACSA apparently immediately realised the Nicaraguan duplicity shortly thereafter that, in Texan parlance, they had been 'rode hard and put away wet' by the Nicaraguans during the intervening four years, and promptly dispatched them to Miami via a broker where they were sold on, as shown in Chapter 7, to subsequent owners, who were oblivious – or did not care – about their rather tattered condition.[44]

A fourth aircraft, assumed to have been GN 56, however, was acquired somehow by 1 February 1952,[45] when she reportedly was lost when she crashed on top of a hill west of the Bonanza Mine while being flown by a FAN crew, Capitán (P.A.) Tulio J. Norori and Sub.Tte (P-PA) Max Egner R. Unfortunately, the identity of the aircraft has escaped verification. However, it appears that there may have been yet another aircraft in this mix – possibly the mysterious personal aircraft of Somoza himself. Some weeks after the three FAN crews had ferried the Costa Rican aircraft home, the tight-knit FAN staff was shocked to receive the news that three Fuerza Aérea Hondureña (FAH) pilots were shortly to arrive at Las Mercedes to take possession of the C-47 AN-ADP, which was the last FAN C-47 in the inventory at the time. Without so much as a word to his own troops, Somoza had abruptly sold the aircraft to the Honduran government for $60,000 cash. This left the FAN without a solitary organic DC-3 or C-47 by the date of the AOB for 29 February 1952, and it was this series of calamities that essentially obliged the 'shotgun' wedding of the FAN and LaNICA – one source going so far as to report that the air force was obliged to 'rent' the aircraft when needed.

This reality has been rather confused over the intervening years by the loss of another C-47 on 14 August 1952 while being, again, flown by a FAN crew, Tte (P.A.) Victor M. Zúñiga, Tte (P.A.) Felipe Quintanilla and an unidentified NCO. This aircraft disappeared in bad weather while on a flight between Las Minas and Managua while carrying a large load of rubber and was not found until a year later. In fact, this was a LaNICA aircraft and not FAN.

And then there were None

The loss of what is assumed to have been GN 56 in February 1952 left the FAN with a zero balance of DC-3 or C-47 aircraft.

In an obvious move to finally establish its own dedicated transport element, the FAN submitted a formal request for the sale of no fewer than five C-47s (and six North American F-51Ds) via the Reimbursable Military Air provisions of MDAP on 20 July 1953.

The USAF, finally replying to this request on 17 September, conveyed the disappointing news that, due mainly to the demands of the ongoing Korean Conflict, no C-47s or F-51Ds were available for sale via RMA.

Interestingly, however, in the AOB for February 1954, the USAF noted that the FAN had seven C-47s, but with the name LANICA in parenthesis thereafter – as well as a single North American Navion. Clearly, the service continued its day-to-day operational relationship with the 'civil' airline, and this conclusion was reinforced in the AOB of 30 June 1954 when, under the 'transport' section of the AOB, the observer specifically stated that 'FAN pilots were flying seven C-47s and a Cessna 180 owned and operated by LANICA'.

The AOB for August 1954, however, made no mention of the LANICA fleet, showing the FAN with three operational transport types: the venerable Fairchild 24-C8E and two Cessna UC-78s.

This situation persisted until 30 December, when the US Embassy reported on a rather peculiar transaction. Dr Rafael Huezo who, at the time was the Nicaraguan Minister of Finance, came to the Embassy and asked the Consular Section to notarise a promissory note for $168,750, with an interest rate of 4.5 per cent, in which half of the principal was to be payable in one year and the other half in two years. The note was payable to the Bank of America National Trust and Savings Association in San Francisco, California, and was

intended to cover part of the cost of purchasing two C-47s for the FAN. Twenty-five per cent of the cost of the aircraft, or $56,250, had already been paid – in cash – from FAN funds and the total cost of the two aircraft was thus $225,000.

This deal may very well have been for yet two more of the shadowy Lee Mansdorf rebuild jobs and, if the deal was actually consummated, the aircraft clearly did not end up on the roster of the FAN because, as late as 1 January 1955, the AOB still reflected a zero balance of DC-3s or C-47s. However, once again, the report language left no doubt about the FAN relationship with LANICA, saying 'LANICA is totally controlled by President Somoza and their aircraft would be used by the Air Force in any emergency. This civil airline has in its possession seven C-47 aircraft available to the FAN.'

The same language was used in the AOB of 22 April 1956, although in this instance the (then) six extant LANICA C-47s were listed as 'Potential Mission Aircraft', with the notation that 'the six C-47s of the International Airline could be mustered to support the Air Force in the event of hostilities'.

The close working relationship with LANICA was once again manifested on 19 January 1957 when AN-AEC, being flown at the time by FAN Capitan (P.A.) Orlando Castellón and Tte (P.A.) Oscar Herrera, crashed into the Concepción Volcano in full flight, killing all on board. According to witnesses, the crew had been observed drinking heavily at San Carlos prior to take-off. The aircraft was on a Bluefields–San Carlos–Managua flight at the time. Some observers even claimed that, because of extremely violent manoeuvres the aircraft was observed to have made prior to impacting the volcano, it seemed as though she was flown into the mountain intentionally.

The AOB of 28 May 1958 again reflected no C-47s whatsoever organic to the FAN, although the weary Fairchild 24-C8E and pair of Cessna UC-78s had finally been discarded and replaced by four FMS-acquired Beech C-45s.

From available images, it appears that at least some of the LANICA DC-3s and C-47s of this period wore both Nicaraguan civil registrations and small GN/FAN serials on their vertical fins, although these have not been conclusively linked. This reality persisted until 4 December 1958.

A MAP delivery, C-47D FAN-412 has escaped identification, although she was noted at Howard AFB, CZ, as early as 6 February 1967. She crashed into the sea in August 1975 having become lost carrying a group of artists. *Dan Hagedorn*

The FAN Tries Again

On 25 February 1959, the FAN once again floated a formal request up through diplomatic channels, this time a request to be authorised to purchase two US Navy surplus R4Ds.

This request apparently did not gain any traction as, by 31 August 1959, the service was reported to have a grand total of one C-47A that had been acquired 'locally' and which, surprisingly, was noted on the AOB as being in 'very good condition'.

However, this aircraft was apparently short-lived with the FAN as, again, by 1960, the AOB reflected no C-47s on strength – noting yet again that the service 'could count on LANICA for its four C-47s and two C-46s' but with the startling additional notation that 'the C-47s are equipped with rocket rail launchers to perform in an offensive role'.

FAN 208 and the Commencement of the Modern Era

Although circumstantial, it appears that the single C-47 noted above 'in very good condition' as of 1960 may well have been the first FAN C-47 to gain a 'modern' Nicaraguan three-digit serial, 208, having previously worn GN 56 briefly. First suggested in service as of 1956 or 1957, but reported concretely as of 9 January 1962, the aircraft suffered damage at Las Mercedes Airport, Managua, on that date and the small USAF Mission reported on 30 June that 'the C-47 [that was] crash damaged is in process of being rebuilt with MAP support'.

Although details are confusing, FAN-208 was supposedly acquired via the United Fruit Company while Nicaraguan Capitan Heberto Sanchez B.[46] was the Air Attaché in Tegucigalpa. Very possibly the first Guardia pilot to be checked out on DC-3s, while in Honduras he gained experience on both civil Douglas B-18s and DC-3s.

FAN-208 was, in fact, one of the aircraft fitted with rocket rails[47] as of 1957 when, in company with several P-51Ds and a solitary F-47N, it was dispatched to destroy an insurgent Curtiss C-46 that, upon landing to discharge revolutionaries some 20 miles east-north-east of Bosco (itself about 50 miles from Managua) became mired in mud. The FAN aircraft then made short work of the C-46 and, in the process, gained FAN-208 the unique distinction of probably having been the solitary C-47 to ever share credit for the strafing destruction of another aircraft on the ground! Initially, FAN-208 was reported to have worn a very small version of her serial on her vertical fin but, later, as pictured, sported full FAN colours and markings.

The well-travelled FAN-208 also apparently had further adventures, apparently in Guatemala and a brief stint with LaNICA before settling down with the FAN. She was also probably one of the few FAN C-47s to have been initially based at Xolotlan Field, where she operated alongside a number of North American AT-6s and Beech AT-11s, and another C-47 – possibly GN 55.

The same report supplied the additional information that 'two MAP-supplied C-47s are programmed for delivery in October 1962'.[48] These two aircraft were, in fact, delivered under MAP Grant Aid (GA) in November 1962 and were formally designated as C-47Ds. Interestingly, these were the very first truly 'militarised' and fully kitted C-47s ever operated by the service.

One of these was apparently lost by 31 December 1962, suggesting that one of the two may in fact have been passed on to Colombia, which enjoyed a priority because of the ongoing, high-intensity insurgency there, while the one retained by the FAN had flown a very respectable 376 hours since receipt. A third – and possibly replacement – Grant Aid C-47 was supplied to the FAN under GA during Fiscal Year 1963, bringing the total strength to three aircraft by 30 March 1963, the FAN by this time having reserialed all of its organic tactical aircraft into the 400s.[49]

By 30 June 1963, the FAN had finally established its own, organic transport force, although the relationship with LANICA persisted to a lesser degree. The service owned four C-47s, although one of them – almost certainly the former FAN-208 – purchased directly by the Government (and damaged in an accident and repaired as noted) was then 'returned' to LANICA 'on loan' until such time as LANICA could restore yet another of its own aircraft and return it to operational status.

In the meantime, the small but energetic USAF Mission had been laying big plans with only grudging support from the host air force. Future MAP planning envisaged a 'transport squadron' consisting of no fewer than six C-47s and eight Cessna U-17Cs. By 31 December 1963, the only direct MAP support being provided to the FAN was that for the four C-47s, including, oddly, the aircraft that had been 'loaned' to LANICA – a rather embarrassing violation of MAP ground rules, and which had almost certainly resulted in the 'return' of the aircraft to FAN control on 10 September. The USAF Mission report claimed that the aircraft had been 'deleted from MAP support during the period of utilisation by LANICA', although in fact this appears to have been a paperwork shuffle to retrospectively make things tidy, legally. Ironically, the Mission, after surveying the aircraft upon its return, immediately recommended that it be retired 'as soon as a replacement can be programmed' due to its age.

To everyone's surprise, in 1963 Luis Somoza held to his promise to step down from the presidency. The family did not, however, step down from control of the country. They managed to orchestrate the election of René Shick to the Presidency, the first years of which were relatively uneventful. Anastasio Somoza continued to command the Guardia Nacional and the FAN and Shick did nothing to challenge his position or his family's constantly expanding domination of the entire economy. By this time, the Somoza holdings included the country's only cement factory, LANICA, the entire national merchant marine, the meat processing plant, and a vast array of other manufacturing and agricultural holdings. In spite of all of this and encouraged by the establishment of the Central American Common Market, the economy showed impressive growth – in some periods actually boasting the highest growth rate in all of Latin America. The supreme irony in all of this, of course, was that it was all achieved while dissent was brutally suppressed and the nation was, in reality, a dictatorship in fact if not in name. Even to this day, some elements of Nicaraguan society look back with nostalgia as the mid-1960s being the 'golden age' of the history of their country.

By 15 October 1964, MAP was still supporting four C-47s, suggesting that, if in fact the 'loaned' aircraft had been retired, it had been replaced by this time, and each was averaging a very good twenty-three hours of flight time per month, and a cumulative total flight time during the preceding quarter of 272:15, of which 155:45 (57 per cent) had been in direct support of Civic Action programmes, the then current 'buzz word' justifying MAP support to governments with less than sparkling human rights records.

Four FAN C-47 pilots had also successfully completed a counter-insurgency (COIN) course presented locally by a USAF Mobile Training Team (MTT). Of the four C-47s on hand, one was noted as 'not MAP provided – source unknown' and this was almost certainly the former, long-serving FAN-208. All were noted, for the first time, as being assigned to what was formally designated as the Escuadron de Transporte/SAR at Las Mercedes and enjoyed a respectable C-2 combat rating.

Calendar year 1964 and 1965 may be regarded as a high water mark for Nicaraguan C-47 utilisation in the role for which they had originally been intended. The small FAN fleet of four aircraft managed to amass a total of 1,745 flight hours during the year and, in the process, transported some 3,717 passengers and 456,785lb of incredibly diverse forms of cargo – all associated with Civic Action initiatives.

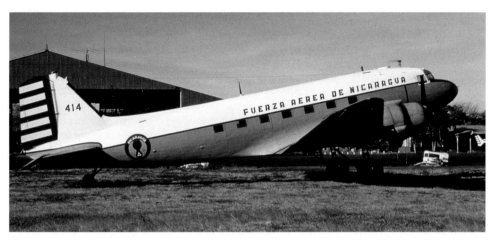

C-47D FAN-414 was unusual in being described as a 'non-MAP gift' from the USAF direct to the FAN, having served there for years as a Mission aircraft. She survived to pass into the hands of the Sandinistas.
Capt. George G. Farinas

Then, in the midst of all of this, Somoza decided he required a dedicated VIP aircraft for his own personal use that, while operated by a picked FAN flight and maintenance crew, was finished in a civil colour scheme and, for reasons that are unclear, a straightforward civil registration (AN-AWT) in sequence. This, the former exotic Douglas C-68, had a storied lineage and, when purchased on 18 February 1965 via Bellomy Aviation, Inc., may well have qualified as the most luxuriously appointed presidential aircraft in Latin America at the time. By the time of acquisition, she was formally described as a DC-3-G202A, but had been extensively refitted inside the main cabin, including an interphone system, three folding card tables, a small round stationary table, six Aerosmith W-14 swivel seats, a three-place divan, a three-place circular lounge at the rear of the cabin, two cold air ducts with reading lights and vents, a cabin partition, five electric fans, and a radio cabinet and bar. The main passenger entrance featured a door draft curtain and partial bulkhead, there were fifteen oxygen masks, a cabin rug, two blankets and – topping off the equipment list, a 24-volt Hoover vacuum cleaner!

By 22 January 1965, the four military configured C-47s on hand were averaging 26:15 hours per month while, during the final three months of 1964, they had flown 315 hours, of which 251:35 (79 per cent) were reported as Civic Action related. One of the C-47s had been unserviceable for three weeks as of that date, however, as it had suffered a take-off accident.

Between January and June 1966, the total C-47 strength remained just four, with three of these being MAP provided, the fourth having been acquired commercially. But despite the health of the economy, it had become obvious to one and all that General Somoza Garcia's youngest son, Anastasio Somoza Debayle, was determined to have 'his turn' as president. The hapless President Shick, powerless to prevent this, reportedly started drinking heavily and, shortly after the Liberal Party convention made Somoza Debayle's candidacy official, Shick died, by all appearance from natural causes. He was promptly succeeded by a staunch Somoza supporter, Interior Minister Lorenzo Guerrero.

The Beginnings of the Sandinista Insurrection

The aroused opposition, probably fuelled by Castro-trained agitators, responded to all of this on 22 January 1967 by calling for a mass march in Managua – and made impassioned and strident calls upon the Guardia Nacional to revolt. The demonstration soon turned in the direction of the Presidential Palace, and the elite GN elements detailed to defend the palace responded by firing on the crowd, killing at least forty in the process – although three Guardia troopers were also slain. In spite of all this, Anastasio Somoza was, in fact, elected, claiming some 70 per cent of the popular vote.

But one of the very first events of his administration was yet another clash with what was by now being called the FSLN (Sandinista National Liberation Front). The FSLN had, in the meantime, already organised well-armed guerrilla elements, and, with the aid of the FAN, the Guardia located and totally destroyed a major guerrilla training camp at Pancasán, making martyrs of several key leaders in the process. Although the Guardia was able to defeat the guerrillas, it was becoming more and more corrupt and unpopular with the common folk who had supplied its troopers.

Between these initial skirmishes and July 1979, some twelve exceedingly brutal years, Nicaragua disintegrated into a pervasive civil war, which has had few parallels in Latin America. A multitude of scholarly books and monographs have attempted, in the intervening years, to describe the tumultuous interlude, focusing for the most part on the politics of the situation, and, with the ultimate triumph of the Sandinistas, as always, such records as may have been created to document the actions of the regime, the Guardia and, in particular, the FAN, which was deeply involved at all levels, were either destroyed, lost or described by the victors that, in a Communist regime, seldom translates to historical veracity.

We do know that the regime – for the first time – finally saw the wisdom of expanding the transport element of the FAN although, by December 1967, the four on hand had been augmented by only one aircraft, and it was something of a puzzle. A VIP-configured aircraft, cited officially as a 'VC-47' but otherwise unidentified,[50] was acquired by this time by Coronel Heberto Sanchez and, although frequently cited as having been utilised by LANICA, so far as can be determined, she never served a day with the airlines and she was in fact an 'Admiral's barge' intended for conveying members of the ruling regime internally and externally – hence her quasi-civil colour scheme and civil registration. The USAF Intelligence Report for December 1967 reported that she was 'flown very little', and that the FAN 'intended to sell it'. In fact, as the insurrection spread, she was pressed into limited service as a trooper and actually survived the insurgency, as noted in the accompanying table, although oddly, she never adopted a FAN serial or national markings.

By 9 October 1968, however, aside from AN-AWT, FAN C-47 strength remained static at four aircraft, and collectively they flew 273:45 hours during the previous quarter. The USAF Mission had assisted in the overhaul and refurbishment of the three MAP-supplied examples, and MAP case NU-MZH was in fact established specifically to acquire three zero-timed C-47 engines for them. By this date, however, the former Escuadrón de Transporte had been merged with the B-26B operating unit to created what was described simply as the Sección C-47, B-26 with four of each on hand and five complete crews for all eight aircraft – although even at this late date, a number of the senior pilots were still routinely flying (and supplementing their FAN compensation) with LANICA.

Last serving the USAFSO as a VC-47D, FAN-415 was yet another 'non-MAP gift' handed over on 23 January 1970 and is unusual here in having a mostly natural metal fuselage but white vertical fin and strake at Managua on 21 January 1972. *Guido E. Bühlmann*

The same four aircraft were still the total complement by 6 April 1969, but only three were in commission, the fourth undergoing what was described as a 'Limited IRAN' conducted by the LANICA workshops. They had collectively flown 387 hours during the previous quarter, however. By 24 July, all four were active once again, and their quarterly flight time had climbed to 415:35.

By 27 October 1969, the four C-47Ds on hand had flown 274:40 during the preceding quarter, the second highest in the entire FAN and, oddly, second only to the hard-working Cessna U-17Cs.

Finally, following repeated official requests, the US finally relented and transferred two former 605th Air Commando Squadron C-47Ds (FAN-414 and 415) to the FAN, although this was under rather unusual circumstances. They were both, according to the official USAF report on the subject, 'provided by the USAF at no cost to Nicaragua, as a "non-MAP gift"', and finally raised the total FAN C-47D inventory to six aircraft, although one of the six was temporarily unserviceable awaiting an engine then being overhauled in the US

Then, between 3 and 30 September 1970, yet another former USAFSO aircraft, this time a VC-47B, formerly with the 24th Special Operations Wing, was similarly transferred to the FAN as FAN-416.

As shown in the table, the FAN, casting around for aircraft to bolster their hard-pressed inventory, managed to acquire at least three more aircraft including, oddly, yet another VIP-configured aircraft, AN-ASP, which, contrary to popular belief, was not the President's aircraft[51] but, rather, that of his son, Anastasio Somoza Portocarrero – from whom her vanity registration was acquired. This aircraft was acquired through the efforts of the FAN Commander sometime shortly after 9 November 1971, aided in this endeavour by one Richard McGuire and the First National City Bank.

Throughout this entire interlude, the activities of the FAN's C-47 fleet actually contributed to the seemingly interminable agony of the country by affording the Guardia simple, rugged, on-demand transport to assorted insurgent hot spots around the country.

By mid-July 1979, as the US attempted to broker a peaceful solution of the civil war and return the country to some form of order, the rank and file of the Guardia finally realised that the end

was near, and the formerly rigid organisation started to disintegrate. This was in no small measure accelerated by the fact that Somoza had fled to Miami on 17 July, but not before convincing the remaining leadership of the Guardia that the US would send troops to crush the FSLN and, in the process, rescue them – so, briefly, they soldiered on. Members of the FAN, cramming as many family members and loyal ground crew as they could into every airworthy aircraft, started bolting ahead of the ground troops for neighbouring countries – notably Honduras. Others, still viable as organised units, started convoys in the direction of Honduras and Costa Rica, where they planned to dispose of their weapons and seek asylum. Hundreds of others, mainly officers and their families, sought asylum in the several foreign embassies in Managua.

Belated regime and US efforts to reopen negotiations with the triumphant FSLN failed utterly when the junta, realising they had nothing to gain from such efforts, instead demanded unconditional surrender by the government and what remained of the Guardia and FAN.

After only forty-three hours in office, the last pre-Sandinista president of Nicaragua, Francisco Urcuyo, fled to Guatemala (he is believed to have flown out on one of the FAN C-47s), and the last vestiges of the Somoza government collapsed. FSLN forces, in a portrait reminiscent of Fidel Castro entering Havana twenty years previously, occupied Managua on 19 July and, the following day, took over the government.

Fighting between scattered, hard-core elements of the Guardia, supported by at least one C-47, continued for weeks. Meanwhile, an untold number of youths had acquired weapons of all kinds abandoned by the Guardia or acquired from the FSLN and roamed the streets of Managua, perpetrating untold violence against anyone even hinted of having supported the regime.

Finally, on 4 August 1979, the very last FAN aircraft to be lost during the twelve-year conflict – a C-47 – was shot down by the FSLN near Condega, Nicaragua – in the process gaining the dubious distinction of being one of only a handful of Latin American C-47s to ever be lost to ground fire.

Yet a third non-traditional 'non-MAP gift' to the FAN was former USAFSO C-47D FAN-416 turned over on 4 September 1970. Seen here at Tucson, Arizona, in April 1976, almost certainly on a spares foray, she was well-maintained at the time. Replete with full COIN radio antenna array, she almost certainly also survived to pass to the FAS when the Somoza regime crumbled. *M/Sgt Ben Knowles via Brian R. Baker*

The Fuerza Aérea Sandinista y Defensa Antiaérea (FAS-DAA)

Although a significant number of FAN aircraft had fled the country as the debacle accelerated, some of these were apparently repatriated and, together with what few intact aircraft remained of the defeated air arm, shortly became assets of a 'new' national air force, with an entirely new national insignia, title and serialing system.

As had happened in Cuba, however, the new air arm immediately found itself hampered severely by an almost total lack of qualified aircrews and mechanics. As in Cuba, however, Communist regimes quickly stepped in to help take up the slack, and, reportedly, politically vetted pilot candidates were recruited and dispatched for fast-jet training in Communist Bloc nations. Cuba also sent 'civilian' engineers to carve out two new, entirely equipped airfields in the country capable of accommodating jets.

Ironically, based on known recruits, the initial cadre of pilot trainees – believed to have been around sixty – was intended to provide the new FAS-DAA with around forty-five to fifty qualified pilots, which just happened to be the mix needed to form a typical Soviet-style air force regiment – and which, not coincidentally, was a far greater number of pilots than the recently defeated FAN had ever maintained.

While this was all well and good, the oft-reported fleets of MiGs and other jets usually dispersed by the Russians and their proxies never materialised, for reasons that have never been properly understood, and so, the freshly minted crews found themselves returning home to man aircraft for which they had not been trained whatsoever: a smattering of Lockheed T-33s, Cessna 337s, Douglas B-26s, North American T-28s, assorted helicopters – and C-47s.

Purchased on behalf of the Ministerio de Guerra y Marina but operated 100 per cent by the FAN, AN-AWT was last described as a 'quasi DC-3 Hi-Per' variant. Aside from the national flag on her vertical tail surfaces, the only clue to her ownership was a coat of arms on the forward fuselage. Every time she was seen, she was in company with a standard FAN C-47, as here at Tocumen International Airport, Panama, on 27 April 1969. She was apparently used by Somoza henchmen to escape to Tegucigalpa, Honduras, and was last noted derelict there in March 2009. *Dan Hagedorn*

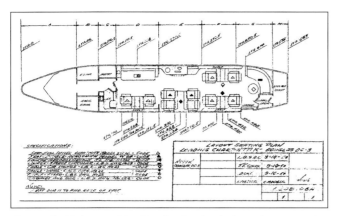

The actual cabin layout of AN-AWT showing the plush appointments and the VIP equipment noted in the text. *Hagedorn Collection*

Another DC-3C-2SC9G operated by the FAN in civil colours of convenience was AN-ASP that, despite numerous references to the contrary, was the personal aircraft of Somoza's son, not the *Caudillo* himself. She was also used to escape to Honduras when the regime fell and was last seen derelict at Tegucigalpa. *Eddy Gual*

The first reported FAS-DAA C-47 was noted airworthy as early, however, as February 1980, when FAS-204, with most of its former FAN markings scrubbed off, but without, as yet the 'new' FAS national markings (which were apparently still being settled upon). FAS-203 was noted at Managua by 6 November 1980, and, eventually, additional C-47s were noted with serials FAS-205, 206 and 210 – strongly suggesting that most of the five former FAN aircraft known to have survived to that point had in fact been absorbed into the 'new' service; this number also agreeing with known FAS-DAA serials. Unfortunately, not a solitary one of these has been positively identified, but can be assumed from their former FAN identities.

Opposition to the new Sandinista regime was not long in coming and, predictably, involved a number of clandestine and shadowy DC-3s and C-47s.

On 26 March 1984, a DC-3 bearing completely fictitious Canadian civil marks CF-ETE crashed near the border between Nicaragua and Costa Rica and was almost certainly flying to the so-called Contras at

the time, ferrying guns and ammunition to anti-Sandinista guerrillas. The aircraft had reportedly had a valid US civil registration since 1979, but the actual identity has not been determined.

Then, on 28 August 1984, another C-47 crashed near Quitali, 65km south of the Honduran border, reportedly with eight people on board. The two-man crew was reported to have been captured.

On 28 August 1986, an FAS-DAA-operated C-47 crashed near Siuna Rosita during what was described as a routine flight, and the two-man crew was killed. The aircraft has not been identified.

Finally, and possibly the very last vestige of Nicaraguan C-47 operations of any kind, as of 1 December 1986, the FAS-DAA reportedly lost two C-47s to unspecified 'mechanical difficulties, bad weather or combat losses'. They were both described as having been camouflaged at the time. Aeronica, the successor to LANICA, also possessed two DC-3s or C-47s at that time and, incredibly, the associated intelligence report stated that 'both could be equipped with bomb racks'.

Right At least five C-47s survived FAN service to pass into the hands of the FAS, including FAS-203 seen here at Managua bearing evidence of her former USAF service and one of the first versions of the rather unusual FAS national insignia. *via George G.J. Kamp*

Below Right The last FAN C-47 to be acquired before the fall of the Somoza dynasty was FAN-418 on 13 February 1976, a MAP C-47D. This aircraft suffered the rare fate of being shot down by insurgents over Esteli sometime after February 1976. *Eddy Gual*

Below: Significant in having a 'five-star' placard, curtained windows and a DC-3C-style air stair, FAN-417 was a commercial acquisition in the US by May 1976, and may best be described as a VC-47H hybrid. She is believed to have survived to pass to the FAS. *Eddy Gual*

LaNICA (LANICA,) Aerovias Inca de Nicaragua S.A. and FANSA Douglas DC-3 and C-47 Series Aircraft Known Operated by FAN Crews or on FAN Missions

Nicaraguan Registration	Previous Identities	Built As	MSN	Notes
AN-ACN	41-1868 NC-54310	C-47-DL	6090	LaNICA between 1947 and 1957. Known operated by FAN crews and on military missions on numerous occasions. To N5522A in 1957.
AN-ACR	43-15654 NC-66006	C-47A-85-DL DC-3C-S1C3G	20120	LaNICA and ferried from Brownsville on delivery by Raymond Norton 9 Aug 46. Known operated by FAN crews and on military missions on numerous occasions but had actually passed to FAN custody by 24 Nov 55 and may have actually been operated by them with quasi-civil marks AN-ACR as no known FAN serial. To N16774 3 Sep 63 and then to FAE-20120 29 May 68.
AN-ACS	–	C-47	'42856'	LaNICA between 1947 and Mar 48 and not subsequently reported. The actual identity of this aircraft is unknown.
AN-ACT	42-92994 NC-66131	C-47A-20-DK	12856	LaNICA delivered Mar 47 but also cited as MSN 3293. Last reported Jul 53 and known to have been flown by FAN crews and on military missions.
AN-ACX	–	C-47	–	LaNICA. Reported during 1947, fate unknown. Suspected of having been lost while being flown by an FAN crew.
AN-ACY	–	C-47	–	LaNICA. Reported during 1947, fate unknown.
AN-ACZ	41-18537 NC-9922H	C-47-DL DC-3C-S1C3G	4662	LaNICA bought 4 Aug 47 from the Ford Motor Company for $20,000 which, in turn, had bought it from the RFC 25 Jan 46 – for $20,000! Ford did the conversion to DC-3C-S1C3G by 15 Jan 47. Known operated by FAN crews and on military operations on numerous occasions. Damaged beyond repair 27 Aug 48.
(NC-56800)	41-18497 NC-88713 NC-56800	C-47-DL DC-3C-S1C3G	4589	Leased by FANSA by Apr 48. Owner Harry Wheeler claimed she was 'impounded at Managua 18 Oct 48 for non-payment of airport fees'. Wheeler claimed he could 'clear this up' the same date and that he then intended to move the aircraft to Venezuela, where he intended to sell it. Almost certainly one of the aircraft used, with markings obscured, to support Nicaraguan incursion into Costa Rica in Apr 48. Despite previous claims, had no association with LaNICA. Written off 11 Mar 49 at Puerto Cabezas probably in FANSA or FAN hands. The US registration was not formally cancelled until 18 Aug 54.
(NC-53192)	41-38719 NC-53192	C-47-DL	6178	Leased by FANSA c.Apr–Jun 48 via Charles Mathews & Cia., Inc. and AAXICO and, despite previous claims, had no association with LaNICA. Almost certainly one of the three C-47s used, with markings obscured, to support the Nicaraguan incursion into Costa Rica in Apr 48. Returned to the US by 9 Mar 49 still as NC-53192. Later to N91230.
(NC-17079)	42-23609 NC-17079	C-47A-30-DL	9471	Leased by FANSA c.Apr–Jun 48 via Charles Mathews & Cia., Inc. and AAXICO and almost certainly one of the three aircraft used, with markings obscured, to support the Nicaraguan incursion into Costa Rica in Apr 48. Returned to the US by 9 Mar 49.
AN-ADJ	42-32835 NC-54727	C-47-DL	9061	LaNICA from Jun 51. To N5515A 21 Jan 58.
AN-ADK	41-18677 NC-60003	C-47-DL DC-3C-S1C3G	6083	LaNICA by 1949 via PAA and had been converted to DC-3C-S1C3G configuration by 12 Aug 46. Interestingly, the US registration for this aircraft was not cancelled until 9 Jun 64! Known operated by FAN crews and on numerous military operations. Fate unknown but this may have been the aircraft lost on 31 Oct 54 while being flown by FAN crew Capitan Salvador López and Tte Antonio Mejia in an emergency landing at the Siuna Mine. A fire had broken out in the cargo area while the aircraft was carrying 6,000lb of petrol that had been loaded at Alamikamba.
AN-ADM	44-76390 NM-43 CU-T9 HK-???	C-47B-25-DK	15974/32722	LaNICA by 1949. Known flown by FAN crews and on numerous military missions. Supposedly named Managua. Last reported Jul 53. Fate unknown.
AN-ADP	41-18690 NC-54075	C-47-DL	6096	Aerovias Inca de Nicaragua S.A. It appears that this may have been the aircraft, mentioned in the text, as seized by a local bank when this operator went into bankruptcy on 3 June 50, briefly held by the FAN, and then abruptly sold to Honduras on 4 Sep 51 to become FAH-301.
AN-ADQ	42-23350 NC-88875 (HK-???)	C-47A-5-DL DC-3C-S1C3G DC-3A-S4C4G DC-3C-C404G	9212	LaNICA by 1948 but the FAA registration file for NC-88875 says she was not cancelled until 23 Oct 51 for the reason that she was being exported to Colombia via Frontier Airmotive of Brownsville, TX. The aircraft underwent a number of conversions between 1946 and 1951, as shown, but had been 'converted from freight to plush interior' c.30 Aug 47, suggesting a use other than airliner. Believed flown by FAN crews. Last reported Feb 60 when she suffered unspecified damage.
AN-AEB	–	C-47	–	LaNICA by Jul 53. Reported written off 21 Sep 57. Believed flown by FAN crews.
AN-AEC	42-92504 BuA17142 TI-1003	C-47A-5-DK R4D-5	12312	LaNICA. Written off 23 Jan 57 Ometepe Isle, Lake Nicaragua.
AN-AEF	–	C-47	–	LaNICA by Sep 57. Believed flown by FAN crews and flown on military missions.

FAN-Owned and Operated Douglas DC-3 and C-47 Series Aircraft

GN/FAN Serial	Previous Identities	Built As	MSN	Notes
GN 53	NC-34925 TI-17	DC-3A-345	4957	Impounded and incorporated into the GN 24 Apr 48. Finally returned to Costa Rica in Jul 51.
GN 54	*42-92279* *FL635 (RAF)* *YS-34* *C-209* *YS-34*	*C-47A-15-DK*	*12062*	Impounded and incorporated into the GN 24 Apr 48. Finally returned to Costa Rica in Jul 51.
GN 55	41-18381 NC-51182 XA-XYZ-1 TI-18	C-47-DL	4419	Impounded and incorporated into the GN 24 Apr 48. However, did not return to Costa Rica in Jul 51 (was apparently replaced by another aircraft) and, instead, became AN-ADJ and then FAN-208 (q.v.).
GN 56	–	C-47	–	
FAN-208	41-18381 NC-51182 XA-XYZ-1 TI-18 GN 55	C-47-DL	4419	Written off 9 Jan 62 on landing at Las Mercedes, Managua, while being flown by Tte Orlando Torres Lanuza and Mario Amaya with thirty-five passengers on board, flying a LANICA route from Corn Island! All on board walked away. According to witnesses, the aircraft aborted a very challenging landing at Corn Island, and the crew elected to return to Managua, where it made a wheels up landing after dumping fuel. It had been flying with LANICA at the time for almost a month, illustrating the very incestuous relationship between FAN and the airline.
FAN-410	*44-76951*	*C-47B-35-DK* *C-47D*	*16541/33289*	MAP delivery Nov 62. Became 'Air Force One' with a five-star placard. Survived as late as 9 Jan 79 and probably passed to FAS as FAS-210.
FAN-411	*45-996* *0-45996*	*C-47B-45-DK* *C-47D*	*16999/34261*	MAP delivery 14 Dec 62 but in- country in November. Written off 4 Dec 70 when it crashed into the Turrialba Volcano in torrential rain. Tragically, she was conducting a humanitarian mission at the time to Panama where a sick woman, the mother of a wealthy Nicaraguan land owner, was to be picked up and transported home.
AN-AWT	NC-30005 42-14298 NC-20752 N20752 N777K CU-N654 N10315 XB-GEL N9089R	DC-3A-414 C-68-DO DC-3A-S1C3G DC-3-G202A	4174	Purchased 18 Feb 65 via Bellomy Aviation, Inc. and first noted as AN-AWT in Dec 67. Had no connection with LANICA whatsoever, despite export declarations, although frequently cited as such. Apparently also utilised to escape by unknown persons to Tegucigalpa, Honduras, where she was noted derelict as late as Mar 02.
FAN-412	–	*C-47D*	–	MAP delivery. First noted 6 Feb 67 at Howard AFB, CZ. Written off off Amapala, Nicaragua, date given as either 2 Aug 75 or 30 Aug 75, the former appearing most likely. She crashed into the sea 300m from the shore near Tamarindo after becoming lost during a flight from Mexico to Nicaragua carrying a group of artists. Minutes earlier, the aircraft had attempted to land at Ilopango (Tegucigalpa, Honduras) and San Miguel, but bad weather and nightfall at both alternates precluded the crew from finding either location.
FAN-414	43-15497 0-15497	C-47A-85-DL C-47D	19963	'Non-MAP Gift' 29 Jan 70. Last reported in Feb 79. This aircraft almost certainly passed to the FAS.
FAN-415	43-49110 0-49110	C-47B-10-DK C-47D VC-47D	14926/26371	'Non-MAP Gift' 23 Jan 70. This aircraft had served for years as the USAF Mission and Attaché's aircraft to Nicaragua. As of 21 Jan 72, she was unusual in having a natural metal fuselage and wings, but white vertical fin and fin fillet. Written off 21 Sep 74 when she crashed in bad weather at lake Xolotlán while conducting a relief mission to Chinandega and León, which had just been devastated by Hurricane Fifi.
FAN-416	43-48499 0-48499	C-47B-1-DK VC-47B C-47D	14315/25760	'Non-MAP Gift' 4 Sep 70, a former 24th SOW, USAFSO aircraft. Last reported 9 Jan 79 and almost certainly passed to the FAS.
AN-ASP	41-18457 NC-67825 NC-69040 N321HA	C-47-DL DC-3C-S1C3G DC-3-S1036 DC-3C-2SC9G	4519	Purchased *c.*9 Nov 71. Often cited as 'Air Force One', this was in fact the personal aircraft of the President's son. Noted at Santa Cruz in open storage by 1978. Apparently made airworthy and used by unknown persons to escape to Honduras, where its very tattered remains were noted on the dump by Mar 02.
FAN-417	42-92925 BuA17181	C-47A-20-DK R4D-5 R4D-5Z VC-47H C-47H TC-47H	12780	Apparently, a commercial acquisition 19 May 76. Last reported 9 Jan 79 and almost certainly survived to pass to the FAS.
FAN-418	43-49556 0-49556	C-47B-15-DK C-47D	15372/26817	MAP 13 Feb 76. This aircraft had been in Latin America with the USAF since 1949! Shot down over Esteli sometime after Feb 79.

Although of very marginal quality, images of FAS C-47s are quite rare – and they did not survive in service for long. This aircraft was also photographed at Managua and appears to be about to receive new service titles over the broad white fuselage cheatline. *via George G.J. Kamp*

Certainly a candidate for the most unusually camouflaged of all Latin American military C-47s, this otherwise anonymous FAS example was photographed at Managua as late as January 1987. *via Carlos Planas*

FAS-DAA Douglas DC-3 and C-47 Series Aircraft

FAS-DAA Serial	Previous Identity	Built As	MSN	Notes
FAS-203	–	C-47	–	First reported 6 Nov 80 and as late as 22Jun 83, by which time she was camouflaged with white '203' in small numerals on her vertical fin and an abbreviated Nicaraguan flag over the middle third of the rudder. She also had black titles on her fuselage reading 'Fuerza Aérea Sandinista'.
FAS-204	–	C-47	–	First reported in Feb 80.
FAS-205	–	C-47	–	
FAS-206	–	C-47	–	
FAS-210	*44-76591* *FAN-410*	*C-47B-35-DK* *C-47D*	*16541/33289*	

Left: Something of a controversial aircraft, this machine, pictured at Managua around January 1987, bears a colour scheme very similar to AN-ASP, which is known to have escaped to Tegucigalpa, Honduras, where it was last known derelict. The story goes that the Sandinistas wanted to lay claim to having 'captured' the aircraft and its escapees. It was every inch an FAS asset by this time. *via Carlos Planas*

Below left: The host of shadowy aircraft utilised in Central America in support of the CONTRA forces may never be understood, as nearly all of them were sanitised beyond recognition. This FDN-operated C-47 sustained damage after being sabotaged by Sandinista forces at El Aguacate airfield, Honduras, and is clearly beyond redemption. *via Mario Overall*

Below: Another mystery aircraft, this C-47 was used by the Sandinistas for flying arms and supplies into Nicaragua during the civil war. By the time this photo was taken, she was already part of the FAS inventory. *via Xiofano*

CHAPTER SEVENTEEN

Panama

I T WAS ONE OF THOSE DAYS that is etched indelibly into the memory.

Your co-scribe Hagedorn, as a young GI, had just alighted on 21 October 1964 from the jarring journey via native bus from the Canal Zone to the Paitilla Airport (known rather grandly, but only on its signage as the Aeropuerto Marcos A. Gelabert) on what was then a rather thinly populated, extreme south-eastern boundary of Panama City, to make his weekly scout of aviation activities at the rather lazy general aviation field.

Rounding the modest TASA terminal, where sporadic third-level operations were being carried out with a few Beech 18s, I was brought up short by a vision I had not expected whatsoever: a brand-spanking new Cessna Model 185C clearly bearing quasi-military markings 'GN-001'. Then, to my left and just in front of the aircraft, I noticed that a small house that had previously been vacant had been completely refurbished and painted since my last visit and had a sign in front proclaiming that this was the site of the Destacamento Aéreo No. 1, Guardia Nacional.

I did not appreciate it at the time, but I was witness to something very rare in the aviation world: the actual birth of an air force.

Panama had, in fact, experimented with a small air arm at least twice before: once in 1931 when the Guardia acquired a pair of armed Travel Air A14D Speedwing Sportsman Deluxe biplanes and a Keystone K-84 Commuter amphibian, ostensibly for an internal mail service.

Seen at Miami on 14 January 1969, HP-11 was a very out-of-sequence Panamanian civil registration, destined to become the first FAP C-47 – but, as noted in the narrative, she actually received code FAP-202, suggesting she was the second! She was very much an airline configured aircraft at this point, leading to her temporary service as Panama's first 'Air Force One'. *ALCOSS*

The government soon found that this modest effort was rather more expensive to maintain than had been anticipated and, as well, US officials in the hated Canal Zone took a very dim view of armed aircraft being operated locally over which they had no control. The surviving aircraft were soon sold on to the civil register and the service folded.

Then, as the war-surplus glut of very inexpensive yet relatively modern aircraft became apparent in late 1945 and 1946, the sitting government, ever intent after the war in asserting Panamanian sovereignty, once again experimented with creating a small Guardia aviation detachment at Paitilla (then known as the Aeropuerto Nacional) with several surplus Sixth Air Force (Canal Zone-based) surplus Vultee BT-13A, a Cessna UC-78 and a modified Beech AT-11 of questionable provenance. This enterprise, too, foundered – the public explanation once again being inadequate funding but, in fact, due to official disapproval from the Canal Zone defence authorities.

Panamanian politics throughout this period was based almost entirely upon a love/hate relationship with the Canal Zone. In fact, the career opportunities, training and largesse emanating from the CZ had helped create in the country one of the first viable middle-class constituencies in Central America. Despite this reality, every candidate for high office throughout the period based their campaigns, directed mainly at the poor rural campesinos in the hinterland, on a never-ending litany of virile rhetoric deploring the affront to the dignity and sovereignty of the country that the Canal, its residents – and prosperity – displayed in their midst on a daily basis.

With the basic colour scheme still drying, this was the former HP-11 at the landmark former Pan American nose hangar at Tocumen airport, which had been acquired as the FAP's primary operating base. The rudder markings have not yet received the two stars, red and blue, parallel. *Hagedorn*

Although the first to arrive, and initially marked as FAP-202, for a period in early 1970, the serial was deleted entirely and replaced by the Panamanian coat of arms on the rear fuselage, and the FAP titles replaced with 'Presidencia de la Republica', as seen here at Tocumen on 17 January 1970. The aircraft is probably best described as a 'DC-3C-like hybrid'. *Hagedorn*

Confusingly, the second C-47 acquired by the FAP received the codes FAP-201 and was named 'Urracá' complete with accompanying nose art, as seen at Tocumen on 30 December 1969. *Hagedorn*

Earlier, however, like the Cessna U-17Bs and Fairchild-Hiller FH-1100s in the inventory at the time, FAP-202 had been painted with full FAP titles and had been christened '11 de Octubre' as seen here on 30 December 1969. *Hagedorn*

A full-length view of FAP-201 on 30 December 1969. She was easily picked from a line-up as she was the solitary Panamanian C-47 to have an RDF 'bullet' atop her forward fuselage. *Hagedorn*

The empennage of *FAP-201* at first had the coat of arms of the Guardia Nacional applied to both sides of her vertical fin, but this was later painted over. *Hagedorn*

When FAP-201 performed a blistering low pass at Tocumen on 17 January 1970, by this point still named 'Urracá' but with a slightly modified nose art, most spectators missed the fact that, besides the fact she had large 'FAP' titles inboard under her starboard wing, she had also been inscribed in large letters under the centre section 'Bilboa' and, just inboard of the oddly placed national insignia under the port wing, 'Macho'! *Hagedorn*

This stance was pervasive and, viewed first-hand by Hagedorn with a young family, was brought home on countless occasions in the dead of night when the 'alert phone' rang and the US military establishment garrisoned in the Canal Zone reacted (with loaded weapons and live ammunition) to yet another in a seemingly endless series of incidents and provocations, most of which appeared to be designed to inflame what, in honest retrospect, now appears to have been American self-righteousness.

As my weekly excursions to Panamanian airfields became facilitated by the acquisition of a 1955 Chevrolet four-door sedan (I was the sixth owner), it soon became clear that Panama was, in fact, going to have its own air force – the Canal Zone leadership be damned.

A second-hand Cessna 180 (GN-002) was noted by April 1968 and then, starting in the summer of 1969, USAF stations in the Canal Zone – notably at the major Howard Air Force Base – were startled when Fairchild-Hiller FH-1100 light helicopters started making high-speed, low-level incursions into Canal Zone airspace. This observer witnessed three of these first-hand, the FH-1100 flying due west at low altitude directly over the main runway at Howard AFB while flight operations were under way, without so much as a word to ATC. The Panamanian news media had announced as early as March 1969 that the Guardia had established what was being termed the Fuerza Aérea Panameña

(FAP) to operate these 'ambulance' helicopters, and defended the overflights of Canal Zone bases on the grounds that the aircraft were rushing to accident scenes to rescue victims. FAP-101, the first of the FH-1100s, was indeed equipped with two stretchers on the port side but, significantly, when FAP-102 was inspected on 12 August 1969, she had a rudimentary gun mount on the starboard skid for a .30 calibre weapon and was named 'Espiritú de la Revolución'. These features seemed rather odd for an ambulance aircraft.

Somehow, an accommodation was reached with the Panamanian government, which insisted it had every right to fly its aircraft wherever and whenever it wished. As so often, the US officials who confronted this serious situation reached the conclusion that it was probably best to accept the reality and to undertake measures to professionalise the emerging air arm and bring it 'into the fold' of USAF military assistance – a strategy that invariably appealed to the local military-minded leadership, many of whom had in fact been trained at the Inter-American Air Forces Academy at Albrook AFB, CZ, literally over the hill from Panama City.

Soon, the FAP established its permanent first station at the old Pan American nose-hangar at the rather distant Aeropuerto Internacional de Tocumen east of Panama City, and the acquisition of an amazing and cosmopolitan array of aircraft commenced.

A large crowd and the media had turned out for what was almost certainly the shortest delivery flight of any MAP-supplied C-47s! Here, C-47D 0-24405, followed by sister-ship 0-15970, arrive at Tocumen airport, still wearing full USAF livery, on 17 January 1970. Note that although the base fairings for the astrodomes is still evident, the Plexiglas domes themselves have been removed. *Jimmy Stark*

C-47D 0-15970 after shut down and with Guardia and FAP officers welcoming her crew at Tocumen on 17 January 1970. Note the Guatemalan Lockheed AT-33As lined up in the background, which gave a spirited aerial demonstration the same day to help the Panamanians celebrate the birth of the newest air force in Central America. *Hagedorn*

The second MAP-supplied C-47D, 0-24405, just after being shut down at Tocumen on 17 January 1970. The terminal is in the left background and a civil DC-3 and COPA HS 748 sit on the apron on the right. *Hagedorn*

The earliest known image of the former C-47D 0-15970 after being painted in full FAP livery as FAP-203, seen here at Tocumen on 20 March 1970. Note the antenna array. *Jimmy Stark*

First to arrive, on 10 January 1969, was what appeared, at the time, to be an exceptionally 'out-of-sequence' civil DC-3, bearing the Panamanian civil marks HP-11. The aircraft was noted being masked for respraying at Tocumen not long thereafter. Then, within the space of two weeks, what was clearly the same aircraft was photographed at Tocumen in full FAP markings but without a serial number, bearing only the titles Presidencia de la República and the Panamanian coat of arms on the rear fuselage. Until 2013, the identity of this mysterious aircraft – the first FAP C-47 – remained unknown, but it is fully documented in the accompanying table. By 30 December 1969, the aircraft had gained serial FAP-202 and the presidential titles had been deleted in favour of full FAP titles on the upper white fuselage.

This aircraft was followed by another aircraft, acquired from commercial sources in Venezuela around 17 January 1969 and, between 16 and 21 February, it had gained the marks FAP-201. In the weeks that followed, these aircraft were observed at Tocumen clearly undergoing crew training as they rather comically taxied erratically and haltingly and conducted endless touch-and-go landings. At one point, one landed and, while rolling out, departed the main runway at speed and executed a slow-motion ground loop, but was apparently undamaged in the process.

Then, to the astonishment of scribe Hagedorn, who was witnessing this phenomenal growth both officially and unofficially, with virtually no preamble, two Howard AFB-based Douglas C-47s flew to Tocumen almost precisely a year later, on 17 January 1970 – which must certainly rank as the shortest MAP delivery flight in history, where they were handed over to the FAP, and these were joined a year later by another aircraft, for a total of five – not four – Panamanian military C-47s.

To everyone's surprise, a second increment of US-supplied aircraft arrived in 1970 in the form of four Cessna U-17Bs, which were quickly assimilated, complete with 'nose art' and individual names, followed by the first two Bell UH-1H Hueys. These were followed between 1971 and the end of the decade by a VIP-configured Convair Cv-580, Douglas DC-6B, de Havilland Canada DHC-6 Twin Otters, ex-US Army de Havilland Canada U-1A Otters, a Lockheed L-188C Electra II, Britten-Norman BN-2As, a Cessna 402B, a Cessna 172, an Aero Commander 560A and a Beech 95-B55 Baron – as well as several other short-lived aircraft.

Geographically, Panama is unusual in that – contrary to common wisdom – the country actually extends, either east or west, from the central national capital and the all-important Canal, and not north and south. Aside from Panama City and Colón at either end of the Canal, the other cities in the country are rather modest, David at the extreme western frontier near Costa Rica being the next largest. Consequently, the growing FAP inventory was a force with little to do, and few destinations. The fleet was primarily employed, to no one's surprise, to support the Guardia and its nationwide garrisons, soon to become the Fuerzas de Defensa Nacional or Panama Defence Force – the closest thing the country has ever had to an Army in the conventional sense.

C-47D FAP-203 again, by this time notable for its interesting array of antennas on the forward upper fuselage and, slightly different than the last image as of this 20 August 1970 view, with the addition of a diagonal band on her vertical fin with 'TAM' inscribed on it. *Jimmy Stark*

The FAP, as a condition of its MAP agreement, did in fact employ the aircraft in so-called 'nation-building' projects, as well as on numerous mercy and regional resupply flights. But as these almost all moved westward (the area east of the Canal, consisting for the most part of the incredibly inhospitable Darien Province having very low population density), even these were hardly sufficient to warrant such a transport-centric organisation.

The Guardia did engage the FAP fleet in a modest paratroop experiment but, again, the topography of the national territory really did not lend itself well to even company-size paradrops, and as a result those few troops so trained evolved instead into a form of special forces.

The C-47 fleet did eventually commence making international flights, ostensibly to acquire needed supplies and parts, ranging as far afield as Miami with crews who had previously been captains and first officers on COPA and RAPSA DC-3s, long-since retired and replaced by more modern types, and who were apparently awarded Reserve commissions in the Guardia to facilitate the process. The service certainly did not possess any multi-engine trained pilots of its own as of 1969–70.

It soon became apparent that, despite the 'free' delivery of the quartet of MAP C-47s, the aircraft were hardly cheap to operate and, in any event, were beyond the airlift needs of the service. As a result, one had already been surplused and sold to a government entity, although the other three soldiered on sporadically until February 1984, making the FAP experience with the type the briefest of any established air arm in Latin America – a scant fifteen years. However, they also earned the distinction, seldom recognised, as the only Latin American air arm to not suffer the loss of a C-47 while in service, a credit to the crews and maintainers.

Finally, this chapter would not be complete without mention of a derelict C-47 fuselage, with crudely painted-out USAF titles, found in the Guardia Nacional compound on the east side of Tocumen airport, alongside an equally anonymous North American AT-6D as of 30 December 1968. Hoisted up on empty 50-gallon drums, close examination could not disclose her identity or why she had come to be in the Guardia compound. By March 1969, she was gone.

The second January 1970 MAP-delivered C-47D, 0-24405, gained code FAP-204 and was seen at the busy FAP nose hangar on 27 March 1970. Note the longer-chord air intake fairing on top of the engine cowling, one of the recognition points on most C-47Ds. *Jimmy Stark*

FAP Serial	Previous Identity	Built As	MSN	Assignments and Notes
FAP-201	42-24249 FL528 NC4683U YV-C-AGI YV-T-JTP	C-47A-50-DL Dakota III	10111	Delivered by 16 Jan 69. Named 'Urracá' by Sep 69. Sold 13 Feb 84 to N4683U.
(HP-11) FAP-202 C-47 202	42-100779 TI-104 C-170 C-205 NC79989 XA-HUG N75885 HP-11	C-47A-70-DL 'DC-3C-like hybrid'	19242	Delivered between 10 and 19 Jan 69, initially as HP-11. Then painted with serial FAP-202 by 21 Feb 69, but this serial was temporarily dropped and replaced with Presidencia de la República titles after 17 Jan 70 as well as the name '11 de Octubre' on her nose. By 10 Dec 73 she had been remarked with service titles and had regained serial FAP-202. Last reported at San Jose, Costa Rica, Feb 78. Reported to HP-560 in 1971, but this appears to disagree with the known spotting reports and photographic evidence.
FAP-203 TAM-203	43-15970 0-15970	C-47A-90-DL C-47D	20436	MAP 17 Jan 60 ex-24th SOW, USAFSO. Noted at COOPESA, San Jose, CR, 22 Feb 72 for overhaul. Last reported in service 10 Dec 73. May have been one of two being overhauled at COOPESA c.Jan 75.
FAP 204	42-24405 0-24405	C47A-60-DL C-47D	10267	MAP 17 Jan 70 ex-24th SOW, USAFSO. Last reported 10 Dec 73, Sold to N58296 18 Oct 84.
FAP-205	(42-108938) BuA17218	(C-47A-25-DK) R4D-5 C-47H C-47L	13228	MAP? After 7 May 72. Although FAP-205 is assumed, no photos of her wearing these marks have surfaced. Noted at COOPESA, San Jose, CR, being overhauled Jan 75. Sold to N89BJ.

The derelict fuselage of a former USAF C-47 found in the Guardia Nacional compound on the east side of Tocumen airport as of 30 December 1968. The hulk had been completely sanitised and was sitting next to an equally obscure derelict North American AT-6D fuselage. *Hagedorn*

CHAPTER EIGHTEEN

Paraguay

ALTHOUGH NOT CONFRONTED with some of the geographic challenges facing other Latin American nations, even at that the nearly landlocked central land mass of Paraguay is actually divided into two main – and totally different – regions.

The Oriente of nuclear Paraguay, east of the Río Paraguay, consists of fertile, undulating country, much of which is still heavily forested. An escarpment, running roughly north–south, nearly bisects this region, the eastern half of which is a heavily forested plateau varying in height from 1,000 to 2,000ft above sea level. The roughly triangular region to the west of the Río Paraguay and north-east of the Pilcomayo River is the infamous Chaco, an almost dead-level plain, rising slightly towards the west. Although relatively fertile in the immediate vicinity of water sources, the Chaco degenerates rapidly into scrub jungle, and even this becomes progressively sparser towards the north-west.

An essential understanding of this often forgotten and resource-poor nation is that, in a word, Paraguayans are a proud people. Her aviators and aviation heritage date back to 1912 and, of course, her stubborn and gallant defence of her barren Chaco wastes in the brutal Chaco War with Bolivia, which finally erupted fully in 1932, is the very stuff of aeronautical legends.

Following the Chaco War, which saw the Paraguayan Aviación en Campaña or, more formally, the Arma Aérea Paraguaya mature very rapidly into a force to be reckoned with, as so often happens,

the brutal sacrifice of the flower of many of her brightest and best resulted in a period of near exhaustion, and until the Second World War and a modest infusion of Lend-Lease aircraft, commensurate with her ability to contribute to the Allied cause, Paraguayan military aviation was a shadow of its Chaco glory.

Indeed, as late as April 1945 when, rather remarkably, a Paraguayan Lend-Lease requisition for a single Beech UC-45F twin was approved on political grounds (effectively becoming Paraguay's second 'Air Force One'), the air arm had operated a grand total of only one other multi-engined aircraft: a venerable Italian Breda Ba-44 biplane, acquired in March 1933 – and which, miraculously, survived as late as October 1947.

But a bit earlier, on 12 July 1944, seeking a means to maintain day-to-day proficiency, provide at least some modest internal air and mail capability, and not least, help justify Lend-Lease requisitions, the Paraguayan Army created the Línea Aérea de Transporte Nacional (LATN) employing a truly cosmopolitan array of aircraft. The US Air Attaché at the time described the service as 'spasmodic', at best, but it was a start. While the accomplishments of the airline during its first few years were, after a fashion, experimental in nature, the experience gained unquestionably brought home to aspiring Paraguayan airmen the fact that the country needed larger and more appropriate aircraft and, concurrently, trained crews to man and maintain them. In essence, the seed had been planted for the eventual acquisition of DC-3s or C-47s for what was, at the time, the Military Aviation and redesignated as the Arma Aérea Paraguaya (AAP), although still very much under the direct control of the Army.

An aircraft with a scrambled provenance, exactly where and when T-27 was acquired remains obscure. Here, her fuselage code is much smaller than it should be, while the code on her vertical fin is larger than standard! On top of this, whoever applied her titles misspelled 'Aéreo' to read simply 'Aero'. The shadow of a roundel can just be seen on the fuselage, suggesting a possible RAF past, and this image was definitely taken in California. Her name, 'Mcal F.S. López' is barely visible on her nose. *Dustin A. Carter*

T-21 again after she had been painted in nearly definitive TAM colours, the former broad, civil cheatline giving way to the distinctive red lightning bolt. After being damaged in a storm, she was withdrawn by November 1976 to use as a paratroop trainer. *Dr Antonio Sapienza*

The second Paraguayan C-47 was T-23, purchased in Burbank, California – probably from the Charlie Babb organisation there, but her actual identity, as described in the table accompanying Chapter 18, is rather obscure. Seen at Asuncion on 28 February 1972 in her seventeenth year of service, she survived to pass to new marks FAP-2003 by February 1980 but made her final flight that May. *Georg von Roitberg*

Nearly into her third year of service in this 5 December 1955 image at Bella Vista, Paraguay's first military DC-3, T-21, still bears vestiges of her former US civil colour scheme. She was delivered as a DC-3A-G202A but incorporated some unusual characteristics, among them an RDF loop atop the extreme forward cabin roof. Her name, 'Silvio Pettirossi', is just visible on her nose. *Dr Antonio Sapienza*

By 15 May 1952, the entire inventory of AAP consisted of a grand total of seventeen aircraft, comprising seven Fairchild PT-19As (the survivors of eighteen or nineteen delivered under Lend-Lease during the war years), three North American AT-6Cs, three nearly new Beech 35 Bonanzas, two Vultee BT-13As and single examples of the Beech UC-45F and AT-11, the latter converted to a transport. At about the same time, steps had finally been set in motion to locate, acquire and enter into service the first DC-3, as it had become clear the country could expect no assistance in acquiring any from US military aid or surplus sources.

This self-reliance was necessary because, following the bitter civil war of 1947, chronic political instability in the semi-isolated country did nothing to moderate US State Department insistence that, until the situation in Paraguay headed towards a government more amenable to US interests in seeing the evolution of more democratic governments in the Latin America, she was not to be considered as a viable recipient for the post-war American Republics Projects largesse. As a direct consequence, only Paraguay and Argentina were denied the usual mix of aircraft witnessed nearly everywhere else in the region. The coup d'etat by the Army in 1954, which installed its Commander in Chief, General Alfredo Stroessner in power, further hardened the State Department line towards Paraguay. With his mandate confirmed by the elections of 1954, 1958, 1963, 1968, 1973 and 1978, Stroessner ruled the country for nearly thirty years. While Stroessner's iron grip in fact provided the country almost thirty years of unprecedented political stability, which actually helped foster economic development, his control did not necessarily require or depend upon a large, combat-capable air force.

As a direct consequence, Paraguay became the very last traditional South American air arm to acquire DC-3s, her very first example having been acquired commercially in the US, a former TWA aircraft, at a cost of $150,000, and delivered in January 1953, remaining the solitary example as late as 30 June 1954. This historic aircraft was assigned serial T-21, following on a long chain of 'T' (for Transporte) aircraft types that had commenced during the Chaco War with T-1, then skipping every other number until T-21 was reached. Shortly thereafter, a USAF Mission to the AAP was arranged, one of its underlying objectives being the creation, finally,

of a professional, well-trained and appropriately equipped air arm tailored to the actual needs of the country. By early 1954, the Mission had set up a nine-month long 'Pre-Mechanics' training programme, the very first of its kind in the AAP, as well as beginner English-language training for both officers and crews. They also facilitated arrangements for seven AAP pilots to be trained in Brazil and one in Peru. One officer, Capitán Herbert Leo Nowak, had just returned from completing three intensive courses at the Air University, Maxwell AFB, AL, including the USAF Squadron Officers Course, Primary Instructors School and Instrument Instructors School, and two more AAP officers were selected to attend the same trio of courses. Nowak, not surprisingly, was then detailed as the A-3 (Operations) Officer for the AAP.

One of the limiting factors governing Paraguay's acquisition of DC-3s and C-47s was the pure and simple fact that, as late as 1954, there was only one paved runway in the entire country, and this was at the International Airport at Asunción. There were about twelve small, privately owned grass fields elsewhere in the country and three other small grass fields belonging to the armed forces scattered around. Although Coronel Abdón Caballero Álvarez was, on paper, the Chief of the AAP it she acquired its first DC-3, his position was largely titular, and a recent graduate of the USAF Command and Staff School, Tte.Cnel Epifanio Ovando, was the defacto leader as Chief of Staff.

LATN figured prominently in all of this, and the officers who had been trained in the various USAF schools had not failed to observe the benefits of a well-established airlift capability. In fact, the US Assistant Air Attaché at the time, LTC Charles V. Greffet, went so far as to say that 'the actual purpose of the AAP in operating this airline is to be able to earn sufficient funds to maintain their one DC-3 and to buy additional aircraft and spares'. That single, hard-working DC-3, T-21, was kept busy almost constantly flying semi-scheduled routes every Tuesday from Asunción to Concepción, thence to the small town of Pedro Juan Caballero and return and, on every Friday, from Asunción to Filadelfia (Chaco) and return.

By 1 January 1955, the in-country flying training programme of the AAP was essentially at a standstill due to age and deterioration of the few trainers still airworthy but, more importantly, to a shortage of fuel – nearly all available fuel going to keeping the revenue-earning DC-3 flying. The USAF Mission had arranged for four AAP cadets to be trained in the US, however, and two had only just returned home. Five more were undergoing DC-3 transition training in Brazil and two others were taking DC-3 transition training with the Fuerza Aérea Argentina at El Palomar. The USAF Mission also provided C-47 training using their own mission aircraft. This left a grand total of only five AAP active duty pilots actually on active duty, in country, to fly the DC-3 routes.

Perhaps to the surprise of all concerned, General Stroessner announced in late 1954 that he had authorised the acquisition of three additional DC-3s and C-47s in the US, one of these due to arrive on 30 January 1955 and the other two following in February. Interestingly, the negotiations for these aircraft were being conducted by none other than Paraguayan aviation pioneer and notable Nicolás Bo with Fleetwings, Inc., while at the same time conducting talks for the acquisition of the AAP's first two Bell 47G-2s and four Beech 35 Bonanzas. In the event, however, these were apparently delayed and did not actually reach Paraguay until June. The crews then being trained in Brazil and Argentina were clearly planned to man these and, almost overnight, DC-3s and C-47s became the most important type in the AAP/TAM[52] inventory (LATN had actually splintered off from TAM but continued to operate separately) and, indeed, its crown jewels. Bought at Burbank, CA, for about $100,000 each, these aircraft are represented on the accompanying table.

By 18 January 1956, the by then restyled TAM was routinely operating all four of its DC-3s and C-47s, one of which was designated as the personal VIP transport for Stroessner, although also apparently pressed into service on route services when needed. Meanwhile, servicing of the small fleet was being carried out catch-as-catch-can in five totally inadequate and ancient hangars at the principal operating field, Campo Grande, where, in the words of the British Air Attaché, Air Commodore Hobson, 'the crudest possible kind of workshop organisation tackles even the most complicated repairs'. Apparently, however, the AAP was finally attracting some much-needed funding as, on 28 February 1956, they sent a telegram to their Ambassador in Washington asking for quotes on acquiring various quantities of either reconditioned North American AT-6Cs or AT-6Ds and 'the availability and cost of six DC-3s'. However, in spite of these overtures, by year's end 1956, the AAP could still only count a total of four DC-3s and C-47s on hand.

By 1957, TAM had acquired a fifth C-47 and, although on paper always available for internal security and military requirements, it was in fact devoted almost entirely to carrying passengers and freight on a commercial basis. TAM had finally managed to qualify twelve DC-3-rated pilots and was making fourteen scheduled flights each week to Encarnación, Mariscal Estigarribia, Concepción, Bella Vista, Pedro Juan Caballero, Pilar, Puerto Pinasco, Puerto Sastre and Puerto Guaraní. They were averaging seventy-one flying hours per month, and each rated pilot was flying an average of sixty-five hours per month. Incredibly, even with a fleet of only five, the airline was turning in a 69 per cent in-commission rate. Its relationship with LATN by this point was, to say the least, curious, as the AAP could hardly afford to operate two competing services. Described by intelligence reports of the time as leading a 'nebulous' existence, it remained ostensibly a civilian organisation, as opposed to TAM, which was entirely military. However, its director, Coronel Epifanio Ovando, who by this time was also the Commander in Chief of the AAP, was aided by his two top executives, both of whom were also serving officers in the AAP. In this connection, it is worth noting that the highly regarded Chief of Staff of the AAP, by then Mayor Herbert Nowak, named earlier, was killed on 21 August 1957 while 'stunting' in one of LATN's Consolidated PBY-5A Catalina's (ZP-CBB), although precisely how one stunts a 'Cat' remains a puzzle. In addition to that aircraft, LATN by then possessed one other PBY-5A (serial T-29, in the midst of early C-47 serials), which had only recently been overhauled to first-class condition in Brazil, the old UC-45F, no fewer than ten Beech 35 Bonanza variants, three assorted Aeroncas, one Piper J3C-65, a Stinson of unknown flavour and three Noorduyn UC-64s.

Another view of T-27, also taken at the same location, showing the position of her starboard lower wing national insignia. At one time, these were worn in only two locations: as shown and on the upper port wing. However, by the 1970s, the roundels were usually in all four wing positions. *Dustin A. Carter*

With her colours once again transformed by the time of this October 1978 view, T-27 now has regulation-size codes on her rear fuselage, but none on the vertical fin, and her christening name has disappeared. She has also been fitted, unusually for a Paraguayan C-47, with dual RDF 'bullets' and wears the insignia of the TAM on her nose. Note also that her cowlings and accessory covers have been painted grey and that the yellow star that should be in the white field of the tail stripes has faded almost entirely due to weathering. *ALPS*

By 1958, the relationship between the AAP, TAM and LATN had become even more confusing. Epifanio Ovando had been promoted to brigadier and was wearing three hats: he was the Commander of the first and *jefe* of both TAM and LATN. Although he had gained some notoriety early in his career as a pilot, he had come to realise, through loyalty to Stroessner and family connections, that – in the words of US Assistant Air Attaché LTC Charles H. Shaw – the 'transport squadron is the real bread-and-butter section of the Paraguayan Air Arm'. DC-3 and C-47 pilot strength had, by then, risen to nineteen, although by 31 August 1959 the service still had only five airworthy aircraft (although the USAF rated all five as 'combat ready'), and it was making money, although in its spare time it was also devoting some time to training the first company of paratroopers for the Army.

Although the DC-3s and C-47s acquired over the years by Paraguay led a more-or-less pacific existence, there were moments. For instance, during the low-intensity actions against Communist insurgents in 1959 and 1960, a number of C-47s were used to transport Army troops to the Alto Parana and Itapua regions, aided by at least one PBY-5A. Although a closely guarded secret from that period, some of the insurgents who were captured alive were, reportedly on the direct orders of Stroessner, dispatched from C-47s over forested areas – and allegedly Stroessner directed that all of them be dealt with in the same manner.

In spite of the rumours and innuendo regarding these actions, Paraguay finally became eligible for MAP offsets in 1962 and, perhaps to no one's surprise, the first two aircraft acquired were C-47s, two being delivered in October. Two aircraft that had been in the inventory since 1955 had been damaged in a violent storm on 3 October, although the AAP shops was going to attempt to rebuild one of them. The USAF Mission C-47D was also damaged and, unable to recover the aircraft so remotely located in Panama, it was donated to the AAP and rebuilt locally, becoming one of four additional MAP Grant Aid aircraft (becoming T-45, T-47, T-49 and T-51) to substantially rejuvenate TAM's fleet by April 1964.

The first MAP-supplied VC-47D, the former USAF 45-1076 (0-50176) became T-37 in March 1964. Reserialed as FAP-2009 in 1980, she was written off on 26 September 1994. *via Dr Gary Kuhn*

Oddly, this C-47A, also a MAP delivery, was received on 1 October 1962 as T-41 – ahead of T-37, strongly suggesting that there may have been two aircraft with the serial T-37. She displays some markings anomalies: her code is not repeated on either the nose or vertical fin and, once again, her engine cowling has been painted light grey. *Air-Britain #72*

By April 1964, the C-47 operating unit was being cited as the 1° Escuadrón de Transporte and the USAF, at the time promoting the merits of the hemisphere-wide Civic Action concept, went so far as to record for posterity that this unit was 'continuing to contribute to the economic development of the country by providing low cost internal air service to isolated areas which are otherwise inaccessible or which require travel time via surface transportation'. The unit was busily engaged in maintaining a regular schedule, which included the following destinations and frequencies:

One of the single largest infusions of aircraft into the Paraguayan inventory occurred in June 1967 when five ex-USAF C-47s were handed over during a huge celebration at Campo Grande, and these became T-53, T-55, T-57, T-59 and T-61. Here, Gen. Adrian Jara, left, takes the salute with Stroessner himself while one of the 'new' C-47s, already in fully marks, displays the US and Paraguayan flags behind. The black panel under the nose is a common MAP recognition feature. *Southern Command News*

Destination	Flights per Week
Concepción	9
Pedro Juan Caballero	4
Encarnación	3
Pilar	2
Bella Vista	2
Rosario	3
San Pedro	3
Itacurubí del Rosario	1
San Juan Neopomuceno	2
Puerto Presidente Stroessner	1
Puerto Pinasco	2
Filadelfia	1
Mariscal Estigarribia	1

In addition, active consideration was being given to providing the AAP with a C-47 specifically kitted out as a flying dispensary, which was to join a Cessna U-17A that had been supplied for the same purpose.

However, this did not come to pass. Of the DC-3s and C-47s being flown on the above services, seven and, not long thereafter, a total of eleven were MAP-supported for spares as well as ground handling and support equipment. The C-47s were averaging some 127 hours each, and this was achieved with only ten fully qualified crews. However, even at this late date, the FAP was still unable to provide in-country training for the C-47 pilot crew members due to heavy workload imposed on those on active duty in keeping up their schedule, the lack of a properly equipped training aircraft, and no purpose-built instrument trainer. The service had dispatched thirteen candidates to the US, and they were undergoing basic flight, instrument and C-47 transition training, with three more following in February 1965. One C-47 that was, at the time, undergoing repair (almost certainly the former USAF Mission aircraft, which was expected to be ready around 3 October 1964), had been identified as a potential training aircraft when the freshly minted crews returned.

The third of the 'new' MAP C-47Ds handed over in 1967, T-57 was formerly C-47B-1-DL 43-16391 (0-16391) but had been withdrawn from service by 29 October 1976 after only a relatively brief nine years of service. *MAP*

A very well-travelled aircraft, TAM T-63 was one of the three aircraft donated to Paraguay by Argentina in May 1969. Formerly USAAF C-47A-20-DK 42-92988 and then CF-DSW in Canada, she had flown with both ZONDA and Aerolineas Argentinas as LV-ABY after conversion to DC-3C configuration, and then with the Fuerza Aérea Argentina as T-08. Seen here awaiting passengers at Asuncion on 28 January 1972, she survived to be reserialed as FAP-2015 but reportedly made her final flight on 19 January 1979 as T-63. *Georg von Roitberg*

Appearing marked identically to all other TAM fleet aircraft of the 1960s and '70s, this is a truly historic aircraft – none other than the former Air France DC-3-294 F-ARQJ, which had been in continuous service in Argentinas a T-145 and T-16 from 1941, the oldest military DC-3 in Latin America. Here, she poses as T-65 after being donated to Paraguay in May 1969, complete with the TAM badge on her nose. Incredibly, she served on to become FAP-2017 and made her last flight on 13 February 1983 in her forty-second year of service! *Dr Antonio Sapienza*

By 30 June 1966, the total AAP C-47 inventory stood at nine aircraft, five of which had been MAP Grant Aid supplied, as noted, one donated outright (the former Mission aircraft) and three that had been acquired commercially. On the Air Order of Battle for the six-month period ending in December 1967, the service was shown with a mix of a total of fourteen DC-3s and C-47s, all of which were active. The report noted curiously that T-25 (which it cited as MSN 2183) and T-49 (cited as 43-49639) had been either written off or stricken from the inventory for some other reason during the same period – although

TAM
Transporte Aéreo Militar

nearly every other source gives the loss of T-25 as some time in 1964! This may have in fact been merely an administrative accounting measure that had finally caught up with reality.

The MAP delivery of five C-47s in 1967, which became T-53, T-55, T-57, T-59 and T-61, was, at the time, one of the single largest influxes of 'new' aircraft into the inventory in the history of the service, and so was attended by a huge celebration. The US Ambassador at the time, Benigno C. Hernandez, formally presented them to Stroessner in person on 10 August at Campo Grande. At the conclusion of the ceremony, all five took off

The 'official' TAM escudo, not known to have been worn on the aircraft other than as a component of the other badge pictured next. *Dr Antonio Sapienza*

Serving as backdrop for pilots of the Paraguayan aerobatics display team, the Escuadrilla Aguila, which performed magnificently with AT-6Ds, this TAM C-47 displays the unit insignia on her nose as of 23 August 1969. The only variation was in having the lower quadrant marked with either 1º or 2º Escuadrilla. *Dr Antonio Sapienza*

A more-or-less standard TAM aircraft, T-69 was a VC-47D (43-49887) delivered on 27 August 1970, and written off as FAP-2016 on 27 August 1980 at Lambaré. She was one of the few TAM C-47s, however, to mount a swept-blade radio antenna. *George G.J. Kamp*

with Paraguayan crews and, joining seven other veterans already in service, made what was at the time one of the largest fly pasts, of twelve aircraft, ever performed in the country, led by Coronel Epifanio Cardozo, commander of TAM at the time.

By September 1968, the Military Assistance Program was supporting only two types in the AAP inventory: C-47s and Cessna U-17As. The C-47s were, by this time, averaging 37.6 hours each per month, although this had increased to 38.7 per aircraft by 31 December with a total of fourteen on strength, all of which were by this time MAP-supported

Argentina donated three very weary DC-3/C-47s to the AAP in June 1969 to temporarily bolster the TAM fleet even further, but these were soon found to be maintenance-intensive and exceptionally high-time aircraft, and the USAF Mission was forced to admit that their acquisition had actually inhibited serviceability, average time per aircraft for the first

quarter following their arrival plummeting to just 23.8. The service had meanwhile formalised its organisational infrastructure and, by June 1973, DC-3s and C-47s were nominally assigned to the either the 1a or 2ª Escuadrilla of the 1º Grupo de Transporte alongside a smattering of other transport types. The C-47 in Paraguayan military service reached its apogee between 1969 and 1975 when no fewer than eighteen and a maximum of twenty-four were in the inventory.

By early August 1987, Paraguayan use of the venerable DC-3 and C-47 was in rapid decline, and a total of seven were noted in various stages of repair at Campo Grande on the 8th of that month, of which six were natural metal or painted white and one had been camouflaged. By 1 April 1992, seventeen airframes were noted derelict.

The last known incident involving a Paraguayan military C-47 occurred on 8 July 1995 when an unidentified aircraft was obliged to make a forced landing due to engine failure.

An exceptionally rare image of two Paraguayan C-47s and a PBY-5A, T-29, 'in the field' during operations against Communist insurgents at Puerto Presidente Stroessner airfield in 1959, as described in the narrative. The C-47 at centre appears to be T-25. *Dr Antonio Sapienza*

Yet another MAP VC-47D, T-77 was the former USAF 43-48700 and was delivered in March 1974. Here, she shares the apron at Asuncion with a PBY-5A, two DC-6Bs and another C-47. *Carlos Fortner via Dr Gary Kuhn*

The 'T-' Serials – 1953–80

FAP Serials	Previous Identity	Built As	MSN	Assignments and Notes
T-21	NC-33680 43-1981 NC-30079 N30079	DC-3-454 C-49J DC-3A-G202A	6264	Purchased in Burbank, CA, in Jan 53. It was christened as 'Silvio Pettirossi'. This aircraft was granted permission to overfly Brazilian territory in 1958, Oct 59 and Nov 59. Noted as late as 23 Nov 76 but had been withdrawn from use due to damage from a storm. The hulk was reportedly being used as a training aid for paratroopers.
T-23	N4667V	C-47B DC-3A	'15378'	Purchased in Burbank, CA, in Jan 55, this aircraft did not arrive in Paraguay until around 25 Apr 55. It is a puzzle, as there are no known DC-3As or C-47Bs with the previous identity N4667V and the MSN is also untraceable as such. Historian John M. Davis found in examining the FAA file for N4667V that this 'MSN' was an 'invented' number cited on a USAF surplus sales document in 1954. N4668V to N4670V, which followed, were also all sold at the same time and all with equally unreliable 'MSNs!' All four aircraft had been sold as '14,000 pounds of aluminum scrap!' It was at some point christened as Gral. Stroessner. T-23 was issued clearances to overfly Brazilian territory in 1958, Jul 59, and Sep 59.She was last reported on 23 Nov 76 before becoming FAP-2003 (q.v.).
T-25	NC-25608 XT-5xx N8338C N1791B	DC-3A-269B	2183	This aircraft was delivered in Jun 55 from Burbank, CA, although her last US registration was not cancelled until 30 Apr 56. This aircraft was also christened as 'Presidente Stroessner'. She was granted permission to overfly Brazilian territory in 1958, Nov 59 and again in 1960. She was reportedly written off on the ground by fire in an accident at Encarnacion in 1964. However, the USAF MAP V-12 report for the period Jul to Dec 67 states that this aircraft was either written off or stricken from the inventory during that six-month period.
T-27	42-100783	C-47A-70-DL	19246	This aircraft was christened as 'Mcal. F.S. López'. A Paraguayan C-47 with this serial was granted authority to overfly Brazilian territory in 1958, again in Aug 59 and as late as 1960, establishing an earliest date for the use of the serial. Although cited as MSN 19252 based on existing Paraguayan records, this aircraft conflicts with an aircraft that last saw service with the Burmese Air Force and as N2271F in Apr 78. It should have been an aircraft acquired by the FAP in Burbank and delivered in Jun 55, in service by Apr 56 and as late as Feb 80. To FAP-2005 (q.v.).
T-35	BuA4702 NC-91028 N91028	R4D-1	4362	In service by 1958, when she was granted authority to overfly Brazilian territory (and again in Apr 59 and 1960) and as late as Feb 80. One source states that she made her last flight as T-35 on 14 Oct 81 but another states she passed to civil marks ZP-CCG with LAP in either 1971 or 14 Oct 82. To FAP-2007 (q.v.). T-35 was used by LAP between 1970 and 1974 with the civil registration ZP-CCG. In 1974 it was returned to TAM. In 1980 was reserialed as FAP 2007.
T-37	45-1076 0-50176	C-47B-50-DK C-47D VC-47D	17079/34346	MAP on 20 Mar 64. Oddly, however, a Paraguay C-47 with serial T-37 was granted authorisation to overfly Brazilian territory in 1960! This may have been an error for T-27, however. Last noted on 12 Feb 80 and reportedly written off on 26 Sep 94 but also reported as having gone to FAP-2009 (q.v.). In 1980 was reserialed as FAP 2009.
T-41	42-100539 0-100539	C-47A-65-DL	19002	MAP on 1 Oct 62. Noted in service on 19 Apr 75. Last known flight as T-41 on 16 Aug 81. To FAP-2004 (q.v.).
T-43	42-23655 VHCHE 0-23655	C-47A-30-DL TC-47A C-47A	9517	MAP on 1 Oct 62. To FAP-2011 (q.v.). This aircraft sojourned to Río de Janeiro's Galeao airport on 11 Jun 1973 and was wearing the badge of the 1º Grupo de Transporte, 2ª Escuadrilla by that time. She was noted in service as of 23 Nov 76 and according to one source made her last flight on 10 Dec 76.
T-45	43-48675 KJ905 43-48675 0-48675	C-47B-5-DK Dakota III C-47D	14491/25936	MAP on 27 Mar 64. To FAP-2006 (q.v.), although exactly when she took up these marks is unclear as she was reported in service with TAM.

In 1980, the FAP decided to commence an entirely new four-digit serialing system for all aircraft in the inventory – and apparently included some aircraft that were, although nominally still intact and on the Order of Battle, rather less than airworthy. FAP-2005 was the former veteran T-27 acquired in the 1950s. She made her final flight on 3 November 1980 and was on the dump by November 1996.
Carlos Fortner via Dr Gary Kuhn

FAP-2010, formerly T-81, a C-47D, reveals something most unusual in a Latin American military C-47: she still has the insulation bunting on the inside of her cargo door. Seen in January 1996, as of 2001, she was the final airworthy Paraguayan C-47. Note that the yellow star on her rudder has all but faded away. *George G.J. Kamp*

T-47	44-76594 KN454 44-76594 0-76594	C-47B-30-DK Dakota IV C-47D	16178/32926	MAP on 24 Mar 64. She was noted in service on 19 Apr 75 and reportedly made her last flight as T-47 on 23 Oct 75. Noted withdrawn from service as such at Campo Grande on 5 Nov 84. To FAP-2013 (q.v.).
T-49	43-49639 0-49639	C-47B-20-DK C-47D	15455/26900	MAP on 17 Mar 64. Crashed at Pedro Juan Caballero on 2 Jun 65 but was not formally stricken from the inventory until sometime between Jul and Dec 67.
T-51	45-1110 45-1110A 0-51110	C-47B-45-DK C-47D C-47B C-47D	17113/34380	This was the former USAF Mission aircraft surveyed following an accident in Paraguay in Feb 64, donated to the FAP and rebuilt locally. Noted still in service as of 23 Nov 76. Reserialed as FAP 2008 in 1980.
T-53	45-946 0-50946	C-47B-45-DK C-47D AC-47D EC-47D C-47D	16949/34208	MAP on 14 Jun 67. She was noted in service on 19 Apr 75. Noted at Campo Grande as such on 5 Nov 84 withdrawn from use. Supposedly to FAP-2018 (q.v.) but remains, as T-53, noted on the dump as of 9 Jul 96. This C-47 made its last flight on 12 Jan 74.
T-55	43-49564 0-49564	C-47B-15-DK C-47D	15380/26825	MAP on 8 Jun 67. Noted in service on 19 Apr 75. Supposedly to FAP-2025 but remains noted on the dump as T-55 by 9 Jul 76. However, this C-47 is also authoritatively reported to have made its last flight on 2 Nov 77!
T-57	43-16391 0-16391	C-47B-1-DL C-47D	20857	MAP on 5 or 6 Jun 67. Noted in service on 19 Apr 75 and at Campo Grande on 12 Feb 80 as such. Supposedly to FAP-2024 but remains noted on the dump as T-57 by Nov 96. She had made her last flight on 29 Oct 76.
T-59	45-1077 0-51077	C-47B-50-DK C-47D AC-47D EC-47A C-47D	17080/34347	MAP 18 Jun 1967. Noted derelict by 23 Nov 76 and on the dump as T-59 9 Jul 96. For some reason, it did not receive a four-digit serial. WFU in 1975.

Formerly T-69, and an August 1970 MAP C-47D acquisition, FAP-2016 rests next to one of the three DC-6Bs acquired in 1975 in this February 1986 view. The DC-6B wears a quite prominent yellow star on her rudder markings, while that on the C-47 is all but indistinguishable. *Carlos Fortner via Dr Gary Kuhn*

This view of C-47D FAP-2023 in February 1986, the former T-85, shows that she was wearing her national roundel on the upper port wing only. She had gone to the dump by July 1996. *Carlos Fortner via Capt. George G. Farinas*

T-61	45-998	C-47B-45-DK	17001/34263	MAP on 12 Jul 67. Noted derelict by 23 Nov 76 as T-61 although reportedly to FAP-2012
	0-5998	C-47D		(q.v.). She actually made her last flight on 6 Dec 73 as T-61.
		VC-47D		
		C-47D		
T-63	42-92988	C-47A-20-DK	12850	Donated to Paraguay by Argentina on 28 May 69. In service as of 23 Nov 76. Last reported
	CF-DSW	DC-3C		Feb 80. She made her last flight, apparently as T-63 on 19 Jan 79 but was in fact remarked
	LV-ABY			as FAP-2015.
	T-08 (FAA)			

One of the last two C-47s acquired by Paraguay, FAP-2032 did not arrive until 14 May 1984, the former Brazilian FAB C-47 2090. A very high time aircraft, she managed to remain active until at least 1999 and, in fact, outlasted one of her replacements, a Lockheed L-188 Electra II, just visible withdrawn from use in the right background. *George G.J. Kamp*

Above: One of only two Paraguayan C-47s to be camouflaged, this is FAP-2030, the second of two donated in this configuration by Chile in December 1981. She did not retain the camouflage long. A C-47A-10-DK, she was the former FACh-969. She made her last flight in 1999. *Dr Antonio Sapienza*

Right: The end of the line for Paraguay's faithful DC-3 and C-47 fleet, part of the boneyard at Campo Grande. Note that the second aircraft canopy framing and nose markings differ from the next aircraft, and that her former TAM unit insignia has been painted over. The nearest, camouflaged, aircraft is FAP-2030. *Dr Antonio Sapienza*

T-65	F-ARQJ FAA T-145 FAA T-16	DC-3-294	2112	A truly historic and long-lived aircraft. Donated to Paraguay by Argentina by 28 May 69. Noted in service at Buenos Aires-Aeroparque, Argentina, by 25 Jul 72 and at Campo Grande on 5 Feb 79. Last noted May 80, to FAP-2017 (q.v.). In 1980, reserialed as FAP 2017. Last flight 13 Feb 83.
T-67	42-92394 FZ633 PP-JAC PP-YPV T-22 (FAA)	C-47A-1-DL Dakota III DC-3C	12190	Donated to Paraguay by Argentina by 28 May 69. Last reported being used as a paratrooper training aid. Last flight in 1975. No four-digit serial was allotted in 1980.
T-69	43-49887 0-49887	C-47B-23-DK C-47D VC-47D VC-47B VC-47D VC-47B VC-47D	15703/27148	MAP on 27 Aug 70. This aircraft had seen continuous service with USAFSO in USAF Mission work from Jan 48. Noted in service on 5 Feb 79. To FAP-2016 (q.v.) in 1980.
T-71	43-48496 0-48496	C-47B-1-DK C-47D	14312/25757	MAP on 9 Nov 70. Another former USAFO aircraft, which had been in Latin America since Jan 63. Noted withdrawn from service as such at Campo Grande on 5 Nov 84. Reportedly reserialed as FAP-2014 (q.v.) in 1980 but her last flight was recorded as on 22 Dec 78.
T-73	44-76442 0-76442	C-47B-25-DK C-47D	16026/32774	MAP on 9 Nov 70. A former USAF 605th Air Commando Squadron, USAFSO aircraft. Noted in service on 26 Feb 75. Administratively reserialed as FAP-2022 (q.v.) in 1980 but not actually worn, as her last flight was on 24 Jun 72.
T-75	43-49349 0-49349	C-47B-15-DK C-47D TC-47D C-47D	15165/26610	MAP on 17 Jan 74. In service on 19 Apr 75. To FAP-2019 (q.v.) in 1980.
T-77	43-48700 0-48700	C-47B-5-DK C-47D VC-47D	14516/25961	MAP on 5 Mar 74. Noted at Campo Grande as such on 12 Feb 80. To FAP-2021 (q.v.) later that year.
T-79	43-48807	C-47B-5-DK C-47D TC-47D VC-47D C-47D	14623/26068	MAP on 6 Mar 74 and still in service on 23 Nov 76. To FAP-2026 (q.v.) in 1980.
T-81	44-76298 0-76298	TC-47B-25-DK TC-47D C-47D	15882/32630	MAP on 11 Mar 74. Noted at Campo Grande on 5 Feb 79. To FAP-2010 (q.v.) in 1980.
T-83	45-1050 0-51050	C-47B-45-DK C-47D	17053/34320	MAP on 24 Mar 74 and noted airworthy on 12 Feb 80. To FAP-2020 (q.v.) in 1980.
T-85	45-1106 0-51106 0-1106	C-47B-50-DK C-47D VC-47D C-47D	17109/34376	MAP on 6 Apr 74. Noted at Campo Grande as such on 5 Feb 79. To FAP-2023 (q.v.) in 1980.

The '2000' Series – 1980 until Retirement of Type

FAP Serial	Previous Identity	Built As	MSN	Assignments and Notes
2003[53]	N4667V T-23	C-47	'15378'	First reported on 12 Feb 80. TAM. Last flight on 27 May 80, noted withdrawn from service at Campo Grande n 27 May 80 and noted on the dump by 9 Jul 96.
2004	42-100539 T-41	C-47A-65-DL	19002	First reported in May 80 and withdrawn from use 16 Aug 81, when she made her final flight. Noted on the dump by 9 Jul 96.
2005	42-100789 T-27	C-47A-70-DL	19252	First reported in May 80. TAM. Last flight on 3 Nov 80. Withdrawn from use at Campo Grande 3 Nov 80 and noted on the dump by Nov 96.
2006	43-48675 KJ905 43-48675 0-48675 T-45	C-47B-5-DK Dakota III C-47D	14491/25936	First reported on 28 Jan 79 with TAM, possibly still as T-45. Last flight on 24 Feb 81. Noted withdrawn from service at Campo Grande by 5 Nov 84 and on the dump by 9 Jul 96.
2007	BuA4702 NC-91028 N91028 ZP-CCC T-35	R4D-1	4362	First reported in Feb 80. Noted withdrawn from use in 1982. On the dump by 9 Jul 96.
2008	45-1110 45-1110A 0-51110 T-51	C-47B-50-DK C-47D	17113/34380	Reserialed as 2008 in 1980. This aircraft suffered an accident at Bahía Negra on 7 Apr 87 and was written off.
2009	45-1076 0-51076 T-37	C-47B-50-DK AC-47D EC-47A C-47D	17079/34346	First reported May 80. Still in service in 1993. Written off in Bahia Negra on 26 Sep 94.
2010	44-76298 0-76288 T-81	TC-47B-25-DK TC-47D C-47D	15882/32630	First reported in May 80. As of Nov 01, she was the last airworthy FAP C-47. Last flight in 2003. Preserved in mint condition at Ñu-Guazú AFB.
2011	42-23655 VHCHE 0-23655 T-43	C-47A-30-DL	9517	This aircraft made her final flight on 10 Dec 76 and was noted stored at Campo Grande by Jul 96 less engines and outer wings.
(2012)	45-998 0-5998 T-61	C-47B-45-DK C-47D VC-47D C-47D	17001/34263	This serial was apparently assigned but not actually taken up, as T-61 was noted as derelict at Campo Grande by 23 Nov 76.
(2013)	44-76594 KN454 0-476594 T-47	C-47B-30-DK Dakota IV C-47D	16178/32926	This aircraft made her final flight on 23 Oct 75 and was last noted at Campo Grande on 5 Nov 84, still marked as T-47. Therefore, it is not clear if marks 2013 were ever actually worn or merely assigned retrospectively. The serial was assigned but probably not actually painted on since this C-47 was WFU as T-47 in 1975.
(2014)	43-48496 0-48496 T-71	C-47B-1-DK C-47D	14312/25757	This serial was apparently issued but not actually taken up, as T-71 was WFU as such and later was noted on the dump at Campo Grande on 9 Jul 96.
2015	42-92988 CF-DSW LV-ABY T-08 (FAA) T-63	C-47A-20-DK DC-3C	12850	Noted withdrawn from use on 19 Jan 79 when she made her final flight, probably as T-63, but remarked as FAP-2015 and stored at Campo Grande by Sep 96 with no engines or wings.
2016	43-49887 0-49887 T-69	C-47B-15-DK C-47D VC-47D VC-47B VC-47D C-47D	15703/27148	First reported on 11 Feb 80, she was written off in an accident at Lambaré 27 Aug 80.
2017	F-ARQJ FAA T-145 FAA T-16 FAP T-65	DC-3-294	2112	Contrary to some reports, this serial was in fact assigned in 1980 and painted on the aircraft. Its last flight was on 13 Feb 83, the end of the road for a truly historic aircraft after more than forty-three years of continuous service.
(2018)	45-946 0-50946 T-53	C-47B-45-DK C-47D AC-47D C-47D EC-47D C-47D	16949/34208	This serial was apparently not taken up, as T-53 was noted on the dump at Campo Grande 9 Jul 96.

2019	43-49349	C-47B-15-DK	15165/26610	First reported in May 80 but written off in an accident on 1 May 84 near Concepción.
	0-49349	C-47D		
	T-75	TC-47D		
		C-47D		
2020	45-1050	C-47B-45-DK	17053/34320	First reported in Feb 80, last flight was on 30 Dec 83 and on the dump at Campo Grande by 9 Jul 96. Operated by TAM.
	0-51050	C-47D		
	T-83			
2021	43-48700	C-47B-5-DK	14516/25961	First reported in Feb 80 and as late as 1982 in service, but withdrawn from service that same year. Noted on the dump at Campo Grande by 9 Jul 96.
	0-48700	C-47D		
	T-77	VC-47D		
(2022)	44-76442	C-47B-25-DK	16026/32774	This serial was assigned but apparently not taken up, as T-73 was noted on the dump at Campo Grande as such on 9 Jul 96.
	0-76442	C-47D		
	T-73			
2023	45-1106	C-47B-50-DK	17109/34376	First reported in Feb 80 and made her final flight on 6 Oct 83. Noted on the dump at Campo Grande by 9 Jul 96.
	0-51106	C-47D		
	0-1106	VC-47D		
	T-85	C-47D		
(2024)	43-16391	C-47B-1-DL	20857	This serial was assigned but not taken up, as T-57 was noted on the dump at Campo Grande marked as such by Nov 96.
	0-16391	C-47D		
	T-57			
(2025)	43-49564	C-47B-15-DK	15380/26825	Reportedly noted on the dump at Campo Grande by 9 Jul 76 still wearing T-55, but also reported to have made her final flight as such on 2 Nov 77!
	0-49564	C-47D		
	T-55			
2026[54]	43-48807	C-47B-5-DK	14623/26068	Withdrawn from service in 1982.
	0-48807	C-47D		
	T-79	VC-47D		
		C-47D		
2028	44-77083	C-47B-35-DK	16667/33415	Donated to Paraguay by Chile on 10 Dec 81 and arrived in a camouflage colour scheme devised in Chile. She was written off in an accident in Puerto La Victoria (Chaco) on 24 Nov 94. She was dismantled and brought to Ñu-Guazú Base to be used as a gate guardian since 1999, and is still there. Noted missing her vertical fin and wings at Campo Grande by 4 Nov 96.
	0-77083	Dakota IV		
	RNethAF X-8			
	RNethAF ZU-8			
	0-77083			
	FACH 964.			
2030[55]	42-92725	C-47A-10-DK	12557	Donated to Paraguay by Chile on 10 Dec 81 and arrived in a camouflage colour scheme devised in Chile but was repainted after a few months of operation as such. Last flight in 1999. This aircraft was camouflaged at some point.
	FACH 969.			
2032[56]	43-49837	C-47B-20-DK	15653/27098	Delivered on 14 May 84 and noted in service on 4 Nov 96. WFU in 1999 and noted derelict by Oct 03.
	KN230	DC-3C-S1C3G		
	PakAF C-402			
	N4724V			
	YV-C-ARC			
	PP-ASN			
	PT-AYC			
	PP-ENB			
	FAB-2090			
2034	43-49661	C-47B-20-DK	15477/26922	Delivered on 14 May 84. This aircraft was written off in an accident in Lagerenza (Chaco) on 21 Nov 87.
	FAB-09			
	FAB-2018			

The Paraguayan Navy

Although Paraguay is usually thought of as being totally landlocked, it is, in actuality, bisected by a major river from which it in fact derives its very name – and most of its frontiers are also delineated by navigable rivers. Perhaps to some readers' surprise, therefore, the country has maintained a Navy since its independence.

The Navy had, in fact, established a small air arm as early as 1929 and, when full-scale hostilities broke out with Bolivia over the Chaco in July 1932, the tiny Aviación Naval concentrated its little-known but significant contributions in the region of the Alto Paraguay. The inevitable post-war decline was moderated by small numbers of aircraft in the 1930s and even the Second World War under Lend-Lease, but it was not until the late '40s and early '50s that the service became slightly more rounded, acquiring multi-engine equipment in the form of Grumman JRFs and a number of fairly capable land-based monoplanes, including two Vultee BT-13s, a couple of North American AT-6A Standard aircraft and even a few Republic RC-3 Seabees.

Then, in November 1979, the Argentine Navy donated their former C-47A-25-DK, 5-T-26/psn 0278 (MSN 13469) to the Paraguayan Navy, and it was noted bearing Armada Nacional titles by May 1980. It was briefly used by the Servicio Aero Naval (SAN) for one year, being withdrawn from use sometime in 1981. Apparently seldom flown, she was noted derelict alongside a large number of former FAP DC-3s and C-47s in 1991. Issued serial T-26, she has often been reported as an FAP aircraft in error as a direct result.

Above: The single largest aircraft ever acquired by the small Paraguayan Naval air arm, here the Argentine Navy crew and Paraguayan reception committee pose by C-47A-25-DK MSN 13469, the former Argentine 5-T-26, PSN 0278, when she was donated to Paraguay in November 1979. *Dr Antonio Sapienza*

Left: The official crest of the Grupo Aéreo Transporte Especial (G.A.T.E.), which, while very grand, is not known to have ever adorned any of the service's C-47s or DC-3s. *Dr Antonio Sapienza*

Below left: Still wearing most of her former Argentine Navy markings, 5-T-26/26 awaits her final identity in late 1979. *Dr Antonio Sapienza*

Below: An exceptionally rare image, the solitary Paraguayan Navy C-47, T-26, after being painted briefly in its markings. As a one-of-a-kind aircraft, she presented the small Navy maintenance staff with enormous logistics challenges, and the fact she is devoid of her engines in this image is probably symptomatic. She was in service for barely a year. *Dr Antonio Sapienza*

CHAPTER NINETEEN

Peru

P ERU HAS ENJOYED an extraordinary relationship with the benefits of aviation since the very earliest epoch and can justifiably lay claim to having employed aircraft in nearly every conceivable capacity to the benefit of her national aspirations as one of the great Latin American powers.

The third-largest nation in South America, Peru lies entirely within the tropics and, while her geographical challenges may not be as daunting as some of her neighbours, more than half of her population resides in the Sierra, or central highlands, the lower western approaches to the mighty Andes. However, besides the coastal desert, the largest of the three primary zones of the country is known as the *selva*, which takes up some 63 per cent of the total land area of Peru, but which contains only roughly 8 per cent of the population. This region, covered for the most part by impenetrable tropical jungle while being intersected by many rivers, to this day remains only partially explored and is often viewed as having enormous economic potential.

Peru was one of the first Latin American nations to recognise the inherent value of aviation in exploiting its hinterland, and as a direct consequence was one of the first to acquire aircraft specifically intended, from the outset, to conduct transportation, exploration, communications and cargo flights. As early as 1927, six Keystone K-55 two-place biplanes and two K-55As were bought new for use by what was known at the time as the Navy's Servicio Aéreo a la Montaña, some with floats and others with conventional landing gear,

The earliest known image of a Peruvian military C-47, serial 424 was MSN 9220, acquired surplus via the RFC at Bush Field, Augusta, Georgia, in July 1946. Seen here in front of the Lodwick Aircraft Industries hangar at Lakeland, Florida, wearing most unusual Peru Transportes Aéreos Militares titles, she was almost certainly overhauled by Lodwick after acquisition and before flying home. *David W. Ostrowski*

for pioneering work on the San Ramon–Masisca–Iquitos line. These were joined, before the Second World War, by Boeing Model 40Bs and other between-the-wars, single-engine transports.

By the Second World War, the separate Navy and Army air services had been merged into the Cuerpo Aeronáutico del Perú (CAP) and, with the late 1930s' acquisition of a number of Italian Caproni Ca-135 and Ca-310 twin engine bombers and attack aircraft, as well as Ca-111 dedicated transports, the service had gained more multi-engine aircraft experience than almost any air arm in Latin America, being nearly on a par with Argentina.

During the Second World War, Peru benefited substantially from Lend-Lease, and was one of only a few nations to receive twin-engine aircraft. The Munitions Assignment Board (Air) approved Peru to acquire a Beech C-45 on a 'cash basis' in September 1944 – an exception to the normal requisition process – but also approved Peru to receive six Cessna AT-17s and a single UC-78B between October 1944 and January 1945. Peru also submitted a requisition on 4 May 1945, for four brand-new Douglas C-47Bs, and the MAB (Air) actually issued a Case Number for this action (PU-664). However, as the war was nearing its climax, the Foreign Economic Administration (FEA) interceded and requested that the action be withdrawn. This may have been because rumours were already circulating in Washington at the time about a Lend-Lease follow-up programme (which, in fact, became 'Hap' Arnold's pet project for Latin America, the ARP) and the FEA reasoned that Peru could probably negotiate a better deal than 'as new' costs that Lend-Lease would incur.

Believed to have been the first of the second series of Peruvian C-47 serials, 301 (47-301) was formerly serial 483, an ARP-supplied aircraft that joined the inventory in 1947. Seen on the apron at Limatambo with an FAP Grumman SH-16B Albatross and a Douglas B-26B in the background, this dates the image as being after November 1963. Note that the serial on the fuselage has clearly been painted over a previous serial and that the national insignia is worn on the upper port wing only, the individual serial number being on the upper starboard wing. *via Amaru Tincopa*

With her serial, 307 (53-307), barely visible on the after fuselage – but repeated under the port wing, this former VC-47B had actually been the USAF Attaché's aircraft to Chile and had suffered an accident at Talara, Peru, on 25/26 May 1953. She was essentially abandoned in place but rebuilt locally after being nominally gifted to Peru under the provisions of Grant Aid, probably by the Panagra shops. By the time of this 1962 view was wearing a most unusual colour scheme, being assigned at the time to the Grupo Aéreo 31. *FAP via Amaru Tincopa*

Described as a DC-3-R2000, FAP-315 (60-315) was a former Panagra aircraft and FAP-697. She wears what had become the standard FAP DC-3 and C-47 colour scheme by 1972. *via Amaru Tincopa*

It thus transpired that Peru was the ultimate recipient of at least six C-47s under two known ARP projects, No. 94492-S (covering, unusually, three aircraft in exact serial sequence, 45-1003, 45-1004 and 45-1005) and 94493-S, each apparently covering three aircraft between March 1947 and February 1948. However, initially, the Interim Program allocation for Peru, as of 14 March 1946, had cited five C-47s on Project 72015[57] as of 12 September 1947, while another document cited a total of eight. Adding to the confusion, an ARP document dated 1 December 1948 listed Peru as only getting six! As elsewhere, however, the first three were actually in country with the USAAF ARP training Cadre as early as 17 January 1946, the first of a substantial number of DC-3s and C-47s that were to follow from a variety of sources.

Apparently deciding that, while the ARP arrangements were satisfactory as far as they went, like other Latin American air arms, the Peruvians wasted little time in seizing upon the often-foggy world of post-war surplus dealers. On 12 November 1946, before the first three ARP C-47s had even been formally handed over (that had not yet occurred by 24 October) the Peruvian Embassy in Washington had requested US State Department clearances to ferry two surplus Beech UC-43, three ex-Navy GB-2s and a single C-47 from the US to Peru. The identity of this aircraft can only be speculated. This may, in fact, have been the aircraft identified curiously as a 'DC-47' which had actually arrived in Lima on 19 August 1946[58] and identified as being destined for the relatively newly created Transportes Aéreos Militares (TAM).[59] However, it may also have been FAP-424, which was apparently acquired from the surplus park at Bush Field, Augusta, Georgia around 25 November, and then for some reason flown on to Bolling Field, DC, departing from there to Lima on or about 30 November 1946.

On 4 January 1947, the Peruvian Government acquired the remains of Panagra DC-2-118A NC-14270 (Fleet Number P-29, MSN 1303) and, still later, on 7 July, the remains of NC-13729, a DC-2-112 (MSN 1255, Fleet Number P-35) for use at a central trade school. Although strictly speaking not CAP assets, the service certainly benefited from their tuition as training aids through the modest numbers of maintenance personnel who were detailed there for instruction.

Between 1 January 1949 and the end of July 1950, the by now renamed Fuerza Aérea del Perú (FAP, officially renamed as such 18 July 1950) maintained a constant total of eight C-47s (three C-47As and five C-47Bs), although known serials suggest that losses and replacements must have occurred during the same interval, as more than eight aircraft have been identified. One was known lost on 24 February 1949 at Cuzco when a main tyre blew out on take-off on a flight bound for Lima and, of twenty-two on board, only four survived. The principal operating unit during this period was the 41 Escuadrón de Transportes, which maintained its headquarters at Limatambo but had a semi-permanent detachment at Iquitos that, besides the stalwart C-47s, possessed five biplane de Havilland D.H.89 Rapides (at least two of which were operated on twin floats, the survivors of eight acquired in 1946), four indigenous Faucett F-19s (two on floats), a mix of five Consolidated PBY-5As and OA-10s, and a single Beech UC-43. By the end of 16 June 1950, the unit had a total of nine C-47s but, of these, six were non-operable for one reason or another (one C-47A and five C-47Bs), still assigned to the 41 Escuadrón, by then a subordinate to the 2° Región Aérea and, for some reason, reflected in USAF intelligence documents as the '41st Military Training Squadron', now with a mix of the C-47s, only two OA-10s and single examples of the Beech AT-11 and AT-7. The D.H.89s had apparently been temporarily detached to other duties.

FAP-315 and 307 once again but wearing the cheatline and scheme in use around 1960–63 somewhere in the hinterland. Note the 'crank' in the cheatlines just aft of the cargo and entry doors. *via Amaru Tincopa*

Peruvian C-47s operated under primitive field conditions throughout the country, and FAP-356 or 366 seen here on 16 June 1970 is on a grass field somewhere high in the foothills of the mighty Andes. *via Amaru Tincopa*

FAP-355 (62-355) was a July 1962 MAP delivery and poses handsomely wearing yet another variation on the cheatline arrangement at Limatambo in 1965. Note the complete absence of any markings under the starboard wing, although the location of the former USAF insignia has obviously been scrubbed off. *Gordon S. Williams*

FAP-355 again but as she appeared in 1969, with a much modified cheatline, at Limatambo. *MAP1983-96 #12*

TAM lost an unidentified C-47 on 18 January 1951.[60] The aircraft had departed Limatambo at 1600hrs that date en route to Arequipa and crashed near a small town named Chala, in Parinacochas Province, killing all fifteen on board. The pilot was Tte Carlos Peña Vásquez, with co-pilot Alférez Victorio Mosto. Among the passengers was another serving FAP officer, Capt. Alfredo Mercado. Evidence at the crash site suggested that Vásquez had attempted a forced landing. At the time, this was the most tragic accident in FAP history.

That same year, the 41 Escuadrón remained the principal operating unit, and by then possessed a mix of four C-47As and four C-47Bs, with surprisingly a total of six D.H.89s, three Faucett F-19s, two OA-10s and single examples of the AT-7, AT-11 and a brand-new de Havilland Canada DHC-2 Beaver. Things remained essentially the same as of 1 July 1952, although by then there were four C-47As and five C-47Bs.

FAP C-47 strength had increased slightly to a total of nine (four C-47As and five C-47Bs) by 30 June 1954, all still assigned to the 41 Escuadrón de Transportes with a mix of other types, but by December one of the C-47Bs had been lost. However, the FAP purchased two veteran DC-3As (N19913 and N30008) from Panagra on 8 November 1954, providing a welcome infusion to the unit.

Apparently, a replacement C-47B had been located by 31 December 1956, as total strength by that time showed three C-47As and six C-47Bs and this remained unchanged through June 1957, although a British-produced Air Order of Battle for 31 December 1955 had briefly shown

the FAP with a total of ten C-47s. By 1 June 1958, however, one C-47 had been lost, probably the TAM/Grupo de Transporte No. 41 aircraft written off on 4 March 1957 at Yurimaguas, Yureto, dropping the aggregate total to eight once again.

Finally, the Military Assistance Program (MAP) started to augment the Peruvian C-47 inventory starting in 1962 and, with the advice of a very active USAF Mission, the rather static FAP C-47 strength, which had hovered around eight or nine aircraft from 1946 clear through the 1950s, started to climb exponentially, as reflected in the accompanying tables.

On 4 February 1960, the FAP's Transportes Aéreos Militares (TAM), was split into two distinctly separate operations: SATCO (Servicio Aéreo de Transportes Comerciales) and TANS (Transportes Aéreos Nacional de la Selva), with the latter operating generally smaller aircraft types as an essentially feeder service, although it had been in existence since 1951.

When SATCO operations commenced in 1960, it had three Curtiss C-46s and seven assorted DC-3s and C-47s[61] (although this had grown to twelve C-47s and seven C-46s by April 1964, and was not MAP-supported) and served Lima and Iquitos and a host of smaller cities on the lower eastern slopes of the Andes. Coastal routes, both north and south from Lima, were also operated. In May 1973, SATCO transformed into AeroPeru and the emphasis shifted to international services, replacing Aerolíneas Peruanas, which had gone bankrupt in 1971. SATCO is known to have operated at least thirteen DC-3s and C-47s.

This aircraft was, for some reason, described as a C-47E when MAP delivered in June 1962 to become FAP-356 (62-356). She was lost on 18 March 1983 in poor weather in Arequipa Province with all five crew members. *via Amaru Tincopa*

No fewer than five FAP C-47s share a remote grass strip in the foothills of the Andes near Ancash on 16 June 1970 alongside an uncamouflaged DHC-5 Buffalo. The second and third aircraft in the middle of the image are FAP-364 (64-364) and FAP-356 (62-356). *via Amaru Tincopa*

Another MAP-supplied aircraft, FAP-357 (62-357) was built as a C-47A-30-DL. She is unusual in having Day-Glo on her wingtip undersides but exhibits serious weathering on her white upper decking. She had become OB-R-1149 with TANS by 29 May 1979. *via Amaru Tincopa*

By May 1963, the FAP had reorganised its transport element once again, and the majority of the C-47s on strength, including most of the MAP aircraft expected during 1963 and early 1964, were assigned to Grupo de Transporte 42 operating as SATCO.

By December 1963, the FAP DC-3 and C-47 inventory had grown to eighteen, all of which were active, with two 'new' aircraft having been acquired via MAP on 28 May. Four years later, at the end of December 1967, this had declined, due to attrition, to sixteen, of which fifteen were active.

By 30 September 1964, with the infusion of MAP-supplied C-47s that was unparalleled anywhere else in Latin America, the FAP C-47 was reinvigorated and, together with the relatively new Grumman HU-16Bs, were the most heavily utilised aircraft in the service, mainly on Civic Action duties, reaching an average of 42.30 hours per aircraft per month, with all sixteen aircraft receiving MAP Grant Aid support and being operated by the Escuadrón de Transporte No. 841 along with one commercially acquired DC-3, a DC-4 and three C-46s. This did not, however, include DC-3s and C-47s that the FAP had acquired commercially. These, significantly, included all the aircraft being operated by SATCO which, by that date, included six C-47s, five DC-3s, two DC-4s and seven C-46s. These intensive Civic Action scheduled flights materially aided social and economic growth in the hinterland and, of these, the three routes connecting destinations in the Amazon Basin were the most significant, these all having commenced in July 1964. These comprised:

- Connections between Iquitos and Yurimaguas, Tarapoto, Saposoa, Bellavista, Juanjuí, Uchiza and Tingo María on a weekly basis
- Another weekly service connecting Iquitos with Pucallpa, Puerto Inca, Puerto Victoria, Puerto Bermúdez and San Ramón
- A bi-weekly service operated from Iquitos to Pucallpa, Manú and Puerto Maldonado

A MAP-supplied 'flying dispensary' (*avión dispensario*), the former 43-15283 (which became FAP 64-367), an element of Peru's commitment to the hemisphere-wide Civic Action Programme initiative, also entered service on 14 July 1964, and was, for a time, based out of Iquitos, serving exceptionally isolated communities in the deep interior, including the Colonia Penal del Sepa, Saposoa, Pucacaca, Picota, Bellavista, Juanjuí, Uchiza, Tocache, Puerto Inca and Puerto Bermúdez with both medical and dental services. By 31 March 1965, with the addition of the medically equipped C-47, the inventory had returned to a total of sixteen aircraft, of which thirteen were operative and these flew a very respectable total of 1,722 flight hours during the preceding quarter, with MAP providing spares support for all sixteen aircraft. Of these, twelve were assigned to the Escuadrón de Transporte No. 841 based at Lima, an element of Grupo Aéreo Mixto No. 8 while the other four were assigned to the Escuadrón de Transporte No. 421 at Iquitos. This organisation remained unchanged by 30 June, although by then only eleven of the sixteen DC-3s and C-47s on strength were airworthy, although they did fly a total of 1,432:07 hours during the three-month period.

Shown taxiing at Limatambo, FAP-359 (63-359) was another MAP acquisition, arriving on 16 May 1963. Oddly, her fate is unknown. *Jorge Chavez*

The three-digit serial of FAP-367 is just barely visible on the upper starboard wing of this January 1964 MAP-supplied C-47A-80-DL. This was the wide-ranging medical dispensary aircraft noted in the text, and despite her special equipment she wore no special markings to denote her status. *Harold G. Martin*

Yet another MAP delivery, FAP-368 (64-368) arrived on 12 February 1964. Obviously very weathered, she became OB-R-1151 with TANS on 29 May 1979. *Amaru Tincopa*

Although improvements and in-service modifications to C-47s supplied under MAP to Latin American operators following delivery are generally ignored in most discussions, it is significant to understand that, for nations that enjoyed having their MAP-supplied C-47s supported by a local USAF Mission, occasional retrofits and improvements dictated by Change Orders and TOs were often implemented when funding allowed. For example, by October 1968, all of the surviving MAP-supplied C-47s in the FAP had received Group A and B kits for the Class V modification for their AN/ARC-44 radios dictated by RCN Y6YY16. It is interesting to note that the USAF Mission regarded all fifteen of the surviving aircraft as being 'to C-47B/D standard' by this time, and the fleet had flown some 1,581 hours, combined, during the previous quarter. On the other hand, nearly all of them also shared the same inherited problems as well. Most of the MAP-supplied C-47s, for instance, had the AIC-2 interphone system installed. A few, however, had the improved AIC-3. The

problem was that none of them had the MX-1646 headset-microphone adapter installed, which would have enabled the use of the H-101 headset-microphone. The C-47s that had the AIC-3, in an actual retrogression, had to have them replaced by the earlier AIC-2 of the AIC-10 interphone system in order to facilitate the installation and use of the brand-new AN/ARC-44s. The FAP's ingenious depot engineers, however, figured out how to make the necessary connections, thus making these aircraft virtually unique, from a communications point of view, in the world.

The US Military Assistance Plan for Peru for the Fiscal years 1971–75 reflected the commitment to maintain FAP C-47 strength at an average of fifteen aircraft, and this was largely achieved.

One of the last major redeployments of FAP C-47s came about on 20 May 1979 when five, all former SATCO aircraft, and possibly the last of the airworthy examples, were formally transferred to TANS as OB-R-1147 to OB-R-1151. These had been the former OB-R-539, FAP64-366, FAP62-357, FAP64-365 and FAP64-368.

When the last FAP C-47 flew, reportedly in December 1991, it was being replaced by Ukrainian-built Antonov An-26 and An-32 aircraft.

A trick of exposure, this telephoto view of FAP-370 (64-370) appears to have a deep green cheatline, when in fact is was deep blue, which was standard as of her 4 March 1964 MAP delivery. This aircraft was lost four years later on 29 October 1968 while being operated by Grupo Aéreo Mixto 8 near the San Ramón airfield, Chachamayo. She is unusual, however, in wearing narrower than normal rudder stripes. *Air-Britain #72*

Here, C-47A-90-DL FAP-371 (64-371) sits on the apron at Limatambo next to LANSA YS-11A OB-R-895 in 1969. Her serial, repeated on her upper starboard wing, is in larger numerals than usual. *MAP 1984-108 #158*

Contrast this view of FAP-373 (64-373) with that of the previous image of FAP-371. The numerals used were of different size and character, and the red/white/red rudder striping was entirely different. *George G.J. Kamp*

Right: This map shows many of the remote airfields regularly utilised by the FAP C-47 fleet, including the 'hospital' ship, FAP-367 as of 1964, as Peru's contribution to the region-wide Civic Action Program. *USAF*

Below: The earliest-known image of one of the SATCO aircraft, in this case DC-3A-279B OB-R-536, which had previously been FAP-305 (49-305) and OB-XAC-536. *Javier Goto W.*

The First CAP Serials

CAP Serial	Previous Identity	Built As	MSN	Assignments and Notes
401	–	–	–	Although this serial has been reported by a number of sources, no candidates for her have been located.
403	–	–	–	ARP. Delivered as early as 27 Feb 47. An aircraft with this serial was granted authority to fly from Lima via the Panama Canal Zone to Miami on 3 Mar 47. Crashed on 16 Nov 54 on a TAM flight from Pucallpa to Lima at Mount Yerupajá under the command of Mayor Gustavo Yábar Marmanillo and co-pilot Tte Sergio Pinillos, with three other crew and one passenger. The remains were located on 20 Nov.
404	43-15591	C-47A-85-DL	20057	ARP allocated on 25 Sep 47 and departed Kelly Field, TX, that date with formal handover on 18 Feb 48. However, an aircraft with this serial was granted authority to fly from Bush Field, Augusta, Georgia, via Miami to the Panama Canal Zone on 25 Nov 46! If this MSN is correct, became FAP-486 (q.v.).
424	42-23358	C-47A-5-DL	9220	Acquired via RFC at Bush Field, Augusta, Georgia, on or about 18 Jul 46. An aircraft with this serial was granted authority to fly to Peru from Bolling Field, DC, on 30 Nov 46. This aircraft was in service with TAM by 26 Apr 48 when she was used as a Presidential aircraft, conveying him to Pisco incident to the opening of a new airfield there. To FAP 47-319 (q.v.) by 1960.
482	45-1005	C-47B-45-DK	17008/34271	ARP Project 94492-S on 20 Jan 46 but did not depart Kelly Field, TX, en route on actual delivery until 19 Mar 46. Apparently officially handed over on 27 Mar 47. An aircraft with this serial was granted authority to fly to Bolling Field, Washington, DC, on 3 Jul 47.
483	45-1004	C-47B-45-DK	17007/34270	ARP Project 94492-S on 17 Jan 46 and departed Kelly Field, TX, en route to Peru on 19 Mar 46. Apparently officially handed over on 27 Mar 47. Last reported in Jun 60. To FAP 47-301 (q.v.) by 1960 but also reported to SATCO 13 Jun 60 as OB-XAF-539, OB-R-539.
484 (1)	45-1003	C-47B-45-DK	17006/34269	ARP Project 94492-S on 19 Jan 46 and officially handed over 22 or 27 Mar 47. Written off on 24 Feb 49 en route from Cuzco to Lima under the command of Tte Arturo Schutt Basagoitia. Fatal to twenty-two of those on board although, miraculously, the co-pilot, flight engineer and two passengers survived.
FAP 484 (2)	–	–	–	While operating with TAM, a C-47 with this serial disappeared on the morning of 8 Jan 58 while en route across the Andes from Rioja to Cajamarca with four crew and six passengers aboard under the command of Capt. Fernando Castrat Montes with co-pilot Tte Oscar Hurtado Vargas Machuca.
485 (1)	42-24293	C-47A-50-DL	10155	ARP initially allotted on 19 Sep 47 but not officially handed over until 16 Feb 48 although one source cited 26 Mar 48 to TAM. An aircraft with this serial was ferried from Kelly Field, TX, to Lima sometime around 20 Jan 48, however and an alternate handover date of 26 Mar 48 is also cited by some sources. With TAM by 26 Mar 48. An aircraft with this serial was granted authority to fly via the Panama Canal Zone to Miami, FL on 19 Sep 49. She must have been lost prior to 1955 when this serial was allocated to the second aircraft to wear it, see below.
FAP 485 (2)	42-68791 NC-50617 NC-19913	C-53D-DO DC-3A-S1C3G	11718	Acquired from Panagra, the acquisition reported in US State Department correspondence as early as 23 Sep 54 but as the US registration was not cancelled until 11 Nov 54, the actual date of acquisition has been suggested as 8 Nov 54. To FAP 55-302 (q.v.) in 1960, then OB-XAA-534, OB-R-534 with SATCO from 13 Jun 60.
486	43-15591 FAP-404	C-47A-85-DL	20057	This aircraft was ferried from Kelly Field, TX, to Lima (in company with 485 (1) and 487) sometime around 20 Jan 48 although some sources give the actual handover date as either 18 Feb 48 or 26 Mar 48. Was serving with TAM by 26 Mar 48. An aircraft cited as serial 786 (but believed an error for serial 486) was granted authority to transit the Panama Canal Zone en route to Brownsville, Texas, en route to Miami, FL. To FAP 48-303 (q.v.) by 1960.
487 (1)	42-100711	C-47A-70-DK	19174	ARP allocated on 22 Sep 47 and delivered from Kelly Field, TX, sometime around 20 Jan 48 in company with 485 and 486. Apparently not officially handed over until 18 Feb 48, however.
FAP 487 (2)	NC-30008 N30008	DC-3A-414	4177	Acquired from Panagra 8 Nov 54 but this acquisition was actually reported in US State Department correspondence as early as 23 Sep 54. To FAP 55-304 (q.v.) by 1960.
488	NC-28334 N28334	DC-3A-279B	4800	Acquired from Panagra on 9 Jun 49 for $30,000 and assigned to TAM. An aircraft with this serial was granted authority to transit US territory from Kelly Field, TX, including the Panama Canal Zone, en route to Lima on 29 Jan 53. To FAP 49-305 (q.v.) by 1960.
489 (1)	–	–	–	A C-47 with this serial was serving with TAM by 26 Mar 48 and was apparently delivered at the same time as 485 (1) and 486.
489 (2)	NC-25652 N25652	DC-3A-279A	2192	Acquired from Panagra in 1950, US registration cancelled 8 Sep 50. To FAP 50-306 (q.v.) by 1960.

As can be seen, a number of the early serials worn by CAP C-47s were subsequently reissued to other aircraft acquired after the service had actually transitioned into the FAP in 1950.

Following these early '400' series issues, however, the FAP adopted a very confusing succession of C-47 serialing conventions that, by the 1960s, included a form of 'Fiscal Year' prefix system similar to that used by the USAAF, some of these being in fact retroactively assigned to aircraft that had actually been acquired much earlier. However, it should be noted that these prefixes were not actually painted on to the aircraft, which carried only the three-digit serial proper in large numerals, the prefixes apparently being used for administrative purposes only. For ease of reference, we have elected to list these arbitrarily by their 'root' three-digit serial, in numeric order as follows.

FAP C-47 Serial Systems and SATCO Quasi-Civil Marks After 1950

FAP Serial and Quasi-Civil *SATCO* Marks	Previous Identity	Built As	MSN	Assignments and Notes
'13'	–	DC-3	–	An aircraft with this very unusual code was reportedly in use as a Presidential aircraft *c*.16 Aug 63 but has not been otherwise verified.
47-301 OB-XAF-539 OB-R-539 OB-R-1147 OB-1147	45-1004 CAP 483	C-47B-45-DK	17007/34270	Assumed this serial by Jun 60. Noted at Lima as 301 on 31 Jan 77. To SATCO as OB-XAF-539 on 13 Jun 60 and then TANS in 1973. Withdrawn from service in 1977 but apparently resurrected for TANS as OB-R-1147 and registered as such 20 May 79, later changed to simply OB-1147.
55-302 OB-XAA-534 OB-R-534	42-68791 NC-50617 NC-19913 FAP 485 (2)	C-53D-DO DC-3A-S1C3G	11718	Assumed this serial by Jun 60. To SATCO.
48-303 OB-XAG-540 OB-R-540	43-15591 *CAP-404* CAP 486	C-47A-85-DL	20057	Assumed this serial by Jun 60. To SATCO as OB-XAG-540 on 13 Jun 60. Reported lost on a flight from Callao 9 Jun 67.
55-304 OB-XAB-535 OB-R-535	NC-30008 N30008 FAP 487 (2)	DC-3A-414	4177	Assumed this serial by Jun 60. To SATCO as OB-XAB-535 on 13 Jun 60. Withdrawn from use by 1974.
49-305 OB-XAC-536 OB-R-536	NC-28334 N28334 CAP 488	DC-3A-279B	4800	Assumed this serial by 13 Jun 60. To SATCO as OB-XAC-536 on 13 Jun 60.
50-306 OB-XAD-537 OB-R-537	NC-25652 N25652 FAP 489 (2)	DC-3A-279A	2192	Assumed this serial by 13 Jun 60. To SATCO as OB-XAD-537 on 13 Jun 60. Reported derelict at Lima by 12 Sep 71 as OB-R-537.
53-307 OB-XAU-654 OB-R-654	43-48725	C-47B-5-DK C-47D VC-47D VC-47B	14541/25986	This aircraft had originally been assigned to US Air Attaché in Chile in Sep 45 and, following an accident at Talara, Peru, on 25–26 May 53, the USAF found it uneconomical to recover, and sold her remains 'as is' to the FAP on 16 Oct 53 ostensibly under a Grant Aid arrangement. She was then rebuilt and added to the FAP inventory in 1953. To SATCO by Jun 63. Reported lost to an accident 24 Dec 64 at Yurimaguas, Loreto

A fine study of OB-XAD-537 while with SATCO at Lima on 1 July 1965. A DC-3A-279A, she became OB-R-537. Note the curtained windows and very high state of maintenance. *Gordon S. Williams*

Left: Evidencing her evolution to the final quasi-civil registration series worn, here OB-R-653, a C-47D, unloads cargo via wheelbarrow at one of her flag stops with SATCO as of 1970. She was lost in the mountains on 20 April 1972.
R. Wasche

Below left: Formerly FAP-307 pictured earlier, here is VC-47B OB-XAU-654 in full SATCO colours and markings after June 1963. She did not survive long, being lost tragically on Christmas Eve 1964 at Yurimaguas, Loreto.
via Amaru Tincopa

Below: A starboard view of the same aircraft, OB-XAU-654, under power showing the exceptionally clean aircraft not long before her demise.
Will Blount

58-311 OB-XAT-653 OB-R-653	45-1099 0-51099 FAP-677	C-47-50-DK C-47D	17102/34369	This aircraft was previously FAP-677 (q.v.), having been acquired in 1958, with a considerable CAC and USAF history in Latin America dating from Jan 48. It gained serial 58-311, confusingly, only in 1960. She passed to SATCO on 31 Jan 63 and was last reported in Aug 67. Reported crashed on 20 Apr 72 on a mountain named Killukichu in northern Peru en route to Tarapoto near Moyobamba (a scheduled stop). Six killed.
60-314 OB-XAP-581 OB-R-581	41-20060 NC-54311 FAP-696	C-53-DO DC-3S-S1C3G	4830	Purchased from Panagra on 18 Feb 60 and initially FAP-696 (q.v.) but reserialed as 60-314 the same year. To SATCO by 6 May 61 and noted at Barranco in Dec 80. Reported preserved, possibly at Campo de Marte, in Lima.
60-315	42-68844 NC-49550 FAP-697	C-53D-DO DC-3-R2000	11771	Purchased from Panagra. First reported on 20 Apr 72 at Lima and again on 3 Dec 73. Noted at Pisco, Peru, in poor condition as '315' in Apr 87 and then at Pucallpa in Apr 96. Apparently recovered and registered as OB-1345 28 Dec 89 with TAS.
316	–	C-47	–	Reported *c.*Sep 71.
47-319 OB-XAE-538 OB-R-538	42-23358 CAP 424	C-47A-5-DL	9220	Assumed this serial in 1960. To SATCO as OB-XAE-538 on 13 Jun 60. This aircraft crashed on 30 Nov 66 at Chachapoyas.
61-320 OB-XAK-568 OB-R-568	(43-49422) BuA50807 NC-67797 PP-XCJ PP-SDF PP-AAA PP-ATJ PP-YQH OB-LHZ-568	(C-47B-15-DK) R4D-6	15238/26683	Taken up, and a very well-travelled aircraft, in 1961. To SATCO on 6 May 61. Destroyed in an accident 30 Nov 66 at Chachapoyas, Amazonas (?).
62-355	43-15066 0-315066	C-47A-80-DL	19532	MAP on 31 Jul 62. Known with Grupo 8 by 5 Dec 62 and as late as Apr 72.
62-356	43-15543 0-15543	C-47A-85-DL C-47E	20009	MAP on 22 Jun 62. Known with Grupo 8 by Sep 66 and reported crashed on 18 Mar 83 in Arequipa Province in poor weather and her five-man crew were all killed.
62-357 OB-R-1149	43-48012 0-348012	C-47A-30-DL	13828/25273	MAP on 27 Aug 62. Last reported in service on 5 Feb 77. To TANS and noted at Miami as FAP-357 24 Jul 75 but then as OB-R-1149 on 29 May 79, registered to TANS as such. Reportedly preserved at the FAP museum at Las Palmas, Lima, by Sep 97 as FAP 357 if the serial number is reliable.
62-358	43-48081 0-348081	C-47A-30-DK	13897/25342	MAP on 31 Jul 62.
63-359	42-100806 0-100806	C-47A-70-DL	19269	MAP on 16 May 63. One source cites this aircraft as the former 43-15213.

63-360	43-15213 0-315213	C-47A-80-DL	19679	MAP 23 May 63.
361	–	C-47	–	Reported in 1977.
64-364	43-16064 0-16064	C-47A-90-DL	20530	MAP on 4 Jan 64. Known in service with Grupo 8. Noted in service on 26 Feb 72. Apparently survived to be sold surplus to N81602 and then CP-2178 in Bolivia by Aug 88.
64-365 OB-R-1150	43-30682 0-30682	C-47A-DL	13843	MAP on 13 Jan 64. Noted in service on 29 May 79. To OB-R-1150 with TANS on 29 May 79.
64-366 OB-R-1148	42-24132 0-24132	C-47A-45-DL	9994	MAP on 3 Jan 64. To OB-R-1148 with TANS on 29 May 79.
64-367	43-15283 0-315283	C-47A-80-DL	19749	MAP on 27 Jan 64. Crashed on 4 Jun 66 at San Ramón, Chachamayo Province. This was the medical 'dispensary' aircraft noted in the text.
64-368 OB-R-1151	42-93792 0-93792	C-47A-25-DK	13743	MAP on 12 Feb 64. Noted at Collique in Aug 71. To OB-R-1151 with TANS on 29 May 79.
64-369	43-15711 0-315711	C-47A-90-DL	20177	MAP on 18 Feb 64. Known to have served with Grupo 8. Noted at Lima on 18 Aug 73 and again on 31 Jan 77.
64-370	42-93167 42-93167A 0-93167	C-47A-20-DK	13049	MAP on 4 Mar 64. While serving with Grupo Aéreo Mixto 8 this aircraft crashed on 29 Oct 68 at or near the San Ramón airfield, Chachamayo.
64-371	43-16100 0-16100	C-47A-90-DL	20566	MAP on 13 Mar 64. Known in service with Grupo 8 by 20 Apr 72.
64-372	42-93820	C-47A-25-DK	13774	MAP on 17 Mar 64.
64-373	42-100531 0-00531	C-47A-65-DL	18994	MAP on 4 Mar 64. Known with Grupo 8 by 1964 and as late as 31 Jan 77 at Lima.
OB-XAA-534 OB-R-534	42-68791 NC19913 N19913 FAP-485	C-53D-DO DC-3A-S1C3G	11718	Rgt to SATCO 13 Jun 60. Reported derelict at Lima as OB-R-534 by 12 Sep 71.
FAP-539 OB-XAF-539 OB-R-539	45-1004 FAP-483	C-47B-45-DK	17007/ 342702*192*	Almost certainly a corruption of OB-R-539 (see FAP-483). Reported by an Argentine source but not verified.
FAP 552	–	C-47	–	First cited as in service by 24 Jan 56. Reported with SATCO as of Jul 60.
FAP 554	–	C-47	–	Reported on 4 Feb 62.
FAP-667	45-1099 0-51099	C-47B-30-DK C-47D	17102/34369	A former CAC aircraft that had been in Latin America since Jan 48. Salvaged by the USAF on 30 Nov 56, the remains were acquired by the FAP and completely rebuilt by 1958. Reserialed as 58-311 (q.v.) in 1960.
FAP 673	–	C-47	–	Reported in service *c*.28 Oct 64.
FAP-696	41-20060 NC-54311 N54311	C-53-DO DC-3S-S1C3G	4830	Purchased from Panagra on 18 Feb 60 and almost immediately reserialed as 60-314 (q.v.). Although quoted in some sources as initially having been given serial FAP-496, there has been no verification of this.
FAP-697	42-68844 N49550	C-53D-DO DC-3-R2000	11771	Purchased from Panagra in 1960 (US registration cancelled 13 Apr 60) and almost immediately reserialed as 60-315 (q.v.).
FAP-???	43-16080 OB-I-818	C-47A-90-DL	20546	This, formerly operated by a Peruvian governmental airport agency, CORPAC, reportedly passed to the FAP in September 1975, making her one of the last C-47s acquired. However, no FAP identity has been traced and she may, at best, have been used merely as a spares source hulk.

Peruvian Navy

As noted earlier, the Peruvian armed forces maintained a separate Naval and Army air arm until the two were merged to form the CAP in 1929.

However, as Peru has always maintained one of the most professional and well-rounded deep-water (and riverine) navies in Latin America, powerful forces within that establishment lobbied successfully for the return of an organic Naval air arm and, in 1963, this was basically started from scratch as the Servicio Aéronaval de la Marina Peruana. Initially equipped with Bell 47 helicopters, the service eventually gained fixed-wing and dedicated anti-submarine warfare aircraft.

Both the US Navy and US Marine Corps unquestionably had a hand in all of this, as both of those services had had unusually strong ties to the Peruvian Navy, going back as far as the 1920s. Indeed, as early as February and July 1946, the US Navy had briefly toyed with a form of 'American Republics Project' of its own for the four

principal regional naval powers, Argentina, Brazil, Chile and Peru, placing advisory teams and Missions intermittently with each. In a document entitled 'Interim Project for Supply of Naval Aircraft to Latin American Countries' dated 8 February and 18 July 1946, the USN proposed providing the Peruvian Navy with four R4D-5s and, in the process, reinvigorating a naval air arm there. The US State Department took a very dim view of this, however, and apparently managed to terminate the entire concept.

On 31 October 1966, however, the Navy acquired what is believed to have been its first large post-war fixed-wing aircraft when C-47A AT 502, a rather weary former Faucett aircraft, was reconditioned and purchased – the first of apparently at least ten former airline DC-3s and C-47s acquired for the service.

Used in direct support of the fleet, both at its coastal stations, on the rivers and the small Lake Titicaca presence, little is known about the actual service of these aircraft.

Peruvian Navy AT 503, believed to have been former Dakota IV KN367 and Peruvian civil OB-R-200, with her deep blue cheatline once again portrayed, via the use of Agfa chrome film and a telephoto lens, as green. *Air-Britain #72*

Navy AT 510 is believed to have been DC-3A-S3C4G MSN 4801 and the former OB-R-551 with Cia. Faucett first reported in Peru in September 1969. Her fate is unknown. *MAP1983-96 #13*

Aéronaval Code	Previous Identity	Built As	MSN	Assignments and Notes
AT 502	42-24118 NC-18664 HC-SGG OB-PAB-246 OB-R-246	C-47A-45-DL	9980	Acquired from Cia. Faucett on 31 Oct 66.
AT 503	44-76405 KN367 VMYBU OB-PAT-200 OB-R-200	C-47B-25-DK Dakota IV	15989/32737	First reported in 1967 and ex Cia. Faucett. This aircraft is believed to have been wrecked at Lima between Jan 76 and Jun 80 and then broken up.
AT 510	NC-28335 N28335 OB-PBK-551 OB-R-551	DC-3A-279B DC-3A-S3C4G	4801	Last with Cia. Faucett and cancelled in 1964 as OB-R-551. First reported as AT 510 in Sep 69.
AT 511	43-49144 N6494C OB-LHC-499 OB-M-499	C-47B-10-DK C-47D	14960/26405	Candidate only.
AT 512	NC25655 YV-AVI YV-C-AVI YV-C-ARF N3929C N625ST N777V N778V	DC-3A-228C	2195	Suspected as purchased by the Peruvian Navy by 28 Aug 71. Last reported on 20 Apr 72 at Lima. Suggested as having previously been AT 502.
AT 513	43-49144 N6494C? OB-LHC-499 OB-M-499	C-47B-10-DK C-47D	14960/26405	Probably a rebuilt/composite aircraft, acquired by the Navy 21 Dec 70 although another source claims it did not pass to the Navy from the airline until Apr 84, which seems most unlikely. Suggested as having previously been AT 503.

Although often cited as a DC-3A-228C, Peruvian Naval AT 512 clearly has a C-47 cargo door in this view and a most unusual radar nose, not seen on any other Latin American C-47. However, she also has curtained windows, suggesting a passenger interior! Some reports suggest she was previously AT 502, but this appears highly doubtful. *via Ken F. Measures*

AT 521 wears what is believed to have been the final colour scheme of Peruvian Naval C-47s, light grey over off-white undersides. Gone are the prominent rudder stripes, replaced by a simple tricolour, and note also the modification by the time of this 11 June 1988 image taken at Collique of the Naval national insignia. Believed to be MSN 17061/34328, she has also been nominated as MSN 13177, but that was more likely AT 520. *Javier Goto W.*

AT 520	42-93283 CF-DME N2719A N7147C OB-PBJ-544 OB-R-544	C-47A-20-DK	13177	Ex-Cia Faucett to the Navy on 16 Apr 84 in derelict condition. However, a spotting report cited her as seen on 18 Aug 73 and as late as 11 Mar 79!
AT 521	45-1058 NC-63351 OB-PAQ-167 OB-R-167	C-47B-50-DK	17061/34328	Acquired from Cia. Faucett in Feb 67 or 15 May 67.
AT 522	–	–	–	First reported on 29 Oct 73 and as late as 8 Dec 73 at Lima.
AT 523	–	–	–	First reported on 8 Dec 73.
AT 524	–	–	–	First reported on 31 Mar 79.
AT 528	*43-49099* *N87657* *OB-PBO-676* *OB-R-676*	*C-47B-10-DK* *C-47D* *SC-47D*	*19415/26360*	This aircraft was derelict when sold or donated to the Navy on 16 Apr 84 and is the only airframe that is a candidate therefore for AT 528, which was first reported on 4 May 85 and again in Aug 85.

Unfortunately, the identity of this Navy C-47, one of the last known as of Christmas 1993, is unknown, but the view does reveal the character of the undersurface off-white camouflage, and the location of the naval version of the national insignia under the starboard wing. *Javier Goto W.*

A fascinating although slightly blurred line-up of no fewer than four Navy C-47s at Limatambo. At least one of the aircraft, the most distant, is a C-53D or DC-3. *via George G.J. Kamp*

An important aircraft in the story of the evolution of Peruvian Naval use of C-47s, US Navy C-47J BuA17251 was assigned to the US Naval Mission to Peru in 1963. Seen here on 1 July 1965, note the unusual placement of the US national insignia under the starboard wing. *Gordon S. Williams*

CHAPTER TWENTY

Uruguay

THE SMALLEST OF THE ORIGINAL independent states of South America, the beautiful nation of Uruguay, where more than 50 per cent of the entire population lives in the vicinity of the capital, Montevideo, has enjoyed an exceptional aviation heritage from the very earliest days, and although small, has managed to maintain both a conventional air force and a naval air arm continuously.

Often cited as a 'buffer state' between neighbouring giants Argentina and Brazil, Uruguay supported the Allied cause during both world wars and, even though often characterised as casting a wary eye on her two more powerful neighbours, had maintained her own delightful identity unmenaced overtly.

However, in the early 1950s, the country was extremely sensitive to the overly expansionist objectives of Argentina's Juan Domingo Perón, who made no secret of his ambitions to incorporate the independent states that had arisen from the Viceroyalty of La Plata into what he saw as a Greater Argentina. Uruguay consequently received US military aid that, in retrospect, seemed out of all proportion to her actual defence needs, with a clear view towards resisting Perón's overtures.

With this seemingly never-ending tension of the 1950s, after the fall of Perón, Uruguay's internal political and economic conditions came under the increasing pressure of inflation that, predictably, eroded the value of the country's currency. This then led to reductions in the hitherto extraordinarily lavish social services that Uruguayans had long enjoyed – indeed, often touted as a model for Latin America – and this then provoked labour unrest from the 1960s onward and, to the astonishment of most well-educated Uruguayans, an epidemic of urban terrorism by the so-called Tupamaro guerrilla movement, which had its roots in the disillusioned urban middle-class youth of the country.

Faced with the alarming breakdown of long-established national institutions, the armed forces – which had hitherto taken enormous

pride in being the least politicised and professional in all of Latin America – effectively seized power in 1973, although ruling through a puppet civilian regime. The good news was that the services had, in fact, reversed the slide towards anarchy and actual national collapse. The bad news was that it came at the cost of severe repression of the flower of Uruguayan youth, the best educated in Latin America.

Against this backdrop, the country was one of the last to transition its air arm, the Aeronáutica Militar Uruguaya (AM), an element of the Army, to an actual independent, autonomous air force, not becoming the Fuerza Aérea Uruguaya (FAU) until 4 December 1953.

Unlike nearly all of her mainland South American neighbour states, Uruguay has long maintained a comprehensive rail network and an adequate road system, as well as a remarkably well-developed internal air transport network and, per capita, one of the largest civil aircraft registers in Latin America. With no daunting geographical barriers, and with only modest distances to contend with, her military air transport requirements were not nearly as compelling as elsewhere.

Certainly a candidate for the most attractively marked Latin American military C-47, 507 is seen being inspected for the first time at Carrasco on 3 September 1965 with what was known at this juncture as the Colegiado and other dignitaries present, as Uruguay did not have a 'President' in the traditional sense at the time. The Colegiado was the Presidente of the Partido Nacional made up of representatives of the Colourado and Nacional (Blanco) parties. Note the FAU Lockheed F-80C and T-33A in the background. *via Eduardo Luzardo*

A Second World War veteran of the Sixth Air Force in Panama, Uruguay's first C-47A-30-DK, serial 507 (43-48007) troops the colours at Carrasco (BA1) in her eighteenth year of service in 1965 after having been converted locally to VIP Presidential configuration by the Regimiento de Mantenimiento. Note the air stair deployed on the port side. *via Eduardo Luzardo*

Because of her 'buffer' status, Uruguay had enjoyed an unusually lucrative Lend-Lease experience during the Second World War, which transformed the AM into a truly modern and professional service. Following the war, and again with the approval of the US, both the military and naval air arms prospered, becoming, in fact, one of only two naval air arms in Latin American aviation history to ever operate single-seat fighter aircraft.

As the Second World War appeared to be nearing its end in favour of the Allies, as early as November 1944, the AM started laying plans for the expected post-war surplus glut, with a view towards expansion of the modest Lend-Lease deliveries she had received. The Uruguayan Embassy in Washington made no secret of the fact that officials there would be interested in negotiations with any firm that could possibly supply Lockheed C-60 Lodestars with which to equip a projected airborne infantry element, as well as additional Vought OS2U-3 Kingfishers for the Navy, PT-19s, PT-23 and PT-26s for both the AM and the Navy – and DC-3 'types' for the AM.

Uruguay had operated several twin-engine aircraft prior to the arrival of her first ARP-supplied C-47s in 1947 but not many and, as a consequence, her cadre required assistance in making the transition to what were, at the time, the largest aircraft the service had ever operated. Only ten Uruguayan crews had received training in the US during the Second World War, and none on multi-engine aircraft. Her influx of new types under ARP included one Beech UC-45B and eight AT-11 twins (which were issued serials 501 to 506) as well as additional AT-6 and Fairchild PT-26 aircraft – and four C-47s. Because of the funding situation and lack of fully trained Uruguayan crews, the actual sequence of the ARP deliveries is rather confusing. A report on the Interim ARP Project Status dated 12 September 1947, for instance, declared that Uruguay was to get two under Project No. 94543-S, both to come from stocks held in the Caribbean Air Command in the Panama Canal Zone. An even earlier document, dated 14 October 1946, stated that the aircraft to be covered by Project 94543-S covered just one aircraft, 43-48007!

Initially, the first increment of C-47s, G3-507 and G3-508, were assigned to what was known at the time as the Grupo Aeronáutico No. 3 (Bombardeo) and they served alongside new Beech AT-11s and North American AT-6Cs and AT-6Ds. By 1948, however, the unit had lost the AT-6s, but still had the two C-47s, UC-45B number 506, Fairchild PT-26 number 648 and eight AT-11 'bombers', numbers 100 to 102, and 104 to 108.

Oddly, however, the first documented report of a Uruguayan military C-47 operating abroad came from Brazil, where, in November 1948, two were authorised to transit Brazilian territory en route home – but these were cited as serials 107 and 108, which do not match any known C-47 AM serials of the day, these having been assigned to AT-11s. This agrees with a report dated 1 December 1948, which stated that Uruguay, to that date, although authorised three C-47s, had in fact only received two. Since both of these serials are in fact known to have been assigned to Beech AT-11s, it must be assumed that the request for transit cited the aircraft type in error, or they were worn only for the purposes of ferrying from the US, as no Uruguayan C-47s are known to have otherwise operated with such serials.

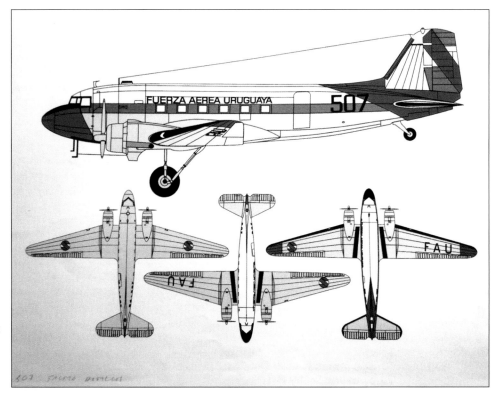

Marking details of the VIP conversion of FAU-507. The side view shows her profile, with the stylised half-wing aft of the cockpit not yet added, nor the serial repeat in small numerals on her nose. The three overhead views show the evolution of her markings from delivery, with the national insignia in all four wing positions, through an interim 'white-top' scheme, to the definitive scheme at right.
Pedro Otto and Fernando Cerovaz

Above: FAU-507 again, but late in her service life, her VIP air stair having been replaced by a conventional cargo door and now bearing a variation on the famous *Tortuga* (cargo-bearing turtle) nose art on her nose. She had been withdrawn from use by March 1972 after an adventurous career spanning nearly thirty years. *Nery Mendiburu via Dr. Gary Kuhn*

Left: The *Tortuga* nose art in one of several variations as it appeared on FAU-507 as of June 1961 at Paysandú, Uruguay, comprising a hunch-backed turtle with an enormous strapped package on his back, walking with a cane in his right 'hand', and with 'Urgente' plastered on the cargo pack! *Nery Mendiburu via Eduardo Luzardo*

Thus, it fell to G3-508 to make the first official foreign sojourn of an FAU C-47 when, on 10 April 1948, the Grupo Commander, Mayor Alberto L. García and his crew flew the President of Uruguay and his accompanying delegation to Bogotá, Colombia, to attend the IX International American Conference. Both G3-507 and G3-508 were subsequently utilised again in September 1948 to convey the President and his staff to Rio de Janeiro, returning on the 9th. Further C-47 excursions followed into 1949 to Paraguay and Ecuador, the latter flying aid to earthquake survivors in Quito.

Between 1 January and 1 July 1949, however, Air Order of Battle reports showed the AM as possessing only one C-47, increasing to two by 1 January 1950. During this same period, each three-month periodic report also stated, in every instance, that 'three other C-47s are on order, not yet delivered', and since another report dated 1 November 1948 stated 'the Uruguayan Air Force has secured appropriation funding for the purchase of two C-47s from the US', it would appear that the arrival and actual transfer dates for the ARP C-47s was much more protracted than previously thought.

US State Department records indicate that Uruguay bought one C-47A at Kelly AFB, TX, on 11 March 1949 on Contract W-ANL-(MP-I)-466 Uruguay 33 Part 1 and two others, at Davis-Monthan AFB, AZ, on the same date on Part 2 of the same contract.

C-47 G3-507 continued her adventures in January 1950, this time flying all the way to the US via the Atlantic coastal route, arriving at Bolling Field, Washington, DC, on the 29th with six weary passengers – crews for the new North American B-25Js the FAU was due to acquire. She was followed to Bolling by G3-508 in February. Both had returned home by March.

The FAU then acquired two C-47s via ARP, numbers 509 and 510, which had been reconditioned at Glendale, California, following actual handover at Kelly AFB, TX. This work delayed their actual arrival following what has always been reported as the 'official' delivery date into 1950.

Meanwhile, G3-507 and 508 continued their yeoman work as quasi-VIP transports, providing the mode for the Ecuadorian delegation to Uruguay to memorialise the 100th anniversary of one of the founding fathers of modern Latin America, General José Artigas, in September, and then returning them home.

On 3 March 1951, Grupo de Aviación No. 4 (Transporte) was stood up and, with the arrival of the North American B-25Js and F-51Ds at inception, was equipped with C-47s serials 507 to 511, Beech UC-45B serial 506 and Ryan Navions numbers 1903 and 1904.

Uruguayan C-47 strength remained remarkably constant from the introduction of the type in 1947 through to 1960 – more than thirteen years – at between four and five, the latter figure cited on the Air Order of Battle for 30 June 1954. Of these, four were assigned to Grupo 4 at Montevideo and the other was in the hands of the materiel depot and rated 'not combat ready'. These numbers remained unchanged through December 1956, including the single inactive example.

The FAU took a bold move in 1954 when, following the civil unrest in distant Costa Rica in 1954–55, Uruguay's diplomatic representatives at the Organisation of American States (OAS) offered two of its C-47s for use in patrolling the contested areas of Costa Rica in conjunction with the OAS Committee that was investigating the situation there. Back home, FAU officials, rather taken by surprise by this offer, interpreted existing Uruguayan law as requiring

Two different aircraft wore the serial 508 in FAU service, the first, a 1947 ARP delivery, was written off early on at Salta in October 1950. This is T-508, also wearing CX-BJD, a September 1970 MAP delivery while serving with TAMU. *Nery Mendiburu via Dr. Gary Kuhn*

A very rare view of T-508/CX-BJD with her three .50 calibre guns actually mounted, two in one window and one in the other. Note that the dorsal astrodome has been covered over and is surrounded by a host of special antennas in this 1981 view. *Gustavo Figueroa via Eduardo Luzardo*

T-508/CX-BJD once again after conversion to gunship configuration. Note that the two aft-most cabin windows, where three .50 calibre machine guns had been positioned, have been blanked off. The 'whip' antenna on the upper port cabin roof was a clear indication of USAF Mission involvement in this conversion. She also wears a variant of the *Tortuga* nose art and her lower extremities have been painted light grey. *via Capt. George G. Farinas*

The 'G4-' prefix to serial 509, a Second World War Ninth Air Force veteran aircraft and 1948–49 ARP delivery to Uruguay, but only after numerous diversions, as noted in the accompanying table. She had been G3-509 and assumed the G4- prefix around 1960. She made her final flight as simply FAU-509 on 20 March 1974. *Nery Mendiburu via Dr Gary Kuhn*

G4-509 poses on the apron at BA1 (Carrasco) in the late 1950s wearing a version of the *Tortuga* emblem on her nose, as detailed in the accompanying image. *Nery Mendiburu via Dr Gary Kuhn*

Congressional approval prior to the dispatch of military personnel and equipment outside the country. As a result, Uruguayan Congressional approval was requested to send not only two of the FAU's highly prized C-47s, but two F-51Ds to Costa Rica to support the OAS mission there. Apparently to the surprise of the FAU leadership, the House of Representatives approved the action within a few days, something of a record at the time. As this was annual vacation period nationwide, however, a quorum could not be obtained in the Senate and, as a result, the project was delayed until the uprising had ended, putting this entire matter to rest. C-47s 509 and 511 were utilised and made the trip via the Pacific route, flying first to Mendoza, Argentina, then to Santiago, Chile. They then flew up the coast to Antofagasta, Chile, Pisco in Peru, Guayaquil and Esmeralda in Ecuador and finally, via Albrook AFB, CZ, to San José, the Costa Rican capital. They amassed some sixty-seven hours of flying time during the exercise.

From 9 May 1956 on, all Uruguayan military C-47s were adorned with the titles Fuerza Aérea Uruguaya on their upper fuselage sides.

The Aircraft Overhaul Company (also cited as Aircraft Technical Services, Inc.) of Dallas, Texas, received an FAU contract to overhaul two C-47 on 20 September 1955, 42-100558 and 42-100838. A third aircraft, 43-15079, was to have originally been included under this contract but apparently there were not sufficient funds available. A little more than four years later, the FAU made a formal request to buy three C-47s under the MAP provisions. This was followed by another contract with the same firm to recondition FAU-510 and 511.

Although of poor definition, the *Tortuga* emblem on the nose of G4-509 reveals significant variation from the norm, including a smaller 'load' and what appears to be a much larger 'Urgente' placard, as well as a coloured, circular surround when photographed at Carrasco in 1960.
via Eduardo Luzardo

As in neighbouring nations, Uruguay decided in 1961 that the air arm should put its transport capability to practical use for the good of the country, and, as a direct result, Transporte Aéreo Militar Uruguayo (TAMU) was formally launched on 10 August. The first official mission under this designation was to the Aeroparque aerodrome in neighbouring Buenos Aires, Argentina, to help celebrate Air Force Day there.

Between July and December 1963, FAU C-47 strength, with the advent of MAP deliveries, had taken a dramatic turn, with a total of fourteen assorted aircraft on the Order of Battle, of which four were inactive at the time. Of these, one was awaiting the results of a complete survey, one was down for periodic inspection and two others were undergoing IRAN. Of the total of fourteen, five had been acquired by the FAU via other than MAP means. MAP and USAF Mission support was highly effective, and often quite personalised. For example,

USAFSO's 5700th Airbase Wing Quality Control section dispatched USAF Staff Sgt Jones on Temporary Duty with the FAU to assist the service in ensuring that all of the MAP-supported aircraft were in compliance with Technical Orders 1C-1-610 and 1C-1-613 – a seemingly inconsequential matter, but an indication of the extent that the USAF was willing to invest in supporting the Latin American C-47 fleet. As a direct result of this visit, FAU-516 was returned to service by January 1965 and three other C-47s were in line to receive the same attention. To that date, the AM and FAU had acquired a total of sixteen DC-3s and C-47s of all variants, fourteen of which remained in service and of these, six were assigned to Grupo 3 (Transporte) including the veterans 509, 513, 514 and 517, and eight others to Grupo 4 (Transporte), both stationed at Carrasco and both with eight fully qualified crews. Both were rated 'C-1', Combat Ready.

By 1964, both C-47 operating units – together with a mix of minor types – were pooled to provide the equipment for Transporte Aéreo Militar Uruguayo (TAMU), which the USAF Mission likened to the USAF's MATS. A portion of this force was held on continuous alert status for air transport support in the event of natural disaster or emergency relief requirements. It also served as an executive governmental transport organisation as well as movements of high-priority cargo to remote areas of the country, many of which were not served by commercial airlines. By the second quarter of 1965, Grupo 3 and 4 had flown fifty-eight hours with C-47s in direct support of health and sanitation initiatives, and a total of 196 hours since the start of the year.

These flights did much to enhance the public image of the FAU, as many of them involved flights of what would normally be known as an air evacuation nature, bringing critically ill patients – many making their very first flights – to Montevideo for treatment. The service operated in conjunction with the Ministerio de Salud Pública by transporting inoculation teams with vaccinations, drugs and other medicines to remote villages as a part of the several national health programmes. Both of the operating units were, by this time, devoting some 25 per cent of their activities to Civic Action programmes.

Grupo de Aviación No. 3 (Transporte) made one of its final long-range missions aboard C-47 FAU-517 to Mexico City on 22 January 1966, completing the flight and returning home having flown some seventy-four hours over the thirteen-day period via the Pacific route.

Compare this view of C-47A-25-DK (MSN 13744) FAU-509 with her scheme while marked as G4-509. Her titles are far more robust, her individual serial higher and much larger and she wears a more modern RDF blister atop her forward fuselage. She also has a much more muscular version of the *Tortuga* on her nose in this period Paysandú view. Note also the erosion of her port wing leading edge. *Nery Mendiburu via Dr Gary Kuhn*

An unidentified FAU C-47 suffered major damage sometime between January and June 1966, but the exact aircraft has not been identified. At the time, the AOB showed a total of fifteen C-47s. This remained unchanged until June 1966, even though two aircraft had been MAP recovered and redeployed from the Netherlands.

Air Order of Battle data for the period July to December 1967 still showed a total of fifteen received, but only fourteen on strength, of which thirteen were active.

By 1968, Grupos 3 and 4 were operating with a mix of C-47s and at least a few veteran AT-11s converted to transport configuration. The USAF Mission assisted the FAU in securing the services of a special Installation team who had arrived in country on 2 October 1968 for the express purpose of modifying one of the FAU MAP-supported C-47s to accommodate a Class V Photographic Modification. The installation took about six weeks to complete, although it is not clear which aircraft was involved or exactly why this very unusual installation had been requested. Between July and September, an FAU C-47 was also treated for corrosion and repainted with the assistance of the Mission.

By late September 1969, Grupo 3 (Transporte) had been reduced to just five C-47s on strength but had added a single Beech A65 Queen Air (purchased in March) and its Combat Readiness rating had dropped to C-2. However, Grupo 4 (Transporte) with eight C-47s (and also with a new Beech A65 Queen Air) had dropped to C-3 due to a very low in-commission rate, only three of the aircraft having been flown during the preceding three-month period.

Above: G5-510 was a 1949 ARP delivery, the former C-47A-65-DL 42-100558. Seen here at BA1 (Carrasco) on 22 March 1957 in her eighth year of service, she wears a very early version of the *Tortuga* insignia and evidence of significant erosion on her antiglare panel. Note also her wartime 'cheek' antennas just ahead of the mail/baggage door. *via Eduardo Luzardo*

Above: FAU-510 again, but some ten years later, as photographed at Carrasco on 19 July 1967, displaying yet another interpretation of the *Tortuga* emblem. Note the two 'balloons' near the right 'hand' holding the cane, the significance of which are not known. *4_DSV_FAU via Eduardo Luzardo*

Below: By way of contrast, here is a very early view of G4-510 taken not long after ARP delivery in 1949. Still in essentially 'stock' configuration, G4-510 can just be seen in the distant background. *Eugene M. Sommerich*

Left: A much later view of the veteran FAU-510 visiting Aeroparque in Buenos Aires, Argentina. Her dorsal astrodome is now gone, replaced by an RDF 'bullet', and she bears yet another variation on the *Tortuga* emblem on her nose, probably operating for TAMU by this juncture. *Air-Britain #72*

Below: The last incarnation of T-510, the second aircraft to be assigned this serial, now wearing joint registration CX-BJG. A 1970 MAP delivery, she arrived with all of the trappings of a VC-47D but was briefly kitted out as a gunship with a single .50 calibre gun in her aft-most cabin window. She is seen here on 19 December 1995 in her fifth year as a gate guard at BA1 (Carrasco). Although she has nose art, it is not believed to have been worn in actual service but applied after being posted on the gate. *George G.J. Kamp*

The first of two aircraft to be assigned serial 511, this one is the ARP C-47A-75-DL, MSN 19301 which arrived in January 1949. She is seen here at Grand Central Airport in California incident to the delivery of the FAU's North American F-51D Mustangs. She served on until stricken on 26 June 1970. Sharp-eyed observers will note that the diagonal stripe on her rudder insignia is sloped in the wrong direction, and that she still has her Second World War-vintage gun-port windows! *Chalmers Johnson via Warren M. Bodie*

The second aircraft to bear the serial 511 was also marked CX-BJH, a MAP-supplied C-47D (45-1111) that had served in Panama before delivery around September 1970. Note the absence of service titles as she taxies out, and that the lower extremities have been painted light grey. She crashed at Artigas on 10 February 1978, as described in the narrative. *Nery Mendiburu via Dr Gary Kuhn*

By 31 March 1970, Grupo 4's long association with the C-47 had come to an end, and its C-47s at the time – FAU 507, 510-512, 515, 516, 518 and 519 – were transferred out, consolidating all thirteen surviving aircraft in Grupo 3, having partially re-equipped with the two new Fokker F-27s and the single Beech A65.

In June 1970, the FAU C-47 fleet once again stepped up to aid the Uruguayan Red Cross in efforts to bring relief to the earthquake victims in Peru. On the 5th, FAU-512 of Grupo No. 3, piloted by Mayor (PAM) Julio Uria and his crew made the long trip, followed by FAU 515, not returning home until the 20th.

By the middle of 1970, the R-1830-92 engines fitted to most of the FAU's C-47s had started becoming a problem. Because of personnel and funding issues, the usually efficient FAU Depot had only been able to overhaul a single R-1830 all year. The USAF Mission privately noted that this was due almost entirely to increased security measures that had recently been imposed on enlisted FAU ranks, added to similar steps that had been taken earlier. Despite its best efforts, including emergency requisitions, the USAF Mission was only able to facilitate the overhaul of three additional engines. In spite of this, total FAU C-47 inventory still hovered around eleven, but these had flown only 739 hours in the quarter ending June 1970.

G4-511 once again as she appeared on 26 October 1957 at Arapey, Salto, following her forced landing there – with, among other things, damage to the precise area of the legendary *Tortuga* nose art!
5_DSV_FAU via Eduardo Luzardo

FAU-512, a November 1960 MAP delivery, is unusual in sporting Day-Glo bands around the rear fuselage and most of her nose. The rectangular areas under the cockpit window are her former USAF data blocks for 43-48131. She was stricken from the inventory on 16 July 1974 with 10,825 hours on the clock. *Nery Mendiburu via Dr Gary Kuhn*

C-47D G3-514, a September 1961 MAP acquisition (note the black panel below the nose) displayed a much larger than usual impression of the *Tortuga* as well as the legend '23 de Octubre' when she was flown to Brazil in 1966 to celebrate the fiftieth anniversary of pioneer Alberto Santos-Dumont's first flight at Bagatelle in Paris in 1906. She is seen here on 15 March1969 still wearing the titles. *Roberto Grasso via Eduardo Luzardo*

The usually authoritative Air-Britain publication *Aeromilitaria* for June 2014 reported that Uruguay received three former 24th Special Operations Wing, USAFSO aircraft in 1970, the first of which was 43-16074 (formally stricken from the USAF inventory on 4 September that year), apparently to have become the third FAU-508, and that she was already detached to Montevideo. However, this aircraft in fact went to Argentine instead, leading to no end of confusion. The other two, 43-48275 (FAU-510) and 45-1111 (FAU-511), were stricken on 27 October 1970.

In December 1973, the two operating Grupos still counted ten C-47s between them, and were, at the time, the most numerous airworthy types in the air arm.

Then, on 10 February 1978, the otherwise splendid record of the C-47 in Uruguayan military service was probably tarnished forever by what was, at the time, the worst air disaster in the country's aviation history. During an emergency landing near Artigas, while en route there from Montevideo on a commercial TAMU flight, FAU-511 with at least thirty-eight passengers on board (including twenty-three adults and fifteen children) were killed as well as the captain, Mayor (Av.)

Roberto A. Ferradás, and his crew of five. Ferradás was the brother of the pilot of the FAU Fokker F-27 (purchased in March 1970) that had crashed in the Andes in October 1972, with the infamous and harrowing aftermath.

At least one FAU C-47 had been camouflaged by May 1978 and was being used to train the Uruguayan Paracaidistas Militares.

As the remaining FAU C-47 fleet entered the twilight of their service in Uruguay, their annual flight hours reflected the reality of their ever-increasing obsolescence. In 1981, they managed a fairly respectable 1,246:10 but in 1982 this dropped to just 335:08. In 1983 it dropped even further, to just 234:20 but made a brief resurgence in 1984, the last known year of operations, with 372:09, all of these hours having been accumulated while assigned to Grupo No. 3.

As of 1985, the last year they were reported, Grupo de Aviación No. 3 (Transporte) still possessed, among its mixed inventory, C-47s FAU-508, 514 and DC-3s FAU-523 and 524.

A very special thanks to Uruguayan aero-historian Eduardo Luzardo and our mutual friend, the legendary Tte 1º (Av.) Juan Maruri.

Shown during her final flight over the Rio de la Plata estuary on 27 May 1988, when she was referred to as 'El Veterano', C-47D T-514 by that date was also assigned registration CX-BKH but only her nose codes have survived. She is today preserved at BA1 (Carrasco). *FAU via Eduardo Luzardo*

FAU-515 was a C-47D supplied to Uruguay under MAP on 6 December 1961 and is seen here at the Aeroparque in Buenos Aires, Argentina, on 18 August 1967. *Andreas Keleman*

A MAP Grant Aid delivery in April 1962, G4-516 displayed yet another incarnation of the *Tortuga* nose art as of October 1968.
Roberto Grasso via Eduardo Luzardo

Delivered at the same time as G4-516, and also under Grant Aid, former Dakota IV FAU-517 is unusual in having no cheatline at all separating her white upper decking from the natural metal lower extremities. She had her final flight on 7 June 1974. *Nery Mendiburu via Dr Gary Kuhn*

AM/FAU Serial	Previous Identity	Built As	MSN	Assignments and Notes
507 G4-507 G3-507	43-48007	C-47A-30-DK	13823/25268	A former Sixth Air Force aircraft assigned to the Canal Zone on 2 Aug 44, this aircraft actually served in Uruguay with the USAAF Air Attaché as early as 3 Sep 46 but was not turned over to the AM following training by ARP Cadre until 6 Oct 47 on O/DGAM #7784. She was granted permission to overfly US territory, via San Juan, Puerto Rico, on 26 Jan 50. She is noted as having been issued permissions to overfly Brazilian national territory in 1958, May 59 and 1960. She was converted to a VIP interior by the Regimiento de Mantenimiento by 3 Sep 65. This aircraft enjoyed a remarkably long service career, serving successively with the Grupo 4 and Grupo 3 (from 6Apr 70) until noted withdrawn from use at the FAU cantonment area at Carrasco on 5 Mar 72. Officially stricken on Orden No. 1748 dated 22 Jun 77.
508 (1) G3-508	43-15079	C-47A-80-DL	19545	ARP/FLC allocated on 18 Sep 47 and officially handed over on 6 Oct 47. She was converted to an executive VIP interior by the Talleres de la Aeronáutica Militar around Sep 48. She was granted permission to overfly US territory on 26 Jan 50 via San Juan, Puerto Rico, and again on 23 Feb 50. This aircraft was written off on 27 Oct 50 at the Aeródromo de Salta while being handled by 1°Tte Atilio Bonelli and Sgto Washington Galarza, no injuries. Grounded due to severe structural damage and not finally stricken until 27 Jul 61.
508 (2) T-508/CX-BJD	43-16075 0-16075	C-47A-90-DL	20541	MAP on 4 Sep 70. A former USAFSO 605th Air Commando Squadron aircraft, this aircraft has often been reported, in error, as having gone to Argentina. She had, in fact, already been detached to Montevideo as early as 15 May 70, but had to wait until September for the formal handover. Joint marks T-508/CX-BJD with TAMU were taken up on 24 Sep 70. She was formally assigned to Grupo de Aviación No. 3 on 14 Oct 70. However, when she visited São Paulo-Congonhas airport on 16 Apr 74 (in company with FAU-511) she was noted only as FAU-508. She was converted to a gunship around Nov 79, mounting three .50 calibre machine guns. She suffered damage on 29 Oct 82 while being handled by a mechanic at Carrasco but was repaired. She made her final flight on 28 Dec 82 but was not formally stricken until 28 Jul 87 with an incredible 18,982 hours total time.

Seldom illustrated, here is an apron scene at BA1 (Carrasco) showing at least five FAU C-47s with 517 – now with a standard cheatline – nearest.
via Edwardo Luzardo

509 G4-509 G3-509	42-93793	C-47A-25-DK	13744	A Second World War Ninth Air Force veteran, this aircraft was originally intended for Peru (22 Sep 47), then Uruguay (17 Jun 48) and then Bolivia (1 Mar 49) under ARP, and is an excellent example of how the various Latin American recipient air arms were shuffled by the Caribbean Air Command to deal with circumstances in the field as they developed. She was finally allotted to Uruguay on ARP project 72017 as early as 29 Sep 48 and as late as 16 Nov 49 under the terms of the Interim Program and departed Kelly Field, TX, on delivery on 21 Nov 49. She first went to Glendale, CA, where she was reconditioned prior to final delivery around 18 May 50, but is known to have accompanied the FAU's new F-51Ds home around 31 Aug 50 when she was apparently marked as G3-509! She was granted permission to overfly Brazilian territory in 1958, Sep 1959 and 1960. She was granted permission to overfly US territory marked as G4-509 on 16 Feb 60. She suffered a landing accident on 14 Jul 65 at Carrasco due to mechanical failure but was repaired. Endured another incident on the ramp at Carrasco on 1 Nov 71 due to human error but was repaired. She made her final flight on 20 Mar 74 and was officially stricken on Orden No. 1748 dated 22 Jun 77.
510 (1) G4-510	42-100558	C-47A-65-DL	19021	The earliest US document linking this aircraft to Uruguay is dated 12 Jan 49. Allocated to Uruguay under ARP on 3 Apr 49 and delivered on 25 Nov 49 ex-Davis-Monthan AFB but not actually handed over until 11 Apr 50 following reconditioning at Glendale, California. She was granted permission to overfly US territory, marked as G4-510, on 16 Feb 50, however, which challenges the 'official' handover date. By 31 Aug 50, however, she was marked as G3-510 and was one of three C-47s accompanying the new Uruguayan P-51Ds home. Current and active as of Apr 56, she was refurbished in Dallas, TX, that year. She was given permission to overfly Brazilian national territory in 1958, May 59 and 1960. She suffered a taxiing accident on 19 Jul 67 at BA1 Carrasco while being tested by a mechanic but was repaired. She was stricken on 26 Jun 70.
510 (2) T-510/CX-BJG	43-48275 0-48275	C-47B-1-DK C-47D VC-47D	14091/25536	MAP on 27 Oct 70 but handed over on 5 Nov 70. A former 24th SOW, USAFSO aircraft. First noted as T-510/CX-BJG at Aeroparque, Buenos Aires, Argentina, on 4 Jan 77. This aircraft was also converted to a gunship with one .50 calibre machine gun c.Nov 79. Final flight on 22 Apr 80. Officially stricken by Orden 1997 dated 20 May 81. Noted withdrawn from use by Nov 82. She was displayed marked as T-510/CX-BJG at the 75th Anniversary of the FAU 17 Mar 88 – but with the wings of CX-BHP and was noted serving as a gate guard at Carrasco by 22 Nov 90. This aircraft was reported in an all-white colour scheme with FAU titles at Carrasco on 4 Dec 98. She is now displayed at Brigada Aérea I at Carrasco, Canelones, in rather casually applied markings.
511 (1) G4-511 G3-511(?)	42-100838	C-47A-75-DL	19301	ARP. The earliest US document linking this aircraft to Uruguay is dated 12 Jan 49. She was granted permission to overfly US territory, marked as G4-511, on 16 Feb 50, the earliest known report, although she was not officially taken on charge until 11 Apr 50. By 31 Aug 50, however, she was reportedly marked as G3-511 and was one of three C-47s accompanying the new Uruguayan P-51Ds home, but as the accompanying photo proves, she actually retained marks G4-511 at that time. She was refurbished in Dallas, Texas, in 1955–56. This aircraft was still current as of 31 Oct 57, although she had suffered an accident on 26 Oct 57 at Arapey, Salto, when she was obliged to make a forced landing with officials on board due to engine failure. She overflew Brazilian territory in Nov 59 and visited São Paulo-Congonhas airport, Brazil, on 16 Apr 74 (in company with FAU-508) and noted only marked as FAU-511 at the time. Officially stricken on 26 Jun 70.
511 (2) CX-BJH	45-1111 0-5111	C-47B-50-DK C-47D	17114/34381	MAP on 27 Sep 70 ex-24th SOW, USAFSO, but officially handed over between 5 and 9 Nov 70. Collided with a PLUNA aircraft at Carrasco on 15 May 71 during severe weather but was repaired. Another exceptionally long-serving C-47 with very extensive service in Latin America commencing in May 1946 (see Chapter 1). This aircraft crashed on 10 Feb 78 at Artigas as noted in the narrative. Officially stricken by Orden 1817 dated 28 Aug 78 with 16,828 hours total time.
512 G4-512	43-48131 0-48131	C-47A-30-DK	13947/25392	MAP on 22 Nov 60 but officially taken up on 29 Nov 60. Assigned to Grupo 3 on 6 Apr 70. Officially stricken on 16 Jul 74 with 10,825 hours total time and her fuselage passed to the Batallón 14 de Paracadistas of the Ejército Nacional near Toledo, Canelones, which painted it in a spurious camouflage scheme – the only Uruguayan C-47 to be so treated.

This C-47A-70-DL, the former 42-100768, became FAU-521 following MAP delivery in July 1963. She eventually was remarked as T-521/CX-BHR and her nose section is now preserved at the Museo Aeronáutico in Montevideo.
Nery Mendiburu via Dr. Gary Kuhn

This C-47D, FAU-522 was an exception to the usual high degree of FAU maintenance when seen at Paysandú in November 1966, following her March 1965 MAP delivery. She still has traces of her former USAF titles on her nose and her previous USAF serial just visible on her vertical fin.
Nery Mendiburu via Eduardo Luzardo

FAU-522 following her landing accident at Rivera on 29 July 1967, following which she was stricken with only 1,337 hours service in Uruguay. This rather weary aircraft had actually been in Latin America exclusively since 1946! Note the very prominent shadow of her former USAF titles and the erosion of her white upper decking. *FAU via Eduardo Luzardo*

This view of FAU-522 reveals the shadows of her former abbreviated USAF seral '0-48472' on her vertical fin. Although the damage does not appear overly severe, apparently that to the undercarriage and engine mounts proved beyond local repair capabilities. This was the first of two aircraft to bear the serial FAU-522. *7_DSV_FAU via Eduardo Luzardo*

The port wing of the second FAU-522, the former PLUNA CX-AFE, clearly establishes her lineage – and the fact that her port upper wing national insignia had, for some reason, been painted on rather far inboard. Note DC-3 FAU-523 in the background, also a former PLUNA aircraft, CX-AQC. *5_DSV_FAU via Eduardo Luzardo*

Clearly marked as FAU-522, this is the second aircraft to bear this serial, the former PLUNA CX-AFE acquired in May 1971. She is seen here following an accident at BA1 on 7 April 1972. *4_DSV_FAU via Eduardo Luzardo*

The former PLUNA DC-3 CX-AQC MSN 9226 became FAU-523 and, eventually, was coded T-523/CX-AQC, as seen here. Seen in 1981, she bears a caricature Dino of the animated cartoon *The Flintstones*, known as *Los Picapiedras* in Uruguay, on her nose and her engine cowlings have been painted aqua blue. *Eduardo Luzardo*

A close-up of the Dino emblem associated with the Grupo Avn. No. 3 painted on the ribbon beneath it and, under that, in black, the titles 'Uruguay'. *via Eduardo Luzardo*

513 G4-513 G3-513	43-15151	C-47A-80-DL	19617	MAP on 22 Nov 60 officially taken up on 29 Nov 60. Serial changed with assignment to G3-513 on 7 Jan 63 when assigned to Grupo 3. Withdrawn from use due to severe corrosion in 1963!
514 G4-514 G3-514 T-514/ CX-BKH	43-16138 0-16138	C-47B-1-DL C-47D	20604	MAP on 7 Sep 61. Initially assigned to Grupo 4 on 7 Sep 61. Reassigned to Grupo 3 on 7 Jan 63. She suffered a landing accident on 3 Mar 67 at Carrasco due to pilot error but was repaired. By 15 Mar 69, in addition to the famous caricature of the 'Tortuga', this aircraft was also named '23 de Octubre' on her nose. This aircraft visited Rio de Janeiro-Galeão, Brazil, as simply FAU-514 on 11 Nov 73. Converted to a gunship around Nov 79 by installation of one .50 calibre machine gun. Last reported airworthy in Dec 04 but also reported deployed as a 'decoy' as early as 10 Dec 95. However, she was reported in an all-white colour scheme at Carrasco, with FAU titles, on 4 Dec 98. This was the final airworthy FAU C-47 and was, during her final period of service, referred to as El Veterano, with her last flight on 27 May 88. She is preserved at BA1.
515 G4-515	44-76438 0-76438	TC-47B-25-DK TC-47D C-47D	16022/32770	MAP on 6 Dec 61. Reassigned to Grupo 3 on 6 Apr 70. Last reported on 10 Sep 72. Officially stricken by Orden 1997 dated 20 May 81.
516 G4-516 T-516/ CX-BHP	43-48347 KJ824 RNAF X-15/ ZU-15	C-47B-1-DK Dakota IV	14163/25608	MAP Grant Aid on 6 Apr 62. A MAP redeployment from the Netherlands, most documents record the delivery as 31 Aug 62, which may account for a period of rehabilitation by OGMA in Portugal before actual delivery to Uruguay. Reassigned to Grupo 3 on 6 Apr 70. Joint TAMU marks T-516 and CX-BHP were taken up on 29 Jul 70. Officially stricken by Orden 1997 dated 20 May 81 with 9,539 hours total time. This aircraft had been withdrawn from use by Nov 82. Confusingly, however, T-510/CX-BJG on display at Carrasco has 'CX-BHP' painted under her port wing!
517 G4-517 G3-517 T-517	44-77079 KN696 RNAF X-17/ ZU-17 44-77079	C-47B-35-DK Dakota IV	16663/33411	MAP Grant Aid on 6 Apr 62. A MAP redeployment from the Netherlands, most documents record the delivery as 31 Aug 62, which may account for a period of rehabilitation by OGMA in Portugal before actual delivery to Uruguay. Transferred to Grupo 3 on 7 Jan 63. Made her final flight on 7 Jun 74. Officially stricken by Orden No. 1748 on 22 Jun 77.

A fine study of the last FAU DC-3, T-524/CX-AIJ MSN 4471 – the oldest variant used by the service taken after her acquisition in mid-1971. She suffered a ground accident at BA1 on 17 October 1982 and was withdrawn from use. Her conversion from C-47-DL configuration was carried out in a non-standard fashion and when seen was unusual in having been fitted with a weather radar in her nose. *Airline Photos #865*

During 1978, engineers of the FAU installed a radar nose on T-524 with the titles, most unusual for a Latin American military C-47, 'Equipado con radar' on her nose. It is believed the installation was made to provide the service with a limited sea-search capability. *via Eduardo Luzardo*

Believed to have been taken incident to her final flight, this is T-524/CX-AIJ on final approach to BA1. Note that she wears no national insignia or service acronym under her starboard wing and that her rudder stripes are severely eroded. *Gustavo Figueroa via Eduardo Luzardo*

518 G4-518	43-48722 0-48722	C-47B-5-DK C-47D	14538/25983	Apparently acquired via FMS at Davis-Monthan AFB, AZ, on 19 Dec 62 with 14,221 hours total time already on the clock. Reassigned to Grupo 3 on 6 Apr 70 but, with total time at 16,853 was probably not flown subsequently. Last reported in 1972. Officially stricken on 16 Jul 74.
519 G4-519 T-519/ CX-BHQ	44-77099 KP217 0-4099	C-47B-35-DK Dakota IV C-47D	16683/33431	Apparently acquired via FMS/Fairchild on 19 Dec 62. Reassigned to Grupo 3 on 6 Apr 70. Assumed joint marks T-519/CX-BHQ with TAMU on 29 Jul 70. She suffered a taxiing accident on 17 Apr 71 when she struck FAU-512 due to human error and was repaired. Last reported in 1980. However, officially stricken from the inventory by Orden No. 1748 on 22 Jun 77.
520 G3-520	43-49362 0-349362	C-47B-16-DK C-47D VC-47D	15178/26623	MAP on 31 May 63. Some FAU records cite the identity of this aircraft as 43-49363, however. Assigned to Grupo 3 on 20 Jun 63. She suffered a landing accident on 29 Aug 69 at BA1 Carrasco due to human error but was repaired. Officially stricken on 16 Jul 74 with 12,607 hours total time. Noted derelict at Carrasco by May 80.
521 G3-521 T-521/ CX-BHR	42-100768	C-47A-70-DL	19231	MAP on 17 Jul 63 and assigned to Grupo 3. Experienced a ground accident while on the ramp at Carrasco on 12 Oct 69 due to human error but was repaired. Assumed joint TAMU marks T-521 and CX-BHR on 29 Jul 70. Made her final flight on 4 Jul 79. Officially stricken by Orden 1997 on 20 May 81. The cockpit and cabin section of this aircraft is now preserved in the custody of the Museo Aeronáutico.
522 (1) G3-522	43-48472 0-48472 48472	C-47B-1-DK C-47D	14288/25733	MAP in Mar 65 but not handed over until 2 Apr 65, although yet another report gives the date as 6 Sep 65! This aircraft had extensive service in Latin America, commencing as early as Nov 46 (see Chapter 1). She was lost in an accident on 29 Jul 67 at the Rivera airport when she landed with excessive speed. She had amassed only 1337 hours in FAU service. She was officially stricken on 30 Jan 68.
522 (2)	44-76219 CX-AFE	C-47B-28-DK	15803/32551	Originally acquired at the Miami FLC Centre for PLUNA. Transferred from PLUNA to the Grupo 3 of the FAU on 19 May 71. Often cited in error as FAU-509 (2). Suffered an accident on 7 Apr 72 at BA1 (Carrasco) when she hit personnel on the ground due to human error and was repaired. Officially stricken on 16 Jul 74. Remains noted at Carrasco by May 80.
523 T-523/ CX-AQC	42-23364 NC-79023 CX-AQC	C-47A-5-DL DC-3	9226	Originally acquired by PLUNA in Nov 55 as CX-AQC transferred to the FAU on 19 May 71. Final flight on 30 Mar 82. However, she was damaged on 17 Aug 82 at Carrasco while stationary due to human error. Officially stricken on 16 Jul 86.
524 T-524/CX-AIJ	41-18409 NC-54206 CX-AIJ	C-47-DL DC-3	4471	Originally acquired by PLUNA in Apr 47. Passed to the FAU between 19 May 71 and 25 Jun 71. Had weather radar installed c.Nov 77, accounting for her unusual nose. Final flight on 14 Jun 82. Noted withdrawn from use by Nov 82 following a ground accident at Carrasco on 17 Oct 82. Officially stricken from the inventory by Orden CGTA 2602 on 16 Jul 86.

Rarely photographed 'in the field,' this is USAF Mission to Uruguay VC-47D '0-48275', which served the Mission intermittently from December 1952 to as late as July 1968. She passed to an unidentified MAP recipient on 27 October 1970. *Germán Perez via Eduardo Luzardo*

CHAPTER TWENTY-ONE

Venezuela

COMPLETELY WITHIN THE TROPICS and the sixth largest nation in Latin America, Venezuela can be generally said to not be as defined by geography as many of her neighbours.

As, until fairly recently, the world's third largest oil exporter, the country and her armed forces have, since the wells started producing in the late 1930s, benefited enormously from the associated revenues, although the general populous, not so much. Ironically, much of this largesse has been directed towards development of the best and most comprehensive highway network in all of Latin America, although large sections of the hinterland still remain without effective surface communications.

Venezuelan military aviation got a late start compared to other major Latin American nations and through the 1930s was very much an instrument of the ruling tyrant, Vicente Gómez, one of the bloodiest dictators in Venezuelan history. His reign persisted until 1935, although, ironically, the relative stability that his rule visited upon the country can arguably be said to have resulted in the exploitation of the country's vast oil resources and laid down the basis for all that followed.

Gómez was followed by a series of progressive, if not democratic, presidents, but in 1945, a military coup placed the leftist Acción Democrática party in power under Rómulo Betancourt, and it was shortly thereafter that Venezuela's armed forces, especially her air arm, which had benefited modestly from Second World War Lend-Lease, finally emerged from the hodge-podge of its first twenty-five years of existence operating a mix of French, Italian and US aircraft and finally launched on the path towards professionalism and modernisation.

By the late 1940s the oil revenues had revolutionised the economy and the military government of Coronel Marcos Pérez Jiménez sought to ensure the continuing loyalty of the armed forces with lavish defence spending, and Venezuelan military aviation – and, indeed, the entire country – entered into what many now regard as the 'golden age' of modern Venezuela.

The first US Air Mission arrived on 4 April 1944 to find that, prior to their arrival, most Venezuelan pilots had not been permitted to make-cross country flights unless accompanied by at least one senior officer – a hold-over from the very strict constraints of the Gómez regime. The Mission was also surprised to learn that, so far as they could determine, no Venezuelan cadet pilot had ever been 'washed out' for lack of flying ability – and they promptly recommended cutting six. The Chief of the Mission commented that, 'this is the first time that any pilots have been eliminated and it has caused the others to be a little more on their toes. Being something of a "family affair" in this Air Force, in the past the only system of elimination had been for a pilot to kill himself – whereupon he was immediately eulogised.'

Although preserved until recently in very good condition at the FAV Museo Aeronáutico at Maracay marked as the first Venezuelan military C-47, '4AT1', this aircraft is almost certainly a former Venezuelan governmental C-47 that never served a day with the service. The markings as worn are a curious mix of accuracy and supposition. Among other things, the national insignia on the fuselage is too small, as is the seldom-seen unit badge on the nose. *Coronel (Av) Luis H. Paredes*

The earliest known photo of a genuine Venezuelan military C-47, 5-A-T-1 (with the first numeral, '5' for some reason scrubbed off) bears the 1940s-style 'wingless' national insignia in all four wing positions. She was one of the first batch of ARP-supplied aircraft. *Jesus A. Aveledo*

An unusual obstacle to early US Mission objectives in what was, by any standard, an oil-rich country, soon manifested itself. The Mission had started a programme to provide refresher training to all accredited pilots – including a number who had, significantly, gained multi-engine experience flying as first officers on Linea Aérea Venezolana (LAV) routes in Lockheed Model 10s – and a schedule of flying time was established. However, when everything was in readiness, it was found that an acute fuel shortage would preclude more than 50 per cent of the schedule. Incredibly, crude oil was shipped by surface vessel to the island of Curacao for refining, shipped back to Puerto Cabello – and then transported to the interior by truck.

Until 22 May 1944, Venezuelan service aviation had been officially known as the Aviación Militar Venezolana (AMV, although it had also been known as the Aviación Militar Nacional briefly) but was then renamed as the Servicio de Aeronáutica but, via Decree No. 85 of 10 December 1945, was renamed as the Fuerza Aérea Venezolana (FAV).

So far as can be determined, the first known instance of Venezuelan interest in acquiring C-47s was associated with Lend-Lease Requisition VZ-168, which was staffed to cover two 'used' C-47s by the Munitions Assignment Board (Air) on 25 June 1945. However, this requisition was apparently shelved at the direct request of the US State Department, the file having been marked as 'Pending' repeatedly, and with the end of hostilities, was not acted upon.

Following on its Lend-Lease allotment, Venezuela became eligible for the Interim Program of the American Republics Project (ARP) and, by 8 February 1946, was slated to receive a total of thirty-five aircraft of all types, including fifteen Republic P-47D Thunderbolts, its first truly modern fighters, four North American B-25Js, five Beech AT-11s, one UC-45F – and no fewer than ten C-47s.

By 8 May 1946, the initial allotment had been changed, with the number of P-47Ds dropping – for the time being – to just six – but now with six AT-11s, no UC-45, six North American AT-6s, just three B-25Js, but adding six Boeing-Stearman PT-17s. The number of C-47s projected for ARP assignment remained unchanged at ten, significantly the most numerous of all types offered. However, an ARP report dated 27 December 1946 showed a total of only six!

However, as the ARP programme evolved, on 12 September 1947, Venezuela was shown to be programmed for four C-47s on Project No. 94548S (also cited as Project No. 72013) – all of which were to be drawn from examples then in the custody of the Caribbean Air Command in Panama but with the added notation 'short two, with an estimated availability of 20 September 1947', which clearly reinforces the notion that a total of six were delivered.

The first actual Air Order of Battle citing C-47s as on strength, however, was that for 5 May 1948, which reflected a total of only four C-47s, with four others awaiting delivery in the US, implying that the number programmed had once again changed from ten, to six, to eight.

An evocative view of the early FAV apron and hangar devoted to the growing C-47 fleet. Unfortunately, the aircraft facing the camera is unknown – although she has an RDF 'bullet' atop her forward fuselage, but 2AT1 is in the immediate background, while the two beyond her are thus far unserialed. As there are also five B-25Js in the right background, these are probably ARP deliveries circa the late 1940s. *via Hélio Higuchi*

The 'old' escorting the 'new', with 6AT1 and 6AT11 flanking the second Fairchild C-123B, 4CT2, dating this image to around the autumn of 1958. *via Hélio Higuchi*

A US report entitled 'Status of Foreign Military Aid, Cumulative to 1 December 1948', however, noted once again that Venezuela had to that time acquired a total of ten C-47's!

Between November 1948 and September 1949, the FAV exercised its new fleet of C-47s intensively, successfully completing some 246 round trips to an astonishing number of internal missions all over the country, amassing in the process some 2,458:10 flight hours – by far the most ever flown in any comparable time span previously. In the course of these missions, the C-47s lifted some 269,609kg of assorted cargo and mail, and carried 6,439 passengers. What is less obvious was that, of this impressive set of accomplishments, it included the transport of large numbers of Army troops from Caracas to Maracaibo during the unrest that occurred around 1 December 1948.

On 3 May 1949, a new 'DC-3' for the FAV accompanied ten reconditioned North American AT-6D Standard aircraft heading south through Managua, Nicaragua, from the US. By 1 June 1949, the total on hand showed twelve but exactly a month later, on 1 July, the FAV Air Order of Battle reflected a total of thirteen C-47s on strength with the rather surprising notation that ten more were on order from a firm in the US, and this remained unchanged until 1 April 1950.

A new dimension was added to the Venezuelan armed forces in 1949 when, availing themselves of another capability for their C-47s, the Compañía de Paracaidistas was formally organised and constituted on 7 November. Having been flown intensively since delivery, it is no wonder that, by 1 June 1950, all thirteen C-47s on hand were in need of 5,000-hour overhauls.

By 4 October 1950, the FAV C-47 strength had reached thirteen aircraft, although where the three aircraft beyond the ten delivered under ARP originated is not clear. It seems likely that they were acquired from TACA de Venezuela when that organisation wrapped up around this time. However, of the thirteen on hand, no fewer than six were inoperative for one reason or another, but three more were

on order from commercial interests in the US Interestingly, all were assigned, as of this time, to a hybrid unit known as the Grupo Mixto de Bombardeo y Transporte No. 10 based at Boca del Río, Maracay, with, in addition to the C-47s, fourteen North American B-25Js, the presidential Douglas C-54 and a single Vultee BT-13. The unit had thirty officers and 111 enlisted ranks.

By 7 May 1951, the FAV transport force was stretching its wings and demonstrating its ability to fly its C-47 fleet to foreign destinations as well, making flights to Lima, Peru; Mexico City, Mexico; the Panama Canal Zone; Port-au-Prince, Haiti; Curacao; Quito, Ecuador and Bogota, Colombia. Significantly, the flights to Albrook AFB, Canal Zone, were all to transport FAV officers and NCOs to the USAF School for Latin America there, while most of the others were for diplomatic purposes.

As the C-47s were received, they were initially assigned two-digit serials (known are '20', which was supposedly current on 14 March 1949, and '21', but there must have been a period of transition, as a photo exists showing '20' next to '4-BT-1' at the same time) but at the urging of the US Mission, the service was reorganised and the aircraft were subsequently assigned to one of the two Escuadrillas, 'A' or 'B' of what was known by this time as the Escuadrón de Transporte T-1 (also seen as 'No.1' on some aircraft by the late 1950s), and were issued straightforward serial codes from '1' to '8', followed by an 'A' or 'B' then the unit designator, 'T-1' within each. Known codes, such as 1-AT-1, etc., are shown in the accompanying table. Initially, these codes were almost always painted on the aircraft with the hyphens in place, and there are at least two documented images showing the hyphens being more numerous, as '5-A-T-1' and '4-B-T-1'. Later, however, as some aircraft were repainted, the codes were painted on without them, leading to some confusion as, for example, 4-BT-1 subsequently appeared to be '4BTI'. Besides fourteen C-47s on strength with the unit as of 28 February 1952, the unit was also operating the presidential C-54 and a single Ryan Navion.

Part of the second increment of ARP-supplied C-47As and C-47Bs, 2BT1 was one of the first aircraft noted wearing the unit serial code without the earlier hyphens in this January 1964 image taken at Baltimore, Maryland. Note the tail of one of the Fairchild C-123Bs, also with 'old' style codes, at left. The C-47 retained its wartime 'gun' windows even at this late date, and her lower extremities were highly polished. *Dr Gary Kuhn*

This aircraft, seen at the Dutch Naval facility at Hato Field, Curacao on 8 June 1961, has clearly had an air stair-type modification made to her former forward cargo door, and bears an unidentified unit insignia on her nose, plus prominent Day-Glo panels. She had been centrally involved in the incident described in the narrative. *Jerry Casius*

The first known FAV C-47 loss occurred shortly before Christmas 1952, when an aircraft with twenty-six passengers aboard crashed on take-off at Boca del Río, Maracay, having lost an engine at a critical moment. Incredibly, everyone aboard survived. This loss reduced C-47 strength to twelve, suggesting that one other had somehow also departed the inventory by this time.

An unidentified FAV C-47 crashed on 12 July 1952 on a mountain near Los Teques while being commanded by Sub.Tte Ruperto Salazar, co-pilot Alférez Ciro Ramírez and Flight Engineer Sgto Técnico Julio C. 'El Chato' Salas.

By 14 May 1954, C-47 strength had increased to fourteen (comprising thirteen C-47As and one C-47B) with the arrival of two (of five) which had been acquired commercially in the US from Aerodex in Miami, with the other three to arrive by the end of June (2) and August (1), although the USAF Mission only rated twelve of them as 'combat ready', and with only ten qualified crews.

Much has been made over the years regarding the Military Assistance Program (MAP) and the collateral Mutual Defence Assistance Program (MDAP), and it has always been assumed that, like most Latin American nations, Venezuela was party to the benefits of these. However, as evidenced by the private purchase noted above

of five reconditioned C-47s from Aerodex in Miami, Venezuela preferred to go it alone and thus, as of January 1955, no mutual security agreement existed between Venezuela and the US. As a direct consequence, all aircraft and munitions acquisitions from the US were on a strictly reimbursable basis.

This stance, ironically, enabled Venezuela to engage her air arm and its aircraft as it saw fit, without US constraints commonly attached to MAP-supplied arms. This manifested itself around 6 January 1955, when at least seven FAV C-47s, flying in formation – possibly the largest such formation to ever make an international flight with the type in the region – conducted what was euphemistically referred to as a 'training' flight to Managua, Nicaragua, followed by a mass flight of five more on 10 January. Clearly ferrying arms to Somoza for one of his adventures, cited elsewhere in this volume, the USAF Air Attaché in Venezuela at the time was instructed to journey to Boca del Río Airbase on 14 January to ascertain the whereabouts of the FAV C-47 fleet. He found all eleven 'missing' on 7 January and four 'missing' on 14 January, although every other known FAV aircraft, including B-25Js and F-47Ds, were accounted for on both days. Reports that the aircraft were scrubbed free of Venezuelan national insignia and markings for these flights have escaped verification.

FAV DC-3s and C-47s, unlike many of their sister services elsewhere in Latin America, did not wear service titles on their usually white upper decking. This is believed to be 7-BT-1 and, in the extreme left background, the solitary FAV presidential C-54 can just be seen. Note also that by the time of this photo, the acronym 'FAV' was being worn on the lower port wing. Jesus A. Aveledo

Here is 7BT1 in a 29 June 1959 configuration bearing the seldom-seen unit emblem on her nose of the Escuadron de Transporte No. 1 while visiting Meacham Field at Fort Worth, Texas. Why the FAV decided to delete the hyphens from their unusual unit codes is unknown. *E.C. Manly via Brian R. Baker*

But that was not all. While clearly used to ferry arms to Nicaragua, several of the C-47s were apparently also used, staging from Managua, to carry out arms drops via parachute to Nicaraguan troops in the vicinity of Quesada, Costa Rica, on 11 and 12 January.

This semi-clandestine episode, which demonstrated the Venezuelan C-47 operating organisation's ability to complete a rather complicated mission, was reinforced by the comments of Maj. Vincent A. Braun, Assistant USAF Air Attaché, in his overall summary for the period 1 September 1954 to 31 August 1955. He said that 'probably the most well-trained and most effective unit of the air force in accomplishing their assigned mission is the Transport Squadron T-1. This unit is the most active in the air force and has become quite efficient in troop transport and paratroop drops.' In retrospect, this extraordinary use of the Venezuelan C-47 fleet may, in the view of a number of historians close to the subject, have had an unintended consequence. If, as seems likely, the aircraft were indeed 'sanitised' of their national insignia, titles and serial codes during this operation, this may have been the juncture at which their previous identities became so murky as to become impossible to reconcile.

FAV C-47 strength had grown by around December 1956, when a total of eighteen were on the inventory (although only fourteen were 'combat ready'), some of these almost certainly acquired from civil airlines in the country, although this had decreased to fourteen again by 1 June 1958.

The FAV sent two of its C-47s on an urgent mission to Mobile, Alabama, in the US on 20 June 1957 to take delivery of a quantity of ammunition to be used in a massive fire power demonstration, the Semana de la Patría (Independence Week) celebrations to be held the following month.

Modernisation finally came with the eighteen Fairchild C-123Bs delivered between February and July 1958, immediately following the abortive revolt by Army and FAV units of 1 January, in which the solitary involvement of the FAV's C-47 fleet consisted of two aircraft making repeated, low-level passes over Caracas starting at about 1100hrs. While not exactly terrifying, it achieved the anticipated psychological impact with the props in coarse pitch. The FAV decided to split Escuadrón de Transporte T-1 between the new aircraft and its existing C-47s, with the C-47s (and the single C-54) staying with T-1 while the C-123Bs went to a new T-2 – but with the predictable shift of most of the qualified pilots to the new aircraft. This resulted in the seldom recognised reality that, although the FAV now had more than thirty transports, it also had nearly twice as many aircraft as it had pilots to man them.

Surprisingly, following the receipt of all of the C-123Bs, the FAV almost immediately dispatched nine of the fifteen C-47s still in the inventory of T-1 to a contractor in Los Angeles, California, where they were to be completely overhauled – although it was suspected that this was merely to put them in good enough condition to be sold to help finance the C-123 purchase!

By July 1959, although fairly well equipped, the aftermath of the 1958 coup attempt was proving to be prolonged, with ripple effects in the command structure and stagnation at unit level, even though it resulted in the end of the dictatorship that had been in place since 1948. Following his overthrow, the country was ruled by a 'Civilian-Military Junta', followed by elections in December that brought Betancourt to the presidency. The subsequent stability brought conditions within the operating units back to some semblance of normality, which lasted until early 1960. But then, in April 1960 yet another, this time unsuccessful revolution, led by a retired FAV officer, accompanied by retired Army and Navy officers, once again set the FAV into turmoil, resulting in the FAV being put on more or less constant alert until December 1960.

FAV C-47 4-BT-1 (by 8 June 1961 marked as '4BTI') then gained dubious notoriety when she was being used to fly seven Venezuelan Army officers to Caracas to face court martial for their part in a failed coup attempt against President Betancourt. Somehow, they managed to overpower their armed guards during the flight and, in the process, the aircraft commander and flight engineer were wounded. They then compelled the co-pilot to fly them to the Dutch Naval Air Service facility at Hato Field, Curacao, where they hoped to gain political asylum.

After landing at Hato unannounced in the afternoon, the seven officers scrambled out of the aircraft and ran for the scrub alongside the ramp, and there was more shooting. As luck would have it, Dutch Marines were on a field exercise close to the airfield and managed to round up everyone. On 10 June, 4BTI was allowed to return to Venezuela. The seven officers were not granted asylum but, instead, were flown to Holland on a commercial KLM flight. After spending two months in quite comfortable accommodation at a hotel in Arnhem, and meanwhile having somehow been joined by their families, they were asked politely to leave the country and several of them fled to fascist Spain, where they joined a fairly large group of anti-Betancourt refugees already in residence.

The 'lowest' of the peculiar four-digit serials assigned to FAV aircraft starting in the early 1960s, FAV-0130 came down in a swamp and river area somewhere in the interior in 1967. It is not known if she was recovered. *via Nick J. Waters III*

The standard colour scheme for all of the FAV's C-47 fleet varied only slightly during most of the 1960s and '70s and the aircraft were, according to the USAF Mission, very well maintained. FAV-1162 was photographed at Miami some time prior to May 1968. *Air-Britain #72*

Sometime around 1965 or 1966, as the political situation once again stabilised, the FAV made a service-wide decision to reserial all of its aircraft, permanently dropping the previous system and replacing it with what were apparently completely random four-digit numbers, although the new series did not appear overnight. This has resulted in massive confusion for historians as, according to some FAV sources, apparently no effort was made to document previous FAV or other identities at the time. Indeed, the Venezuelan penchant for security has resulted in the fact that, despite the best efforts of your scribes and legions of native historians, not a solitary FAV C-47 has been definitively linked to an actual identity, the only such instance in this entire volume.

At the same time, monthly C-47 utilisation of the fifteen aircraft on hand had dropped to probably its lowest level at just seventeen hours per aircraft per month. However, as depressing as this might appear, it was still the highest in the FAV as, for example, the C-123Bs averaged only 11.25 hours while the important training fleet of

Hunting Jet Provosts and Beech T-34s only achieved 10.5 and 10.9 hours respectively. An FAV C-47 is known to have crashed in December 1966 when it hit a mountain in Tachira State, and four on board were all killed.

With attrition, FAV C-47 strength was fairly steady at fifteen aircraft as of December 1967, although first efforts were starting to dispose of the fleet as the far more capable Fairchild C-123Bs – and C-130s being forecast – assumed more and more of the domestic and foreign air transport missions. Peak FAV C-47 strength was probably reached between June 1968 and July 1969, by which time eighteen had been acquired in total, but of these, only fourteen were still active, the other four having been 'lost' to other causes.

By 1981, the few remaining C-47s on strength were all assigned to Escuadrón de Transporte 1, an element of the Grupo de Transporte 6[62] based at Base Aérea 'El Libertador' at Palo Negro, operating alongside Lockheed C-130Hs, but they were seldom flown and were finally phased out shortly thereafter.

In service as early as February 1967 as FAV-1250, this C-47A was transferred to civil marks with LAV in 1972, the reverse of the normal migration pattern. She is pictured here at Caracas in 1972 not long before the transition, her rudder markings appearing rather faded. *Paul Hayes*

A testament to the obvious pride that the service took in its fleet that visited foreign destinations, FAV-1544 was photographed gleaming at Howard Air Force Base, Canal Zone, in August 1969. She had been withdrawn from service by 1978. *Hagedorn*

FAV-1544 again, minus her engines, at Caracas on 10 October 1972, sitting amidst a bevy of LAV (Aeropostal) DC-3s and obviously at the centre of ground vehicle activity, it appears that the aircraft is being defuelled. Note that in this view, some three years after the preceding image of 1544, her serial numbers are much bolder, but her markings otherwise remain identical. *Derek Monk*

FAV Code	Previous Identity	Built As	MSN	Assignments and Notes
1-AT-1	43-48003	C-47A-30-DK	13819/25264	A Sixth Air Force veteran, this aircraft had been one of those positioned at Natal, Brazil, for deployment under the ARP Interim Program on 18 Sep 46. It was probably delivered from there to Venezuela on 25 Sep 46, although some sources cite it came from Kelly Field, TX. By Dec 72, it had passed to LAV as YV-C-ANQ.
2-AT-1	43-16129	C-47A-90-DK	20595	ARP assigned on 28 Aug 47. Was modified for aerial survey duties with the Cartografia Nacional. By Mar 72 had become YV-C-ANH with LAV.
3-AT-1	42-92105	C-47A-1-DK	11869	ARP assigned on 28 Aug 47 but did not depart the Canal Zone on delivery until 30 Sep 47.
4-AT-1 *4AT1*	42-93165	C-47A-20-DK	13046	ARP assigned on 22 Aug 47. Departed Kelly AFB, TX, on delivery on 13 Nov 47.
5-A-T-1 *5-AT-1*	42-24040	C-47A-40-DL	9902	ARP assigned on 5 Sep 47 but did not depart Kelly Field, TX, on delivery until 13 Nov 47. Reported in service in 1951 and noted with old-style roundel on her fuselage and the titles 'Ministerio de la Defensa' like 6-BT-1 noted elsewhere.
6-AT-1	42-24183	C-47A-50-DL	10045	ARP assigned on 5 Sep 47 but did not depart Kelly Field, TX, on delivery until 13 Nov 47. This aircraft was granted authority to overfly Brazilian territory in 1960. It was reportedly outfitted as a VIP transport, possibly accounting for the delay in delivery.
7-AT-1	42-92090	C-47A-DK	11852	ARP assigned on 22 Aug 47. Departed Kelly AFB, TX, on delivery on 13 Dec 47.
8-AT-1	42-23597	C-47A-30-DL	9459	A Sixth Air Force and 20th Troop Carrier Squadron veteran, this aircraft was delivered to Venezuela under ARP from Albrook Field, CZ, on 28 or 30 Aug 47, although the official handover date appears to have been 5 Dec 47.

As a USAF Air Policeman looks on, FAV personnel load C-47A FAV-1570 at Howard AFB, CZ, on 1 July 1968, with a number of Air Commando personnel in attendance as well. *Hagedorn*

In standard C-47A cargo configuration, FAV-1593 is marked identically to the other frequent Venezuelan visitors to USAF facilities in the Panama Canal Zone, when relations between the two countries were close and fraternal. Even the antenna arrangements on FAV C-47s were remarkably consistent. She was at Howard AFB on 10 May 1967 (co-author Hagedorn's twenty-first birthday!) when photographed. *Hagedorn*

Appearing at first glance to be virtually identical to the two previous C-47As, FAV-1660, upon close examination during her visit to Howard AFB on 17 March 1968, was found to have had a passenger-type air stair installed in place of her forward cargo door. She made a very spirited departure that day, apparently very lightly loaded. *Hagedorn*

1-BT-1	45-1129	C-47B-50-DK	17132/34399	Although initially assigned to the US Air Attaché in Caracas on 17 Jun 46, this aircraft was apparently made a part of the ARP package by 11 May 48. It suffered an accident on 9 Jan 48 at Maracay while being flown by one of the ARP Cadre, Frank P. Bender, but was apparently repaired. This aircraft was granted permission to overfly Brazilian national territory in 1958.
2-BT-1	42-100537	C-47A-65-DL	19000	ARP on 18 Dec 47. Last reported in Jan 64. Known to YV-C-ANS.
3-BT-1	*42-100605*	*C-47A-65-DL*	*19067*	ARP Project No. 94548 ex CAC 5 Sep 48.
4-BT-1 *4BT1*	–	DC-3 (conv)	–	In service by Dec 49 and as late as 8 Jun 61 when she was used to transport seven Venezuelan Army officers to Curacao after they had been arrested as conspirators in a failed Apr 60 coup. See main text.
5-BT-1	–	–	–	–
6-BT-1	–	–	–	Reported in service in 1951. This aircraft is known to have worn the old 'wingless' national roundel on its fuselage and the titles Ministerio de la Defensa early in its service life and was outfitted for VIP duties.
7-BT-1 *7BT1*	*41-18669* *NC-57667* N57667	*C-47-DL* DC-3	*6030*	Known to have been acquired by the FAV from the L.B. Smith Aircraft Corp. of Miami in Aug 54. Noted at Meacham Field, Fort Worth, TX, on 29 Jun 59 with unit insignia on her nose. Last reported on 4 Sep 60.
8-BT-1	*42-68760* NC-45381	*C-53D-DO* DC-3C-S1C3G	*11687*	MSN 11687 is known to have been sold to the FAV sometime after 27 Jun 52 and 8-BT-1 appears to be the best candidate, probably with a VIP interior. Noted in service in Jul 54 marked as '8-B-T-1'. This aircraft was granted authority to overfly Brazilian territory in 1960.

A little-known event late in the service lives of the FAV C-47 fleet, a number of the survivors were camouflaged using MAP-supplied, Vietnam-era three-tone shades – and, oddly, for the first time, full service titles, in black characters, along the fuselages. Fuselage insignia were dropped, however, in favour of small Venezuelan flags, just as on combat aircraft such as Canberras and Mirage series aircraft. This, FAV-1840, was almost certainly the last airworthy operational FAV C-47 when photographed in November 2000. Note the blade antenna atop the forward fuselage, also unusual in the fleet. *API*

Arriving with a group of FAV officers to attend a special meeting at Albrook AFB, CZ, on 7 May 1968, FAV-1923 had VIP-style interior passenger fittings, but her access door was hinged, the aft section having been faired over. She was also unusual in having a light blue nose cone rather than flat black. *Hagedorn*

0030	–	–	–	–
0130	–	–	–	Reportedly crashed into a river in 1967.
0131	–	–	–	Crashed while landing and ran into a river sometime between Oct and Dec 67.
1023	–	–	–	Current in Oct 78.
1127	–	–	–	Noted at Howard AFB, CZ, in Aug 66 and as late as 1973.
1162	–	–	–	Noted at Howard AFB, CZ, on 30 May 68.
1250	–	–	–	Noted at Howard AFB, CZ, in Feb 67. Transferred to civil marks with LAV in 1972.
1311	–	–	–	Transferred to civil marks with LAV in 1972.
1330	–	–	–	Noted in service at Caracas on 2 Jan 74.
1544	–	–	–	In service at Caracas on 10 Oct 72, 28 Oct 73 and 2 Jan 74. Noted withdrawn from use by 1978.
1547	–	–	–	Current in Oct 78?
1570	–	–	–	Noted at Howard AFB, CZ, on 1 Jul 68.
1593	–	–	–	Noted at Howard AFB, CZ, in May 67.
1633	–	–	–	Transferred to civil marks with LAV in 1972.
1660	–	DC-3	–	Noted at Howard AFB, CZ, on 17 Mar 68. Noted withdrawn from use at BA 'El Libertador', Palo Negro, Aragua, by Jan 91.
1840	–	–	–	Noted in Hangar No. 2 at BA 'El Libertador' in Apr 98 being restored to flight condition and camouflaged in Vietnam-era colours, almost certainly the last airworthy FAV C-47.
1923	–	DC-3	–	Noted at Howard AFB, CZ, on 5 May 68 and current on 12 Jul 76. Reportedly last operated by the FAV's Escuadrón Legendario.
2111	–	–	–	–
2122	–	–	–	–
2315	–	–	–	Noted at Howard AFB, CZ.
2458	–	–	–	Being processed for disposal between Jul and Dec 67.
4984	–	–	–	Preserved at the Museo de la FAV at Maracay and by Jan 91 believed originally coded 4AT1 there.
5984?	–	C-53	–	Reported at the Museo de la FAV at Maracay by Jan 91 but may be a spotting error for 4984 above.

Although nominally the final airworthy FAV C-47 at the time she was seen here, FAV-1923 once again had by this time added service titles on the upper decking and a large numeral '4' aft of the fuselage national insignia, denoting her as the fourth aircraft in the special Escuadrón Legendario, having long since been withdrawn from unit service. Note her exceptionally highly polished engine cowling and the fact that her lower extremities by this time had been painted light grey, USAF-style. *Jesus A. Aveledo*

Although FAV-2122 was one of the 'highest' of the random number serials spotted in FAV service, she was also one of the first observed, lending credence to the total lack of chronological significance of these numbers. She is otherwise in typical markings. *Jesus A. Aveledo*

Believed to have been the first Venezuelan Navy C-47, ARV-12 sports an airline-style cheatline and curtained windows, suggesting VIP intentions. She also has a larger than normal skylight over the aft lavatory. The 'wings' on the national insignia are more abbreviated than seen on Air Force aircraft. *Stephen P. Peltz via George G.J. Kamp*

Apparently a very early C-47, FAV-4984 was the 'highest' random number serial known assigned to a Venezuelan C-47, but is believed to be a completely spurious number, this aircraft subsequently being refurbished and repainted as '4AT1' – the first aircraft illustrated in this chapter at the FAV museum at Maracay. As seen here around February 1981, her two middle cabin windows had at one time been enlarged downwards, then blacked off entirely, and a large, vertically rectangular patch of some sort can be seen on the forward fuselage, just aft of a ventilation intake. Her underwing starboard national insignia is too small, incorrectly positioned, and much too far inboard as well. *Dr Roberto Gentilli*

Venezuelan Navy

Although Venezuela experimented with a small naval aviation element in the 1920s and '30s, it was not until the late 1970s that a concerted effort was launched to create a small air arm to support the modest service.

A second attempt was noted around December 1945, probably aided by the arrival of a small US Navy Mission, but this came to nothing, as the 'free' aircraft hoped for could not be organised.

Since the Navy could not demonstrate any obvious internal security role, important to often tenuous ruling entities, budgetary support for a naval air arm had to be absorbed from internal redirection of existing funds.

With a Marine establishment in excess of two understrength battalions, the Navy did, however, play a major part in the coup that finally toppled dictator Pérez Jiménez in 1958 and, almost certainly as a direct consequence, a third battalion was authorised, as well as

rather ambitious negotiations the preceding year to acquire a surplus, 25,000-ton British aircraft carrier.

In the early 1960s, the first aircraft were actually acquired and, by 1974, had achieved sufficient stability to be designated as the Servicio de Aviación Naval Venezolana.

Although mainly acquiring rotary-wing aircraft to be operated between bases and aboard surface vessels, by 1984 the Navy had about twenty-six aircraft of all types, including a dedicated transport unit known as Escuadrón TR-02. Besides other types, this unit operated at least three known DC-3s from early on, almost certainly former LAV civil examples, and the last two of these were finally retired around the end of 1982.

Very little is known about these aircraft, and our table includes details thus far confirmed.

Either a C-53D or DC-3C, the second known Navy aircraft was coded ARV-14. Her parallel blade antennas atop the fuselage are noteworthy, as is the RDF 'bullet' located ventrally under the nose and the service insignia on her port nose. Besides a red (or Day-Glo?) nose cone, she also has the same colour on her prop tips, wing tips and horizontal tail surface tips. *Paul Hayes*

Something of a mystery aircraft, Navy C-47B TR-0102 is not believed to have any relationship to the other two known aircraft, ARV-12 or ARV-14. In this view, taken prior to March 1982, her service titles are painted far aft on the fuselage and her partial code, '0102' is repeated on her nose, and her lower extremities are painted light grey. The blade antenna atop the fuselage and absence of an astrodome are also noteworthy. *via George G.J. Kamp*

ARV Serial Code	Previous Identity	Built As	MSN	Assignments and Notes
ARV 12				Reportedly acquired in 1964 and in service by 1968. Withdrawn from use by Feb 83. Reportedly to TR-0102 (see below) but not confirmed.
ARV 14	*42-23530* *NC-86598* *N91233* *N153A*	*C-47A-5-DL* *DC-3*	*9392*	Believed in service as early as 1972. Withdrawn from use by Feb 83. To YV-2183P?
TR-0102	43-48017 KG734 YS-36 TI-119 YV-AZC YV-C-AZC ARV-12?	C-47A-30-DK Dakota III DC-3C-S1C3G	13833/25278	Acquired ex-LAV after Jan 58 and noted in service *c.*Oct 78. To YV-2184P and YV-147C by Nov 98.
TR-0202				Reportedly acquired 1967. Withdrawn from use by 1981.

ARV-14 again under way at a coastal airfield. So far as can be determined, she wore no wing insignia whatsoever.
Guido E. Buehlmann #25360 via Roger Eberle

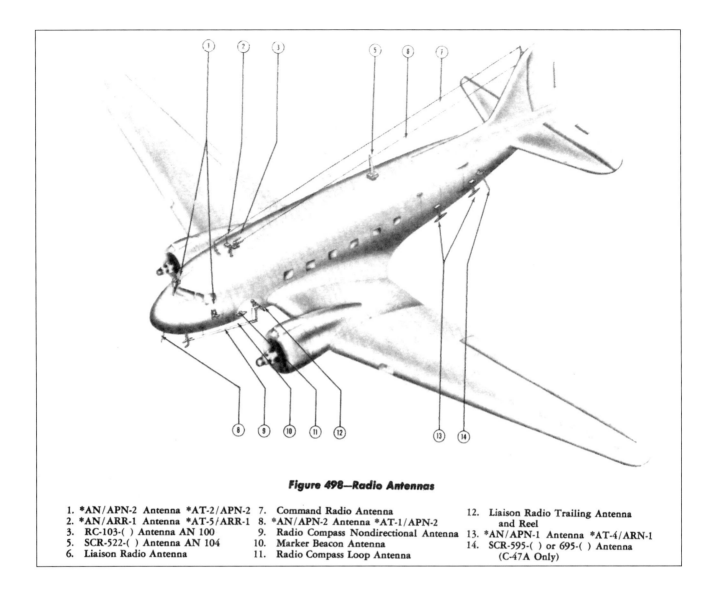

Figure 498—Radio Antennas

1. *AN/APN-2 Antenna *AT-2/APN-2
2. *AN/ARR-1 Antenna *AT-5/ARR-1
3. RC-103-( ) Antenna AN 100
5. SCR-522-( ) Antenna AN 104
6. Liaison Radio Antenna

7. Command Radio Antenna
8. *AN/APN-2 Antenna *AT-1/APN-2
9. Radio Compass Nondirectional Antenna
10. Marker Beacon Antenna
11. Radio Compass Loop Antenna

12. Liaison Radio Trailing Antenna
    and Reel
13. *AN/APN-1 Antenna *AT-4/ARN-1
14. SCR-595-( ) or 695-( ) Antenna
    (C-47A Only)

Appendix

THROUGHOUT THIS VOLUME, particularly in the tables we have appended to the end of each country chapter, we have undertaken to annotate, to the best of our ability, the evolutionary designations of each individual aircraft.

While we recognise that, in a great number of instances, these designations (or lack thereof) may in fact be arbitrary in the minds of some readers, we concluded early on that it was incumbent upon us to make the attempt.

From the time that all of these aircraft were originally built by Douglas, the original customers, whether the wartime USAAF, US Navy, British Commonwealth, or original commercial operators, found it necessary to assign very specific designations to each and every aircraft.

This drawing shows the locations of most of the antennas for radio gear installed on factory new C-47-DL, C-47A and some C-47B aircraft – some of which in fact carried over to post-war C-47D aircraft. Note that of these, the only one specific to just one variant, the C-47A, was number 14, the SCR-595 or SCR-695 Antenna on the extreme rear lower port fuselage. USAF T.O. AN 01-40NC-2 revised to 9 January 1950

These designations aided the initial maintainers and operators in understanding what to expect in the way of standard, factory-fresh equipment, accessories, engines, radios and other ancillary gear on each aircraft.

One of the most frequently asked questions regarding the C-47 family is how one differentiates between the denoted variants. The USAAF, in particular, went to considerable lengths to define these and, for the convenience of readers, they are summarised here.

C-47-DL – Was the first major 'block', and the first fully militarised version of the corporate DST/DC-3 family that had preceded it. These were built, initially, with two 1,200hp Pratt & Whitney R-1830-92 engines and differed principally from the generally similar DC-3A in incorporating a number of modifications to adapt the design for military cargos of a very wide variety.

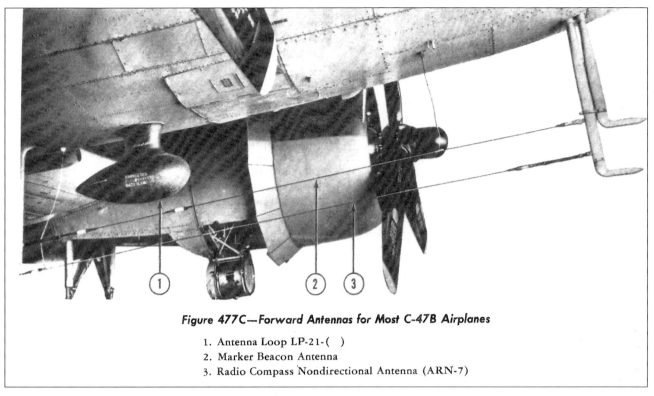

Figure 477C—Forward Antennas for Most C-47B Airplanes

1. Antenna Loop LP-21-( )
2. Marker Beacon Antenna
3. Radio Compass Nondirectional Antenna (ARN-7)

This view shows the 'Antenna Loop LP-21-()' which we have usually described in our captions as an 'RDF Bullet', common on *most* C-47B aircraft as delivered. The other two, the marker Beacon Antenna and the Radio Compass Nondirectional Antenna (ARN-7), differed from those on C-47-DLs and C-47As only upon very close examination! *USAF T.O. AN 01-40NC-2 revised to 29 June 1950*

This included, in most of the C-47-DLs, the distinctive two-panel cargo door on the port side, which featured a forward, standard door and a reinforced strengthened fuselage floor with tie-downs. Not usually noted, and visually impossible to detect, the C-47-DLs had a 6in greater span than the DC-3A and the fuel tank arrangement differed, with a total capacity of only 804 US gallons, as opposed to the DC-3A's 822. A total of 965 C-47-DLs were built, and the first rolled out in November 1941, before Pearl Harbor, which comes as a surprise to many, although she was not in fact handed over to what was till the USAAC until 23 December.

C-47A-DL and C-47A-DK – The C-47A series was, by far, the most prolific version of the entire family, with no fewer than 2,954 built in Long Beach, California (the C-47A-DLs), and 2,299 in the Douglas plant in distant Oklahoma City, Oklahoma (the C-47A-DKs). Together, they accounted for nearly 50 per cent of the entire Douglas production of the DSTs, DC-3s and military and naval versions. It seems odd, in retrospect, that the USAAC/USAAF saw fit to issue the 'A' suffix to these aircraft, as their differences from the earlier C-47-DLs were relatively minor, that being the fitting of a 24-volt instead of a 12-volt electrical system that noticeably improved cabin heating. There were many post-war modifications, including SC-47As, HC-47As, VC-47As, etc.

C-47B-DL and C-47B-DK – Once again, the USAAFs decision to issue a new suffix letter seems odd in retrospect, as the major difference between these aircraft and the C-47As was in the fact that they were powered by two 1,200hp Pratt & Whitney R-1830-90Cs, which featured two-stage blowers and further improved cabin heating systems. These were specifically altered for the demands of the China Burma India (CBI) theatre and high-altitude flight over the 'Hump'. Ironically, the actual performance of these engines proved disappointing and a very large number of them that survived the war into USAF and MDAP/MAP service were modified to become C-47Ds by the simple

expedient of deleting the blower. A total of 300 C-47B-DLs were built but a very respectable 2,932 C-47B-DKs. The last production aircraft, in fact, was 45-1139, a C-47B-50-DK.

C-47D – As noted, this designation was arrived at by the modification of the engine blowers of many C-47Bs although, oddly, a few C-47As were also redesignated post-war to C-47Ds as well. There were many variations on this designation, including a surprising number of VC-47Ds, RC-47Ds, SC-47Ds, TC-47Ds and HC-47Ds to name just a few.

C-53 – While the C-47s were intended from the outset to be cargo haulers, the C-53 series were built specifically as troop transports and, while popular in the post-war surplus market because of their relatively simple conversion to passenger aircraft, were a decided minority in Latin American military service, the majority of which were built originally as 'straight' C-53s or C-53Ds.

While it is true that the significance of some of the 'Block Numbers' that were interspersed in the C-47A and C-47B series during the war, and associated nomenclature, the significance of these quickly broke down or were modified at Depot, Numbered Overseas Air Force level or via the inevitable flurry of Change Orders and Technical Directives that followed, they nonetheless largely served their purposes. These are too technical for our purposes here, and mainly involved relatively minor internal equipment or instrument/radio equipment changes.

Post-war, however, as large numbers of aircraft became available for surplus – or for continued operation by major powers – the more or less rigid wartime guidelines inevitably started to become, in truth, increasingly irrelevant: a DC-3 was a DC-3 and a C-47 was a C-47, or so some maintain. Frankly, none of the Latin American recipients appear to have been concerned with these distinctions in the slightest, other than when it came time to hazard the MAP spares and supplies system, at which point the significance became all too apparent!

Figure 501P—Forward Antennas for Very Late C-47B Airplanes

1. MN-26-C Loop Antenna, Manual Radio Compass
2. Antenna (Transmitting), AN/APN-1 Radio Altimeter
3. Antenna (Transmitting), AN/APN-2 Navigator's Radar
4. Antenna (Receiving), AN/APN-2 Navigator's Radar
5. Antenna, Marker Beacon
6. Sense Antenna, Manual Radio Compass
7. Antenna, ARN-7 Automatic Radio Compass
8. LP-21-( ) Loop Antenna, Automatic Radio Compass
9. AN-104-B Antenna, V.H.F. Command Radio
10. Antenna (Receiving), AN/APN-1 Radio Altimeter

Above: This image shows the very distinctive ventral nose MN-26-C Loop Antenna, Manual Radio Compass and other antennas found only on very late production C-47Bs, examples of which are found in a number of our illustrations. *USAF T.O. AN 01-40NC-2 revised to 15 January 1946*

Right: Although only a very few Latin American military C-47s were ever fitted with skis, the arrangement used is shown in these detailed illustrations. *USAF T.O. AN 01-40NC-2 revised to 20 February 1948*

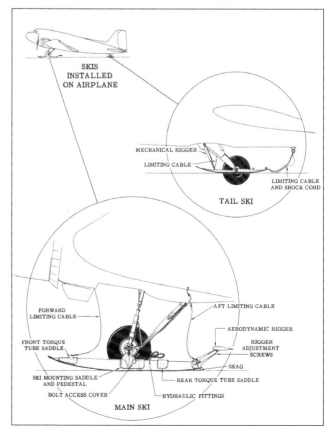

In fact, however, what actually happened was that the major US military operators, the USAF, US Navy, US Marine Corps and US Coast Guard, continued to invest in the notion, well into the 1970s, that modifications to wartime designations did in fact have worthwhile meaning: many C-47As and C-47Bs of the USAF, as noted, became C-47Ds, VC-47Ds, EC-47Ds, AC-47Ds etc. Likewise, the Navy issued suffixes to R4D-1 designations to denote special functions or equipment additions. In the British Commonwealth, although far less definitive, the use of Dakota III and Dakota IV meant something at the operating level.

Truthfully, a decided lack of visual recognition features, compared to other major production aircraft types, makes telling a C-47-DL or a C-47A from a C-47B or C-47D exceptionally challenging to even the most practised eye. Such features as existed during the Second World War quickly became obscure as many aircraft were modified by a surprising number of post-war contractors, including TEMCO, Witbeck, Aerodex, Pacific Airmotive, Aviation Maintenance Company and many others, who responded to customer demands and modified aircraft at will – often not even subject to US Approved Type Certificate specifications, as the aircraft were not intended to be entered on to the US Civil Aircraft Register in any case.

To make recognition even more challenging, a significant number of Latin American DC-3s and C-47s were modified 'in country', further diluting the significance of most wartime and even post-war MDA or MAP designations. Panagra in Lima, Peru, for example, is believed to have modified and overhauled a number of former DC-3As and C-47s for the FAP, while elsewhere, notably in Argentina, Brazil, Chile, Colombia, Ecuador, Mexico, Paraguay and Uruguay, service depot and maintenance organisations performed not only ancillary equipment changes, but rather remarkable conversions from cargo to VIP transport configuration as well. No two of these were like similar modifications performed in the US or elsewhere. Such changes are poorly understood and documented but, more importantly, but with very few exceptions, they did not result in any local changes in designation: a MAP- or ARP-supplied C-47A converted to presidential or VIP use remained, on the books, just another C-47A. Thus, in some cases, while we may identify an aircraft as a C-47B (technically), it may in fact be closer to the classic definition of a DC-3C, quite a different aircraft.

Despite all of this, there were some common denominators, at least at first, and we have populated this annex with several images and drawings that may aid in identifying at least a few of these.

And Finally, Those Basler BT-67 Conversions

The old saying that 'it takes a DC-3 to replace a DC-3', has been taken to heart since around January 1990 by Basler Turbo Conversions of Oshkosh, Wisconsin.

Although a number of attempts had been made previously to re-engine and otherwise strengthen the basic DC-3 or C-47 airframe,

the Basler success in producing at least sixty-six known conversions has been predicated, to a large extent, upon the process by which the company acquires candidates for its rebuild.

Details are proprietary, but stated simply, Basler had conducted unprecedented market research, resulting in the location and identification of aircraft – and operators – that could afford their conversions, which, in some instances, can range from a low of $4.5 million per airframe, depending on equipment choices, to a high of around $6.5 million, with the customer often supplying surplus airframes as part of the bargain for Basler to use as parts sources or outright total rebuilds for yet other potential customers.

Needless to say, long-time Latin American C-47 operators found the Basler formula exceptionally attractive as, besides the promise of extended service life on already 'owned', dedicated and very capable transports that resulted, and tailored by Basler to their specific geographic requirements, there were also strictly tactical, combat gunship variants as well.

The typical Basler conversion's most obvious modification are the engines, Pratt & Whitney (Canada) PT-6A-67Rs turboprops that, besides their efficiency, power and fuel convenience, literally bring the otherwise sturdy airframes well into the twenty-first century of aviation technology.

Other changes are not as obvious, but usually include customer-specified interior equipment, the standard lengthening of the fuselage, radical strengthening throughout, customer-specific upgrades to avionics and communications gear and, upon close examination, modifications to each aircraft's wing leading edges and wing tips.

This three-view drawings describes most of the panel lines and air intake found on most later C-47A blocks, as well as the standard cargo door arrangement. *Nick J. Waters III*

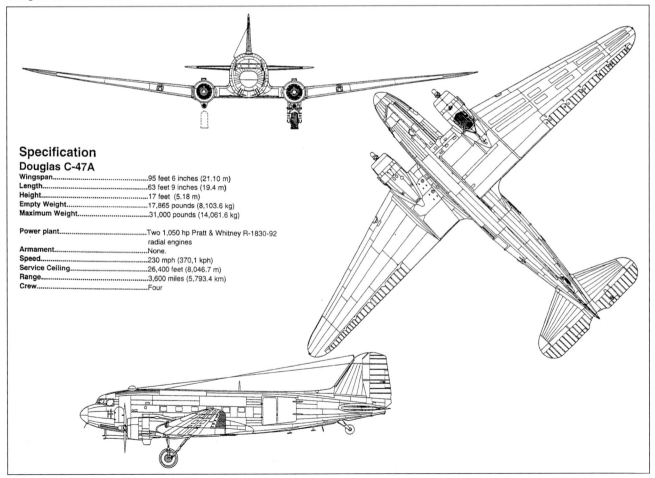

Specification
Douglas C-47A

Wingspan	95 feet 6 inches (21.10 m)
Length	63 feet 9 inches (19.4 m)
Height	17 feet (5.18 m)
Empty Weight	17,865 pounds (8,103.6 kg)
Maximum Weight	31,000 pounds (14,061.6 kg)
Power plant	Two 1,050 hp Pratt & Whitney R-1830-92 radial engines
Armament	None.
Speed	230 mph (370,1 kph)
Service Ceiling	26,400 feet (8,046.7 m)
Range	3,600 miles (5,793.4 km)
Crew	Four

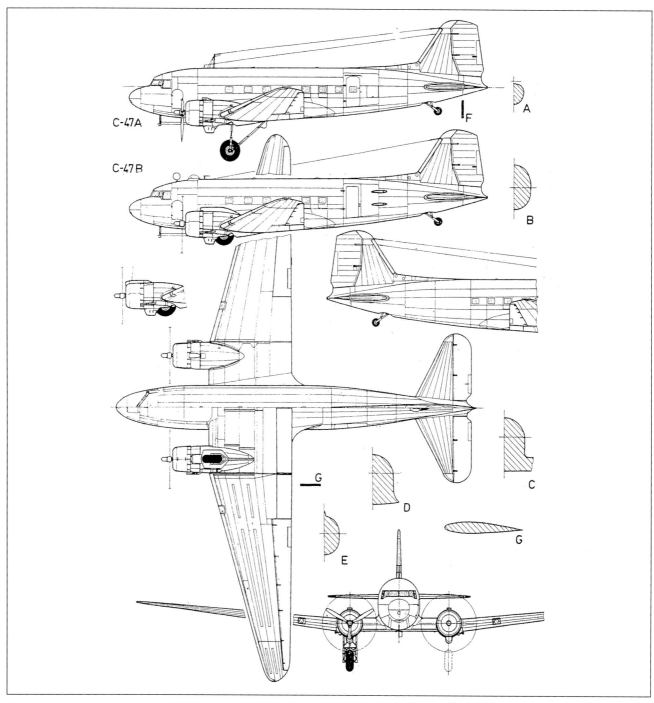

These drawings show, at top, an early C-47-DL and early C-47A fuselage configuration, as well as the much shorter engine air intake, The cabin entry configuration was often retrofitted to Latin American C-47s of all variants for strictly passenger use. Below that is the C-47B configuration most commonly seen. *Dr David Montgomery, BYU*

Although the power and reliability of the PT-6As has become nearly legendary, they are in fact thirstier than the old recips, and as a result, because of weight and balance issues with the longer fuselages, etc, the former standard fuel tanks have thus had to be reduced in capacity. As a result, while range used to be around 1,160 miles with recips, with the PT-6As, with a forty-five-minute reserve, it is only 950 – good enough, however, for virtually any Latin American military operator and a worthwhile sacrifice. Basler does offer an extra, long-range fuel tank option, which can extend standard range to 2,140 nautical miles, but it is not clear if any of the Latin American military operators have opted for this.

The purpose-built gunship version is an exceptionally durable aircraft, although obviously more expensive, and although Colombia is known to have acquired such aircraft, the exact number of other such conversions in Latin American service – whether Basler originated or local conversions – is an unusually fluid equation.

To date, besides civil operators, BT-67s are known to have been acquired by Bolivia, Colombia (both the Air Force as well as the National Police), El Salvador, Guatemala, Malawi, Mali, Mauritania, Thailand and – it is reported – certain US military agencies.

Time will tell, but it is almost certain that the longevity of the DC-3 and C-47 in Latin American military service will owe much to the Basler conversions, a development that could hardly have been imaged in 1941 when Argentina acquired her first military DC-3.

In Appreciation

It will quickly become apparent to even the most casual reader that this volume has been very much a labour of love and respect by your scribes.

But it will come as no surprise that our fondness for the DC-3 and C-47 is shared by an extraordinary number of aviation enthusiasts worldwide, and that an astonishing number of these folks have stepped up to assist us in myriad ways in ferreting out even the most obscure of details and imagery in support of our objective.

We have been so fortunate, first and foremost, to have enjoyed the lifelong friendship – and supreme patience – of Mr John M. Davis of Wichita, Kansas, who has endured a barrage of complex and challenging requests for his unsurpassed qualities as an analyst of our most obscure and sometimes overly enthusiastic postulations. His DNA is inextricably woven throughout this volume, and we quite frankly could not have done it without his way-finding, incomparable sense of humour, and uncanny ability to synthesise aircraft service lives.

In the US, we are also extremely grateful for obscure details on aircraft movements researched in great detail by historian Matthew Miller, and for the encouragement and supply of assorted support documents by Dr Gary Kuhn, also known to us as members of the Latin American Aviation Historical Society (LAAHS) as 'tio Gary!' Dr George Cully provided responses to a number of 'urgent' requests for assistance at the USAF Historical Research Agency at Maxwell AFB, AL, as did Dana Bell at the National Archives at College Park. Mr David W. Ostrowski, former editor of the sorely missed *Skyways* quarterly, contributed numerous images from his incredible photo archive that added significantly to a number of chapters.

Elsewhere, we want to express our sincere thanks to Guido E. Bühlmann of Switzerland for sharing a number of exceptional photographs with us that we could not locate anywhere else. His support for our projects over the years has been just outstanding.

Our colleagues Sr Javier Mosquera, Guillermo Gebel, Atilio Marino and Angel Bertogna in Argentina very generously shared the fruits of their outstanding work on Argentine Army and Air Force DC-3s and C-47s with us and, in the process, enabled us to jointly put a number of long-standing myths to rest once and for all. Their book on the subject, *Douglas DC-3/C-47 en la Fuerza Aérea Argentina* from Avialatina (Buenos Aires, September 2010, ISBN 978-987-24081-1-4) is a 'must have' for any student of the subject, and highly recommended.

Likewise, lifelong friend and internationally recognised dean of Argentine Naval aviation, Jorge Félix Núñez Padín, shared with us his pioneering research into the use of C-39s, DC-3s and C-47s in the Argentine Navy and helped immeasurably in also settling some vexing and very oft-repeated myths that gave us enormous satisfaction. His book on the subject, *Douglas C-39 & C-47 Skytrain, Serie Aeronaval #36*, is very highly recommended for anyone desiring further details on this.

In Bolivia, our friends Sub.Ofc. Ramiro Molina Alanes and Jonathan Olguin, who have laboured in isolation for many years to assemble a coherent record of military aviation in their homeland, provided what has been arguably the very best possible assistance in sorting out the extremely complex FAB history of the C-47 that has thus far been achieved. Their work and sympathy for our project has been invaluable.

The chapter devoted to Brazil, which we are delighted to regard as perhaps the most definitive account thus far published, owes its accuracy and depth to one person: the late, great Brazilian aero-historian Capt. Carlos Dufriche, who laboured in isolation for nearly his entire life collating primary documents that were, at the time, available to him from the FAB. More recently, his sterling labours were assisted by the next wave of Brazilian aviation historians, notable Hélio Higuchi, who assisted, in particular, with some exceptionally rare imagery and interpretation of unit insignia. Via Hélio, we also benefited from the work of Aparecido Camazano, who has conducted extensive research into Brazilian military C-47 aircraft.

When we commenced work on the Chilean chapter, we rather smugly felt that our research, combined with published resources, would make this a relatively complete and tidy section. How wrong we were! Astonishing input from Dr Sergio Barriga Kreft and Sr Pedro Turina, the latter a colleague from the National Air and Space Museum, enabled us to not only radically adjust the Chilean chapter but also to understand that long-held assumptions are not necessarily reliable. Our profound thanks to both of these wonderful gentlemen and scholars. In addition, we must mention our good friends Álvaro Romero and Mario Mangliocchetti, who made available to us the files of the Museo Nacional Aeronáutico y del Espacio, in Santiago, and pointed us in the right direction when dealing with elusive subjects.

The chapter on Colombia, a major military (and civil!) C-47 operator, was, to say the least, challenging, and while the results of our efforts still leave an uncomfortable number of open questions, we believe it adds to the common pool and, perhaps more importantly, suggests direction for additional research. Two Colombian historians were exceptionally generous with the fruits of their own extensive labours, Dr Gustavo Arias and Douglas Hernández of Revista TRIARIUS.

Since the advent of the Castro regime, coherent research into the relatively modest Cuban utilisation of military C-47s has been restricted almost entirely to records located at the National Archives up to that moment and such Cuban governmental Memorias that had been published prior to 1958. However, the indefatigable and, frankly, intrepid efforts of lifelong friend and colleague Capt. George G. Farinas provided an outstanding sounding board and priceless additional details that could not have been found anywhere else. Special mention must also be made of the sterling efforts of Capt. Irving Silva and Master Sgt Enrique Saavedra, who supplied information on Nicaraguan use of these classic aircraft that could not possibly have been obtained anywhere else.

The study and historiography of military aviation in the Dominican Republic after the end of the Trujillo era has benefited enormously from the efforts of our friend and fellow aviation historian Dax Roman, who provided corrections and additions to our own work on the FAD use of C-47s.

In Ecuador, our fellow SAFO member Capitan Jorge Delgado and his invaluable secretary, Srta Andrea Garcia Saeteros, helped us work through a myriad of problem aircraft, and most importantly, provided details regarding the double-hijacking of two TAME C-47s that we had missed completely.

Mexico, where the FAM use of a large number of DC-3s and C-47s remains disappointingly undocumented, is not because of any lack of effort by two outstanding aero-historians, who also contributed quite without condition to this project – despite the fact that both Dr Alfonso Flores and Santiago Flores have been assembling information for their own independent projects for years. We hope that what we have jointly crafted will aid their ongoing efforts. José Antonio Quevedo also assisted with some excruciating details.

The chapter dedicated to Paraguay is, for all practical purposes, a 100 per cent complete survey, and we owe this extraordinary – and exemplary – contribution to the literature almost entirely of our friend and colleague Dr Antonio Sapienza. Tony shared from his own research and collection in the very highest traditions of collegiality, and we could only wish that historians and researchers of his calibre were more numerous!

In Peru, yet another challenging section, the field work by Amaru Tincopa and Ing. Javier Goto Watanabe over the years proved exceptionally helpful, although admittedly more work remains ahead of us.

Our chapter devoted to Uruguay, also nearly 100 per cent complete, is the result of outstanding work pioneered there by the late Nery Mendiburu and Tte. 1º (Av.) Juan Maruri and to the exceptional contributions of friend and aero-historian Eduardo Luzardo, without whom this section would have indeed been much the poorer.

Our coverage of military C-47s in Venezuela can, at best, be described as a primer on the subject, and we sincerely hope that what

we have presented will spur on additional research into the use of these aircraft in this troubled nation. We enjoyed the support, nonetheless, of a number of enthusiasts and students of the subject that, individually, provided what they could, and we are thankful therefore for the aid of Enrique Martín of Organisación Rescate Humbolt, Gerard Casius, Alfredo Schael, and Fabian Capecchi.

Finally, regarding the chapters dedicated to the Central American nations, our work would have been impossible without the invaluable help of our good friends and excellent aero-historians: Amado Aguiluz, Jurgen Hesse, Marco Lavagnino, Mario Alfaro, Douglas Cornejo and Mario Ávila, who went out of their way to provide us with answers to difficult questions and hard to find images. In fact, these chapters are a testament of their impressive work along the years.

But above all, we owe our profound thanks to Charlotte Stear, Editorial and Production Manager, and Harriet Hirshman, at Crécy Publishing and the entire staff of that great publishing house for their faith in us and in seeing the intrinsic value of telling this story.

1   Oddly, however, records found in the office of the former USAFSO Command Historian, the late Fred Young, in 1967, showed that the two C-33s were in Panama as early as 14 August 1939 – possibly on a 'pre-deployment' sojourn.

2   The first had been a Douglas C-1C, AC26-422 received in May 1927, followed by two Y1C-21 Dolphins in the mid-1930s (AC32-283 and AC32-284), a single Y1C-26A Dolphin (AC32-409) and at least one C-29 Dolphin (AC33-292.)

3   Punta Vargas is an extremely remote location, and exactly why a USAAC C-33 would have been anywhere in the vicinity is puzzling. It is a considerable distance from the more likely location of this incident, Puntarenas.

4   This aircraft returned to CONUS on 9 May 1941 to Olmsted Field and served on into the early war period until wrecked at Brookley Field, Alabama, on 13 January 1942.

5   Apparently, the Defence Supplies Corporation (DSC) had actually taken possession of a total of four mixed former LATI Savoia-Marchetti aircraft, and it was proposed that all of these be incorporated into the 20th TCS!

6   This suffix was dropped, however, on 12 April 1944.

7   There is evidence that this may not have been the first such mission. The 20th TCS also made a 'special' flight to La Paz on 26 April 1943 and another on 14 October 1943. The 1944 operation was by no means the first time that Bolivia had interned Axis nationals. On 11 June 1942, sixty-eight 'Nazis' were arrested in La Paz and dispatched by train to Arica, Chile, where they were loaded aboard the SS *Shawnee*. They were described as 'volunteers'. Of these, ten (of a total of ninety-eight) had been specifically identified by the FBI, and whose detention and removal had been requested to be 'expedited', but the Bolivian Government 'had completely failed to cooperate'. The President, Penaranda, had promised concerned FBI officials – who had overall responsibility for Counterintelligence in Latin America – that eighteen more would be sent to Lima by plane on 12 June, to join those on the *Shawnee* there but, in the event, apparently only six were thus transported – described as 'the less dangerous'.

8   Although a number of these C-49Hs are shown on Sixth Air Force records, no unit of assignment is cited, suggesting that they may in fact have been flown by Air transport Command crews on high-priority, quasi-civil routes in the Sixth Air Force zone of operations on mainly former civil routes.

9   There is photographic evidence that suggests the detachment, in order to avoid confusion with Unit Numbers of the parent organisation, assigned its aircraft individual letters 'A' through at least 'E', the latter having been known worn on the nose of the single C-39.

10 Throughout official USAF documents held by the USAFHRA, the designations of these units are variously cited as Foreign Mission Squadron or Group, while in other instances as Foreign Missions Squadron or Group. It is not clear which was technically correct.

11 The acronym MSN will be utilised throughout this work to denote the Douglas-issued serial number for all aircraft. Although 'C/N' has gained wide general use internationally, commencing in Great Britain, and is certainly interchangeable, the US Aeronautics Branch of the Department of Commerce first started using 'MSN' on all of its registration documents, forms and correspondence as early as 1927, as did the US armed forces, which acquired Douglas twins, in order to differentiate these numbers from strictly Army-issue military serial number or Navy Bureau of Aeronautics serial numbers.

12 This was unquestionably a reference to DC-2-118B CX-AEF, MSN 13561 and DC-2-124 CX-AEG, MSN 1324, which had been acquired by PLUNA around December 1942 and which the airline was anxious to replace with DC-3s or converted C-47s.

13 Argentina had actually filed a rather comprehensive Military Assistance request, case No.Argentina-11, between 3 August and 26 October 1951, to provide equipment for the conversion of T-20. This includes skis for the aircraft, special gyros, safety and survival equipment, sleds, heaters, snow-shoes and training for two pilots in landing with skis.

14 The ferry registrations used by Argentina at this time make a fascinating study. This aircraft, along with LV-XFS to LV-XFY, actually transited through Albrook Field, Panama Canal Zone on 13 February 1947 en route home, along with nine demilitarised C-54s and eight Beech AT-11s with similar ferry registrations, all having arrived there from California.

15 This loosely organised 'unit' eventually involved four FAA C-47s and DC-3s (T-19, T-23, T-26 and T-89), two Army C-47s (ETA-101 and ETA-103) and five Aerolineas Argentinas DC-3s (LV-ABZ, LV-CAN, LV-ACP, LV-ADG and LV-AFE).

16 Not to be confused with the British airline using the same acronym, this Argentine incarnation of the term signified the Base Oficial de Aviacíon Civil, later known as the INAC.

17 This included the assignment, like the US Navy, of what was essentially a Bureau of Aeronautics-like 'permanent' serial number to each aircraft, which remained with the aircraft throughout its service life, while temporary unit 'codes' were applied in generally large characters and numerals elsewhere on the aircraft. Although not an official term, these have come to be referred to as 'PSN's' denoting 'Permanent Serial Numbers'.

18 A persistent legend has gained some currency that claims that the Navy acquired a sixth ex-AVENSA C-39 that was subsequently found to be in even worse condition than the other five, and that it was used for spares. Said to have been issued PSN 0108, MSN 2063 a former USAAC C-39 AC38-506 and Pan American via the DSC by 18 September 1944, this aircraft was last reported at the Brownsville, Texas, Pan Am maintenance base as a spares source. The PSN 0108 is known to have been assigned to a North American AT-6A, however. The issue, however, is far more fundamental: AVENSA is only known to have acquired five C-39s, and the only other possibility is that the Navy acquired the alleged sixth aircraft from TACA de Venezuela or somehow from Brownsville via Pan Am, which also operated a few.

19 The official capital of Bolivia is Sucre, some 164km north-east of Potosi.

20 For full details of the astonishing activities of this aircraft see co-author Hagedorn's book on the P-38 in Latin America from MMP.

21 Besides those that appear in the following table, other candidates appear to have included C-47A-90-DLs 43-15661 and 43-15678, both of which went to MAP from Miami on 20 May 1964.

22 ARP records at the National Archives indicate that at one point the US was thinking of making as many as forty-six C-47As available to Brazil via this programme.

23 Of these, twenty-seven were covered by the so-called Interim Program on Project 94539-S and two C-47As were covered by Project 72012.

23 Although of these, four were apparently purchased directly from the FLC in May 1946 for $120,000.

24 These included the one marked as 'C-47 EDL', 2014, 2022, 2025, 2030, 2038, 2041, 2043, 2044, 2052, 2064, 2071 to 2073, 2076, 2077, 2081, 2082, 2084 to 2086 and 2092.

25 These included C-47 2035, 2038, 2043, 2046, 2056, 2082, 2085 and 2086.

26 In addition to the above, these included 2017, 2020, 2039, 2069, 2080, and EC-47 2088.

27 Oddly, however, the Air Order of Battle for the FACh dated 15 January 1946, reflected one C-47 on strength and 'nine more on order for LAN', suggesting that one of the earliest LAN C-47s may have, in fact, been detailed to the air force prior to the arrival of the dedicated ARP aircraft.

28 C-47B-10-DK 43-49043 (MSN 14859/26304) was apparently originally intended for ARP to Chile. It had arrived in the Canal Zone after 6 June 1946 and suffered an accident on 20 September 1947 at Los Cerrillos while being flown by a serving USAAF officer, Donald C. Dickson Jr, and home station was cited as 'Quintero', from whence the ARP cadre was operating. It is officially recorded as having been handed over to the FLC for surplus sale on 23 July 1948, so may have been acquired by Chile as a hulk or spares source.

29 These were USAAF serials 44-77258, 45-1026 and 45-1034.

30 The waters are rather muddied by the little-known fact that the Colombian Government purchased a single wrecked C-47 from the Foreign Liquidation Commission (FLC) on 30 June 1946 for $5,500. It can only be assumed that this was intended for the FAC, possibly as a training aid, but the actual reason for this unusual acquisition remains unknown. This was, incidentally, the very first month of FLC operations.

31 The US had informed Latin American ARP recipients that a typical, low-time C-47B supplied under the programme, which had cost the USAAF $35,019.03, could be made available to Latin American air arms for $26,262.78.

32 This may have been the C-47 that collided with a training aircraft (reportedly a civil Luscombe 8A) and which was destroyed by fire on 25 May 1948 at BA Madrid, possibly FAC-662. The four-man crew of the C-47 were all killed, as was the single pilot aboard the Luscombe.

33 Although often cited as 'Nicaraguan Air Force' aircraft, the FAN in fact owned no organic C-47s at this juncture, and so these were almost certainly a combination of LaNICA and FANSA aircraft commandeered for the task and probably crewed, at least in part, by serving or Reserve FAN crews.

34 There is one other possibility. C-47B-50-DK, MSN 17116/34383, USAAF 45-1113 had been assigned to the Division of Military Intelligence, Ecuador, on 25 October 1946, a style of entry covering the 'cadre' and training period for ARP aircraft. However, it was reported instead to Guatemala on 14 December 1949 and reclaimed on 31 January 1950, suggesting that she was either diverted north or that she had suffered an accident in the midst of the ARP training phase and was thus never assigned to a recipient nation.

35 According to a Mexican Order of Battle document generated by the US dated 31 January 1947, Mexico had 'completed negotiations for the purchase of seven C-47s and they will probably be delivered by June 30, 1947', suggesting that the ARP Project number was merely a document of conveyance.

36 The FAM subsequently acquired commercially twenty North American T-6D Standard aircraft directly from the manufacturer.

37 The continued Mexican infatuation with F-51Ds was a seemingly endless topic of discussion amongst the senior FAM leadership. By 30 June 1950, such an acquisition had been predicated upon the sale of the Republic P-47Ds then on hand, and in fact the Peruvian Air Attaché in Washington traveled to Mexico City to discuss the possible purchase of their P-47s. The USAF Liaison Office to Mexico had advised 'strongly against a changeover to F-51s due to the supply and maintenance problems it would entail, but to no avail'. Ironically, it was probably USAF demand for F-51Ds in Korea that finally quieted the persistent requests.

38 At this juncture, the airline acronym was invariably presented thus, and not with all capital lettering, as LANICA, until substantially later, chronologically.

39 It is the belief of your scribes that the three aircraft involved may well have been NC-56800, NC-53192 and a third, unidentified, FANSA-operated DC-3.

40 Most sources cite all three as having been LACSA aircraft, but this is not possible, as only two survived by that point, as noted in Chapter 7.

41 These two US civil registered aircraft were very nearly joined by a third, C-47 41-18497, NC-56800 on 12 November 1948. Still in the custody of the War Assets Administration (WAA) Sales Centre in Miami at the time, it was somehow spirited away by 'owner' and pilot Harry R. Wheeler, who then flew her – single-handedly – to Managua, Nicaragua, where the FAN promptly seized the aircraft on the grounds that Wheeler owed the government money. The US Embassy intervened, and a USAF crew was dispatched from the Panama Canal Zone to fly it there and prepare it for return to Miami. Wheeler clearly was trying to sell the aircraft to the FAN quite illegally and, in the bargain, settle whatever debt he had with the Somoza regime. The possibility that he had been prompted to do all of this by Somoza's henchmen in the first place cannot be discounted.

42 For the record, the captains of the aircraft when returned to Costa Rica was Mayor Roger Bermúdez, aged just twenty-nine – at the time the Deputy Commander of the FAN, and Capitans Jorge Zogaib and Francisco Ullóa. According to one source, the crew were 'worried to death' during the flight, as they were well aware of the fact that some key components had been switched out. In fact, and possibly due to this ruse, Bermúdez resigned his commission after returning to Nicaragua. Indeed, during final approach to land at La Sabana at San José, one of the engines on the aircraft being flown by Capitan Ullóa packed up, but despite this, the young aviator managed to bring her in safely. To add insult to injury, Somoza managed to demand – and get – $40,000 from the Costa Rican government for the maintenance and repair of these aircraft before they were repatriated!

43 LACSA, by this point, saw little profit in attempting to rehabilitate the aircraft locally as, late in December 1948, after the revolution and the issue of the three impounded aircraft had been put on the back-burner, two converted C-47s were brought to Costa Rica by LACSA to add to the single aircraft operated at the time by them which was on lease from PAA, during the last seven months of 1948. Two of these aircraft were returned to PAA later in the year and two C-46s were purchased to replace them.

44 The FAN AOB as of this date may be worth noting at this point, as it still reflected no DC-3s or C-47s whatsoever. The force totaled exactly thirty-one aircraft of twelve different types, the most numerous of which were ten assorted North American AT-6 variants. The next most numerous type were five Vultee BT-13s, four Fairchild PT-19As, two each Lockheed P-38L/M Lightnings, Consolidated PB4Y-1 Liberators, Waco UPF-7/PT-14s, and single examples of an ancient Waco WHD, CCF G-23, Fleet 10F, Douglas A-20G, Fairchild 24-C8E and Cessna UC-78. There were twenty-one commissioned pilots, twenty-one other non-rated officers, three other NCO airmen and seventy-seven enlisted ranks for a total of 122 personnel. There were also ten cadets in training, expected to graduate on 27 May 1952.

45 Who just happened to be the Military Aide de Camp to President Somoza as of 1950.

46 According to Capt. Irving Silva, these comprised three rails under each wing, apparently configured to accommodate 2.75in rockets. Who installed these and when remains an open question.

47 Based on known MAP offsets, these aircraft may have been 44-76951 – also linked with Colombia – and 45-996 but these have eluded verification.

48 The Douglas B-26Bs included FAN-400 to 404 and then 420 and 422. Since the 'lowest' known DC-3 or C-47 serial in the 400s was FAN-410, it is assumed that the serials between 404 and 410 were assigned or reserved for North American T-28As, although 413 and 418 are also known to have been issued to T-28As. FAN-418 was apparently reissued to a C-47 when the T-28As were reserialed into the low 200s.

49 A truly exotic aircraft, this rather weary airframe had started life as a DC-3A-414, NC-30005, in December 1941, but never served a day as such, having been acquired by the Defence Supplies Corporation that month and issued to the USAAC as a C-68, 42-14298, subsequently serving with the RAF briefly.

50 The President, in fact, used C-47 FAN 410 as his preferred mount, including a 'five-star' placard on her vertical fin and nose.

51 LATN is often confused with the Transporte Aéreo Militar (TAM). In fact, they operated concurrently, although obviously to differing destinations depending on the probable traffic. TAM was formally constituted as such in March 1954, while LATN had been in existence since 1944.

52 'New' series codes FAP-2001 and 2002 were assigned to surviving Consolidated PBY-5As.

53 Serial FAP-2027 was assigned to a CASA C-212.

54 Serial FAP-2031 was assigned to a CASA C-212.

55 Serial FAP-2033 was assigned to a CASA C-212.

56 Project 72015 originally included, amongst others, 42-100552 and 42-93793 for Peru. However, these were instead offered to Mexico and Bolivia, respectively, as noted elsewhere and, to add to the confusion, 42-100552 was also offered to Cuba at some point. However, it appears to have actually ended up in Mexico.

57 This unusual armada actually departed Bush Field, Augusta, Georgia, for home on 3 August, suggesting a stop at USAAF stations in the Panama Canal Zone – or elsewhere – along the way. On delivery the UC-43s became CAP-428 and 429, while the GB-2s got codes 430 to 432. This obviously suggests that the 'DC-47' may have been CAP-424.

58 Born out of Escuadron de Transportes 41, TAM was officially stood up on 28 February 1947.

59 Some sources have cited the date of this loss as 20 January, but the 18th was the actual date. It should be recalled that TAM at this juncture was the commercial-type enterprise operated by 41 Escuadrón at this juncture.

60 The DC-3s and C-47s, formally registered to SATCO on 13 June 1960, were the former FAP-485, 487, 488, 489, 47-319, 483 and 486, which became, respectively, initially OB-XAA-534, OB-XAB-535, OB-XAC-536, OB-XAD-537, OB-XAE-538, OB-XAF-539 and OB-XAG-540. On 31 January 1963 these were joined by the former FAP-677 and 53-307, which became OB-XAT-653 and OB-XAU-654.

61 This Grupo was stood up on 27 July 1961 when the FAV started augmenting its C-47 fleet with the first of eighteen brand-new Fairchild C-123Bs.

Index

British Combat Aircraft in Latin America

Santiago Rivas

In the aftermath of World War II, Britain had some of the world's most advanced military aircraft, and the decision to start selling its most modern warplanes to Latin America gave it an advantage over the United States who had been the main provider of planes to Latin American air forces until that point. This was one of the main reasons why many so many South American air forces chose to buy British combat aircraft right into the 1970s.

In many South American countries, their first jet combat aircraft were British, while the Argentina's Avro Lancasters and Lincolns gave it the most potent bomber force in Latin America. BAC Canberras had five South American operators, and as the only jet bombers in use in the region they saw action several times. Combat activity by British types include Argentine planes used during the 1955 revolution and ironically Argentine Canberras in action against British forces during the Malvinas/Falklands War. Exported Brtitish aircraft also saw action over the Bay of Pigs in Cuba, in the Peruvian conflicts with Ecuador, during the Chilean 1973 coup d'etat, as well as in various internal struggles.

Meticulously researched and featuring numerous illustrations, *British Combat Aircraft in Latin America* is a remarkable book and a fascinating study on a little known aspect of military aviation history. Though British combat types is now almost gone from the skies over Latin America, their legacy will last for a very long time.

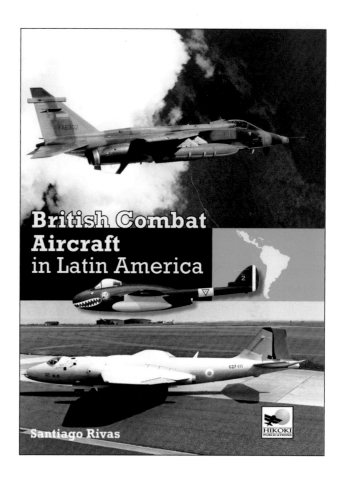

624 pages, hardback
ISBN: 978 190210 9572 £44.95